A Storm of Songs

A STORM OF SONGS

India and the Idea of the Bhakti Movement

JOHN STRATTON HAWLEY

Harvard University Press
Cambridge, Massachusetts
London, England
2015

Printed in the United States of America

First Printing

Library of Congress Cataloging-in-Publication Data

Hawley, John Stratton, 1941– author.
A storm of songs : India and the idea of the bhakti movement / John Stratton Hawley.
pages cm
Includes bibliographical references and index.
ISBN 978-0-674-18746-7
1. Bhakti—Social aspects—History. I. Title.
BL1214.32.B53H42 2015
294.509—dc23
2014026466

To my academic patit-pāvan, who have rescued me when fallen:

Aditya Behl
Shrivatsa Goswami
Monika Horstmann
Rachel McDermott
Rupert Snell

Contents

Acknowledgments ix

Transliteration and Pronunciation xiii

Introduction 1

1. *The Bhakti Movement and Its Discontents* 13

2. *The Transit of Bhakti* 59

3. *The Four Sampradāys and the Commonwealth of Love* 99

4. *The View from Brindavan* 148

5. *Victory in the Cities of Victory* 190

6. *A Nation of Bhaktas* 230

7. *What Should the Bhakti Movement Be?* 285

Notes 343

Bibliography 381

Index 423

Acknowledgments

And the last shall be first. As I come to the end of the decade-long project that has resulted in the book before you, I have the pleasure of thanking some of the people and institutions who have made it possible. Not all, by any means: how could I possibly record the full extent of the kindnesses and conversations that have gone into the making of this book? If you remember such a conversation and do not find your name in the list below or in the text and its notes, please accept my silent thanks.

I am grateful to the National Endowment for the Humanities, the American Institute of Indian Studies, the Andrew W. Mellon Foundation, and Barnard College for grants that made it possible for me to travel to India, and to Barnard for the leaves that allowed me to accept them. I am also indebted to the Leonard Hastings Schoff Fund of The University Seminars at Columbia University, which has provided support for aspects of the book's publication. Members of the University Seminar on South Asia discussed the final chapter with me on September 15, 2014.

In India I have been the recipient of many kindnesses from the India International Centre, the Sri Caitanya Prema Samsthana, the Indira Gandhi National Centre for the Arts, the Nehru Memorial Library, the Indira Gandhi Center for the Arts, the National Museum, Prof. Seniruddha Dash and the staff of the New Catalogus Catalogorum, the Indian Institute for Advanced Study, the Oriental Institute of Baroda, the Rajasthan Oriental Research Institute, the Vrindaban Research Institute, the City Palace library and museum in Jaipur, Rabindra Bhavan and the Hindi Bhavan at Shantiniketan, Vrajesh Kumarji Maharaj and his staff at the Sarasvati Vibhag Library in Kankroli, and numerous other manuscript collections across the country. The Indian Council of Philosophical Research, the Indian Council of Historical Research, and the Kanakadasa Adhyayana Peeta and Kanakadasa Samshodhana Kendra of Mangalore University have made it possible to engage with colleagues at Tirupati, Banaras, and Mangalore. Students and faculty at a number of universities and colleges will recognize sections of this book and, I hope, detect their contributions to it: Banaras Hindu University; the College of William and Mary; Harvard University; Indiana University; McGill University; Northwestern Michigan University; Oxford University; Princeton University; Smith College; SOAS, University of London; the State University of New York at Stony Brook; the University of Toronto; the University of California, Berkeley; the University of California, Santa Barbara; the University of Florida; the University of Mysore; the University of Pennsylvania; the University of Texas at Austin; the University of Venice; and Wellesley College. Behind the names of each of these institutions lie not only the funds that made it possible to visit them, but the deeply valued friends who arranged it all and have kept in touch from then until now. In many cases—but hardly all—my endnotes are my witness. Individual scholars who work apart from institutions such as these have also played important roles. I think especially of Shyam Manohar Goswami and K. G. Subrahmanyam, whose guidance and expertise have been crucial.

A special word of thanks goes to friends, students, and colleagues (these categories overlap!) who have read all or portions of the book in draft and provided me with invaluable comments and criticism: Justin Ben-Hain, Patton Burchett, Allison Busch, Margaret Case, Bharati Jagannathan, Linda Hess, Joel Lee, Rembert Lutjeharms, Christian Novetzke, Francesca Orsini, Heidi Pauwels, Srilata Raman, Ajay Rao, Davesh Soneji, Ramya Sreenivasan, Shiv Subramaniam, Anand Venkatkrishnan, and my consummate, brilliant editor-wife, Laura Shapiro. I am also indebted to the wonderful circle of friends and colleagues who responded to the book as a whole at the Madison South Asia meetings in 2014. Then there are those who played a special role in helping me interpret languages I cannot read or cannot read as well as I ought to be able to do: Purushottam Agrawal, Gil Ben-Herut, Hena Basu, Prithvi Datta Chandra Shobhi, Abhijit Ghosh, Brian Hatcher, Jon Keune, Joel Lee, Gurinder Singh Mann, Rachel McDermott, Vasudha Narayanan, Christian Novetzke, Stefano Pellò, Dalpat Rajpurohit, Neelima Shukla-Bhatt, and my daughter Nell. To

Robyn Beeche, Isabelle Lewis, and Neeraja Poddar I am grateful for photography and cartography and the expertise that those two words only barely suggest. Students in graduate seminars at Columbia have helped me think through many of the issues that presented themselves along the way. These students are also my teachers, and there is nothing to compare with the week-in week-out warmth they have offered over the years as we argued and probed and appreciated and expanded one another's worlds.

Rupert Snell and David Shulman provided excellent, detailed, and helpfully divergent feedback as readers for Harvard University Press. Sharmila Sen and Heather Hughes at the press have been superb in their various capacities, as have Anne Sussman and Kathleen Richards. Perhaps Sharmila will remember that moment over a cup of coffee at Burdick's when she asked me whether there was a next book in my queue and went on to wonder, to my amazement, why she shouldn't publish it.

I dedicate the book to a Gang of Five without whom I could not have made it to this day—old friends, deep friends, scholars to the core.

Transliteration and Pronunciation

Words from many Indian languages come together in this book, and I hope to honor the transliteration practices that are standard for each. Speakers of the languages that stretch across northern India from Gujarat to Bihar tend to drop the sheva that is assumed as part of a Sanskrit syllable unless another vowel is indicated. I will do the same, and invariably so if the sheva falls at the end of the word (Skt. Tulasīdāsa > Hindi Tulsīdās). Medial shevas are more difficult. If audible in speech, then I retain the medial *a* (Nandadās, not Nanddās); otherwise not. Bengali, also a member of this Indo-Aryan group, does retain the final sheva in speech (often as *o* rather than *a*), but because in this book Bengali terms so frequently arise in contexts where Hindi words are also being discussed, I transliterate them uniformly, dropping the final *a* as I would for the much more frequent Hindi.

The Dravidian languages of south India uniformly pronounce their implied *a*'s, so in that case I retain them. I write the name of the Kannada poet Kanakadāsa in that way rather than as it would be pronounced in Hindi (Kanakadās or Kanakdās). Similarly, if a word is Sanskrit and is being discussed in a context where Sanskrit is to the fore—rather than as an object of Hindi speech (Rām, *sampradāy*)—I retain all vowels (Rāma, *Sampradāyapradīpa*). I also follow the standard transliteration scheme for Tamil names, but Tamil terms borrowed from Sanskrit are retained in that form (*bhakti,* not *patti*). Actually, the word bhakti is special: since it has become common in many European languages I write it without diacritics. By extension I do the same for bhakta (the person affected by bhakti)—after the fashion of such ordinary words as karma, guru, and dharma.

Other words and names, especially those designating places and languages, have also acquired standard anglicized forms, and these usually do a fair job of representing the ways such words are actually pronounced (Krishna, Mathura, Chaitanya, Brajbhasha, Babur, Chamar). I retain these ordinary usages even if they diverge from the more "correct" form of transliteration that appears in more technical contexts (Kṛṣṇadās, *Mathurā Māhātmya, Caitanyacaritāmṛta, bhāṣā, camār*). In the case of less well-known names (Galtā, Navadvīp) I display the appropriate diacritics. The Indian administrative system has settled on Vrindaban and Varanasi to designate the cities I call Brindavan and Banaras. I prefer the latter spellings since they are closer to local usage and ordinary pronunciation *(brindāvan, banāras)*—and in certain contexts, they too are official (Brindavan Gardens, Banaras Hindu University). If this seems an unruly thicket, well, it is. My hope is that the conventions I have adopted will enable readers to "pronounce" the trees in this forest and recognize that they do in fact belong in the same wood.

Some special difficulties remain. The *t* that appears in formal Tamil transliteration sounds more like the English *d* than a *t*. Hence the name of the poet-saint Nantaṉār is pronounced Nandanar, and Āṇṭāḷ sounds roughly like Andal. The Tamil *c*, as in Cēkkiḻār, is a sibilant, so it sounds like the English *s* (Sekkilar). When one moves to Indo-Aryan languages such as Hindi and Sanskrit, however, that same lone *c* should be pronounced as if it were the English *ch*. Hence the spelling Chamar has historically been used to render the Hindi term formally transliterated as *camār*. Finally, it is well to remember that a century ago it was common practice to render the neutral Hindi, Punjabi, or Bengali *a* with the English *u*, as in Punjab and Keshub. In both these words the *u* should be pronounced like the *u* in "punch" or "but." Normally I would employ *a* in such instances, but because Punjab and Keshub have become conventional I retain them.

A Storm of Songs

Introduction

"SWEET MERCY"

May 10, 1933, on the third day of Gandhi's fast against untouchability

Raidas, the sweeper, was tanner by caste
  whose touch was shunned by the wayfarers
    and the crowded streets were lonely for him.
Master Ramananda was walking to the temple
          after his morning bath,
  when Raidas bowed himself down before him from a distance.
  "Who are you, my friend" asked the great Brahmin
    and the answer came,
    "I am mere dust dry and barren,
      trodden down by the despising days and nights.
  Thou, my Master, art a cloud on the far away sky.
   If sweet mercy be showered from thee
          upon the lowly earth,
  the dumb dust will cry out in ecstacy of flowers."
    Master took him to his breast
      pouring on him his lavish love
    which made a storm of songs
      to burst across the heart
        of Raidas, the sweeper.

A storm of songs: that is how Rabindranath Tagore described the poetic output of the important sixteenth-century saint Ravidās—or Raidās, as he is also called.[1] Ravidās was a Dalit (the word means "oppressed"), a member of the vast underclass of Indian society that did and still does its dirty work and was until recently called Untouchable. In Tagore's imagination it was the touch of a Brahman, albeit a uniquely unconventional Brahman, that stirred the parched dryness of Ravidās's life situation into a welcome storm of songs. These were bhakti songs, songs of deeply felt religious emotion. They were the medium though which Ravidās was no longer isolated, exiled, but a living, breathing member of India's religious whole.

"Bhakti," as usually translated, is devotion, but if that word connotes something entirely private and quiet, we are in need of other words.[2] Bhakti is heart religion, sometimes cool and quiescent but sometimes hot—the religion of participation, community, enthusiasm, song, and often of personal challenge, the sort of thing that coursed through the Protestant Great Awakenings in the history of the United States. It evokes the idea of a widely shared religiosity for which institutional superstructures weren't all that relevant, and which, once activated, could be historically contagious—a glorious disease of the collective heart. It implies direct divine encounter, experienced in the lives of individual people. These people, moved by that encounter, turn to poetry, which is the natural vehicle of bhakti, and poetry expresses itself just as naturally in song. There is a whole galaxy of bhakti poets who have been moved to song in the course of Indian history, and their songs are still sung today, everywhere across the subcontinent and in all its major languages. In Hindi there's Kabīr and Sūrdās, Ravidās and Mīrābāī. In Tamil there's Nammāḻvār and Āṇṭāḷ. In Marathi, Nāmdev and Tukārām. In Punjabi, Bābā Nānak, who became the first of the Sikh Gurus. All of these are bhakti poets. They come from both sexes and all social stations. They are understood to be the voice of the people's religion, broadly, and they are held to have had a distinctive history, one that bound them together as a group. In Tagore's picture of the encounter between the Brahman and the Dalit, the touch of Rāmānand and his words of searching friendship initiated Ravidās into that great company. The storm of songs that broke across his heart made him a part of a larger monsoon that has been called the bhakti movement.

This book is about the idea of the bhakti movement. In its final, fully articulated form, the bhakti movement idea coalesces in the twentieth century, in Tagore's own lifetime, but it refers to a much deeper past. It says that all the poets we have just mentioned were woven together in a single fabric of shared identity before God that extends throughout India's long medieval period (ca. 500–1700 C.E.)—this despite the fact that their regional languages might initially have seemed to separate them. Singers travel, they go on tour, and then as now people living in India could speak more than a single language, so it was actually no mystery that these bhakti poet-singers and others who sang their songs after them could be understood as they moved around. As they traveled, we are told, they shaped a history that made India's many regions connect at a grassroots level.

Sanskrit too could be understood all over India—it was India's refined supralocal language, like Latin or Greek, but you had to be educated to take in its meanings. These bhakti poets fashioned a different kind of translocal movement, one that spoke the mother tongue—or rather, the mother tongues. And there was a pattern to it. Among India's regional languages, Tamil, which is spoken in the far south, was the first to be written down. Tamil was pictured as being the root of the bhakti movement, and indeed, we know that Tamil bhakti poets were already active in the sixth and seventh centuries. But they were just the beginning. As the great poet and critic A. K. Ramanujan once said, these Tamil poets lit a fuse that refused to go out before it had ignited the whole subcontinent, first sparking poetry in the neighboring region of Karnataka, then spreading northward to Maharashtra and Gujarat until finally it ignited the Hindi- or Urdu-speaking regions of north India and beyond.[3]

The rope of this fuse extended from the sixth century to the sixteenth or seventeenth—a full millennium. Thus the bhakti movement performed its work of national integration both in space and in time—"from region to region, from century to century," as Ramanujan put it, "quickening the religious impulse."[4] Spatially, it knit together India's many regional literatures. Temporally, it formed a bridge that spanned between the classical period and its modern counterpart. Socially, it put Dalits in touch with Brahmins.

But what about the hundreds of millions of Muslims who live in South Asia? Are they too a part of this picture? As many told the story, the answer was a wholehearted yes. Kabīr, indisputably one of the greatest of India's bhakti poets, had a Muslim name. Particularly in west and north India, Sufi poets too became part of this religion of the heart, and they too traveled. Some who tell the bhakti movement story have made the case that other religious sensibilities were also involved—Buddhist, Jain,

Christian—but the question of Muslims' participation in the great sweep of the bhakti movement is key. Certain ideologues, both Hindu and Muslim, have wanted to deny this common bhakti religiosity in favor of a Hindu-Muslim split they hold to be intractable, perennial. This kind of thinking provided the basis for the bloody partition of South Asia into India and Pakistan at the moment of their independence in 1947, and later it justified the demolition of the great Babri Mosque in Ayodhya when armies of militant Hindus attacked it on December 6, 1992. The slogans heard from loudspeakers on that day proclaimed that Hinduism was India's real religion and that the god Rām, who was born in Ayodhya and ruled from there in righteousness, was its paradigmatic king. Though it too appeals to a Hindu majority, the idea of the bhakti movement makes a very different claim—that India's true religion lies beyond the reach of business-as-usual organized religion, whether the organizing is done by Hindu Brahmins or Muslim *qāzīs*. This bhakti religion is higher, deeper, available to all without exception; it forms the central thrust of Indian religious history, its core reality.

Of course, other answers have also been given to the question, "What is India's real religion?" Some have said it is local religion, the religion of India's villages and its village-like urban enclaves—an array of demigods, family gods, and specific practices that can never fully translate into regional or national forms. Others have pointed to the tantric side of things—mantras, yantras, and yogic self-transformation. Still others have emphasized spirit mediums, possession, and healing practices—realms of religious action that defy the borders established by polite, public religion. But with each of these there remains the question of whether it is *India*'s real religion—the religion of the nation as such, something not just dispersed through the national religious consciousness but serving to strengthen it by connection and make it resilient. The claim has been that bhakti alone performs this function. Outsiders like the great linguist George Grierson sometimes confused it for personal monotheism, and modern-day Hindus have often followed suit, but in the idea of the bhakti movement we have the affirmation that the nature or number of the deity/deities concerned is secondary.[5] What matters is the heartfelt, intrinsically social sense of connectedness that emerges in the worshipper. That socially divine sense of connectedness traces a pulmonary system that makes the nation throb with life.

The word "bhakti" is notoriously hard to translate. The Sanskrit term *bhakti* is an action noun derived from the verbal root *bhaj-*, meaning broadly "to share, to possess," and occupies a semantic field that embraces the notions of belonging, being loyal, even liking. References to bhakti by the grammarian Panini reveal this range of meanings in the fourth century B.C.E., but suggest that even then the word's most important usage was in the domain of religion. Panini speaks of "bhakti to Vāsudeva," that is, Krishna. Typically such devotion is shared with other bhaktas (that is, those touched by bhakti), to the extent that it has sometimes been said that the most basic bhakti of all is bhakti to one's fellow bhaktas. This strengthens the hand of those who would reach for a word like "participation" in an effort to convey in English what bhakti is all about.[6]

Despite the human focus, a conviction about the deep and sometimes surprising, even upsetting agency of God in creating communities of bhaktas is also part of the picture. Across the whole span of north India today, one of the most common designations for divinity is *bhagavān*, which means in its Sanskrit origins "one who shares out" and thus designates the giver of blessings. The greatest of these blessings is often said to be the presence of God per se. In reviewing this nexus of Sanskrit meanings J. A. B. van Buitenen has said, "The vast concept of sharing allowed of specialization, and meanings developed in two directions: offering someone else a share in something; and accepting or adopting something as one's allotted share. The latter usage evolved further into 'declaring for, choosing for.' It is the last of these meanings that governs later uses of the word *bhakti*."[7] True enough, but van Buitenen could also have gone on to say that the former usage is the one that gives us the word *bhagavān* in modern vernacular parlance: God who shares.

In an important article, John Cort, a scholar of Jainism, has quoted this passage and questioned its preoccupation with etymology. Cort's objection is twofold. First, the search for a unitive etymology obscures the fact that, as he says, "Bhakti is not one single thing." Second, it downplays the fact that bhakti is "primarily what bhaktas have said it is" rather than being some primordial entity enshrined in ancient Sanskrit usage—the sort of thing that only scholars have access to.[8] Cort urges us instead to understand bhakti as being a spectrum extending from "sober veneration" at one extreme (the Jain register) to "frenzied possession" at the other, this being a defining feature of much early south Indian Hindu bhakti.[9] Better still, he says, "we need to think in terms of mutually interpenetrating fields of influence" when we consider the historical sweep of bhakti in South Asia.[10] Only this will enable us to perceive the complex patterns of relationship that connect Jains, Buddhists, Vaishnavas, Shaivas, and many others—and not only along vectors suggested by the labels we have just adopted.

I applaud everything Cort has just said, yet I do see a problem. What are we to say when bhaktas themselves insist on the notion that bhakti is a single thing, something with a single, unitary history? That, in fact, is precisely what began to happen at a certain point in Indian history, and the power of that notion is very much with us today. We encounter it not only in English but in other languages widely used in India. To be sure, there are significant variations by language and region, but almost always one finds the idea that bhakti exerted a unifying force over Indian history and culture that lasted from the sixth century at least until the sixteenth, and did so in an arc that swept from south to north.

This bhakti movement idea has become so widespread that nowadays it functions as historiographical common sense. We meet it in textbooks used in India at all levels and in many languages, in books about Hinduism and South Asian history that are produced abroad, on the Internet, in repositories of collective wisdom that range from the *Encyclopedia Britannica* to *Wikipedia*, in school curricula and examinations, in manuals that prepare candidates to compete for positions in the Indian Administrative Service, on television and All India Radio, and in countless conversations between real live people, whether bhaktas or skeptics or some mixture of both. As an idea about history, thus, this idea has itself become an important fact of Indian history. The guiding themes of the bhakti movement are believed to present a formidable challenge to the ritually oriented Vedic traditions preserved by the Brahman caste that have so often been seen as lying at the core of Hindu religion.[11] To wit,

(1) The bhakti movement is characterized by the singing of devotional songs composed in vernacular languages by poets who have attained the status of saints.
(2) It celebrates a sense of the mutual companionship on the part of many of these poet-saints.
(3) It displays a tendency to consider both sexes and all strata of society as potential devotees.

(4) It trumpets the cultivation of personal experience as against external or ritual punctiliousness, or at least clearly prioritizes the former in relation to the latter.[12]

None of these defining themes can pass the test of Brahmanical, Vedic religion—or rather, to put it the other way around, all of them contest the authority of Brahmanical or upper-caste ideas, practices, and institutions. The bhakti mirror shows Brahmanical Hinduism in a cruel light—or rather, some would say, shows it for the cruel thing it actually is. No wonder, then, that on more than one occasion the servants of Brahmanical religion have reached for that bhakti mirror and tried to change its angle of vision, co-opting bhakti and making it their own. And yet, there is more to the story than co-optation. Other Brahmin actors felt the bhakti impulse deeply enough to train its mirror willingly on the regressive habits associated with the class to which they themselves belonged. This is what Rāmānand is said to have done, displaying the progressive, dissenting disposition that in Tagore's vision made him ready to embrace Ravidās. For Brahmins such as these, as for all the others, bhakti was liberation—a genre of performed self-knowledge that enabled them to situate themselves in the broader social and political fabric in genuinely new ways. If bhakti was a movement, as its historiographical devotees insist, they were a part of it.[13]

How could they not be? For many who have told the story of the bhakti movement, bhakti appears as an independent, living being, something that rides above distinctions of power and status with an agency all its own—a persuasive, at times overwhelming presence that can move through history and shape it to its own ends. To see things thus is to challenge a major way in which Hindus have conceptualized the religious heritage that makes them who they are: *sanātana dharma,* the idea that Hinduism, often interpreted not as a doctrinal system but as a way of life, is uniquely stable, reliable, unmoving; something perennial and eternal.[14] Bhakti, by contrast, feels to Hindus like something that characteristically moves, travels, and develops. In the image of the bhakti movement we meet a bhakti that is organic and has a life of its own. It is capable of change and development; indeed, it has moved history.

One of the most significant ways in which it has moved history, say partisans of the bhakti movement idea, is by prioritizing vernacular speech, giving ordinary people the literary and musical voice they craved.

According to the bhakti movement paradigm, it was the radical perception that the legitimate demands of religion had to be expressed in speech people could actually understand—and that they themselves generated—that brought India's vernacular languages to the fore in the millennium that began in 500 C.E., challenging the hegemony of Sanskrit. This is a further implication of the first item on the four-point list we have offered just above.

This view of history—that bhakti is about deep social reform, that its natural vehicle is vernacular speech, and that bhakti therefore generated the turn from Sanskrit to the vernaculars in the course of Indian history—has recently come under a withering attack in the writings of Sheldon Pollock. Pollock argues that the first expressive uses of Indian vernacular literatures (or at least those to which we have access through written records) occurred not in some independent realm of bhakti but in court settings and with political or aesthetic, not religious, intent. In his masterwork *The Language of the Gods in the World of Men,* Pollock states:

> If the vernacular polity created in southern Asia during the first five centuries of the second millennium remains obscure as a structure for exercising power, there is no doubt that the vernacularization project was initiated (in many cases) and prompted and practiced (in most cases) by those who exercised such power. This judgment is . . . completely at odds with scholarly opinion, which holds that religious consciousness and especially the religious movement now called devotionalism *(bhakti)* constituted the engine of the vernacular revolution . . . The standard interpretation, then, of the relationship of religion and vernacularization, especially the *bhakti* axiom, rests on a foundation of both general and particular imprecision. We seem to have been misled by yet another Protestant presupposition . . . about the role of the Reformation in the growth of vernacular languages. In addition, substantial and long-term primary evidence, such as that supplied by the development of Kannada, demonstrates positively that the general consensus is erroneous. These data also suggest, more broadly, that a religious transformation of vernacular culture and consciousness, where it does occur, is typically secondary to, and only made possible or necessary by, a foregoing political transformation.[15]

In pursuing this challenge to "scholarly opinion"—that is, the bhakti movement idea—Pollock elaborates a new framework for understanding how "the vernacular millennium" came to be in India. Delving into the specifics of dynastic history and literary formation across what he calls the Sanskrit cosmopolis, he shows how each major regional vernacular developed independently, though according to a pattern that was often loosely shared from region to region. The principal drive, in each case, was a ruler's desire to mobilize the specificities of Place (Pollock capitalizes "place" in deference to the particular literary history of the term *deśī*) in the service of greater political cohesion and the desire on the part of him and his courtiers to perform the same work of cohesion in the literary realm, as well.[16] This knowledge/power way of framing things may not relegate bhakti entirely to the sidelines in each case, but certainly it sets bhakti on a playing field where other concerns tend to be dominant. Pollock is often at pains to show how the religious register has been overemphasized in earlier treatments of vernacularization, and he does not fail to point out that even when the vernacular option was there, some bhakti authors continued to choose Sanskrit as their medium.[17]

Pollock's challenge to the existence and agency of the bhakti movement is a major one, and we will need to consider its implications before we conclude (in Chapter 7). For the moment, though, let us just take it as a further impetus to understanding how this mistaken idea—from Pollock's point of view—gained the sort of traction that makes it necessary for him to beat it back. How did the idea of the bhakti movement become such an important intellectual force? Where did it come from? When? Under what circumstances, political and otherwise? In what languages and owing to the efforts of what groups and individuals? To answer these questions is the task that lies ahead. In doing so, we will see how the idea of the bhakti movement is itself a product of history.

We will begin with the twentieth century, when the idea of the bhakti movement fully crystallized. The mid-twentieth century was, of course, the moment in which India gained its independence, and in compelling ways the magnet of independence was crucial for shaping the notion of the bhakti movement. Yet there was a colonial background as well, particularly in the writings of British intellectuals such as George Grierson and J. N. Farquhar. So was this idea indigenous or not? Conceptually, was it a product of Indians or others? Linguistically, was it a child of English or something that emerged from one of India's homegrown languages, perhaps Hindi? In Chapter 1 we start at the end of the bhakti movement story—seemingly the moment of its triumph—and delve into such discontents as these, ultimately coming to rest on Hazariprasad Dvivedi, the brilliant Hindi literary critic who was more than any other person responsible for giving us the idea of the bhakti movement in its present, canonical form.

Then we move back, searching for the foundations on which this persuasive historiographical edifice rested, not so much at the level of fact but of concept. In Chapter 2 we investigate what we might call the inner master narrative of the master narrative of the bhakti movement: the story of how bhakti, lovingly portrayed as a hypostatic female being, made the historic transit from south to north. This tale has an encompassingly literary sensibility—it emerges in a celebration of that great Vaishnava text, the *Bhāgavata Purāṇa*—but it also has a real-world edge. We will see how this earlier kernel of the bhakti movement story, like its more fully developed twentieth-century cousin, makes sense only in light of a major emerging political formation. This time it is not the creation of the Indian nation in a contest with the British, but the consolidation of the Mughal state four centuries before. That means, of course, that this was not a southern idea, as might seem dictated by its content, but a northern one.

The early modernity of Mughal rule proves crucial to another major constituent of the bhakti movement story, as well. This is arguably the central lode in the ore, and it occupies the three central chapters of our book. I speak of the motif of the four *sampradāys* (Skt. *sampradāya*), four traditions of teaching and initiation that were later believed to have provided the central channels of communication by means of which the bhakti movement flowed from south to north. Here we have a different version of the story of south-moves-north, but once again we discover that it is northern in its origins and not southern. Again the Mughals are involved, but now we can see much more clearly the imprint of their chief collaborators, the Kachvahas of Āmer. We will bring this complex into view from two vantage points—first Galtā, in the immediate vicinity of Āmer (Chapter 3); then Brindavan, much closer to the center of Mughal power (Chapter 4). Then finally we will see what happened to the concept of the four *sampradāys* as the Mughal star began to fade but that of the Kachvahas remained bright (Chapter 5). After the death of the emperor Aurangzeb, the Kachvaha Raja Jaisingh II (r. 1699–1743) envisioned a new sort of imperium, whose core he laid out in the planned city of Jaipur, built to be his capital. In his efforts to control the religious politics that swirled around him, Jaisingh seized upon the concept of the four *sampradāys,* giving this early formulation of the bhakti movement narrative its first chance to carry institutional weight in what we so perilously call the real world.

The impact of the concept of the four *sampradāys* was long-lasting, as we discover when we return to twentieth-century developments in Chapter 6. At this point we are equipped to engage Tagore and his circle with new seriousness, moving eastward from the Mughal/Kachvaha axis marked by Galtā, Brindavan, and Jaipur to Bengal, which had by then become the headquarters of British power. There we set up shop in Shantiniketan, the little town where Tagore established the utopian educational institution he called Viśva Bhāratī, "India's, the World's" or in a different sense "All of India." As that title suggests, we will feel the magnetism of the modern nation-state, even if Tagore himself had reservations about the concept. More important for our story, actually, is Hazariprasad Dvivedi, who came from a village northeast of Banaras and would return to Banaras not once but twice in the course of his professional career. Yet it was as a member of the faculty at Shantiniketan that Dvivedi first articulated his understanding of the *bhakti āndolan,* the Hindi analogue to English's "the bhakti movement." As we learn in Chapter 1, Hindi's national aspirations were crucially important as the concept of the bhakti movement began to take on lasting form. We see this again in Chapter 6, but discover that the Bengali background also made a difference. In surprising ways we find that the great Bengali reformer Rammohan Roy, founder of the Brahmo Samaj and the man frequently dubbed "the father of modern India," also has a role to play in our story—not personally but through his successors.

As we move through these several articulations of the bhakti movement idea—the crystallized modern form and its prototypes—we will also have to deal with what is left out, marginalized, or downright othered. Where are Muslims? Where are Dalits? Where are independent communities such as the Sikhs, who are often claimed to be a part of the bhakti movement and who sometimes make that claim themselves? And what about the south? The north, we will see, is the prime mover, but at what point does the south become an active participant in generating the great narrative that casts this region in such a crucial role?

We will touch upon each of these issues as we move along, but they take center stage in our final chapter, "What Should the Bhakti Movement

Be?" There we will also have to face one last question, the ultimate one. Does an awareness of the historical contingencies that have produced the idea of the bhakti movement mean we have to consign it to the dustbins of history, or can we take that very historical embeddedness as a sign that this is a concept worth saving? What in good conscience can be salvaged from a story that is in a certain sense dated but that continues to mean so much to so many? Chapter 7 brings us up to the present day, showing how this great monsoon of an idea keeps sending out squalls and downpours—a storm of songs to the last.

1

The Bhakti Movement and Its Discontents

The Bhakti Archive

The bhakti archive of India—its corpus of vernacular religious songs ready to be sung at any moment—provides the country with a sense of shared richness that has no peer. Individual gems of Sanskrit poetry may be cut finer, but vernacular bhakti digs deeper into the national soul. Bhakti poems in many Indian languages are sung and recited in homes, in the bazaar, in temples, on cassettes and CDs, in movies, in singing groups, in the fields, on the job. They are on the tongues of millions of individual Indians as they face a personal challenge or feel a moment of joy. They utter humor and protest, suffering and satisfaction; they bring to mind beloved realms of story; they are addressed to many gods, to one god, or none. And there are life stories of the singers to match.[1]

This living bhakti archive was an immense resource in the cause of national integration. It led everywhere—a gorgeous, finely woven fabric just waiting to be donned by the new nation-state. But why did it need to be narrativized to do so? Why did these expressions of bhakti, coming from all around the subcontinent and from many points in time, need to be consolidated into a single, seemingly definitive narrative as the first decades of the twentieth century progressed?

At a certain level the answer is simple. Nations need histories, as has been stressed in a spate of scholarly studies pioneered by Benedict Anderson's *Imagined Communities* and Eric Hobsbawm and Terence Ranger's *The Invention of Tradition*.[2] Yet the Indian situation was more specific: Indians required a particular kind of history. Taught in British schools, their intellectual leaders were conditioned to expect a broad historiographical scheme that followed a tripartite progression from ancient to medieval to modern.

That framework proved hard to displace. What was easier to do was to reshape the medieval that lay at its core. Rather than assigning the long period between classical Gupta splendor and the latter-day greatness of British modernity to a long intervening lull in which Islamic polities were dominant, as British historians had done, their Indian counterparts worked to make the middle period more distinctively their own. The British largely told the story of their country's rise to power in India as a benevolent alternative to a weakened Mughal state. Both regimes were foreign in origin, imposing themselves almost necessarily over the weak, balkanized mass that was India itself. Nationalist historians could not accept this. They required a sense of the medieval that gave indigenous coherence to this crucial period, even if its political impact was less than clear. Not only must it serve as a realm that could be interpreted as resisting a rule that was ultimately foreign (some granted that the Mughals eventually became quite domesticated), it had to have sufficient internal coherence to give birth at the same time to a distinctly indigenous modernity. It had to presage the independent Indian state and prepare its way. Appropriately narrativized, bhakti could do this job—and without overly alienating Indian Muslims, many of whom could be seen as forming part of the broader bhakti domain. After all, it was India—and specifically Indian bhakti—that made Indian Islam so different from what was to be seen in the Middle East.[3]

And so the stage was set, but before we pull back the curtain we need to introduce ourselves briefly to the songs themselves. To do that, suppose we start with Ravidās, whom we have already met. In the poem by which he is perhaps best known—attested already by the end of the sixteenth century—Ravidās speaks, so to speak, with his body. His makes his leatherworker's stigma a part of the poem and shares it with his Lord, whose good name ironically depends on it. He wonders what the difference between them is anyway:

> You and me, me and you: What difference does it make?
> It's like gold and a golden bracelet, water and a wave.
> You who have no limits, if I didn't sin
> how could they call you Redeemer of Fallen Men?

You're Leader, Controller, the one who rules within,
  but lords are known by their people, people by their lord.
This body: I'm praying. Turn your thoughts to me.
  Ravidās: Who else can explain what this mixing means?[4]

In another poem, similarly, Ravidās makes his lowly caste occupation serve as the specific theater of bhakti, turning the things of this world on their head:

I've never known how to tan or sew,
  though people come to me for shoes.
I haven't the needle to make the holes
  or even the tool to cut the thread.
Others stitch and knot, and tie themselves in knots
  while I, who do not knot, break free.
I keep saying Rām and Rām, says Ravidās,
  and Death keeps his business to himself.[5]

Where do such poems come from? Not just from the experience of a particular individual—the usual explanation—but from long-shared genres and a deep history of oral intertextuality. Tagore was exploring this reality in "Sweet Mercy" when he attributed Ravidās's inspiration to Rāmānand, a Vaishnava ascetic of the most expansive sort who was reputed to have been the great messenger between southern and northern bhakti traditions. If we let this hagiographical link be our cue, we can quickly see the kind of thing Tagore could have had in mind. The great ninth-century poet Nammāḻvār, artistic paragon of the Śrī Vaishnava *sampradāy* to which Rāmānand is held to have belonged, gave us the following meditation on the mystery of the self's elusive dual/nondual involvement with the Lord, the sort of thing that was exposited by Ravidās in "You and Me." Here are Nammāḻvār's Tamil words in A. K. Ramanujan's translation:

You dwell in heaven
  stand on the sacred mountain
  sleep on the ocean
  roll around in the earth

yet hidden everywhere
  you grow
  invisibly:

moving within
    numberless outer worlds

playing within my heart
    yet not showing your body

will you always play hide and seek?[6]

If we look elsewhere in the great treasury of south Indian bhakti poetry, we can also find precedents for "I've never known how to tan or sew." One interesting example is provided not by a Dalit poet simultaneously announcing and renouncing his stigmatized body and caste occupation, but by a woman poet who implicitly announces her gendered body while at the same time renouncing what the world thinks has to go with it: a decent regimen of garbing. This is the voice of the twelfth-century Kannada Shaiva poet Mahādevīakkā, who insisted on going about in public with no clothes:

People,
male and female,
blush when a cloth covering their shame
comes loose.
                When the lord of lives
lives drowned without a face
in the world, how can you be modest?

When all the world is the eye of the lord,
onlooking everywhere, what can you
cover and conceal?[7]

The four poems we have just heard, with their intriguing pair of parallels, provide us with only a tiny sample of the echoes that sound across the range and depth of India's bhakti archive, but even this sliver suggests the power of the resource upon which some of the architects of independent India hoped to draw as they advanced the cause of national integration by appealing to this countrywide bhakti legacy. And the more we know about this archive, the stronger seems its appeal. Beyond poems of contestation like these, and beyond the much broader genus to which they belong—poems that appeal to personal experience—lies a vast repertoire of bhakti compositions that open onto a different sort of narrative experience: widely known stories that appear in the *Mahābhārata* or *Rāmāyaṇa,* or tales of Krishna such as those that occupy a great swath of the *Bhāgavata Purāna*. We generally think of the epic texts where these tales appear as having been composed in Sanskrit, and the shoe certainly fits in the case of the *Bhāgavata Purāna*, but these have vernacular analogues as well—not just because the Sanskrit epics were translated into regional languages in the course of the second millennium C.E. but because the stories they contained had always had lives in the languages people actually spoke.

In Hindi a distinction is commonly made between *nirguṇ* and *saguṇ* aspects of bhakti poetry—"without attributes" and "with attributes." These terms derive from a long-standing theological contrast between two ways of conceiving divinity—apophatic and world-infusing—and the contrasting stances that devotees must cultivate to approach the Deity in these very different modes. In regard to bhakti poetry, however, the contrast comes to have a related meaning: a contrast between the poetry of ordinary life ("attributeless" in this sense: lacking the plot of a divine narrative) and poetry that situates itself in the charmed ("attributeful") realm of divine play or *līlā*—stories of how Rām and Sītā, Krishna and Radha, Shiva and Shakti, or a host of other divine figures lived their lives for a time as earthly beings. Bhakti poets speaking every major Indian language have piped into these *līlās*, creating a polyglot repository of devotional story that can be heard from one end of the country to the other. Poems of this sort complement poems we can imagine as reflecting the individual experience of Ravidās, Nammāḻvār, Mahādevīakkā, or any number of other poet-saints.

We can work back from sixteenth-century north India in this mode too, just as we earlier did with Ravidās. We might begin, for example, with a poem of Sūrdās in which he assumes the persona of a cowherding woman *(gopī)* who is concerned about a friend—perhaps Radha—who has been deserted by Krishna and is left forlorn. He must have chased off after another beauty, she suspects. Despite the fact that Sūrdās speaks through this woman of Braj, he must also register his own identity, as the Hindi genre in which he works demands, and he does this by "signing" what would originally have been an oral composition in the final verse:

> Hand on her cheeks, Mother, arm around her knees,
>   she's writing lines with her fingernails.
> She sits with her worries and thoughts, lovely woman,
>   and contemplates his Love-god's mouth and clothes.

Her eyes fill with tears. She heaves a set of sighs.
    Herder girl, she damns the way so many days have passed
With the lotus-eyed one so far off in Mathura,
    whose virtues even thousand-hooded serpents do not know.
Kānh has made a lie of the time he said he'd come.
    If at night she sees more lightning, friend,
        how will she survive?
Sūrdās's Lord has come in a flash and gone,
    a dancing street performer—
        many costumes, many roles.[8]

We do not have to search long to find a parallel for this poem from the earlier south. Take Nammāḻvār. In the poem that follows, unlike that of Sūrdās, the personal presence behind the female persona he adopts is not indicated by an overt signature, but his identity is well understood by those who hear him, since his poems have been so carefully collected and are often performed in a liturgical moment where his role as an exemplary devotee is being celebrated. Here he speaks as a longing *gopī:*

Evening has come,
    but not the Dark One.

The bulls,
    their bells jingling,
    have mated with the cows
and the cows are frisky.

The flutes play cruel songs,
    bees flutter in their bright
        white jasmine
    and the blue-black lily.

The sea leaps into the sky
    and cries aloud.

Without him here,
    what shall I say?
    how shall I survive?[9]

In songs such as these, bhakti poets of all regions and periods bivouac on the broad plain of shared Hindu narrative, and there are analogues from the Sufi side of things as well. Those Sufis tended also, however, to celebrate the fact that the world itself is structured as a testament to the imprint of its Creator. A Hindu poet who takes an interest in the fabulous domain of story—a *saguṇ* poet—may also stop to marvel at how the world is positivity shot through with divinity in its own terms, even before we discover a narrative line to expound and embroider that fact. Thus Tulsīdās, another sixteenth-century figure from north India, spoke for many when he said,

> Knowing the whole world to be infused with Sītā and Rām,
> I make my obeisance, pressing palm to palm.[10]

This couplet comes from the opening sections of Tulsī's renowned *Rāmcaritmānas* (Spiritual Lake of the Acts of Rām), which he composed in the Avadhi dialect of Hindi, following the pattern of earlier Sufi epics. In many ways their impact on him is clear.[11] Whether he was also aware of other vernacular *Rāmāyaṇas* that had been composed throughout the subcontinent before he attempted his own, we do not know, but by now it will come as no surprise that a Tamil *Rāmāyaṇa* composed by Kampaṉ preceded Tulsī's by four centuries. In recasting the *Rāmāyaṇa* as an Avadhi text, Tulsīdās drew not only on other vernacular versions but also on a plurality of Sanskrit ones. The borders between spoken languages and Sanskrit are not firm in this arena: both could give expression to sentiments and stories such as these. And the same could be said of the very porous borders separating "secular" eroticism—the poetry of court or courtesan—from the narratively embedded "divine" love poetry we have just been considering. Such connections—between languages and periods, between religious communities both Muslim and Hindu, and between sacred registers and secular—all served to enhance the value of bhakti as a resource in the cause of national integration, and to suggest that it had been doing that work for centuries.

The Great Integrators

To see how this vast bhakti archive was specifically marshaled in the service of nation-building, we can do no better than to turn to a moment at the end of 1964 when Indira Gandhi, then the minister of information and broadcasting of the central government of India, called upon the great Sanskritist V. Raghavan to deliver the Sardar Vallabhbhai Patel Memorial Lectures in New Delhi. In these high-profile lectures, Raghavan took on the task of showing "the great role of consolidation" that had been played over the course of centuries by India's poet-saints.[12] Unlike the hollow "conferences and resolutions" that resounded in the public life of his own day, said Raghavan, these agents and exemplars of the bhakti movement had been able to achieve the real integration—the emotional integration—upon which the territorial integration of India had relied and would continue to rely.[13] Here was the idea of the bhakti movement full force.

In his first of his two Patel Lectures, Raghavan took his listeners on a long and loving historical circumambulation of India, which, using traditional Hindu terms, he called a "*pradakshiṇa-yātrā* of Bhārata in the company of the saints."[14] It began and ended in Tamilnadu, in the far south, and it proceeded in a clockwise direction, as any *pradakṣinā* must by definition do, keeping the object of veneration—in this case, India itself—on one's right. In achieving this full circle, Raghavan did have to let chronology take second place to geography at one important point—when he had arrived at Bengal, in the east. He had led his hearers from the Tamil poet-saints of the sixth through eighth centuries up the west coast through Maharashtra, Gujarat, and Sindh (thirteenth through seventeenth centuries), into the Himalayas as far as Kashmir (Lālded, fourteenth century), down to the Punjab (Nānak and the Sikh Gurus, sixteenth century and following), across the Gangetic plain to sixteenth-century Assam (Śaṃkaradeva, sixteenth century) and into Bengal, where he ended with the eighteenth-century Shākta saint Rāmprasād. Then he regrouped, noting that Rāmprasād had his Vaishnava side too, which gave him his segue to the ecstatic Chaitanya (ca. 1500) as a predecessor and the much earlier Bengali poet Jayadev—a writer of Sanskrit, yes, but with famously vernacular overtones. Since the *Gītagovinda* had spawned a series of traditions of performance and commentary in the Dravidian languages of the south, that fact allowed him to continue his journey until he arrived where he had begun, in his own native Tamilnadu. This was a tour de force—even to the point of exercising a little force over history to make the circumambulation come out right—and it made it seem that Raghavan himself was but the most recent in the ancient and honorable company of religious troubadours he described. He called them in his title "The Great Integrators: The Saint-Singers of India."

Dr. Raghavan's audience far exceeded the group of dignitaries and educated citizens of the capital who assembled to hear the lectures

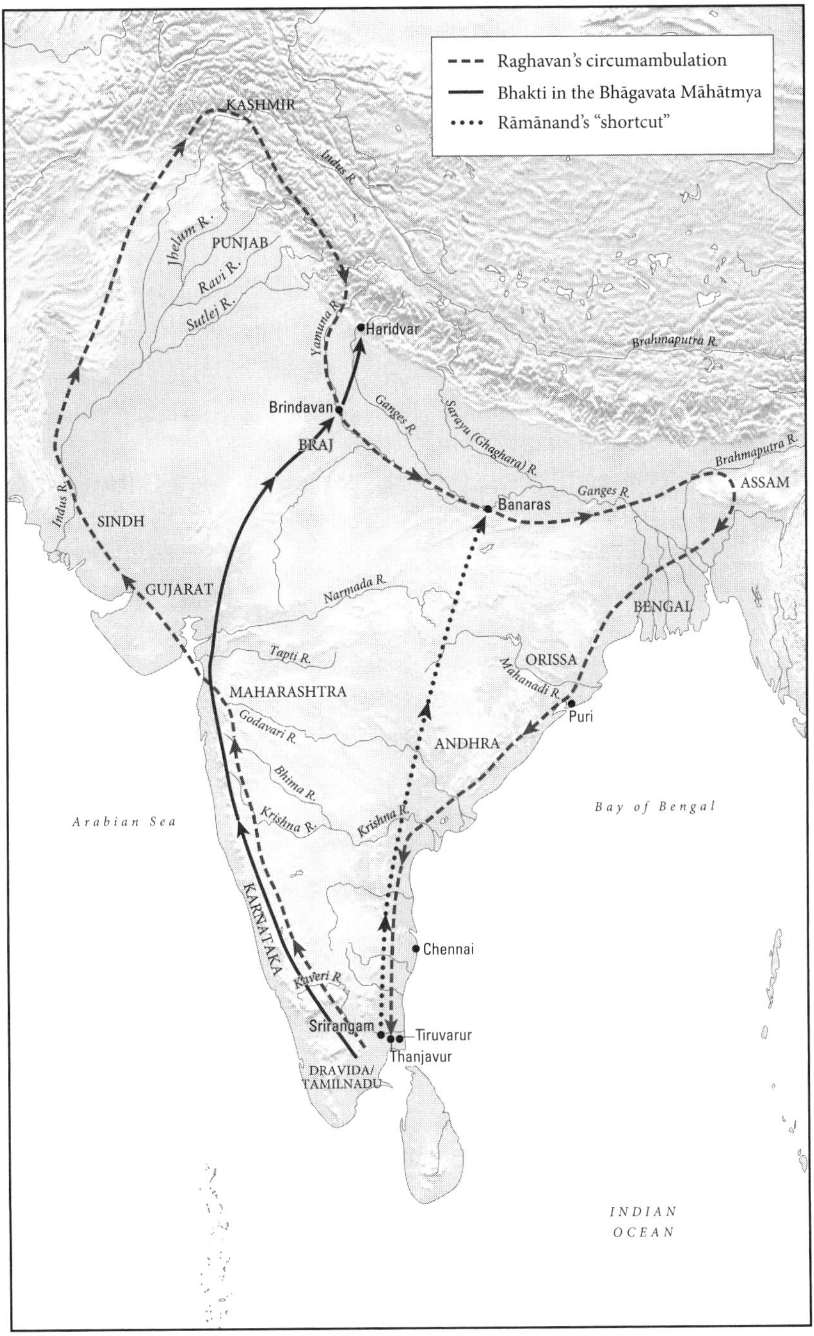

Map 1. The bhakti movement: three trajectories. Courtesy of Isabelle Lewis.

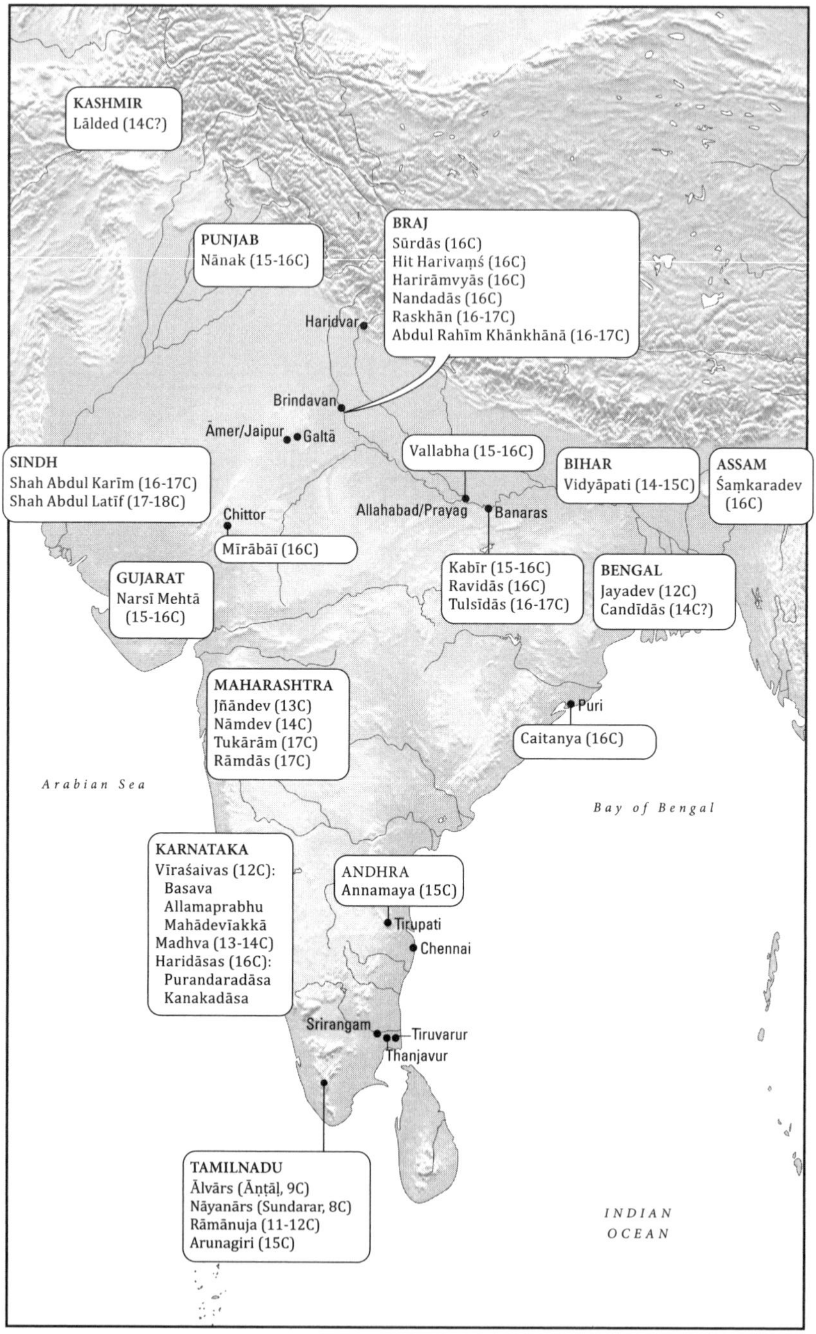

Map 2. Major figures in the bhakti movement narrative according to V. Raghavan. Courtesy of Isabelle Lewis.

themselves. Not only did the Ministry of Information and Broadcasting subsequently publish these lectures with a seventy-five-page anthology of selected compositions attributed to these singer-saints—in English translation—but it immediately broadcast large portions of the lectures to all parts of the country over All India Radio.[15] Hence they were heard a thousand miles away from Delhi in Chennai, for example, where Raghavan was professor of Sanskrit at the University of Madras, or even further south in Tiruvarur, where he had grown up.

In his preface to the published version of the Patel Lectures, Raghavan drew special attention to these origins:

> When at school in my native place Tiruvarur—an ancient centre famed in the annals of South Indian history, devotion and the arts of music and dance—I was drawn into the *bhajana-goshṭīs* which went round the town, particularly in *Mārgaśīrsha* (December–January), singing devotional songs in different languages, prayer formulas *(nāmāvalis)*, etc. . . . No one could be a votary of Karnatak music without coming under the influence of the religious and spiritual message of the repertoire of that art; nor could one study the history of Indian music, or even of Indian literature, without having to study at the same time the devotional movements that had swept the country.[16]

Thus we form the impression that Raghavan's fabled Sanskrit learning was only incidental to the task at hand—a second order of creativity. India's spoken languages mattered more:

> The south Indian institution of *Harikathā* or *Kālakshepa,* especially of Tamilnadu, offers the best illustration, where in the course of a Tamil discourse, the life of a Telugu, Marathi, Hindi or Bengali saint is expounded; among the songs sung are Telugu *kīrtanas* of Tyāgarāja, Kannada *padas* of Purandaradāsa, *sākis, daṇḍīs* and *ovīs* from Mahārāshtra saints, Mīrā's lyrics, as also songs of Kabīr and quotations from Tulasi's *Rāmāyaṇa.* In *bhajan-mandirs* and special festivals for *kīrtan* in Tamilnadu, the same wide variety in the recitals of the songs of the saints from all parts of the land can be heard.[17]

It wasn't that Raghavan thought Sanskrit had failed to play a role in this exuberantly vernacular realm. He specifically spoke of the mutual influence of "the learned and popular traditions" and noted that there were times when persons able to move in both mediums offered a special service by translating Sanskrit works into the spoken tongue.[18] He especially mentioned the *Bhagavad Gītā* and the *Bhāgavata Purāṇa* in this regard, since their translators (he mentioned Jñānadev of Maharashtra and Śaṃkaradeva of Assam) had had a major impact on history. Furthermore, he reflected, "owing to the one-sided nature of the records" we do not know as much as we should about the vernacular literary activities of many figures whose Sanskrit works are preserved.[19] But even more than this Sanskrit-to-vernacular translation activity, Raghavan was interested in vernacular-to-vernacular processes of transmission—the sort that he himself had witnessed as a boy growing up in Tiruvarur.

Like others who have told the bhakti movement story, especially in a quasi-political context, Raghavan's purpose was to paint a sweeping panorama of India's democratic instincts as they had existed before the word "democracy" was coined.[20] Bhakti, he said, is "a democratic doctrine which consolidates all people without distinction of caste, community, nationality, or sex"—and the bhakti movement is the story of that consolidation over the course of centuries. He gives due weight to other features of "this song-literature of the saints": a shared emphasis on the name of the Lord and on the guru; a clarity about the true, simple form of worship; a "reformist zeal and denunciation of sham and deception as also of empty formalism"; and a "sense of the unity of all paths" and concomitantly a certain "*advaitic* tone and the preference for monism." But at the end of the day he is most pointedly attentive to the bhakti movement's socially inclusive nature, and occasionally he makes his case for catholic diversity in an even stronger way: "The large galaxy of saints from all over the country is made up largely of those who arose from the non-literary classes." Here then we have a shared formation of consciousness that naturally served, when the time came, to undergird the nation in its current form. It had great significance in "preparing the ground for centuries for the evolution of an increasing sense of equality, and in the bringing up of the masses and educating them in the essential culture of the land."[21]

I have already hinted that from its earliest conception the idea of the bhakti movement was a northern effort to ground its own institutions and practices in a southern past that it believed to be older and somehow more authentic than its own. Here too we see the same pattern. The capital, where Raghavan spoke, was and is located in the far north. Raghavan was from the south, and carried with him the particular cultural capital of that region, including especially the prestige of its tradition of unbroken

Sanskrit learning. Yes, he was emphasizing the vernacular aspect of things, but few of his listeners would have lost sight of the fact that Professor Raghavan was probably the world's most famous Sanskritist. Yes, he acknowledged that the north had also had a special role to play in generating the bhakti movement: before he began his historical circumambulation he spoke of the impetus of the Buddhist Siddhas in the east and northeast, and of the commanding figure of Gorakhnāth, "who popularized Yoga."[22] But his core narrative—both in its inception and at its conclusion—was anchored to a southern base. Anyone in the central administration concerned about national integration, that well-funded cultural shibboleth, would have been pleased to see this southern ingredient stirred so effectively into the broth of a national entity whose capital and official language (Hindi) were located so far north.

In subsequent chapters of this book, we will delve into the history of how several premodern formulations laid the basis for the modern idea of the bhakti movement and were incorporated into it as the twentieth century advanced. In each case, we will see, fresh political configurations served as relevant background for what happened in the realm of ideas. Here we see the same pattern in spades. After all, it was the daughter of the nation's first prime minister who invited Raghavan to give the Patel Lectures. A narrative that would support the state by drawing India's religious minorities into a wide-tent vision of the bhakti movement—especially if it did not bear the Hindu label explicitly—was clearly what she sought.[23] Such a narrative could be majoritarian without being exclusive. Raghavan's portrait of "the great integrators" expressed eager appreciation for the hospitality shown by Hindus to other religious groups—their "spirit of tolerance" to be found in their songs—and their tendency to encompass rather than exclude, and did so without hinting at anything that could be construed as narrowly brahminical. Impeccably educated, famously liberal, deeply southern, and patently Brahman, Raghavan was perfectly suited to the task of putting forth a narrative of Hinduism from the ground up, Hinduism in a bhakti mode—Hinduism, in fact, beyond Hinduism.

He told the story with elegance and clarity. Vaishnava and Shaiva singer-saints had been equally important in getting the movement rolling, both groups being eager to reclaim Tamilnadu against Buddhists and Jains for "the older faith"—that is, the "Vedic, Purāṇic and devotional path." Then, by means of a quotation from the Shaiva saint Māṇikavācakar, Raghavan pulled the great philosopher-theologian Śaṃkara into the narrative as a person of great genius and personal charisma, as well as being a hymnist in his own right. His Vaishnava counterpart Rāmūnuja followed seamlessly afterward (their deep philosophical differences went unmentioned), and Raghavan accepted the notion that it was through Rāmānand, whom he connects to Rāmūnuja as "a follower of the devotional school of Vedanta," that we came to have "the *Bhakti* movements of the north, Kabīr, Tulasi and others owing allegiance to him."[24] As we shall see in Chapter 3, to claim Rāmānand as a shortcut from south to north was actually to say quite a mouthful.

Yet this notion of a Śrī Vaishnava tradition that connected Rāmūnuja to Rāmānand and thereby headed directly northward was actually not the principal focus of the plot that Raghavan wanted to develop. He spent far more time celebrating a second Śrī Vaishnava trajectory—more literary and liturgical in tone—that connected these Tamilians with other parts of the south in a more elaborate sequence, the first steps along his circumambulatory path. In this more detailed account, we learn how the *āḻvārs* and *nāyaṉmārs*, Vaishnava and Shaiva bhaktas of the sixth through ninth centuries respectively, drew from different social groups as well as different regions of Tamilnadu: they were integrators in more than one way. Later, by good fortune, they were "salvaged and organized" into parallel Vaishnava and Shaiva devotional anthologies under the helpful umbrella of royal patronage in the Chola period. Well known in Śrī Vaishnava circles and to the Smārta Shaiva community into which Raghavan had been born, these liturgical collections are called the *Divyaprabandham* and the *Tevāram,* and Raghavan was particularly interested in the sheer number of compositions that were gathered there. He also took note of subsequent mandates, which came quite soon, that they be regularly performed, and was pleased to observe that the *Tevāram,* the Shaiva hymnbook anthology, is "the earliest corpus of south Indian music compositions."[25]

Drawing attention to several particularly significant Tamil composers and performers of later centuries, he then crossed the border to Karnataka and there, once again, focused on two distinctive groups of Vaishnava and Shaiva singer-saints, the Haridāsas and the Vīraśaivas. He distinguished the Haridāsas' preference for the performance of *pada* lyrics from the "sententious prose" of the Vīraśaivas: their *vacanas*.[26] Like many others throughout the twentieth century, Raghavan found the Vīraśaivas particularly praiseworthy for challenging caste distinctions—a crucial "democratic" motif, as we have seen—while the Haridāsas stood out for being a "popular movement" of a somewhat different kind. Like the Vīraśaivas, "the Dāsas also popularized the practice of holy mendicancy, going about with the *tambura* on the shoulders, bells on feet, and *chiplas* for rhythm on hand, singing the *Padas* and receiving handfuls of rice *(uncha-vṛtti)* from willing householders."[27]

At that point Raghavan allowed the momentum of the movement to swing farther west and north—through Maharashtra to Gujarat, Sindh, Kashmir, and Punjab—before heading south and east again, as we have seen. In regard to Maharashtra he particularly noted the guru-pupil association between the bhakta Rāmdās and the famed the Maratha king Śivājī, whose daring exploits against the Mughals have been acclaimed as heralding India's thirst for independence from the British. (Subsequent scholarship has thrown both this and Śivājī's connection with Rāmdās into dispute.)[28] Raghavan also celebrated the Maharashtrian saints' use of the "devotional institution of musical *Saṅkīrtan,*" which "had far-reaching effects."[29] In so saying, he was probably not referring to the public practice of singing and chanting that Chaitanya championed under that name in the north and east, though the connection is thought-provoking, but to the widely felt influence of the great fourteenth-century Marathi *kīrtan* performer Nāmdev. This, he suggested, ultimately connected to the musical practices adopted at the Maratha court of Thanjavur several centuries later, where his narrative would culminate.[30]

In regard to the north, Raghavan quotes George Grierson, the legendary British scholar-administrator who directed the Linguistic Survey of India, to the effect that the words of two men "can still be heard in every village of Hindustan. These are Tulasi Das [Tulsīdās], the abandoned child of a beggar Brahman tribe, and Kabir, the despised weaver of Benares."[31] Both of them, says Raghavan, were pupils of Rāmānand—again, that southern link—and looking forward, he makes mention of Kabīr's influence over a number of communities, beginning with the Sikhs and Dādūpathīs, communities formed in the sixteenth century, and extending right up to the Radhasoamis, who began their work three centuries later.[32] Other figures also come in as significant—the Brajbhasha poet Sūrdās, especially, who is mentioned right after the philosopher-theologian Vallabhācārya. This is probably not by chance since the poet is normally (if falsely, in my view) considered to be the philosopher's pupil. Raghavan also makes a point of saying that "many of these popular singer-saints" of north India "became the apostles of a synthesis and *rapprochement,* aided by common points in *advaita* and Sufism.[33] His penultimate step was to move east to Bengal and Orissa, "the land of Krishna and Shakti," before turning his attentions again southward, as we have seen.

His circumambulation ended at Thanjavur, deep in the Tamil country but a place where Marathi, Telugu, and Tamil speakers met in performances hosted by the great king Serfoji II (1777–1832). Raghavan was one of the first scholars to understand the formative role Serfoji played in bringing north and south together, though he stressed even more the agency of the poet-performers themselves at court. Doubling back over the same terrain in a more thematic fashion in his second lecture, pointing out shared images and performance practices, Raghavan also laid stress on the movement of these singer-saints in a literal sense. Their "genius for mass-contact," he said, and the "vow of austere mendicancy that they took" meant that they were constantly on the road making pilgrimages.[34] Raghavan was struck by the analogy to the *Bhārat-darśan* (See India) tours of his own day, but he emphasized that there was a gap between these and the deep emotional and moral component that caused the bhakti singer-saints to travel in search of "self-elevation." Gandhi had remarked that "our leading men travelled throughout India either by foot or in bullock carts," Raghavan recalled, so it is little surprise that eventually, after paying homage to Śaṃkara as pilgrim and hymnist, he shone his light on Gandhi himself, who also functioned in these roles.[35] Then drawing to a conclusion, he stepped back in such a way as to reveal Gandhi's global impact, ceding the stage to Arnold Toynbee, who had given the Maulana Azad Memorial Lecture in Delhi only a few years before.[36] At some length Raghavan quoted Toynbee's appreciation of Gandhi's "inexhaustible spiritual strength."[37] Thus the father of the nation, with his pilgrimages and his spiritual struggles and his favorite Vaishnava hymn (Narsī Mehtā's *Vaiṣṇava Janato*), emerged in Raghavan's portrait as the greatest modern "great integrator" of all—not just for India, in fact, but for the whole world.

The Legacy in English

Raghavan's lectures marked a high point in twentieth-century articulations of the bhakti movement idea, but they built on much that had come before. Raghavan himself referred to one of these—the famous little book *Rise of the Maratha Power,* written by Mahadeo Govind Ranade, a founder of the Indian National Congress and judge in the Bombay High Court. It was published only months before Ranade's death in 1901.[38] In this book, as the title would indicate, Ranade enters into a discussion of only those "saints and prophets" who inhabited his own region, Maharashtra; and although he is comfortable with an idiom that speaks in terms of movements, he does not trace out a bhakti movement that would encompass all of India or, indeed, use that phrase. Still, Raghavan found particular value in a sentence that looked out across a wider domain, of which he quoted the first clause: "It may safely be said that the growth of the modern vernaculars in India is solely the result of the labors of these saints, and that the provinces, which showed the most decided tendencies in the way of reform, also showed the most healthy development of their vernacular literature."[39]

This assertion, we recall, is just what has worried Sheldon Pollock, but for Ranade and Raghavan it was uncontested common ground. Yet in the prose that immediately precedes the passage Raghavan quotes with such approval, Justice Ranade says something that would have caused Raghavan concern: "The struggle between the claims of the classical Sanskrit and the vernaculars, of which we hear so much in these days, is thus an old conflict . . . The saints and prophets . . . laid Sanskrit aside as useless for their work, and spent all their energies in the cultivation and growth of their mother tongue."[40] Looking back after more than six decades, Raghavan was at pains to downplay this dichotomy, as Pollock was later to do. And Raghavan took implicit issue with Ranade's view that these "reformists" opposed monastic ways of being since they appreciated "the sanctity of family-life."[41] But most intriguing of all their disagreements is a motif whose importance Pollock particularly flagged. Raghavan was far less preoccupied than Ranade with drawing out parallels between what Ranade called bhakti's "reforms" and—note the term—the Protestant Reformation in Europe.

Ranade had, in fact, introduced all of the themes to which we have so far drawn attention in the course of assaying a large, overriding comparison between the religious and cultural histories of India and Europe. His argument against Sanskrit, as he spoke for his Maharashtrian "saint and prophet" predecessors, was against "the thraldom of scholastic learning." This he saw as being closely akin to the Protestant reformers' attempts to set aside "the oppressive preponderance of the classical Latin in which all the best books were till then written."[42] And he saw an analogy between the sense of common humanity that emerged on the pilgrimage from all parts of Maharashtra to Pandharpur and the sense of shared human dignity that led to the Protestant reformers' rejection of clerical privilege in distributing the Eucharist. In this regard, for example, Ranade referred to the last ritual of the Vārkarīs' pilgrimage to Pandharpur as the moment when they observed "the Lord's Feast."[43] He also analogized polytheistic worship in India to the image and saint worship of the Roman Catholic Church, and depicted the bhakti reformers' deep allegiance to their own "favorite form of the divine incarnation" as an instinct for true monotheism, just the sort of thing that had inspired the activities of the Protestant reformers, especially the strictest among them. Here and elsewhere was a manliness—he did not shrink from the word[44]—that caused religion and politics to march together as two sides of a single movement, in India no less than in the early modern Europe.

Not surprisingly, Ranade allowed the storied bond between Rāmdās and Śivājī in the cause of a united "*Dharma* (religion) of Maharashtra" to serve as his point of departure as he developed this line of thought. Here was something special, he said. Because of it and also because of the great profusion of Marathi saints over a longer period of time, Ranade insisted that the "similar movement [that] manifested itself much about the same time" in northern and eastern India—he mentioned Nānak, Chaitanya, Rāmānand, Kabīr, Tulsīdās, Sūrdās, Jayadev, and Ravidās in referring to it—could not quite be compared "with the work done by the saints and prophets of Maharashtra." The religious movement that had coursed through Maharashtrian history ever since the time of Jñāndev prepared it "in a way no other nation in India was prepared, to take the lead in re-establishing a united native power in the place of foreign domination." The domination he had in mind was "the Mahomedan yoke" that had spread across India in the wake of successive invasions by "Afghans, Gilchis, Turks, Usbegs, and Moghuls." Its answer was the Maratha Confederacy that began to form around the turn of the seventeenth century and created a political infrastructure that would, in the century prior to the consolidation of British hegemony, extend from Dvaraka to Haridvar to Jagannath Puri to Rameshvaram, the four compass points of "the Indian Continent," and still served as the foundation of civil order under Victoria, "the Queen-Empress of India."[45]

Obviously an Elphinstone College education and the career path Ranade had chosen shine through in what he has to say, and his understanding of history also reflects the particular vortex of Marathi nationalism that swirled around the Bombay in which Justice Ranade lived. Raghavan's formation, though equally elite, had been different, and it took place at a different time. Both men spoke with enormous confidence about the special potencies of the religious histories to which they believed themselves specifically heir—Maharashtrian on the one hand, Tamilian on the other. And they promulgated a similar though not exactly equivalent litany of features that would characterize the movements of which they spoke. These included, in Ranade's case, a stress on vernacular usage, a protest against "the old spirit of caste exclusiveness," an elevation of "the Shudra classes," an attention to the status of women, a suspicion of "rites and ceremonies, and of pilgrimages and fasts, and of learning and contemplation" in comparison with "the higher excellence of worship by means of love and faith," and even "a plan of reconciliation with the Mahomedans."[46] All this sounds familiar, and finds its place in Raghavan's catalogue as well, but for Ranade it is a mainly regional affirmation while for Raghavan it is national. Or to put more accurately, the nations they envisioned were not the same size.

For all they shared, the terms had changed significantly between the time of Ranade and that of Raghavan, and with it the frames in which they located the religious movements they both sought to describe. Ranade saw analogies between what had been experienced in Maharashtra and what had happened elsewhere in India, but they were not part of a single thrust as they were for Raghavan. For Ranade, in fact, what brought them parallel to one another was at least as much their synchronicity with what was happening in Europe as the force of the analogies that could be located in between religious communities in various parts of India itself. This may possibly explain the intriguing fact that Ranade identified the first Marathi reformer, Jñāndev, as belonging to the fifteenth century, when the Protestant Reformation was beginning to gather steam, rather than to the late thirteenth century, when Jñāndev is ordinarily thought to have flourished. Ranade's whole narrative breathes a spirit of comparison with Europe. Even the distinctiveness that Ranade perceived in pan-Indian bhakti, its shared tendency to contemplate "the bright side of divine Providence," came into focus by virtue of its contrast with the darker proclivities of "the Shemitic religions" that ruled the day in Europe and elsewhere—their "awe and trembling" before "a judge who punished more frequently than He rewarded."[47]

As Ranade summoned his powerful English, he clearly imagined British readers in addition to Indian ones—this in a way that would have been far less marked in the case of Raghavan. Raghavan's Toynbee was an invited guest, and Toynbee's point of reference, in turn, was that most famous of Indians—Gandhi—not anyone living in Europe. The nation for whom Raghavan's spiritual narrative of national integration was appropriate was an entity that was still being imagined in Ranade's time. As he laid out "the moral interest" of the story of Maratha resiliency, whose basis he understood to be distinctively and broadly Hindu, Ranade could only gesture in the direction of "those who can see far into the future of the possibilities open to a Federated India."[48] Was that perhaps the reason why he failed to articulate a unified picture of India's bhakti past—a single bhakti movement rather than a cluster of more or less analogous "religious upheavals"?[49] Does the present dictate the past to such an extent that he could not?

The intellectual historian Krishna Sharma, whose book *Bhakti and the Bhakti Movement: A New Perspective* appeared in Delhi in 1987, took quite a different view of these matters. To her perception the idea of the bhakti movement emerged considerably before the achievement of an independent India, and was the product of exactly the class of people to whom Justice Ranade was speaking—Europeans, especially the British among them, and their Indian protégés. From her point of view the most important of these were the Indologists. It was their imprint, she argued, that caused bhakti to be conceived in a thoroughly Vaishnava way, since the Vaishnava strand in Hindu theology corresponded most comfortably with Protestant Christian conceptions of God. It was their historicism, she said, that produced a conception of bhakti as history. Not surprisingly, therefore, it was their understanding of leading motifs in European history, most notably the Protestant Reformation, that shaped their understanding of what was going on in India at roughly the same time. This utterly deformed and obscured the theological and historical realities of India itself.

Krishna Sharma was the first scholar to take a critical look at the idea of the bhakti movement, and what she found was anathema. Analogies of the sort Ranade saw between Indian bhaktas and their contemporary Christian cousins deserved to be subjected to a much closer inspection than they had typically been given, and the whole preoccupation with these purported analogies ought to be summarily rejected once their foreign origins and biases had been made clear. All that seemed manly, hopeful, and virtuous to Ranade seemed submissive and deeply regretful to Sharma. The idea of vernacular religious movements, as in Ranade, or of a single bhakti movement, as for Raghavan, historicized something that was actually timeless in her view. Even if one wanted to move forward with a national "history of religion" for India, the sort of thing Raghavan was so clearly attempting, what would be the point in doing so if that history turned out to be alien to the core?

Sharma put her finger on a fundamental problem—the historicization of bhakti in the way that subsequently came to be accepted as fact—and let us make clear just who she thought she was exposing by blowing the whistle in this way. The likes of Ranade and Raghavan were actually not her primary targets; they do not even appear in her index. Rather it was the great Indologist Ramakrishna Gopal Bhandarkar (1837–1925) and an impressive array of Europeans whose methods and assumptions, if not always their conclusions, Bhandarkar shared. Principal among these were Horace Hyman Wilson, Albrecht Weber, Franz Lorinser, and Monier Williams, whose works most relevant to the subject at hand had been published between 1828 and 1877.[50] Last but not least on this list of invidious European eminences was a man we have already mentioned because he was cited so appreciatively by Dr. Raghavan: George Grierson (1851–1941), author of *The Modern Vernacular Literature of Hindustan* (1889) and later director of the Linguistic Survey of India. According to Sharma it was the personalist, monotheist, Protestant Christian conception of deity these men shared that led them to conceive—or rather, misconceive—of bhakti in the way they did, and it was especially Grierson who historicized this conception in such a manner as to give us "the bhakti movement": "By establishing a link between the medieval bhaktas and the

Vaishṇava acharyas, Grierson was able to describe the whole phenomenon of the medieval religious resurgence as the Bhakti movement in terms of Vaishṇavism."[51]

Indian thinkers, says Sharma, never found the strength to challenge this "artificial formulation."[52] By her lights Ranade and Raghavan would have to belong to the group whom she implicates in this charge, and I am sure she would have been eager to be seated subversively in the auditorium of All India Radio as a member of the Delhi audience that heard Raghavan give his lectures in the last month of 1964. But that was impossible. She was on research leave from her teaching position in the history department of Miranda House at the time—away in London, at the School of Oriental and African Studies, deeply involved in writing the thesis that would emerge two decades later, with only minor revisions, as her book.[53]

Let us return to the matter of Grierson, Sharma's bête noire. Grierson's writings on bhakti did indeed have enormous influence, as Sharma observed, but so far as I can determine, and contrary to what she implies more than once, Grierson never made use of the concept of the bhakti movement as such. It is odd that she does not seem to recognize this fact, since on other occasions she carefully notes that European Orientalists made use of formulations that were closely similar to the idea of the bhakti movement without being precisely the same.[54] But she is strangely uncritical when it comes to Grierson, her ultimate target, the man who took "the theories put forward by the aforesaid authors" and finally "bound [them] together in a neat system."[55]

What Grierson actually says on the subject was most influentially articulated in the entry he wrote on "Bhakti-Mārga" for a volume of James Hastings's widely circulated *Encyclopaedia of Religion and Ethics* that was published in 1910. There the famous linguist indeed spoke about "the greatest religious revolution that India has ever seen," but he called this transformation "the Bhāgavata reformation of the Middle Ages" or "the Bhāgavatism of the reformation."[56] Considering the impact that his words would have, both on those who largely accepted them and on those who just as firmly rejected them, it is worth hearing in considerable detail what Grierson had to say:

> It was in Southern India that the lamp of Bhāgavatism was kept burning [after the time of the *Bhagavad Gītā*], though with but a feeble light, and

> it was in the South that it revived through the teaching of the four great leaders whose names have been mentioned [Rāmānuja, Madhva, Nimbārka, and Viṣṇusvāmī]. Then arose Rāmānanda, and within half a century Bhāgavatism became the leading religion of India. Yet there is as great a difference between the monotheism of the *Bhagavad-Gītā* and that of Rāmānanda as there was between the teaching of Plato and that of St. Paul. It now became as fully the right of the despised classes, of Musalmāns and of unclean leather-workers, as of people of repute. From Rāmānanda's time it was to the poor that the gospel was preached, and that in their own language, not in a form of speech holy but unintelligible. No one who reads the Indian religious literature of the 15th and following centuries can fail to notice the gulf that lies between the old and the new. We find ourselves in the face of the greatest religious revolution that India has ever seen—greater even than that of Buddhism, for its effects have persisted to the present day. Religion is no longer a question of knowledge. It is one of emotion. We visit a land of mysticism and rapture, and meet spirits akin, not to the giant schoolmen of Benares, but to the poets and mystics of mediaeval Europe, in sympathy with Bernard of Clairvaux, with Thomas à Kempis, with Eckhart, and with St. Theresa. In the early years of the reformation, the converts lived and moved in an atmosphere of the highest spiritual exaltation, while over all hovered, with healing in its wings, a Divine gospel of love, smoothing down inevitable asperities, restoring breaches, and reconciling conflicting modes of thought. Northern India was filled with wandering devotees vowed to poverty and purity. Visions, trances, raptures, and even reputed miracles were of every-day occurrence. Rich noblemen abandoned all their possessions and gave them to the poor, and even the poorest would lay aside a bundle of sticks to light a fire for some chance wandering saint. Nor were these converts confined to the male sex.[57]

This is remarkable prose, but considering what Krishna Sharma was later to make of it, it is also remarkable that it fails to articulate clearly a concept of the bhakti movement or even of the "Bhakti religion," as she claims it does.[58] Here we have not movement but revolution. In an earlier passage Grierson does indeed offer a sketch of what he somewhat endearingly calls "the four churches of the reformation," that is, the sects (or teaching traditions: *sampradāys*) associated with the names of Rāmānuja, Madhva, Nimbārka, and Viṣṇusvāmī. But he does so largely in schematic terms; the historical aspect, while present, is relegated to a smaller typeface.[59] As for the Christian frame of reference, it goes without saying that there is scarcely an effort to disguise it. And this is substantive, not just stylistic: "Whence did Rāmānanda receive the inspiration that produced this marvelous change?" asks Grierson. His answer takes us back to the presence of "large colonies of Nestorian Christians and Jews" on the Malabar coast from the sixth century onward; to Syrian Christians who came in the seventh century; to Jesuit missionaries present in the second half of the sixteenth century; and then, overall, to the following assertion: "We thus see that from the first centuries of our era, Christianity has always been present in India, and that, both in the North and in the South, Hindus had every opportunity of becoming acquainted with its tenets."[60]

Grierson's interest in Rāmānand in particular and in the worship of Rām in general leads him to explore that realm further, as we shall see, and he notes the analogy between "the institution of the *mahāprasāda,* or sacramental meal" in the Śrī *sampradāy* and the Christian Eucharist, opining that such parallels—or "coincidence," as he says on this occasion—

> cannot be mere matters of chance. The consecrated elements are even reserved for administration to the sick, and the communion, which is shared in only by those who feel themselves worthy, is followed by a love-feast attended by all members of the sect present at the time.
>
> But it is in the literature of the Śrī *sampradāy* church that we find the most evident reminiscences of Christianity. Kabīr, one of Rāmānanda's twelve apostles, speaks of the Word in language which is but a paraphrase of the opening verses of St. John's Gospel, and quotes sayings of our Lord almost verbatim.[61]

This was obviously a lot for Indian historians of their own religious traditions to swallow. Ranade apparently responded to sentiments like this in one way, emphasizing the positive thrust of parallels such as those Grierson had identified, but others—Krishna Sharma provides a fine example—found Grierson's comparativist (or was it imperialist?) perspective much harder to accept. Either way, though, it is important to point out that a clearly expressed notion of the bhakti movement is actually lacking in Grierson's words. His image of the religious history of bhakti corresponds in only the most general way to what V. Raghavan laid out in his Patel Lectures; and neither here nor anywhere else in his writing does Grierson develop an idea of the bhakti movement that identifies it by that label, though Krishna Sharma implies that he does. How did she get this idea? To understand that, we have to move into an entirely different domain of conversation about the bhakti movement—a domain that is carved out not in English but in India's other candidate for being regarded as the national language, Hindi.

Crossing into Hindi

In northern India, Hindi is not just a language but a world. Those who belong to it may or may not have the ability to pass into the realms defined by additional spoken languages, but the linguistic border that makes the greatest difference of all is the one that separates Hindi from English. Schools are either in one medium or the other, looking across the fence by law—children are required to study at least a little of both—but often without too profound an effect. Despite the amazing phenomenon of Hinglish, so prominent in the metropolitan spaces of north India and increasingly over radio and television, there remains an important disparity between people who are primarily educated in Hindi and those thoroughly schooled in English. The Hindi equivalent to the English concept of bhakti movement—*bhakti āndolan*—is a significant feature of education in Hindi, certainly through secondary school and subsequently as well for those who choose Hindi itself as an educational specialization at the university level. In Hindi even more than in English, the rubric of the bhakti movement, as *bhakti āndolan,* is simply common sense. Because that rubric constitutes part of the generally accepted history of the language of everyday communication in much of northern India, the bhakti movement typically matters more to Hindi speakers than to their English-speaking compatriots. And we must not forget that while Hindi is not a part of everyday speech in other parts of India to the extent that it is in the north, its presence elsewhere is often at least as real as that of English, particularly among less elite segments of the population. For one thing, Hindi is mandated for instruction in schools throughout the country.

Let us begin, then, in the schools. The National Council of Educational Research and Training (NCERT), headquartered in Delhi, while technically not a wing of the Ministry of Education, has for many years functioned as the main agency for the production of textbooks in use in public schools throughout India. The eleventh-grade textbook called *Medieval India* (or in its Hindi version, *Madhyakālīn Bhārat*) is written for use in history classrooms. Its original version was produced in 1978 by the well-known historian of medieval India, Satish Chandra; a parallel text for use in the seventh grade was composed a decade later by the equally eminent Romila Thapar, who had interrogated the "Muslim desecration" narrative of the great Shiva temple at Somnath.[62] A revised version of the upper-level text *Medieval India* was produced in 2002 by a strong critic of Thapar's book on Somnath, Meenakshi Jain of Delhi University. This revision was published in the wake of the electoral victory of the Bharatiya Janata Party (BJP) over its main rival, the more left-leaning Congress Party, in 1998.[63] In Jain's *Medieval India,* the section entitled "bhakti movement"—or in Hindi, *bhakti āndolan*—appears as part of a chapter devoted to "Cultural and Religious Trends," which separates earlier chapters offering a broadly political history of the pre-Mughal period from later ones devoted to the events that followed, these being told largely from the standard Mughal perspective.

Several facets of Meenakshi Jain's portrait of the bhakti movement, which varies only minimally between its English and Hindi versions, deserve our attention. First is the overall positioning of the bhakti movement narrative. Internally, Jain gives us an exposition of the bhakti movement that moves from south to north starting in the sixth century, as we have come to expect. Its defining feature is "the emphasis on a loving relationship between the devotee and a personal god." Jain also informs us that "its popular poet-saints [Hindi: *kavi sant*] composed devotional hymns [*bhakti pad*] in the regional vernaculars and promised salvation to all classes [*sabhī vargoṅ ko mukti kā āśvāsan diyā*]. The leaders of the bhakti movement came from all strata of society [*bhakti āndolan ke netā samāj ke sabhī vargoṅ se the*]."[64]

So far, this is standard fare, and what comes next is scarcely less so. The following section carries forward the bhakti movement narrative by focusing on the Vārkarī Panth in Maharashtra, in the context of which we also hear about the distinction between *nirguṇ* and *saguṇ bhakti.* Then comes a section entitled "Saguṇ Bhakti," which takes us still farther north into the Hindi-speaking regions and Bengal.[65] This concludes with three paragraphs on Shaiva bhakti—this includes Gorakhnāth—and prepares us for "The Birth of Sikhism." There are a few concluding words about "Other Sects" such as the Dādūpathīs and the *sants* in general, and we get a line about the importance of the *Bhāgavata Purāṇa,* whose date of composition is estimated as having been in the tenth to eleventh centuries according to scholarly opinion. That, in a nutshell, is what eleventh-graders are supposed to learn about the bhakti movement, and it is a most important supplement to the otherwise largely political history with which it is surrounded.

Partly because of that encompassment, perhaps, Meenakshi Jain wants to make sure that her narrative of the bhakti movement is rightly understood in several key respects. In doing so, she sees herself as correcting a series of popular misimpressions. One is that the bhakti movement arose as a response to Śaṃkara—or as she calls him, incorporating the normal honorific, Śaṃkarācārya. She is evidently concerned that bhakti not be seen as rejecting the monistic "illusionism" *(māyāvād)* often associated with his name, since she says that he "is known to have authored several works of a profoundly devotional character."[66] In short, Śaṃkara is a bhakta too, which enables her to sidestep the question of whether there was ever any acrimony between the Shaivas whom he is popularly taken to represent and their Vaishnava counterparts—or, for that matter, between an elite philosopher and representatives of a more inclusive social range. In the story she wants to tell, all Hindus stand together under the capacious canopy of bhakti.

Jain's second explicit caveat in introducing the bhakti movement points in a different direction, as she makes clear in her very first words on the subject: "The bhakti movement has often been presented as a Hindu response to the egalitarian message of Islam and its spread among the lower classes. But this seems to be an inadequate assessment, as in the Hindu scheme bhakti (devotion) is an essential constituent of *sādhanā* (religious pursuit). It was mentioned in the *Śvetāsvatara Upaniṣad* as well as the *Bhagavad Gītā,* where Lord Krishna said even the humblest devotee could reach him through simple devotion."[67]

Here we get a sense of how the bhakti movement must figure in a wider narrative frame that, for the "medieval" period in Indian history, especially in the north, has to be concerned in a major way with the political successes of Islamic rulers. Jain's message is that while the rulers may be Muslim, we should not understand that the embracing of Islam on the part of any in the rank and file followed from its egalitarian appeal. Jain rebuts this view explicitly, saying there is no evidence that the "so-called tyranny of the caste system" stimulated conversion to Islam on the part of the Indian masses. To the contrary, "foreign nobles" who came into the country with these Muslim conquests "were contemptuous of Hindu converts" and exemplified an "extreme racialism" that continued "well into the seventeenth century." The bhakti movement could therefore hardly be explained as a response to the appeal of Islam, for conversions to Islam in the Sultanate period "were restricted to certain urban professional and vocational groups." It was really the British, she says, who put forward "the idea that Islam fosters social, as opposed to religious equality," not the Muslims themselves, either in word or in practice. Hence there is no place to look but the bhakti movement itself for a class-comprehensive view of what religion is all about. The phenomenon of the bhakti movement shows bhakti to be an organic force in Indian history that exists independent of anything Islamic. As for the "Sufi movement" *(sūphī āndolan),* which appears at the end of the section, its nature is no more to be attributed to its contact with Hinduism than the other way around. Sufism and Hinduism are independent entities, which interacted "only after most of [Sufism's] distinctive traits had already developed."[68] As the bhakti movement shows, this was also the case in regard to Hinduism.

Reading these caveats, one senses the perils of the medieval period from the point of view of a BJP-approved historian, and how the bhakti movement must be carefully defined and protected to serve its proper role in the face of more liberal interpretations of it that had been put forward by historians of a different stripe. Or perhaps, to some extent, Meenakshi Jain was forced to offer these clarifications simply because of the overall political context within which the bhakti movement had to be placed in her own larger narrative—the preceding and succeeding chapters organized largely by means of the Sultanate/Mughal divide.

Of course, not every depiction of the bhakti movement has been oriented in such a way. Certainly Raghavan's view of it was far more irenic with respect to Islam, and even Ranade, for all his fascination with Rāmdev and Śivājī, insisted that the Maharashtrian "religious movement" he described "suggested and partly carried out a plan of reconciliation with the Mohamedans."[69] In other curricular tellings of the bhakti movement story, we feel this dialogical emphasis far more powerfully than in that of Meenakshi Jain. A case in point is provided by the most recent history texts published by NCERT. In these the category "medieval" all but disappears as a strict periodization is reworked to produce a thematic approach. Among these Theme Six, which is intended to stretch from the eighth century to the eighteenth, is boldly entitled "Bhakti-Sufi Traditions." As these interlinked traditions are described, the language of "bhakti movements" is not altogether abandoned, but there is a shift toward the concept of "traditions" as these cults, sects, practices, and communities are described. When they are considered as a group, we tend to hear metaphors such as "mosaic" and "fabric"—or "path," as in the case of nonelite usage from the period itself—and an emphasis on processes of perpetual change keeps alive the sense of movement that had been explicit in the earlier formula.[70]

With the educational materials produced by NCERT for use in northern India, as we have seen, we find ourselves standing on the frontier between English and Hindi. Some interesting adjustments occasionally have to be made to translate from one language to the other. In Meenakshi Jain's book, for example, salvation, that quintessentially Christian term, gets glossed as *mukti,* a "release" that many of the great voices in north Indian bhakti thought to be a false aim of faith. Meanwhile *sādhanā,* the sense of personal discipline and refined practice so deeply imbedded in Hindu ways of thought, comes across in English as "religious pursuit," which sounds more disembodied than its Hindi counterpart.[71] On the whole, despite some awkwardness, the two languages with their differing religious backgrounds stand equal and do not impede effective translation back and forth. Things necessarily change, however, if we move somewhat more deeply into the Hindi-speaking realm, especially if we cross the line from general studies of Indian history into the domain defined by the Hindi language itself.

Much has been written about the way in which the standard language of modern Hindi usage—*khaṛī bolī hindī*—emerged not because of its own self-evident shape and weight, but in response to the demands and opportunities of a particular historical moment.[72] It had to be grammaticized and supplied with a master dictionary, and it had to accrue a normative conception of its own history. All this happened in the decades just prior to and following the turn of the twentieth century, and it happened more than anywhere else in the learned centers of the central Gangetic plain—in institutions like the Hindī Sāhitya Sammelan of Allahabad (1910) and the Kāśī Nāgarīpracāriṇī Sabhā in Banaras (1893). And there was a definite religious dimension to the process as proponents of Hindi sought to distinguish their language from Urdu not just by script but by cultural heritage—the one being more Hindu, the other more distinctively Muslim. We will turn to these matters in greater detail in Chapter 6, but for now let us look at some of the fruits of this process of linguistic precipitation and let them guide us back toward questions we left open at the end of our consideration of Krishna Sharma's book.

Suppose we choose Allahabad University as our vantage point—a great university with an even greater past, and located smack in the middle of the "Hindi belt." In exams that bring to a conclusion the second year of the B.A. curriculum in Hindi, Allahabad students must face two batteries of questions. One set concerns individual poets who count as exemplars of the language in its early forms—Vidyāpati, Kabīr, Sūrdās, Tulsīdās, Jāyasī, Bihārī, and Ghanānand. The other set of questions takes up the history of the language more broadly, moving from the period of its origins through the bhakti period (*bhakti kāl,* 1375–1700 C.E.) and into the subsequent mannerist or courtly period (*rīti kāl,* 1700–1900), until one arrives at the modern period, which becomes the focus of a different set of exams. As is well known, this template for parsing out the history of the language was established by Pundit Ramchandra Shukla with the publication of his *Hindī Sāhitya kā Itihās* (History of Hindi Literature) in 1929. The work was originally intended to function as an introduction to the *Great Hindi Dictionary (Hindī Śabd Sāgar),* which was published in the same year and by the same institution, the Nāgarīpracāriṇī Sabhā of Banaras. Once released, however, it came to have a life of its own—a sort of eternal life. It is still the backbone of college curricula in Hindi today, with trickle-down effects through the lower grades, as well.

If one enters the bookshops that cluster near the entrance to Allahabad University, one finds an array of curricular materials for sale—the books on various syllabuses, of course, but also study guides that help students approach these books and prepare for their exams in a more specific way. One such book is the *Navīn Hindī Gāiḍ* (New Hindi Guide) written by Dr. Śiv Mūrti Pāṭhak and published locally in Allahabad itself in 2004. In the section that concerns the *bhakti kāl,* references to the bhakti movement *(bhakti āndolan)* are frequent. The concept is assumed as axiomatic; only the processes by which it came into being and developed *(uday aur vikās)* are put forward as topics appropriate for the student's inquiry. Sample questions are listed, and the guide provides in condensed form the answers that major scholars in the field have given to those questions.

The first question to emerge is whether the bhakti movement arose in response to changes in India's political climate or, rather, in accordance with a complex of literary, religious, and social factors that are internal to the domain of bhakti itself. Especially in regard to the former option, the ideas of a much earlier generation of European scholars are mentioned—Albrecht Weber, George Grierson, Arthur Berriedale Keith, and H. H. Wilson, roughly the same group to whom Krishna Sharma so strenuously objected. That they all flourished well before Shukla wrote his masterpiece is not incidental. They are fossils displayed to perform the educational task that fossils serve, casting the light of contrast on a very different present. A more crucial challenge, however, comes from more recent scholars like Tara Chand, Humayun Kabir, and Abid Husain, who chalk the bhakti movement up to the influence of Islam. Such a view, suggesting the importance of political frameworks, may sound helpful from the point of view of modern-day political expediency, says Pāṭhak, the author of our guide, but it is historical nonsense. The hope of drawing Muslims and Hindus together in a single state, he implies, is no excuse for ignoring the great distance between Islamic monotheism and the great Hindu philosophical systems.[73]

Pāṭhak rejects such views—both the foreign comparisons and any sense that politics dictate culture. He despises misleading conceptions such as these, seeing them as a plot *(durabhisaṃdhi)* to play down the importance of that which was indigenously Indian.[74] In contrasting tones and various degrees of strength, we have already seen such an organically cultural and specifically Indian view put forward in the writings of V. Raghavan and Meenakshi Jain. Within the realm of Hindi literary critics, Pāṭhak could well have cited Ramchandra Shukla as his authority in this regard, but instead he emphasizes the way in which Shukla's eventual successor as chair of the Department of Hindi at Banaras Hindu University argued these matters out: Hazariprasad Dvivedi. As we shall see, both Shukla and Dvivedi also turn out to be relevant in the case of Krishna Sharma.

Shukla was eager to dispatch Westerners' view of the development of bhakti on the grounds that such a view prioritized a certain "mystical" *(rahasyātmak)* conception of religious truth, as against the corporate and deeply aesthetic sense of participation that he believed to be more central to the bhakti movement.[75] In his long essay *Bhakti kā Vikās* (The

Development of Bhakti) he does not come out and say he is trying to undo the view of the subject that Grierson took, but he does make extensive use of the very encyclopedia in which Grierson published his "Bhakti-Mārga" essay in an effort to turn Western preconceptions back upon themselves. He takes Rufus Jones's entry on "Mysticism" in the *Hastings Enyclopaedia of Religion and Ethics* and Nicol Macnicol's essay on "Mysticism (Hindu)," which follows it, and shows how a preoccupation with a distant divinity made known to man in the upper reaches of inner experience prejudices a true understanding of what the mainstream path of Hindu bhakti—the *saguṇ bhaktimārg*—is all about.[76] To see bhakti and its development through the lens of the history of Western mysticism is to distort and upend it. Certainly there should be no suggestion that Hindu bhakti owes its excellence to any Sufi influence; rather, in regard to the *premākhyān* genre, it was the Sufis who adopted Indian forms of religiosity.[77] The virtue of bhakti is its corporate sensitivity and, indeed, its corporality, by contrast to the sentimentalism *(bhāvukatā)*[78] that is apt to infect mysticism—by rights, a Western phenomenon and not an Indian one—because of its denigration of the body. Macnicol may find in certain Hindu saints "the desire to draw near to God, to find Him in personal, inward experience," but for Shukla the treasure is elsewhere, in the close harmonization between the religiosity of bhakti exemplars and the forms of worship dear to common people.[79]

As we have said, however, Pāṭhak does not choose to follow Shukla in dealing with the inadequacy of Western views of the animating spirit of the bhakti movement, though it would seem to suit his perspective well. Perhaps the reason is that Shukla's clearest articulation of his argument comes in *Bhakti kā Vikās* rather than in his general *History,* which students would be expected to know. Instead Pāṭhak turns to Dvivedi for a vigorous defense of an indigenist reading of the history of bhakti, and Dvivedi's perspective is distinctly different from Shukla's.

That difference has been marked in the title of Namvar Singh's influential book on Dvivedi, *Dūsrī Paramparā kī Khoj* (In Search of a Different Lineage, 1982). Rather than focusing obsessively on *saguṇ* poets such as Sūrdās and Tulsīdās, whom Shukla took to be almost self-evidently the literary paragons of the Hindi language, Dvivedi tried also to thread a past for bhakti through Kabīr and other *nirguṇ* poets, tracing it back through the "Nāth Sampradāy" associated with Gorakhnāth and way back to the Buddhist *siddhas,* in roughly the manner that we have seen in Raghavan. In this way he proposed a complementary genealogy to that put forward by Shukla, or rather, attempted to right a *saguṇ* imbalance that he found there. All this was to articulate a more convincingly organic sense of the literature produced by the classical poets of Hindi's "bhakti period" *(bhakti kāl).* That the religious and literary history of all of India deserved to be considered an appropriate part of Hindi's greater literary (and religious) past was a matter that did not come in for intense scrutiny. It was as the national language that Hindi's cause was being advanced. Obviously it would need to have a national—even if not a specifically Hindi-speaking—past commensurate with that role.

In bringing all this to bear on questions that might face B.A. students at Allahabad University, Pāṭhak drew attention to two particular contributions Dvivedi had made to the discussion. First, he went back over Dvivedi's answer to the question of whether the rise of Hindu bhakti ought to be attributed to the presence of Islam in the Indian subcontinent. Dvivedi answered in the negative by posing the following question: if an interaction with Islam had been responsible for the rise of the bhakti movement, why had that movement not followed the same trajectory as had been traced by the advent of Islamic peoples in India? To simplify somewhat, why had bhakti not moved from west to east, beginning in Sind, rather than from south to north, beginning in Tamilnadu? In the same spirit Pāṭhak asked the following: if some sort of bhakti chemistry was to be expected in the wake of Islamic expansion, why had there been no similar reaction in other parts of Asia and Europe, where Muslim rule had also spread? No, for all its connections with Sufi modes of expression, bhakti had to be at base an indigenous thing.[80]

Implicitly Pāṭhak may also have been relying on Dvivedi when he dealt with the synergy between Muslims—who were, he insisted (contrary to what Meenakshi Jain would argue), less caste-conscious than many Hindus—and the Naths and Siddhas, so as to prepare the ground for a *sant mārg,* a "saints' path." This *sant mārg,* he wrote, was not strictly *nirguṇ* in its persuasion, following the logical distinctions that philosophers like to make. Rather, it was some sort of mix between that and *saguṇ bhakti,* after the manner of a common bhakti mentality. Sufi poets, said Pāṭhak, had made use of Hindu images and figures of speech in their romances *(prem kahānīs),* thereby doing their part to wipe away cultural dualism in the cause of intercultural understanding. Logically this would have to mean, as it had for Dvivedi, that the primary direction of processes of influence moved from Hindus outward to Muslims—or, to put it in literary terms, from Hindi outward toward more distinctively Muslim media such as Persian. In this view, Avadhi, the common language of Sufi *prem kahānīs* and that great masterpiece of Hindi literature, the *Rāmcaritmānas* of Tulsīdās, remained at base a Hindi form of speech rather than any kind of importation from the Muslim west. But Pāṭhak put it more summarily. Working forward from a famous passage in Dvivedi, he affirmed that, whatever role Muslims may have played in the formation of a common *sant* mentality, bhakti had always been a thoroughly Indian plant, from the moment it appeared in the south as a tender sapling *(biravā)* and throughout the course of its later development.[81]

For the rest, Pāṭhak anticipated Meenakshi Jain in emphasizing that the Āḻvārs of south India were actually unconcerned about Śaṃkara's *advaita* philosophy—again, bhakti is not reactive—and emphasized its organic unity by pointing to the analogy between Āṇṭāḷ in the ninth century and Mīrābāī in the sixteenth, as if their separation in space and time were a matter of no moment in the face of bhakti's irresistible unifying bond. Of course, that common bond was strengthened by those who specifically dedicated themselves to organizing and solidifying the bhakti tradition. He offered as an example the work of Nāthamuni, the major Śrī Vaishnava anthologist and systematizer whom Pāṭhak saw as part of the greater Rāmānandī tradition, with its impact on his own north India. To this first major Vaishnava stream he added a second, which consisted of the *sampradāys* that remained after one subtracted the Rāmūnuja/Rāmānand line: Madhva, Nimbārka, and (replacing Viṣṇusvāmī) Vallabha. Hence we have here, as with Raghavan, two broad arcs of bhakti: the direct south-north connection articulated along the Śrī Vaishnava/Rāmānandī line and the more complex and, for Raghavan, circuitous connection that formed the south-north connection in a more leisurely way. Here, though, by contrast to anything Raghavan intended to argue, all this was laid out as background to and in some way part of the cultural history of the Hindi language—and, by implication, the land that served as its home. No place was more home to that home than Allahabad, where the story was being told—confluence of the Ganges and the Jamuna, and of Hindi and English as well.

Krishna Sharma challenged just this sort of conception of the bhakti movement well before it was published, but she was writing from a different place and for a different language community. She was writing from Delhi in English. Yet I believe it is impossible to understand her access to the idea of the bhakti movement without factoring in exactly the tradition of Hindi scholarship that Pāṭhak was summarizing for students at Allahabad University—and thereby perpetuating. Even in Krishna Sharma's Delhi, even in the polyglot capital where English was king, the local undercurrent of Hindi and Punjabi was strong—then, as it still is today. Both Shukla and Dvivedi exercised important influences on her work, and in rather different ways. Yet it is important to grasp that, aside from their particular formulations of what was at stake in the idea of the bhakti movement, these men represented and helped to create the strong institutional base upon which this idea stood—the sort of institutional traction that is evident when we see students in places like Allahabad, Banaras, Agra, and yes, Delhi, worrying about the bhakti movement as they prepare annually for their B.A. exams. This was and is knowledge that matters, supported by government agencies and structured by academic departments. Faculty are paid to know about the bhakti movement and students are penalized if they don't.

This didn't mean there was no room for argument as Krishna Sharma encountered the concept. To the contrary, it meant that there was precisely room for argument—and the institutional paradigm would support it. Krishna Sharma joined that argument as a member of the faculty of Miranda House at Delhi University, and when she did so she almost necessarily made a point of acknowledging her debt to Ramchandra Shukla, the man whom she credited for separating out the *nirguṇ* and *saguṇ* streams or currents, as he called them *(dhārā)*. These, in Shukla's *History*, formed the main arteries by means of which the literature of bhakti was transmitted, and served to locate its various branches *(śākhā)*. Sharma lauded Shukla for having been the first scholar to press the *nirguṇ/saguṇ* distinction—a major qualification of the bhakti movement rubric he had inherited from the Orientalists, she said—but she regretted that "even in Hindi scholarship, the two groups are always linked together in all general accounts of the Bhakti movement and its antecedents."[82] Her purpose, she said, was effectively to strengthen Shukla's work by providing "a *raison d'être* for the *polarisation* of the two groups." The italicization is hers: only this polarization, she felt, would unravel the enigmas that had been caused by mistakenly welding the two together as if they formed a single bhakti movement.[83]

One way to gauge the disastrous consequences of this "artificial formulation," she said, was to see its effects on Marxist historians, so important to Indian intellectual life. She showed how on this account they had produced contradictory readings of bhakti's social force. On the one hand were Marxists who pointed to bhakti as the ideological backbone of the feudal system, emphasizing the way it exalted the virtue of servitude. Sharma mentions D. D. Kosambi and R. S. Sharma as exemplifying this position; Ranajit Guha continues the line.[84] On the other hand, and utterly opposed, were Marxists who stressed the fact that bhakti provided a language in which to protest the inequities and indignities of the caste system. Among the latter group, Sharma singles out Irfan Habib for particular mention, since he is regarded as the architect of the theory that bhakti took hold in north India in the period of bhaktas like Kabīr because they emerged from a class of urban artisans that had quickly grown far more consequential in society at large because of changed economic circumstances in the late Sultanate and early Mughal period.[85]

Sharma principally wanted to display this major contradiction in Marxist analysis, but along the way she also faulted Habib for trying too hard to establish a class base for *nirguṇ bhakti,* suggesting that his effort to align Nānak with Dādū and Kabīr on the basis of their shared occupational affiliations was misleading. Habib does point out that Kabīr was a weaver, Dādū was a cotton carder, and Nānak a grain merchant. Yet to suggest that this represents a single class location, broadly speaking, is to gloss over the fact that Nānak, unlike the other two, was a member of the upper castes—a *khatrī*—and as such could hardly serve as an example of an ideological formation that "belonged mostly to lower classes." Other scholars, not necessarily Marxists, erred even more egregiously by attempting to associate Chaitanya with this group. Altogether, such awkwardnesses showed the difficulties of trying to resort to a social or materialist model without paying sufficient attention to "the religio-philosophical content of the Bhakti movement."[86]

Sharma proposed an alternative, one that challenged the coherency of the bhakti movement to which even she sometimes loosely referred. For her, it was actually "the Nirguṇ tradition" that, as "a continuous factor in the religio-intellectual history of India," provided the larger context that made it possible to explain the emergence of a figure like Kabīr. He was, she said, "a definite stage" in its outworking. That tied him not to the Vaishnava figures who had conventionally been grouped as the acharyas of the "four *sampradāys*"—Rāmānuja, Madhva, Nimbārka, and Vallabha, in her formulation—but to a tradition that was entirely independent of it and always existed as a potentiality in Indian intellectual history. Its most famous proponent—indeed, its most effective popularizer—was Śaṃkara.[87]

Before Kabīr came along, that is. Sharma depicted Kabīr as her "case study" for the "medieval movement of Nirguṇ bhakti" as a whole. He and those like him "gave shape to a new popular cult, namely, that of the Nirguṇa-pantha" (*nirguṇ* path) that stood squarely within the Śaṃkarite tradition.[88] Actually, however, Kabīr was for Sharma more than just a case study. For it was he who succeeded in transferring Śaṃkara's "impersonal concept of God" into popular speech, and in doing so "he also carried it to its logical conclusion," refusing any compromise with *saguṇ* ways of thinking such as could be observed even in Śaṃkara, who was capable of distinguishing between higher and lower levels of truth that would accommodate them both.[89] Here she operates less as a historian than as a philosopher, and she credits Shukla and the tradition of Hindi scholarship he spawned as having laid the groundwork that enabled her to make this radical move. She praises Shukla for taking the first great hammer to the unitive edifice of the bhakti movement, but she faults him for not going far enough. As she might have pointed out, Shukla made explicit use of that unitary formulation, which was not surprising, given that his metaphor of streams suggests a confluence somewhere along the way. What impressed Sharma, though, was that Shukla had made such consistent use of the *nirguṇ/saguṇ* tension in bringing order to his *History of Hindi Literature.* Later writers like Pāṭhak were to perpetuate the theme of this tension, along with the idea of there being a strong and persistent analogy between *nirguṇ* and *saguṇ bhakti,* as they took up commentarial roles in the great Ramchandra Shukla tradition.

Dvivedi and the Ganga-Jamuna Sari

Even more important along these lines, however, was Hazariprasad Dvivedi, whose writings on Kabīr and the Nāth *sampradāy* played a significant role in shaping Sharma's thinking, as they had the thinking of many scholars of her generation. In fact, owing to his vivid prose style, Dvivedi's influence was hardly confined to an academic context. Many read his work on the *Nāth Sampradāy* (1950), but his book on Kabīr, called just that—*Kabīr* (1942)—almost had the status of a best seller. Sharma did dispute one of Dvivedi's major conclusions about Kabīr, namely, that his association with Rāmānand as a guru aligned him with bhakti of a Vaishnava stripe as practiced in south India, but other aspects of Dvivedi's work were fundamental to her own project. Two emerge in particular—one that she acknowledges explicitly and one of which she may possibly have been unaware.

The first of these was Dvivedi's effort to provide an intellectual lineage for Kabīr by relating him to the Nāth Yogī community that carried forward the legacy of Gorakhnāth. The spadework in this regard had actually been done by Barthwal, the young scholar who took considerable pride in the fact that the central argument of the paper he had delivered on this subject to the Sāhitya Pariṣad of the Nāgarīpracāriṇī Sabhā had been "universally accepted by scholars of Hindi."[90] But to Krishna Sharma's mind it was Dvivedi who fully documented the great extent to which Kabīr spoke the language of the Nāths and provided sociological and literary data to show how such a connection would have been widespread in the weaver *(julāhā)* community to which he belonged. Sharma accepts this, yet she objects, as she had in the case of Irfan Habib, to any sort of sociological reductionism: Dvivedi had thought the *jogīs* who patterned themselves after the Nāthpanthīs were a particular *jāti* within the weaver community. Rather, she urged that Kabīr's famous statement that he was neither Hindu nor Muslim was to be chalked up to his "spirit of universalism in general." Nonetheless, the sort of work Dvivedi did allowed Sharma to develop an intellectual lineage for Kabīr that connected him in real terms with a general "*nirguṇ*-izing" trend that could be seen in certain north Indian Vaishnava circles and was evident in the enormously influential text *Yogavāsiṣṭha*. This allowed her, despite her respect for the force of intellectual conviction per se, to give a general description of social if not strictly sectarian history that would render irrelevant—and in fact, false—the unitive construct of the bhakti movement, the "unitary approach" she so abhorred.[91]

Sharma's second debt to Dvivedi, as I have hinted, may have been an unconscious one, but it is at least as important as the first. This is the very concept of the bhakti movement itself. As we have seen, Sharma held that this concept had precipitated in the thinking of George Grierson in the first decade of the twentieth century. But the words "bhakti movement" are nowhere to be found in Grierson's prose, and I would argue that there is also a fair distance between the organic conception of the bhakti movement that emerges in later writing, both in Hindi and in English, and what we find in Grierson. For such a concept, in fact, we must turn to Dvivedi, and we can see it in the way he read—and perhaps misread—Grierson.

A particular passage was crucial. This was the passage to which Sharma had made reference when she credited Grierson with having crystallized the concept of the bhakti movement and criticized him for having done so in strictly Vaishnava terms. She said, we recall, "By establishing a link between the medieval bhaktas and the Vaishṇava acharyas, Grierson was able to describe the whole phenomenon of the medieval religious resurgence as the Bhakti movement in terms of Vaishṇavism."[92] Yet I have been unable to trace the concept "bhakti movement" to any of Grierson's writings, including those Sharma cites in this very passage. Where did she get the idea that he promulgated a theory of the bhakti movement when his own terms of reference were somewhat different?

I wonder if she got this impression from reading Dvivedi, who spoke of just the sort of "Vedanta-inspired bhakti" *(vedānt-bhāvit bhakti)* that Sharma was trying to restore to its rightful place in history. He believed, as Sharma did, that Kabīr—that plain-speaking Muslim-born proletarian giant of fifteenth- (or perhaps sixteenth-) century Banaras—had played a pivotal role in introducing the form of bhakti that took root in the religious consciousness of ordinary people living in north India. Dvivedi's epoch-making book *Kabīr,* to which Sharma sometimes refers, was one of the main places where he made these arguments. Assessing Kabīr's place in Indian religious practice, in the very passage where he spoke of "Vedanta-inspired bhakti," Dvivedi found occasion to quote Grierson, as Krishna Sharma was later to do in the passage we have just quoted. In Dvivedi's Hindi, Grierson comes across as saying the following:

> *grierson ne kahā thā, bijlī kī camak ke samān acānak is samast (dhārmik matoṅ ke) andhakār ke ūpar ek naī bāt dikhāī dī. yah bhakti kā āndolan hai.*[93]

Here Dvivedi is quoting a striking passage from Grierson's article "Modern Hinduism and Its Debt to the Nestorians," published in the *Journal of the Royal Asiatic Society* in 1907. According to Dvivedi, Grierson says, "Suddenly, like a flash of lightning, there came upon all this darkness a new idea." The darkness to which Grierson refers was the darkness of "gods, demigods, and deified heroes"—and the new idea? If we skip an important sentence that intervenes (more on that in a moment), we hear Grierson give a clear answer: "This new idea was that of *bhakti*."[94] This, apparently, was what came over into Dvivedi's translation as "the bhakti movement"—*yah bhakti kā āndolan hai:* "This is the bhakti movement."

Grierson goes on to specify what he means by "this new idea." He says, in a formulation he was later to borrow for his article for Hastings's *Encyclopaedia of Religion and Ethics,* "Religion was now no longer a matter of knowledge. It became a matter of emotion. It now satisfied the human craving for a supreme *personality,* to whom prayer and adoration could be addressed."[95] We can easily see where Grierson is going with this—just the sort of thing Krishna Sharma thought was so objectionable, the infusion of theistic Christian paradigms into the representation of Indian religious history. Indeed, that is the sentence Dvivedi allows to fall out of his translation. Grierson attributes this new impulse in the history of Indian religion to the advent of the Nestorians in the Indian subcontinent. Dvivedi disputes this idea—one that Grierson himself later modified—but note this: when Dvivedi enters this important caveat, he retains the idea of an all-encompassing *bhakti* movement. *Yah bhakti kā āndolan hai.*

For Dvivedi, of course, there was a difference: the bhakti movement he embraced had no tinge of Christian influence. That was an explicit point of departure from what the earlier Grierson, at least, had claimed. But there was another difference as well, one of which Dvivedi—like Sharma after him—was apparently unaware. Grierson had not actually spoken in terms of a movement in the first place. That happened only in translation—across the fence in Hindi.

We can see this transformation elsewhere in Dvivedi's handling of Grierson—slightly earlier. In 1940, as he laid out his *Hindī Sāhitya kī Bhūmikā* (Introduction to Hindi Literature), Dvivedi also wanted to set his own thinking in relation to Grierson's. He quoted a passage from Grierson's well-known entry on "Bhakti-Mārga" in Hastings's *Encyclopaedia of Religion and Ethics,* the one we earlier quoted at length. There the famous linguist had spoken about "the greatest religious revolution that India has ever seen," the bhakti transformation that made Hindu religion "no longer a thing of knowledge but of emotion." Dvivedi brought this passage over into Hindi, but when he did so, he made it thoroughly a matter of "movements." So here we have that sleight of hand—conscious or unconscious—once again. Dvivedi rendered "revolution" as *āndolan,* the term that was just then coming into standard use as a way to say "movement" in Hindi. Grierson had injected an element of comparison when he said that this "religious revolution" was "greater even than that of Buddhism," but Dvivedi, in paraphrasing, went further, saying that this *bhakti āndolan* was of a magnitude that set it above all the other, lesser *āndolans* in Indian history. This included that of the Buddhists, as Grierson had said, but again Dvivedi made those Buddhists into a movement. He took Grierson's simple noun "Buddhism" and converted it into "the movement of [the] Buddhist religion" *(bauddh dharm kā āndolan).*[96]

Even earlier in the process of thinking this out, Dvivedi had paused to offer a short checklist of the characteristically new points of view that had "suddenly burst forth" in the fifteenth century—the idea that the human lover of God (the bhakta) is greater than God *(bhagavān),* for example, or that the chief purpose of life is not release from the cycle of rebirth *(mokṣa)* but intimate love *(prem)*—and he credits Grierson for perceiving the great significance of this moment. But watch him closely once again. This time, in a famous departure, Dvivedi goes on to say that what Grierson saw as a sudden burst of rain would not have been possible if the clouds hadn't been gathering for years. Observe the logic: once again bhakti is a continuous movement—*bhakti āndolan* in the full sense of the word.[97] It is a long-gathering monsoon. It rolls on. A storm of songs, writ large?

Surely Dvivedi's distinctive articulation of the bhakti movement idea had a fair amount to do with his perception of himself and of his times. There he was, after all, participating in the gathering storm of Indian nationalism—all this was happening in the decade or so leading up to 1947—and because he was a historian of Hindi literature, with its major devotional component, bhakti was a big part of what he brought to the struggle. It was his own deep personal momentum. Hence I would urge that it was someone like Dvivedi rather than someone like Grierson who consolidated and perhaps even invented "the bhakti movement" as a single, simple, coherent notion. To be sure, it is Grierson who gets to frame the Linguistic Survey of India and mount the high platform of the *Encyclopaedia of Religion and Ethics,* but it is Dvivedi who is reacts intimately, viscerally to what he was reading not just in English but in Hindi.

There is another aspect of the Hindi-writing past to consider, as well. This takes us back to Ramchandra Shukla, Dvivedi's most illustrious predecessor as head of the Hindi Department at Banaras Hindu University. As we know, Shukla had written a long essay called *Bhakti kā Vikās* (The Development of Bhakti). Interestingly, he had not used the language of *āndolan* there. Perhaps the development of which he was speaking was too central in his sense of the *Geist* of Hindu/Indian cultural history to permit him to do so. In Shukla's usage the word *āndolan* still trailed a good bit of its earlier usage—a sense of swinging or oscillation—and that didn't quite match his image of bhakti as a great highway *(mārg)* of Indian religious culture, the road in which all other roads ought to converge.[98]

Yet in one passage, subsequently to be very influential, the chance to speak of such a swinglike motion in relation to what we could roughly call bhakti did arise, and then *āndolan* was on the tip of Shukla's tongue. This occurred in his subsequently canonical *History of Hindi Literature* (1929). There Shukla spoke of a "movement of Vaishnava religion that extended from one corner of India to the other in the fifteenth and sixteenth centuries of the *vikramī* era."[99] This was not lost on Dvivedi. Shukla's phrase "from one corner . . . to the other" resurfaces not once but twice in the section of Dvivedi's first book called "Hindi Literature and Vaishnava religion."[100] This book, *Sūr-Sāhitya,* was published in 1936.

Of course, Shukla had his forebears, too. In framing the passage at hand, he doubtless had in mind the sort of portrait of pan-Indian Vaishnavism that had been put forward by his own illustrious Banarsi predecessor Bharatendu Harishchandra (1850–1885), whose works he had just been editing at the time.[101] In fact, this is a thread that leads back to the end of the sixteenth century, as we shall see, but it is only when we arrive in the late 1920s and 1930s and then, conclusively, in 1940 that talk of *māls* (garlands of bhaktas) and the *sampradāys* (traditions of teaching and reception) changes to a discourse of "movements." By then, people like Dvivedi and Kshitimohan Sen and the members of the Progressive Writers' Association had been talking: the sound of the nationalist movement—*rāṣṭrīya āndolan* or *svatantratā āndolan*—echoed in the land. So when Shukla published the second, revised edition of his *History of Hindi Literature* in Banaras in 1940—the same year and city in which Dvivedi's *Introduction to Hindi Literature* appeared—he does indeed make reference to the *bhakti āndolan* (or as he says, *bhakti kā āndolan*) as such. To quote the line in full, "The wave of the movement of bhakti [*bhakti ke āndolan kī jo lahar*] that came from the south created in the sensibilities of certain persons a shared bhakti path [*sāmānya bhaktimārg*] for Hindus and Muslims alike, as was appropriate to the situation in north India."[102] Once Shukla said it, in an austere tome that is still in India the backbone of just about every college curriculum in Hindi, it was gospel.

Indeed there is a case to be made that the idea of the south-to-north course of Vaishnava bhakti as a movement first became something of deep significance not in English but in Hindi—as *āndolan*. Dvivedi, the initial energizing voice, was widely read, and he was to become a major player in two curriculum-building institutions where bhakti mattered most: Shantiniketan and Banaras Hindu University. Yet as we have seen, English was also important, even to those who wrote in Hindi, and from a strictly chronological point of view there is one more cluster of writers to take into account. First there is J. N. Farquhar, a missionary scholar whose book *An Outline of the Religious Literature of India,* published in 1920, Sharma cites. No overriding concept of a bhakti movement extending throughout India appears there, but Farquhar does make use of the phrase "bhakti movement" on two more specific occasions—first in regard to Maharashtra, then with regard to Gujarat. He does not bother to standardize his usage: one time he capitalizes the term bhakti, the other time he does not.[103] In this same unsystematic way the phrase "bhakti movement" also appears in Farquhar's *Primer of Hinduism,* published in 1912, where he says *en passant,* in the middle of a paragraph, that "the whole *bhakti* movement in the north owes a great deal to Rāmānanda." In his *Modern Religious Movements in India,* published in 1915, he gives the concept of "movement" title billing, but here again he speaks more often of movements than movement. Really his concern is with "the fresh religious movements which have appeared in India since the effective introduction of Western influence," which he holds primarily responsible for their genesis. Any predecessors are incidental to his subject and would, in a way, distract from it. This seems to underscore the fact that Farquhar's use of the term "bhakti movement" elsewhere seems more a reflex of general reference rather than the postulation of a single bhakti movement connecting all of India. That sense of the term—against which Sharma was arguing—is present nowhere in his writings.[104]

A second author to consider is Frank Ernest Keay. His *Introduction to Hindi Literature,* written in Jabalpur and published in 1920 by the Association Press, an arm of the Indian YMCA, where Farquhar served as literary secretary, was the second English treatment of this subject. The first, not coincidentally, had been written by none other than Grierson—

his *The Modern Vernacular Literature of Hindustan* (1889). In introducing his chapter on "Early Bhakti Poets (1400–1550)" Keay speaks of "the growth of the Vaishnava movement in North India" as if it had had a predecessor elsewhere, but he never tells us where. Even in his discussion of Rāmānand, who "took up his residence in Benares and made that the headquarters of the new movement," there is no direct mention of the southern connection to Rāmānuja that is familiarly claimed for Rāmānand and of which Keay was probably thinking. After all, his subject is Hindi literature: he is much more interested in the Sikh *Gurū Granth* of 1604, which gives us, he says, "some of the earliest specimens we possess of Hindī poetry of the *bhakti* movement."[105] This is the one time Keay uses the phrase. On the one hand it shares a commonly suggested broader usage; on the other it is, as with Farquhar, unspecific.

Finally, and I believe most importantly, there is Ishwari Prasad's *History of Medieval India,* published in Allahabad in 1925 by a member of Allahabad University's influential and distinguished history department and widely adopted in B.A. curricula elsewhere.[106] Here the tone and scope are quite different from what we meet in Farquhar and Keay. As Prasad concludes a discussion of "religious reform" and "the revival of the bhakti cult" in north India in the fifteenth and sixteenth centuries, he observes that "the domination of the Muslims did not utterly extinguish Hindu spirit and manliness." How does he know? First of all, he mentions the armed resistance to Muslim rulers that was offered by "Hindu chieftains and Zamindars all over the country"; and second, there was the emergence in the north of men like "Ramanand, Chaitanya, Kabir, and Nanak, who will stand for all time to come as beaconlights to guide frail humanity which is only too prone to fall into error and superstition . . . [This] proves the virility and vigour of the Hindu mind." Just earlier he had explained: "Excluded from the secular sphere of the state, the Hindu genius found an outlet in religion, and the new school of reformers tried to purify a system which was encrusted with superstitious rites and practices, so completely at variance with the true spirit of religion."[107]

"The virility and vigor of the Hindu mind" must have been much on Prasad's mind, for he also used this phrase when he introduced a discussion of "leaders of the *Bhakti* movement" like Rāmānuja, in south India.[108] Prasad saw such leaders of the bhakti movement both in the south and in the north.[109] The organic bond between them is not yet as forcefully articulated as it would be by Dvivedi, but one can see a definite consolidation by comparison with his sources—both on the English side (Grierson, Bhandarkar, Farquhar, and Keay) and also, if more sparsely, on the Hindi (the Miśrabandhu). Did Dvivedi read or talk with Prasad? His footnotes provide no clue. Yet Dvivedi was certainly connected to the Allahabad historians. R. P. Tripathi, one of the important mentors of his own teacher Rāhul Sāṃkrityāyan, in Banaras, was Prasad's great rival in the Allahabad history department and served as the principal architect of its characteristic emphasis on thought and culture. This is precisely the concern that comes across so clearly in the last chapter of *History of Medieval India*, "Civilization of the Early Middle Ages," the one that concerns us here. It is notably absent elsewhere in the book. Did Prasad include it only because Tripathi's efforts had put "thought and culture" on the syllabus for the first time? Perhaps: this was a textbook and it must cover the materials. But if that was how it happened, and if it had anything to do with Prasad's renowned ability to repeat verbatim what he had heard or seen, then we may have here the echo not just of what he might have read—in Ranade, for instance—but also of a more general level of public utterance that he may have heard around him. His contribution was to connect this talk of virility to the bhakti movement.[110]

As for Dvivedi, with his indirect ties to Allahabad, the man we know he was reading and responding to directly was Grierson. Here Hindi engages with English, and with considerable respect, but it worked the other way around, too. As Vijay Pinch has shown, Grierson was much shaped by Hindi-writing Indians such as the great Rāmānandī commentator Sītārāmśaraṇ Bhagavānprasād "Rūpkalā." Rūpkalā's life's work, eventually published in 1914, was a definitive edition of and commentary on the *Bhaktamāl* of Nābhādās. As it unfolded, this project had a major impact on Grierson. He devoted three articles to Nābhādās's *Bhaktamāl* in the pages of the *Journal of the Royal Asiatic Society*—his "Gleanings from the Bhakta-Mala" (1909–1910). Instructed at least in part by Rūpkalā, Grierson elsewhere declared the *Bhaktamāl* essential for "a just comprehension of the religious attitude of modern Hinduism."[111]

In all, then, we have a complexly bilingual and bicultural story, not the simple product of Orientalist conceptions, as Krishna Sharma had concluded. The European imprint on the concept of the bhakti movement was real, but it was only half the picture. The other half came from India itself, and in various ways. It came from European missionaries like Farquhar and Keay, who spent long, formative years there and were deeply concerned with the vernacular languages that most Orientalists tended to undervalue. And it came from Indians like Prasad who were thinking and writing in English, but whose lives and careers had far deeper local meanings than the name of that language would suggest. Prasad was renowned at Allahabad for his ability to quote page after page of English prose from memory—his command of Gibbon's *Rise and Fall of the Roman Empire* was legendary—but while many of his peers and students habitually wore jacket and tie and the manners that went with them, Prasad showed up in clothes with a more purely Indian accent—a "Bengali's coat," a shirt with a round collar, and a Nehruvian *ṭopī* cap. A home visit to "Punditji," as he was familiarly called, found him surrounded by his English books but clad in the still more traditional *bandhī* and *dhotī.*[112] Finally, as this sartorial momentum may suggest, the idea of the bhakti movement came not only from English but from Hindi—and even Bengali, as we shall see in Chapter 6. The *bhakti āndolan* was a crucial aspect of the cultural work of nation-building that preoccupied many north Indian intellectuals in the first half of the twentieth century, so the close tie to Hindi, a major vehicle of that work and one of its aspirations, seems in retrospect entirely natural.[113]

Where does this leave us? Seen from one angle, it leaves us with a self-proclaimedly nativist story of national interiority that turns out be a fabric partly woven of imported thread—perhaps even spun on an imported loom. Here is a supposedly homespun *khādī* garment that turns out to be at least partly a product of the imperial factory—like Gandhi himself. But there's another side to it. Not only are the primary salesmen and principal consumers of the bhakti-movement garment Indians, they are also important agents of its design. India, Indians, and Indian languages turn out to be at least as important as England, Englishmen, and English in the generation, maintenance, and marketing of this major idea of cultural and religious history.

In the end, there is no way to keep the two aspects entirely separate. Here we have a Ganga-Jamuna sari, as Aditya Behl once said in another context. It's woven such that if you turn it one way, it's one color; but if you let the light strike it from a different angle, suddenly the sari changes hue. And yet, like the reality to which the idea of the bhakti movement is intended to point, the garment is one.

2

The Transit of Bhakti

As we sleuthed our way through the twentieth century in the chapter just concluded, trying to discover how the modern idea of the bhakti movement took shape, we found ourselves in the pages of several very well-known texts—Ranade's *Rise of the Maratha Power,* Shukla's *Hindī Sāhitya kā Itihās* (History of Hindi Literature), and a trio that emerged from the hand of Hazariprasad Dvivedi. We visited stores where many thousands of students buy college textbooks and we listened to Raghavan's lectures along with millions of his countrymen. But nothing written or spoken about the bhakti movement in any of these contexts is as instantly recognizable to many Indians as another formulation, which is our subject in this chapter. This time bhakti speaks for itself—or rather, herself, since the Sanskrit word *bhakti* is feminine in gender, and bhakti's feminine gender is also preserved in most of India's spoken languages. Here is what Bhakti says:

> I was born in Dravida,
> grew mature in Karnataka,
> Went here and there in Maharashtra,
> then in Gujarat became old and worn.
> There, under the spell of these awful times,
> my body was riven by schismatics.
> For long I went about in this weakened condition,
> accompanied in lethargy by my sons,
> But on reaching Brindavan I was renewed,
> I became lovely once again,
> So that now I go about as I ought:
> a young woman of superb appearance.[1]

This passage, often called to mind by the mention of its opening phrase alone, has often served as the symbol and epitaph for more extended expositions of the bhakti movement. Although Professor Raghavan did not quote it when he launched into his Patel Lectures, these verses give us in nutshell form the first half of the circumambulatory narrative to which he appealed. Bhakti originates in the deep south—very likely the Tamil country itself, as Raghavan asserts, although the term "Dravida" as used in this passage may originally have had a somewhat wider reference. Then she moves northwest into Karnataka, as Raghavan confirms; thence northward into Maharashtra—the hint of various places in the phrase "here and there" is intriguing; then farther northward along the western coast of India into Gujarat, where she encounters a set of difficulties to which Raghavan does not allude. Finally, in the culminating moment, Bhakti leaves the coastal regions and crosses half the continent in a northeasterly direction to reach Brindavan, the area renowned as the wilderness *(van)* of the basil plant (*vṛndā* > Brindā) where Krishna spent his youth, performing marvelous acts of heroism, mischief, and spellbinding love. Brindavan lies on the banks of the Yamuna not far north of the ancient city of Mathura. There Bhakti is rejuvenated, which accounts for her sparkling appearance in present time, despite the fact that she has been traveling for quite a while and is actually quite ancient (*jīrṇatām*—"old and worn").

There is more to the story, and more of that anon. For now, though, let us be content with this part of the narrative, since it is by far the most famous segment of the whole. People in many parts of India know the initial phrase *utpannā draviḍe sāham,* "I was born in Dravida," and even if they are not be able to quote much of the passage that follows, they often have a good sense of what it says. They may not know where it came from, but thanks to Gita Press, India's premier publisher of inexpensively available religious books, that too is gradually entering the stream of public awareness. Gita Press's standard edition of the *Bhāgavata Purāṇa,* which is probably as influential as the *Bhagavad Gītā* itself among Vaishnava texts, includes as a preface another, much smaller text, whose purpose is to announce "the greatness of the *Bhāgavata Purāṇa.*" Those very words, in Sanskrit, comprise its title—*Bhāgavata Māhātmya*—and it is here, in the warm glow of the splendor of the *Bhāgavata Purāṇa,* that Bhakti utters her famous words of self-disclosure. Hence every reader of Gita Press's *Bhāgavata Purāṇa*—often accompanied by a Hindi or English translation—begins with these memorable words; and whenever it is expounded, as it is all over India, performers are apt to direct their audience's attention to these words from the *Bhāgavata Māhātmya,* very much as if they formed part of the *Bhāgavata Purāṇa* itself.

In the chapter that lies before us we will attempt to determine when, where, and why the "born in Dravida" narrative was fashioned. We will speculate about what the *Māhātmya*'s author intended when he spoke of the transformative effect exerted on bhakti by Brindavan, since that spot—eternally Krishna's—was the site of a major development effort in the course of the sixteenth century. Indeed, that effort took place in close proximity to the Mughal throne and sometimes with its active cooperation, contrary to anything one might imagine from reading the *Māhātmya* itself, so wrapped in its Vaishnava envelope. We will expand the envelope, therefore, and ask what the *Bhāgavata Māhātmya*'s narrative might have meant not just to the knowledgeable Hindus for whom it was evidently composed, but for any Muslims we might imagine as having been within earshot. Why press this question? The answer is plain. While Dvivedi, Raghavan, and others believed that the bhakti movement was capacious enough to embrace India's many Muslims and that Muslims played a part in creating it, this idea has been rejected by others. In its *Bhāgavata Māhātmya* form we can see why this would have been so. And yet, as we shall also see before the chapter is at an end, an influential group of Islamically inclined historians has championed the idea of the bhakti movement and even asserted that Islam was very largely responsible for its origin and growth. It would be hard to derive such a notion from the words of the *Bhāgavata Māhātmya* itself, but its appeal to Brindavan as the great force for renewal in bhakti's long story may actually justify it.

Bhakti in the Bhāgavata Māhātmya

The *Bhāgavata Māhātmya* is brief—a mere six chapters in all—but it plays upon the vastly larger document whose glories it sings. Allusions to the *Bhāgavata Purāṇa* abound, and this is so from the beginning. The author of the *Bhāgavata Māhātmya* transports us into the web of interconnections that launched the *Bhāgavata Purāṇa* itself. Gently, often implicitly, he reminds us of the several dialogues that the Purana had offered to explain its own origins. He situates his own account among them.

Two of these dialogues are more or less off-screen in the parent text, but no less significant for that reason. These are the dialogues in which the "*Bhāgavata* wisdom" is revealed by Krishna, the Supreme Person, to the world-encompassing deity Brahmā (BhP 2.9–10), and in which Brahmā expounds the *Bhāgavata* to the curious, musical, perennially peripatetic sage Nārada, who is a special patron of bhakti (BhP 2.5–7).[2] There is also a hint that Nārada had already known the *Bhāgavata* in some form in a past life, hearing it from sages who recited these Krishna stories *(kṛṣṇakathāḥ)* when they interrupted their wanderings and settled down during the rainy season (BhP 1.4.26–30). These past conversations form the background for two additional dialogues that occupy the author of the *Bhāgavata Purāṇa* more directly: one transpires between the seers Sūta and Śaunaka, the other between the sage Śuka and king Parīkṣit. These provide us with the situations that furnish us the manifest text. The former serves as its frame story, comprising the Purana's first and last books (BhP 1, 12); the latter supplies it with the narrative that constitutes the interior books (BhP 2–11).

The author of the *Bhāgavata Māhātmya* takes this rich dialogical dough and kneads it once again, with new results. He tells us that he is bringing to light a previously neglected encounter that will make us appreciate just how valuable the *Bhāgavata Purāṇa* is in the dark *kali* age into which we are now plunged. True, the Purana had proclaimed its own value—like other Puranas, it is not shy on this point—but the author of the *Māhātmya* thinks he ought to add to this, revealing the spectacular results that can be had when the *Bhāgavata Purāṇa* is recited in a certain way. He revisits the frame story in which Sūta imparts his wisdom to Śaunaka, acknowledging the dialogue between Śuka and King Parīkṣit as he does so, but this time he has Sūta report something new: a dialogue between Nārada and Bhakti that Śuka had heretofore kept secret (BM 1.24). It is in the context of this crucial secret that Bhakti makes her appearance in the *Māhātmya* and utters her famous words. What she says to Nārada in that moment will ultimately cause him to hear the *Bhāgavata* yet one more time—this time, not from Brahmā but from Brahmā's sons, the four eternal youths familiarly called "Sanaka and the rest."[3] In the course of doing so, he will renew his compact with the great text—doubtless something worthwhile in its own right, but an event that turns out to be even more important for the fate of Bhakti and those who depend on her.

The scene is a dramatic one. Nārada has come to earth with the conviction that it is the best of all worlds; but as he roams from place to place, even the most sacred and celebrated among them, he discovers that things are seriously amiss. The world has been cast into bondage by the *kali* age, which the *Māhātmya* describes as being the friend of all that opposes dharma (*kalinādharmamitreṇa,* BM 1.30). Lying is rampant. No one cares for the poor; instead they care only for their own bellies. Those who ought to show the ways of truth are infatuated with falsehood instead. Everything is upside down. Renunciants live the lives of householders, and just as the *Bhagavad Gītā* had observed in a similarly dire moment (BG 1.40–42), the roles that women play in this brave new world tell a sorry, revealing tale. Wives rule the house, not their husbands; wives' brothers provide what passes for wisdom; people sell their daughters out of greed; couples quarrel all the time. As for the sacred places Nārada has been visiting, he can report that they and the rivers that flow by them are controlled by outsiders who have destroyed great numbers of temples. The word he uses to name these evildoers is *yavana,* a term that initially referred to Greeks or Westerners but later came to connote Muslims, as undoubtedly it does here. Yet the rot in the society Nārada observes is hardly caused by external forces alone. As he presents his tale of woe, Nārada returns to two key indexes of social health—or in this case, sickness. Women, he says, live by prostitution, and Brahmins sell their Vedic expertise for financial gain (BM 1.31–36).

Yet there is a ray of hope. In the midst of this depressing Bosch-like landscape, a familiar subject of Puranic lament, Nārada's eye is drawn to a remarkable sight—a young woman of astonishing beauty surrounded by a bevy of lovely female companions. She seems to inhabit a charmed realm, to boot, for Nārada encounters her on the banks of the river Jamuna (Skt. Yamunā), where the playful actions *(līlā)* of Hari—that is, Krishna—had transpired. Even so, there is nothing charming in her mood, for she is obsessed with the condition of two aged, insensate men who lie beside her, gasping for breath. She tries to nurse them back to life, but the attempt leaves her desperate. Nārada is drawn magnetically to her side. "Who are you?" he asks.

The young woman, of course, is Bhakti, and she volunteers just this information in the words we have already heard. She goes on to identify the women who faithfully attend her as being India's rivers—"the Ganges and so forth" (*gaṅgādyāḥ,* BM 1.46). As for the old men, she explains counterintuitively that these are her sons Jñāna and Vairāgya—knowledge and renunciation, the disciplines of wisdom and self-control. Since Bhakti has enveloped them with her maternal protection, denizens of the present world-age perceive them as being her sons, and indeed the bond that ties them together is strong. They ought to be equal partners, these three—it has been so ordained in the *Bhagavad Gītā,* though there renunciant action is called *karma,* not *vairāgya*—but we see that nothing could be further from the truth in present time. Bhakti feels the weight of this awful imbalance: the distress of Jñāna and Vairāgya prompts a deep anxiety in her.

Nārada resolves to try to help her. The sight of her disorientation makes him return to his catalogue of the ills of the present age, but through it all he assures Bhakti that her own powers, being connected with an overwhelming consciousness of the presence of Krishna and the uttering of his names, ought to be sufficient to revive Jñāna and Vairāgya. In the *kali yuga,* he says, bhakti alone confers liberation (BM 2.21). This affirmation has an ironic twist, for in the very course of making it, Nārada says that *jñāna* and *karma* (read *vairāgya*) have become useless in the cause of attaining Krishna, who is the ultimate key (2.18).

This does not sound hopeful. Nonetheless, responding to Bhakti's desperate plea, Nārada tries his hand at resuscitating these spent forces. He chants the Vedas, Upanishads, and the *Bhagavad Gītā* in the ears of Jñāna and Vairāgya, but it is no use. They scarcely stir. A voice from heaven tells him not to give up, however—he's on to something with this chanting—and eventually, after he has consulted the paragons of faith that do still inhabit this world (*sādhus* and *sants,* BM 2.32, 3.26), and after he himself has tried a stint of renunciation at Badrikāśram, the Himalayan retreat classically dedicated to that purpose (2.44), Nārada realizes that only a chanting of the *Bhāgavata Purāṇa* holds any promise of bringing Knowledge and Self-Abnegation back to life. This makes sense since, as the author of the *Māhātmya* soon has Nārada explain, the *Bhāgavata Purāṇa* is the sum and essence of all the texts he has just been busy intoning. It supersedes them (2.64–73). If only Jñāna and Vairāgya can hear a chanting of the *Bhāgavata Purāṇa* they will be able to join Bhakti and dance in every heart (2.62–63).

In the third chapter of this little epic, they do just that. Nārada sponsors a reading of the *Bhāgavata* at a place not far from Badrikāśram—

Haridvar, where the Ganges gushes out from the mountains onto the plain below. Yet the performance he orchestrates is no ordinary one. Nārada has learned from the four sons of Brahmā that in the *kali* age the *Bhāgavata Purāṇa*'s special potency can best be experienced when it is recited end to end over a seven-day period (BM 3.47). This is what Nārada arranges to have happen.

It is a joyous scene. Gods and sages gather, sharing in the huge éclat. Various categories of sacred discourse are also in attendance—Vedas, Upanishads, shastras, mantras, tantras, and the seventeen remaining Puranas. So are the guardians of space—the great pilgrimage sites, the directional quadrants, lakes, mountains, and streams—and a gamut of beings from women to celestial musicians to ascetic seers and demons. As the story comes to a crescendo, the sons of Brahmā take their special seat at the center of the assembly, preparing to recite the *Bhāgavata Purāṇa* to Nārada (BM 3.10–22). What we actually hear from their lips, however, is not the actual text of the Purana. Rather, they speak about its glory, for that is the *Māhātmya*'s special mission to relate. This occupies a great deal of the third chapter (3.23–52), including a reminder of how Krishna infused the *Bhāgavata* with his own presence when he departed from this world (3.53–65).

Finally comes the moment we have been waiting for, when the Purana itself will be recited, but since that happens in and as the *Bhāgavata* itself, what we now hear is not the actual text but evidence of its presence. This is provided by the fact that Bhakti returns to the scene. Our narrator remarks that she is "nothing but love," and when she suddenly appears, she has her two youthful sons in tow (BM 3.67). "How did she get here?" the others ask, the implication being that they had not seen her taking her seat along with the other guests. The sons of Brahmā are quick to explain this miracle. Bhakti, they say, has emerged from the substance of the story itself (*kathārthato niṣpatitā,* 3.69). Indeed, she confirms that this is so: she has been nurtured to full flower by the "juice" of the exposited text (*puṣṭā . . . kathārasena,* 3.70).

Apparently the stated goal of the *Māhātmya* has been achieved: all is well, thanks to this seven-day performance. But the odd thing is that, while Jñāna and Vairāgya are shown to be present with Bhakti, no explicit attention is paid to them. Their remarkable rejuvenation, which had seemed to be the driving force of the plot, apparently goes without saying.

If there is a concern for anyone else beside Bhakti, it is for "the servants of Hari" (*haridāsa,* BM 3.72), Krishna's devotees. After Bhakti emerges in the great epiphany, she asks where she should reside: she does not want the revivifying force of the *Bhāgavata Purāṇa* to dissipate. The answer she receives from Brahmā's eternally youthful sons is that she should establish her dwelling in the consciousness of Vaishnavas (*vaiṣṇavamānasāni,* 3.71). After all, as the *Māhātmya* had earlier explained, she is the one dearest to Krishna, dearer to him than even his own life, so it is she to whom all souls in this world must have access, even those who have only "the meanest homes" (2.3). Yes, we may reflect, the *Bhāgavata Māhātmya* is dedicated to singing the Purana's greatness, but Nārada was hardly wrong when he sang Bhakti's own *māhātmya* to her face (2.22).

If on the shores of the Jamuna Bhakti had seemed to lose the luster that would naturally accompany such greatness, it was really only an illusion. It is true that she resides eternally with Krishna, but she had found it necessary to manifest herself in a shadow form (*chāyārūpam,* BM 3.8) so that she could take under her wing the two forces that in earlier ages had joined her in granting liberation to denizens of time and space—Jñāna and Vairāgya. Her silent partner in the enterprise of saving them is Krishna, who, as he departed from this earth to recover his own intrinsic form, infused himself into the *Bhāgavata Purāṇa* to such a degree that it became a tangible image of himself (*vāḍmayī murtiḥ pratyakṣā vartate hareḥ,* BM 3.62). That is how, thanks to Nārada's plot-enabling curiosity (he often plays this role), Bhakti's earthly doppelgänger manages to succeed in her task.

As we come to the end of these first three chapters there is a considerable sense of satisfaction, both narrative and theological. We have heard of Bhakti's travels and travails, and her primacy has been vindicated in a story that takes advantage of India's physical landscape and seems to refer to its bhakti history—the "born in Dravida" passage. Moreover, a particular ritual conception of what the *Māhātmya* regards as India's most significant bhakti text has been announced and justified at great length: a week (Skt. *saptāha,* Hindi *saptāh*) wholly dedicated to reciting and hearing the *Bhāgavata,* a *bhāgavat saptāh.* Why then does the author of the *Māhātmya* feel it necessary to continue for another three chapters?

Parsimoniousness of expression is hardly the hallmark of Puranic discourse, but even so it is hard to miss the fact that the narrative loses some of its tight coherence at this point. As the fourth chapter commences, in fact, the hypostasized figures of Bhakti and her two "sons" utterly disappear from view. Nārada persists, but he seems to be looking beyond this trio as he asks in a general sort of way just who might be purified by a seven-day "sacrifice" of the verbal sort (*saptāhayajñena kathāmayena,* BM 4.9)—a *yajña* such as we have just observed (4.10; cf. 3.6, 3.30). The sons of Brahmā respond by telling a tale of "primordial history" (*itihāsam purātanam,* 4.15) that takes us back to a moment when an archetypically evil figure called Dhundhukārī was rescued from unending perdition by a *bhāgavat saptāh.* His righteous half-brother Gokarṇa was responsible for this good deed, so avidly remembered. The story of Dhundhukārī and Gokarṇa is a flashback, and this chronological fact has its geographical counterpart. Whereas the first three chapters of the *Bhāgavata Māhātmya* plot a generally northward trajectory, chapters 4 and 5 take us back to the south. Only as they conclude do we loop northward to Ayodhya and Citrakūṭ—Rām's country, it would seem.

Then in the sixth chapter we shift gears again as the sons of Brahmā take up another potential question: Just how should a seven-day recitation of the *Bhāgavata Purāṇa* proceed? What ritual precautions should be observed? That leads back into a scene that is meant to be similar to what we experienced at the conclusion of chapter 3. By pure narrative logic, it should actually be the same, but there is a little slippage. Once again the gods and certain significant mortals assemble and Bhakti, Jñāna, and Vairāgya break out dancing, but the gods are different this time—Krishna himself (he is called Hari) leads the pack—and so are the human beings, who are now identified as bhaktas. Moreover, two new results are announced. Hari grants the boon of his presence in all subsequent *bhāgavata saptāhs* and the sage Śuka appears—emerging as if from the *Bhāgavata Purāṇa* itself to install Bhakti, Jñāna, and Vairāgya in a formal way in the text that from a philosophical point of view is meant to reconcile them (BM 6.91). All's right with the world.

In the end, as a sort of coda, Śaunaka comes back on stage to ask Sūta about the exact chronology of the three *saptāhs* that the *Māhātmya* has by now described (BM 6.93–103). Sūta aligns them nicely, explaining how each began on the ninth day of the waxing half of a different lunar fortnight; each would then have concluded on the full-moon day. The first of these was Śuka's recitation to Parīkṣit—the *Bhāgavata Purāna* per se. The second was Gokarṇa's recitation to Dhundhukārī and other residents of Karnataka; this happened two hundred years later. Finally there was the moment when the sons of Brahmā performed the *Bhāgavata* for Nārada, Bhakti, and the others at Haridvar; that was thirty years later still. Thus the author of the *Bhāgavata Māhātmya* does his best to rationalize the text as it draws to its conclusion. Along the way, however, we experience some of the lilting, disparate, dialogue-generated momentum that we associate with the diction of the Puranas. It is tempting to think that the three major parts of the text—Bhakti's transit, the drama of Gokarṇa and Dhundhukārī, and the prescription of how a *bhāgavat saptāh* ought to be performed—may originally have existed independently of one another, but manuscript evidence hints at such a possibility only in the case of the third.[4] Otherwise the *Māhātmya* seems always to have been transmitted as a single unit.

The Text in Space and Time

In earlier writing I have pursued a range of clues provided by the *Bhāgavata Māhātmya* that would enable us to specify the identity of its author. Other scholars have tended to read the "born in Davida" pericope in isolation from the *Māhātmya* as a whole, which has led them to focus on the pivotal importance of Brindavan and to suggest that the text must have been written in or shortly after the sixteenth century either by a Vallabhite (Krishna Sharma seems to lean in this direction) or a Chaitanyite (Jean Filliozat, in this). I have urged, by contrast, that we keep Haridvar firmly in view, since it and not Brindavan is clearly the culmination of the story. Building on James Lochtefeld's observation that leaders of ascetic orders in Haridvar could on occasion patronize Brahmins, I have tried to take adequate account of the fact that the *Māhātmya* is so focused on the present state of scholars and renunciants *(jñāna, vairāgya)*.[5] When it specifies a Brahmin as the ideal expositor of the *Bhāgavata Purāṇa*, as it does so pointedly in its final chapter, this need not exclude Haridvar's ascetics from the larger picture of who might have been responsible for the text's composition. Unfortunately the location that the *Māhātmya* suggests as the place where this act of patronage might have occurred—*ānandavan*, the forest of bliss—turns out never to have designated a specific locale in or near Haridvar and therefore the home of a particular group or order. Rather, it functioned as a name for the city as a whole.

This broad indeterminacy, however, should not lead us to despair. We can be quite sure that the *Bhāgavata Māhātmya* was composed somewhere in north India, very likely in the latter half of the seventeenth century or the early years of the eighteenth. This is clearly indicated by the *Māhātmya*'s earliest dated manuscripts. These burst onto the scene in 1714. Seven copies survive from then until 1731, three written in a single year (1724). None of these reveals where it might have been scribed or the community responsible for doing so, but the collections where they are now housed—Baroda, Jaipur, Jodhpur, Nathdvara (which houses two copies), Kota, and the British Library—show that they must have circulated in northern India. One manuscript, coming from a Brindavan collection, claims a date some three centuries earlier—V.S. 1405, that is, 1347 or 1348—but the odd appearance of the numbers themselves (there has been overwriting) together with a set of related considerations makes it impossible to trust this date. Baroda, Kota, and Nathdvara all suggest a Vallabhite connection, and undoubtedly that community took an interest in the text; but nothing in its dedicatory formula confirms that it originated there, as would have been normal if this was the case. The familiar Vallabhite term *brahmasambandh* does tantalizingly occur (BM 1.22), but not in its normal sectarian meaning, and the text's pointed references to dancing and singing in Brindavan, where the Vallabhites have no historical home, point if anything toward the Chaitanyites. Overall it is hard to read the *Bhāgavata Māhātmya* as a document belonging to either sect (we will examine their histories and personalities in Chapter 4), even though it mentions the importance of maintaining clear lines of transmission according to *sampradāy* (1.76). It seems rather to take a more comprehensive view.

As its general place and time of authorship and its internal narrative structure make clear, the *Bhāgavata Māhātmya* shows us a north looking self-consciously to the south for its legitimacy. We know that the same thing happened at the court of the great Kachvaha king Jaisingh II, as will be shown in Chapter 5. We also know that great infusions of Maharashtrian Brahmins into the intellectual life of Banaras in the course of the seventeenth century led to a new sense that Brahmins of north and south have an important interregional relationship. A sense of the prestige of the south is also reflected somewhat earlier, in the conviction that Vallabha and Nimbārka both came from Tailangana Brahmin families, and in the paradigm of the four *sampradāys,* which first gets articulated at the end of the sixteenth century (see Chapter 3). Still earlier we witness Chaitanya's effort to recruit Gopāl Bhaṭṭ from the chief priestly family at Srirangam, perched on an island in the Kaveri in Tamilnadu, so as to place his Brindavan initiative on a proper ritual footing, as would become evident in the new Rādhāramaṇ temple there. Thus the overarching account suggested in the *Bhāgavata Māhātmya* does seem to have been built on earlier foundations, but they were disparate.

At present, alas, it is not possible to specify exactly where or when the *Bhāgavata Māhātmya* might have been composed, and the author of the *Māhātmya* may not have been eager for us to discover that information in any case. He was projecting a bigger picture instead. He seems to have wanted us to ask just how far north we should travel so as to look southward in the most convincing way. His answer, ultimately, is Haridvar. Wherever our author sat, Haridvar would have represented the place that was as far north as you could go without actually entering the mountains. It lies just this side of the ethereal Himalayan realm of Badrikāśram, whose consciousness of its connection to the whole of India, including its southern regions, was registered in temples built way back in the ninth century.[6] But Haridvar is the pivot. Looking one direction, it is the doorway to the realm of Hari and the gods; looking the other, it opens to the Gangetic plain and the entire subcontinent beyond. Time and again the myths of Haridvar celebrate this focal position on the great north-south axis.

If the specific geographical setting that produced the *Bhāgavata Māhātmya* remains unclear, however, we can be more definite about the social and religious milieu out of which it came. Performing the *Bhāgavata Purāṇa* was a growth industry in sixteenth- and seventeenth-century north India. In Braj, a man named Ghamaṇḍī (or alternatively, Nārāyaṇ Bhaṭṭ) is said to have created something like the kernel of the *rās līlā* Krishna dramas we recognize today—or perhaps they were already there before these south Indian aficionados arrived.[7] Gurū Nānak knows about enacted Krishna stories *(kahāniyāṅ)* something like this, and doesn't like them one bit.[8] Then there are the Ahīrs whose performances of the Krishna story figure importantly in the *Kanhāvat* said to have been written by Malik Muhammad Jāyasī in 1540.[9] All these float around somewhat unclearly in the *Bhāgavata*'s general ambience, but we can also be more concrete. A decade before Jāyasī a man called Lālac "Halvāī," writing from Hastīgrām near Rae Bareilly, specifically created an Avadhi shortening of the tenth book of the *Bhāgavata*. Before the end of the century (1595), we also had a vernacular commentary on the eleventh book by Caturdās, and when Eknāth produced his famous Marathi treatment of the eleventh book in the sixteenth century, he was sitting in Banaras.[10]

The tenth book, the famous *daśama skandha,* must have risen to almost canonical status by then—and particularly the five "core" chapters describing the *rās līlā* proper, that is, Krishna's amours with the *gopīs*—since just about then Harirāmvyās, in Brindavan, was shaping his *rāspañcādhyayī* on the five famous chapters extending from 29 to 33. Narsī Mehtā had already produced similar works in Gujarati, and Nandadās was about to do so again in Brajbhasha (ca. 1560–1570).[11] Nandadās also produced what one might call an actual "translation" of the tenth book of the *Bhāgavata,* his *Bhāṣā Dasam Skandh,* which he seems to have abandoned after he completed the twenty-eighth chapter. "Why did he stop?" we might ask. Was it because this brought him to the section of the text with such obviously—and already well-celebrated—dramatic possibilities that he skipped the rails and went over into the more interactive genre of *rāspañcādhyayī,* which comes out almost as a *nāṭak* in his hands?[12] Nandadās's *Rāspañcādhyayī* is one of his best-known works.

We would apparently have to wait another century in north India—until 1687—before we got a "faithful" *bhāṣā* version of the complete Sanskrit original of the *Bhāgavata*'s tenth book—this, at the instance of Bhūpati. At the beginning of his work, Bhūpati tells us that he is producing it not just in *bhāṣā,* but specifically in Brajbhasha.[13] And his was not the only text of its kind that circulated at this moment in time. Another Brajbhasha *Bhāgavat Dasam Skandh,* this one richly illustrated in the Malva or Bundelkhandi style, shows up in 1686 and 1688, the former giving us episodes from the first half of the tenth *skandha;* the latter, from the last.[14] Still another appears in 1703.[15] There are numerous parallel works in other vernaculars—Kannada, Gujarati, Malayalam, Bengali, Orissi, and Assamese—and we also have versions of the *Bhāgavata* not only in Sanskrit but, very importantly, in Persian.[16]

I can well imagine now this remarkable profusion of *Bhāgavatas* by the late seventeenth century in north India—and the performative mêlée that it implies—might have produced a certain anxiety in groups of Brahmins who understood the *Bhāgavata Purāṇa* to be their own special domain. And then there is the social component. Bhūpati was not a Brahmin but a Kāyasth, and in this he was not alone. A Gujarati named Keśav Kāyasth had composed a *Kṛṣṇakrīḍākāvya* in the late fifteenth century, and you may remember that Lālac was a *halvāī:* he or someone in his family sold sweets. Lālac too was a Kāyasth, and it was another Kāyasth, a man by the name of Āsānand, who took it upon himself to finish the *Haricarit* that Lālac had begun. He had made it to chapter 45 in 1614, when he stopped.[17] Against this polyglot, poly-caste backdrop, did certain Brahmins want to reassert their own particular capacities and training—and thereby reassert the power of the original text?

In asking this question, we have to be careful to distinguish between the particular way the *Bhāgavata Māhātmya* demands that the great Purana be performed—who has the right, for whom, under what circumstances—and the simple fact of its being performed in the course of seven days. For the latter we may have a bit of earlier evidence, coming from the Vallabha *sampradāy,* though it sits on a philological quagmire. The *Vallabhadigvijaya,* which dates itself to March 1601 according to the printed edition and is ascribed to Yadunāth, a grandson of Vallābhācārya, says that Vallabha performed *bhāgavat saptāh.*[18] The *Caurāsī Baiṭhak Caritra,* another Vallabhite document, follows suit. The problem is that despite what they intend to convey, both of these are late texts—the *Caurāsī Baiṭhak Caritra* apparently dating to the eighteenth century and the *Vallabhadigvijaya* to the end of the nineteenth.[19] More interesting for our purposes, therefore, is another, far less well-known Vallabhite text, the *Sampradāyapradīpa* of Dvivedī Gadākhya, which dates itself to 1553 and which will be a major focus of Chapter 5. Unless I have missed the reference, it does not attest to Vallabha as a performer of *bhāgavat saptāhs* (although we do have good evidence that Vallabha was deeply interested in and knowledgeable about the *Bhāgavata*), but it does say that Keśav Kāśmīrī, the leader of the Nimbārka community in sixteenth-century Brindavan, was known in precisely this guise.

If we step back from the seven-day frame, we quickly see how widespread devotion to the performance of the *Bhāgavata* was in other sixteenth-century Brahmin communities. Take the Chaitanyites, for example. Rūp Gosvāmī's guru-brother Raghunāth Bhaṭṭ is remembered as having recited a portion of the *Bhāgavata Purāṇa* on a daily basis "at the assembly of Rūp Gosvāmī," as the *Caitanyacaritāmṛta* puts it—probably at the temple of Govindadev.[20] And Gadādhar Bhaṭṭ made a similar commitment, not only to Govindadevjī but to Rādhāramaṇjī, Gopīnāthjī, and Madanmohan. Gadādhar Bhaṭṭ's descendents keep that vow alive till this day.[21] These are just examples: the list is long indeed. In the face of all this—perhaps especially the vernacular activity—we can well imagine a degree of anxiety on the part of Brahmins who might have been eager to assert (or reassert) their particular way of performing the great Purana.

Who might these Brahmins have been? The geography that the *Bhāgavata Māhātmya* adopts in its fourth and fifth chapters provides a clue. Looking outward from a base in the north, as established in the first three chapters, we find ourselves surveying quite a different part of the country in a prior time: Gokarṇa and its environs in Karnataka. The text tells us that the virtuous Gokarṇa, who saved his brother from death through a seven-day recitation of the *Bhāgavata Purāṇa,* lived on the upper reaches of the Tungabhadra River, which is not terribly far, as the crow flies, from the ancient Shaiva Gokarṇa. What seems to have happened is that place has been transformed into person. The name designating a great lodestone of southern Shaiva pilgrimage practice has been co-opted in such a way that it now applies to a hero of Vaishnava religiosity. This would have had a certain delicious appeal to Vaishnava ascetics living in Haridvar, since they had long been embattled with their Shaiva rivals and had tended to be on the losing side of the conflict, but it would also have made sense as a new twist on a general pattern according to which the prestige of Gokarṇa was leveraged so as to participate in and amplify the sanctity of north Indian pilgrimages centers such as Banaras and Mathura.[22] I think the author of the *Māhātmya* belonged to a community of north Indian Vaishnava Brahmins who felt besieged by a profusion of *Bhāgavata Purāṇa* performance practices that they no longer controlled, and who therefore turned to the south to shore up their authority as purveyors of the *Bhāgavata*'s special power. They turned to Gokarṇa as others had done, but in a new, narratively inventive way.

Had they recently migrated northward from southwestern India, carrying with them memories that were fresh in mind, or did they make up their image of the south in a much more approximate way, perhaps never having had any close connection to that place? It is hard to tell. Their migration from south to north is not impossible to imagine. One thinks, for comparative purposes, of the networks that tie the Nambūdari Brahmins who officiate at Badrināth to their Shaiva kinsmen in Kerala, or of the Vīraśaivas, originally from Karnataka, who are ensconced at Kedārnāth not far away. But one should also consider the *agnihotṛ* Brahmins who maintain a tradition of *bhāgavat saptāh* at Gokarṇa itself.[23] They are Shaiva, but they intermarry with the Mādhva Vaishnava families of Udupi, and they trace their devotion to the *Bhāgavata* to its miraculous powers. Family tradition has it that seven generations ago no male child was forthcoming—the same interval that is given before the birth of Dhundhukārī and Gokarṇa. In the family story as in the *Māhātmya,* a seven-day recitation of the *Bhāgavata Purāṇa* turned the tide.[24] By my estimate, this crucial event might have transpired sometime around the turn of the eighteenth century, and it was precisely then, as we have seen, that manuscripts of the *Bhāgavata Māhātmya* began to appear. But this occurred in the north, not the south, and the *Māhātmya* projects not a direct image of this family's remembered migration—from north to south—but an inverse one, from south to north.

What is one to conclude? It is hard to know whether *Bhāgavata Māhātmya* was composed by a group of northern Brahmins who once had southern origins and felt the power of that pedigree threatened by others' recently articulated claims to the *Bhāgavata Purāṇa,* or whether we are dealing with a set of strictly northern Brahmins who, similarly pressured, wanted to invoke the sense of deep, unbroken history that was offered by the cultural mystique of the south. Either way, this was a text that emerged from a Brahmin community living somewhere in north India between the mid-seventeenth century and the early years of the eighteenth.

The Built Brindavan and Mughal Bhakti

I have been stressing the importance of Haridvar in imagining the conditions under which the *Bhāgavata Māhātmya* might have been composed, but there is something important to be said about Brindavan as well. When the author of the *Māhātmya* works Brindavan into that crucial "born in Dravida" passage, he is speaking of a site that had, by the time he wrote, emerged as a fixed, built locale. At another level, Brindavan, the adolescent world of Krishna, is always and eternally present, but clearly it was not this perennial, ineffable Brindavan that brought Bhakti back to life in the *Bhāgavata Māhātmya*. There she is pictured as wandering around in time and space as we know them. When the *Māhātmya*'s author speaks of Brindavan, he means the Brindavan that was created more or less *ex nihilo* by kings, generals, and high officials associated with the court of the Mughal emperor Akbar (r. 1556–1605). This new theater of Hindu-Muslim collaboration at the imperial level made possible, among other things, the largest temple in all India that was ever designed as a single structure—the Gauḍīya temple of Govindadev, completed in 1590 (Figure 1)[25]—and the *farmāns* suggest that the Mughal administration also understood the Gauḍīya *sampradāy* as its official conduit for many other building projects in Braj. A retrospective *farmān* issued to Govindadev in 1598 described what Tarapada Mukherjee and Irfan Habib have called "the entire scheme of grants" that had by then emerged from the throne.[26]

When Bhakti says in the *Bhāgavata Māhātmya* that she "became lovely once again" *(navīn eva surūpinī)*—that she was positively and beautifully renewed—she is undoubtedly referring not just to the new aestheticism that recast the Braj countryside in Krishna's image,[27] but to the major program of land grants and temple construction by means of which bhakti was deliberately built for all to see. Rūp Gosvāmī, the architect of a philosophical system that expanded aesthetic theory in such a way that it culminated in bhakti, was not just an academic but simultaneously the principal officer *(adhikārī)* of the first temple of Govindadev. In that role he evidently managed grants made to Govindadev by Rājā Bhagavāndās of Āmer. Direct imperial support for this temple and the sister temple of Madanmohan is first documented in a *farmān* dated January, 1565, less than a year after Rūp's death, and within a decade of Akbar's ascent to the Mughal throne.[28] Bhagavāndās's son Mānsingh, who became Akbar's most important general, expanded this legacy by authorizing and supporting the construction of the massive new temple that was constructed on the same site in 1590.

Govindadev was hardly the only temple in town, and the project of massive renovation—actually, innovation—of which it served as capstone seems very probably to correspond to the sort of renewal Bhakti had in mind as she spoke her fateful words in the *Bhāgavata Māhātmya*. The connection to the *Bhāgavata Purāṇa* is also worth noting. We have already mentioned the fact that Raghunāth Bhaṭṭ, another of the six *gosvāmīs*

Figure 1. Brindavan and Mathura as depicted in the dining hall of Jaisingh II's palace at Āmer (ca. 1710–1720). At central left, the temple of Govindadev, with spire intact and its subsidiary Garuḍa shrine. Above on the shore of the Jamuna, the temple of Madanmohan, also recognizable by its spire. Right: Mathura in the vicinity of the city's Delhi gate. Courtesy of the Archaeological Survey of India. Photo by Robyn Beeche from the archive of the Sri Caitanya Prema Samsthana, Brindavan.

Chaitanya sent to Braj, is said to have recited the *Bhāgavata* "at the assembly of Rūp Gosvāmin."[29] Context suggests, not surprisingly, that such performances transpired in front of the deity whom Rūp served—Govindadev—and that may be part of the reason why the central space in the expanded temple of Govindadev is so sprawling (Figure 2).

Krishna Sharma argued that the bhakti narrative expressed in *Bhāgavata Māhātmya* 1.48–50 may have emerged from the Vallabhite community in just this period, but this is probably mistaken. Contrary to what she seems to have believed, and contrary as well to the impression given in the *Caurāsī Vaiṣṇavan kī Vārtā,* the Vallabhites had no firm foothold in Braj until 1577. It was only then that the *sampradāy* obtained its first *farmān* from Akbar—twelve years after the first known grant to the

Figure 2. Interior of the temple of Govindadev, Brindavan, showing especially the *jagmohan* or assembly hall (1590). Photo by Robyn Beeche.

Gauḍīyas. Moreover, this *farmān* granted Vallabha's son Viṭṭhalnath control over lands in Gokul on the east side of the Jumuna, not in Brindavan itself, on the west. As if in response to the obvious fact that the newly "official" Brindavan was rising at a dramatic spot on the river's right bank, the Vallabhites argued that Brindavan was really to be found not there but near Mount Govardhan, where, at some point during the sixteenth century, they seem to have staked a claim, displacing the Bengalis.[30] The way in which Bhakti speaks of her experience in Brindavan makes it very likely she had in mind not the Vallabhites' "Brindavan" but this commonly assumed and importantly Gauḍīya alternative—the one with so many Chaitanyite monuments, the one celebrated in Nārāyaṇ Bhaṭṭ's foundational pilgrimage account of Braj, the *Vrajabhaktivilāsa* of 1552. Nārāyaṇ Bhaṭṭ's initiation was apparently Chaitanyite.[31] If this is the Brindavan to which the *Bhāgavata Māhātmya* refers, how does this help us flesh out the meaning of its south-to-north narrative?

It is hard to see Brindavan's sixteenth-century architectural profile as a straightforward expression of the south-to-north progression that Bhakti claims for herself in the *Bhāgavata Māhātmya*.[32] True, one could locate isolated examples of architectural forms used in Brindavan that could have been suggested by prior Gujarati practice, but the far more evident pattern is that Brindavan's architectural signature aligns it with other monuments erected as part of the imperial Mughal network. The use of red sandstone seems to mark that specifically. The Mughals only allowed that material to be used in buildings that received the imperial stamp of approval and were intended to be seen as registering that fact.[33] If the temple of Govindadev looks toward the south in any way, it is not to the Tamilian glories of Srirangam, as might have been suggested by the theological heritage claimed by Govindadev's Gauḍīya servitors, but southwest toward Saurashtra.[34] Srirangam was never a part of Mughal domain; after 1572, Saurashtra was. John Burton-Page has even argued that a specific migration of skilled craftsmen and builders from Gujarat to the Agra region after the demise of Sultan Bahadur Shah may have been involved. He and George Michell propose that members of the same work crew who erected the Agra fort, Fatehpur Sīkrī, and other major buildings dear to Akbar may have been recruited by the Kachvaha ruler Mānsingh, his close colleague and chief general, to construct Govindadev.[35]

The *Bhāgavata Māhātmya,* we recall, suggests that the bhakti heritage transmitted from the Dravidian south in a northwesterly direction faltered after it traveled "here and there" in Maharashtra. In Gujarat it was torn apart by persons the text calls *pākhaṇḍas* (BM 1.49). Probably something like self-interested "schismatics" is meant; later Bhakti laments the fact that Vaishnavism *(vaiṣṇavatā)* has lapsed and that people no longer follow the *sampradāys* (1.76). But there also seems to be a concern about *yavanas*—"Muslims" or "Turks," in all probability—for these are the people, Nārada says (1.34), who have come into control of ashrams, *tīrthas,* and rivers in the *kali yug* and who have destroyed many temples, as well. Bhakti supplies the *kali yug* as context—*ghorakaler yogāt,* "the force of these awful times" (1.49)—when she describes what happened to her in Gujarat.

Indeed Gujarat had passed into *yavana* control in the period to which Bhakti seems to be referring, but architecturally, at least, the results were not as crushing as the text seems to imply. In fact, Gujarat was the place where the local or "Hindu" imprint on Muslim buildings was most marked. Could this actually be an aspect of what Bhakti means in speaking of her old age and dismemberment—that in Gujarat some glorious Hindu temple tradition passed into Muslim hands? It seems a long shot, and the passage remains enigmatic. What is striking, though, and entirely unacknowledged in the text, is that when Bhakti was dramatically and beautifully "reborn" in Brindavan—when Vaishnavaness *(vaiṣṇavatā)* came back into focus—it was also under a *yavana* star. This was the firm Mughal-Rajput alliance that allowed Akbar to succeed in an ongoing series of struggles. Hindus at the Mughal court were massively responsible for the stability and expansion of the empire; and the empire, in turn, served as the protective casing for the new Hindu jewel that it enshrined near the center of its crown—Brindavan.

Architecturally, however, as the temple of Govindadev shows, the heritage was much more continuous. When read against the history of temple architecture, then, the bhakti narrative given in the *Bhāgavata Māhātmya* takes on a curiously different meaning from the ones that have usually been assigned—bad Jains, bad Shaivas, bad Advaitans, or bad Sultans. The aging and fraying that Bhakti associates with Gujarat in her autobiography emerges not so much as a tale of religious loss as of dynastic succession—Muslim dynastic succession. True, the "through line" of Vaishnava temple-building that connected Tamilnadu, Karnataka, and Maharashtra was largely broken—the sort of continuity that was maintained by the incorporation of the worship of Viṭṭhal of Pandharpur into temple life at

Vijayanagar and Tirupati.[36] But another line of connection remained intact—or rather, perhaps, substituted for it. If there was rupture, as the story itself suggests, there was also rebirth. The part that escapes the *Bhāgavata Māhātmya*'s story is that *yavanas* were the agents not just of dismemberment but of reaggregation. The sultans of the Deccan (not Gujaratis, by the way) were responsible for the demise of Vijayanagar in 1565, and the story is sometimes remembered as a Muslim-Hindu conflict, but whatever the truth of that claim—recent scholars have tended to discredit it—it is clear that farther north, Yavanas and Hindus worked hand in hand. Through the effects of intermarriage, in fact, some of the most important of these Yavanas—the emperor Jahangir, for example—were half-Hindu.

It is hard to find in the architectural background of Brindavan any close analogue to the westerly pilgrimage route the *Māhātmya* says Bhakti chose as a means of getting from the Dravida country to the banks of the Jamuna. There may have been a Gujarati component, both stylistically and in terms of Govindadev's actual work force, but it hardly stands out to the exclusion of others. As George Michell has observed, the octagonal sanctuaries of the great temples of late-sixteenth-century Brindavan (Figures 1 and 4) and the grand *mahāmaṇḍapas* laid out in a cruciform plan connect much more vividly to prior structures in Gwalior, Orccha, and Orissa, later replicated in Bengal.[37] And more than anything else, there is the massive presence of what Pika Ghosh has called "Mughal fashion"—an absolute "flaunting" of the red sandstone the Mughals loved. Red sandstone has a very long history in the Mathura region, but its deployment here has numerous Mughal touches. "Krishna's residence," Ghosh goes on to say, "was modeled in part on that of the emperor," just as the emperor, with his daily *darśans,* returned the compliment.[38]

It was this broad system of complementary resonances that made it possible for Brindavan—the built Brindavan—to be born at the heart of the Mughal state. The pious saw it not as birth but as rebirth, an unearthing and revival of the Brindavan where Krishna and Radha had spent their youths. The *Bhāgavata Māhātmya* historicizes this picture and thereby fundamentally changes it, claiming the south as the land of origins, but we must not let that close our eyes to the fact that without the commanding force of the Mughal-Rajput machine—political, military, and cultural—it would have been impossible for the *Māhātmya* to speak of Brindavan as it does. Brindavan would have remained a *van,* a wilderness. This Mughal-Rajput project was a northern phenomenon, so the *Māhātmya*'s effort to plot its effects—the glorious Brindavan—on a north-south axis is an act of generous redirection, to say the least.

At the time the *Bhāgavata Māhātmya* was written, Brindavan was a real place situated in a real, complex, and doubtless well-known history, but that very history evidently caused its effects to be partial in the eyes of the *Māhātmya*'s author. Bhakti danced there, yes, but her sons remained untouched. The political and intrafamilial concordat between Mughals and Rajputs that shaped the earthly Brindavan, while making it possible for this remarkable site to emerge in historical time, simultaneously prevented it from exemplifying the full integration of heart, mind, and body *(bhakti, jñāna, vairāgya)* that certain Hindus continued to believe would have been ideal. Hence there was a need for what Haridvar represented: a place where gods and humans could gather in a purely Vaishnava mode (the presence of Shaivas notwithstanding), a place where a man like Parīkṣit could still be king, a place where Brahmins—Brahmins of the bhakti persuasion—could fully call the shots. Situated between heaven and earth, between learned *vairāgīs* and learned Brahmins, and being therefore a forest of bliss *(ānandavan),* Haridvar had enormous resources to give to the cause—even if, as the story itself tells us, it takes a continual renewing of the authorizing text, the *Bhāgavata Purāṇa,* to make this ideal Haridvar come to life in the real world. It is right and proper, then, that Haridvar remained at the limit of the *Bhāgavata Māhātmya*'s conceptual geography. It is the telos that waits to be realized whenever a *bhāgavat saptāh* is performed. It is more than Bhakti's ever-compromised present; it is her ever-future goal.

Hindu Allusions

Clearly the *Bhāgavata Māhātmya* presents us with a spectacle of narrative geography that is meant to rise above the sordid or at least soiled pages of history. But at the same time it seems to trade on the substance that "real history" provides. The trouble is that it does so partially. It builds an arc from south to north that would make little sense if Brindavan had not emerged into the light of history as it did under Rajput-Mughal patronage. Yet as we have seen, that south-north arc obscures what we might playfully think of as the east-west dimensions of the tale: those that brought together Hindus (Indus-ites) and Yavanas (Greeks, for which read Turks or Muslims) in a political/religious enterprise that eluded the complete control of either. In the remaining pages of this chapter, moving beyond Brindavan, let us consider the full range of moments in the history of Hindu religion that the author of the *Bhāgavata Māhātmya* might have had in mind as he composed the "born in Dravida" narrative—the sorts of things that could have made his portrayal ring true to a knowledgeable audience. Then we will look the other way from Brindavan—toward the Islamic world implied by Mughal rule. However much the author of the *Bhāgavata Māhātmya* wanted to ignore it, this Islamic ambiance substantially shaped the bhakti that flowered in north India during the second millennium C.E.

On the Hindu side, suppose we start at the high end, with philosophy and theology. Working within the *Māhātmya*'s clearly Vaishnava frame of reference, the obvious move would be to identify the great theologian Rāmānuja (d. ca. 1160) with bhakti's initial development in the Dravida region. His commentaries on the *Brahma Sūtras (Śrībhāṣya)* and the *Bhagavad Gītā,* along with his independent treatise called *Vedārthasaṃgraha,* articulated a philosophy of qualified nondualism *(viśiṣṭādvaita)* that has remained supremely influential since the time of their composition. Rāmānuja participated in a philosophical lineage that had flourished for at least a century: in this succession Yāmuna is his most eminent predecessor. Along with Yāmuna, Rāmānuja came to be honored retrospectively with the title *ācārya,* recognizing his seminal importance as a preceptor in this own right and putting him on a par with the formidable Śaṃkarācārya (ca. 800 C.E.), who also bore the name.

Yet from the point of view of the *Bhāgavata Māhātmya,* with its interest in Dravidian origins, Rāmānuja's specific debt to the Tamil country and its Āḻvār hymnists is at least as important as his philosophical credentials. He is firmly associated with the Śrī Vaiṣṇava theological and ritual perspective called *ubhayavedānta,* "the Vedanta of both," which sets this sung tradition of Tamil bhakti parallel to the teachings of the Sanskrit Veda. Moreover, he is credited with taking on the management of the imposing temple of Vishnu at Srirangam on an island in the Kaveri River and instituting there a number of significant theological and administrative reforms.[39] Tradition says that it was the grandfather of Rāmānuja's preceptor Yāmuna, the tenth-century teacher Nāthamuni, who first established the practice of singing the hymns of the *āḻvārs* alongside the Vedas at Srirangam, and who created the anthology that made this possible in a consistent, enduring way.

If Rāmānuja and his Śrī Vaishnava tradition can be imagined as the backdrop for the affirmation that bhakti was "born in Dravida," then Madhvācārya (d. 1317?) and his dualist *dvaitādvaita* philosophy would logically stand behind the idea that bhakti came into its full maturity in Karnataka.[40] Madhva established an important monastery dedicated to Krishna that took up its place opposite the two ancient Shaiva temples at Udupi, not far from the Arabian Sea near modern-day Mangalore, and is remembered as having institutionalized this important innovation by ordaining his brother and seven of his followers to carry on his work as renunciants. Aside from the fact that this eventually led to the creation of a complex of eight *maṭhs* (monasteries) in Udupi itself, there was considerable impact throughout southwest India as the Mādhva *sampradāy* became a truly missionizing order. Again there is a vernacular connection, for the Haridāsas (servants of Hari) of this period, minstrels who traveled throughout the region singing in Kannada, are closely associated in memory with the Mādhvite order. Indeed, the earliest known singer-saint among them is Naraharitīrtha, who is considered to have been a pupil of Madhva himself. The association between high philosophy and popular song can also be seen two centuries later in the great Mādhvite theologian Vyāsatīrtha, who left us at least the occasional hymn. It may be recalled that we met the term *haridāsa* in the *Bhāgavata Māhātmya* (3.72). Probably it carries a general meaning, but it is thought-provoking that the *Māhātmya* takes us to Karnataka not twenty verses after mentioning this term, and that the editor, at least, feels free to reinsert it in a heading that appears just as the passage in question concludes (*haridāsā ucuḥ,* 5.71). Perhaps we have here a hint of the regional Haridāsa tradition, after all.

As for the *Māhātmya*'s remark that bhakti "wandered here and there in Maharashtra," it would be tempting to interpret that as a reference to the Vārkarīs, who do just that in the course of their once-yearly pilgrimage from all over the Marathi-speaking region to Pandharpur and its great temple of Viṭṭhal. The Vārkarīs literally wander with the saints—and sing their songs as they go. They coalesce in huge bands that walk toward

Pandharpur carrying palanquins that contain silver images of the footwear associated with each of Viṭṭhal's principal bhaktas—the poet-singers who, more than any other group, are thought of as having actually forged Maharashtra into a linguistic unity. This picture of the formation of vernacular literary history has been greeted with suspicion by Sheldon Pollock, we recall, and challenged on other grounds by Christian Novetzke, but it was embraced wholeheartedly by Mahadeo Govind Ranade.[41]

In suggesting a possible link between the *Bhāgavata Māhātmya* and the Vārkarīs there lurks a chronological question. The Vārkarī pilgrimage circuit in its full, modern form may only have come into being after the time of Tukārām, perhaps in the late seventeenth century.[42] Yet it surely had antecedents, even if in a simpler form; and like its Kannada and Tamil cousins, this Maharashtrian Vaishnava tradition also has its philosophical bhakti heroes. Jñāneśvar, author of the first great Marathi commentary on the *Bhagavad Gītā*—popularly called for that reason the *Jñāneśvarī*—probably completed his work in the thirteenth century, which makes him a rough contemporary of Madhva, and Eknāth wrote his *Eknāthī Bhāgavata,* based upon the eleventh book of the *Bhāgavata Purāṇa,* in the sixteenth century. This means that they both answer not only to the theological demands of the "born in Dravida" account—they are Krishna devotees working with the two cardinal Bhāgavata texts—but more or less to its chronological demands, as well. And each of them has a palanquin that travels to Pandharpur with the Vārkarīs twice a year.[43] If the author of the *Bhāgavata Māhātmya* was thinking of Vārkarī journeys when he spoke of Bhakti's going "here and there" in Maharashtra, he might well have understood Eknāth and Jñāneśvar to be involved.

Finally there is the ticklish matter of Gujarat, so prominent in our thoughts about Brindavan. What is the reason for the *Bhāgavata Māhātmya*'s opprobrium, its insistence that bhakti experienced difficulties there, becoming "old and worn" in the process? Chronologically speaking, the story of the northward progress of Krishna bhakti ought to continue in glory. It is commonly held that Narsī Mehtā, Gujarat's most important poet, belonged to the fifteenth century—just the right timing.[44] Certainly he was a devotee of Krishna, and it is hard to believe that other aspects of his devotion, more *nirguṇ* in tone, would have made him seem not "bhakti enough" in the eyes of the author of the *Bhāgavata Māhātmya.*[45] Another possibility is that he thought Shaivas or Jains or Muslims were too important in Gujarat's religious landscape, but the shoe never quite seems to fit. Some Gujaratis have gone so far as to argue that the term *gurjari* (BM 1.48), which would plainly seem to refer to Gujarat on both geographical and linguistic grounds, is really a reference to another place entirely: the grazing lands of the Gurjars some distance to the north.[46] This seems a desperate attempt to restore self-esteem, but it underscores the mysteriousness of the passage and the perceived importance of the text.

I can think of only two plausible ways to extricate ourselves from this morass. One path is simple and broad: to abandon the claims of historical geography and say that the author of the *Bhāgavata Māhātmya* got boxed into positing this Gujarati nadir so that he could announce the summit that would succeed it. What he really has his eye on is Bhakti's rejuvenation in Brindavan. This, after all, is a pilgrimage narrative—clockwise in the traditional fashion—and as the journey continues, it gets arduous. Or to see matters against the background of a different sort of canvas, one might take this as an instance of a wider pattern to which Sheldon Pollock has drawn attention in seventeenth-century intellectual life: an assertion of the importance of being new *(navya)*. That which has gone before has to be old by contrast—by definition, if for no other reason—and the term *jīrṇa* is naturally enough invoked to name it so.[47]

The second possibility is a more focused one. This is Shrivatsa Goswami's suggestion that the person who wrote the *Māhātmya* was sufficiently well attuned to the historical realities of sixteenth-century Brindavan that he adopted the point of view we might have expected from someone closely associated with the Kachvaha-Mughal political machine. On that understanding we would have here a reference to the tensions that had descended upon Saurashtra in the pre-Mughal period—commercial and political more than specifically religious. These contributed importantly to the possibility of a Mughal victory in Gujarat under the leadership of Mānsingh Kachvaha in 1572–1573, and that, in turn, benefited Brindavan (see Chapter 4).[48]

If we discount this enduring puzzle about Gujarat, we seem to emerge with a fairly convincing reconstruction of what might have been in our narrator's mind when he had Bhakti explain to Nārada where she came from. The *Bhāgavata Māhātmya*'s "born in Dravida" pericope obviously has to represent a considerable simplification of history. Among numerous other things, its broad northwesterly sweep pays no attention to the fact that in sixteenth-century Vijayanagar, at the apogee of empire under King Kṛṣṇadevarāya, it was actually Śrī Vaishnavas who held the strongest hand, and that this was something relatively new.[49] We had been thinking that the *Māhātmya*'s narrative passed the baton of south Indian bhakti leadership from Śrī Vaishnavas to Mādhvas to Vārkarīs, but here we are back in the hands of the Śrī Vaishnavas! Have we perhaps missed a major point? Could it be that the author of *Bhāgavata Māhātmya* was actually thinking of Śrī Vaishnavas the whole while? This may seem a tempting possibility, but it makes no room for Maharashtra, where the Śrī Vaishnavas were not active until much more recent times, and it is even somewhat hard to reconcile with the prominence of Brindavan in the narrative. There is a ritual connection to Srirangam at Brindavan's temple of Rādhāramaṇ, but no Śrī Vaishnava temple as such was erected in Brindavan until the mid-nineteenth century.

Other problems also appear. If we try to square the *Māhātmya*'s view of the transit of bhakti with the evolving religious preferences of Vijayanagar kings, for instance, we find we almost have to reverse our sense of the geography of her maturation. We move from an earlier devotion to local and regional Shaiva deities and monastic formations—Virūpākṣa at Vijayanagar itself and the Srngeri *maṭh* farther south—through a period in which Jains and Mādhvites also became established in the capital, and on toward a full-fledged enthusiasm for the Śrī Vaishnavas. Broadly, this would take us not in a northwesterly direction but on an arc from the Malabar southwest to the Tamil southeast. Nor does there seem any way to connect the *Māhātmya*'s plot line with the fact that the great temple at Tirupati played a crucial role in all this, or with the emerging glories of the Telugu language, to which it does not seem to allude. Others interested in appropriating the luminous legacy of Kṛṣṇadevarāya, as happened at Madurai in the late sixteenth century when his "autobiography" the *Rāyavācakamu* (Tidings of the King) was written, had no reason to downplay either this linguistic dimension or the geographical slant that went with it. They were interested in bringing the Vijayaganar legacy southward rather than claiming it spread to the north.[50]

Our author's viewpoint is different. Almost surely he writes from the north. Given that this is so, and conceding the caveats we have just registered, it is striking that one could actually conjure up a fair amount of evidence from the Vaishnava history of south and west India that would flesh out what he might have meant when he had Bhakti give her famous autobiographical sketch to Nārada. In general terms one can indeed see why Jean Filliozat said that Bhakti's words nicely summarized the course of bhakti's history "from its flowering in the Tamil country to its rebirth on the banks of the Yamunā at the hands of Chaitanya's disciples."[51]

Some scholars have gone on to expand the claim, making this vision of the south-to-north path of bhakti pertain not only to Vaishnavas but to Shaivas as well. This was what A. K. Ramanujan did so pointedly in *Speaking of Śiva,* and not entirely without cause. It may be hard to verify that Rāmūnuja traveled from Tamilnadu to the Karnataka city of Tonnur and there converted the Hoysala king Bittideva (r. ca. 1106–1142) from Jainism to Vaishnavism, bestowing upon him the name Viṣṇuvardhana.[52] But if this event did indeed occur, it transpired not long before the Vīraśaivas were to flourish in and around Kalyāṇa in the Chalukya-Kalachuri domain, not very far away. Can we see in such a pattern a shared Vaishnava-Shaiva bhakti momentum? Later, it seems—in the sixteenth century—prominent Haridāsas such as Purandaradāsa and Kanakadāsa knew something of the Tamil songs that had been sung by the *āḻvārs,* Vaishnavas of an earlier period. This may come as no surprise given how the *āḻvārs* were esteemed by the Śrī Vaishnavas who came to exert such influence at the Vijayanagar court just then, but it is striking that this memory of the Tamil bhakti saints also appears on the Shaiva side of the line—this time, of course, a memory not of *āḻvārs* but of *nāyaṉmārs.* Perhaps one Vīraśaiva *vacana* in fifty makes such a reference—or so, at least, modern editions make it seem.[53] In similar fashion, when Harihara chronicled the lives of these Vīraśaiva saints in the early thirteenth century, he understood their flourishing to be a recent development in a much longer Shaiva lineage that especially featured the Tamil *nāyaṉmārs.* Interestingly, Harihara did not group these recent Kannada-speaking saints under the term "Vīraśaiva," nor did he refer to their utterances as *vacanas,* and this helps assure us that his distinction between exemplary Shaivas of an older *(purātana)* generation and the newer *(nūtana)* Kannada saints he celebrated—and also the bond that held them together—were hagiographical facts of his own making, not something later Vīraśaivas wrote back into the record he had established.[54] In similar fashion the *Basava Purāṇa* of Somanātha, composed in Telugu in the thirteenth century, shows an awareness of the *nāyaṉmārs,* even though they may appear under different names from those we know in the great Tamil hagiographic compendium called *Periya Purāṇa.*[55]

What was happening in Tamil itself adds further dimensions to this story. Although you would never know it from Ramanujan's account, relationships between Tamil Shaiva and Vaishnava elites were often strained and fraught with enmity, with the Shaivas by and large holding sway. Nonetheless—or perhaps in consequence—the independent Shaiva and Vaishnava bhakti canons developed in roughly parallel ways. Māṇikkavācakar and Nammāḻvār play complementary roles as the poets who completed the *nāyaṉmār* and *āḻvār* traditions respectively by adding their own impressively weighty bodies of poetry to what had gone before. Both do so in the course of the ninth century. There is also a parallel in the process by which these collections were effectively canonized and brought into sung temple usage. Nampi Āṇṭār Nampi accomplished that work of systematization in the Shaiva case, giving us the first full-fledged Tamil bhakti canon, the *Tēvāram,* probably in the course of the eleventh century. Nāthamuni performed a parallel task somewhat earlier—his *Divyaprabandham* of four thousand *āḻvār* poems known in Tamil as *Nālāyiratiyaprapantam.* In both cases, somewhat later on, this work of collation came to be represented in sectarian accounts as having been caused by the discovery of lost manuscripts from an earlier period that suddenly came to light, as if begging to be recognized for the canonical creatures they had been all along—revelation.

When we come to hagiography similar vectors emerge. The *Periya Purāṇa,* where the lives of *nāyaṉmārs* are gathered in the comprehensive form that would remain authoritative to this day, was prepared in the mid-twelfth century by Cēkkiḻār, while its Vaishnava analogue, the *Guruparamparāprabhāvam,* followed a century later. Yet here there was a difference of language: the Shaiva document was written in Tamil while the Vaishnava one adopted the mixed Tamil-Sanskrit medium known as *maṇipravāḷa.* And the number of saints involved are also quite different. There are only twelve *āḻvārs,* while the *nāyaṉmārs* number sixty-three—or, counting Māṇikkavācakar, sixty-four. Sixty-three remains the official sum because it corresponds to and was intended to eclipse a collection of sixty-three exemplary Jain lives, the *Triṣaṣṭilakṣaṇa Mahāpurāṇa.*[56]

Despite such discrepancies one can see how strongly the Shaiva and Vaishnava Tamil traditions resemble each other in their structural formation and in the chronological sequences by means of which these structures came to be discovered and displayed. Yet it is only in recent times—in the twentieth century itself—that we find any general effort to represent *nāyaṉmārs* and *āḻvārs* as forming two aspects of one common bhakti stream or movement. Certainly this was far from the intent of the writer of the *Bhāgavata Māhātmya,* who was if anything eager to suppress the idea that Shaivas and Vaishnavas might form parts of a single bhakti enterprise. By calling his chief protagonist from the Karnataka region Gokarṇa, in fact, he seemed to want to siphon off Shaiva greatness for greater Vaishnava glory.

Or maybe it was just his clouded memory. After all, he probably wrote the *Bhāgavata Māhātmya* hundreds of miles from the Karnataka coast and the headwaters of the Tungabhadra—in north or northwestern India. But Muslims must have played an impressive role in his lived environment, so that is a different matter indeed. If it weren't for the general silence of Hindu writers about Islam, and if it weren't for the fact that the author of the *Bhāgavata Māhātmya* was so clearly writing to promote a Vaishnava point of view, we might actually marvel at the effort it must have cost him to ignore the Muslim contributions to bhakti history. This Islamic penumbra came immediately into view when we looked in detail at Brindavan, so why is it absent in the *Bhāgavata Māhātmya?* Was it that the *Māhātmya*'s Bhakti, speaking in Sanskrit and swathed in the garb of Krishna, simply couldn't give utterance to such a thing? This may be, but if so, her Vaishnava chastity contrasts broadly to what Krishna wears when he walks onstage to perform his central role in the *rās līlās* of Brindavan: Mughal clothes.

Muslim Exclusions

In the Sanskrit intellectual world there is a long history of principled ostrich-ism—xenology, as Wilhelm Halbfass has called it—with regard to anything that might exceed its purview, especially anything that originated outside India.[57] This is so not just in the higher realms of pure philosophy but also in the freer rhythms of Puranic discourse, and the *Bhāgavata Māhātmya* clearly participates in that pattern. Along about the sixteenth century, however, cracks in the system began to appear, letting us know that the presence of Muslims—*mlecchas, yavanas, śakas* (Scythians), or *turuṣkas* (Turks)—was on the minds of even the most rarefied theoreticians of philosophy and theology. This happened in the south with the sophisticated polymath Appayya Dīkṣita, and it certainly happened in the north, in the treatises of Madhusūdan Sarasvatī and Vijñānabhikṣu, Advaitans of contrasting persuasions.[58] In the writings of Madhusūdan, who lived in Banaras, the teachings of the new outsiders—Muslims—were for the first time explicitly aligned, if still a bit offhandedly, with those of Cārvākas, Jains, and Buddhists—*nāstikas* who had long been seen as standing outside the boundaries of constructive thought by virtue of their failure to engage with and defer to the Veda.[59] That was in Sanskrit. In vernacular writings one could see the interpenetrations far more clearly, whether one had in mind literature that could have been performed at court or bhakti poetry more likely to have been heard in temples or streets.[60]

We should not think it was only Hindu intellectuals who often held their Muslim counterparts at arm's length. Muslims also played an active role in keeping the worlds of Muslims and Hindus conceptually apart. In fact, as came to be so deeply resented by certain Hindu apologists of the early twentieth century, Muslim thinkers played a crucial role in taking the Persian term "Hindu" and endowing it with religious meaning, thereby producing the very existence of "Hindu" as a common category of identity in the first place.[61] This seems to have begun in the fourteenth century when, ironically, Persian writers started praising India as an ideal locale for the practice of Islam. They may have done so, Carl Ernst has suggested, in response to the depredations that Mongols had visited on the Islamic kingdoms of central Asia. Such invasions encouraged many Muslims to move farther south, which in turn gave urgency to the task of sorting out India's Muslim inhabitants from their non-Muslim peers. The latter were for the first time seen in distinct and generically religious terms—unfavorable ones. In the eyes of Persian writers these people were, like the Mongols, idolaters or unbelievers, and their general designation as Hindu came to have a newly collective religious force.[62] In the *Hindū-Turk Saṃvād* ascribed to Eknāth, a Marathi dialogue in the *bhāruḍ* genre, both parties to the debate accede to a higher truth after many mutual insults and are reconciled.[63] Kabīr, in his Hindi lyrics (*pads*, i.e., *śabdas*), uses the same device of literary balancing but puts it to a different purpose: he excoriates the religious leaders of both communities evenhandedly in the name of a bhakti that eludes them both.[64]

If Eknāth or Kabīr is a central figure in one's conception of what has to be meant by "the bhakti movement," then it is obvious that the *Bhāgavata*

Māhātmya's effort to describe the history of such a reality can only be understood as a partial snapshot of the whole. Taking into account the region and time when the *Māhātmya*'s construction of bhakti history emerged, however, this Vaishnava foreshortening and its elision of Islam seem striking. We have already seen that a denial of the legitimacy of vernacular transmission and non-Brahmin performance might be inferred from the *Māhātmya*'s insistence on the power of the Sanskrit *Bhāgavata* and its meticulously guarded ritual domain, but a great deal else would also be denied, even specifically in regard to the worship of Krishna at Brindavan. Brindavan belonged inescapably to the broader world of Mughal bhakti, and there the crossovers between Muslims and Vaishnavas were plainly to be seen. Two of the most prominent sixteenth-century Krishna poets composing in Brajbhasha, for example, were called Raskhān and Rahīm—the latter, in fact, a high Mughal official.[65] Conversely, toward the end of the following century, poets with Krishnaite names like Śrī Gopāl and Brindāvan Dās joined other Hindus in gathering around the remarkable Sufi poet Mīrzā 'Abd al-Qādir "Bīdil" in the Mughal capital at Delhi. They took him as their *sheikh* and began to produce a memorial literature about him and his circle that followed Persian canons (Hindi *tazkirā;* Ar., Pers. *taẕkira*). Only in the eighteenth century were members of Bīdil's salon sorted out in memory as having been Muslims or Hindus.[66]

The full scope of expressive religiosity in north India thus developed in an environment that could be called "linked families of cultural practice." Aditya Behl has introduced this phrase in the course of explaining how *premākhyān* poetry as a Sufi genre partook generously of idioms native to India while also drawing on motifs and styles that circulated more widely around the western reaches of the Indian Ocean.[67] The term can also fittingly be used to describe the complexly connective tissue of literary religiosity that pertained within north India itself. We have just given two examples where these linkages are to be seen—Muslim bhakti lyrics and the presence of Vaishnavas in *tazkirā* commemorative compendia—yet these are just the tip of the iceberg. There are many others, as well: musical traditions that Muslims and Hindus shared, not just in courtly spaces but more strictly religious ones; spiritual leaders who could be identified alternately as *pīrs* or *svāmīs* depending on who was doing the naming; parallels and crossovers that connect Muslim and Hindu hagiographical traditions; communities such as the Kabīr, Dādū, and Bāṅvarī Panths, which developed as Hindu although their founding figures were in some obvious sense

Muslim; devotional groups who self-consciously positioned themselves between Vaishnavism and Islam, borrowing ritual conventions and narrative motifs from both; and treatises written with the explicit purpose of translating indigenous Hindu concepts and deities so that they could be understood in an Islamic frame of reference.[68] No one imagining the historical reality of bhakti on the basis of the *Bhāgavata Māhātmya*'s narrative of Bhakti's journey could possibly have suspected any of this. Indeed the story of her trajectory suggests, to the contrary, that for all her travels and sufferings she remains who she was at the beginning—a southern girl, someone who hailed from a region relatively untouched by the *yavanas* of the present *kali* age. Was that precisely our author's purpose?

If we join Filliozat in concluding that verses 48–50 of the first chapter of the *Bhāgavata Māhātmya* may be read as a parabolic account of important developments in the history of popular and philosophical Vaishnavism up to the sixteenth century, then we must do so with the awareness that this account disregards a great deal else that made Krishna bhakti what it became in that century in Brindavan—and beyond. This is no small caveat. As we have seen, what makes the *Bhāgavata Māhātmya*'s historicizing program believable is that it builds upon a historical Brindavan where bhakti had indeed been brought to life in a new way. But this was the Mughal Brindavan, not some southern clone, and it participated almost par excellence in the web of Hindu-Muslim connections we have been describing.

Of course, what the *Bhāgavata Māhātmya* suggests about the interregional logic of south-to-north Vaishnavism is not the only way to recount the saga of the bhakti movement. Whole histories have been written to tell this story from a radically different point of view—a Muslim one. Surprisingly, though, even those histories have often retained the general arc that the *Bhāgavata Māhātmya* so deftly sketches. Consider, for example, the widely read account of medieval Indian history that was published in 1936 by Tara Chand of Allahabad under the title *Influence of Islam on Indian Culture*. Chand devotes two full chapters to "Hindu Reformers of the South," starting with the *āḻvārs* and *nāyaṉmārs* and concluding with the Vīraśaivas and Siddhars—almost fifty pages of text—before he goes on to say, "The movement which started there continued to develop in the North. The religious leaders in Mahārāśtra, Gujarat, the Panjab, Hindustan and Bengal from the fourteenth century onwards deliberately reject certain elements of ancient creeds and emphasize others and thus attempt to bring about an approximation between the Hindu and Muslim faiths. At the same time Muslim *Sufi* orders and Muslim writers and poets show a strong tendency to assimilate Hindu practices and doctrines, in some cases going so far as to adopt even the adoration of Hindu gods."[69]

The development of such a "synthetic" Indian culture—I use Tara Chand's term—is no small thing, considering that "the character of Muslim consciousness is as different from that of the Hindu as possible"—the one having been disciplined in west and central Asia and the Maghrib by "scanty rainfall," "howling wastes of sand," and "the immensity of the cloudless sky overhead," while the other, in its "plastic exuberance," imbibed the natural fecundity of the Indian tropics.[70] Even so, Tara Chand argues, it would be almost impossible to explain the strikingly new directions in the bhakti aspect of Hindu religion from the ninth to the fourteenth century if it were not for the massive influence of Muslim settlers and travelers in south India. He observes that the "reforming shears" of bhakti were in all cases "applied to the very parts anathematized by Islam," and in his two most persuasive examples from south India, "the evidence leaves almost no doubt that the *Vīrśaivas* and the *Siddhārs* were largely influenced by Islam."[71] In north India, of course, the pattern becomes clearer still.

Tara Chand was not the only historian to enunciate such a view. Some forty years later, well beyond the elations and despairs of independence and partition, Muhammad Hedayatullah reiterated many of the same themes as background to his study of *Kabir: The Apostle of Hindu-Muslim Unity* (1977). Hedayetullah, like Tara Chand, repeatedly acknowledges that he cannot provide the documentation that would show how this causation actually occurred. He states, for instance, "It may be asserted without any doubt that Nāmdev's sayings betray Ṣūfī influence on him, though we have no specific evidence on his acquaintance with Ṣūfīs."[72]

Leaping ahead another generation, we arrive at Shahabuddin Iraqi's *Bhakti Movement in Medieval India: Social and Political Perspectives*, published in 2009. Here too we find the old south-to-north narrative, but under the pressure of all that causative inspecificity, presumably, it has been confined to a much more limited role. Iraqi focuses on examples where he believes the "cross-breeding" of bhakti and Sufi beliefs can be documented, as in the case of the Kashmiri poet Lālded and her pupil Sheikh Nuruddīn. That cross-fertilization shows up, he says, in the very name by which the *sheikh* is popularly known: Nand Ṛṣi. Iraqi also draws attention to the existence of both Sufi and Vaishnava Bauls in eastern India, and relishes the fact that the Vaishnavas among them say their first guru, a Hindu, "received the Baul faith from a Muslim woman called Madhava Bibi."[73] Obviously, both these examples supplement the "classic" south-to-north account of the bhakti movement in important ways.

As he approaches his conclusion, Iraqi leaves that narrative entirely behind and focuses on a "Bhakti movement in medieval northern India" that was "almost the same . . . as Sufism." It "started as a protest against orthodoxy" and its most "radical saints were particularly [arrayed] against the institutional structure and practices of Hinduism and Islam both." Iraqi devotes the bulk of his book to individuals such as Kabīr, Nānak, and Dādū, and to groups such as the Prānnāmīs and Satnāmīs—representatives of "the *Nirguna* school" who were "not bound to any of the four popular Vaishnava sects"—the four *sampradāys* that often structure narratives of bhakti's progress from south to north. He proposes a different story, connecting these northern *nirguṇīs* to the south on the basis of the low-caste position he thinks they shared with the *āḻvārs*. More striking, however, is the vivid awareness of an Islam that can be documented among *nirguṇ bhaktas* such as these, which displays an evolving "common culture" in which Sufis and *sants* shared key concepts and genres. Iraqi notes that there was a great fascination for conversations between Sufis and yogis, even if we cannot be sure about the historical veracity of many of the accounts in which they are embedded, especially any claims about conversion between one group and the other.[74]

Shahabuddin Iraqi is a member of the faculty of Aligarh Muslim University, whose historians tend to be frankly Marxist in their commitments. He shares with them a conviction that the most important leaders of the bhakti movement came from the lower levels of society. This movement, because of its message of social protest, could be valued all over India, even if it did not often achieve the social revolution one wishes it had been able to deliver. In that way, at least, the bhakti movements of north and south India, though separable—the northern more deeply infused with Islam than the southern—remain linked, and it is hard for historians such as these to give up the idea that the presence of Muslims living in the south mattered there, too. Certainly they did in the north, where the implicit egalitarianism of Islam (*pace* Meenakshi Jain) had an obvious effect on figures such as Dādū and Kabīr, producing what another Aligarh scholar describes as a real turning point *(moḍ)* in the bhakti movement.[75] Many historians interested in this dimension of things are Muslim, of course, but by no means all; and it is well to recall that the person who started the ball rolling—Tara Chand—was not Muslim but Kāyasth. Caste-wise, his reasons for embracing the idea of a composite Indian culture were rather different, although it is true that in a Hindu-majoritarian society the interests of Kāyasths often converged with those of Muslims. As we recall, the views of his Allahabad contemporary Ishwari Prasad, a Brahmin, were somewhat different.

Looking back, we see that the overarching resonance between the broad "bhakti movement" story at which the *Bhāgavata Māhātmya* hints—a story that creates a religious narrative for as much as a millennium leading up to the seventeenth or eighteenth century—and the expansion of the Muslim presence in South Asia during just that period remains harder to establish than a raft of particular connections between Hindus and Muslims that come into view once one reaches a certain point in "the story of bhakti." Take the poetry of the Brindavan region itself. It would be going much too far to say that there was a complete blurring of Sanskritic and Persian registers in vernacular poetry of the sixteenth century—at that time *pads* attributed to Sūrdās, for example, are almost devoid of Perso-Arabic words—but the mix can often be quite striking in others.[76] Poets such as Keśavdās (*fl.* 1580–1612) and Ānandghan (d. 1757) self-consciously negotiated the transition from one realm to the other, and much of this happened in the world of royal culture. Keśavdās left behind the Sanskrit orbit in which his family had excelled at the Orccha court of Rudrapratāp and his son Madhukar Shāh; chose instead to serve Madhukar's son Vīrsingh through Brajbhasha; and then at the end of his life wrote a paean to Jahangīr in which, for one surprising moment, he has the Mughal emperor perform *pūjā* to Hindu gods.[77] As for Ānandghan, he seems to have oscillated between the Nimbārkī monastery at Salemabad and the nearby court of Kishangarh, subsequently withdrawing to an ascetic life in Brindavan. His lyrics exhibit a Brajbhasha diction that would have been appropriate to any of these places, but he also composed a longer, Persian-inspired *'iśklatā* (Love's Vine) in Punjabi. The Sufi associations of *'iśk* were not, of course, accidental, and his persistent habit of addressing lyrics to Sujān, "the wise," in his Brajbhasha lyrics often left it unclear whether he meant a divine lover (Krishna) or a human one. In the latter instance was it a male or female—perhaps, as legend has it, a Muslim courtesan at the Mughal court in Delhi?[78]

In the course of the sixteenth or seventeenth century, it seems, a poet whose identity we do not know lampooned the reputation of the famous Sufi poet Malik Muhammad Jāyasī by producing in his name a *premākhyān* romance devoted to none other than Krishna. If the Krishna legends and their performers were in part the butt of his joke, so too were Nāth Yogīs, and not least the excesses of the *premākhyān* genre itself. What is interesting is that Krishna bhakti could be embraced in a single field with the others. The *Kanhāvat* did not begin to approach Jayasi's *Padmāvat* in popularity—only a few copied manuscripts have survived—and that is no wonder, it being a far less polished work. But there is no hint that this literary failure occurred because anyone felt the *Kanhāvat*'s genre, being Sufi, was inappropriate to its self-proclaimedly Vaishnava subject.[79] In other cases the Sufi-Vaishnava overlap was self-consciously engaged, but the celebrated poetry of lovers' separation in both Sufi and Vaishnava streams created echoes that ricocheted freely between the two. Both Persian and Indic poetic genres expected descriptions of heroes, heroines, and deities to proceed systematically from toe to head, or the reverse *(sarāpā; nakh-śikh, śikh-nakh)*; that too created echoes. So it was no great stretch when certain poets reached for special effects by drawing pointedly on Persian and Indic lexicons in the same composition.

If moods, registers, figures of speech, literary conventions, and poets themselves could travel between the domains that we would today label Hindu and Muslim in some all too binary way, how could Bhakti herself fail to make the journey? The *Bhāgavata Māhātmya*'s account vaguely suggests the old Sanskrit formula tracing the journey of a messenger—a cloud, say, or a goose—from one region of India to another, refashioning it in obvious ways as a specifically Vaishnava story. Yet some who heard it may also have conjured up the great Sufi tale of Ratansen's journey from Chitor in the northwest to Singhaldvīp (Sri Lanka) in the far south, and of the beautiful princess who lived on that island, Padmāvatī. In both the *māhātmya* and the *premākhyān* there is a prominent element of allegory.

Of course, Bhakti is not Padmāvatī, but the land over which she journeys is an India they share. It is not just the India that Kālidāsa could imagine to suit the ambitions of the Guptas way back when he wrote the *Meghadūta* in the fifth century, but the India that Tughluk and Mughal rulers sought to unify a millennium later. It was also in some sense the India of Vedāntadeśika's fourteenth-century *Haṃsa-saṃdeśa* (Message of the Goose) and of the circumambulatory tours that are celebrated in the roughly contemporaneous *Śaṃkaradigvijaya* (Śaṃkara's Defeat of the Quadrants) and its imitators. The historical and geographical landscapes each of these texts evoke are hardly coterminous, but they share a continental aspiration.[80]

The author of the *Bhāgavata Māhātmya,* working within the performative space provided by his parent Purana, sought to stake out a distinctive version of this Indian whole. In doing so, he created a framework that has seemed intriguingly persuasive to a number of recent interpreters; I have attempted to trace these resonances under the heading of "Hindu allusions." By the same token, however, he removed his account from anything that could be construed as a welcoming invitation to interpreters who stress the correspondences between Hindu and Muslim registers of Indian religious and literary expression. Only his invocation of Brindavan provides that hook, and not because he wanted it to do so. The author of the *Bhāgavata Māhātmya* was hardly eager to advertise its Mughal associations. He sees Brindavan, rather, as a—perhaps the—principal node in a purely Hindu line. It has been left to us to reveal the shortcomings of this perspective.

That notwithstanding, the three much-quoted verses (1.48–50) from the *Bhāgavata Māhātmya* seem to capture a great deal of the inner spirit of the bhakti movement story, and have been acclaimed for doing just that. But since when? I have no direct evidence that this connection was perceived before 1940. It was then that Surendranath Dasgupta, aware of the southern associations of the *Bhāgavata Purāṇa* itself, used the *Bhāgavata Māhātmya*'s "parable" as a way of making a place for the *āḻvārs* in his massive history of Indian philosophy—quite a controversial move, considering that these were poets, but he saw them as the basis for the Viśiṣṭādvaita (qualified nondualist) school that grew up among Śrī Vaishnavas. Dasgupta was sure that the *āḻvārs* must have been what the *Māhātmya* meant when it said that bhakti was born in Dravida.[81] As for what happened subsequently, he emphasized the fact that bhakti's sojourn in Gujarat and north India—before she got to Brindavan, that is—was a tale of "great misery." The farther she got from the south, the harder the going became. Jñāna and Vairāgya expired, he notes, and he doesn't mention the *Māhātmya*'s conviction that they revived, perhaps because south India was his almost exclusive concern in volume 3 of *A History of Indian Philosophy*. Yet for others that revival, like Bhakti's own in Brindavan, was at the heart of the narrative, the sign that north and south were in this together. And perhaps the Brindavan moment was also a sign that Hindus and Muslims shared this story, though you would never know it from what the *Māhātmya* itself has to say.

3

The Four Sampradāys and the Commonwealth of Love

When the idea of the bhakti movement jelled in the 1920s and 1930s—partly in English, partly in Hindi—it identified as the essential substrate of Indianness a long and cumulative current of religious poetry and song. The *Bhāgavata Māhātmya*'s image of a bhakti that stretched deep into the south and came to life much later in Brindavan was a fitting symbol of that indomitable, deeply musical reality. Yet as we have seen, this Brindavan, which did indeed flourish in the sixteenth century, was made possible by something of which the *Bhāgavata Māhātmya* gives us little hint: political formations broadly, and especially the Mughal state.

This structural dimension comes into sharper focus in a second major concept of bhakti's movement through time that twentieth-century thinkers inherited from precolonial sources. This is the idea of the four *sampradāys*—Vaiṣṇava teaching traditions that served to connect Hindu bhaktas of the Mughal and post-Mughal north with a south whose religious and cultural moorings were believed to be deeper and more secure. These *sampradāys* drew their power, we are told, from the fact that they served as vessels for an uninterrupted transmission of religious teaching and practice. In fact, the very word *sampradāy* could be interpreted as meaning just that.[1]

In this chapter we will explore the rubric of the four *sampradāys*. We have already alluded to the way in which George Grierson translated this idea for readers of Hastings' *Encyclopaedia of Religion and Ethics* as the "four churches of the reformation," each with its separate "leader" *(ācārya)*. Here, however, our primary guides will be Hazariprasad Dvivedi and his mentor Kshitimohan Sen, colleagues at Shantiniketan and true fathers of the idea of the bhakti movement. As we know, the name Tagore gave to the university he founded at Shantiniketan was Viśva Bhāratī—"All of India"—and the notion of the four *sampradāys*, encased in the larger concept of the bhakti movement, was put forward by Dvivedi and Sen as an important statement of how the country had sustained its all-India unity over the centuries. As in the case of the "born in Dravida" motif, however, this history of south-to-north progression turns out to be the history of a wish—a northern wish that required the invention (or perhaps reinvention) of an earlier south. Still, it illuminates in various ways a web of perceived connections across the full breadth of northern India that one might indeed, on reflection, call a movement or series of movements. One might also think of calling it a commonwealth of love.

The Three-Storey House of the Four Sampradāys

In its ideal form, the notion of the four *sampradāys* has an impressive structural rigor, and we meet this rigor already in its classic formulation, the one to which Dvivedi and Sen refer when they make it the backbone of their bhakti movement thinking several centuries later. It comes from the *Bhaktamāl* (Garland of Devotees) of Nābhādās—or Nābhā, for short. This extensive work was composed in Brajbhasha, an influential literary stream of Hindi, sometime around the turn of the seventeenth century in an environment about which we will soon be learning more.[2] The motif of the four *sampradāys* occurs in the *Bhaktamāl*'s twenty-seventh chapter, first in a six-verse stanza called *chappay*, Nābhādās's preferred mode of exposition, and then in the *dohā* (couplet) with which he concludes it. *Dohās* otherwise appear only at the opening and close of the *Bhaktamāl*, so this is a rare form of emphatic punctuation, seemingly intended to mark the beginning of the whole second part of the text, where Nābhādās catalogues the bhaktas who lend coherence and sanity to the present world-age. Here is the passage, with the first verse of the *chappay* also appearing at the end, as is customary in the original, since it functions as a refrain:[3]

> Earlier Hari took on twenty-four bodies—
> so, in this *kali* age, four formations:

Śrī Rāmānuja—ocean of life-giving nectar,
noble wishing-tree for all the earth;
Viṣṇusvāmī—the boat that takes you across
to the opposite shore of the sea of rebirth;
Madhvācārya—the rain-cloud of devotion
that fills your barren pond;
Nimbāditya—Āditya, the sun whose fire
disperses the fog of knowing nothing.
In life and deed they've laid out teaching traditions
of God's religion for all time.
Earlier Hari took on twenty-four bodies—
so, in this *kali* age, four formations. *(chappay)*

Rāmānuja follows Ramā's approach,
Viṣṇusvāmī, that of Shiva,
Nimbāditya, of Sanaka et cetera,
and Madhva, that of four-faced Brahmā. *(dohā)*

In these lines Nābhādās gives us a template for the religious history of the world. The first tier of his conceptual edifice, the part pertaining to the time that has elapsed with the onset of the *kali* age, is supplied by the gods themselves, but we must remember that from Nābhā's perspective the gods' greatness derives not so much from their divine status as from the fact that they themselves are bhaktas—bhaktas who inhabited a prior, more perfect era of world history. Three of the four deities he mentions in the *dohā* just quoted also appear at the head of the list of "twelve principal bhaktas" whose mercy sustained that earlier epoch.[4] The disastrous *kali* age has intervened, but one redeeming feature keeps it aligned with its longer, better past: a quartet of flanks or formations (*byūh* < *vyūha*—the word originally had a military valence) by means of which Hari continues to act in something like the way he had before, when he periodically took up the cause of righteousness by infusing himself into twenty-four successive avatars. The four *vyūhas* of the present age are the acharyas who form the basis of the four *sampradāys,* and Nābhā associates each of these greats with one of the deity-devotees who was active in primordial time. His own preceptor Rāmānuja, for example, is aligned with Vishnu's consort Śrī—or as he calls her here, for euphony, Ramā.

Anantadās, a Rāmānandī contemporary of Nābhā's, also makes it plain that he knows the rubric of the four *sampradāys,* and interestingly, he too uses the notion to suggest something of a protective edifice. To be associated with—or literally, come inside *(bhītari āvai)*—one of these four bhakti communities is not only to be given a reputable family but to be made secure:

> People who come within the four teaching traditions—
> such bhaktas are pleasing to Hari.
> They'll always be accounted as of good family,
> finding release, or at least not being lost.[5]

Following Nābhādās's *dohā,* we can think of the foursquare logic of these *sampradāys* as comprising a two-tiered structure. One storey pertains to the distant past—mythical time, one might say—and the other inhabits history, the *kali yug.* But as one makes one's way further into the *Bhaktamāl* it becomes plain that the *kali yug* has been subdivided so that a third storey also appears. All the acharyas Nābhā names in his classical formulation lived in the south, but their influence continued in the north. In the *Bhaktamāl* we see this most clearly in the case of the *sampradāy* to which Nābhā himself belonged. He explains that Rāghavānand, who belonged to Rāmānuja's lineage, made his way to Banaras and there became the guru of Rāmānand, who in turn became the guru of twelve notable disciples. In an important flashback Nābhā explains that Rāghavānand and Rāmānand were able to strike out in this new direction because they were supported by another four-part scaffolding, this one provided by four religious leaders (*mahant,* "abbot") who had been guru-brothers of Rāmānuja. Nābhā likens them to the four elephants who anchor the world at each of its cardinal points.[6] Thus in this one instance, at least, the overall solid structural logic of the four *sampradāys* is also replicated on a smaller scale, as often happens in the exterior design of Hindu temples.

Yet it seems the building is still under construction: the community of teaching transmission that Rāmānand established was only one of the four sectors of the edifice. Nābhā is much less forthcoming about the structural details associated with the other three *sampradāys*—he offers a complex and even sloppy picture—but by the time this paradigm had been inherited by those who shaped the parlance of the bhakti movement in the early twentieth century, it was well understood that each of these four classic southern flanks might generate a northern form. The writings of

Kshitimohan Sen and Hazariprasad Dvivedi provide good examples. Both men believed that the line of Viṣṇusvāmī had been extended by Vallabha—there was no dispute on that. In other respects, however, emphases could differ. Dvivedi considered that Nimbārka's *sampradāy* connected to the community formed in Brindavan by the poet Hit Harivaṃś. Nimbārkīs themselves, by contrast, usually stress the importance of Keśav Kāśmīrī Bhaṭṭ, also a resident of Brindavan, in depicting their *sampradāy*'s northern aspect. As for Madhva, both Sen and Dvivedi felt that the connection sometimes claimed to exist between him and Chaitanya was open to question, but in the simple fact of registering this opinion they implicitly acknowledged that others accepted it as valid.[7]

As we can see, then, the girders anchoring these northern teachers and their communities to a presumed southern past were sometimes shaky, both in actuality and in their conception. Yet the striking thing is that even so, the overall four-*sampradāy* structure had a definite, long-lasting appeal. We might represent it as follows:[8]

The Time-Structure of the Four *Sampradāys*

Upper: Recent/North	Rāmānand	Vallabha	Keśav Bhaṭṭ or Hit Harivaṃś[9]	Chaitanya
Middle: Classic/South	Rāmānuja	Viṣṇusvāmī	Nimbārka (Nimbāditya)	Madhva
Lower: Primordial	Śrī	Rudra/Shiva	Sanaka, etc.	Brahma

The Four Sampradāys within the Bhakti Movement Narrative

When Hazariprasad Dvivedi tells us in his *Hindī Sāhitya kī Bhūmikā* (Introduction to Hindi Literature, 1940) that "simply put, the Vaishnava philosophies of the south provided the basic inspiration for the bhakti movement," it is the second of our three "storeys" that he has in mind.[10] Dvivedi explains that something fundamental happened in the history of Indian religion in about the twelfth century, when these *sampradāys* began to take shape—a moment of clarity that was to give shape to the entire history of Indian religion and literature from that time forward. As we saw in Chapter 1, however, Dvivedi took sharp issue with Grierson as to why this change occurred. If, as Grierson said, Hindu religion took a sudden, momentous turn from doctrine to emotion at that point—from *jñāna* to *bhakti*—it was not because of the long-standing influence of Christianity in the subcontinent. Indeed, as Dvivedi pointed out, the *jñāna* aspect had never been lost. He also dismissed the even more ridiculous idea (so he said: *upahāsāspad*) that Islam had anything to do with it—the notion that Hindus took refuge in the hard-to-attack realm of religious singing after Muslims destroyed their temples.[11]

Dvivedi saw no need to go over the same territory he had covered in his Sūrdās book as he laid out his basic picture of the bhakti movement in *Hindī Sāhitya kī Bhūmikā,* but he did stop to say a word about why the long-standing tendency toward imaginative devotional expression *(paurāṇik ṭhos kalpanāeṅ)* that India had always nurtured came into focus with such seeming suddenness starting in the eleventh century. The cause was to be found in the personal force of the acharyas of the four *sampradāys.* They were expert in the systematic procedures of traditional learning *(śāstrasiddh),* yet deeply opposed to its most influential expression at that time. For they all shared two perspectives: they recoiled at the Advaitan *(māyāvād)* notion that human beings ultimately dissolved into God *(bhagavān meṅ līn),* and they affirmed the belief that, contrary to this passive view of the relation between humanity and divinity, God had projected himself actively into manifest forms *(avatār)* as time went by and the need arose. In both respects they accepted and revivified "the ancient Bhāgavata religion *(prācīn bhāgavat dharm).*"[12]

In saying all this, Dvivedi draws repeated attention to the fact that these acharyas were not only Vaishnavas but southerners. It is almost as if this southernness was a necessary aspect of "the ancient Bhāgavata religion"—even if Śaṃkara, also a southerner, got it wrong from their point of view. Like Nābhādās, Dvivedi focuses particularly on Rāmānuja and his lineage. In his exposition Rāmānuja was not just the first acharya chronologically speaking and the first of the four in importance and ranking, but in some unstated way paradigmatic of them all. Dvivedi repeats the familiar notion that Rāmānuja released the path of bhakti from any bondage to caste,[13] and connects that to his participation in a tradition that had been established centuries before him by the *āḻvārs.* The *āḻvārs* are absent in the *Bhaktamāl,* but Dvivedi, following the lead of Kshitimohan Sen, whom he explicitly acknowledges on this point, pulls them to the fore and makes them stand at the front rank of a *vaiṣṇav āndolan* that later split into two contrasting groups, the Teṉkalais and the Vaṭakalais.[14] Dvivedi saw the entire sectarian drama of the four *sampradāys* as playing itself out against the background of the deep religiosity of the *āḻvār* poets—their *bhaktipūrṇ upāsanā-paddhati* (devotion-filled spiritual path). They thus emerge as the *fons et origo* of the bhakti movement, the head of a stream that would continue to bubble through the religious history of the deep south long afterward, even though it was the four acharyas who gave the movement its philosophical bite and institutional resiliency.[15]

Except in regard to the *āḻvārs,* Dvivedi acknowledges his debt to Nābhādās's *Bhaktamāl* in laying this out this view of bhakti history, quoting at some length from a *Bhaktamāl* commentary published by Rāmānuj Harivardās in 1875.[16] His object in doing so is to highlight the specific nature of the south-to-north transition, in which the socially and devotionally radicalizing work of Rāmānuja was later replicated in the person of Rāmānand—far away from Kāñcī in Kāśī, that is, far away from Kanchipuram in Banaras. Dvivedi pictures Rāmānand as bolting from the caste preoccupations that had crept back into the Śrī *sampradāy,* throwing its membership open once again to all. In the same spirit, he says, Rāmānand composed his poetry not in Sanskrit but in the spoken language *(deśbhāṣā meṅ kavitā likhī)*—Hindi, this time, not the *āḻvārs*' Tamil.[17]

In picking up this line of thought, Dvivedi participates in a broader intellectual tradition that had developed in the Rāmānandī community, gradually taking the populist radicalism that had been thought of as belonging first and foremost to Rāmānand's guru, Rāghavānand, as in Nābhā's *Bhaktamāl,* and transferring it to Rāmānand instead. Rāmānand then becomes the chief vehicle for the great south-to-north transition in bhakti history: Dvivedi propounds the same Rāmānandī "shortcut" to the north that would later be echoed in the lectures of V. Raghavan. He says it is well known that bhakti arose in the south, that Rāmānand brought it to north India, and that Kabīr, upon becoming Rāmānand's pupil, spread it far and wide. In a footnote Dvivedi lets us know that he is paraphrasing a Hindi *dohā.* Its exact provenance is unknown, but its sentiments are plainly Rāmānandī. Its opening phrase suggests that it builds upon and redirects the "born in Dravida" discourse that was apparently first articulated in the *Bhāgavata Māhātmya* (Surendranath Dasgupta drew upon it in the same year, 1940), but the rest of its content is clearly Rāmānandī:

bhaktī drāviṇa upajī lāye rāmānanda
paragaṭa diyā kabīra ne saptadīpa navakhaṇḍa

Bhakti was born in the south; Rāmānand bought it forth from there;
Kabīr revealed it to the seven continents and all nine parts of ours here.[18]

It is striking that in expositing the four *sampradāys* Dvivedi feels no obligation to tarry too long in the domain of the founders themselves. What interests him far more is the third storey of the bhakti house we have envisioned, the one that took form in the north. Hence, under the heading of the Śrī *sampradāy,* we hear of Rāmānand's twelve disciples, especially Kabīr; then via Kabīr's son Kamāl we move on to Dādū, whom Dvivedi takes to be his pupil; and finally to an entirely different face of the Rāmānand tradition—Tulsīdās. At the end of the section he credits Nābhādas for his expansive bhakti vision and notes that Nābhā's *Bhaktamāl* has been translated into many languages. Dvivedi has Bengali and Marathi especially in mind—the latter, apparently, a reference to Mahīpati's massive eighteenth-century hagiography, the *Bhaktavijaya,* even though it is much more than what we usually think of as a translation.

Thus Dvivedi uses the rubric of the four *sampradāys* as his structure for envisioning the bhakti movement even though, as already in Nābhā, these four bear uneven structural weight. They serve explicitly as Dvivedi's headings as he launches into his exposition of the bhakti movement, and they retain their marquee status for quite a while. Madhvācārya's Brāhma *sampradāy* requires only a single paragraph to deal with, since, as Dvivedi observes, it has no obvious connection to Hindi literature. Some have aligned Chaitanya with Madhva, he explains, but he laments the fact that in Hindi scholarship this claim has received no sustained treatment.

Then he moves on to the Rudra *sampradāy* of Viṣṇusvāmī. In doing so, he fully accepts the connection to Vallabhācārya, tossing off an aside to the effect that other branches of Viṣṇusvāmī's *sampradāy* aren't of any importance. Is this a smokescreen to cover up the fact that Nābhādās regards Jñāndev, Nāmdev, and Trilocan as belonging to the Viṣṇusvāmī line?[19] Dvivedi's narrative is much more direct. It takes him via Vallabha's son Viṭṭhalnāth to Sūrdās and the "eight seals" *(aṣṭachāp)*—again, a rubric that sets Dvivedi apart from Nābhā and reveals the extent to which he accepts Vallabhite teachings. He is aware of the considerable dose of imagination that infuses the great Vallabhite hagiographies where 84 and then 252 bhaktas are presented as being devotees of Vallabha and his son Viṭṭhalnāth, but he passes off this element of ahistoricity with a kindly gloss. Such stories serve as apt commentaries on the emotional mentality of India's Middle Ages *(madhyayug)*—its "era of bhakti" *(bhakti-kāl),* as he elsewhere calls it—so it is no surprise, he explains, that elements in these stories are easily transferred from one bhakta to another.[20] A motif like the "eight seals," however, which also owes its origin to the Vallabhite *vārtā* literature, passes by without any questions being asked about its historicity.

Next Dvivedi takes up the Sanakādi *sampradāy,* that is, the one associated with Nimbārka, but at that point he begins to depart more substantially from the great paradigm, perhaps because he was not much interested in the literary heritage of those who call themselves Nimbārkīs. He switches almost immediately to poets of the Radhavallabh *sampradāy,* especially Hit Harivaṃś, but he is aware that the reality of their connection to Nimbārka, though sometimes claimed, is dubious, so he also gives the Radhavallabhīs their own heading before proceeding on to groups that can claim no place under the four-*sampradāy* umbrella but nonetheless need to be taken into account in any broad treatment of north Indian religion and its literary correlations.

The first of these is the Sikhs, though interestingly Dvivedi avoids this clear sectarian marking when he describes Gurū Nānak and the bhaktas assembled in the *Gurū Granth Sāhib,* singling out Nāmdev for particular attention. The second such group is the Sufis. Because of their multiple resonances to the poetry of Hindu bhaktas, Sufi works of literature present the most fundamental challenge to a taxonomy built largely around the four southern *sampradāys.* Dvivedi therefore works hard in one or two exemplary instances to overturn any impression that distinctive features of Sufi genres were inventions of the Sufis themselves. People tend to think, for example, that the alternation of *caupāīs* with *dohās* so characteristic of *premākhyāns* such as Malik Muhammad Jāyasī's famous *Padmāvat* began there, while the truth is that certain purely Indic counterparts came first. Similarly, he points to the fact that Sufi poets made use of narratives indigenous to India, thus rooting themselves in "the people's movement [known as] the bhakti way" *(jan-āndolan bhaktivād).*[21] This is hardly an attempt to fit Sufi works of literature to a girdle molded after the four *sampradāys,* but looking back over this chapter on "The Bhaktas' Tradition" *(bhaktoṅ kī paramparā),* one sees that he allows little to rival the four *sampradāys* as institutional channels through which the history of his "people's movement" might have flowed.

Dvivedi's use of the four-*sampradāy* formula had a major impact on later articulations of the idea of the bhakti movement, especially in Hindi, yet he was hardly the only thinker of his time to adopt it. With interesting variations, we also have his friend and senior colleague Kshitimohan Sen, who posited a "Neo-Bhakti cult" (Bgl. *naba bhaktivād*) that could ultimately be traced back to the ancient Dravidians and "other pre-Aryan settlers of the land." Its first flowering was visible in the poems of the *āḻvārs,* but it became a full-fledged "philosophy," he said, with Rāmānuja, Madhva, Viṣṇusvāmī, and Nimbārka filling out the picture.[22] Sen laments the fact that the author of the *Bhaktamāl* failed to do justice to "the South Indian *bhaktas*" who are so important to any full treatment of the subject.[23] Frederic Salmon Growse's remarkable *Mathurá: A District Memoir,* published in Allahabad half a century earlier (1874), also makes a contribution, and historically speaking, R. G. Bhandarkar's magisterial handbook *Vaiṣṇavism, Śaivism, and Minor Religious Systems,* published in Strassburg in 1913, was uniquely important in English-language scholarship. Ishwari Prasad seems to have relied upon Bhandarkar more than anyone else as he worked his way into the particularities of the bhakti movement, though he abandoned the great man's punctiliousness as he addressed a somewhat different and rather more general readership.

The position of Viṣṇusvāmī in Bhandarkar's narrative is especially interesting. Unlike the three other Vaishnava acharyas, he does not warrant a section of his own. This may be because so little is known about what he thought, but if so, Bhandarkar does not concede the point. Rather, he folds Viṣṇusvāmī into his exposition of Vallabha, stating twice on the same page that Vallabha's "Vedāntic theory" is the same as Viṣṇusvāmī's. It would be hard to guess that this "earlier author" is actually the fourth acharya in the set, even though Bhandarkar tries to evaluate Nābhādās's claim that Jñāndev, Nāmdev, Trilocan, and Vallabha were his successors—as he says, "follower[s] of his system (Sampradāya)."[24] Bhandarkar's hesitation on this point was very likely the reason for Prasad's, and his unmarked segue from the southern acharyas to northern figures, via Rāmānand, was also a precursor to Prasad.

Then there was J. N. Farquhar, who published *A Primer of Hinduism* shortly before Bhandarkar's *Vaiṣṇavism, Śaivism,* and seems to have been utterly unconcerned about any inadequacies in the four-*sampradāy* paradigm. He includes a fascinating diagram in which he attempts to parse these four *sampradāys* so that two come out to be Rāmaite while the remaining two are Krishnaite. As we know, Ramchandra Shukla was to adopt a similar division not long afterward. A notable feature of Farquhar's account is that he applies the dominant European frame of sociological analysis to his Indian material, with the result that the original "churches" of the south yield to "sects" as they move to the north, and they, in turn, to "sub-sects."[25] H. H. Wilson had found it natural to use the notion of "sect" some seventy-five years earlier, and Grierson had seemed to contrast it to "church," but only in Farquhar does the relationship between these two categories come into open view as a way of explaining the connection between the second and third storeys of our four-*sampradāy* "house."

Needless to say, the four *sampradāys* were hardly absent in Hindi writing about bhakti of the period. For instance, one finds a brief treatment of the subject in the hugely influential *Miśrabandhuvinod* (The Miśra Brothers' Delight, 1913), named after its authors, the three Miśra brothers who were literary doyens for a generation. They speak of "four chief branches of Vaishnavism" *(vaiṣṇavamat meṅ cār pradhān śākhāyeṅ)* and are notably more interested in the "sub-branches" *(upaśākhāyeṅ)* that formed in the north than in the southern roots. Those pertain to Chaitanya, Vallabha, and, as the Miśras imply in another passage, Kabīr. Aligning Chaitanya with the Mādhva *sampradāy* (see Chapter 5), and Vallabha with what they call the Vishnu (not Viṣṇusvāmī) *sampradāy,* they are nonetheless more interested in these men's relationship to one another than to their supposed southern gurus. The Miśra brothers call them "classmates" *(sahapāṭhī).*[26] Elsewhere the Miśra brothers take southern narratives of how the Vaishnava acharyas co-opted Śaṃkara's rationalism and defeated the Buddhists and Jains and embed them in a broader story of bhakti's galvanizing response to Muslim attacks on Indian culture that began with Mahmūd of Ghaznī. Certain of the southern acharyas are great heroes in this regard—Rāmānuja's battles against the Jains are mentioned, as is Nimbārka's trip to Bengal to purify its Vaishnavism of Śākta influences—but the Miśra brothers make little effort to connect these aspects of their stories to the rubric of the four *sampradāys* as such.

The Miśras mention several *Bhaktamāl* commentaries written after that of Priyādās,[27] but it is striking that they are silent about the massive, recently published commentary that was to become so determinative for the field. In 1913 Sītārāmśaraṇ Bhagavānprasād "Rūpkalā," a member of a distinguished family of performers of the *Bhaktamāl,* swept into print with his elaborate edition of the *Bhaktamāl,* in which he enfolded the commentary that had almost inevitably accompanied the *Bhaktamāl,* the *Bhaktirasabodhinī* of Priyādās (1712), into a much more extensive commentary of his own. Rūpkalā's eight-hundred-page work, a version of which was known to Grierson, was reprinted a number of times in the three decades that intervened between 1913 and the date when Dvivedi published his *Hindī Sāhitya kī Bhūmikā* (1940). In one elaborate chart, somewhat like Farquhar, he amplifies the information given in the *Bhaktamāl* and *Bhaktirasabodhinī* so that his readers will know the lineaments of all four *sampradāys,* something they might have expected since, as we shall see, the four-*sampradāy* rubric had actually been put forward as an instrument of state policy in the early decades of the eighteenth century by the remarkable Savāī Jaisingh. Undoubtedly it was in the widely circulated literature that surrounded the *Bhaktamāl* and in its oral recitation that the notion of the four *sampradāys* came into prominent view as an integral part of the narrative of the bhakti movement.

Plainly this was so for Dvivedi, yet when Ramchandra Shukla published his *Hindī Sāhitya kā Itihās* in 1929, he slid by the idea of the four *sampradāys* and focused instead on a parallel or two that he saw between Vallabha and Rāmānuja, but it was really the parallel positions of Vallabha and Rāmānand—innovators in the north—that caught his attention.[28] This is an important point, since it was not just the Rāmānandīs but also the Vallabhites who had developed a particular interest in putting forward the four-*sampradāy* rubric. The portrait of Viṣṇusvāmī that Shukla gives in his essay on Vallabhācārya shows that he knows both sources.[29]

Shukla, we remember, was writing in Banaras, and was deeply enmeshed in the intellectual elite that made Banaras such a force in the construction of Hindi and Hindu history as it emerged in the early twentieth century. As such, he was heir to the great Hindi litterateur Bharatendu Harishchandra, whose work he was involved in editing so that it could take its proper place on the new stage of Hindi history that he and his colleagues at the Nāgarīpracāriṇī Sabhā were busy building. One of Harishchandra's most influential essays—his "Vaiṣṇav Sarvasva," written between 1876 and 1879—featured the motif of the four *sampradāys* prominently, but did so from a distinctly Vallabhite point of view. This comes as no surprise, since Harishchandra was himself the scion of a prominent Banarsi Vallabhite family. Harishchandra also brought into view a set of subsidiary *upasampradāys*—"sub-sects" in Farquhar's later term, though the names Farquhar and the Miśra brothers were to assign to these sub-sects do not exactly match Harishchandra's.[30] In Chapter 5 we will learn about the textual tradition that Harishchandra was mining as he laid all this out. For now we may simply observe that, influential as it was, Nābhādās's celebrated *Bhaktamāl* and its associated traditions of commentary were not the only reason that the notion of the four *sampradāys* became so fundamental in structuring that of the bhakti movement. There was an independent Vallabhite source. Yet time and again it is Nābhādās to whom we must return as we try to appreciate where the idea of the four *sampradāys* came from and how it became so crucial in imagining—perhaps even generating—the bhakti movement. In fact, Harishchandra composed a long poem he called "The Latter Half of the *Bhaktamāl*" *(Uttarārdhabhaktamāl),* thereby styling himself Nābhā's latter-day successor.[31]

Nābhādās and the View from Galtā

Tradition is unanimous in believing that Nābhādās composed his great work at Galtā, one of the most remarkable geological formations in eastern Rajasthan. Galtā is a gorge. If you enter it from the bottom, the only direction accessible by road, you wind your way through scrub woods into a narrow valley that suddenly opens up to cream-colored monastic buildings and a set of great tanks continually replenished by fresh water. These recede tier by tier in the distance above you, ever more closely flanked by the mountains with their occasional caves, and if you climb all the way to the top you find yourself suddenly gazing down at the great city of Jaipur. Jaipur's most splendid east-to-west artery, passing along the southern wall of the palace compound that stands at the center of the city, aligns itself from far below with the temple to the sun, Sūrya, where you stand. It is a magnificent sight.

But Galtā would have looked quite different around 1600, when Nābhādās wrote his *Bhaktamāl,* and Jaipur would have been nothing but an open plain. At that point the Kachvahas' capital lay just to the north in the mountain fastness of Āmer, and the great tanks and *maṭhs* of Galtā with all their Mughal-style architectural finery had not yet been built. Nonetheless, the connection between these two places had indeed been forged, laying the groundwork for all that was to come. For it was in the first half of the sixteenth century that the first Rāmānandī abbot of Galtā became, in effect, the *rājguru* to the Kachvaha king Pṛthvīrāj (r. 1503–1527), conferring on him the deity that would most clearly mark the entry of the Kachvahas into a configuration of Vaishnava worship much more elaborate and cosmopolitan than anything mandated by the Rāmaite ancestry the royal family had always claimed. Sītārāmjī, as this deity is called, is primarily worshipped in the form of a *śālagrām* stone that Kṛṣṇadās Payahārī presented to King Pṛthvīrāj, and the inclusion of both Sītā and Rām in the divine name is significant. It signals an amorous dimension that Kṛṣṇadās Payahārī was evidently responsible for introducing into the Rām-oriented worship and self-conception of the Kachvaha kings and queens. The other deity he brought to the Kachvahas—also in the shape of a *śālagrām* stone—was more martial: Vishnu as Narsīṃha, the man-lion.

The story of how Kṛṣṇadās Payahārī came to reside in a cave along the side of the water-fed gulch at Galtā is a dramatic one. He is said to have done battle there with a yogi called Tārānāth, who had, with his Nāth Yogī following, been its prior resident.[32] Or at least one could speak loosely of this confrontation as a sort of battle. Actually, as the story goes, there was no need to fight. When Kṛṣṇadās appeared at Galtā, starting what Tārānāth perceived to be a turf war, Tārānāth summoned his yogic powers and set upon Kṛṣṇadās in the form of a tiger or lion, but Kṛṣṇadās merely responded with a dismissive quip. "What a jackass!" he said, and sure enough, in a fast-backward of yogic potency, that was the form to which Tārānāth was immediately reduced. After that, he and his Shaiva band retreated to the upper reaches of the wilderness surrounding Galtā, while the gorge itself was inhabited by the Rāmānandīs.[33]

This tale seems intended to epitomize a definitive moment of transition in which the yogic traditions of Galtā became domesticated through a network of associations that made them part of a Vaishnava ecumene of considerable breadth. In the language of Nābhādās, the rubric of the four *sampradāys* was what made such associations intelligible, anchoring them in a ritual and historical landscape that extended throughout India and very importantly included the south. Later, perhaps as late as the nineteenth century, Nābhādās himself was said to have emerged from a community that had southern origins—in the Tailangana country along the Godāvarī River—which would have shown, if a bit indirectly, that Nābhā knew whereof he spoke.[34] The preponderance of the legendry that surrounds him, however, suggests that he was more or less a local boy, hailing from somewhere in Rajasthan. And the only thing we know for sure, since he himself provides us this information, is that Nābhā was the pupil of Agradās (also called Agradev), and Agradās, in turn, of Kṛṣṇadās Payahārī.[35]

Whether the four-*sampradāy* formula predates Nābhādās in the teachings of the Rāmānandīs among whom he lived, we cannot tell. We also do not know exactly what they called themselves. As yet we have no evidence that the label Rāmānandī was applied to the Galtā community until the 1730s,[36] and judging by what Nābhā himself has to say, together with the usage of Anantadās, roughly his contemporary, it seems the term Śrī may have been the designation of choice. But whichever title was preferred, it is clear that in sixteenth-century Galtā the idea of the four *sampradāys* did indeed circulate. Part of its appeal surely had to do with the new cosmopolitanism of the Kachvahas, who became the Rāmānandīs' patrons at just that point in time, while Kṛṣṇadās Payahārī was abbot. Indeed, as the story goes, the Kachvaha king was present on the scene at the critical moment when Kṛṣṇadās vanquished Tārānāth. Prior to then, it seems, the Nāth Yogīs had played an important role at court, but at the moment of his humbling Tārānāth gestured to Kṛṣṇadās and said to Rājā Pṛthvīrāj, "This is now your guru."

A weathered painting on the wall of the cave of Kṛṣṇadās at Galtā refers to this event. Kṛṣṇadās Payahārī's image is daubed with sandalwood *tilaks* and at the time this photograph was taken, framed by a cloth declaring the name of RĀM. Tārānāth, who wears the heavy bone earring of a *kānphaṭa* Nāth Yogī, stands at Kṛṣṇadās's left (our right), and behind him is the worshipful presence of King Pṛthvīrāj. This is interpreted by modern-day Rāmānandī *sādhus* as registering the fact that these two eminences became supporters of the Rāmānandī tradition at the same time. Meanwhile, at Kṛṣṇadās's right (our left) and also seated, as he is, we find his disciples Kīlhadev and Agradās. These three take their place at the focal point of a lineage of Rāmānandī acharyas that on the one hand

Figure 3. Painting in Kṛṣṇadās Payahārī's cave, Galtā (early nineteenth century?). Photo by John Hawley.

stretches downward and forward toward the present day, and on the other hand reaches backward and upward to its divine origins in Vishnu and Śrī themselves. The lion of our story also takes his peaceful, submissive place in this composition just below the image of Tārānāth.[37]

Obviously this painting restricts itself to the Rāmānandī *sampradāy* in depicting the relations of patronage and dependency that tied the throne of Āmer to the gods and religious communities that surrounded it, but as we recall from the last chapter, the Kachvahas' religious involvements were actually much more wide-ranging, even so far as Vaishnavas themselves were concerned. The four-*sampradāy* formula was one way to make sense of that fact—and indeed, during the reign of Rājā Savāī Jaisingh (r. 1699–1743) this became its central purpose. The sixteenth century witnessed no such attempt to give political agency to the four-*sampradāy* rubric. Still, its appeal to a broad span of Vaishnava activity reminds one in a general way of how, at just the time Nābhādās and Anantadās composed their bhakti treatises, the Kachvaha rulers Bhagavāndās and Mānsingh were making major efforts to erect some of the greatest Vaishnava monuments ever to grace the Braj country.

In the case of Rājā Mānsingh, these efforts were preeminently associated with the Gauḍīya *sampradāy*. It is doubtful that the Gauḍīyas felt any need to forge a connection between themselves and the four-*sampradāy* scheme until late in the seventeenth century (see Chapter 5), and yet it is interesting that they, like the Rāmānandīs, understood their relation to the wider Vaishnava ecumene through a link to the Śrī (or Śrī Vaishnava) *sampradāy*. Through the leadership of Gopāl Bhaṭṭ, the Brindavan Gauḍīyas patterned their ritual canons in crucial ways after Vaishnava observances at Srirangam, allowing them to be modified by conventions that had been established at Puri. Formally Sanātan Gosvāmī, the brother of Rūp, was also involved in preparing the text where such matters are recorded, but both brothers are clear in acknowledging their primary debt to Gopāl Bhaṭṭ, who actually came from Srirangam. The Gauḍīyas' Bengali connection, however, may have impressed Mānsingh equally. As if to incorporate the power of east India into his own, Mānsingh amplified the pantheon worshipped in the family fortress at Āmer by bringing back an image of the goddess Śilādevī when he returned victorious from his military campaigns in Gauḍ.[38]

Mānsingh's broad geographical reach as a chief player in Akbar's imperial venture is otherwise evident, too. He more than anyone else, through his military victories in Gujarat in the 1570s, was responsible for securing the great road that connected the Mughal heartland along the Jamunā with the Arabian Sea. It passed directly through the Kachvaha domains near Āmer; a fine view could be had from the top of the Galtā gorge. Later a more direct road to Agra and Abkar's new capital at Fatehpur Sīkrī would be constructed at the bottom of the gorge.[39] So both literally and metaphorically, Galtā in the late sixteenth century straddled the terrain on which the great new Mughal axis intersected with earlier forms of regional power that the Kachvahas had exercised. We have spoken already of the Kachvahas' patronage of Galtā starting in the early sixteenth century. By the end of the reign of Akbar early in the following century (1605), the Mughals had followed suit, assigning to the *mahants* of Galtā the revenue earned from a substantial acreage in the *ṣubā* of Ajmer.[40]

It is this broad context that we should locate the Rāmānandīs' articulation of the idea of the four *sampradāys*. Certainly it does not replicate or directly legitimate the new imperial formation. As we will see in Chapter 5, it probably drew its initial cogency from a rather different source—ideas of foursquare monastic security and power that were pioneered at Vijayanagar no earlier than the fourteenth century and seem in time to have had a more general impact among various groups of Brahmins and ascetics.[41] Yet we have no evidence that the idea of four Vaishnava *sampradāys* grew up anywhere but in the north. It is unknown in documents that emerge from the south until quite recently, and even today if one asks knowledgeable southerners to identify the four *sampradāys*, one is apt to be greeted with a blank expression.

Why then the north—and why the Rāmānandīs in particular? On the one hand, because their ranks were so inclusive and expanding so rapidly, they more than others needed a history that would validate them, anchoring them in a past they themselves were in the process of creating. On the other hand, as the sixteenth century proceeded and the Āmer court became part of a political, conceptual, and customary world that could not have been envisioned at its beginning, it was incumbent upon the Rāmānandī gurus to expand their sights similarly. Given the increasing competition for patronage that came from groups like the Gauḍīyas in the imperial heartland of Braj, where the Kachvaha rulers now spent much of their time and money, a continental vision of where the Rāmānandīs belonged—as first among equals—seemed requisite. Nābhādās's vision of the geographical and historical depth that the four *sampradāys* provided offered just this, and his notion of the general cogency of bhakti and the importance of its spread supplied a dynamic countervailing force. What the *sampradāys* contributed by way of structure and longitude, the common spirit of bhakti answered in dynamic latitude.

The oil painting in Kṛṣṇadās's cave was probably fashioned at some point in the early nineteenth century, and it makes no explicit reference either to the rubric of the four *sampradāys* or to the Mughal presence. Only one *sampradāy* is pictured, and only one king. Yet this painting does provide a vision of the sort of settled religious order that proved amenable to the aspirations of those who gave form to the Mughal state. Kṛṣṇadās Payahārī holds a string of *tulsī* prayer beads, and his scions Kīlhadev and Agradās sport artful *tilak* marks and carefully sewn bags concealing their own *tulsī* rosaries. They radiate a focused, formally seated decorum as they regard their guru. Contrasting such rhythms to the slyer, sometimes more agitated moods of Nāthpanthī asceticism, Vijay Pinch has made the case that Vaishnava religiosity—conceived along the lines of bhakti, emphasizing canons of mutual service, and paying obeisance to a single overarching divine presence (most often named Hari or Rām in the language of Nābhādās and others)—nicely served the needs of the new Mughal imperium.[42] Perhaps it is fitting, then, that Pṛthvīrāj's dress anachronistically anticipates the Persianate style that would come into such favor in Mughal circles at the end of the sixteenth century—not at the beginning, when he ruled.

Another aspect of Pinch's work is relevant, too. In a forceful essay on Nābhādās himself, Pinch argues that the theology of the *Bhaktamāl* displays a central structural tension between the strictly imitative guru-to-pupil lineage system represented in the old idea of ascetic *sampradāys* and a much more liberal, egalitarian commonwealth of bhaktas. In his view the rubric of the four *sampradāys* carries forward an old model of ascetic lineages—imitative and intrinsically conservative—but he goes on to argue that Nābhādās navigates within it in such a way that the Śrī *sampradāy,* Nābhā's own, turns out to be anything but hidebound in its traditionalism. He speaks of Nābhādās as developing a "poetic progression from Ramanuja to Ramanand" in which parables of early Rāmānandī *sādhus'* radical devotion to their fellow bhaktas and to their gurus' commands prepare the way, in this specific tradition, for the moment when Rāghavānand and later Rāmānand would make the equally radical move of initiating low-caste recruits into the order.[43] I am not sure Pinch is able to build an airtight case in regard to the actual poetics of this progression, but there is no question about the fact that Nābhādās uses his magnum opus as a way to articulate a far more extreme view of what bhakti entails than the institution of a *sampradāy* might lead us to expect. This is true not only within the confines of the Śrī *sampradāy* as Nābhādās understands it, but even more so in parts of the *Bhaktamāl* where Nābhā allows the power of bhakti to flow in channels quite undisciplined by the four-*sampradāy* format he trumpets.

Pinch points out that Nābhādās's view of the Rāmānandī or Śrī *sampradāy* may jibe well with Nābhā's own position within it. Subsequent Rāmānandī authors, at least, held that Nābhādās was just the sort of person other Śrī Vaishnavas had barred from their community, but whom Rāghavānand welcomed—a *śūdra* and a particularly low-born one at that. According to Prīyādās, Nābhādās belonged to "Hanumān's clan" *(hanūmān vaṃś).*[44] The phrase may simply refer to the devotion that ascetics typically accord Hanumān or to a set of clans belonging broadly to the *kṣatriya* group who live between Rajasthan and Kathiavad, but it may also denote Nābhā's very humble origins as a member of the corpse-handling *ḍom* caste. H. H. Wilson was told that in Marwari the expression *hanumān-vaṃśī* is a euphemism for a *ḍom,* and Narendra Jhā points out that when Nābhādās refers to the bhakta Lākhājī as being of the monkey clan *(vaṅsani maiṅ . . . vānaro),* Priyādās glosses it as *ḍom.*[45] Prīyādās explains that Agradās and Kīlhadev found the child Nābhā abandoned in the forest and rescued him from certain starvation by bringing him into the Rāmānandī order. They allowed him to live among the *sādhus* resident at Galtā and educated him there—but only as a layman, so to speak. Thus in his own person Nābhā stood at the point of intersection between an older, upper-caste vision of how Vaishnava tradition should be transmitted from generation to generation and a newer one in which representatives of every social station could also be involved, and in fact were. Pinch characterizes this transition as one in which the notion of *sampradāy* was transformed from "a vessel containing sacrosanct tradition" to a new kind of "field of social memory"—just the sort of field that the *Bhaktamāl* itself represents.[46]

James Hare has taken matters further, arguing that Nābhādās, without abandoning his own sectarian moorings, imagined "a new kind of religious community" that "spans boundaries of *sampradāy,* region, caste, and gender" and also "exceeds temporal boundaries."[47] However difficult it may be to articulate exactly what such a community might mean, given the fact that the *Bhaktamāl* is such a dispersed narrative, Hare is certainly right to bring to the fore aspects of Nābhādās's writing where he moves entirely beyond the four *sampradāys.* There bhakti's characteristic "movements" not only animate and change the history of a particular sectarian order, as Pinch points out, but they also float free of these institutional channels. We see this especially when Nābhā praises bhaktas who belong to the sixteenth century itself, as he tends to do in fully three-quarters of his work. The text has an unfinished quality, as if another flower could always be strung onto the garland, and indeed, it comes down to us in versions of somewhat unequal lengths.[48]

Given its conceptual prominence, it is striking that the logic of the four *sampradāys* does not figure more pervasively in Nābhādās's *Bhaktamāl.* Only bhaktas who belong to his own Rāmānandī *sampradāy* are actually introduced according to that plan, and there too we confront a hiatus between Nābhā's exposition of the core lineage up to Kīlhadev and

Agradās (§§29–40) and his portraits of five *sant* poets whom he claims to have been pupils of Rāmānand (§§58–62, cf. §35). The remaining figures in this group of twelve disciples are not treated. Kabīr is one of the disciples who does appear (§59), but when Nābhādās uses Kabīr's name to introduce Padmanābh, who is represented as being one of his disciples (§67), it is only after an additional four *chappays* have passed. These intervening *chappays* are connected not by the logic of disciplic succession within a *sampradāy* but by another logic altogether. When one hears the list of bhaktas who are praised in those verses—Sukhānand, Surasurānand, Surasurī, and Narahariānand (§§63–66)—the resonances between the sounds of their names makes it is clear why Nābhā might have remembered them as a group. Or again, when he introduces Viṣṇusvāmī, it is not because he follows the logic of the four *sampradāys,* but because he is listing bhaktas whose names begin with the syllable "Vi"—or rather, in Brajbhasha, "Bi": Bilvamangal, Biṣṇupurī, Biṣṇusvāmī (§§45–47).

Indeed, if the four *sampradāys* were his model, we would have expected quite a different exposition of Viṣṇusvāmī's sectarian progeny. When Nābhā gets around to introducing Viṭṭhalnāth and Kṛṣṇadās, who are respectively Vallabha's most important son and devotee, we hear nothing about a *sampradāy, mārg* (road) or *paddhati* (path, system)[49] and there is no mention of Viṣṇusvāmī himself, whom he had earlier portrayed as standing at the head of Vallabha's lineage. Later, when he describes Viṭṭhalnāth's sons Giridhar and Gokulnāth (§§124–125), he prefers the simple term *vaṃś* (Brajbhasha *baṃs:* clan, family). And most striking of all, a *chappay* on Vallabha himself is absent from Narendra Jhā's critical edition. The widely used version of the *Bhaktamāl* compiled by Sītārāmśaraṇ Bhagavānprasād "Rūpkalā" seems to supply it, but even so there are ambiguities. This Vallabha is actually called Braj-Vallabh, and seems to have been inserted to bolster the idea that Vallabha—not just his son and grandsons—was part of the Braj landscape. As we shall see (Chapter 4), this is doubtful.[50]

As we can see, then, Nābhādās was only partially interested in structuring his *Bhaktamāl* along sectarian lines. Other groupings also drew his attention—the simple alphabetical fact that names sometimes suggest each other, or the knowledge that certain bhaktas shared ties to a given region. He was also interested in poetic associations that were formed through bhakti's most characteristic act—singing.[51] But against the background of what he says about the four *sampradāys* one fact stands out: the bhaktas who take their place on Nābhādās's garland almost never come from south of the Vindhyas. But for the rarest exceptions—notably the brothers Tattva and Jīvā, who ruled, he says, in the south (*dakṣiṇ deś,* §68)—the bhaktas Nābhā memorialized spoke languages that circulated in the Mughal world. Śamkara and Bilvamangal do appear in his roster, but the fact that they were southerners goes unmarked. By contrast, however, Nābhā locates Chaitanya and Nityānand definitively in Gauḍ (Bengal); and Narsī Mehtā, similarly, in Gujarat (§§71, 102). And he has much to say about bhaktas ranging across the spectrum from Banaras to Braj to Rajasthan, sometimes noting the place where this or that bhakta was active.

So if we step back from the important *yug*-bridging passage where Nābhā explains the four *sampradāys* and also from his exposition of the Rāmānandīs, which follows directly thereafter, we find ourselves in a world where bhakti echoes across the breadth of northern India, but not beyond. Of course, that is a huge realm, but considering the impact that Nābhādās's exposition of the four *sampradāys* had on later writers, right up to the present day, it is striking that this field of bhakti activity does not embrace the south. Nābhādās's *kali yug*—his sense of the present age—seems clearly based in the linguistic, religious, political, and doubtless commercial flows that connect west, east, and especially north India. Nābhā does not use such directional terms to describe this broad domain. Only the south earns an explicit directional name of this type, maybe precisely because it seemed so mysterious and distant.

Galtā's Greater Orbit

The geographical correlates of the four *sampradāys* come across quite differently in the words of Anantadās, who was Nābhādās's guru-nephew within the Rāmānand *sampradāy* and almost certainly his contemporary. He introduces the idea only once—as he approaches the end of his lengthy *Pīpā Parcaī* (Introduction to Pīpādās)—and in doing so, he says the following:

> People who come within the four teaching traditions—
> such bhaktas are pleasing to Hari.
> They'll always be accounted as of good family,
> finding release, or at least not being lost. (35.25)

As one can see, Anantadās does not actually exposit the concept of the four *sampradāys (cāri saṃpradā);* he merely assumes a knowledge of it on the part of his listeners. But the way he weaves it into his text—probably initially a performed, oral text—helps us understand what he takes to be its significance. Like Nābhā, he uses it to introduce his own *sampradāy,* but the force of his doing so is to explain how he has been granted the friendly gaze of Hari by being accepted into the "good family" that was offered him when he was initiated into the Rāmānand *sampradāy* by Vinod, a pupil of Agradās. This, then, serves to reassure his hearers of the value of the tale he has composed: those who take it to heart by hearing and reciting it will enjoy a similar liberation, he says (35.28–29). Thus the trope of the four *sampradāys* seems to exert a sort of summary magic for Anantadās, rather than providing a frame of reference for the bulk of his text, as it does for Nābhā.

In the case of both writers, however, something important stands to be learned from what comes before. Nābhā links the four-*sampradāy* concept to the praise formula with which he began his exposition of bhaktas who have peopled the world from the start—the very first *chappay* in his *Bhaktamāl,* which follows his prefatory *dohās.* This *chappay* offers praise to the twenty-four embodied forms through which the Lord has historically "played" *(līlā)* in the world, beginning with the ten avatars of Vishnu (§5). Nābhā recalls these twenty-four after many *chappays* in which no mention is made of them, and does so precisely at the point when he commences his narrative of the *kali yug,* as we have seen. By means of this primordial linkage he makes it clear that the force once exerted by these twenty-four avatars is now supplanted by that of the founders *(gurumukh)* of the four *sampradāys* (§27), even if in subsequent parts of the text their agency seems very largely to extend only to the Rāmānand *sampradāy* itself.

Anantadās sets the stage for his mention of the four *sampradāys* by a different means, plotting things out along the meridian not of time, but space. After he completes the story of Pīpā per se in the last chapter of his *Pīpā Parcaī,* he appeals to the rubric of the four directions to give his narrative further structure. Earlier he had explained at length how Pīpā's sphere of bhakti influence extends as far west as Dvārakā (7.12–12.14; 35.1–10)—this is one of the main emphases of his story—but now mentions other bhaktas, associating them with the east (Kabīr and Raidās), south (Nāmdev), and north (Dhanā, 35.12–13). These are followed by a larger tally of bhaktas who have no specific association with the points of the compass, making a total of sixteen in all (35.12–17).[52] We also have a passage (35.18–24) that expands the lens even further, to an indeterminate number of other bhaktas *(jan)* who people the *kali* domain (*kali paisār*, v. 18). And that brings us to what seems like a sort of summation: the couplet we have already quoted in which the four *sampradāys* are announced (35.25). At that point the rubric of the four directions is replaced, as if in a moral sense, by that of the four *sampradāys*.

In Anantadās's usage the four *sampradāys* are not meant to correspond to the four points of the compass any more than they are in Nābhādās's thinking, but in the broad geographical sweep that he gives us and in the four-*sampradāy* gloss that follows, Anantadās seems to be suggesting that the bhaktas he proclaims provide the hidden structure of a foursquare cosmos. Anantadās's own literary efforts are not strictly delimited by the bhakti geography he spells out here—a journey to Puri seems implied in his *parcaī* of Angad, who does not appear in the list given above—but it is striking that the *parcaīs* he has left us do represent all four bhakti compass points. In addition to Angad, his *parcaīs* give us portraits of Pīpā, Dhanā, Kabīr, Raidās, and Nāmdev.

There is no explicit sense of a "bhakti movement" drawing the group together, and as the manuscript record shows, these *parcaīs* did not always travel together.[53] Yet it is significant that in more than one of these stories we hear not only about mutual connections to Rāmānand but about travel that was inspired by a desire on the part of one of the bhaktas to encounter another. This suggests that the pull of bhakti is strong enough to overcome physical distance; indeed it reshapes the meaning of distance as such. For example, the Jhālī queen whom other writers call Mīrābāī travels from Rajasthan to Banaras in search of a bhakti guru, encountering Kabīr but preferring Raidās. Similarly Rāmānand receives a letter from Pīpā in Banaras and responds by taking Kabīr and Raidās with him on a pilgrimage westward—not just to Dvārakā, where Krishna dwells, but to stop and see Pīpā in Gagraunī along the way. As they travel, ordinary people in every village come forward to catch sight of Kabīr. When Pīpā decides to stay on in Dvārakā rather than returning eastward with his traveling companions, Kabīr and Raidās worry that he has succumbed to the delusion of being attached to places of pilgrimage. Rāmānand, however, seems to understand the issue as a personal one—Pīpā's desire to be with Krishna for a little longer—for he accepts Pīpā's resolve and observes that for Hari's people, ties of love bridge the gap of separation. Sure enough, when Pīpā returns from Dvārakā to Gagraunī later in the story, his connection to the city he has left behind remains vivid. One day, sensing that a fire has suddenly broken out in Dvārakā, he rubs his hands together and extinguishes it. A team of experts is sent to confirm this bhakti miracle[54]

Then there is the matter of social distance. Nābhādās's bhaktas also represent a considerable range of backgrounds within society, but Anantadās points to this far more directly. Even within the span of the last chapter of his *Pīpā Parcaī* we hear him identifying Dhanā as a *jāṭ*, Bhuvan as a *cauhān*, and Sen as a barber. Pīpā himself is king of Gagraunī, and Rankā and Bankā, whose names identify them generically as paupers, are nonetheless said never to have begged (35.13–16). Angad, we learn elsewhere, was a robber. All this makes one think back to the metaphor that Nābhādās chose to characterize the work of Rāmānand. In this *kali* age, Nābhā says, he was a great bridge-builder, as Rām himself had been with respect to the island of Lankā way back in the *dvāpar* epoch. Where did this new bridge lead? To the saving realm of Rām himself, in the view of the commentator Rūpkalā, and away from the terrors of this world—and no doubt this is so. But a more social dimension may also be implied. This is a bridge to society as a whole, since Nābhādās makes a point of saying in the prior *chappay,* devoted to Rāghavānand, that the world of people who would become the recipients of his and Rāmānand's actions would be a wide one, comprising all four caste divisions and all four stations along the road of life (*cāri barana āśrama sabahi,* §34.5).

In all that we have said so far, we have implied that Anantadās and Nābhādās may both have been resident in Galtā, perhaps at the same time. Two things complicate this picture, however. First, we do not have an early biographical tradition locating Anantadās there. He may have been more peripatetic—a singer, by trade—though it is still likely, if so, that he would have received his initiation during a visit to Galtā. In the case of Nābhā, by contrast, we do have a clear tradition that he dwelt at Galtā: Priyādās provides this information at the beginning of his *Bhaktirasabodhinī* commentary, and local memory recalls the exact place *(nābhādās kā sthān).*

That introduces our second complication. At some point Nābhādās's guru Agradās may possibly have left Galtā and established his own monastery at Raivāsā some hundred kilometers to the north, in the Arāvallī hills on the other side of Āmer. If so, did this perhaps coincide with the moment when Kīlhadev, not he, was chosen to succeed Kṛṣṇadās Payahārī? We do not know. Nor do we know whether Nābhādās went with him, although present residents of the monastery are eager to claim their connection to the celebrated Nābhā.[55] If indeed Nābhādās joined Agradās in pioneering the new community at Raivāsā, he would presumably have been part of a cohort focused on a life of mental and physical cultivation that directed itself particularly toward the amorous side of Rām—his relation to Sītā. Agradās was famously a gardener,[56] and it is worth asking whether there is an intrinsic connection between cultivation of this sort and the flower-filled bowers that are so typically envisioned as the favorite habitat of Radha and Krishna or, in his case, Sītā and Rām. In any case, as his *Dhyānamañjarī* makes clear, Agradās shared wholeheartedly in the eroticized world of *mādhurya bhakti* (honey love) that so powerfully formed the piety of Brindavan and more broadly Braj, even if his own efforts at imaginative realization as a *rāmsnehī,* someone caught up in the love between Rām and Sītā, focused largely on Ayodhyā.[57] Nābhādās's connections to Braj are also vivid, as we have seen, but unlike Agradās the *rāmsnehī* mood does not provide the impetus for his connection. His Vaishnavism is broader, more catholic, more eclectic, whether he wrote from Raivāsā or Galtā or both.[58]

It was this newly cosmopolitan world that Nābhādās's vision of bhakti sought to ensoul, as "the view from Galtā" would have predicted. The precise way in which it did or did not dovetail with *rāmsnehī* devotional practices in the Rāmānandī community of his day has yet to be determined, but they too, however inward-looking as a set of visionary exercises, were very much a part of public, cosmopolitan Mughal religion. They reflect the political stability and infrastructural advances that came into play in the course of the sixteenth century—the "early modernity" that has been emphasized in recent scholarship.[59] Anantadās must also have participated in this world, but the voice he projects has a more bardic tone. He spins out his yarns with the delight of an oral storyteller, and the locale he claims is more specifically Rajasthani that it was for Nābhādās. True, he keeps a wider world in mind, as we saw when he invoked the four points of the compass, but in the verses that immediately follow this passage he makes it clear that the bhaktas he knows best come from places like Bāndhau, Rāysen, and Chittor.[60] His sense of bhakti also has a somewhat more specific flavor than that of Nābhādās. In the classic formulations of Ramchandra Shukla and Pitambar Datta Barthwal, it is strictly *nirguṇ*.[61]

Anantadās's bardic sensibility was carried forward in later works that characterized themselves as belonging to the *parcaī* genre. One that has a special interest for us is a text called the *Premāmbodh* (The Ocean of Love), which was written in a language that we could broadly call Brajbhasha but comes down to us only in the Gurmukhi script that Sikhs introduced into the Punjab. The author concludes his work with a *caupaī* that dates it specifically to V.S. 1750, the equivalent of 1693 C.E.—our oldest manuscript follows not long afterward—and other indications in the text make it almost certain that this was a poem intended to be performed at the court of Guru Gobind Singh in Anandpur.[62] There in the Shivālik range just south of the Himalayas proper, Guru Gobind Singh's father, Tegh Bahādur, had established his base of operations—his capital—in 1665. The list of bhaktas immortalized in the sixteen *parcaīs* comprising the *Premāmbodh* draws substantially from those who had been praised by Anantadās, and they are typically linked together in patterns such as the ones Anantadās liked to feature, though without ever making Rāmānand the point of connection between them, as Anantadās often does. The lives of these saints are told in a specific sequence—one *parcaī* leads on to the next—and in introducing the whole set the author articulates a definite theological point of view, as Nābhādās does when he begins the *Bhaktamāl*. All of these *parcaīs* are intended to display the field of force on which life's game is played, where the vectors are love, lover, and beloved. Notably, however, the poet feels free to throw in a fair amount of humor, even scandal—jokes one could not fully savor if one lacked a sense of the way these tales had erstwhile been told.[63]

The rubric of the four *sampradāys* has little relevance to such a mood, and it also obscures the layered processes of transmission that these insider jokes seem to imply. When the author of the *Premāmbodh* gives us a Mīrābāī who is married to Giridhar Krishna right off the bat, for example, without all the longing that is so familiar elsewhere in her hagiography, and then has her refuse to consummate her marriage because her bridegroom hasn't yet spoken the name of Rām, only a knowledge of the broader Mīrā tradition makes it possible for us to appreciate the clever way the *Premāmbodh* twists the tale.[64] Indeed it is hard to know how Mīrābāī ought to be placed in relation to the four-*sampradāy* paradigm, and Nābhādās doesn't try to solve the problem when he strings her name onto his hagiographical garland. The point to notice, as we have seen, is that he includes her in his roster even so. Rāmānandīs like Nābhā, who put forward the notion of the four *sampradāys,* also traveled in a world where, to their perception, bhakti constituted a much more widely traded currency.

It is important to observe that such a world was not constituted by hagiography alone. Anthologies of compositions attributed to many of these saints were also a fundamental aspect of the network that made them cohere. Sometimes the poems these bhaktas were remembered to have sung gave shape to the biographies that emerged around them, and vice versa. The network is dense and complex, and the Sikhs were a significant agent in creating it. Early on in the formation of their community—and precisely as a means of forming it—the Sikhs developed an intricate system of anthological practice that made it possible to locate the compositions of their own gurus within a wider range of songs ascribed to others—the *bhagats,* as Sikhs called them, adopting the Punjabi vocalization of the Sanskrit term *bhakta.* These include, as part of a longer list, the bhaktas we also know from the writing of Anantadās: Kabīr, Dhannā, Trilocan, Nāmdev, Jayadev, Raidās, Sen, and, until she was ejected for reasons of theology or gender or both, Mīrābāī. The libraries of devotional song that were created at monastic *maṭhs,* both within individual books and as collections of those and similar books, also formed a significant aspect of this memory-building practice, as did those amassed in various royal courts. In both cases and more broadly—in homes, schools, and temples, especially as the ideals of Mughal culture spread—books were an important form of cultural and even physical capital. Not all such books concerned bhakti, but many did.[65]

It would be a mistake to think that the idea of the four *sampradāys* had much of a role in structuring such practices. Its relatively easy-going appeal to a broad cosmopolitan history might well have seemed inadequate to the task faced by as self-consciously institutionalizing a community as the early Sikhs. For them the cultivation of a fixed and capacious canon of performance, the collection of a body of relevant biography, and the building of libraries where these could be guarded and displayed were matters of considerable priority. And it is possible that a preexisting collection of Nānak's own poetry, perhaps one that he himself created, lay at the core of such efforts.[66]

It is striking that the Rāmānandīs, especially at their Galtā headquarters, failed to produce an anthological canon such as the Sikhs developed. Theologically speaking, the two communities were not that remote from one another. Yet for some reason the Rāmānandīs seem not have considered the musical performance of *dohās* and *pads*, the coin and currency of many provinces in bhakti's wider kingdom, to be a feature of their shared identity. This is so despite the high profile that Nābhādās accorded to singing in his *Bhaktamāl*. Could the problem have been that poetic expression in the form of *pads* and *dohās* was not a central aspect of Rāmānand's own work and person? Only a few Hindi *pads* have been attributed to him, and our access to these comes from collections created by bhaktas who were not themselves Rāmānandīs.[67] Or was it perhaps the influence of Agradās? His *Dhyānmañjarī* is an entirely different sort of work, its meter being *rolā*, possibly following the pattern provided by Nandadās's *Rāspañcādhāyī*, and its focus was restricted to the visualization of Ayodhyā.[68] Would this have deterred Rāmānandīs from becoming active anthologizers of *pads* and *dohās* more broadly—in the way the Sikhs were, for example, and as happened in other sorts of settings, both private and public?[69] Some mysteries are hidden here, and one hopes that further research will resolve them. The main point is that the idea of the four *sampradāys*, capacious as it is, fails to take in the full web of connective bhakti tissue that was actually being assembled in north India in the sixteenth and seventeenth centuries.

Rāghavdās and the Four Panths

One community, however, did succeed in marrying the concept of the four *sampradāys* to an avid anthological practice. This is the Dādūpanth, headquartered from the early decades of the seventeenth century at Naraiṇā, halfway between Āmer and Ajmer; another important seat was at Bhairānā, somewhat to the east. The Dādūpanth formed around the prolific sixteenth-century singer-saint Dādū Dayāl and generated a *guru-śiṣya* succession that remains in force today. Dādūpanthīs created anthologies of bhakti poetry that were no less extensive than the Sikhs'. Upwards of 3,800 *dohās, pads,* and other poems make their way into the *Sarvāngī* of Rajabdās, which was compiled at some point during the last three decades of the sixteenth century, when Anantadās and Nābhādās were also active, and Dādūpanthī anthologies such as Rajab's were organized just as systematically as their Sikh counterparts.[70] While the Sikhs prioritized *rāg,* sorting the compositions of the Sikh Gurus first under that heading and following them with songs attributed to the *bhagats,* the Dādūpanthīs preferred to organize their anthological corpus by theme *(ang),* initially without insisting that the compositions of Dādū had to outnumber those of other bhaktas such as Kabīr. Monika Horstmann has attributed this difference in approach to the presence of a vital sermonizing tradition in the early Dādūpanth—anthologies would be convenient resources for preachers—while a homiletic tradition such as this was less central in Sikh gatherings.[71]

Yet the two communities did not develop in total isolation. An immediate disciple of Dādū, Bābā Banvārī Hardās, preached in Haryana and the Punjab, founding a branch of the community called the Uttarādhās that became a natural conduit for contacts with the Sikhs; thus Dādūpanthī anthologies were known in the Punjab.[72] The terms *khālsā* and *dvārā* were used in both communities—to describe the *panth* on the one hand and its places of meeting on the other—and it may even be that the almost simultaneous display and standardization of their scriptural anthologies in 1604 is no accident.[73] By the turn of the eighteenth century, when Guru Gobind Singh stood at the helm of the Sikh *panth,* it was natural for the leader of the Sikh community to stop at Naraiṇā as he traveled farther south toward Nanded. He may even have been in the company of the Mughal emperor Bahādur Shāh.[74]

We find ample evidence of this Dādūpanthī-Sikh connection in the writing of Rāghavdās, a Dādūpanthī who not only created a conceptual frame that made it possible to link his own community with those that bore the name of Rāmānand but did so in such a way as to prioritize the name of Nānak, as well. Rāghavdās styles Nānak and Dādū as the sun and the moon in his sky—complementary radiances.[75] Rāghavdās worked as an anthologizer of bhaktas, not *bhajans.* His model, both from the standpoint of organization and of content, was the *Bhaktamāl* of Nābhādās, which he pointedly acknowledged as his source and inspiration. In his own *Bhaktamāl,* Rāghavdās expanded and updated what he found in Nābhā's, adding many bhaktas who figured in the history of the Dādūpanth. But he did not stop there. He also worked with the rubric of the four *sampradāys* to make it do better justice to the bhakti panoply that Nābhādās had laid out, and went on to use it as a model for another quartet that would set the frame for a great deal of his text: the four *panths*.[76] These he compared specifically to the four *sampradāys,* their forerunner, but by giving them a name and narrative place of their own, he also acknowledged their independence from the earlier formation. The *panths* he had in mind were those associated with the names of Nānak, Dādū, Kabīr, and Haridās (Nirañjanī), in that order. In most cases, if not all, he was adopting their own nomenclature when he did so—these *panths* called themselves just that—but the act of pulling them together as a group of four may well have been his own invention. It made him a historian of Vaishnavism in a comprehensive way, updating Nābhā's rubric such that it would be adequate to the world Rāghavdās saw around him and in which he himself took part.

Obviously this was a major advance in theorizing the four *sampradāys*—or at least a major innovation—and for this reason, before we explore its details and ramifications, we must pause and ask just when it occurred. In this, Rāghavdās would seem to help us: unlike Nābhādās, he does us the favor of dating his *Bhaktamāl.* Yet he does so in such a way that there have been persistent debates about the date to which he was referring. His phrase *saṃvat satrahai sai satrahotarā* has been interpreted as signifying three different dates: V.S. 1717, 1770, and 1777. These correspond respectively to 1660, 1713, and 1720 C.E. Of these, the first is the most persuasive. For one thing, it accords nicely with the fact that Rāghavdās goes no farther than the third generation after Dādū (d. 1603) in describing bhaktas of the Dādūpanth, although he himself is conventionally listed in the fifth.[77] For another, only the date of June 30, 1660, correlates with the day of the week (Saturday) and lunar timing (*śukla pakṣ* 3, *āsāḍh*) that appear as part of Rāghavdās's colophon, as given in the oldest manuscript at our disposal (scribed in 1804 C.E.), the one that serves as the basis for the edition by Agar Chand Nahta: *Rāghavdās kṛt Bhaktamāl.* To Monika Horstmann goes the credit for pointing this out.[78]

There is, however, a major unsolved puzzle if we opt for the 1660 date. As Winand Callewaert observes, Rāghavdās mentions Guru Harkishan among Guru Nānak's successors, and Guru Harkishan did not take the throne until October, 1661.[79] On the other hand, if we head for one of the two eighteenth-century dates it may seem odd that Rāghavdās does not go on to list all ten of the Sikh Gurus, since the last of them, Guru Gobind Singh, did not die until 1708. There are, admittedly, other aspects of the text that may seem easier to square with an eighteenth-century date than a seventeenth-century one—Rāghavdās's decision to regard Chaitanya and the Gauḍīyas as members of the Mādhva *sampradāy,* for example (§§218–232)—but the calendrical alignment to which Monika Horstmann has drawn attention is hard to gainsay. On balance, it seems most plausible to read Rāghavdās's date as indicating the summer of 1660. Thus well within a century of its composition, Nābhādās's *Bhaktamāl* was capable of generating a commentarial tradition that attempted to channel the subsequent movements of bhakti so that they conformed to the design of the original text yet also, at the same time, amplified it.

Rāghavdās begins by embroidering on the metaphors that Nābhādās had originally supplied for the four *sampradāys.* Calling them implicitly to mind, he reshapes them as follows:

Madhvācārya is the root of a wish-granting tree
  ample with every art.
Viṣṇusvāmī nurtures the very world,
  filling its lake with the nectar of deathlessness.
Rāmānuja is love's desire,
  touchstone touching the feet of Rām.
Nimbāditya, a manifest treasury
  of jewels fulfilling every clever thought.
Brahmā, Brahmā's sons, Shiva, and Shakti—
  bhakti brings these to a conclusion.
These four *mahants* take the form of sheldrakes
  and Rāghavdās longs for them all. (§114)

Shiva, Brahmā, Lakṣmī, Sanaka et cetera—
  these are the preeminent teachers;
And their pupils: Call them now bhakti's abundance,
  steadfast resources to cut the filth of the *kali* age.
Viṣṇusvāmī's philosophy pertains to Shiva,
  Madhvācārya's to Brahmā,
Nimbāditya's is for Sanaka et cetera,
  and Rāmānuja's is worthy of Ramā.
Honoring their doctrines, each for each,
  these teaching traditions stay pure.

Intoning their virtues, Rāghav reaches his goal—
that bhakti should pervade the earth. (§115)

It may be just an accident that when Rāghavdās introduces the southern acharyas in his second *chappay,* characterizing them as "pupils" of the original divine teachers, he uses the term *sikh.* But the term certainly has what for Rāghavdās would have been a modern ring—a ring, precisely, to the Sikhs. Later, in a similar way, when it comes time to introduce the motif of the four *panths,* he tacks back and retrieves someone else's language. This time it is Nābhādās's characterization of the four acharyas as four *vyūhas* (formations). Rāghavdās proceeds to map that ancient Pāñcarātra concept onto the founders of these new traditions, the four *panths* (§341.6). He describes the four *mahants* as having manifest in broad daylight an inner light that was implicit from the beginning (§341.1–4), and he reinforces the connection by using the venerable term *sampradāy* (*sampradāi,* "teaching tradition," §341.5). Not only that, he stops to invoke the four original acharyas in two complete *chappays* (§§343–344) before launching into his exposition of the four *panths,* which follows. By the same token, however, he brings the legacy of the ancient acharyas into the present day, via the *mahants* of the four *panths,* by invoking a concept of all-pervading light that goes well beyond the confines of Vaishnavism. The word he uses, unlike any other in the passage, comes from Arabic and has great importance throughout the Muslim world: *nūr* (§341.3), meaning "light." We capitalize it in translation:

Conceiving the realm of that which has properties,
people have conjured up every sort of name,
But there's also a formless, propertyless thing—
one and indivisible—that conquers all the world:
The Light. Its brilliance is everywhere—
the flame that is lit wherever wisdom lives,
Beyond all shape, a place where nothing meets,
measureless, kindled by itself.
Setting down beautiful teaching traditions
that sing the One without blemish or stain,
Like four battle flanks, these four religious leaders
manifest themselves for the Formless. (§341)

Nānak has the form of the sun,
the ruler whose radiance shines everywhere;

Kabīrdās is Indra, the deity whose rains
bring forth lovely ponds from barren earth;
Dādū has the very form of the moon,
nourishing all with the immortal drink it makes;
And Jagan the Nirañjanī is like Varuṇa:
with Hari he slakes every living being's thirst.
These four religious leaders, four points of the compass,
have charted four paths to the Formless:
Nānak, Kabīr, Dādū, Jagan—
Rāghav speaks their names as if they were gods. (§342)

Rāmānuja's system of doctrine
descends from Śrī Lakṣmī.
Viṣṇusvāmī's system of doctrine
was originally sung by Shiva.
Madhvācārya's system is the wisdom
that was first thought out by Brahmā.
Nīmbāditya's system of doctrine
comes from the four youths—Sanaka and the rest.
The doctrinal systems of the four teaching traditions
have emerged in the way the avatars once did;
These four religious leaders of the three-property realm—
their systems lead to the Blemishless One. (§343)

Madhvācārya's thought belongs to Brahmā;
Viṣṇusvāmī's, to the Lord of Umā;
Nīmbāditya's, to Sanaka and so forth;
Rāmānuja's, to Ramā.
Madhvācārya is a very wishing tree;
Viṣṇusvāmī, chiselled like a philosopher's stone;
Nīmbāditya, thought-jewel for every direction;
Rāmānuja, lakhs of wishing cows for the *kali* age.
The four thought-systems of these four teaching traditions
offer shelter like ever-ready umbrellas,
But Nānak and Dādū Dayāl, says Rāghavdās,
shine like the sun and the moon. (§344)

The strength of the connection in Rāghavdās's mind between the four *sampradāys* and the four *panths* is evident. Yet both here and in many stanzas to come he makes it clear that these four latter-day progeny of the old tradition are also different from their ancient forebears. They are specifically a *nirguṇ* fold (§341.6, §345.6, §345.6, etc.), and with that we have the enunciation of an idea that was too useful to be forgotten. In northern India, as we know, the broad distinction between *nirguṇ bhakti,* Rāghavdās's concept, and its *saguṇ* cousin was to become the chief tool for sorting out differences in the larger bhakti family. Here, it seems, is where the old philosophical distinction between *nirguṇ* and *saguṇ brahma* first came to be used as a way to parse out various proclivities in the world of bhakti.

On the other hand, Rāghavdās does not create a complete bifurcation between bhaktas of the *nirguṇ* persuasion and those who are *saguṇ* bhaktas at heart. Rather, he speaks of the leaders of the earlier dispensation—the four *sampradāys*—as directing their attention to "the three-property realm," the field where the three aspects of phenomenal existence, the three *guṇas,* interact. That becomes the platform for the search for "a formless, propertyless thing—one and indivisible—that conquers all the world," namely, the Light *(nūr)* that is luminous and makes possible the knowledge of all phenomenal things, yet has no distinct attribute itself. This realm he does indeed designate with the word *nirguṇ,* but his focus is less on a binary distinction between it and its phenomenal analogue—he refrains from using the term *saguṇ,* which would have emphasized that binary—than on the matter of genealogy: how the earlier and seemingly more constrained systems of thought have generated a more expansive progeny. In his final metaphor, the umbrellas of the four *sampradāys,* sheltering against the threatening clouds of the *guṇas,* yield to the sun and moon of the four *panths,* whose brightest lights are Nānak and Dādū. In this image *nirguṇ* is not so much without qualities as beyond them.

In setting forth this vision of bhakti history as something that continues to unfold toward its telos, Rāghavdās might have been justified in feeling the implicit approval of his mentor. As we have seen, Nābhādās made a crucial place for the liberality of Rāghavānand and Rāmānand in sketching the history of his own *sampradāy* (Nābhādās §§34–35). Both of them, as compared with predecessors, chart a sort of progressive "bhakti movement." The difference is that Rāghavdās structures his entire opus in such a way as to prepare for this progressivist crescendo. He concludes his *Bhaktamāl* with a hundred or so *chappays* devoted to the four *panths,* beacons to the present age, and to the lineage of the Dādūpanth itself, to which he returns after he has given a general description of its position among the four *panths*. Nābhādās, by contrast, does nothing of the sort: he develops the notion of the four *sampradāys* and before long drops it. Rāghavdās repairs this, ordering his "garland" in such a way that many of the bhaktas Nābhā had described without sectarian reference can now be understood as falling clearly within the boundaries of the four *sampradāys*. Perhaps part of the reason he finds it advantageous to do so is that he wants no loose ends as he rises to his finale—the four *panths*. Developing as they do out of the four *sampradāys*, these four should stand on the firmest "vulgate Vaishnava" footing possible.

We should not underestimate the creativity Rāghavdās displays when he locates Vaishnava bhaktas who lived from the fifteenth century onward (of course, Rāghavdās supplies no such dates) within the rubric of the four *sampradāys*. He sticks to Nābhādās's order, but he uses it to comprehend a great deal more than Nābhādās had done. In regard to the Rāmānandīs, for example, he integrates Tulsīdās into the list, whereas Nābhādās had strung him onto his garland independently, connecting him to Vālmīki, not Rāmānand (Rāghavdās §§170–171; Nābhādās §122). In regard to the Viṣṇusvāmī *sampradāy*, he follows Nābhādās in placing Jñāndev, Nāmdev, Jayadev, Trilocan, and Haridās in that orbit (§§199–204, 213)—by contrast to what later historians of the bhakti movement would do. He also follows Nābhā in placing Vallabha there, but then moves distinctively beyond him by also integrating Vallabha's disciples and progeny into the list that begins with Viṣṇusvāmī (§§207–212). Surprisingly, though, he concludes this roster of Viṣṇusvāmī-ites with the names of Mīrābāī and Narsī Mehtā (§§214–217). By contrast, the Puṣṭimārgī hagiography *Caurāsī Vaiṣṇavan kī Vārtā,* dating to the mid or late seventeenth century, goes to great lengths vilifying Mīrābāī and making sure that she not be understood as a Vallabhite. Probably it was her association with Gujarat that made the Puṣṭimārgī association seem natural to Rāghavdās: by the time he wrote, Vallabhites had a strong base there. This would also explain why Rāghavdās categorized Narsī Mehtā as a Vallabhite.

In regard to the Mādhva *sampradāy,* Rāghavdās raises a very important issue. He places there the entire company of bhaktas commonly called the Gauḍīya *sampradāy,* starting with Chaitanya and Nityānand themselves and continuing with many, many more until he comes at last to Sūrdās Madanmohan or, as he calls him, Madanmohan Sūrdās, who is quite a separate poet from the one known simply by the name of Sūrdās.

To assert this connection between the Gauḍīyas and the Mādhvites raises important theological and historical issues, as we shall see in Chapter 5. There is some controversy about when the Madhva-Gauḍīya alignment was first proposed and how widely it was accepted. There is also the interesting fact that Rāghavdās seems to pause after Sūrdās Madanmohan to deal with several sets of bhaktas and *sādhus* that he evidently found it hard to place anywhere else (§§238–241).

Then, finally, it's on to the Nimbārka *sampradāy*. That too brings some surprises, since Rāghavdās places in this category a considerable group of singers whom we normally would not think of positioning there—not just Hit Harivaṃś and Harirāmvyās (§§255–257) but the famous poets Keśavdās, Paramānanddās, and Sūrdās (§§260–264). In the *Caurāsī Vaiṣṇavan kī Vārtā* the latter two are emphatically claimed for Vallabha's *sampradāy*, not Nimbārka's. Interestingly, Rāghavdās seems also to place under the Nimbārkī umbrella the Sanskrit poet Bilvamangal, a figure about whom we will have more to say later (§265). Perhaps the reason for Bilvamangal's being placed here is that the story of his life had already come to be coupled with that of Sūrdās, as we know it did in subsequent centuries. After all, it is Sūrdās whom he follows on the list.

If all this seems self-evidently mistaken to modern-day readers, let us beware. Vallabhite hagiographers were ultimately very successful in persuading the general public that Sūrdās should be regarded as a pupil of Vallabha. Thanks to them, he takes his place as one of the founding members of the "eight seals" *(aṣṭachāp)* who are the liturgical foundation for the *sampradāy*. Yet the fact that this later came to be regarded as a matter of common sense does not make it true. The Vallabhite claim to Sūrdās is in fact no stronger than Rāghavdās's proposal that he could best be regarded as a Nimbārkī. Historically speaking, there is no good way to align the historical Sūrdās—or Bilvamangal, for that matter—with any *sampradāy* whatever.[80] It was later hagiographers who made it so, laying important chunks of the groundwork for what would in time be called the bhakti movement.

In our brief survey of the ways in which Rāghavdās carried forward the notion of the four *sampradāys* into a new setting and a new generation, we have found him to be intent upon systematization and expansion. He extended the reach of Nābhādās's paradigm internally, by bringing under its sway bhaktas whom Nābhā himself had portrayed independently;

and he extended it externally by cloning from it the new rubric of the four *panths*. Many of the bhaktas whom Rāghavdās encompassed under the heading of the four *panths* clearly made names for themselves after Nābhādās completed his *Bhaktamāl*. No wonder he omitted them. But for others this was not so. Nānak and Dādū are cases in point: why did Nābhā not include them? One might excuse him for failing to notice the presence of Dādū Dayāl on grounds that Dādū's status as a great bhakta was only beginning to emerge in Nābhā's own day. As for Nānak, perhaps he was active in regions too far north for Nābhā to become aware of him. Yet both of these explanations seem unconvincing. The realm in which Dādū traveled was quite close to Galtā, and his following apparently considerable; and the political and anthologizing activities of Nānak's *panth* make it unlikely that he would have been unknown to Nābhādās. This causes us to ask whether the reason for Nābhā's silence about these two had instead to do with a principle of selection—a preference for bhaktas who were more straightforwardly Vaishnava in their orientation, even if Nābhādās was generous in his sense of what that word could mean. If *nirguṇ* bhaktas had not been explicitly drawn into the Vaishnava realm by a prior association with Rāmānand, Nābhādās seems to have preferred to exclude them, counting as black the gray area that other communities might see as being closer to white. He also omitted Shaivas and Nāths, even as famous a one as Gorakhnāth.

Rāghavdās, in any case, was far more inclusive. He made room for a string of Shaiva *saṃnyāsīs* and for Nāth Yogīs going all the way back to Matsyendranāth (§§266–288). He treated Dādū, Nānak, and their successors and communities in detail. And in carving out a section of his *Bhaktamāl* for *nirguṇīs,* he included quite a number of bhaktas who bore Muslim names. There was, for example, Rajab, the anthologizer of whom we have spoken. Dādūpanthī biographers claim that Rajab came into the *panth* as Rajab Ali Khān, member of a notable Paṭhān family resident in Sāngāner, not far from Galtā, and closely involved in the military affairs of Bhagavāndās and Mānsingh Kachvaha. Then there was Dādū himself, who almost certainly came from a Muslim family and gave his sons Muslim names. Recent historians from inside the *panth* have had a tendency to obscure this fact, but such sensitivities were foreign to Rāghavdās. One may legitimately take issue with certain aspects of Dominique-Sila Khan's argument to the effect that the missionary activities of Nizāmī

Ismaīlīs, subsequently erased from the historical record, were to a great extent responsible for developing the larger *nirguṇī* ecumene in which the Dādūpanth participated—a social and religious world in which distinctions between Muslims and others were muted or downright meaningless. Yet there is no doubt that such an ecumene existed.[81] For Nābhādās it fell almost entirely beyond the Vaishnava pale. Only his description of Kabīr briefly suggests it: he mentions the fact that Kabīr addressed both Hindus and Turks (i.e., Muslims).[82] For Rāghavdās, however, the Vaishnava face of this *nirguṇ* ecumene seemed much more luminous. The rubric of the four *panths* created a way to embrace it—and, in effect, to Vaishnavize it.

Of course, it is important to remember that the rubric of the four *sampradāys,* even when replicated and extended by means of the four *panths,* did not for Rāghavdās exhaust the universe of bhaktas any more than it did for Nābhādās. There were always others who remained uncategorized—*sants* and *sādhs,* as he sometimes called them (e.g., §§290–291). The difference lay in the fact that those who remained outside the orbit of the four *sampradāys* were a far smaller and more marginal lot than they had been for Nābhā. By working with the material his intellectual mentor had laid out, Rāghavdās vastly expanded the reach of the four-*sampradāy* formulation, both internally and beyond. In adopting and elasticizing it, he played an important part in establishing it further. Perhaps this was part of the reason why Rāghavdās's Dādūpanthī contemporary Sundardās, a far more satirical and purely poetic presence, felt free to call it into question.[83] Did he perhaps have Rāghavdās's opus in mind when he put forward the following comment on the whole enterprise? And did he perhaps further cement its importance in doing so?

> Are you a Rāmānandī—someone who joys in Rām?
>   Then leave the joys of baser things,
>   Sing the name of Rām,
>   And keep the joys of Rām in your mind.
> Are you a Nimbārkī—from a *nīm* tree he saw the sun?
>   Then leave behind your bitter lusts
>   And drink of immortality.
>   Let that satisfy your thirst.
> Are you a Madhvācārī—your guru, the apostle of sweetness?
>   Then let your thoughts be sweet ones.
>   In your heart sing only sounds
>   Where sweetness, sweetness reigns.

Are you a Viṣṇusvāmī—having Vishnu as master?
Then know there is nowhere where Vishnu is not.
Sing to Vishnu, Sundar says,
In Vishnu be contained, content.[84]

Into Persian and Back

The Dādūpanthī developments that we see in Sundardās and especially Rāghavdās make sense against the background of a world in which the *bhaktamāl* genre was being claimed in other contexts, as well. For example, Francesca Orsini and Stefano Pellò have drawn attention to a *Bhaktamāl* written in 1682 in the city of Ghazna, now in Afghanistan, by a certain Rām Sonī, whose pen name is Navanīt, the freshly churned butter so dear to Krishna.[85] Readers of Rāghavdās's *Bhaktamāl* would have felt at home with the stories of many figures who appear in the first half of Rām Sonī's garland. More to the point, perhaps, the same could be said for readers of Rāmānandīs such as Nābhādās and Anantadās. In this Afghan *Bhaktamāl* we start with Rāmānand and, once we move past Jayadev (§2), we find ourselves amid bhaktas whom the Rāmānandīs had long claimed to be their guru's disciples: Nāmdev, Kabīr, Pīpā, and so forth (§§3–11). Rām Sonī seems to accept this Rāmānānd-centric view of things. Speaking of Rāmānand, to whom he gives the title Gosāiṅ, he says, "The *ā'īn* of *bairāg* (i.e., the institution of *vairāgya,* the general Vaishnava term for asceticism) that is now spread all over the world was drawn from the *ā'īn* (again, institutes) of Gosain."[86] It is not impossible that Rām Sonī is referring to a network of Rāmānandī *akhāḍās* that he knows of because such an *akhāḍā* had been established in Ghazna itself, but if that is so, he certainly sees a wide orbit. He inserts the Afghan Bazīd among the "classic" Rāmānandī bhaktas whom we know from Anantadās (§6) and moves on to the Punjabi Nānak when he is through (§12). Then it's on to such familiar figures as Mīrā, Narsī, Dādū, and Mādho(dās) before, roughly halfway down his roster of forty, he pushes forward to a number of *Bhaktamāl* newcomers—Punjabis such as Bābā Lāl and other figures with names like Devrāj *sarraf* (the money changer), Bhagat (bhakta) Harmilāp, and Valī Rām (§§25, 29, 32, 36). In describing the activities of one of these newcomers, Rām Sonī mentions the emperor Aurangzeb (§38).

Obviously we find ourselves in a more northern, more Islamicate world than we have so far been accustomed to inhabiting. Indeed, the language of the text and the script in which it is written are Persian. Orsini and Pellò make it clear that this is not just a matter of language, but of culture. Certain conventions associated with the Persian biographical genre called *tazkirā* are strongly felt: an emphasis on poetic expression rather than storytelling; an interest in the keeping and revealing of secret wisdom (*'irfān, ma'arifat*); and a prologue in which the attributes of Allah are witnessed in the world at hand—in this instance, in the lives of a whole range of figures who emerge from Hindu lore.[87]

Here then is a *Bhaktamāl*—its title loudly proclaims it so—fashioned in such a way as to conform to the expectations of a literary genre that runs parallel to that of the *bhaktamāl* and therefore appealing to cultured members of a linguistic and religious community where it was not born. Or was it? The paradigm of the four *sampradāys* suggests that we should be looking for predecessors of the Hindi *bhaktamāl* genre in the languages and religious communities of south India, but we have found that the landscape is far more complex. The Sufi ambiance of Hindi lyrics and hagiographies is also to be reckoned with, not only when *bhaktamāls* are self-consciously translated into *tazkirās,* as here toward the end of the seventeenth century, but much earlier too, as in the *premākhyāns* to which we drew attention at the end of the last chapter. When Nābhādās refrained from including Sufis such as Bābā Farīd on his list of bhaktas, then, we once again wonder whether that simply followed as a reflex of the world in which he lived—no one there knew about Bābā Farīd—or whether it was an act of conscious self-policing.[88] One can similarly ask whether the *Premāmbodh,* presumably performed at the court of Guru Gobind Singh, is to be taken as an expression of a larger genre in which *tazkirās, bhaktamāls,* and the Sikhs' own *janamsākhīs* were equal participants or instead as a "translation" of a relatively well-defined *parcaī* tradition across the permeable boundaries of language and script. Orally, one might expect, these boundaries would have been much less formidable than on a manuscript page, although one should not underestimate the pull of language and genre boundaries in any literary medium.

We should be clear, however, that the motif of the four *sampradāys* falls away in both the *Bhaktamāl* of Rām Sonī and its rough contemporary, the *Premāmbodh*. And that causes us to ask whether the four-*sampradāy* rubric always disappears when accounts of bhaktas begin to emerge in domains where their "Indic" autonomy had less than full play, as would have been the case both in Ghazna and in the Anandpur of Guru Gobind Singh.[89] The answer: not entirely. In fact, one of the most famous early witnesses to the idea of the four *sampradāys* comes from the massive *Dabistān-i-Mazābib* (School of Religions), a work written in the middle of the seventeenth century by Mūbad Shāh (a.k.a. Saiyid Zu'lfiqār al-Husainī), who was an adherent of the Āzar Kaivānī branch of the Zoroastrian Pārsī community. Like Rām Sonī's *Bhaktamāl*, the *Dabistān* was written in Persian, but its prologue aligns it not so much with the greater Islamic world as with that of pre-Islamic Iranian religion.[90] Its purpose, too, is quite different. Mūbad Shāh dedicates himself to providing a digest of what we today might call "world religions," of which those based in India are only a portion—but, from his point of view, a very important portion.

In the course of providing an account of the religious life of the Hindus, evidently assembled from both oral and written sources, Mūbad Shāh devotes a chapter to groups he calls Vaishnavas and Vairāgīs. For him these categories correspond roughly to the distinction between laypersons and renunciants. This sounds like a clear and well-balanced approach, but Mūbad Shāh seems to feel a certain degree of taxonomic discomfort as he pursues it. He notes that while the Vairāgīs "profess to be Vaishnavas," they actually draw their membership from "whoever among the Hindus, Muselmans, or others, wishes."[91] Evidently he is bothered by the "catholicity" or "vulgateness" that could so easily go with the concept "Vaishnava" in the bhakti environment both he and we have been charting.

Mūbad Shāh uses the rubric of the four *sampradāys* to give structure to his descriptive accounts of both Vaishnavas and Vairāgīs. In fact, he uses it in such a way that it bridges the two. Although he does not mention the term itself *(cār sampardā)* until the beginning of his discussion of the Vairāgīs, he makes it clear that he understands this list of "four classes" to pertain as well to the Vaishnava communities he has already sketched—"as before said," to use his own words.[92] This fulcrum-like moment is actually the only time Mūbad Shāh provides a list as such (the four sequential nouns given in Column 2 below), but it corresponds tolerably well to what he has already explained about the Vaishnavas in a more discursive way (drawn together in Column 1):

The Four *Sampradāys* in the *Dabistān*[93]

[Vaishnavas]	[Vairāgīs]
Madhu acārī	Rāmānuja
Rāmānandī	Nimānuja
Harbayāntī	Mādhoācārac
Rādha-balabī	Rādha-balabī

It is likely that the term Mūbad Shāh heard as "Harbayāntī" actually designated the Nimbārkīs, and that the name Nimānuja refers to the same group.[94] One can understand how a verbal report might have produced these deformities, especially if the interlocutor was not himself a member of the Nimbārka or Nimbāditya *sampradāy*. The disparity between Rāmānandī and Rāmānuja in the terminology of self-designation used by the Rāmānand *sampradāy* is a familiar one, but it is intriguing that at least some of Mūbad Shāh's sources, if we can trust his report, seem to have conflated the Vallabhite community with that of the Rādhāvallabhīs. Mūbad is interested in the fact that members of this sect do not observe the *ekādaśī* fast on the eleventh day of each lunar month as other Vaishnavas do, and that they "deliver their wives to the disposition of their preceptors and masters, and hold this praiseworthy."[95] The former fits the theology of Hit Harivaṃś and the Rādhāvallabhī community, not the Vallabhites, while the latter sounds surprisingly like a reference to a feature of Vallabhite practice that became the butt of severe criticism a century later in the so-called Maharaja Libel Case of 1861. It could also, however, refer to the fact that the ascetical wing of the Rādhāvallabhī community did not entirely dissociate itself from a householder's lifestyle. Rājā Savāī Jaisingh of Āmer and Jaipur was to find this particularly objectionable in the early years of the eighteenth century.

The list of conversation partners that Mūbad Shāh gives at the end of his section on the Vairāgīs suggests that part of his information came from an interview with a Rāmānandī *vairāgī* called Nārāin Dās that took place in Lahore in 1642 (A.H. 1052).[96] He also reports as relevant three conversations he had in Gujarat in 1640,[97] but the fact that these were with members of the Pīrānā community of Satpanthīs and that they are reported at the very end of the section on *vairāgīs*, where the four-*sampradāy* frame is no longer explicitly in play, suggests that these informants were probably not among the sources for what Mūbad Shāh tells us about the four *sampradāys* themselves. His Rāmānandī informant, by contrast, seems just right for this role. And given the great interest in the Mādhvite community that became manifest among Chaitanyite theologians at the time of the disputations surrounding Savāī Jaisingh, one is impressed by the relatively ample theological detail Mūbad Shāh is able to supply about the Mādhvites more than half a century earlier. It far exceeds anything he has to say about the Nimbārkīs or (Radha) Vallabhites, where we find a paucity that matches his unsure grasp on their names.

Thus at the same time Mūbad Shāh is endeavoring to make the four *sampradāys* work as his overarching framework, he also gives us hints that he commands only a partial view of the whole. It is a tribute to his ethnographic honesty that he does not try to convince us of more than he knows, stretching the canopy of the four *sampradāys* over more than it was intended to cover. His conversation with a Rāmānandī makes it natural for him to move on from his listing of the four *sampradāys* into an exposition of Kabīr, but he doesn't stop there. Kabīr brings Nāmdev to mind,[98] and from there he quickly moves on—via Parrah Kaivān, an important figure in his own Āzar Kaivānī community—to other Vairāgīs associated with the Pīrānā Khojās of Gujarat, whom he had visited in 1640.

So by the time Mūbad Shāh has finished with the Vairāgīs and is ready to move on to the materialist Cārvākas—an astonishing leap, and one that shows how unapologetically he navigated between oral and written sources—he has revealed the appealing range of the four-*sampradāy* concept yet also displayed its limitations. Or more accurately, perhaps, he has displayed its fuzzy borders. If Mūbad Shāh's informants used this idea as a way to relate laypeople to ascetics, he was evidently glad to follow suit. But he also seems to recognize that the four-*sampradāy* rubric doesn't entirely capture the full range of what might come in under the heading of Vairāgīs; and he notes the limitations of the latter concept too, since it leans more specifically toward Vaishnavism (he mentions the doctrine of the avatars) than would be indicated by the full range of self-identified "Vairāgīs" whom he surveys.[99] He stops short of asserting independent sectarian identities for Kabīrpanthīs, Pīrānā *satpanthīs*, and Punjabi devotees of Nāmdev by focusing instead on individual exemplary Vairāgīs (we might say bhaktas or *sants*), but it is striking that he allows himself to stray well beyond whatever boundaries might be implied by the idea of the four *sampradāys*. Given this and his occasional caveats along the way, it seems plausible that we should read this narrative sequence not simply as run-on prose but as something more artful in its desire not to be overly constrained by the categories he employs. Indeed, as we have seen, he may have come by this honestly—through the habits of Rāmānandīs themselves.

Mūbad Shāh's report in the *Dabistān* gives us the remarkable chance to see how the notion of the four *sampradāys* might have come across in actual conversation in the middle of the seventeenth century. It seems clear from his linguistic approximations that he is not working from a text. Rather, he gives us a glimpse of how this category might have served as a rough-and-ready framework for understanding bhakti history in the social world of his day, especially in a Rāmānandī orbit. Ironically, however, it seems to have been outside the Rāmānandī community that the notion of the four *sampradāys* became almost canonical. For all that we have said about Nābhadās and Anantadās and the Dādūpanthīs Rāghavdās and Sundardās, it was evidently a man named Priyādās, the most celebrated commentator on Nābhādās's *Bhaktamāl,* who more than anyone else carried the idea of the four *sampradāys* into common usage in the eighteenth and nineteenth centuries.

Priyādās was a Gauḍīya. He tells us that his guru was Mādhodās and that he wrote his great work in Brindavan in 1712. As would have been standard for a commentary—again, an oral dimension may have been crucial—the *Bhaktirasabodhinī* commentary of Priyādās seems to have been transmitted in a form that tied it intimately to the root text itself. Rather than being an addition tacked on at the end, it was interleafed with the parent text throughout. Manuscripts of Nābhādās's *Bhaktamāl* did circulate independently after Priyādās composed his commentary, but they were few and far between.[100]

Since Nābhādās was so parsimonious in giving us actual narrative for the bhaktas he describes, Priyādās's much more generous *kavitts* have deeply colored most people's understanding of the *Bhaktamāl* itself, as if Nābhādās had meant to imply the rest of the story that Priyādās supplies.

In fact, some scholars have argued that this was exactly the situation. H. H. Wilson, for instance, found Nābhā's text to be almost unintelligible if read simply by itself.[101] But if this is so, it has a telling effect, since Priyādās does not comment on every *chappay* in the *Bhaktamāl* and omits the *dohās* altogether. Even among the *chappays* that he does comment on, he gives far greater attention to some than others. As a consequence the "received" *Bhaktamāl* ends up being skewed toward what occupied Priyādās. This was doubtless partly a product of his personal interests, but it must also have reflected his awareness of the written works of others, for instance, the *parcaīs* of Anantadās.

The motif of the four *sampradāys* provides an illustration of the unevenness of Priyādās's comment. When Priyādās comes to the *chappay* in which these four are announced in the *Bhaktamāl* (§27), he fails to supply additional information for two of the founding acharyas, Viṣṇusvāmī and Madhva. Did he perhaps not know them? For Nimbārka (or Nimbāditya), too, he has but a single *kavitt* to contribute, and this is strictly in the cause of explaining how Nimbāditya got his name. It is only Rāmānuja whom Priyādās illuminates to any considerable extent.

Priyādās skips over the *chappay* that explains the lineage Rāmānuja inherited within the Śrī *sampradāy;* it goes all the way to Lakṣmī herself. But he does give us three *kavitts* that elaborate on the *chappay* referring to the famous moment when Rāmānuja mounted one of the *gopuram* towers at Tirukkottiyur—such a prominent part of the architecture of that temple—and shouted to all within earshot the secret initiatory mantra that had been vouchsafed to him by his guru. A nice feature of this narrative in the *Bhaktirasabodhinī* is a story-within-the-story that involves the great Jagannāth temple at Puri. Priyādās tells us that Rāmānuja went to see Krishna enthroned there, taking along all thousand of the pupils who had responded to his open-air revelation of the great Nārāyaṇa mantra. But the local temple officiants didn't appreciate the ritual etiquette practiced by Rāmānuja's band. They were sloppy in the way they attended to their eating implements—and who knows what else that portends! The Lord Jagannāth, however, cared only for the quality of their bhakti, which was superb. Perhaps he was acting as their protector, then, when he ordered his avian vehicle Garuḍa to transport the Srirangam group home while they slept. In the morning they awoke, amazed to find themselves once again in familiar surroundings. They never had cause to be further disturbed by the punctilious Brahmin *paṇḍās* of Puri—nor the latter by them, one might add.[102]

The story is interesting, in that it touches on a familiar theme in the *kavitts* of Priyādās: the running conflict between the world of devotional freedom that bhakti authorizes and the brahminical culture with which it continues to interact. In adjudicating the claims of both parties in this dispute, Priyādās is less one-sided than Nābhādās. In the example at hand, he lets the *paṇḍās* of Puri have their say, turning Jagannāth himself into a sort of mediator. Jagannāth Krishna affirms his connection to the bhaktas from Srirangam—the great new bhakti message—but he does so without calling into question his relationship to those who act as his principal, traditional servants at Puri. Thus Priyādās is far more evenhanded in his treatment of the familiar Brahmin-versus-bhakta trope than, say, Anantadās, and certainly more so than Nābhādās himself.[103] Or should we just come out and say that he is more conservative? The great drama in this story happens at night, but the canons of power and propriety that have always governed Puri continue to do so by day—not just that day, presumably, but many days to come.

Later on in his *Bhaktirasabodhinī,* Priyādās takes up other expressions of the same tension, this time in relation to Rāmānand rather than Rāmānuja. It emerges often in the stories of certain bhaktas whom Nābhādās and Anantadās had claimed as being his disciples: Kabīr, Raidās, Dhanā, Sen, and Pīpā. In Priyādās's telling, Rāmānand's high-caste standing has the effect of brahminizing such bhaktas. The most dramatic example arises in what he reports about Raidās, also known as Ravidās. Priyādās says that Raidās was sentenced to be a lowly leather-worker *(camār)* in this life because of a ritual infraction he had committed in the one just previous. In the course of serving his guru Rāmānand—the relationship spans both lives—Raidās offered him food that he had accepted from a person of insufficiently high caste. *Camār* though he may have become in this life, however, Raidās remains a Brahmin on the inside, as becomes clear in Rāmānand's willingness to reinitiate him once reborn and in the story of how Raidās's inner sacred thread was revealed as he ate with a bunch of thread-wearing Brahmins who vowed to exclude him. A similar story of Raidās's past life as a disciple of Rāmānand is also told by Anantadās, but there one has no hint of the guru's finicky dietary habits: we're only told that Raidās ate meat and suffered the consequences.

Priyādās, by contrast, opens a window in the *Bhaktamāl* that serves to integrate it far more fully into the status-conscious, pollution-savvy gastronomic practices that loom so large in many expressions of Vaishnava life. This is a very different Rāmānand from the one Nābhādās describes. Priyādās offers no overt repudiation of the conviction that Rāmānand served as a bridge from brahminical culture to the world of the lower castes, yet he embeds this bridge in a scaffolding that does nothing to challenge the social and religious differences represented by the *varṇāśrama dharma* system—and in fact he sometimes protects them from the radical challenge that bhakti mounts.

We must remember that the great majority of such stories cannot have been invented by Priyādās. A number of them appear already in the *parcaīs* of Anantadās, though often in somewhat different forms. Yet their recruitment into the sectarian context out of which Priyādās wrote seems to have made a difference, reinforcing the brahminizing narratives that were already abroad in Rāmānandī contexts toward the end of the sixteenth century, even if not in the writing of Nābhādās himself. Priyādās was a Chaitanyite living in Brindavan and closely associated, as was his guru Manohardās, with the temple of Rādhāramaṇjī, whom he mentions in his verse.[104] Not all the leadership roles of the Gauḍīya *sampradāy* in Brindavan were occupied by Brahmins, but most were, and certainly this was so at the temple of Rādhāramaṇjī. As we saw in the last chapter, that temple had a very specific blood and ritual legacy tying it to the Śrī *sampradāy* of Srirangam. In fact, it is not unlikely that Priyādās absorbed his story of Rāmānuja's liberality from his Gauḍīya connections as much as from the stories that moved about in Rāmānandī circles.

Owing in no small part to the broad popularity of Priyādās's commentary, with its literary attraction and narrative interest, the *Bhaktamāl* was read, copied, and recited with great frequency throughout the eighteenth century and beyond. It must have played a major role in keeping the motif of the four *sampradāys* in people's minds. Yet it is striking how little leverage the notion of the four *sampradāys* exerts over the *Bhaktirasabodhinī* as a whole. It seems to have been far more productive as an idea within the Dādūpanth, and as we shall see, the policies of Rājā Jaisingh II were to have a further effect on keeping the notion of the four *sampradāys* in the public eye—and, of course, in the eyes of those directly involved in the sectarian formations to which it referred. Even so, it is likely that no other stream of influence rivaled that of the *Bhaktamāl*—now amalgamated with the *Bhaktirasabodhinī*—as a means of keeping the idea of the four teaching traditions alive.

Priyādās's subtle reshaping of some of Nābhādās's more radical ideas about the force of bhakti doubtless helped the upper castes of his own and subsequent generations to regard the *Bhaktamāl* as something they could embrace and propound. Although Priyādās seems to have had no penetrating interest in the notion of the four *sampradāys* as such, then, his position in relation to the *Bhaktamāl* as a whole served ultimately to shore up the brahminizing, philosophizing, even Sanskritizing potential of this major idea within it.

And what about the commonwealth of bhaktas? That idea hardly faded into nonexistence. Harishchandra, for example, in his latter-day *Bhaktamāl,* went well beyond the specific lineage-geography of the four *sampradāys.* He gave considerable attention to other sorts of regional connections than those implied by the south-north axis of the four *sampradāys.* Thinking of bhaktas like Kabīr and Raskhān, he even allowed that "Muslim servants of Hari" *(musalamān harijanan)* could have a value exceeding that of countless Hindus.[105] This openness to Muslims and low-caste people as part of the bhakti story reminds us of the view from Galtā—or, even more, Naraiṇā. It reminds us of the Sikhs, the Dādūpanthīs, and the protean network that formed around the speech and legacies of Nāmdev and Kabīr.

In another way, however, the Muslim dimension points us back toward Brindavan. Priyādās's perspective on the four *sampradāys* was shaped in a place that had for a century and a half enjoyed the institutional privileges bestowed upon it by the Mughal state. It is odd but telling, then, that Muslims remained as absent from the *Bhaktirasabodhinī* as they had been from the *Bhaktamāl* itself. This too was an element of its social and religious conservatism: the domains stayed separate. Priyādās made no effort to clone the four *sampradāys* into a rubric that would change all that, as Rāghavdās had done. His view of the four *sampradāys* was very different from what may have developed at Galtā and certainly was operative in Dādūpanthī centers such as Bhairānā and Naraiṇā. Priyādās's view was truly a view from Brindavan, and as we are about to see, he was not the only one looking.

4

The View from Brindavan

IN THE CHAPTER JUST concluded we saw that the plot behind the plot of the four *sampradāys* took us not to the south, where the story itself suggested we should look for its origins, but to the north, where it points—specifically, to the bhakti communities that formed in eastern Rajasthan in the course of the sixteenth century. One of these communities—the Rāmānandīs—was decidedly monastic in its conception of itself, just as the four-*sampradāy* paradigm seemed to mandate. The other, by contrast—the Dādūpathīs—had a lay component as well. One might think that a strictly world-denying ascetic environment would have served as the likely habitat for a *nirguṇ bhakti* version of the four-*sampradāy* idea, but it actually happened in the mixed environment represented by the Dādūpathī Rāghavdās.[1] Conversely, the Rāmānandīs were much more comfortable with the kinds of worship that focused on images and invited participation in the narrative worlds to which they gave access. It was this broader vision of bhakti that shaped the *Bhaktamāl* of Nābhādās.

Such a mindset facilitated the Rāmānandīs' connection to royal power, and not surprisingly Nābhādās lay quite some emphasis on the motif of monarch-as-bhakta.[2] As for the Kachvahas themselves, they needed the power of the gods to be firmly ensconced in their midst as icons who could be served in rituals of state and honored with *pūjā*, but they also felt a need to tap into the wellsprings of power that had long been associated with ascetical practice at Galtā. The Rāmānandīs responded to that desire in ways that would befit their new role at court. By representing themselves as heirs to the ancient Śrī *sampradāy*, these monks claimed for themselves the ritual potencies of the great Vaishnava Pañcarātra tradition and deflected any criticism that they were somehow newcomers on the block, even when the story of Kṛṣṇadās Payahārī's relatively recent confrontation with Tārānāth seemed to say just that. Their belonging to one of the four *sampradāys*—indeed by most accounts the oldest—put Kṛṣṇadās's victory in a deeper historical context and conferred on the Rāmānandī order a dignity commensurate with its new connection to the Kachvaha state. The fact that the community derived a fair amount of its quickly expanding power from the practice of liberally recruiting members from the lower castes also gave special urgency to the task of asserting a tie to the Brahmins of ancient Srirangam. It would render their bhakti not only venerable but pure.

Hence while there is little justification for thinking that the idea of the four *sampradāys* emerged from the south itself, there is every reason to understand how it might have germinated at Galtā. Perhaps part of the reason Rāghavdās took it up in the course of the seventeenth century is that the Dādūpanth too, just then, was beginning to develop a degree of military muscle that would bring it into a new sort of conversation with the Kachvaha state. It might have been useful—for both sides of the conversation—to have these bhakti warriors comfortably situated in the terrain charted out by the concept of the four *sampradāys*.

Yet these Rajasthani voices, explicitly interlinked, were not the only ones eager to put forward an argument about how the communities to which they belonged could be traced to one of the four *sampradāys*. Claims were also made on behalf of some of the religious communities who had established themselves in Braj in the course of the sixteenth century. We saw in Chapter 2 how the Braj they helped constitute—specifically its spiritual center at Brindavan—came to be envisioned as magnet and conduit for what would later be called the bhakti movement. Before long we shall also see that both the Gauḍīyas and the Vallabhites, principal players in the new drama being staged in Braj, joined the Rāmānandīs and Dādūpathīs in asserting a connection to the four *sampradāys*. Indeed, if our sources are to be believed, they were actually the first to do so, even before Nābhādās proposed this connection on behalf of the Rāmānandīs.

In Chapter 5 we will discover how all this came to be, considerably expanding our conception of how, when, and why the idea of the four *sampradāys* was embraced from various sides, and how that concept, in turn, created a platform for later ideas about the bhakti movement. But before we can do this, we need to understand a good bit more about the dramatic acts of migration—"bhakti movements," you could say—that contributed so fundamentally to the creation of Brindavan and the rest of Braj in the course of the sixteenth century. Were these transpositions what actually undergirded the south-to-north progression that gets enshrined in the idea of the four *sampradāys*? And if not, what might have lain behind the Vallabhites' and Chaitanyites' desire at a certain point to connect their own histories with that master narrative, causing it to be considerably more persuasive than it otherwise might have been?

Mughal Brindavan

In the course of the sixteenth century, Brindavan fairly exploded onto the religious landscape of north India. As the century began, it may not have been much more than the forest to which its name entitles it—the verdant retreat evoked in texts like the *Bhāgavata Purāṇa* and a raft of others, home only to wandering herds of cattle. So at least was it recalled—"all jungle and uninhabited"—in a legal document *(parwānā)* issued by the Mughal governor of Agra, Mukhtār Khān, in 1709.[3] Earlier Mughal records, however, bear testimony to the existence of small settlements at places such as Barsānā, Govardhan, and Arīṭh, the last bearing a name that carries a memory of the confrontation between Krishna and the bull-demon Ariṣṭha. Early in the century it was renamed Rādhākuṇḍ, as mendicants from Bengal and elsewhere came to settle there. By the 1540s, when the great Chaitanyite *gosvāmīs* Raghunāth Dās and Jīv Gosvāmī bought land there, it was quickly becoming a major beachhead for a new form of Krishnaism. And by the end of the century settlements such as Rādhākuṇḍ constituted, in the words of the Mughal historian Irfan Habib, "a well differentiated village society."[4]

But had it yet been fully remapped as the holy domain of Krishna? In 1594 the Kachvaha ruler Mānsingh, who wanted to acquire land in Brindavan, found himself dealing with an association of peasant headmen *(pañc)* who lived in a village called Dosāīch and two hamlets nearby called Nagū and Bhanān.[5] This is one indication among several that the religious identity soon to be indelibly stamped on these places—the great *paurāṇik* idea of Brindavan, Krishna's playground—had not altogether overtaken the preexisting villages and hamlets of Braj, even their legal names. Yet we do know that immense changes were under way. Dosāīch was by then home to the massive temple of Govindadev, the largest monument in India that had ever been designed as a single structure. It had been consecrated four years earlier, in 1590, as the centerpiece of Mānsingh's desires for this new Brindavan—his and those of his father Bhagavāndās, who ruled on the throne of Āmer until his death in 1589. The land purchase of 1594 only added further drama to the major real estate transformation in which the Kachvahas participated, with far-reaching effect. A century later these new acquisitions would serve as the treasured retreat of Rājā Jaisingh II, a child prodigy whom the emperor Aurangzeb dubbed *savāī* (not just a single exemplary human being but "one and a quarter"), who became the architect and builder of Jaipur, a city he founded from scratch, and who was the greatest Kachvaha ruler of all time. To say this is no small thing. It puts Jaisingh a step ahead of even Mānsingh himself.

It is hard to imagine a place where old local conventions and new imperial realities could have made for a sharper set of contrasts than they did in Braj during the time of Mānsingh, who held the Kachvaha throne from 1589 to 1614 and was Akbar's most trusted general and governor from the 1570s onward. If the political transitions of the sixteenth century were breathtakingly rapid, this was hardly less true in the religious arena, especially in Braj. Speaking of the earlier part of the sixteenth century, Charlotte Vaudeville has argued that "prior to the arrival of the Vaiṣṇava reformers in Braj, there was hardly any Krishnaite shrine in the whole rural area."[6] Yet at century's end, in 1598, a *farmān* could be issued from the court of Akbar, then located in Lahore, making it clear that the temple of Govindadev was to be regarded as the central point of reference in an extensive inventory of major religious sites that crisscrossed the area. Thirty-five temples receiving grants and guarantees from the Mughal throne were listed on the back of this *farmān,* and of this total more than half—eighteen, to be precise—were to be found in Brindavan itself. In comparison, only six belonged to the old mercantile and pilgrimage center of Mathura not far away.[7]

Some of the most important temples in Braj—that of Hari Gopālrāy (or Haridev) at Govardhan and those housing the deities Madanmohan and Govindadev in Brindavan itself—reflected the direct patronage of the Kachvahas, with whom the Mughals had become so closely intertwined in battle, marriage, and administration. Evidence of the last of these connections is provided by the fact that the *farmān* of 1598 records itself as having been prepared during the watch *(caukī)* of Rāmdās Kachvaha, a favorite among Akbar's court officers.[8] It was commissioned by none other than Abu'l Fazl, Akbar's principal advisor, historian, and record keeper, and it evidently reflected the views of an elite group of four Brahmins whom Abu'l Fazl trusted to help him make sense of a religious complex that had grown so rapidly as to require legal review and conceptual systematization. The result was not only the reaffirmation and consolidation of earlier commitments but the extension of the state's patronage to many other sites that appeared on the list, for a total commitment of one thousand *bīghās* according to Akbar's newly expanded definition of the term.[9] These were heady times.

The great octagonal *śikhara* of the Govindadev temple, which apparently rose to a height of some three hundred feet until it was dismantled in circumstances we still do not fully understand (the rest of the temple, except for the *garbhagṛha* over which it stood, was left standing), would have been visible at a great distance.[10] This was so not only because of the height of the temple itself but because of the hillock on which it stood, located not far west of the River Jamuna. This site may have had earlier associations with a goddess. As reckoned at the Govindadev temple itself, she was the goddess Vṛndā, who is associated with the *tulsī* plant sacred to Vishnu.[11] Her hill was not the only high point in Brindavan's landscape—another, even more dramatic, had been claimed as the site for the sister temple of Madanmohan—but these two promontories are quite exceptional in the general sweep of Brindavan's riverine landscape. Utterly different from Galtā, we have here a vast alluvial plain, flooding generously during the monsoon (Figure 4). Doubtless Brindavan became a sort of boomtown during the reign of Akbar, but not a densely populated one. Its new buildings, whose architecture was nicely consistent though not strictly repetitious, were laid out at a comfortable distance from one another. They must have represented striking additions to a pastoral and agricultural scene that they modified but did not destroy.

The great urban concentration remained elsewhere—at Mathura, the ancient city lying on the right bank of the Jamuna seven miles to the south of Brindavan. The highest point in Mathura's terrain had achieved its eminence in part because of the rubble that had been deposited there by the remains of city after city, built and rebuilt over the course of fully two

Figure 4. Brindavan waterfront on the Jamuna, showing the temple of Jugal Kiśor. Photo by Robyn Beeche.

millennia.[12] It is possible that this hill—this tell—may have supported a major temple to Vishnu for many of those years. If so, it was the one great precursor to the plethora of impressive temples built for Krishna in the Braj countryside as the sixteenth century advanced.

But was this Mathura temple actually dedicated to Krishna? The historical record is far from clear. We know from the report of the Jesuit Antonio Monserrate that there was an exciting hubbub of activity at the site when he visited there sometime between 1580 and 1582. According to Monserrate, Brahmins insisted on the tonsure of "huge crowds of pilgrims from all over India" on the banks of the Jamuna before they would let them worship at the temple that stood at the top of the hill.[13] Only when Vīrsingh Bundelā, king of Orccha and a close ally of the Mughal emperor Jahāngīr, built a new temple on the site in 1618 does its Vaishnava status become clear. At that point, we know, it was called the temple of Keśavdev or Keśavrāy, a title that may refer generally to Vishnu or specifically to Krishna. Probably the temple took its name from earlier structures on the site: the *farmān* of 1598 to which we have been referring does mention a grant to a temple of Keśavrāy in Mathura. Significantly, however, for all the press of pilgrims that Monserrate observed, that grant is considerably smaller than those made to the temples of Govindadev or Madanmohan in Brindavan—the revenue from forty-five *bīghās* of land as against seventy or one hundred.[14] And its focus was probably quite different. To judge by the other looming structure that Vīrsingh Bundelā built in the region, the Chaturbhuj temple he had constructed in Orccha itself, it may very well have housed a four-armed image of Vishnu rather than a two-armed one of Krishna.[15] Nonetheless its glory would have rivaled—and was probably intended to rival—that of Govindadev, whose design Vīrsingh copied for the Chaturbhuj temple in Orccha.[16] The Venetian traveler Niccolao Manucci tells us that its golden spire could be seen all the way from Agra some fifty miles away.[17]

The contrast and indeed rivalry between Mathura and Brindavan is truly significant. Let not all this talk of magnificent buildings with soaring towers obscure the fact that in Brindavan, by contrast to Mathura, the reason for building such structures was actually the pastoral landscape in which they were set: the land where Krishna had roamed, the site of his idylls with Radha, the gopis, and his cowherd friends. If Brindavan took on some of the features of urban grandeur in the course of the sixteenth century, as it undoubtedly did, this was owing to its ties to royal centers located at some remove—Āmer, Agra, Fatehpur Sīkrī—rather than on the site itself. Brindavan was built not to be a capital city but to recover the natural garden that cityscapes, however carefully conceived, tended to destroy. At the same time it was, in its way, a monument to the newly far-flung connections that the Suris and Mughals made possible, for it rose at the center of a newly pacified ring of territories that extended coast to coast and from Kabul to the Deccan. If in an ideal Sultanate or Mughal city the palace garden was intended to serve as the quiet, capacious heart of the urban complex as a whole, then by analogy Brindavan and all of Braj seemed to have been fashioned by their Rajput and Mughal architects as the vast garden situated at the center of the new Rajput/Mughal cosmopolis. And at the heart of Brindavan lay, in turn, a garden: *nidhi-ban*, the "treasury-wilderness" that was most closely associated with the love play of Krishna and Radha.

I do not mean to imply that the Mughal rulers themselves conceived Brindavan as the heart of their empire. That honor would have to go instead to Agra, a city of half a million at its peak and a huge military garrison; or for a while to Fatehpur Sīkrī, Akbar's dream-capital and home to the tomb of Shaikh Salīm al-Dīn Chishtī; or to Delhi, which poets could depict as "a little Mecca."[18] Indeed one would have to acknowledge the whole string of cities that pointed back from Agra to Delhi to Lahore to Kabul—and thereby to the Timurid past. The throne itself was a mobile throne, traveling in response to military and administrative demand. Yet at least from the point of view of the Mughals' firmest allies, the Kachvahas, and in concert with the vision of the religious immigrants of whom we shall soon speak, Brindavan lay at the center of it all. It was the religious reality that turned the iron of trade and conquest to gold. No wonder the old *Mathurā Māhātmya* had to be rewritten in such a way as to shift the emphasis at least somewhat from Mathura to Braj. Once exclusively a paean to the ghats, tanks, and images of Mathura, several of which are forms of Sūrya or Shiva, this text became in its new version a much more Vaishnava document, one that made a place for a survey of the Braj country as a whole, conceived as "forests," and that alluded specifically to the deity worshipped in the temple of Govindadev.[19] Tradition attributes the new improved *Mathurā Māhātmya* to the creativity of Rūp Gosvāmī himself—and who was he? Among many other things, he was the man in charge of the temple of Govindadev, the person to whom the deity is said originally to have revealed himself in 1535.[20]

As we indicated in Chapter 2, however, the temple of Govindadev that Rūp oversaw was the first structure on the site, not the splendid second temple that Rājā Mānsingh caused to be consecrated in 1590. Apparently Mānsingh had it built to fulfill a vow he had taken many years earlier: that if he should return victorious from the campaigns that took him to Gujarat in 1572 and 1573 and perhaps to Mewar in 1576, he would thank Govindadev and his initiating guru Raghunāthdās for their agency in making it all happen. We do not have actual text for this vow—perhaps it was oral rather than written—but it can be reconstructed with some plausibility from the relevant documents that do survive.[21] If Raghunāthdās initiated Mānsingh in front of the Govindadev image he served, it may have been after Rūp's death. Dated written works do not emerge from Rūp's hand after 1550, but in a *farmān* of 1568 we learn he had stepped down as *adhikārī* of the Govindadev temple, passing the role on to his nephew Jīv. The wording of the document suggests that he was still alive.[22]

Rūp's fortunes must have been tied, at least indirectly, to the Mughals—perhaps Babur and Humayun, certainly Akbar. One even wonders whether the earliest *farmān* to have survived in which such a tie is formalized might have been issued in the year 1565 in view of Rūp's advancing age, making sure that the royal connections he had developed would be formalized for posterity. Yet we must remember that a major part of Rūp's life in Brindavan would have transpired not during Mughal times per se but in a period when the Afghans had reasserted their control. The first Mughal ruler, Babur, held the throne from 1526 to 1530; the second, Humayun, from then until 1540, at which point he lost it to the Afghan Suri rulers Sher Shāh and Islām Shāh. Humayun recaptured Lahore and Delhi in 1555 but died shortly thereafter, being succeeded by his son Akbar.

We often forget the contributions that the Suri rulers made to the consolidation of empire that had begun under the Mughals. These were crucial to the Mughals' later success. For one thing, Sher Shāh Surī (r. 1540–1545) excelled in making common cause with a range of leaders we could generally call Rajput, as the Mughals were later to do.[23] Equally important, he devised an exacting system of administrative control and revenue collection, which was perpetuated by his son Islām Shāh (r. 1545–1554). Most celebrated of all perhaps was the excellent network of well-protected roads and caravansarais that he created, which not only reconnected Bengal with the northwest, but tied the new capital at Agra with places as far south as Burhanpur in the Deccan, a system that was critical to later Mughal successes. It was Sher Shāh Surī who built the new highway that connected Delhi and Agra on the right bank of the Jamuna, making it possible to travel quite directly between the two cities, rather than crossing the river and taking the considerably longer route that made use of the great road that connected Delhi to Kanauj and Banaras. Pointedly, this new road had the effect of inserting the great bulk of the Braj country, which lay west of the Jamuna, into the very center of imperial concourse. Brindavan grew up not far away on the shores of that other major artery connecting the two cities, the Jamuna itself.

Finally, there were continuities of personnel that tied Afghan patterns of rule to their Mughal successors. The most important figure who comes to mind is the famous Ṭodarmal, a Khatrī Hindu from Avadh who served in Sher Shāh's ranks and then became chief financial officer to Akbar early on in his reign (1560). Ṭodarmal was later employed by Akbar in a number of other capacities, some of them military. One instantly sees how such things matter to our story when one recalls that in 1584 a seasoned, all but invaluable Ṭodarmal would personally grant the income from one hundred *bīghās* of land to the temple of Madanmohan in Brindavan. He made this grant on behalf of Akbar to Gopāldās, the man who served Jīv Gosvāmī as priest *(pujārī)* not only in the temple of Madanmohan, but also at Govindadev, and was elsewhere referred to as his legal representative *(vakīl)*.[24] It is said that Ṭodarmal too, like Mānsingh, was an initiate of the Gauḍīya *sampradāy,* having been given the mantra by Raghunāth Bhaṭṭ, another of the celebrated "six *gosvāmīs*" who worked alongside Rūp, his brother Sanātan, and his nephew Jīv.[25] Thus we see that it was not only the Kachvahas who mediated between the highest levels of Mughal authority and the religious institutions that were blossoming at Brindavan; others were also involved. Note, too, the geographical distance represented in Ṭodarmal's career. Like Mānsingh, who served from Ahmedabad to Kabul to Bengal, when this easterner came to Brindavan he brought the empire with him.

Immigrants from the South: When and Why?

All that we have just said suggests that the building of Brindavan commenced in the Suri period or during the reign of Akbar. Indeed, for every architectural development of which we have a dependable record, this is true, and it is not wrong to imagine that the immense political and economic advances made from 1540 onward created the conditions that made it possible for Brindavan and other parts of Braj to thrive in a new and newly conceived way. Yet we must keep in mind that in Mānsingh's time Rūp was remembered as having discovered the image of Govindadev in 1535, during Humayun's rule, and it seems to have been during the last phases of the prior dynasty—the rule of Sikandar and Ibrahim Lodi (1489–1526)—that others among the new "Braj pioneers" arrived on the scene. As we saw in Chapter 2, it is hard to draw a straight line between the depiction of bhakti traveling from south to north that we get in the *Bhāgavata Māhātmya,* on the one hand, and the on-the-ground realities of the Brindavan toward which she is said to have been heading, on the other. Yet if our sources can be trusted, there is no denying that many of the bhakti immigrants who built new and lasting institutions in Braj around the turn of the sixteenth century did indeed come from the south. The question—now to pick up the thread from Chapter 3—is whether they did so as vanguards of the four *sampradāys*.

Take, for example, the figure of Nimbārka. If one reads the standard account of how the *sampradāys* of Braj came into being, one meets Nimbārka's name at the head of the roster of Krishna bhaktas who arrived in Braj and established an enduring sectarian presence there. This standard is well represented in a book published in 1968 as one weighty volume in a trilogy devoted to explaining all aspects of the cultural heritage of Braj: Prabhudayāl Mītal's *Braj ke Dharma-Sampradāyoṅ kā Itihās* (History of the Religious Communities of Braj). According to Mītal, Nimbārka made his appearance in Braj at the conclusion of what he calls the early medieval period *(pūrva madhya kāl),* that is, just before the onset of Mughal rule.[26] Mītal tells us that Nimbārka made his residence in Nīmgāoṅ, near Mount Govardhan, a place that takes its name simultaneously from his and from the great *nīm* tree that grows there. Mītal then goes on to list the names of three other prominent figures who inherited Nimbārka's mantle before the time of Akbar: Gāngal Bhaṭṭācārya, Keśav Kāśmīrī Bhaṭṭ, and Śrī Bhaṭṭ. These four Nimbārkī *mahants* comprise almost half of Mītal's pre-Mughal list. Only one other figure dating to this period—Vallabhācārya—joins them in taking a clear place within the framework articulated by the idea of the four *sampradāys*.

Alas, a series of difficulties are embedded in Mītal's reconstruction of history. To begin with, nothing in the work most reliably attributed to Nimbārka, the *Vedāntapārijātasaurabha* (The Fragrance of the Heavenly Tree of Vedānta), which was conceived as his commentary on the *Brahma Sūtras,* betrays a specifically Krishnaite orientation.[27] This text does not even cite the *Bhāgavata Purāṇa,* which may be an indication of its early date but may also signal the lack of a theistic orientation that would align its author comfortably into the Vaishnava frame proclaimed by the idea of the four *sampradāys*. Evidently that came later. Moreover, skipping ahead to the Braj aspects of the story, there is no real reason to associate the *nīm* tree that appears in the name of Nīmgāoṅ with the *nīm* that figures prominently in the story of how Nimbārka/Nimāditya got his name, the one that Priyādās reports.[28] What is critical is the turn to Radha (and, simultaneously, to the vernacular) among some who claimed Nimbārka as their guru—the remainder of Mītal's list—but again, that came much later.

Nothing in the writings that can best be attributed to Nimbārka himself shows any awareness of her.[29]

A similar tale would have to be told about the community's establishment at Dhruv Ṭīlā near Viśrām Ghāṭ in Mathura. Again, there is no reason to associate this place with Nimbārka himself. Its proprietors are able to trace their family's presence there only as far back as the sixteenth century. Of course, that date is extremely significant from our point of view, as is the fact that this sanctuary is located in Mathura, for it is there that one can trace the bulk of the older religious activity that occurred in the Braj region, as against what happened in the newly "colonized" rural parts of the area. Very likely we should think of the Nimbārkī presence on Viśrām Ghaṭ as following from the arrival in the course of the early sixteenth century of Keśav Kāśmīrī Bhaṭṭ, the important Nimbārkī ascetic whose *samādhi* lies a short distance away.[30]

That too makes for an interesting story. The earliest versions of Nābhādās's *Bhaktamāl* neglect to mention Keśav Kāśmīrī Bhaṭṭ, but a *chappay* singing his praise had evidently been added to the *Bhaktamāl* corpus by the time Priyādās wove his *Bhaktirasabodhinī* commentary around the work in 1712. By then memory may have become foggy and it was appropriate to explain how Keśav Bhaṭṭ came to have the moniker Kāśmīrī attached to his name. Priyādās therefore provides us with several *kavitts* in which Keśav's wide travels and philosophical prestige are extolled. In the course of doing so, he also features an encounter between Keśav Kāśmīrī Bhaṭṭ and Chaitanya, which is said to have occurred after the former had subdued the intellectual pretensions of the pundits of Navadvīp, the clan among whom Chaitanya was born.[31]

An equally vivid aspect of the citation for Keśav Kāśmīrī Bhaṭṭ, as given in this stratum of the *Bhaktamāl,* concerns the endpoint of these travels: Mathura itself. The *chappay* attributed to Nābhādās calls Keśav a veritable axe in the cause of his firm devotion to Hari, a weapon capable of chopping off the stems of other religious traditions.[32] One might well take this as a reference to the cogency of Keśav Kāśmīrī Bhaṭṭ's philosophical writing, in which the positions of opponents are engaged—perhaps those at Navadvīp, as Priyādās makes us think—but the *Bhaktamāl* takes things in a different direction. It says that Keśav's warlike personality displayed itself at Mathura itself. There Keśav issued a forceful challenge to the foreigners *(mlecch)* who ruled the place, causing these *qāzīs* to fear the very mention of his name. A *kavitt* of Priyādās associates this confrontation specifically with Viśrām Ghāṭ, using the alternate name Viśrānt Tīr. There, says Priyādās, Keśav Bhaṭṭ, accompanied by thousands of followers, found himself confronted by the sight of Muslims circumcising those who had presumably removed some of their clothes so as to bathe. Keśav flared with anger at these oppressors, told them to remove their own clothes (reducing their sartorial status to that of the religious Hindus), and proceeded to drown them one and all.[33] A later tradition, reported by the commentator Rūpkalā, conjures up further details—a terrible circumcising machine that the Muslim authorities had set up, and its destruction when Keśav Kāśmīrī Bhaṭṭ appealed to the countervailing and even more terrifying power of Vishnu's disk, the deadly *sudarśan cakra.*[34] It may not be incidental that Nimbārkīs regard their founding guru as a manifestation of just this weapon.

We must remember that all these stories were written well after Keśav Kāśmīrī Bhaṭṭ's death and seem to have been added to his biography in stages. A rudimentary statement of how he routed the Turks and *qāzīs* from Mathura occurs in Rāghavdās's *Bhaktamāl* (§245), probably written in 1660, and more elaborate versions of the story may well have circulated in the aftermath of Aurangzeb's destruction of the Keśavdev temple a decade later. There was indeed a *qāzī* in residence at Mathura in early Mughal times, but the city did not become an administrative center independent of Agra until 1629. Nothing in records associated with the Mughal court indicates that there were any major controversies, except for an instance in which a local Brahmin was accused of misappropriating material that had been amassed by the *qāzī* with the purpose of building a mosque. The matter seems to have been handled judiciously, accommodating especially the concerns of members of the imperial harem, perhaps especially those who were Hindu.[35] The real tensions—and they may have been more political than religious in nature—boiled up later, in the course of the seventeenth century. It seems likely, then, that Keśav Kāśmīrī Bhaṭṭ's role in a Hindu-Muslim confrontation was dreamed up after the fact, perhaps as a reflection of the martial sensibilities of at least some Nimbārkī ascetics. Keśav himself probably came to Mathura not as a defender of the faith but for the simple reason that it was a major destination on the pilgrimage routes of his time. He was by then old, as Nimbārkī sources affirm, and simply did not go farther, but the ashram that grew up around him, with its lay patrons, remained.[36]

Later, as Brindavan flourished, Nimbārkī theology turned distinctively to Radha and the order established a center in Brindavan—the Śrījī temple, which remains a major site of worship today.[37] As the name would seem to imply, though it also refers to Śrī = Lakṣmī = Radha, this temple is closely associated in memory with the figure of Śrī Bhaṭṭ, one of whose poems is included in the middle section of the Fatehpur anthology of 1582.[38] Brindavan's highly respected Nimbārkī scholar, Brindavan Bihari, affirms the four-*sampradāy* model, yet so far as I have been able to discover, there is no Nimbārkī text of any considerable age that attests it. All we have is the unchallenged conviction that Keśav Kāśmīrī Bhaṭṭ hailed from a Tailangana family, which, in turn, is said to have been connected to that of Nimbārka himself. So far so good, but the family until recently resident at the Dhruv Ṭīlā site where his *samādhi* lies traces its lineage not to the south but to a Gauḍ Brahmin heritage in the north.

Of course, the matter of southern origins is very significant for our concerns, and this is not the only place where there is a strong suggestion of its importance in generating the great transformations that occurred in Braj sometime around the turn of the sixteenth century. In Chapter 2 we mentioned the figure of Gopāl Bhaṭṭ, whom Chaitanya is said to have inspired to depart for Braj when he met him as a young man at Srirangam, and who belonged to the priestly family of that great temple. We also noted that he represents quite a different connection to the milieu of Rāmūnuja than is suggested by the Rāmānandīs' claims, even though Gopāl Bhaṭṭ, like Rāghavānand and Rāmānand, remained celibate. And there is no question about his impact on the ritual life of Brindavan-style Vaishnavism through his *Haribhaktivilāsa,* even if he himself never became the householder whom those ritual prescriptions, enshrined at the temple of Rādhāramanji and honored elsewhere, would require for temple service.[39]

A similarly great impact on the emerging Vaishnava culture of Braj can be traced to another immigrant whose family had roots in the deep south—Nārāyaṇ Bhaṭṭ, the author of the *Vrajabhaktivilāsa* (Devotional Enjoyments of Braj), a massive work completed in 1552. A late seventeenth-century biography written by one of his descendents, Jānakīprasād Bhaṭṭ, reports that Nārāyaṇ Bhaṭṭ's father hailed from Madurai, the city whose name is the Tamil equivalent of Mathura and whose mythology connects it pointedly to its northern prototype.[40] According to this same account, however, and also according to the *Vrajotsavacandrikā* (Luminous Array of Festivals in Braj), a work reportedly written by Nārāyaṇ himself,

Nārāyaṇ Bhaṭṭ was born in 1531 on the banks of the Godavari, the great river that rises in the western Deccan and flows eastward through the Telugu country before emptying into the Bay of Bengal.[41] A pattern of gradual northward migration is implied. Nārāyaṇ Bhaṭṭ is said to have settled in the region around Mount Govardhan in 1545, apparently joining the ascetics from eastern India who had by then encamped at Rādhākuṇḍ—or, to use the local name, Arīṭh.

The *Vrajabhaktivilāsa* is a remarkable treatise, cataloguing every conceivable forest, grove, or ford in the Braj countryside, connecting each with a deity or character in the life of Krishna, and instructing potential visitors about the mantra to be uttered at each place and the time that would be optimal for offering such an utterance. It is an encyclopedic work—the longest ever composed about the sacred geography of Braj—and it reads, in the words of Alan Entwistle, "not so much as a description of actual circumstances, but as a prospectus for a full reclamation of Braj, making use of any existing objects, however trivial, and inventing the rest."[42] The *Vrajabhaktivilāsa* takes Mathura as its basic point of origin, yet its special focus is farther west. Brindavan is not especially featured, but there may be a connection with the followers of Chaitanya, as Nārāyaṇ Bhaṭṭ's several-year stay in Rādhākuṇḍ seems to imply. If so, however, such a fact could not be deduced from the description of Nārāyaṇ Bhaṭṭ that is offered by Nābhādās, who goes to some lengths to depict him as a *smārta,* someone who strives to keep the entire fabric of traditional brahminical learning intact.[43] Nor is a Chaitanyite orientation evident in the *Vrajabhaktivilāsa* itself. Nābhādās positions his *chappay* on Nārāyaṇ Bhaṭṭ after the one on Kamalākar Bhatt, a Mādhvite, and before the one that depicts Rūp and Sanātan. One might interpret this order as indicating a hinge between sects, but I think it is easier to read in terms of caste and perhaps regional affiliation. After all, if we were to believe that Nābhādās understood Nārāyaṇ Bhaṭṭ as being a member of the Chaitanyite fold—a pupil of Kṛṣṇadās Brahmacārī, who was in turn an initiate of Sanātan Gosvāmī, as Gauḍīya tradition asserts—then it would seem odd that Nābhā should devote a *chappay* to Sanātan's pupil's pupil before he got to Sanatan himself.

It is easy enough to understand how a work like the *Vrajabhaktivilāsa* might have been composed by a newcomer to Braj rather than a native. Here would have been someone who could still see the forest for the trees—and indeed, forests become the principal organizing rubric for this massive work, although specific banyans are also featured. Yet although there seems no doubt about Nārāyaṇ Bhaṭṭ's having been an outsider, it is much harder to locate him clearly within any *sampradāy* rubric, certainly not that of the four *sampradāys,* and thereby imagine a sect-based orientation that might have brought him to Braj. Unlike Gopāl Bhaṭṭ and the six *gosvāmīs,* Kṛṣṇadās Kavirāj and the early Chaitanyite biographers never propose such a thing. Much about Nārāyaṇ Bhaṭṭ remains mysterious. He wrote in Sanskrit and may well have been a speaker of Telugu and Tamil, but as to the means of his livelihood or the exact motivation for his immigration to Braj, it is at present impossible to say.

Other southerners were also active in Braj in the first half of the sixteenth century. Rūp and Sanātan Gosvāmī, younger and older brothers who had a major impact on the building of Braj, were also southerners in a certain sense, as we saw in Chapter 2. If Nārāraṇ Bhaṭṭ's relation to the Chaitanyite project that began to unfold in Braj in the first half of the sixteenth century is somewhat indistinct, that is hardly so with Rūp and Sanātan, and in part for that reason we are heir to much more specific information about their southern roots. We learn from the writings of Jīv Gosvāmī, nephew to Rūp and Sanātan, that they all belonged to a family that traced its origins to the Deccan. There is an element of confusion in Jīv's genealogical report, since he seems to claim that the earliest ancestor whom he lists, one Sarvajña Jagatguru, himself "ruled as a king in the land of Karnāṭa"—that is, Karnataka—but it seems clear that the man to whom he was actually referring was not the king himself but rather, as the title suggests, his guru. As we learn elsewhere in Jīv's writing, this man's name was Viśveśvara Kavicandra and he served as court poet (again, the *kavi* in his name gives it away) to King Siṃhabhūpāla, who controlled a region in the Nalgonda district of modern Andhra Pradesh, not far south of Hyderabad, in the last two decades of the fourteenth century.[44]

Yet much had happened in the six generations that separated Rūp and Sanātan from Viśveśvara. Their branch of the family had long since settled in Bengal, probably coming by way of Orissa, and within Bengal Rūp and Sanātan had themselves been itinerant. After being educated at Navadvīp, they settled at Rāmakeli, near Gauḍ, and took up service in the court of Husain Shāh, who from Gauḍ ruled an area that extended across most of what we today would call Bengal. Clearly Rūp and Sanātan preserved the high levels of training that their brahminical past implied, yet by serving a Muslim ruler they effectively become Kāyasths, as certain others openly called them.[45] It was Chaitanya who reinscribed their Brahmin identities upon them by giving them the names Rūp and Sanātan. When he first encountered them, we are told, they were known to him respectively as Dabīr Khās and Sākar Mallik, and these names may actually not have been personal names but the titles by which these men were known at the Shāhī court of Gauḍ. Sākar Mallik is "honored sir" and Dabīr Khās is "private secretary"—that is, to the shah. In Chaitanyite remembrance Sanātan sometimes gets this title, too.[46]

No doubt these roles made Rūp and Sanātan effective interlocutors with counterparts in the Mughal and Suri courts, but their particular standing at Gauḍ, exalted as it was, may also have encouraged them to move elsewhere—to a place where they could reclaim a fuller measure of their Brahminness. Of course, there may have been other motives, as well. They may have wanted to dissociate themselves from a campaign on Puri that Husain Shāh was then considering. But these brothers' sense of having compromised themselves comes through at several points in their biographies, particularly as counterpoint to their efforts not to lose contact with Karnataka Brahmin families like their own.[47] In the *Bhaktiratnākara* it is said that they resettled a group of Karnataka Brahmins in Bhaṭṭabāṭī, near Gauḍ.[48] This is a later text, written in the eighteenth century, so it is possible that it reflects a sense of implicit apology that is more appropriate to a later time than to the sixteenth century itself. At the turn of the seventeenth century, however—in Kṛṣṇadās Kavirāj's *Caitanyacaritāmṛta*—we meet similar motifs. Kṛṣṇadās tells us at several points that Rūp and Sanātan bewailed their untouchable, outsiders' status as they came before the presence of Chaitanya, obviously believing that their identities as twice-born Hindus had been compromised by their work among Muslims.[49] He also reports that the brothers refrained from trying to enter the temple of Jagannāth Puri for the same reason. Chaitanya for his part, eagerly welcoming them into the fold, nonetheless insists that they divest themselves of all they possessed at Gauḍ before they can earn the right to settle in Brindavan. We do not know what was in the minds of Rūp and Sanātan in their own words, but it seems clear that by moving to Braj they were able to don the mantle of their Brahminness anew, and did so in an environment where just about everything was being made new at the same time.

The Gauḍīyas' Bhakti Movement

It would be a great exaggeration to imagine that all—or perhaps even most—of the singer-saints attracted to Brindavan in the course of the sixteenth century came either directly or indirectly from the south, or that they had clear and demonstrable ties to one of the four *sampradāys*. Quite a number undoubtedly hailed from nearby in the north. This is true for the important figures Haridās and Hit Harivaṃś (whose father is also said to have been employed in a Muslim court—this time at Deoband), and no less so for the third of the "Hari trio," Harirāmvyās.[50] In Vyās's poems, many of which chronicle the connections he perceived to exist between the musical bhaktas who flourished in his beloved Brindavan, there is no hint of the model of the four *sampradāys*. The one possible exception to this rule is his acknowledgment on more than one occasion of a strong connection between a number of Rāmānandī bhaktas: Nāmdev, Sain, Dhannā, Raidās, Kabīr, and sometimes Jayadev.[51] This might seem to imply a knowledge of the belief that Rāmānand traced his lineage to Rāmūnuja and the deep south, but we must not jump to conclusions. It is true that Vyās acknowledges these *nirguṇ* (but for the last!) figures as being a group, but he does so in a way that precisely does not make them into Rāmānandīs. That is where he parted company with his contemporaries Anantadās and Nābhādās.[52] As for the matter of origins more generally, the question of the south does not arise. What we hear instead when appeal is made to the past is a lament over the loss of internal purity—the bhakti that filled Brindavan in the good old days. Such nostalgia has little place in the four-*sampradāy* scheme, though it would have been very much at home in a Sufi *tazkirā*.[53] Given the wider world in which Harirāmvyās lived, this may not be entirely accidental.

Vyās's nostalgia relates in interesting ways to the sense of time that comes to the fore in early records of the community that coalesced around Chaitanya, but the two are by no means the same. Among the Chaitanyites there is also a marked conviction that bhakti achieved a pure form of expression in an era not long past, yet the nature of that past could hardly be anticipated on the basis of Vyās's loyal, almost tender poems of memory. For the Gauḍīya community something much more earthshaking was involved. To have been with Chaitanya was to participate in something utterly incomparable, a process of continuing revelation, the pinnacle of fulfillment, the sort of thing that Christian theologians, reflecting the Gospels' accounts of Jesus, sometimes like to call kairos.[54] The Gauḍīyas' sense of how this kairotic moment could be recovered in the present was also plotted out in ways that make it stand apart from anything we meet in Harirāmvyās. In Chaitanyite memoirs the delicate pallor of nostalgia gives way before a vibrant drama of enactment.

Viśvambhar Miśra—Chaitanya's birth name—must have been an extraordinary person. Historians living in the early twentieth century had no hesitation in calling the excitement he generated among his followers a movement in the broadest sense, and well within a century of his death in 1533 his life had generated a corpus of written memory all but unrivaled in its time: eight biographies were already complete when Kṛṣṇadās Kavirāj composed his crowning *Caitanyacaritāmṛta* sometime between 1590 and 1615.[55] The only possible competitors for this biographical crown would be monarchs such as Babur and Akbar, and let us remember that they had a very different range of resources at their command.

Who was Chaitanya? It is a measure of his charisma that we do not quite know. To some it seems that his "conversion" to the intimate worship of Krishna was propelled by his deep remorse at having, as a young man, to perform postmortem rites for his father at Gayā. Or was it instead the force of meeting at this major place of pilgrimage an ascetic called Īśvara Purī, who is said to have taught him the practice of *saṃkīrtan*—publicly reciting the names of God with a group of companions in a crescendo of singing and dance? In any case, he returned to his natal Navadvip a changed man, took *saṃnyāsa* from an ascetic named Keśav Bhāratī at the age of twenty-four, and was given upon initiation the new name Krishna Chaitanya (Consciousness of Krishna).[56]

Then he began to wander. The story goes that Chaitanya was willing to set limits on his travels for the sake of his widowed mother, who had also lost her older son to the life of an ascetic: he agreed to be based in Puri, where she could see him in the course of making the annual *rath yātrā* pilgrimage from Bengal. But he also used Puri as a base to travel farther. One major journey took him to the south, and another brought him to Braj, probably in about 1514. No one doubts the impact he had—directly or indirectly—on the "invention" of Braj and Brindavan toward the beginning of the sixteenth century, but the belief that his being there caused the true location of various episodes in Krishna's life to reveal themselves for the first time was a theme that became a major part of the Gauḍīya biographical tradition only somewhat later on.

Murārī Gupta's *Kṛṣṇacaitanyacaritāmṛta,* our earliest biography—familiarly called *Kaḍacā,* his "notebook"—was probably written at Navadvip in 1531. It describes the course of Chaitanya's pilgrimage in Braj as if he had largely traced out the story of Krishna's life there, rather than following any known pilgrimage route. If indeed Murārī wrote in Bengal, it is not hard to imagine why he would have used this divine prototype as a way to make sense of what Chaitanya did once he got to the sacred land. He has Chaitanya begin and end his journey in Mathura, just as Krishna had done. Charmingly, he also allows the Master to engage a local Brahmin to be his guide, as any ordinary pilgrim might do.[57]

By the time we get to Kṛṣṇadās Kavirāj's *Caitanyacaritāmṛta* the account has expanded, deepened, and altered. Since Kṛṣṇadās wrote from Rādhākuṇḍ, it also makes sense that its geographical trajectory has changed. Here Chaitanya's route follows the typical pilgrims' map much more straightforwardly, even if he retains the guide that earlier accounts had assigned him. In the *Caitanyacaritāmṛta,* Rādhākuṇḍ is the only site Chaitanya manages to locate in physical space thanks to his intuition about where the *lilas* of Krishna and Radha specifically occurred (later accounts expand the list) but Brindavan also gets a boost. Brindavan—the specific locale, that is, undoubtedly the place where Rūp, Sanātan, and all the other *gosvāmīs* were to settle—displaces Mathura as the climax of Chaitanya's journey. It is the last stop he makes in his circumambulation of Braj as a whole (Brindavan in the larger, more generic sense). Thus the religious focus of the new Braj—the Mughal/Kachvaha Brindavan, so to speak—edges out its more venerable competitor in what was to become, for Gauḍīyas, the canonical account.

By common consent it was on his way back east to Bengal from Braj—at Prayag—that Chaitanya encountered Rūp and Sanātan and urged them to go to the place from which he had just come. They were not the only ones Chaitanya deputized to travel on his behalf: he sends Nityānand from Puri to Gauḍ, for example, and as we have seen, he dispatches Gopāl Bhaṭṭ to Brindavan from Srirangam. These acts among many others discourage us from supposing that Chaitanya's susceptibility to experiences of out-of-body transport meant that he lived the life of a hermit. To the contrary, he was often surrounded by admirers, including quite a number who were rich and influential and who proved to be of great use in advancing the Master's plans. The force of his personality was evidently conditioned and amplified by his participation in the rhythms of some of the great cosmopolitan centers of his day: religious cities such as Gayā, Prayag (later also to be called Allahabad), Banaras, and Puri; the renowned scholarly community active in his own birthplace, Navadvīp; and southern destinations such as Rajamandri and Srirangam. Similarly, one of the greatest challenges in thinking about who he was is to understand the remarkable interplay between his own determined silence as a writer—he has left us only eight Sanskrit *ślokas*—and the prolix world of biography, poetry, and theology that grew up through his direct inspiration or with him as its subject.[58] It is as if the tradition itself became his amanuensis.

Both Chaitanya's silences and his strategies are worth our attention. As to the former, no account of Chaitanya was ever written that did not lay emphasis on experiences that catapulted him from the realm of speech and daily concourse into another world altogether. The incursion *(āveśa)* of Krishna into his life, often in response to some unpredictable cue, could instantly transform the world of boundaries, distinctions, and grammar into a place that was more like a sea than dry land. "Sometimes Chaitanya would weep, bathed in a river of tears, while streams of mucus would run from both nostrils," Murārī Gupta tells us.[59] In the same passage Chaitanya confuses day and night, falls prostrate when he hears the names of Krishna sung, and chokes with emotion when he sings them himself. He trembles and shakes; his hair stands on end; he is all gooseflesh. The conventions of poetry lead us to expect such experiences when a woman—or even a man—is in love, but from all we can tell these aesthetic protocols had an impact not only on the writing of Chaitanya's life but on living it. His life *was* aesthetics. Its primary ritual form, the *nagar saṃkīrtan* to which we have already referred, involved the breaking of boundaries between the inner and the outer, the more private and the more public. As a type of processional practice that joined singing, drumming, and dancing, it affected not only those who performed but those who observed, drawing them into the streets and into the waves and ebbings of ecstasy that made Chaitanya famous—or in some eyes, infamous.

All this may seem utterly free-flow, and indeed that sense of being released from standard rituals, standard social behavior, and the standard dispositions of the body itself served as a core element of the Chaitanya tradition, yet as we have already hinted, such experiences were not without their textual templates. Some of the most important of these cluster in the eleventh book of the *Bhāgavata Purāṇa,* and describe the behavior of the perfect bhakta: "Without the hair of the body bristling, without the heart melting, without being inarticulate due to tears of bliss—without bhakti how can consciousness be purified? He whose speech is stammering, whose heart melts, who weeps repeatedly and sometimes laughs, who unabashedly sings and dances—such a person, united by bhakti with me [Krishna], purifies the world."[60]

We get occasional suggestions that Chaitanya was responding to a physical condition that we today might class as epilepsy. In one vignette Kṛṣṇadās offers precisely this diagnosis, placing it in the mouth of Chaitanya himself.[61] Given the context, one might be tempted to explain it away as a subterfuge, something the Master said to save his traveling companions from being attacked by a group of Paṭhāns, but the text clearly says that Chaitanya had fallen down insensate and that he foamed at the mouth. Vṛndāvandās, similarly, writing at almost the same time as Murārī Gupta, calls Chaitanya's condition a disease of the wind *(vāyu)* and details its classic symptoms: rolling on the ground, slapping the arms about, striking any object in the way, emitting a loud yell.[62] But before we leap to a purely physiological explanation we should remember that this extreme behavior—however much it concerned Chaitanya's friends, however much it sapped his own energies, however much it seems to correspond to well-known if not yet well-understood forms of neural dysfunction—also corresponded to what had been set out as scripture, particularly in that great moment when the literature of Advaita expanded to accommodate the life of musical and devotional ecstasy. In Sanskrit, at least, the *Bhāgavata Purāṇa* was the great result of that revolution, and the ecstasies of Chaitanya were its seal.[63]

Yet this seal had to be resealed—sealed in a textual way. In one respect the remarkably swift production of new literary compositions on the part of Chaitanya's followers echoed the exuberance of the Master's personal style, but in another way these intricate treatises and long narrative poems formed a vivid contrast to Chaitanya's own disinclination to reduce his experience to writing. Seen in this second way, their biographical prolixity and theological sophistication almost seem ways to keep the genie of charisma in the bottle: they *were* that bottle. Chaitanya's charisma was contagious, always in danger of reemerging, but here were statements of divine etiquette that would enable the community to survive and thrive when it did. When the two geographical loci of this remarkable Gauḍīya creativity—Braj and Bengal—threatened to move so far apart that the movement was in danger of splintering, a further measure was required: a single text that could hold the whole together—and by that token reshape it as an ongoing unity, dynamic yet stable.

The text in question was the *Caitanyacaritāmṛta* of Kṛṣṇadās Kavirāj, as Tony Stewart has brilliantly shown in his book *The Final Word*. Only after the *Caitanyacaritāmṛta* had been produced, it seems, did the theologian Jīv Gosvāmī, working in Braj, send out an expedition in which the major works of the Brindavan intelligentsia were made available to Gauḍīya communities living in Bengal. Stewart retells the story of how the Malla king Vīr Haṃvīr, intending to steal these precious documents, stopped the bullock carts on which they were loaded and brought them to his capital. But the result was that the scholars who were shepherding these texts through the jungles of Bengal ended up converting the king to their cause, and he ended up playing a major role in consolidating the transregional Gauḍīya community. Vīr Haṃvīr's initiation involved not only donning of a necklace of *tulsī* beads and receiving the requisite mantra but the touch of the great Gauḍīya books themselves. The city he ruled was also reborn. Renamed Vishnupur, it experienced a great efflorescence in the course of the seventeenth century.[64]

This tale, which may be only roughly historical, gives an institutional plot to what was textually achieved by the writing of the *Caitanyacaritāmṛta* itself—a consummate act of summary and grammaticization whereby not only the many biographies that had preceded it but the great theological tradition associated with the names of Rūp, Sanātan, and Jīv were drawn together in a single work. Kṛṣṇadās Kavirāj accomplished this feat by liberally quoting passages from the theological works to which he was heir—the works of his teachers—and also by sometimes inserting their contents verbatim into the mouth of Chaitanya himself. Thus he ascribed to their ultimate source the authoritative words Chaitanya was said to have commissioned: the writings of the Brindavan gosvāmīs. At the same time, in this work of hybrid Sanskrit and Bengali, Kṛṣṇadās joined the two major voices or registers of the Chaitanyite movement so that they would seem to constitute a single euphonious chorus. That still left out Brajbhasha, the third medium in which Gauḍīya works were written, but with Mānsingh in control of the victorious Mughal forces in Bengal and the moment ripe for a Braj-Bengal reconciliation, this was enough.

In another way, though, the absence of Brajbhasha from this particular moment of textual consolidation points to something significant, whether we think of it in its documentary mode—the *Caitanyacaritāmṛta* itself—or by means of its institutional analogue, as symbolized by the direct line between Jīv Gosvāmī's Sanskrit atelier and the Bengalis who were intended to enjoy its fruits when the bullock carts reached their destination. When we first laid eyes on the built Brindavan, we seemed to see the Bengalis in charge: Rūp Gosvāmī and his legatees at the temple of Govindadev, Sanātan and his at Madanmohan, Jīv consolidating the two. But we also saw that by the end of the sixteenth century these men and the institutions they built were apparently regarded by the Mughal state as standing for a good bit more than the Gauḍīya or Bengali element alone. Yes, there was some sort of unpleasant confrontation between Vallabhites and Bengalis for control of the temple atop Mount Govardhan, but it was certainly possible for Abu'l Fazl to elicit a legal description of who belonged at the highest echelons of the Braj region, religiously speaking, that would treat the entire group as a whole. The poems of Harirāmvyās testify to a similar sense that what had happened in Brindavan was beyond the province of any single sectarian formation. From his point of view some of the deepest meanings were to be found at points of common connection—the friendships that were formed, or the way poets thrived by listening to one another's songs—though he did not shrink from the task of suggesting the existence of such groups as clearly did exist.[65] From Vyās's vantage point it seems that all this happened in the common language, Brajbhasha, or as it might have been called in his own time, simply *bhāṣā*—or at least he never draws attention to linguistic differences.

Conflicts were going to rage about how to assign the proper sectarian identity to Haridās or Harirāmvyās or even Harivaṃś, and eventually, at least, there was also the issue about how a certain *sampradāy* present in Braj should be aligned with the great four-*sampradāy* paradigm—or not. These are difficult matters. Even in the case of those who aligned themselves with Chaitanya, a group so richly documented, we may rightly ask just when the sectarian label Gauḍīya came to be applied. When Gopāl Bhaṭṭ writes his *Haribhaktivilāsa*, he speaks as if he were participating in the Śrī tradition, although we should certainly not minimize the fact that in every chapter he also acknowledges Chaitanya as his preceptor. It is also worth noting that he makes liberal reference to the ritual manual *Kramadīpikā* of Keśav, who is normally if tentatively understood to be the same person as the Nimbārkī acharya Keśav Kāśmīrī Bhaṭṭ.[66]

But for all this Braj catholicity—should we speak of Braj itself as a *sampradāy?*—it is hard to shake the feeling that Chaitanya's distinctive personal charisma was the single most important factor in making his community of followers cohere. The "bhakti movement" he planted had a particular tone—if not in the rituals described in the *Haribhaktivilāsa,* then out on the street. There was his language, too. When he uttered his famous call, *bol!* (speak!), it led one forward to a specific set of names for God that were Sanskrit in origin and had no regional or sectarian definition, yet the call itself was Bengali and all those names were also part of the Bengali lexicon. If Chaitanya's strongest appeal was to a form of religious expression that was intended to be shared in the broadest ways, beyond any distinction of region, class, religious background, or even gender, he nonetheless made that appeal in Bengali and was evidently in large part surrounded by Bengalis.

It was therefore not perverse when the various groups that claimed Chaitanya as their founding inspiration ultimately drew together. Men like Sanātan, Rūp, and Jīv wrote in Sanskrit, of course, appealing to its cosmopolitan normativity, and Rūp, at least, reached out in other ways. He was eager to play up the common theological ground he shared with Vallabha.[67] But even keeping in mind these men's family ties to the Deccan, their special link to Puri and Bengal was not trivial, and by the time an effort was made to vernacularize what their works of high theology had articulated—this was the work of Kṛṣṇadās Kavirāj—the deed was done in Bengali.

If the Gauḍīya tradition took shape as a true *sampradāy* only with production of the *Caitanyacaritāmṛta,* then it made perfect sense that it came to be designated by means of the ethnic and linguistic framework that set it apart from others active in north India—as Bengali, that is, Gauḍīya. Gauḍ Brahmins were spread throughout the Doab, and their facility with Sanskrit connected them to other Brahmins throughout India, but when one left that specifically Brahmin frame of reference, Gauḍ was Bengal, and Chaitanya was firmly rooted there.[68] Similarly the power of the Kachvahas, which helped broadcast his life and message, ranged across the north, but despite the importance of his Kachvaha connections Chaitanya's Bengaliness never left him. There was too much detail in accounts of his life to enable later generations ever to view him without his ethnicity, and his own demotic urges reinforced that fact. One could not remember Chaitanya without appreciating that, for all the Sanskrit in his family background and in his own training, this was a man connected to the people, and those people were largely Bengalis. In the episode where he refers to his epilepsy to save his companions from punishment at the hands of a group of Paṭhāns, the Afghans take note of the fact that Chaitanya is taller and fairer than the group who surround him. One of us, they seem to think: they call him a *pīr.* But Chaitanya leaps to his friends' defense by fingering himself as the odd man out in other terms—as an epileptic—rather than denying their common bond as Bengalis.

The place where Chaitanya chose to spend the greater part of his adult life was not, however, Bengal. It was Puri, and Puri rims the ocean, not the Ganges. Much about this city is truly regional: the image of Jagannāth that is its raison d'être—along with those of Balarām and Subhadrā, who accompany him—must be carved from trees of the Orissan hinterland in a cycle that normally lasts nineteen years. But another side of Puri's distinctive identity is cosmopolitan: it straddles the border between north and south, facilitating communication between these two great realms. Religiously speaking, it is the entrepot that connects Banaras and Prayag to Tirupati, Kanchi, and Chidambaram, and this fact connects to one of the most significant motifs in Chaitanya's biographies: his journey southward. We have spoken of the importance of his trip to Braj; his travel to the south is scarcely less so. This comes as no surprise to anyone who has pondered the cachet of the four *sampradāys.*

There is some confusion in the *Caitanyacaritāmṛta* as to how we should understand Chaitanya's journey southward. When he sets out to give us his *madhya līlā,* the "middle drama" of Chaitanya's life, Kṛṣṇadās pauses to offer us a thumbnail sketch of what is to come. Perhaps this is to commit himself to completing the narrative he is about to offer. Or perhaps he is guarding against the possibility that someone else might tell the story differently if he did not have the chance to finish it himself.[69] In any case his outline has a great deal to do with Chaitanya's peregrinations and those of his designees, especially those who were to colonize (or was it theologize?) Brindavan. Kṛṣṇadās plainly states that upon initiation, Chaitanya went to Brindavan—"three days in the Radha country"—and that his trip to the south came later.[70] At that point he went all the way to Setubandh, that is, the "bridge" *(setu)* that connects south India to Sri Lanka at Rameshvaram. Significantly, Kṛṣṇadās says that Chaitanya encountered two books at this southernmost extreme of his pilgrimage, the *Brahma Saṃhitā* and the *Kṛṣṇakarṇāmṛta* of Bilvamangal, and that he brought back portions of each when he returned to Puri.[71] Later Chaitanya attempts another trip to Braj, but cannot accomplish it: the press of the crowds is too great, and his friends and advisors fear the worst. In effect, Rūp and Sanātan make the journey in his stead.

By the time Kṛṣṇadās lays this all out in the chapters that follow, however, certain things have changed. Chaitanya resolves to go to Brindavan (i.e., Braj) immediately upon taking *saṃnyāsa*, but reconsiders and travels first to Navadvīp to see his mother. She in turn dissuades him from his plan, preferring that her son take up residence in Puri, where she will be able to see him on regular occasions.[72] Thus Chaitanya's initial urge to go to Braj becomes but an intention. He waits until he has completed his southern journey and has been settled in Puri for some time before he undertakes the trip to Braj.[73]

Within the narrative itself we know how to account for this altered sequence: the mother's wish causes the son to defer his own desires. But it is harder to explain the change at the level of the narrator. One possibility is that Kṛṣṇadās was somewhat unsure about how to square the latitudinal axis of the narrative—the connection between Puri and Brindavan—with its longitudinal counterpart, the road from Navadvīp to Singhaldvīp, that is, from Bengal to Sri Lanka. Or was he worried about how to square the authority of Braj (or as Kṛṣṇadās says, Brindavan) with that of Puri—and, by extension, the south? On the one hand it seems obvious that Braj was the place to experience the unity of Radha and Krishna. In the prologue, recall, this Braj journey was to be "three days in the Radha country." On the other hand, though, Chaitanya's true identity as simultaneously Radha and Krishna was actually revealed in the south. It was Rāmānand Rāy who first perceived this reality, and the insight dawned along the banks of the Godavari south of Jīyaḍa, somewhere near modern-day Rajamandri. The crucial breakthrough was to see that Chaitanya himself represented the intrinsic complementarity between *sādhya* and *sādhana*—the object of worship (Krishna) and its path (Radha)—and Kṛṣṇadās Kavirāj devotes an entire chapter to its exposition.[74]

So the south has a revelatory, life-changing importance for the community that was to gather around Chaitanya further north. Yet when Chaitanya is with Rāmānand Rāy at the Godavari, he cannot resist the perception that he is actually elsewhere—on the banks of the Jamuna in Brindavan. One may well ask which of these two places is "more real," but from the point of view of the text itself, they go together. Chaitanya's sense of separation from Braj—ever sharper the farther away he goes—turns to its ecstatic realization, and the power of that very distance enables Rāmānand Rāy to recognize who Chaitanya actually is. In the story that Kṛṣṇadās ultimately gives us, by contrast to the précis he offers in beginning, Chaitanya travels to the south before he goes west to Braj, but as we have seen, the narrator seems initially to have charted it out the other way around. If a south-to-north "bhakti movement" is being described here, then, it works with less than maximal clarity.

There is a second confusion, too. If we take as our starting point the forecast of Chaitanya's journey south as given in the first chapter of the *madhya līlā,* it seems there has been a major change in the positioning of this journey not only with respect to the Braj pilgrimage but with regard to another version of what it means to travel the south. A full-blown *digvijaya* account (literally entailing a "conquest of the directional points," figuratively announcing victory over all the world) has fundamentally altered what once was a straightforward journey from Puri to the tip of the subcontinent and back. Now, we hear, Chaitanya travels all the way around Cape Comorin to Trivandrum, Srngeri, Pandharpur, and as far north as the Narmada before retracing his steps and ending in Vidyānagar, that is, Vijayanagar. And the Vidyānagar to which he returns seems to be not the imperial city itself but the provincial capital where Chaitanya met Rāmānand Rāy in the first place. A line has become a circle.

Most of this circular route is traced formulaically, without elaboration, as if merely to fulfill the expectation that any world-class teacher would naturally undertake such a circumambulation cum victory tour. But even this abbreviated account is a nod to the prestige of the south, where journeys demonstrating philosophical one-upsmanship had typically been conceived as occurring, as if the south were the true terrain of intellectuals. Of course, such debates could also be staged at Banaras or Prayag, as in the instance of the Nimbārkī story about how Keśav Kāśmīrī Bhaṭṭ bested Chaitanya at Prayag. In the *Caitanyacaritāmṛta,* similarly, Prayag serves as the right place for theological confrontation between Chaitanya and Vallabha, and the same is true in Vallabhite accounts. In the one version, Chaitanya is victorious; in the other, Vallabha. But in both Chaitanyite and Vallabhite narratives a southern *digvijaya* rounds out the report, and in the Vallabhite story particularly, as we shall see, the south is where the heavy lifting gets done.

There are many other details one could explore, but for the moment the main theme to extract from these tales and countertales is that for a prince of bhakti, even one whose heart is set on making a trip to Brindavan, a journey to the south matters—and matters in a way that is not always consistent with what happens farther north. As we have seen in other instances, much that is said to occur in the south actually transpired in the imaginations of those living much farther north. Yet the memory of Chaitanya's first encounter with Rāmānand Rāy is vivid, and several more meetings were yet to come—in Puri. All this projects an aura of historical facticity. By the same token, however, it suggests that we might profitably reposition the initial Rajamandri encounter within the larger cycle of narratives that transpire in the general orbit of Puri. It is true that Pratāparudra, the Gajapati king who ruled from nearby Cuttack and whom Rāmānand Rāy served as a regional administrator, did on one famous occasion resign himself to a subordinate relationship with the Vijayanagar throne—it was caused by a defeat at the hands of the great Kṛṣṇadevarāya—but even then he retained clear autonomy around Puri and down the Kalinga coast. Hence even if Chaitanya encountered Rāmānand Rāy on the way to Rameshvaram, he did so primarily within an orbit that bound the Deccan to Orissa.

This was true in a literary way, as well. We are told that as Rāmānand Rāy approached his piercing realization of Chaitanya's divine identity, he sang for him a lyric he had composed in a register of Maithili that has since the mid-nineteenth century been called Brajbuli on account of the fact that its poems universally celebrate the love of Radha and Krishna in Braj. This well-bred genre of Vaishnava verse developed in the wake of and as an implicit tribute to the great fifteenth-century Maithili poet Vidyāpati, and it achieved a considerable geographical reach. We can see this in the fact that the courts of both Gauḍ and Puri—Bengal and Orissa—are witnessed in the two oldest datable Brajbuli poems we possess. These bear respectively the names of Husain Shāh and Pratāparudra in their final verses, whose purpose is to divulge the poet's name and extol that of his patron. Rāmānand Rāy is the author of one of these *pads,* and it is the very poem of which we have been speaking. Others bearing his name also praise Pratāparudra and may also have been performed at court in Puri.[75] In regard to the poem at hand, however, the *Caitanyacaritāmṛta* reports that the suzerain's celebration was either silenced or redirected. The concluding verse, which we know from other collections, does not appear there because, as Kṛṣṇadās tells us, Chaitanya stopped Rāmānand Rāy from singing at just that point. He was so overcome by the song's evocation of a gopi's love for Krishna that in a surge of emotion he covered Rāmānand Rāy's mouth; he could bear no more.[76] We are thus given to believe that Chaitanya understood this Maithili register so intimately that on this occasion, when the love it expressed was overlaid by that developing between him and the poet, he could not stand its poignancy. It is easy to wonder whether Chaitanya's susceptibility to Brajbuli may also have something to do with a broader urge—to discover Braj both for himself and for the others he sent there in his stead.

Finally one has to think about how to evaluate interactions such as the one between Chaitanya and Rāmānand Rāy at a different level. According to Gauḍīya sensibilities, the true depth of these encounters cannot be experienced through linear narration alone. In the *Caitanyacaritāmṛta,* Kṛṣṇadās gives us a sense of this deeper meaning by bringing to bear learned commentary and theological exposition, working primarily with the writings of Rūp and Sanātan Gosvāmī, but it is crucial to be aware that there is also a dramatic element. To a considerable extent Kṛṣṇadās relates these stories in a form that would permit them to be reexperienced as present by living bhaktas. The encounter between Chaitanya and Rāmānand Rāy, for example, is rendered substantially in dialogue, and when we come to the beginning of the final third of the work, the *antya līlā,* we are treated to a scene in which Rūp Gosvāmī appears and is asked just how he goes about fashioning his Krishna plays. This gives a chance for him to quote extensively from his *Vidagdhamādhava* and *Lalitamādhava* dramas, to a very appreciative audience that includes Chaitanya himself.[77] Kṛṣṇadās makes use of other dramas as well, especially the *Caitanyacandrodaya* of

Kavikarṇapūra, written in 1572, possibly at the request of King Pratāparudra decades earlier.[78] This is an important addition. Rūp's dramas concern the *līlās* of Krishna, and Kṛṣṇadās's task is to imply their integral relation to Chaitanya. But Kavikarṇapūra, who focuses on Chaitanya to begin with, spares him the intermediate step.[79]

Like other Gauḍīya writers, Kṛṣṇadās also approaches the life of Chaitanya in dramatic fashion by showing how Chaitanya reenacts *līlās* that initially belonged to Krishna. This happens with utter effortlessness when Chaitanya is a child. He eats dirt, he steals food from his mother, he rides on the shoulder of a thief as if he were encountering the demon Pralamba, and he taunts the neighborhood girls when they bathe and pray for good husbands, just as Krishna had done with the gopis.[80] As an adult, this play-acting becomes more formal. Chaitanya delights in taking female parts when dramas of Krishna are enacted. He chooses the roles of both Rukmiṇī and Radha.

As one might expect, this deep sense of dramatic revelation is even more marked in works that are themselves dramas. The *Caitanyacandrodaya,* for example, is so thoroughly dedicated to its theatrical milieu that it makes use of the device of the play within the play—or as Tony Stewart points out, a play within the play within the play.[81] The logic here is important. On the one hand it is a logic of descent, which matches one of the oldest Vaishnava ideas about how divinity manifests itself in the world—the doctrine of *avatāras*—and on the other it is a logic of role-playing more broadly, wherein all the world's a stage and everything depends upon achieving a certain quality of experience *(bhāva),* just as Rūp explained in his *Bhaktirasāmṛtasindhu.*[82] As for the three levels encompassed in the roles and descents of this particular play, they are first, the allegorical—a conversation between Prem Bhakti (Love-Devotion: Faith) and Adharma (Unrighteousness, the bête noire of the present world-age); second, the historical—interactions between Chaitanya and his group of fellow actors; and third, the transcendent—the concourse between Krishna and the other actors who people his world, paradigmatically Radha. In the course of acting out the *dān līlā* (The Play of the Gift, an ironic title that refers to Krishna's efforts to levy a toll tax on the milk trade of Radha and the gopis), the true relationships between two faces of Chaitanya—his Krishna and Radha aspects—are revealed. And they are revealed not only on the plane of historical reality, but as transformative for the archetypical struggle between bhakti and all that is awry in the world.[83]

Such principled theatricality had a great deal to do with the way in which the Gauḍīya community came to construct its own sense of history. The key to it—the critical middle level in the hierarchy we have just described—was the process of discovering who had played whom as Krishna's world manifested itself around Chaitanya in this-worldly time and space. We see this type of speculation already in the first biographer, Murārī Gupta, and it continued well into the lifetime of Kavikarṇapūra half a century later. Some correspondences between the worlds of Krishna and Chaitanya seemed indubitable—everyone agreed that Nityānand had to be Krishna's older brother Balarām, for example—but about others there was less unanimity. Perhaps the mysterious divine process called *līlā* meant one always had to do a bit of guessing. But about the importance of Chaitanya's crowd of witnesses there could be no doubt. It was not he alone who defined the Gauḍīya community's sense of its own identity but those with whom he interacted. In one regard those interactions were the stuff of immediate drama; in another, they were the means by which one saw the formation of a tradition, a movement, even a sect. And in both regards the question of who was playing whose role was key.

Finally, the Vallabhites

As we have seen, there are many "movements" to consider in thinking about how Brindavan became Brindavan—and Braj, Braj—in the course of the sixteenth century, and not all of them fit under the caption *sampradāy*. But among those that do familiarly bear that name, two are distinctive in the way they rival one another: the Gaudīyas or Chaitanyites on the one hand and the Puṣṭimārgīs or Vallabhites on the other. Their theologies of devotional freedom and radical grace were sufficiently similar that the analogy between them became a matter of explicit comment in the sixteenth century itself, yet like siblings, they sometimes fought. In particular they seem to have come to blows over who should be the proper custodian of the important temple that stood atop Mount Govardhan, with the Vallabhites winning that struggle (perhaps initiating it, as well) while the Gauḍīyas remained preeminent at the sacred body of water nearby, Rādhākuṇḍ. The two communities were also competitors for favor with the Mughal rulers and their Rajput associates, although the Vallabhites often sought their primary support from mercantile sources instead.

The conceptual and imaginary worlds they developed also differed. In regard to Braj, both drew up circumambulatory routes that would encompass the whole and both articulated practices of visualization that would inscribe that whole onto the devotional body of individual meditators, yet on the ground, so to speak, they divided the turf. The Vallabhite strongholds were to be found at Govardhan and Gokul while the Chaitanyites shone in Brindavan, where the Vallabhites apparently had no presence.[84] The Chaitanyites initially favored the ascetic life, after the pattern of Chaitanya himself, although the lineage of Gopāl Bhaṭṭ developed in a different way; the Puṣṭimārg, by contrast, championed householdership as a bhakta's proper mode of conduct in this world, following Vallabha's example. Distinctive patterns of collectivity and literary expression also grew up in the two communities. As we have seen, a sense of shared *līlā* was inescapable on the Chaitanyite side, while for Puṣṭimārgīs it was mediated by a primary orientation toward Vallabha and his progeny. The Vallabhites therefore charted their *sampradāy*'s historical record by means of a genre called *vārtā*—accounts whose central element was always a verbal interaction with Vallabha or, later, Viṭṭhalnāth, the son who served as his principal successor. So if the Chaitanyite and Vallabhite formations were both in some sense "bhakti movements," they accomplished this in strikingly different, almost complementary ways. Even the languages they preferred for vernacular usage were complementary. Brajbhasha, the language of the *vārtās*, became canonical on the Vallabhite side, with Gujarati as a second option, while Bengali emerged as canonical for the Chaitanyites, with Brajbhasha and Maithili (or Brajbuli if one prefers that designation) assuming the secondary role.[85]

There was also a distinctive contrast in tone. At the level of Sanskrit theological treatise and daily ritual pattern, there were and still are significant overlaps, and both communities sponsor the *rās līlās* that are such a distinctive part of vernacular Braj culture. But in the Vallabhite *vārtās*—stories said to have been collected by Gokulnāth, the fourth son of Viṭṭhalnāth—a special kind of humor emerged. It seems to have been designed both to highlight the radical claims of bhakti and to recognize and laugh at its excesses. Indeed, those excesses often featured the particular textures of Puṣṭimārg-style bhakti: an unqualified reverence for Vallabha and Viṭṭhalnāth, a focus on the deities or *ṭhākurs* for whom they cared and who justified their preeminence, and a style of worship that emphasized the sort of lavish display that only wealth made possible. If the Chaitanyites developed a distinctive literary culture focused on dramatic *līlā* and the melting away of sexual difference, with Chaitanya ever the exemplar, the Vallabhites had their down-to-earth, local-style *vārtās* as a vivid counterpart. In these tales Vallabhācārya and Viṭṭhalnāth thread their way through a colorful and sometimes almost sitcom-like array of devotees from many places and backgrounds. Of course, there are also many serious moments as well, some quite poignant.

Certain themes recur in these *vārtās*. Shaivas, for example, are apt to come in for a laugh. In other *vārtās* the foibles of the mercantile class are exposed. Even the Lord himself is not immune. On one occasion, owing to his exacting dietary habits, Śrīnāthjī gets so famished that he has to rouse one of his servants and make him prepare a substitute meal. The manner in which he does so brings a smile: God kicks devotee![86] Yet there is a more serious side. We see it especially in the great labors of the commentator Harirāy, who was constantly trying to tamp down the humor and assert theological control over this vernacular mayhem. The *vārtā* concerning Kṛṣṇadās Adhikārī provides an example or two since women play a big part in his life—and they are not always women of the most sterling repute. One of these was actually a girl of twelve, the daughter of a courtesan (*vesyā*, "prostitute") whom Kṛṣṇadās encountered on a trip he made to Agra so as to gather provisions for the temple. One might wonder at the distance of the journey—why not just go to Mathura, so much closer?—and perhaps the young courtesan, herself in training for the trade, was part of the reason he undertook it, though the *vārtā* does not spell this out. All it says is that Kṛṣṇadās, when he heard her sing, immediately became entranced. The narrator provides his own justification by explaining that Kṛṣṇadās recognized in her a *daivī jīv*—a "spiritual soul," we might say. That was why Kṛṣṇadās took her home to perform before Śrīnāthjī. It all comes out well: she has her *Liebestod*. She was so overcome by the sight of the deity that, as she sang a song of Kṛṣṇadās's about self-sacrifice before the Lord, she left her earthly body behind and assumed her eternal, spiritual one.[87]

The story's bawdy theme is thus already given its devotional logic by Gokulnāth, but for the commentator that is still not quite sufficient. How did the courtesan's daughter come to have such an elevated nature, waiting to be revealed first to Kṛṣṇadās and then to Śrīnāthjī himself? He answers this question by providing us a back story in which he explains that the girl's real identity was that of a gopi called Bahubhāṣiṇī, a female associate of Krishna in his perennial state of play *(nitya līlā)*. In that realm she had allowed a bit of her own saliva to drip into sweets that were about to be presented to the Lord, and had failed to take responsibility for her action. That was why she had been assigned a human birth in the family of a prostitute. Her restoration to the presence of Krishna would be sufficient to undo the curse, however, and that is what happened when she came before Śrīnāthjī. The commentator's searching, systematic logic thus attempts to consolidate and supersede the lighter, more ironic fare given us by his uncle Gokulnāth, especially since it is inserted directly into the text at this point. Yet there is another puzzle. Why had the courtesan's daughter not taken initiation *(brahmasambandh)* from Vallabha or, in this case, Viṭṭhalnāth, a necessary condition for being saved and transported to Krishna's *nitya līlā?* Harirāy rationalizes this fact by appealing to the celestial state she had already attained before the incident with the saliva. And so, all's well that ends well—or in this case, begins well—as the energetically this-worldly moods that fill the *vārtās* and much vernacular bhakti poetry are subsumed and sublimated in a frame of discourse that Harirāy thinks is theologically superior.[88]

The steadying hand of the commentator is apparent not only in the way Harirāy intervenes in individual *vārtās* but in the way he makes them take shape as a whole. It was Gokulnāth who got the collection going, we are told, but Harirāy who finished the job, marking off the eighty-four *vārtās* attributed to Gokulnāth *(Caurāsī Vaiṣavan kī Vārtā)* from the 252 *(Do Sau Bāvan Vaiṣṇavan kī Vārtā)* that were to follow. He did this by placing four poets at the end of the first collection and another four at the beginning of the second. These, taken together, form a powerful suture as the "eight seals" *(aṣṭachāp)* who are said to have stood at the center of Vallabha's and Viṭṭhalnāth's efforts to give liturgical coherence to their fledgling *sampradāy*. The older four among them are regarded as initiates of Vallabha and therefore belong among the eighty-four; the latter are initiates of Viṭṭhalnāth, and appear among the 252. Because of their own firm connection as a phalanx of eight—they have antetypes in the cowherds and cowmaidens of Krishna's *nitya līlā* and are also assigned positions at the eight compass points of the mandala that surrounds the omphalic Mount Govardhan—they bring the two *vārtā* collections, the second precisely three times as large as the first, into stable alignment.[89]

One sees the beauty of this *aṣṭachāp* edifice and appreciates the clarity of theological vision that lies behind it, but one must also recognize that it represents a major distortion of history.[90] Five of these poets, including Kṛṣṇadās, may conceivably have had an association with Viṭṭhalnāth, but in the broader world of Braj their poems are the least celebrated of the lot. The literary weight of the eight seals lies elsewhere—with Sūrdās and Paramānandadās, who are the seniormost and best known in the set, and with Nandadās, who was somewhat younger. In each case it seems to have taken quite some maneuvering to make them into Vallabhites.[91] This effort to rewrite history is important not only because it alters what seem to have been the facts, but because it throws a particular spin on the question of how a bhakti movement comes into being. If bhakti is a vernacular groundswell whose major medium is poetry, especially poetry of the sort that would typically be sung, then this effort to constrain it within sectarian channels—take a poet's agency and transfer it to his supposed guru—does a fundamental disservice to the contagious reality of bhakti itself. It harnesses the energy of song for theological and institutional purposes that are foreign to its inner spirit.

Of course, one may well be suspicious of such a free-flowing view of bhakti—it sounds too romantic, too eagerly demotic—but in this case, at least, we can demonstrate that the guru-pupil rubric came in after the fact. The eight seals were not the eight seals until Vallabhite historians made them so. The most famous of these poets, to whose reputations the nascent Vallabha *sampradāy* was appealing for prestige, were poets who were recalled by others as having much more protean relationships to other Brajbhasha poets—and none at all to Vallabha or Viṭṭhalnāth.

Take Sūrdās, for example. Poetry attributed to him is a "movement" all its own, beginning at some time in the course of the sixteenth century, represented by 239 poems in the first extant manuscript (written at Fatehpur in 1582), and growing steadily to a corpus approaching ten thousand poems in the course of the following centuries. In 1640 it was already called an ocean *(sūrsāgar),* but there was nothing specifically Vallabhite about it.[92] The *vārtā* concerning Sūrdās's life is constructed so as to divert that ocean in the direction of Vallabhācārya. He is said to have encountered Sūr on the banks of the Jamuna, where he was already surrounded by a following of his own, and to have initiated the poet as his disciple. Then some deft prestidigitations are performed on one of Sūr's most famous poems to show how it follows logically from that moment.

The writer of the *vārtā* tries to demonstrate that this poem, which he depicts as having been composed shortly after Sūrdās's initiation, takes its inspiration from the dedicatory verse Vallabha had used as a preface to his commentary on the tenth book of the *Bhāgavata Purāṇa*. Thus pupil mimics guru and vernacular follows Sanskrit. The operative phrase in Sūr's Brajbhasha, *śrī sahasra* (a thousand Śrīs), is said to derive from Vallabha's Sanskrit *lakṣmīsahasra* (a thousand Lakṣmīs), but this is a weak reed, not only because the contexts diverge markedly but because the preponderance of early manuscript evidence for this poem favors a different reading altogether. The word *sahasra* does not occur in manuscripts dating to the sixteenth and seventeenth centuries—except as it is remembered in the *sūrdās kī vārtā* itself.[93]

The commentator Harirāy, writing in a similar vein, tries to strengthen the case by drawing attention to a poem in which Sūrdās says:

> With firmness of faith I cling to these feet.
> But for the brilliance that shines from the crescent-moon
> toenails of the Śrī's Beloved, all the world would be dark.

The word translated here as "Beloved" is *vallabha*, and Harirāy interprets it a proper noun, to wit, Vallabhācārya's name. The word that precedes it, the name of the goddess Śrī or Lakṣmī, then becomes an honorific: Śrī Vallabha. Harirāy goes on to offer an exegesis of other aspects of the poem as well, interpreting the "doubleness" *(dvividhi)* that the poet later describes as a doubleness of perception, a faulty vision that fails to see the relation of identity between the beloved who is Krishna and the beloved who is Vallabhācārya. But Sūr, says Harirāy, saw that the two are really one. This interpretation is clever, especially as it draws in the legend of the poet's blindness, but we must remember that *vallabha* is a common designation for Krishna, which is why Vallabhācārya bears that name in the first place. The plain meaning in this Sūrdās poem is then Krishna, and the doubleness to which it refers is any divergence from his path. It is worth noting, once again, that the Vallabhite record of what Sūrdās sang stands at some distance from what we meet elsewhere. In this case it is not a question of variants, but of the fact that this poem does not even appear in other sixteenth- and seventeenth-century manuscripts.[94]

One can admire the ingenuity with which the authors of the *vārtā* and its commentary approached the task of incorporating Sūrdās retrospectively into the Vallabha *sampradāy,* and one can appreciate how satisfying it must have seemed to members of the Vallabhite community to see that Sūrdās was "one of us," participating in the devotional intensity that became such a notable and praiseworthy feature of the Puṣṭimārg; but we must remember, on the other hand, that the facts of the matter were otherwise. As we have already seen, Harirāmvyās makes no association between Vallabha and Sūr. In fact, Vyās never mentions Vallabha at all. In a similar way, anthologists working outside the Puṣṭimārg—and sometimes earlier—show no awareness that Sūr's poetry ought to be aligned with compositions attributed to poets whom the Vallabhites claimed as belonging to the *aṣṭachāp.*[95]

All this is important because in time the Vallabha *sampradāy* did indeed become an important presence in Braj and elsewhere, and their literary reconstructions greatly shaped what was taken to be the historical record. Vallabhite theoreticians had to work hard to create the illusion of an older, more inclusive Vallabhite presence in Braj, but they succeeded. The Vallabha community spread with apparent ease to Malwa and to the Kathiavar peninsula in the far west, but that was not enough: the image it wanted to broadcast was of having a base in Braj, the symbolic center of the Hindu-Mughal world. The medium mattered, too. By the time the *Caurāsī Vaiṣṇavan kī Vārtā* congealed as a connected text in the mid-seventeenth century, Brajbhasha had become a widely shared language of empire. So when compositions of the *aṣṭachāp* were mandated as those most appropriate for singing before the deities in the *havelīs* (houses, literally, but also effectively temples) of Vallabha's successors, this claimed not only the idiom that would have surrounded that greatest of Brajbāsīs, Krishna himself, but also a language that had become a major vehicle of expression in Mughal and Rajput courts. This was true not just for the poems, but for the *vārtās* as well. They too were a performed genre; they rode the imperial wave in prose.

There was a material dimension as well—trade, travel, and property—and these made other connections to the sinews of empire. Much earlier in the history of the *sampradāy* (perhaps before it really was a *sampradāy*), Vallabha had been content to make his lifelong home not in Braj but in Aḍel. Aḍel is a village located on the southern bank of the Ganges just after the Jamuna joins it at the great confluence in Allahabad or, as the city was called in Vallabha's time, Prayag. If Vallabha journeyed to Braj, it was on pilgrimage, not to establish a home or colony of followers, a *sāmpradāyik* beachhead. That came later, at the initiative of Viṭṭhalnāth (1515–1585?), and very likely in response to political changes. The Mughals had returned to power, displacing the Afghans, and Akbar was at the helm of state. It was then, apparently, that Viṭṭhalnāth decided to set up a residence in Gokul, on the east bank of the Jamuna across the river and slightly upstream from Mathura; a Mughal *farmān* acknowledging this fact appears in 1577.[96] As for the contest over the temple on Mount Govardhan, it is unclear whether that happened shortly after Vallabha's death or, much more likely, in the early years of Akbar's rule. In any case there is nothing to suggest that tales of Vallabha's interest in Govardhan and Gokul, as reported in the *vārtās,* were anything more than expressions of the community's desire to connect sites it later regarded as their spiritual home with the founder-preceptor himself. It is easier to believe the Mughal account, as recorded in the *farmāns* of 1577, 1581, and subsequent years. There it is said that the emperor granted land and cattle-grazing rites to Viṭṭhalnāth (or as he is called, Viṭṭhaldās and Viṭṭhalrāy), who in turn blessed the emperor with his prayers, as if in accord with the standard *duniyā-vilāyat* system.[97] If such a *farmān* could be procured, it suggests by implication that Viṭṭhalnāth and his representatives would also have been free to move and thrive along the imperial highways, especially the great one that led to Gujarat. Perhaps the funds used to buy the property in Gokul, in fact, were recruited on preaching tours to Gujarat by Viṭṭhalnāth or Kṛṣṇadās Adhikārī.

Vallabha, however, was earlier—a contemporary of Chaitanya and Keśav Kāśmīrī Bhaṭṭ. He certainly had serious theological purposes, but it is far less clear that he was actively trying to build a *sampradāy* in institutional ways. When Vallabha speaks of *brahmasambandh,* "bonding with Brahman," in the short treatise called *Siddhāntarahasyam* (The Secret of our Doctrine), he does not seem to be authorizing the ritual that would later become the distinctive mark of membership in the Puṣṭimārgī *sampradāy,* but rather putting forward a mental regimen of unalloyed devotion that had been communicated to him by Krishna himself.[98] It initiates a process of "becoming Brahman" (*brahmatā tataḥ,* 5.8), not becoming a Vallabhite. Doubtless the eight-syllable mantra that later came to be transmitted from guru to disciple in the *brahmasambandh* ceremony—*śrī kṛṣṇa śaraṇam mama* (Lord Krishna is my refuge)—was important to Vallabha (6.9), but it is telling that another formula of the same length mattered at least as much: *kṛṣṇa eva gatir mama* (Krishna alone is my goal). Vallabha gives over almost the entirety of one of his short treatises to this formula (9.1–9), which he connects to the core concept of refuge, as well (*śaraṇam, āśraya*, 9.10–11). Again, no ritual dimension seems to be implied, and in this case the *sampradāy* did not supply one later. In a similar vein we find Vallabha far more ambivalent about the value of householdership than would be suggested by the way in which the *sampradāy* named after him championed that form of life. In two of his pithy treatises, Vallabha does indeed struggle with the obstacles that a life of renunciant wandering can pose to cultivating an awareness of Krishna's freely given grace (11.7, 14.2–6), but he is also attuned to the difficulties that a householder's life can throw in one's spiritual path (11.2–3, 11.8) and recommends a measure of travel on that account (11.8).

All this strongly suggests that the *sampradāy* took on its distinctive forms after the death of Vallabha, not before, despite the manner in which the community has come to understand its own early history. Evidently it was Viṭṭhalnāth who made the Vallabha *sampradāy* a *sampradāy,* not his father Vallabha or his elder brother Gopīnāth. It was Viṭṭhalnāth's householdership that became the magnet around which the community was organized: he distributed images to each of his sons, so that they too would have authority to initiate new members into the sect. When Viṭṭhalnāth established his domicile in Braj, he was creating an institutional base that would be central to the identity of his community, many of whose adherents lived in the far west. Mughal avenues of communication made that possible.

Hints of this new widely dispersed yet Braj-centered formation appear throughout the *Caurāsī Vaiṣṇavan kī Vārtā.* Many are anchored in the activities of Viṭṭhalnāth, but the text is also deeply involved in the task of suggesting that Vallabha also pursued the institutional aims that actually seem to have begun with his second son. Harirāy's *Bhāvprakāś* commentary is especially vigorous in providing details and vignettes intended to strengthen the idea that Vallabha traveled widely and began the task of creating the *sampradāy* himself. A somewhat later composition also called a *vārtā* and also attributed to Harirāy—the *Śrī Govardhannāthjī ke Prākaṭya kī Vārtā* supplies an additional dimension.[99] Unlike the *vārtās* we have so far mentioned, it begins to deal in actual dates, and one of the most crucial of these specifies the time of the would-be founder's birth. The date in question—later it came to be accepted as fact—is the year 1478 (V.S. 1535), and the reason that date was assigned has once again to do with Braj.[100]

It was on this date, we are told, that Śrīnāthjī, the lord of Mount Govardhan, first revealed the facial part of his image, which had theretofore been buried in the earth, to a cowherd named Saḍḍū Pāṇḍe. In doing so, the deity simultaneously initiated a new way the sacred mountain was to be worshiped—in image form—and committed himself to Vallabhite care. That moment, in turn, was said to be the very same one that witnessed Vallabha's own birth. While the *Śrī Govardhannāthjī ke Prākaṭya kī Vārtā* seems to suggest this may somehow have happened in Braj, the dominant story was that Vallabha was born far away in the Campā forest that lay along the road to the Telugu country.[101] After a period in which Śrīnāthjī evidently waited for Vallabha to mature and during which he accepted only milk offerings that were provided by the local Brajbāsīs, he sent for the acharya to come to Braj and serve him, giving him a sort of second birth by offering him solid food. Again, as if to revisit the site of his birth, Vallabha was in the southeastern forests, in Jhārkhaṇḍ—the stories circle back upon themselves—and he responded promptly to the call.

Thus the birth of the person the *sampradāy* claimed as its human founder ("full avatar" though he was) was first aligned with a divine "birth" that occurred at the same time and at the center of sacred space; and this connection was reinforced by the notion that Vallabha began his ritual service to Śrīnāthjī by following a divine command he received at the very place of his birth. As the *Caurāsī Vaiṣṇavan kī Vārtā* puts it, Vallabha goes to Braj to complete the work of mastery *(daman)*—mastery over earlier forms of worship—that the deity had already begun.[102] Here Vallabha is made out to be the human agent most centrally involved in refashioning Braj so that it would indeed be Krishna's paradise—that major sixteenth-century development we have seen so palpably elsewhere.

Obviously this memory of Vallabha's intimate connection to the appearance of Śrīnāthjī and the ritual regimen that would sustain him follows from the Vallabhite community's desire to sink down proprietary roots in the mountain that had long served, along with the River Jamuna, as the defining feature of the Braj landscape—its anchor and *tīrtha*. That Vallabha hailed from the south was important in the ideology of the fledgling *sampradāy*, just as the southern roots of other acharyas mattered to its peers. Not surprisingly, then, the place that was claimed to have been the site of Vallabha's birth—an openly miraculous birth in several respects—connects him to his Tailangana lineage in a much more vivid way than would have been possible if it had been recalled that he was born in Banaras, where his parents mainly lived at the time. Clearly some gesture to the south was important, as if to establish a magnetic periphery, yet the contrary pole mattered equally: the primordially central mountain of Braj. For Vallabhites the field that held these two together could not have been epitomized more persuasively than in the circumstances that gave coordinate birth to the deity they worshipped above all and the man they took to be their founder-god.[103]

In time the Vallabhite community developed a much expanded *digvijay* literature that depicted their founding guru as traveling the length and breadth of India, defeating theological and institutional opponents at every turn. The language of both the *Cāurasī Vaiṣṇavan* and *Śrī Govardhannāthjī ke Prākaṭya kī Vārtās* anticipates the power of this *digvijay* genre by saying that Vallabha had begun just such a "circling of the earth" *(pṛthvī parikramā)* when Śrīnāthjī summoned him to Braj.[104] It is not hard to believe that Vallabha did himself travel and engage in theological disputation on a more limited scale—in Banaras, in Puri, in Orccha, perhaps even as far away as Ujjain—but the image of him as victor throughout the subcontinent is almost certainly just that: imagined.[105] Vallabha was recognized as an eminent figure in intellectual circles during his own lifetime—the Chaitanyites make this clear—but he probably exercised this influence from Prayag and Banaras and not from elsewhere, as the *vārtās* and especially Harirāy's commentary would have us believe. The image of Vallabha's "world victory" tours began to be spread only quite some years after his death, and the same is true for the complementary idea that the center of the Vallabha *sampradāy* belonged firmly in Braj. Viṭṭhalnāth and Kṛṣṇadās were apparently the pioneers of the latter idea, working in the second half of the sixteenth century; it flourished further in the *vārtās,* which came together toward the middle of the following century. Later in the seventeenth century, it seems, notions of *digvijays* and the four *sampradāys* emerged as an integral part of Vallabhite thinking. Through them the memory of Vallabha's faraway Tailangana birth was enveloped in a whole new litany of stories that provided dramatic access to the south and elsewhere. When that happened, the Vallabhites joined the Rāmānandīs, Nimbārkīs, and Chaitanyites in accepting a shared view of sectarian history that would later be seen as the core and centerpiece of an integrated pan-Indian bhakti movement. In the chapter just ahead we shall see how this occurred.

5

Victory in the Cities of Victory

THE TIME-HONORED IDEOLOGY OF Brindavan represents it as a forest or garden—anything but a city. Yet fundamental as this idea was to the formation of Brindavan and surrounding regions in the course of the long sixteenth century, we have time and again seen that these acts of creation unfolded against the backdrop of distinctly more urban, cosmopolitan, and sometimes truly imperial realities.[1] It would be a gross exaggeration to hold that every aspect of Brindavan's early development bore a specific, even intimate relationship to state policy, but as we have seen, many did. Thus it is not accidental that the most massive monument to bhakti ever constructed in north India, Brindavan's Govindadev temple, was built to commemorate success in battle. Although its name proclaimed it to be a retreat or wilderness—a *van*—Brindavan was in many respects a city of victory.

In the present chapter we will see how Mānsingh's "victory city"—a Brindavan whose greatest landmarks asserted the extent of the Kachvahas' contributions to Mughal glory—came to take its place in the mental terrain laid out by the concept of the four *sampradāys*. This happened in the latter half of the seventeenth century and the first half of the eighteenth. At that time representatives of the most cosmopolitan communities who claimed Brindavan as home, the Gauḍīyas and (nota bene!) the Vallabhites, issued documents that put Brindavan implicitly into conversation with two other imperial utopias: the Vijayanagar of King Kṛṣṇadevarāya and the Jaipur of Rājā Savāī Jaisingh II. As it happens, both these cities' names mean precisely "city of victory," although the latter also picks up the name of its ruler, Jai ("Victory") Singh. Thus we get a trio of expressions of imperial power—Vijayanagar with its Seluva rulers, Brindavan with its Mughal-Kachvaha patrons, and the distinctly Kachvaha domain at Jaipur. In real time these came to flourish in chronological sequence, but our interest is more conceptual. We hope to discover the images of imperial order that each represented and how these worked in very different ways to take the idea of the four *sampradāys* to a new level of cogency and influence.

We already know of the impact that the notion of the four *sampradāys* had on the Dādūpathī Rāghavdās, who in 1660 extrapolated it from the Rāmānandī context where it was first articulated so that it could serve as a model for his own. By following the literary example of Nābhādās explicitly, he kept that Rāmānandī imprint clearly in view, but others who wrote after him—and from quite different sectarian perspectives—would not be so scrupulous. They presented this idea as if it were a fact and used it for their own ends. Writing about twenty years after Rāghavdās, a Vallabhite thinker who has come to be called Gadādhar used it to establish Vallabha's preeminence and did so especially by invoking the memory of the great Seluva ruler Kṛṣṇadevarāya. Bringing Vijayanagar into the picture in this way, Gadādhar for the first time provided the south-facing notion of the four *sampradāys* with a specific political context. Somewhat later, in the heady 1730s, Savāī Jaisingh, who also had his southern interests, added yet more political ballast to the concept. He saw in it a powerful resource for envisioning a Vedic Vaishnava polity that could give religious shape to the new imperium he was forging, a kingdom whose axially perfect order was also symbolized in the layout he gave to the capital city he constructed on the plain that lay below the old fort-palace at Āmer. When Jaisingh moved to make the idea of the four *sampradāys* function as actual state policy, it became necessary for the Gauḍīyas to come on board. Since the time of Mānsingh they had enjoyed a special relation to the Kachvaha rulers, but it had never been mediated by any concept other than those of their own making. Now they had to submit to a higher authority, a more generalized picture of Vaishnava religious history. Even so, however, the Gauḍīyas continued to enjoy a special status. Jaisingh wanted to ensconce Brindavan at the symbolic heart of his newly vibrant kingdom, and his means of doing so was to provide for Govindadev, who had been exiled from Braj by the political chaos of the 1670s, a residence that would be right at the center of Jaipur's palace grounds.

Brindavan was to be a garden in the middle of the city after all, and indeed a Mughal garden at that.

Thus in different respects all three of our "victory cities" came to play a role in the further development of the four-*sampradāy* idea as it crystallized in north India during the years that lay on either side of 1700. Brindavan stays in view, a prized point of reference just as it was in the *Bhāgavata Māhātmya*. Yet if we read two crucial texts that give us a sense of the impact of these changes from a sectarian point of view—one Gauḍīya and one Vallabhite, and both claiming a tie to Brindavan—we realize that the impetus for such new developments actually emerged from elsewhere than Brindavan itself. In the pages that lie ahead we will see how this was so.

Kavikarṇapūra, Jaisingh II, and the Question of Sampradāy

In Chapter 4 we made the acquaintance of the Gauḍīya poet Kavikarṇapūra as a fine playwright, a great exponent of the dramatic sensibility that became so central to the Chaitanyite vision of reality, but it was a very different sort of work by the same man that became a crucial vehicle for the historiography of the four *sampradāys*. This compact document is called the *Gauragaṇoddeśadīpikā* (A Lamp to Explicate the Companions of the Golden One). In it Kavikarṇapūra provides a guide to the real identities of the people who surrounded Chaitanya, and does so in a way that contrasts broadly to what he set out in his famous drama, the *Caitanyacandrodaya*—so much so that certain scholars have entertained the notion that the two works might not have been composed by the same author.[2] The *Gauragaṇoddeśadīpikā* consists of 220 verses more or less, depending on the manuscript. Most of these, being *ślokas*, are quite short, but a few are considerably longer, and some verses are quoted from earlier works, notably the *Caitanyacandrodaya* itself. The final verse reports that this composition was completed in *śaka* 1498, that is, 1576 C.E.

The *Gauragaṇoddeśadīpikā* is crucial for our concerns because one of its verses contains a prominent mention of the doctrine of the four *sampradāys*. If that verse is integral to the text, it would have to be taken as roughly contemporaneous with what we have in Anantadās and Nandadās, and would indicate that at least one prominent thinker within the Gauḍīya fold regarded the Gauḍīyas' own particular "bhakti movement" as belonging within the scope of a wider array of bhakti orders.[3] Indeed, many scholars have accepted that this is so, but for reasons I will soon explain, I think the greater weight of evidence points the other way. I believe this verse, far longer than any other in the *Gauragaṇoddeśadīpikā*, was inserted into the text many decades after 1576, at a time when the whole matter of *sampradāy* had become a charged political issue. The rest of the text, by contrast, can indeed be read as one man's attempt to work out his community's sense of its own identity as the sixteenth century entered its final quarter.

Kavikarṇapūra wrote from Bengal, probably from the town of Kumārahaṭṭa, where his father Śivānand Sen was a man of considerable wealth and power, a member of the Brahmin *vaidya* caste.[4] Toward the end of his life Śivānand took up residence in Puri and became an important member of Chaitanya's inner circle—an intimate attendant, according to both Kṛṣṇadās Kavirāj and Kavikarṇapūra himself.[5] Although his son Paramānand Dās, born in 1524, is said to have met Chaitanya in Puri and to have been dubbed "the ear-ornament of poets" *(kavikarṇapūra)* by the Master himself, he seems to have worked from Kumārahaṭṭa, which was home to a thriving community of Vaishnavas, many of them Chaitanya's followers. It had been the birthplace of Īśvara Purī and Vrindāvan Dās, and Jīv Gosvāmī's family moved there after the death of his father, Vallabha. Rembert Lutjeharms, an authority on Kavikarṇapūra, believes that Jīv and Kavikarṇapūra very likely would have met, being of about the same age, but the latter shows no awareness of the former's theological works, perhaps because Jīv composed them in Braj and for a long time did not release them for export to Bengal; or perhaps because Kavikarṇapūra was by instinct a poet, not a philosopher.[6]

It is noteworthy that Kavikarṇapūra seems to think of Chaitanya's circle in Puri as the primary analogue for Krishna's circle in Brindavan. He construes the Puri group as "greater" (*mahattarāḥ*, §18) Vaisnavas than the rest and is unconcerned with whatever this-worldly representations of Chaitanya's charmed circle were being constructed in the Braj of his day, where Jīv and others were hard at work. In laying this out, Kavikarṇapūra makes use of a concept that we first meet all the way back in the *Kaḍacā* of Murārī Gupta and which he himself associates with the earliest period of Gauḍīya self-reflection by crediting it to Svarūp Dāmodar, Chaitanya's amanuensis. This is the idea of the "Five Elements" *(pañcatattva)*, a group comprised by Nityānand, Advaitācārya, Śrīnivās, Gadādhar, and last but not least, Chaitanya (§§12–13). Somewhat later on, Kavikarṇapūra goes on to make a place for other ways of enumerating Chaitanya's associates, listing groups of eight, three, nine, or four bhaktas who also gathered around him. He introduces these in a cluster of verses beginning with §100. In regard to the first of these, Kavikarṇapūra tells us that the eight *siddhis,* supranormal yogic powers originally conceptualized in the *Yogasūtras* of Patañjali, had been actualized at a previous time in Brindavan—as part of Krishna's world, that is to say (§§100–101). He goes on to assert that they have now taken form in eight of the bhaktas who had been attracted to Chaitanya, and he lists them by name: Ananta, Sukhānand, and so on. Once again he specifies Puri as the place where this happened (§102).

There is nothing in any of this to suggest that when Kavikarṇapūra or any of the Chaitanyites preceding him thought seriously about the nature, composition, and history of their community, they found it necessary to make reference to any other group that might be parallel with their own—any other sect or *sampradāy.* All their comparisons were focused instead on the connection between the paradigmatic time when Krishna took up residence in Brindavan and the one in which they found themselves. It also does not seem to have occurred to Kavikarṇapūra that the earthly Brindavan—the Braj of his day, the place where Rūp, Jīv, and others worked—needed to be taken into account as an intermediary point of reference in thinking about the connection between the primordial Braj and its latter-day prosopographic image, Puri.

All of this changes markedly once the idea of the four *sampradāys* enters the picture. At that point we have Kavikarṇapūra claiming that Chaitanya's guru-to-pupil lineage must be traced back to Madhvācārya, and he also supplies the whole intervening succession—fourteen gurus taking us down to Mādhavendra Purī, Īśvara Purī, and Chaitanya himself, or as the text says, Gaura, "the fair one" (§24–27).[7] For the first time, in the course of that exposition, we have a hint that Brindavan or Braj might be thought of as something other than a celestial reality. In emphasizing the point that Chaitanya owed a fair amount of his inspiration via his own guru to Mādhavendra Purī, a point that is made elsewhere in Gauḍīya writings including the *Caitanyacaritāmṛta,* the author of this passage necessarily draws attention to the importance of the Braj country as a living and not just mythic entity, the sort of place one could actually visit. Both Chaitanyite and Vallabhite accounts retain a clear memory of Mādhavendra's role in restoring the worship of Krishna at Mount Govardhan to a new primacy in the last decades of the fifteenth century, though they differ as to which of them properly inherited his mantle.[8] This sounds quite different from anything we have elsewhere in the *Gauragaṇoddeśadīpikā*, which superimposes the primordial, mythic Braj onto the present, earthly Puri.

Indeed, it is. For reasons that I have explained in detail elsewhere, I am convinced that this passage is a later interpolation into the text. The theology is wrong, the outsized size of the crucial verse is wrong, the match of relevant details to the rest of the text is poor or contradictory. There is something fishy about the way in which the four *sampradāys* are introduced—as something that has been prophesied in a text of record: the *Padma Purāṇa*, where, as we know, the relevant passage is not actually to be found. Finally, one can omit the entire passage relating to Chaitanya's association with the Mādhvites (§§23–27), including its four-*sampradāy* component, and still have the text read as a seamless whole.[9]

Why would anyone want to make such an interpolation? The reason is not hard to find. This spokesman for what we can now rightly call the Gauḍīya *sampradāy* wanted to justify his community at court. He wanted to show that it conformed to the new requirements for theological legitimacy that the great Kachvaha ruler Jaisingh II and his advisors were in the process of laying down as the necessary marks of religious legitimacy in the early decades of the eighteenth century. That, I believe, is the period to which this interpolated passage probably belongs, although its author may well have been working with an idea that had begun to form already in the middle of the seventeenth century, as we saw in the *Bhaktamāl* of Rāghavdās. He turned to the document that had come to be regarded as the handiest point of reference for the early history of the Chaitanyite community—a veritable "Who's Who" it was—and updated it so that it could answer any questions about legitimacy of lineage that might be raised in the context of the new specifications that were promulgated at the court of Jaisingh. Perhaps the memory that Sanātan and Rūp Gosvāmī came from a family based in Karnataka had something to do with making it seem plausible that there could have been a Gauḍīya connection to that region via Madhva. Or perhaps the verbal association between the name Madhva and that of Mādhavendra Purī was partly to blame. Something like that seems to have happened in the mind of Rāghavdās, who wrote at a greater distance from the tradition itself. He omits Mādhavendra Purī and gives us a figure called Madhvācārya Madhupurī instead (§225), placing him among the Gauḍīyas. But whatever the circumstances that first produced the idea that there was a tie between the Gauḍīyas and the Mādhvites, it is likely that the writer who expanded the original *Gauragaṇoddeśadīpikā* did so in response to current need—the new policies that had been announced by Jaisingh II.

It was a remarkable moment in the history of Indian politics when Raja Savāī Jaisingh sought to discipline the practice of bhakti in the way he did. He lent the considerable force of state sponsorship and state censorship to the notion that the historical movement of bhakti had been channeled into clearly identifiable institutional forms, all of them Vaishnava. This was no isolated act of institutional and theological rectification, and certainly not an arbitrary one. It played a part in Jaisingh's remarkable effort to align his practice of kingship with Vedic ideals—as expressed most notably in his revival of the ancient horse sacrifice *(aśvamedha)* in 1734 and 1741.[10] For guidance on matters such as these, Jaisingh solicited the advice of a coterie of prominent Brahmin scholars that he assembled from various quarters. He nodded especially to men such as Viśvanāth Bhaṭṭ and Ratnākar Bhaṭṭ, who emerged from the powerful circle of Maharashtrian Brahmins who had recently established their hegemony in the great *muktimaṇḍapa* of the temple of Śiva Viśvanāth in Banaras. That had become the center of a newly strengthened network of Brahmin intellectuals whose influence extended throughout India and even north of the Himalayas into Nepal.[11] Jaisingh's childhood tutor, Jagannāth Samrāṭ, was also Maharashtrian. But other Brahmins too were on his mental horizons. Court records show that Jaisingh valued the opinions of Kṛṣṇadās Bhaṭṭācārya and Lālū Bhaṭṭ, members respectively of the Gauḍīya and Vallabhite communities, and that he consulted Nimbārkīs and Rāmānandīs as well.[12] Hence all four *sampradāys* were included in the councils of state—or would be if Gauḍīya connections to the south could be established, as they were claimed to have been in each of the other three cases.

As to the south, it is worth noting that when Jaisingh conducted his first *aśvamedha* in 1734, he built a temple halfway between Āmer and Jaipur to serve as the base of sacrificial operations, dedicating it to Vishnu as royal giver of boons (Varadarāja) after the pattern of the monarchs of Vijayanagar. He recruited as priests members of the family who officiated in the great temple of Varadarājasvāmī in Kanchipuram, a monument whose most impressive pavilions had been constructed by a late-Vijayanagar patron.[13] Obviously, the south stood for something: an unbroken tie to the ritual traditions enshrined in doctrines that had emerged from Vaishnava Brahmins of the Tamil country. Earlier there had been a Shaiva dimension, as well. Śivānand Gosvāmī, who instructed Jaisingh's father, Bisan Singh, in Śākta Kaula rituals, was the grandson of Śrīnivās Bhaṭṭ, who was born in an *agrahāra* just south of Kanchipuram.[14] Jaisingh may also have been aware that the Vaishnava traditions of Kanchipuram and elsewhere in the Tamil region had received the attention of Kṛṣṇadevarāya and his Aravidu successors, so for Jaisingh they may also have connoted the grand dynastic legacy of Vijayanagar. In any case Kanchipuram's Brahmins connected him to a theological tradition in which a community's leaders were expected to demonstrate their Vedic bona fides by producing a commentary each on three central texts *(prasthāna trayī):* the *Brahma Sūtras* of Bādarāyana, the most highly regarded Upanishads, and the *Bhagavad Gītā.* This expectation was sufficiently widespread that it applied not only to Vaishnavas but to Śaṃkara himself. In fact, many believe he was its archetype.

If Jaisingh was making an appeal to his imperial predecessors in Vijayanagar, we should remember nonetheless that their legacy was somewhat dispersed. After the collapse of the imperial capital at Vijayanagar itself, the Nayaka rulers of southeastern India continued to claim its mantle. Jaisingh's Maharashtrian advisors may have had some sense of this through their connections with southern Brahmins at Banaras, although the general Marathi record of remembering Vijayanagar suggests "profound indifference," as Sumit Guha has shown.[15] There may also have been a link closer to home: the Sisodia rulers of Mewar. Already in the mid-fifteenth century Rāṇā Kumbha seems to have patterned a new series of *rāmnavamī/ mahānavamī/dasehrā* rites after the example that had been established by then in Vijayanagar; these were to be vastly upgraded by Kṛṣṇadevarāya and his Tuluva half brothers in the sixteenth century. Ajay Rao has proposed that these same royal rituals may have had an impact on the way in which Tulsīdās thought of *dasehrā*—or rather, to use the term that echoes most obviously to its initial patrons, *vijayadaśamī*—in Banaras.[16] Through the Rāmānandīs and by virtue of the ruling family's own genealogical claims, the impress of Rām was already well registered in Kachvaha ritual and ideology: Jaisingh signed his own name as "Rām." Whether the example of the Sisodiyas' embrace of Rām-oriented rituals also inspired him, we do not know. If it did, however, he and his advisors simultaneously reached out for a more widely based linkage to the south. Many court documents show that Jaisingh was deeply interested in bridging the divides between religious communities, focusing instead on the common strands that united them. The rubric of the four *sampradāys* provided a handsome means to do just that while also suggesting a many-sided connection to the southern past.[17]

Of course, Jaisingh also had his eye on the present. His newly stringent appeals to theological and ritual orthodoxy occurred precisely in the context of his efforts to build an ideal city that would serve as the hub of a newly strengthened Kachvaha realm. While still Mughal with respect to its formal affiliations—the Kachvahas were in name, at least, a subsidiary entity—this state was actually an independent powerhouse. In many ways Jaisingh was a more substantial ruler than the Mughals to whom he maintained a relationship of respectful service, formally speaking, so the "city of victory" that he built, Jaipur, though named after himself, actually justified its identity in more literal terms. This "City of Victory" was a marvel of urban planning guided by traditional *śāstrik* norms, and at its core—in the garden of his new palace and facing it from the north—Jaisingh built a temple that would play host to the images of Govindadev and his consort Radha.[18] These deities may have fled Brindavan as early as 1669; they had arrived in the immediate vicinity of Āmer in 1707. For a time they reigned over Kanak Brindavan, a freshly built "golden Brindavan" intended through its verdure and water views to replicate the moods of the Braj original. As Jaisingh's plans developed further, however, he repositioned Govindadev and his consort so that they would preside over the very center of the new capital—Jaipur itself.

Obviously his family's venerable connection to Govindadev was of great concern to him, but this deity and the Gauḍīya community who served him also had to be located in a theological framework that met the expectations of other Vaishnava communities whom Jaisingh regarded as being relevant to the proper practice of sovereignty. Hence the matter of the four *sampradāys* became a pressing concern. All the other orders most influential in the immediate vicinity of Jaipur had fashioned themselves in such a way as to claim connections to the south, as the rubric of the four *sampradāys* required. We have seen how this worked in the case of the Rāmānandīs. It also pertained to the Nimbārkīs, who had important centers at Salemābād to the west and Nīm kā Thānā to the north. And it also worked for the Vallabhites, who proposed a connection to Viṣṇusvāmī and had come to play an increasingly prominent role at court: more about that before long.

The Gauḍīyas' position, however, was different. Although they had enjoyed strong Kachvaha support since the days of Mānsingh, at least in regard to the Kachvaha presence in the Jamuna heartland as mediated by Mughal authority, the Gauḍīyas had never had to justify their existence at Āmer itself—and now Jaipur. Given the cosmopolitan standards to which Jaisingh now aspired, and given the formidable role that Govindadev was to play in the conception of the new city, they were for the first time required to do so. Probably with an eye specifically to Govindadev, others at court had persuaded the king that the idea of the four *sampradāys* should be considered an integral part of the cosmopolitan structure by means of which he conceived his own identity and through which he intended to rule. I suspect that the Rāmānandīs, who were the first to conceptualize the four *sampradāys* and who were most in danger of being cast into the shadows by the Gauḍīyas' rising star, were initially responsible for this initiative, although one cannot make that specific judgment on the basis of court records that have survived. What is clear, however, is that to assure the victory of Govindadev in the new "City of Victory," and to consolidate their own position both there and in Braj, the Gauḍīyas suddenly felt that they had to explain how they too belonged to the four *sampradāys*.

It has long been recognized that the theologian Baladev Vidyābhūṣaṇ, whom Jaipuri documents show as being a figure of some importance in Gauḍīya Brindavan in 1741 and 1742, was the person most closely responsible for making this happen.[19] He supplied the Gauḍīyas with a commentary on the *Brahma Sūtras*—his *Govindabhāṣya*—thereby articulating the community's relation to the central articles of Vedic faith in a way that had long since come to be accepted as standard. At the same time, equally important, he attempted to give plausibility to the notion that Gauḍīya theological writings could have emerged from the Mādhvite tradition, a tie that he and certain other Gauḍīyas of his time were beginning explicitly to claim.[20] By now we have a general sense of why these moves were urgent, but the specific stimulus seems to have been supplied by a decree that went out from the court of Jaisingh at some point in the 1730s demanding that organizations expecting to receive state approval as orthodox with regard to lineage and doctrine—orthodoxy was being interpreted in a distinctively Vaishnava way—should supply a document proving that they belonged to the fold. Baladev tells us on several occasions that he writes in response to Jaisingh's inspiration, but we find no mention of Baladev in the court records of Jaipur. Instead we discover frequent references to his distinguished senior colleague Viśvanāth Cakravartī, the head of the Gauḍīya community in Brindavan. It must have been Viśvanāth who commissioned Baladev's work—and that at quite a young age, since Baladev lived well into the seventeenth century.[21] As for the *Govindabhāṣya,* Baladev's best-known composition, it may not have been completed until close to midcentury, but Adrian Burton has shown that his *Brahmasūtrakārikābhāṣya,* a forerunner intended to accomplish the same purpose, did indeed emerge as an immediate response to Jaisingh's decree.[22] Here, in a rarefied atmosphere Chaitanya himself certainly never anticipated and might well not have countenanced, the bhakti movement he inspired was brought into alignment with other sectarian formations at the formal level of philosophical or theological justification—all this, of course, in the cosmopolitan, largely brahminical medium of Sanskrit.

Not all exponents of the bhakti religiosity that had taken distinctive form in Brindavan felt it was right to submit to Jaisingh's demands. The leader of the Rādhāvallabh community famously refused, with the result that certain Rādhāvallabhī leaders were exiled from Brindavan to Kamban for a time; and it was not until much later that a Rādhāvallabhī commentary on the *Brahma Sūtras* was produced.[23] Certain of the Gauḍīya leaders were similarly opposed. Of course, the Bengali branch of the tradition had always been more insulated from intersectarian discussions than their peers in Braj, so it is no surprise that there were grounds for resistance there. But this was so in Braj as well. Deeply embedded in the Gauḍīyas' concept of themselves, after all, was the idea that Krishna was God himself—*svayam bhagavān,* as the *Bhāgavata Purāṇa* had said—and that Chaitanya was his full and complete representation. To some, in fact, Chaitanya seemed a more complete expression of divinity than Krishna himself, since he manifested the presence of both Krishna and Radha in a single body. But there were other grounds. Had not Jīv Gosvāmī taken pleasure in referring to Chaitanya as "the presiding deity of thousands of *sampradāys*" *(sampradāyasahasrādhidaiva)*?[24] No wonder, then, that the Gauḍīya leader Śyāmcaraṇdās, head priest of the Gopīnāth temple in Brindāvan, responded to Jaisingh's initiative by resisting any attempt to associate Chaitanya with some other sectarian lineage—or indeed, with the notion of lineage itself. Here, in a letter addressed to Jaisingh, is how he went about claiming the high ground:

> In order to manifest his most confidential secrets, and in order to savor them himself, Lord Krishna, the prince of Braj, became manifest in this world in the form of Caitanya Mahāprabhu and Kṛṣṇa's emanations, partial manifestations, and weapons manifested along with him as his companions. This conclusion has been reached by his companions with evidence from such books as the venerable Bhāgavata and Mahābhārata, by the fact that he demonstrated a six-arm form, and because he experienced such elevated states of divine love. Therefore it is the power of Mahāprabhu alone which is the source of our *sampradāya*. Scripture says that all *sampradāyas* culminate in Bhagavān alone. Therefore, since Mahāprabhu is himself directly Bhagavān, there is nothing defective with our *sampradāya* culminating in Mahāprabhu. On the other hand, those who suffer the defect of lacking faith and accept that he belonged to some other *sampradāya* have in fact become hostile to him. Such people are condemned by us and are worthy of punishment.[25]

Given such sentiment and given the fact that a derogatory comment about Madhva's views is attributed to Chaitanya himself in the *Caitanyacaritāmṛta*, it is remarkable that the urge to connect these two figures went forward.[26] In fact, in the eyes of many—not least, those who held important political positions—it seems to have succeeded. This must have made it easier for Jaisingh to rule at home and at the same time to bridge the two worlds of Jaipur and Braj, as he regularly did not only in his continuing role in the Mughal court—he had been appointed *sūbedār* of Agra and *fauzdār* of Mathura in 1722—but because he actively developed his own presence in Brindavan. He built a retreat for himself on the banks of the Jamuna. Largely in consequence—after all, Jaisingh was a major figure not just there but in Ayodhya and Banaras and across north India—the concept of a Madhva-Gauḍīya *sampradāy* has been abroad in the land ever since, carrying with it the notion that Chaitanya's teachings form a part of a tradition that began in the south many centuries earlier.

Such a notion is not entirely foreign to the Gauḍīya tradition as it had developed up to that point in time. Shrivatsa Goswami has argued that in different ways both Sanātan and Rūp clearly acknowledge their indebtedness to Gopāl Bhaṭṭ, the southerner among the "six *gosvāmīs.*" Sanātan played an editorial role in the production of Gopāl Bhaṭṭ's ritual text, the *Haribhaktivilāsa,* and Rūp was understood by Jīv Gosvāmī to have conceived his *Bhaktirasāmṛtasindhu* and *Ujjvalanīlamaṇi* as commentaries on the first two treatises among the six that comprise Gopāl Bhaṭṭ's theological work, the *Ṣaṭsandarbha.* Jīv picks up the thread by providing editions or commentaries on the remaining four, which he specifically introduces by saying that the treatises themselves had been composed by "a Bhaṭṭ coming from a twiceborn southern family" *(bhaṭṭo dakṣiṇadvijavaṃśajaḥ)* or simply a "Bhaṭṭ from the south" *(dākṣiṇātyena bhaṭṭena),* and he goes on to situate his own theological persuasions in relation to the positions of those southern greats Śaṃkara, Rāmūnuja, and Madhva. Thus as a philosopher-theologian, Jīv sees himself as standing in the lineage of the "old Vaishnavas" *(vṛddhavaiṣṇavāḥ)* Rāmūnuja, Madhva, and Śrīdhara, and he is aware of the moment when the *Bhāgavata Purāṇa* makes reference to its southern provenance (BhP 1.5.39). But he is very clear about the fact that his own sense of correct doctrine, *acintyabhedābheda* (unthinkable difference and nondifference), marks him out as being quite distinct from these predecessors, and there is never a sense that Madhva has any primacy.[27] Given such a clear sense of the intellectual past on the part of the theologian who did the most to consolidate a unified Chaitanyite position, and given Jīv's equally strong sense of the novelty of that position and its location in Brindavan's theological present, it is remarkable to see that as the eighteenth century dawned, leading figures in the Gauḍīya community felt they had to succumb to the task of providing a more "official" *smārta* version of how the Gauḍīyas could be located in a broader Vaishnava past—a southernness that had been transmitted northward not by intellectual paths alone but by the initiatory links that membership in a *sampradāy* would provide.

We are still somewhat in the dark about how it came to pass that Baladev Vidyābhūṣaṇ became such a perfect apologist for the Madhva-Gauḍīya connection that accomplished this job. Tradition says he was born in Orissa and travelled to Mysore, where he trained as a Mādhva ascetic before taking up residence in a Mādhva *maṭh* in Puri. There he engaged in conversation with Gauḍīyas, was "converted," and proceeded via Navadvīp to Brindavan. None of this can actually be documented, however, and it may have come into currency as a biographical retrojection of the philosophical positions Baladev articulated in his various writings. As Adrian Burton explains, our first clear evidence of him is probably the mention of "Vidyābhūṣaṇ Svāmī" that appears in a court account of a visit on the part of Jaisingh to Brindavan in 1741. If this is our man, as seems likely, he was by then in charge of the temple of Govindadev—that is, the Brindavan monument, not its successor at Jaipur—and other official records put him in charge of the temple of Rādhā Śyāmsundar in Brindavan, as well. Not long afterward, apparently, he did also take up residence in Jaipur, establishing a second temple of Rādhā Śyāmsundar there, too.[28] If we separate what is sometimes claimed about Baladev Vidyābhūṣaṇ's youth from what we actually know on the basis of Jaipuri records, then, we seem to come away not with evidence of any south-to-north trajectory we might wish to document in his person, but rather evidence of the success of the new Madhva-Gauḍīya position within the ritual economy of the Kachvaha kingdom. This, I believe, is what we also see in the amendments that were made to the *Gauragaṇoddeśadīpikā* of Kavikarṇapūra.

So far, we have approached the subject of Jaisingh's interest in rationalizing the relations between various expressions of "approved religion," all of them Vaishnava, and thereby creating a rubric for them to be integrated into state policy as if this initiative followed from a high-minded desire on his part to fashion his kingdom after a model that would be vedically correct. And indeed, that was certainly part of his objective. But the king was also desirous of disciplining and perhaps consolidating the military capabilities of Vaishnava ascetics who populated his realm. Monika Horstmann has argued that a letter written in 1722 by Kṛṣṇadās Bhaṭṭācārya shows that by this point in time the state had seized upon the four-*sampradāy* model as being the correct rubric for dealing with such matters. Evidently this was also the position they took when representatives of the various *akhāḍās* gathered at Āmer for a conference organized by the state in 1718.[29]

What the state tried to do was fourfold: (1) to separate out determinedly celibate *vairāgīs* from those who had established relationships with women, thus creating a means to ensure that all Vaishnavas who took part in state rituals were householders, as the Vedas were held to demand; (2) to dispatch any *sādhus* who refused this "clarification"—some to a compound Jaisingh established with the ironic name Vairāgyapur (Abstinence Town) near Mathura in 1727;[30] (3) to disaggregate the four *varṇas* when food was served in a monastic setting, as if to comply with the Vedas; and (4) to disarm all religious personnel, both celibate and married, thereby reserving the right of arms-bearing to employees of the state.[31] The legitimate orders, with their ascetic and householder branches, would be dignified by their association with the four *sampradāys*, of which they were required to provide plausible evidence. Some orders were alienated or split by this policy; others accepted it only reluctantly. Apparently it never managed to be fully enacted, certainly not in Jaisingh's time, but the impetus to do so gave the formula of the four *sampradāys* a prestige and position of power that it had never had before. Even after the policy had failed and bands of armed ascetics were being employed by the state to serve its military ends—this happened later on in the eighteenth century—a number of these groups represented themselves as belonging to the one of the four *sampradāys* or to one of the *panths* that had been incorporated into the general rubric by Rāghavdās: the Dādūpathīs, Kabīrpanthīs, and Sikhs. The Dādūpathīs were especially important. Starting in the middle of the eighteenth century Dādūpathī ascetics were regularly employed as militia for the Kachvaha state; by century's end they were members of its regular army.[32]

By this somewhat unexpected path, then, the idea of bhakti's being channeled by means of the four *sampradāys* did indeed endure after the rule of Jaisingh, even if its institutional expression was not fully implemented in his own time. This is one of the routes by means of which the concept of the four *sampradāys* became available to theorists of the bhakti movement in the early decades of the twentieth century. Although the state Vaishnavism that Jaisingh established was temporarily threatened by a Shaiva "cabal" in the 1860s, the image of a robust, institutionally articulated bhakti presence that tied southern India to realms farther north nonetheless survived. In fact, when the Shaivas sought to interrogate this state Vaishnavism, they did so precisely according to the four-*sampradāy* rubric.[33] This framework also had an impact on Vaishnava ascetics themselves, who in time—we are not yet sure just when—used it as one of the ways to organize their participation in the great Kumbh Mela celebrations.

Clearly this served to keep the idea before the public eye as well as their own, but since when? Despite the impression of unchanging primordiality that is projected by the practice of the Kumbh Mela, the twelve-year, four-site conception that lends so much of the universality we today associate with this ritual seems to have emerged only in the latter part of the nineteenth century.[34]

The attempt to institutionalize the notion of the four *sampradāys* had palpable effects through other channels, as well. Rāmānandīs and Nimbārkīs carried forward a sense of the importance of the four *sampradāys* through their ongoing associations with one another as ascetics, and even Gauḍīyas came to have a clearly institutionalized ascetic wing. In 1793, for example, a disciple of the aged Rāmānandī *mahant* Bālānand, one of the most powerful figures in Jaipur's history throughout the latter half of the eighteenth century, chose to eulogize him as being "manifest in the four *sampradāys* and causing the world to flourish."[35] Notably, this ascetic path for the transmission of the idea of the four *sampradāys* was never open to Vallabhites, whose householder theology militated powerfully against any such thing. Yet the Vallabhite attachment to this idea came to be profound, and Vallabhites were among the most important voices to be heard spreading the message of the four *sampradāys* as the twentieth century approached. One thinks in particular of the writings of Bharatendu Harishchandra, whom we have already mentioned more than once. How did the Vallabhite connection to the notion of the four *sampradāys* emerge?

Vijayanagar Visions of the Vallabhites

According to certain sources—and contrary to everything we have said so far—it was actually a Vallabhite who was responsible for producing the earliest extant document where the idea of the four *sampradāys* comes into view. The text in question is called the *Sampradāyapradīpa*, a fascinating Sanskrit work that represents itself as having been composed in V.S. 1610 (1553 or possibly 1554 C.E.) by a person who refers to himself with the phrase "Dvivedī Gadākhya," that is, "a Dvivedī called Gada"—or conceivably Gadā. This has been taken as a shortening of the name Gadādhar Bhaṭṭ Dvivedī, by which he is usually known. Gadādhar says he was writing in Brindavan, and if this is so, it casts a fundamentally different light on the history we have been reconstructing so far. Perhaps he anticipates this in his title, for he calls this work the *Lamp to* [or of] *the Sects,* but he is actually interested in demonstrating that the light shone by his own Vallabha *sampradāy* utterly outshines all the rest. For this reason we could also interpret his title as meaning *Lamp of the Sect.*

It is clear that Gadādhar was indeed a Vallabhite.[36] He tells us that he is a pupil of Vallabha's son Viṭṭhalnāth, who probably became the leader of the community said to have been established by his father in the early 1540s. The text is designed to tell the story of how Vallabha became heir to the philosophical and ritual community established by Viṣṇusvāmī, the mysterious acharya of whom we first heard in the *Bhaktamāl* of Nābhādās. Whoever and whenever he was—speculations have ranged widely—all of his writings have been lost; we only know him through the response others made to him, and even that is rather sparse.[37] Vallabha is one of the subsequent thinkers who refers to him in passing, but that only deepens the mystery—first, because there is only this one reference, and second, because it seems rather critical. Why then would someone be interested in tying Vallabha's star to his?

The passage in question occurs in the *Subodhinī,* Vallabha's partial commentary on the *Bhāgavata Purāṇa.* In verse 3.32.37, where the sage Kapila speaks of the fourfold nature of *bhaktiyoga,* Vallabha identifies these with three schools of thought and—by implication—the one that he himself is expounding, the best of all. He speaks of those who follow Viṣṇusvāmī and of the Tattvavādīs (that is, followers of Madhva) and "Rāmānujas"—*viṣṇusvāmyanusāriṇaḥ tattvavādinaḥ rāmānujāśceti.* In the spirit of the passage, he associates these with the three classical *guṇas,* the properties that make the universe what it is. These he apparently gives in ascending order: *tamas, rajas, sattva*—the lethargic/dark, the passionate/red, and the pellucid or truthful/white.

Analysts have differed in their interpretation of this line. Helmuth von Glasenapp tried to show that the designation *tāmasik* (from *tamas*), when applied to the ideas of Viṣṇusvāmī in the manner that Vallabha does, is not necessarily derogatory. For other reasons, too, Glasenapp withheld final judgment on the question of whether Vallabha could have stood in the lineage of Viṣṇusvāmī.[38] G. H. Bhatt, the much-admired Sanskritist who was director of the Oriental Institute in Baroda during the 1930s, argued with Glasenapp and took the opposite approach. He was convinced that Vallabha's characterization of Viṣṇusvāmī—as a dualist—cannot have been meant as a compliment, coming from a self-proclaimed "pure non-dualist" *(śuddhādvaita).*[39] It is hard not to feel that Bhatt's position is far stronger than Glasenapp's, and that makes one react with real surprise when one goes to the *Sampradāyapradīpa* and finds that Gadādhar Bhaṭṭ tells his tale precisely for the purpose of demonstrating that the Viṣṇusvāmī-Vallabha lineage is really the *only* respectable lineage in the world of competing Vaishnava communities.

To make this point, Gadādhar tells a series of overlapping stories that create an echo between what we might call "classic" times—the time when Viṣṇusvāmī was initiated by Krishna himself at the beginning of the *kali yug*—and the time of Vallabhācārya, who is believed to have died in Banaras in 1530. He informs us in no uncertain terms that Viṣṇusvāmī's position in society was important, even if he is unable (or unwilling) to offer us a very specific description. He says that Viṣṇusvāmī's father, whom he does not name, was minister at the court of an equally anonymous king who, following the example of Yudhiṣṭhira in the prior world-age, subjugated all of India through his virtue. This king was from the south—it is specifically called *drāviḍa deśa*—and we learn all this in the first substantive segment of the text, chapter 2.

Later, in chapter 4, after he has introduced the founders of the other three *sampradāys,* Gadādhar shows how Vallabha succeeded Viṣṇusvāmī and in several respects retraced his steps. As for the situation at court, the scene that played host to Viṣṇusvāmī is replicated now at Vijayanagar—or as the text actually says, Vidyānagar (Knowledge City, a term also in local use in the sixteenth century). Vallabha had sought it out on his travels, seeing it, understandably, as a crucial destination. In 1553, when Gadādhar Bhaṭṭ is said to have written his account, Vijayanagar would have been India's greatest city, and it was remembered as such in certain circles, at least, for centuries afterward. A debate held there would have been a debate that really mattered. This too, some centuries before Jaipur, was literally "The City [*nagara*] of Victory [*vijaya*]."

Here is what happened, according to Gadādhar.[40] Vallabha hears that a disputation is proceeding—a debate about the nature of reality that is carried on between the illusionist Māyāvādīs (i.e., Śaṃkarites) and the Tattvavādīs. "Tattvavāda" is a term that was used particularly in the Mādhva *sampraday* as a term of self-designation. Vallabha approaches the door of the debating hall. King Kṛṣṇadevarāya senses intuitively that someone extraordinary is at the door, opens it, and ushers Vallabha to the seat of greatest honor. The Māyāvādīs, who are on the cusp of victory, go over the top at just that point, defeating the Tattvavādīs. But theirs is a pyrrhic victory, for the newcomer roars out a challenge that proves, in its turn, definitive. His *śuddhādvaita* teaching emerges as the true or pure *advaita* this title is intended to designate—truer even than Viṣṇusvāmī's, as Gadādhar later explains in some manuscripts, since it ceases to be preoccupied with matters of correct behavior *(maryādā)* and focuses entirely on love *(premaiva)*. In that way, one could say, it is not *saguṇ* but rather *nirguṇ* in character, in a new, better-than-Śaṃkara way.[41] Kṛṣṇadevarāya instantly declares Vallabha the victor in the debate he has organized and prepares to honor him with a "showering of gold" *(kanakābhiṣeka)*. Some manuscripts clarify—or in any case, add—that this was an offering of gold equal in weight to that of a man *(tulāpuruṣa)*.[42] Accounts from Vijayanagar itself testify to the fact that Kṛṣṇadevarāya and other Vijayanagar kings did indeed sometimes perform the *tulāpuruṣa* rite, but they make no mention of Vallabha in this or any other connection.[43]

Never mind: the story gets better. The person presiding over the debate, Vyāsatīrtha—generally known in Vijayanagar records as Vyāsarāya—is the head of the Mādhva order, as Vijayanagar accounts confirm.[44] Because of his pugnacious theological tractate the *Nyāyāmṛta*, he had become well known in north India—or at least in Banaras—by the turn of the seventeenth century. In our story, Vyāsatīrtha, seeing the likes of Vallabha, beseeches the younger man to replace him on the *sāmpradāyik* throne, and thereby effectively to accept a spiritual coronation that will parallel the physical one the monarch has just promised. That night, however, Bilvamangal, a crucial figure about whom we will soon have more to say, appears to Vallabha in a dream and makes it clear that the young prodigy has come into this world in the service of a divine plan—not to succeed Madhvācārya but to revive the teaching line established even earlier by Viṣṇusvāmī. In fact, says Bilvamangal, he himself has been waiting seven hundred years to see this moment come to pass, when at last people's attraction to the worship of Śiva—Śaṃkara's project—will be at an end and they will return to "God's path" *(bhagavanmārga)*.[45] This path is, of course, a Vaishnava one and specifically concerns the continuation of a lineage of seven hundred Viṣṇusvāmī acharyas, of whom Bilvamangal had been the last. Upon hearing this, Vallabha awakens and knows that he must refuse Vyāsatīrtha's offer so that, as the dream has foretold, he personally can save four lakhs of souls from perdition and be succeeded by sons who will accomplish the salvation of thirty-two lakh more.

There is more. In certain manuscripts the Lord Viṭṭhal himself—or Viṭṭhalnāth, as Gadādhar calls him, using the name of his own guru, Vallabha's son—emerges from the image he inhabits, this presumably being the *mūrti* installed in the great Viṭṭhal temple of Vijayanagar. Viṭṭhalnāth tells Vallabha that he is about to inherit the mantle of Kṛṣṇadvaipāyana Vyās, Uddhav, and, yes, Bilvamangal, accentuating the contrast that has already been established between the Viṣṇusvāmī/Vallabha *sampradāy* and the other three, who are explicitly grouped as such.[46] This is not the only occasion on which the motif of the four *sampradāys* is worked into the narrative of the *Sampradāyapradīpa*. We meet it in each of the three central chapters (2–4) and in fact it is discussed at greatest length in chapter 3. But this is its most dramatic appearance, and it is the one where we can physically, geographically see how one of the four southern lineages managed to get transplanted onto northern soil. Here the anointing of Vallabha occurs at the very apex of southern culture, yet his future is to be played out in the north.

Vallabha was indeed a southerner. His family spoke Telugu, and some manuscripts of the *Sampradāyapradīpa* were in fact written in the Telugu script. But it is important to see that Vallabha was born between these two realms of north and south. His parents, having settled in Banaras, returned via Prayag to the Telugu country when the news spread that an enemy was advancing on the city: his mother was pregnant. Vallabha's birth, which has a miraculous element, occurred in the Campakāraṇya forest on the southward journey, but as soon as the birth rites had been completed his parents headed back to Banaras. Gadādhar goes on to tell of Vallabha's student days there, and reports that doctrinal concerns were responsible for taking him to the south a second time. He studied assiduously in Banaras, but was unable to find competent teachers for Advaita Vedānta ("illusionism," the text calls it), so he went south, hearing it was influential there. Sure enough, it was, as we have seen, and it was Vallabha's victory over the Māyāvādīs that ultimately led to his formal authorization in matters doctrinal—at Vijayanagar.

When this happens, it is not just a southern event but a global one. As Lord Viṭṭhal authorizes the future success of Vallabha, he does so by saying it will endure for as long as Mount Govardhan—that anchor of

Braj—shall stand. This having been heard, it makes perfect sense that Vallabha's response is to return immediately northward—to Prayag and Banaras before proceeding to a number of other sites including, ultimately, Govardhan itself. The mention of Prayag first and foremost jibes with the historical record. Vallabha did in fact primarily conduct his work from his home at Aḍel, just across the river from Allahabad.

In concluding the fifth and final chapter of his composition, Gadādhar affirms that his major effort as a writer has been to establish the correspondence-cum-lineage between Viṣṇusvāmī and Vallabha. But along the way, interestingly, he offers us a somewhat different overview of the text, one that gives due respect to the figure whom Gadādhar depicts as having been such a powerful intermediary between these two: Bilvamangal. Waxing poetic, he tells us that Viṣṇusvāmī is the cruse for the *Sampradāyapradīpa,* the "Sect-Lamp"; Bilvamangal is the wick; and Vallabha is the flame that emerges to emit its radiance.[47] Or perhaps I have mistranslated. Perhaps the title of the work is better rendered *The Lamp of Sects,* as suggested above, since that four-sect characterization provides the broad terrain over which this particular sect sheds its light. In any case, Gadādhar seems to recognize that Bilvamangal is a key player in ways for which the four-*sampradāy* rubric as such hardly prepares us. What is Bilvamangal doing there? Just who is he?

Gadādhar Bhaṭṭ expects us to ask this question. At the beginning of the third chapter, well before we will meet the Bilvamangal who enters Vallabhācārya's dreams at that crucial moment in the fourth, Gadādhar explains that there is actually no single Bilvamangal, but three. One lived in Kāśī and went on to become the poet Jayadev in a subsequent life.[48] A second Bilvamangal belonged to Orissa *(utkala deśa),* he explains, and is known as the author of the *Aṣṭottara-śloka-saṅkhyātmaka-stotra* (108 Hymns of Praise). Finally there is the most important Bilvamangal of all—*our* Bilvamangal, the wick that made it possible for the oil contained in the ancient southern cruse of Indian civilization to shine forth with new radiance in the north in the sixteenth century.[49]

Indeed, there is some truth to this. Though Gadādhar seems to prefer not to mention the fact, but about which he must have known, Līlāśuk Bilvamangal was the author of the *Śrīkṛṣṇakarṇāmṛta,* a work that served as one of the most significant facilitators of south-north Bhāgavata connections. Starting already in the late fourteenth century it had come to be widely circulated and widely acclaimed in the south—in Kanchipuram, in Kerala, and once again in the Mādhva *sampradāy*.[50] By the early decades of the sixteenth century it was beginning also to have a deep impact farther north. We see its importance in the fact that, according to Gauḍīya accounts, Chaitanya regarded it so highly. As we have seen, the *Caitanyacaritāmṛta* reports that it was one of two texts (with the *Brahma Saṃhitā*) that Chaitanya made a specific attempt to acquire in the course of his own travels to south India, his own *digvijaya*.[51] Could we be seeing in Gadādhar's account of Bilvamangal a reflection of the prestige of the *Śrīkṛṣṇakarṇāmṛta* in Chaitanyite circles and perhaps elsewhere?

Monika Horstmann and Anand Mishra have made it clear just how close the Vallabhites and Gauḍīyas were in some of the theological arguments they put forward. The theologians at the helm of these two communities often found it crucial to respond to difficulties that arose in connection with the same scriptural passages, and did so in ways that were also quite similar.[52] Yet their orientations toward one another—as against their responses to the authoritative texts they shared—tended to be quite different: the Vallabhites were distinctly more defensive than the Chaitanyites. Here the critical term of reference among the Vallabhites was *anyāśraya*, the danger of "taking refuge with another." Vallabha himself had not used this term. What he had done instead was to emphasize the importance of seeking refuge with Krishna alone since all other routes to salvation had been blocked by the magnitude of human sin.[53] Vallabha's bloodline successors and those who surrounded them sectarianized this frame of reference. In their usage the term *anyāśraya* warned of the dangers of responding to the spiritual authority of anyone other than the leaders of the *vallabh kul* itself.

If we think of Gadādhar's text with all this in mind, certain connections suggest themselves. Gadādhar is emphatic in establishing that Bilvamangal belonged to the Viṣṇusvāmī-Vallabha *sampradāy* alone—nobody else's *āśraya*—and he may have wanted to drive this point home to counter the fact that Bilvamangal actually had a much wider currency among Brindāvan's theological elite. Did Rūp Gosvāmī quote frequently from Bilvamangal's *Śrikṛṣṇakarṇāmṛta?* Did the Bengalis report that Chaitanya insisted on having a copy to be made of its first hundred verses? Did certain poems of Sūrdās effectively render its Sanskrit verse into Brajbhasha? Never mind. According to Gadhādhar, Bilvamangal was in reality the man who prepared the ground for the preeminent position that Vallabha would—or at least should—occupy among all the other stakeholders in the four *sampradāys*.

The more one thinks about it, the more one suspects that there may have been a particular anti-Chaitanyite thrust here, and some confirmation is provided by the fact that in one crucial passage in the *Sampradāyapradīpa* Gadādhar demotes Chaitanya from the rank of acharya, leader of one of the original *sampradāys*, to being captain of a subsect, an *upasampradāy*. The same fate befalls Nanda—short for Rāmānand—whom Gadādhar locates within the lineage of Rāmānuja.[54] But Chaitanya's position is especially interesting. Gadādhar aligns him with the Viṣṇusvāmī *sampradāy*, and in so doing connects him with the lineage he himself professes. (As we have seen, Kṛṣṇadās Kavirāj does the same with Vallabha.) It may seem odd that Gadādhar does not stop to explain what Chaitanya's relation would then be to Vallabhācārya, but there may be a simple reason. The passage where Gadādhar makes us aware of Chaitanya's secondary position in the hierarchy of the four *sampradāys* comes at the end of chapter 3, and Vallabha is about to appear immediately afterward, at the beginning of chapter 4. Once he does, as we have seen, the reader learns in no uncertain terms why Vallabha is overwhelmingly the inheritor of Viṣṇusvāmī's true glory. Indeed, by the time chapter 4 is at an end, Chaitanya himself will have ratified that truth by submitting himself to a Vallabha whom he recognizes to be Krishna himself.[55]

In saying all this, I do not mean to imply that Chaitanya is in any direct way a principal focus of the *Sampradāyapradīpa*. Gadādhar also shows how figures connected with the Nimbārka and Rāmānand *sampradāys* are either incorporated or sidelined by the Puṣṭimārg. Yet if we interpret the major role he gives to Bilvamangal as an effort to one-up the Chaitanyites' appropriation of him, then only the Mādhva *sampradāy*, as represented in the person of Vyāsatīrtha, could possibly be seen as looming greater in Gadādhar's thinking. Here too, though, we may be walking in the Gauḍīya shadow—the shadow cast by Viśvanāth Cakravartī and Baladev Vidyābhūṣaṇ as they marshaled the figure of Madhva for their own Chaitanyite purposes in response to Jaisingh's new protocols of religious legitimacy. That would seem to point to the fact that the *Sampradāyapradīpa*, like the interpolated passage in the *Gauragaṇoddeśadīpikā*, was composed in the time of Jaisingh. Yet the earliest manuscript we have (Baroda 9570) says clearly that it was copied somewhat earlier—in V.S. 1739, that is, 1682. This forces us to imagine a somewhat different context.

More of that in a moment, but first back to basics. Because of all the evidence we have reviewed, I do not think it is plausible to accept the date offered by the text itself. One might conjure up a sixteenth-century environment capable of producing a real-life Vallabhite called Gadādhar Bhaṭṭ Dvivedī, though the text's expression of sectarian rivalries with the Chaitanyites, Nimbārkīs, and Rāmānandīs makes it far easier to place in a subsequent period; yet it is very difficult to conceive of such a Gadādhar as living in Brindāvan, if so. As we saw in chapter 4, the Vallabhite purchase on the place clearly known by that name, both then and now, was at best tentative in 1553. As for anything having to do with Viṣṇusvāmī, the historical record is blank. The well-known Braj scholar Prabhudayāl Mītal claimed that the Sanāḍhya Brahmin family who now serve the image of Krishna installed in Bhagavāndās's Haridev temple at Govardhan—not the original *mūrti*—belong to the Viṣṇusvāmī *sampradāy* by virtue of an initiation that occurred in the fifteenth century, but they themselves possess no detailed knowledge of him. They speak of having descended through fifty-nine generations from a certain Keśavācārya, whom Bhagavāndās patronized, but this genealogically specific memory seems only loosely connected with any having to do with Viṣṇusvāmī.[56] In the end, one wonders whether they have drawn on the Vallabhites' knowledge of Viṣṇusvāmī to claim a sectarian grounding of their own, thereby justifying a well-entrenched but very local family tradition in terms that would echo in broader terms.

As we have learned, certain Vallabhites have on occasion also felt moved to rewrite history, or at least to consolidate what was remembered in rubrics of their own construction. This sometimes happened for laudable theological reasons, and these have helped justify a tradition of closely guarded and carefully preserved liturgical practice whose benefits extend far beyond the confines of the Puṣṭimārg itself. But the narrative accounts that emerged from such efforts to construct a usable past cannot be taken at face value historically. This is the sort of terrain in which we find ourselves if we study the manuscript records associated with the sectarian records bearing most closely on the *Sampradāyapradīpa*.

Two documents must be reckoned with, both of them far better known in Vallabhite circles than the *Sampradāyapradīpa* itself. The *Caurāsī*

Baiṭhak Carit, depicting in order eight-four places where Vallabhācārya stopped in the course of his supposed pilgrimages, is probably to be dated not to the seventeenth century, as most Puṣṭimārgī scholars believe, but to the mid-eighteenth, judging by the dates of the works that it itself quotes.[57] Its authorship is attributed to Gokulnāth, obviously in an effort to link this text to the earlier "Eighty-Four," but that seems most unlikely. Similarly, there is nothing to suggest that the memorial structures honoring these *baiṭhaks* can be traced to a pre-eighteenth-century date. As for the second document that concerns us, the *Vallabhadigvijaya,* it too must have been written much more recently than the date claimed in the text itself (1601). The *Vallabhadigvijaya,* which sets out the idea that Vallabha accomplished three "world-conquering" journeys and gives details about what he included in each, was probably not written much before the turn of the twentieth century, when it appeared in print. Again we are led to believe that it is to be associated with a major early figure in the tradition—this time Yadunāth, one of Gokulnāth's brothers—but there is no manuscript to support such an idea, as there certainly would have been if this were true. In fact, no known manuscripts predate its appearance in print.[58] I believe the *Sampradāyapradīpa,* though older than either of these, partakes in the same pattern.

When Nārāyaṇ Śāstrī, principal scholar in residence at the Śrīnāthjī temple at Nāthdvārā, tells the story of how Vallabha assumed the mantle of Viṣṇusvāmī, with Bilvamangal bridging the gap of seven hundred years that separates these two figures—a fact he proudly proclaims—he does so with great relish. Like the Gauḍīyas, Nārāyaṇ Śāstrī clearly savors the fact that he is reporting something more than run-of-the-mill history—something verging on the miraculous.[59] And yet, the tale he tells is simultaneously the community's record of itself, and on that account, from his point of view, not to be dismissed as mere fiction. There is no room in Nārāyaṇ Śāstrī's world for any doubts about this seven-hundred-year hiatus—or if doubts exist, it is a welcome test of faith to overcome them, just the sort of move beyond the workaday world of commerce and production that brings pilgrims to Nāthdvārā in the first place. But it was exactly such doubts, focused on the veracity of the story of Vallabha's gold-coronation at the hands of Kṛṣṇadevarāya, that seem to have prompted Kaṇṭhamaṇi Śāstrī and Jaṭāśaṃkar Śāstrī, in reaction, to produce editions and translations of the *Sampradāyapradīpa* that might pass muster in a changed scholarly climate, with a serious introduction and variant manuscript readings and all. Indeed, Kaṇṭhamaṇi Śāstrī was a great scholar, but the faith position he set out to prove was clear. G. H. Bhatt was a different sort of person altogether.

I do think it is possible to conjure up a time and place when the *Sampradāyapradīpa* could plausibly have been written. I have in mind the second half of the seventeenth century, when talk of the *cār sampradāy* was definitely on the rise, as we have seen in the elaboration this motif received at the hands of Rāghavdās. It was then—in 1682—that the first known copy of this scantily attested document appears. I am intrigued by the notion that the *Sampradāyapradīpa* might have been composed some years after the destruction of the temple of Keśavdev in Mathura in 1670, when many of the great deities of sixteenth-century Brindavan were in hiding or on the run. This was a time when the Vallabhites had to make urgent appeals for royal support in a way they never had before. Might the account of Vallabha's victory at Vijayanagar (or as the text says, Vidyānagar) have been intended to persuade some Rajput king to follow suit and acclaim the progeny of Viṭṭhalnāth? A bit of gold wouldn't be out of line either. As for status, to hear the *Sampradāyapradīpa* tell it, a decision to accept Vallabha's primacy would enable his patron-devotee to climb to the pinnacle of the structure that made Vaishnavism what it was—the new security, the new dispensation, the four *sampradāys*.

What evidence do we have for any of this? Nothing direct, to be sure. But to accept this view of the text would put to rest some otherwise troubling worries. First of all, we would no longer have to wonder what a committed, inner-circle Vallabhite was doing in Brindavan in the year 1553. As we have seen, extant Mughal *farmāns* give us no reason to expect that Vallabhites lived there, and there is nothing in the poems of Harirāmvyās, who clearly did live there, to suggest anything different. He mentions Kṛṣṇadās, to be sure, but almost always in connection with Govardhan, and as we have seen, the Vallabhite *vārtā* on Kṛṣṇadās explicitly says that no Vallabhites lived in Brindavan.[60] Why then might the *Sampradāyapradīpa* claim this place as its provenance? Maybe the mention of Brindavan to some western audience was intended to draw on the prestige that had emanated from the built Brindavan of the sixteenth century. Maybe Brindavan was intended to certify the prestigious Braj to which a monarch would be connecting himself if he embraced the Puṣṭimārg.

Initially the author's claim that he was writing "in the vicinity of Śrī Govindadev" *(śrīgovindadeva-sāṃnidhye)* might seem odd. After all, historically speaking, this was the greatest monument of the Chaitanya *sampradāy*. Indeed the Baroda 1580 manuscript omits the phrase, perhaps for just this reason. But maybe the mention of Govindadev in the colophon was intended to strengthen the sense of religious/political authority about which we were just speaking, as suggested by Akbar's *farmān* of 1598, in which Abu'l Fazl made it clear that Govindadev had become the central point of organization for all of the empire's religious philanthropies in Braj.[61] If heard from far enough away, this invoking of Govindadev might have conveyed something about proximity to religious and political power that eluded a specifically Gauḍīya meaning. In Brindavan itself, though, that would have been unlikely. The Gadādhar Bhaṭṭ who really did live not far away was certainly known to be a Chaitanyite.[62]

Then there is the matter of the four *sampradāys* themselves. If the *Sampradāyapradīpa* was intended to be read somewhere in Rajasthan circa 1670, the author of the text might well count on the fact that this rubric would be easily understood. Rāghavdās's deployment of it when he wrote his Dādūpanthī *Bhaktamāl,* probably in 1660, suggests that the Rāmānandīs had by then put it forward in a public way; he was already building on that to advance his idea of the *cār panth*. Sundardās's use of the motif of the four *sampradāys* in the late seventeenth century suggests the same sort of familiarity. So if the man who calls himself Gadākhya was writing in the 1670s or so, he could comfortably appeal to a motif that already had fair currency in Āmer and regions farther west—and, like the Dādūpanthīs, use it to his own purposes.

Other facts also fall into place. First and foremost, as we have seen, the oldest known copy of the *Sampradāyapradīpa* dates only to 1682, and its manuscript history is otherwise sparse. If the *Sampradāyapradīpa* was actually composed only a decade or so before that date, the prior silence would no longer be a mystery. Second and similarly, the oldest text in which a quotation of the *Sampradāyapradīpa* has come to light is Śrīśa Bhaṭṭ's commentary on Vallabha's *Jalabheda,* which dates to the eighteenth century.[63] So far as I know, moreover, the *Sampradāyapradīpa* is not cited outside the Puṣṭimārg until the twentieth century. Third, if this was really a sixteenth-century text, it would have been almost alone in announcing its subject with the term *sampradāy*. Later on, however, one gets such texts as the *Sampradāyabodhinī* of Manohardās, the guru of Priyādās, which we have mentioned in passing. It was written in 1719.[64] Even at that point in time a title beginning with the word *sampradāy* was rare, as the *New Catalogus Catalogorum* makes evident; earlier, if we take away the *Sampradāyapradīpa,* it was nonexistent. The only precedent that has come to my attention is Vedantadeśika's fourteenth-century *Sampradāyapariśuddhi,* written in Maṇipravāḷa.[65]

Finally, there is the whole matter of Kṛṣṇadevarāya. Doubtless he was to some extent known in northern India even in the sixteenth century—the *Baburnāma* refers to him[66]—but a century later, after the fall of Vijayanagar and with a sudden feeling of Mughal threat, this king might have seemed even more magnificent to some. And there is the connected motif of Vallabha's *digvijay.* Might it have had a particular poignancy in a time when the deities of Brindavan had begun to travel on quite different journeys of their own, journeys of exile rather than victory? In Braj, these were the unsettling days when Aurangzeb deposed his father and killed his brother Dara Shukoh, when the Jāṭs in response rebelled, when Abdunnabi Khan reasserted Mughal control as military commander of Mathura, and when Śivājī's Maratha forces struggled to overturn Kachvaha-Mughal hegemony in the heartland. In the aftermath, in 1670, Aurangzeb gave orders that the great temple to Keśavdev in Mathura should be destroyed. Shyam Manohar Goswami, the greatest living scholar of the Puṣṭimārg, has suggested that the *Sampradāyapradīpa*'s "world victory" motif might have been felt persuasively hopeful in times of divine wandering such as these.[67]

Mughal Bhakti and the Wider Meaning of Fourness

For all of the above reasons I think we should look with suspicion on the idea that either of the documents that claim a Brindavan origin for the idea of the four *sampradāys* in the course of the sixteenth century is to be believed. Both the Gauḍīya articulation of this idea and its much more elaborate Vallabhite cousin are far more likely to have been created at a later point in time. The jockeying for position that one saw between bhakti communities of the late seventeenth and early eighteenth centuries caused the Gauḍīyas and Vallabhites to invent ways to situate themselves in what was by then becoming a grand narrative of the bhakti movement south to north. That narrative seems first to have been put forward by the Rāmānandīs, just as its best-known articulation—Nābhādās's—would have led us to believe all along. The systematizing proclivities that were embedded in Dādūpathī culture from its earliest days also played an important role. Just as the Dādūpathīs had been the first to organize bhakti poetry rigorously by theme (*ang*, literally the limb of a larger whole), so did they go to work on bhakti history. It was Rāghavdās who gave us the great compendium in 1660, using Nābhā's idea of the four *sampradāys* as the frame that would enable him to turn chaos into order. He extended Nābhā's idea of the past into his own present day, allowing the movement of bhakti to keep on moving.

This does not mean that Nābhādās's *Bhaktamāl* and the circle of works it directly inspired were the only means by which later generations became acquainted with the idea of the four *sampradāys*. Far from it. If we take what we now know and return to that seminal essay of Bharatendu Harishchandra called "Vaiṣṇav Sarvasva" (see Chapter 3), it becomes immediately clear that Nābhādās's *Bhaktamāl,* though important, is only half the story. The other half involves the *Sampradāyapradīpa*. Not that Harishchandra cites it specifically—instead he names as his source a text he calls the *Viṣṇusvāmīcaritāmṛta*—but most of the details that form his narrative in "Vaiṣṇav Sarvasva" are to be found precisely there. I have not yet been able to locate a copy of the *Viṣṇusvāmīcaritāmṛta* itself, but in one way or another it must have been abstracted from or even equivalent to the *Sampradāyapradīpa*.[68]

Something similar happened in Gauḍīya circles. Once they regarded themselves as belonging to the four-*sampradāy* narrative, thanks to Madhva, they too provided an independent point of access to it in the nineteenth, twentieth, and even twenty-first centuries. Consider, for example, *Hinduism Today,* the energetic magazine that proclaims on the cover of every issue that it is "affirming Sanatana Dharma and recording the modern history of a billion-strong global religion in renaissance." In the summer of 2008, *Hinduism Today* included a page explaining the "Five Schools of Vaishnavism."[69] These were indeed the four *sampradāys,* plus one: Shri Vaishnava, Sanakādi Vaishnava, Brahma Vaishnava, Rudra Vaishnava, and (nota bene!) Gauḍīya Vaishnava. Here the difficult pairing of Madhva and Chaitanya is left behind, but the new five-part formulation suggests how important it was that someone tried to make it work earlier on—and failed. This provides a new solution to the problem of connecting the Gauḍīyas with the four *sampradāys*. For centuries theoreticians of Hindu religion have played with the category of the four Vedas, proposing a fifth to account for a body of text that was difficult to encompass within the original formulation. Now, it seems, this has happened with the idea of the four *sampradāys*, as well.

But what provided the impetus for this Vaishnava idea in the first place? At the general level of motive, the cause is not too hard to guess. In India, as elsewhere in the world, the number four has two fundamental associations. First, it suggests stability. One shove is enough to upend a tripod, but something with four legs is far harder to overturn. Second, the number four has a cosmic ring. It conjures up the four points of the compass that give orientation to all of space. In Indic systems of reference, these two meanings recombine in a series of related constructs that suggest both stability and cosmic reach. There are four divisions of time, the *yugas;* four divisions of remembered speech, the Vedas; and four aspects of a given divinity—the four *vyūhas* of Vishnu and the four faces of Brahmā or of Shiva's ineffable emblem, the *linga*. Finally we have the four divisions of social classification, the *varṇas,* which depict society as an internally differentiated but well-integrated whole. In the same way the four aims of human life, the *puruṣārthas,* chart out the diverging realms of human aspiration while implying that they belong together as a single field, a single cosmos of individual possibilities that derive much of their legitimacy from the fact that they exist in relation to one another.

Thus the idea of four has many resonances, but two "fours" are of particular importance when one asks where the idea of the four *sampradāys* might have come from. One is a foursome that might not have been anticipated on the basis of the foregoing summary: the Sufi practice of tracing individual orders *(silsilās)* to one of the four Caliphs or one of the four sages *(pīr)*. The latter include Muhammad, Ali, Husain, and Hasan al-Basri. Mūbad Shāh makes reference to this practice in the *Dabistān-i Mazāhib* when he speaks about the sorts of things Sufis talk about when they meet. He says that the Sufis' interest derives in part from their awareness that *saṃnyāsīs* and yogis (i.e., Nāths) are preoccupied with such things, even though he does not at that point explain how they use the number four.[70] Given the importance of Sufi orders at the time of which we are speaking and given the fact that so many Rāmānandīs (who give us our first evidence of the idea of the four Vaishnava *sampradāys*) were ascetics—people who as a class were depicted as conversing with Sufis and might have been interested in their forms of organization—one wonders whether the vectors of influence might also have gone the other way, from Sufis to Vaishnavas. In any case we need to be aware of the extent to which the number four was not just a Hindu preoccupation, but served as a principle of organization in Islamic environments, as well: four Caliphs, four sages, four schools of law according to the Sunnis, and four categories of scripture, sequentially arranged—*toret* (Torah), *zabur* (Psalms), *injil* (New Testament), and Qur'an. The concept of the four *sampradāys* may have been born out of a desire to appeal to a notion of scriptural, legal, and organizational authority that would sound plausible not just to Hindus but also to Muslims. Gurinder Singh Mann has argued that this may have been a major reason why Sikhs initially organized their collection of bhakti poetry into four *pothīs* (books)—this in the 1570s—although he concedes that the notion of the four Vedas may also have played a role.[71]

Returning to the Hindu side of the fence—a fence with many holes—there is a final trajectory to be explored as we look beyond the world of Vaishnavism for a context that might have made an idea of the four *sampradāys* seem appealing. Here the object of our curiosity is not a paradigm of fourness articulated by the Muslim "other" but one engendered by that other great Vaishnava "other," the Shaivas. Could it be that the idea of the four *maṭhs* supposedly established by Śaṃkara was what provided the most crucial motivation for Vaishnavas to develop their own idea of the four *sampradāys?*

A confrontation between Shaiva and Vaishnava ascetics and intellectuals is often thought to have played a major role in establishing the primacy of the four *sampradāys* in the time of Jaisingh, and tensions between Shaiva and Vaishnava institutions may have been on the rise in the years leading up to the moment when Jaisingh ascended the throne of Āmer. The received tradition is that when the Vaishnava ascetics gathered in Jaipur in 1734 under the banner of the four *sampradāys,* they were following a precedent that had been set in a conference they convened in Brindavan in about 1713.[72] That gathering, in turn, had as its object the formation of an alliance that could stand up to the Daśanāmīs, who had apparently coalesced into a Shaiva-dominated order of ascetics in the course of the sixteenth and seventeenth centuries.[73] As such, it seems, the

Daśanāmīs were able to join combat with the Vaishnava *vairāgīs* in Ayodhya with a success that deeply concerned those who gathered at Brindavan. These Shaiva ascetics had modes of organization that enabled them to make common cause against the Vaishnavas and defeat them when conflicts arose. The Vaishnavas were therefore in need of establishing similar ties, and the rubric of the four *sampradāys* was adopted to supply the organizational clarity that would enable them to do so.

Thus the story. The difficulty with this reconstruction of how the four *sampradāys* might have emerged as a single, institutionally effective formation is that it is not based on documents that would have been more or less contemporary with the establishing of such a fighting federation in 1713 or so, but on reports that came several decades later. It is possible, therefore, that this Shaivite "other" was invented after the fact. We know that the idea of the four Vaishnava *sampradāys* existed a century prior to this meeting in 1713, but we do not know whether it had anything to do with a desire to "match" the Śaṃkarite Shaivas, the Daśanāmīs. Nābhādās's peaceable integration of Śaṃkara into his narrative sequence would not suggest any such thing—and, by the way, he makes no attempt to associate Śaṃkara with monastic orders.[74] The Rāmānandīs' story of how they constituted themselves at Galtā also calls this narrative into question. Shaivas were at issue, but the opponents in question were Nāth Yogīs, represented by Tārānāth, not *saṃnyāsīs*.

And yet there is something intriguing here, and it takes us back ultimately to the south. We do know that a concept of *sampradāys* was indeed coming into Shaivite usage at just this time, and that it was parsed out according to a four-part scheme. In current usage these four Shaiva *sampradāys* are lineages ascribed to each Daśanāmī ascetic upon initiation; they correspond to the four *maṭhs* that nowadays provide the basic taxonomy for Shaiva asceticism in general. In turn these *maṭhs*, one at each point of the compass, are said to have been established by Śaṃkara himself, and each is held to be associated with a particular tradition of received doctrine *(āmnāya)*.[75] So to modern-day understanding it would seem plain that when the Vaishnavas of the sixteenth century came up with their idea of the four *sampradāys*, they were simply copying an idea that was well known in Shaiva circles.

The historical facts, however, prove different. In a remarkable tome, Matthew Clark has shown that the rubric of the *maṭhāmnāyas* determining the affiliations of Shaiva ascetics and the ancillary idea of four *sampradāys* characterizing each of these respectively (Kīṭavāra, Bhogavāra, Ānandavāra, or Bhūrivāra) can only be traced back to the late sixteenth or early seventeenth century—the very period when we get our first evidence of the idea of the four Vaishnava *sampradāys*.[76] The older tantric notion of the four *āmnāyas*, each corresponding to a point of the compass, may well have been known in royal circles at Vijayanagar, but there is no evidence that the Srngeri *maṭh*, which mattered greatly to the earliest Vijayanagar kings, made this idea its own until sometime near the end of the sixteenth century. Perhaps this happened exactly at the point when Kṛṣṇadevarāya's great interest in Śrī Vaishnavism diminished the position of authority the Srngeri *maṭh* had enjoyed until then. In any case, it was then and not before that the large Srngeri temple to Śaṃkara was built by a patron whose name, rather unusually, we do not know from an inscription. Was it perhaps constructed by the *maṭh* itself?[77] Similarly, was the notion that Śaṃkara established a global network of *maṭhs* anchored at the four points of the compass, one of them Srngeri, an attempt by the abbots of Srngeri to project an image of universal spiritual governance that would appeal in new ways to monarchs like Kṛṣṇadevarāya or his son Acyutarāya—kings so eager to advertise their global sway?

So far we do not know. It is clear that Vyāsatīrtha's pupil and biographer Somanātha, at least, thought there was an atmosphere of contestation between the Advaitan and Mādhvite monastic communities at that time.[78] Was it political and not just doctrinal? That seems likely, and if so, the author of the *Sampradāyapradīpa* is correct in staging the intellectual battle that Vallabha waged against the "illusionist" Śaṃkarites precisely at court—*the* court. Of course, Gadādhar Bhaṭṭ has no interest in pondering whether the idea of the four *sampradāys* owed its origins to anything Shaivite, but he does seem to pick up on the historically correct memory that the earlier Shaiva leanings of the Vijayanagar rulers took a Vaishnava turn under Kṛṣṇadevarāya, even if he stops short of identifying the once-regnant Māyāvādīs as Shaivas specifically. And somewhere in his consciousness lies the memory that the Mādhva community had a special role to play in this drama. Perhaps such a memory was accessible to the Gauḍīyas as well when they mounted their campaign to establish a new form of legitimacy for themselves as participants in the four-*sampradāy* network, using the name of Madhva to do so. In the *Sampradāyapradīpa*, Vallabha demurs when Vyāsatīrtha asks him to take over his own role as *rājguru,* but this is just the sort of succession that politically minded Chaitanyites were later to claim. So there are several possible echoes between the memory of Vijayanagar and the new challenges that Gauḍīyas and Vallabhites met in the second half of the seventeenth century and later.

What would have kept those echoes echoing? Here we must consider what happened in purely intellectual circles as the sixteenth century progressed. Madhva's theological positions, especially as reformulated by Vyāsatīrtha in his *Nyāyāmṛta,* became a sort of cause célèbre among Advaitans, provoking rebuttals from philosophers south and north—men the stature of Appaya Dīkṣita in the Tamil country and Madhusūdan Sarasvatī in Banaras, as well as their pupils and associates. Part of this involved intellectual issues per se, of course, but it is important also to consider two crucial matters of context. First, threats to the substantial tradition of Vijayanagar patronage for Advaitan causes seemed to be posed by Vyāsatīrtha's ascent at court. This would have been a matter of great concern to thinkers associated with the Shaiva *maṭhs* of the south. Second, the forceful articulation of a Dvaita point of view by Vyāsatīrtha—doubtless repeated by Dvaita theorists living elsewhere, for example the Śeṣas of Banaras—caused Advaitan thinkers to circle the wagons and attempt to articulate a unified, "syndicated" Advaitan position, as if to fend off a new kind of threat from the outside world.[79]

Could it be that such a threat to hegemonic Shaiva Advaita was posed not just by the elevation of Vaishnavas over Advaitans at Vijayanagar—first the Mādhvites, then the Śrī Vaishnavites—but also, later, by close Vaishnava connections to the Mughal state? I am thinking of the new axes of patronage that were fast developing in Brindavan in the second half of the sixteenth century and imagining that, as their influence spread eastward in the Bengal campaign led by Mānsingh in the late 1580s, an Advaitan Brahmin establishment in Banaras, wary of such developments, might have found a way to address this anxiety, in part, by attacking Vyāsatīrtha. Here was an outspoken theist who could be opposed without potentially offending Kachvaha-Mughal sensibilities. As for themselves, they largely stood for quite a different approach to Hindu-Muslim dialogue—the sort of nondualism that would later appeal to Dara Shukoh.[80] Again, the hope of patronage and the fear of penalty may be lurking in the background. We know that the Advaitan thinker Kavīndrācārya Sarasvatī was later to receive two Festschrifts from his colleagues when he managed to persuade the emperor Shah Jahan to rescind the pilgrim tax on Banaras.[81]

These are just speculations. A more direct response to the doctrines of Rūp, Sanātan, and Jīv on the part of the Advaitans based at the temple of Śiva Viśvanāth in Banaras would certainly be more convincing proof of such a mindset.[82] *Yavanas* and *mlecchas* are rarely mentioned in the Sanskrit philosophical literature, but Mughal involvement with the various *'ulema* and independent traditions of Islamic scholarship in India might well have made a concerted response to theistic monotheism seem urgent on the part of thoughtful, well-placed Brahmins. The presumption of a single, distinct, all-knowing deity was certainly influential in a way that it had not been in Indian theological debates up to that time. Advaitans almost never addressed this fact by speaking to or of Muslim intellectuals directly, but it is hard to think they could have ignored them, especially when Vaishnavas and Muslims were making common cause in the conduct of state.[83]

As we saw in Chapter 3 and have seen in a different way throughout this chapter, it was apparently in just this environment—the Mughal/Kachvaha environment—that the idea of the four *sampradāys* germinated and grew. Given all that had happened institutionally and theologically in the late days of the Vijayanagar empire, and assuming at least a vague awareness of these developments in places like Banaras and Puri, it comes as no surprise that Madhva and Rāmūnuja figured importantly in the new concept of Vaishnavism that came forward in the concept of the four *sampradāys*. The Mādhvite Vyāsatīrtha had engineered a major success in Vijayanagar itself; King Saluva Narsiṃha's Śrī Vaishnava administrator Kantāṭai Rāmūṉuja Ayyaṅkār had done the same at Tirupati; and by the mid-sixteenth century the two sites were closely intertwined.[84] But it is striking that when a unifying formulation was attempted, as it had been for Advaita by the Banaras intellectuals, this shared vision of Vaishavaness comprised not only the Mādhva and Śrī Vaishnava elements but a larger, foursquare whole. Perhaps the reason was that this happened not in the south, with its close connection to the groups involved, but in the north, where a more general vision might naturally have taken root. It was there, with the dramatic rise of Mughal rule, that new Islamic institutional and intellectual pressures exerted themselves on Brahmin theory and practice.

And it was also there that the state reached out impressively for administrative and intellectual contributions from those same Brahmin literati.

At what level, then, did the four-*sampradāy* Vaishnava synthesis appear? Apparently it was initially not in the scholastic world of Brahminism—the sort of circles that surrounded Jaisingh—nor even in the less *śāstrik* diction of a work like the *Sampradāyapradīpa*. It happened instead at a more vernacular level, both literally and figuratively: among the Rāmānandīs, where Brahmins did not call all the shots. Yet the Muslim-Vaishnava "concordat" was relevant at all levels, and it wasn't always "assimilation at a distance," as Muzaffar Alam has so wisely described it in a somewhat different context.[85] In the world of everyday bhakti we seem to meet a more intimate association among artisans, tradesmen, and farmers. Dādū and Kabīr, respectively a cotton carder and a weaver, were in important ways both Muslim and Vaishnava, and both registers were important to Nānak, a *khatrī*. We also meet this sense of mutual solidarity in the more elevated Vaishnava world symbolized by Brindavan. There the Brajbhasha poet Rahīm becomes relevant—Abdurrahīm Khānkhānā, the high official in Akbar's court who was simultaneously a Muslim and a poet of Krishna—and it is hard to overstate the importance of the administrative "Sultanate" consciousness that helped steer Rūp and Sanātan into their new roles as elite Vaishnavas dwelling in Braj. Rām and Sītā were also on the scene. The Rām-Rasik movement initiated by the Rāmānandī ascetic Agradās made connections with the imaginative world that Tulsīdās projected in his *Rāmcaritmanas;* and Tulsīdās, for his part, composed his masterpiece in a genre—the *premākhyān*—that had served as a premier vehicle for Sufi self-expression on the part of poets like Qutban, Manjhan, and Muhammad Jāyasī. He never mentioned them, but clearly, they were there.[86]

The Mughal ecumene also made it possible for the *bhaktamāl* genre, where the idea of the four *sampradāys* first emerged and where there was an explicit sense of a shared bhakti tradition, to bleed over into the world of the *tazkirā*, the principal Persian genre of poetic memory. We have seen this in the case of Rām Sonī "Navanīt." By the time of Jaisingh II a man with the name Brindāvandās, dubbed "Khwushgū," who lived in the Mughal capital at Delhi, could be so deeply involved in the production of *tazkirās* that the collection of biographical notices he produced would become the standard work for the school in which he participated, the one devoted to his Muslim poet-guru Bīdil.[87] To that extent did the Krishnaite and Persianate poetic sensibilities reinforce one another. It is not that the *bhaktamāl* and *tazkirā* genres were the same—they had separate histories and emphases—but they shared a common concern for the mixed legacy of poetry and biography, especially in a religious frame, which meant they could occasionally converge. Particularly because poetic inspiration was a crucial element in the perceived history of bhakti, this was no small thing. I have even wondered whether the prestige of *tazkirās* in the world that Nābhādās inhabited, with the great shrine of Mu'īnuddīn Chishtī just down the road in Ajmer, may have had something to do with the composition of his *Bhaktamāl* in the first place—as a sort of counter-*tazkirā*.[88]

Tales of the "victory tours" of Chaitanya and Vallabha also suggest resonances between Muslims and Vaishnavas, though in a rather different way. In this case the Yavanas are almost invisible and we feel instead the impress of two deeply Indic paradigms: the royal *rājasūya* sacrifice, in which the "quarters of space" are symbolically secured, and the pilgrimage journey primarily undertaken by Hindu ascetics, which encapsulated symbolically all four corners of the known world. Since the fourteenth century, Śaṃkara's *digvijays* had become the model for such victory tours, and philosophical/theological debates *(śāstrārtha)* had become one of its main features. Hence it is unsurprising that the conquest of Śaṃkara—that is, of the *māyāvādī* view he was held to have espoused—should have become a major purpose of the *digviyaya* put forward in the *Sampradāyapradīpa*. Yet once again, when we consider the actual fields of force that shaped the Deccan when Chaitanya (and perhaps even Vallabha) traveled there, a good bit more seems to be involved. Vijayanagar's fifteenth- and sixteenth-century monarchs wore *kabāyi* and *kuḷḷāyi*—Persianate garments.[89] They employed Muslim horsemen, apparently had no objection to mosques being built in the capital city, and allotted a portion of that city to the population who would have worshiped there.

A text like the *Sampradāyapradīpa* may have aimed itself primarily at success within a Vaishnava marketplace strictly speaking. It may indeed have thought of Vyāsatīrtha as Vallabha's chief competitor—or Chaitanya, as we have seen—and made it all play out within earshot of a very Hindu king. But it also appealed to a vision of truly cosmic competence, and it is hard to think that Muslim/Rajput political formations could have seemed irrelevant to that larger sphere, even if they did not manifest themselves explicitly in the text. To be sure, that text presents us with an alternative reality, a purely Hindu one, but its scale may have seemed necessary as an answer to what the Mughals were able to achieve. We know that Vallabhites were not indifferent to those achievements: on occasion they tried to promote their cause at Akbar's court. We have guessed that the *Sampradāyapradīpa* emerged in a later era when important confrontations had arisen, the period following the destruction of the Keśavdev temple in Mathura, and these may have added further luster—by contrast—to Vijayanagar's remembered glories. By mobilizing the *digvijaya* genre, the *Sampradāyapradīpa* used the memory of Vijayanagar to appeal to a conceptual universe that embraced Indianness as a whole. It was Victory City writ large, and the *Sampradāyapradīpa*'s pitch was that the four *sampradāys,* with Vallabha victorious over all, could make that city's legacy live forever. This, by implication, is what could happen in the city of whatever king might embrace Vallabha's community as primus inter pares in matters of religion.

Splendid as it was, though, this City-of-God account provided only a second-order articulation of a four-*sampraday* ideal that was already current. The *Sampradāyapradīpa* hoped to sound knowledgeable about the intellectual world inhabited by figures such as Madhusūdan Sarasvatī and his Banaras cohort—an aura its author sought to appropriate—but the primary level at which ideals of shared Vaishnava identity had been articulated through the notion of the four *sampradāys* actually lay much closer to the ground. In the writings of Anantadās and Nābhādās we see clearly how this was so. When these two Rāmānandīs appealed to the concept of the four *sampradāys,* which they did in such different ways, they were merely adding value to a sense of the commonwealth of bhakti that they articulated in the main bulk of what they wrote. And they did not invent this conviction of bhakti belonging out of whole cloth. In a more limited form, we also meet it in compositions attributed to the very poet-saints they praised. In a Sūrdās *pad* that circulated in the sixteenth century, for example, the poet asks the Lord to enroll him among those to whose rescue he has come, and the example he offers as being closest to his own is that of Nāmdev.[90] Likewise Dādū (though he was ignored by Nābhādās and Anantadās) was deeply aware of Kabīr, so it made sense for his disciples to call him a latter-day Kabīr. Ravidās appears also to have been conscious of Kabīr.[91] As for the broader picture, it is important to remember that an early anthologist working in the Kachvaha city of Fatehpur in 1582 was pleased to set Sūrdās, whom we normally think of as primarily a *saguṇ* poet, alongside such *nirguṇ* stalwarts as Kabīr, Kānhā, and Ravidās.[92] And many other anthologists, also bridging the *saguṇ/nirguṇ* gap, similarly projected an image of a shared bhakti world.[93]

Not all anthologists agreed with this policy. Two of the greatest anthologies, those of the Sikhs and the Dādūpathīs, were specifically *nirguṇ,* but they too envisioned a liturgical universe that went well beyond the poets of their own specific *panths.* Nābhādās, of course, went further, envisioning a wide world of Hindu bhaktas that seemed to exclude, ironically, only Nānak and Dādū themselves. Nābhā's text in turn became the model for many others: the Brindavan-style *Bhaktirasabodhinī* of Priyādās, the Persian *Bhaktamāl* of Rām Sonī, the Bengali *Bhaktamāl* of Kṛṣṇadās Bābā, the Marathi *Bhaktavijaya* of Mahīpati, the Urdu *Bhaktamāl* of Tulsīrām, and many more, right down to the present day. Indeed the Sikhs and Dādūpathīs come on board. We also have the *Sikhāṅ dī Bhagatmālā,* in Punjabi, and, as well we know, the elaborately systematic Dādūpathī *Bhaktamāl* of Rāghavdās.[94]

We cannot fail to be impressed by just how northern this explosion of texts was, even as Nābhādās genuflected so pointedly toward the south. A remarkable set of poetic anthologies and collective biographies had actually been constructed in the south—by Śrī Vaishnavas, Shaiva Siddhāntins, Vīraśaivas, Mahānubhāvs, even Jains—but the anthologizers and hagiographers who gave us the notion of the four *sampradāys* seem to have been entirely unaware of them. For Nābhādās and Priyādās the south was an ideal instead—an imagined entity, far more a mirror than a quarry. Their idea of the south may have been suggested by the presence of actual southern migrants in the north, especially Bhaṭṭs of various stripes, but if it was, we have no specific indication of that fact. Nābhā lists a number of Bhaṭṭs, but we never hear of a southern connection. Moreover, so far as we can see, neither these Bhaṭṭs nor any other immigrants to the north were the people who first went to work articulating the idea of an overarching, historically progressive Vaishnava bhakti through the rubric of the four *sampradāys.*

No, the idea of the four *sampradāys* was northern, and within that northern span it stemmed from Galtā more than from Brindavan. To be sure, Brindavan emerged as the enduring sign of a newly shared religious consciousness, as so forcefully claimed by Harirāmvyās and the

Rādhāvallabhīs, but perhaps because Brindavan made its own statement about the ingathering of bhaktas, it did not require a vision of continental comprehensiveness in the same way Galtā did. Only later did it too have to be enmeshed in the foursquare universe of the four *sampradāys*—only when its own imperially guaranteed position of privilege had begun to falter in the wake of uncomfortable political strains. Then the protection of Rajput rulers farther west was required in a new way. At that point new formulations of the four *sampradāys* had to kick in—from the Vallabhites on the one hand, from the Gauḍīyas on the other. These added new elements of ornament and expanse to the idea of the four *sampradāys* that had emerged in and around Galtā thanks to the Rāmānandīs and their Dādūpathī neighbors.

Jaisingh played his part, too. While his attempt to institutionalize the concept of the four *sampradāys* did not entirely succeed, we do find that a full century after his death self-proclaimed representatives of the four *sampradāys* still found it possible to act in concert when confronted by newly influential Shaivas in the Kachvaha court. They also sometimes positioned themselves on this high *sāmpradāyik* ground when articulating their authority before the British resident.[95] British officials in Rajasthan became familiar with the rubric of the four *sampradāys* and apparently accepted its basis in custom and legal practice—a recognition that then spread to other parts of British India and complemented what H. H. Wilson had been learning as he consulted with a group of Indian scholar-advisers in Banaras and Calcutta, especially in regard to the *Bhaktamāl*. He personally owned a copy.[96] Nābhādās's vision of a religiously united India certainly jostled with the universalist aspirations of many Christian missionaries, but it received a more sympathetic hearing from administrators and Orientalists such as George Grierson. And then, under the spell of the Raj with its unprecedented subcontinental scope, the four-*sampradāy* idea was effectively born again—reborn as the bhakti movement. This happened in the world inhabited by J. N. Farquhar, Ishwari Prasad, Hazariprasad Dvivedi, and ultimately Tagore. To that world we now turn.

6

A Nation of Bhaktas

Hazariprasad Dvivedi at the Pivot

The figure of Hazariprasad Dvivedi (1907–1979) is by now no stranger to us. He is second in rank only to Ramchandra Shukla as the critic whose breathtaking overview of Hindi's literary past—a past that connected it to all of India—actually produced that past. For our purposes, though, Dvivedi ranks not second but first. It was he and not Shukla who channeled major portions of that past into the story called *bhakti āndolan;* Shukla adopted the idea only later. We have spent the last four chapters showing how two main motifs from the early modern period—the "born in Dravida" story and the notion of the four *sampradāys*—developed in such a way that they could later be folded into the concept of the bhakti movement. More than any other person, it was Dvivedi who produced the sense of history that aligned them in this way, forming a stable, working whole. With him, the machine was ready to leave the shop.

Of course, Dvivedi did not work in a vacuum, and a main purpose of this chapter is to show how this was so. But there was a beautiful sense of pointedness and buoyancy in his writing—a human dimension that set him apart from the more severe Shukla, his great Banarsi predecessor. It has endeared him to Hindi readers ever since. Dvivedi was a novelist, an essayist, a writer of many letters, a research scholar, an administrator, and a host with an informal touch. He wore his bhakti a little more lightly than Shukla, and though both men believed that bhakti was the people's religion, Dvivedi let the force of language and emotion sweep away barriers of literariness and morality that for Shukla remained the measure of true worth. When bhakti "moved" for him, it walked with a wider stride. His Sūrdās roamed more freely than Shukla's, and Dvivedi had no hesitation advancing Kabīr to the front ranks of the march. No doubt, as Shukla observed, Kabīr was less "literary" than Sūr and any number of other poets who belonged to what they both called the "bhakti period," but Dvivedi saw clearly that Kabīr was, as he put it, "a dictator of words" *(vāṇī ke dikṭeṭar)*. How could one refuse to let him speak?[1]

Dvivedi was the first to bring into alignment the various aspects of the bhakti movement narrative that we have identified so far. When he took upon himself the task of introducing Hindi literature as a whole, in *Hindī Sāhitya kī Bhūmikā* (1940), he adopted the formula of the four *sampradāys* and made that the core of a much larger, yet still single and integrative bhakti movement. In this he followed the example of Rāghavdās, though apparently not self-consciously. But it was earlier, in his book on Sūrdās (*Sūr-Sāhitya,* 1936), that Dvivedi first laid out his concept of the *bhakti āndolan,* and not with quite the same sense of duty to the four-*sampradāy* vision of history that his introduction to Hindi literature, *Hindī Sāhitya kī Bhūmikā,* seemed to require. There, instead, he directed special attention to the question of how we ought to position Sūr in relation to Vallabha on the one hand and to the Chaitanyite theologians and their Bengali forebears on the other. In doing so, he seemed to take cognizance of the special rivalry we reviewed in the previous chapter.

Rāmānand, who loomed so large in our third chapter, was also given a place of pride—this time in *Hindī Sāhitya kī Bhūmikā.* There he is the one who emerges as Vallabha's main rival for enduring influence—in fact, he far surpassed him, since Dvivedi accepted that he was the guru of Kabīr and many others.[2] Shukla was less interested in Rāmānand's tie to Kabīr than he was in the mentoring relation he believed to exist between Rāmānand and his fellow Brahmin Tulsīdās, to whom he devoted an entire book.[3] For Dvivedi the equivalent book went the other direction—to low-caste Kabīr.

Finally, it was Dvivedi, not Shukla, who brought the "born in Dravida" story fully to bear on the bhakti movement theme. Characteristically, he did so not only by following the Sanskrit version of the story—our subject in Chapter 2—but by also incorporating the common Hindi *dohā* that made the tale turn on Rāmānand. This was the "shortcut" we observed in Chapter 3. Dvivedi seems to have been the first bhakti movement "theorist" to place this piece in the puzzle. If we add this to all the other motifs we have now mentioned, we see that Dvivedi took account of every major element that had emerged as being relevant to the bhakti movement narrative up until the time he wrote. By the same token his shadow falls in some way across every chapter of our book.

That Sūṛdās, Kabīr, Tulsīdās, and even Gorakhnāth should emerge as such crucial figures in Dvivedi's bhakti movement story says something about the medium into which we have now clearly moved—Hindi, as against Sanskrit, say, or English. Already in our first chapter we began to see how decisive Hindi would be for the institutionalization of the idea of the bhakti movement. After all, it was not just in history curricula that the idea of the bhakti movement came to hold sway, but in curricula governing Hindi literature, as well. And we must remember that Hindi curricula were not confined to the "Hindi belt." Even before independence, Hindi had its advocates throughout the subcontinent.

In a way this was exactly as it should have been, for the medium was a considerable part of the message. Especially for Hindi speakers, Hindi appeared to be the linguistic culmination of the bhakti movement, its telos and true embodiment. The very idea of a movement from north to south in which the spoken language *(bhāṣā)* was prized seemed to make that almost necessary; Nābhādās's *Bhaktamāl,* written in that very *bhāṣā,* helped to pave the way. But the reception the *Bhaktamāl* received suggests a further dimension. As we have seen, versions of it and commentaries upon it appeared in many languages; sections of it were also included among the "Hindee extracts" that were used to educate "Junior Members of the [British] Military Service" at Fort William College in Calcutta.[4] All this helped create exactly the sort of widely shared literary universe that would in time lend plausibility to the idea that Hindi ought naturally to serve as the link language for an emergently independent India. In the spiritual realm, embracing language and religion but not yet politics, that nation already existed in the 1930s, as Partha Chatterjee has argued.[5] The idea of the bhakti movement helped make it so. And in a way, Hindi seemed to be implied in that concept. It was the major vernacular of the region toward which the bhakti movement tended, at least in northern eyes, and therefore, logically, the medium of its literary fulfillment.

This did not necessarily mean, however, that the concept of the bhakti movement had to crystallize in a place where Hindi was the dominant language. Dvivedi's mother tongue was an eastern form of Hindi, to be sure, but he was living in Bengal when he wrote the books about which we have spoken. He had come to teach in Tagore's educational experiment at Shantiniketan. Tagore took a steady and increasing interest in Hindi, although his own literary expression flowed through the two languages that defined the cultural perimeters of the upper crust he represented: Bengali and English. Already in Tagore's youth well-known Bengali intellectuals such as Bankimchandra Chatterji, Rajendralal Mitra, and Bhudev Mukherji had become proponents of the idea that Hindi should displace English and Urdu as the medium of national unity.[6] Tagore was deeply invested in English, but in time he too moved in that direction, championing the cause of Hindi Bhavan (Hindi House) at Shantiniketan. In a reciprocal way Dvivedi, once ensconced at Shantiniketan, found it natural to reach out to Bengali as an important element in Hindi's literary past. He asserted that Chaitanya and his followers had played significant roles in the development of a bhakti expressed in Hindi, and he paid considerable attention to the great Bengali poets Jayadev, Vidyāpati, and Caṇḍīdās. In his Sūrdās book he observed, "It wasn't just that Nābhādās or Guru Nānak called on the name of Jayadev. In the songs of Sūrdās there actually appeared translations of poems by Jayadev. As Pundit Ramchandra Shukla correctly said, 'It is evident that the *Sūrsāgar* is a full if oral outworking of an earlier tradition of song and poetry.' So long before Sūrdās—and by the same token, long before Vallabhācārya—the Vaishnava stream of love [*vaiṣṇav prem-dhārā*] had established itself in this region."[7]

By "this region" Dvivedi meant Bengal—that's where he was sitting when he wrote—and the Bengali connection to Hindi was a special one. Yet the point Dvivedi was making was more general. He saw Sūrdās's Hindi as the culmination of a tradition of sung poetry whose roots connected it to a series of other linguistic registers, some of which had flowered earlier than Hindi. This made the sort of Hindi to which he was referring—the Hindi of a Sūrdās or Kabīr—far more than a regional language. It was potentially national in scope and could therefore bear the weight it was being assigned in nationalist circles, although Dvivedi himself did not champion this cause explicitly. What he articulated instead was a strong sense of "we"—an encompassingly Indian "we," uttered in Hindi—that contravened the European "they." We have seen how pointedly Grierson stood for that foreign other in Dvivedi's mind, and how it was Grierson's Christian bias that Dvivedi felt he had to set right. That Christian misreading of Indian history had led even as intelligent a man as Grierson, someone so deeply interested in India's vernacularity, to get the bhakti movement wrong. Unlike what Grierson claimed, Dvivedi urged that the bhakti movement was in all its expressions indigenous, integral, organic—the very things others were saying about Hindi.

Krishna Sharma, who wrote in English and was later demeaned for the shallowness of her Hindi, objected to this conviction that the bhakti movement "had a unitary character since bhakti (as academically defined) was common to all medieval bhaktas."[8] She appreciated Dvivedi's work on Kabīr, and credited him especially for demonstrating Kabīr's reliance upon the Nāth *panth*,[9] yet Dvivedi's effort to lay out the beliefs that *sants* of the medieval period had in common—his precisely stated purpose in chapter 7 of *Hindī Sāhitya kī Bhūmikā*—was just the sort of thing she regarded as anathema. But Dvivedi had his reasons. He believed that there was indeed a great sense of bhakti commonality, following from the fact that Vaishnava religion came very close to expressing "the people's religion" *(lok dharm)*.[10] For him, Kabīr was definitely a part of that picture. Sharma thought Kabīr belonged in a different lineage—Śaṃkara's—and she held Orientalists like Grierson responsible for spreading a view of Indian bhakti that would locate him and his *nirguṇ* ilk anywhere else: an artificial sense of monotheistic unity that obscured the role of Advaita Vedanta as queen of the theological sciences. Dvivedi too saw Grierson as the enemy, but for exactly the opposite reason. The great linguist had failed to appreciate the internal continuity of historical Indian bhakti in all its unitive, indigenous fullness.

With respect to both content and language, Hindi was a sign of the unity for which Dvivedi and so many other nationalists hoped: an organic unity sufficiently rock-bound that it could accommodate a fair amount of internal difference. Sharma, speaking well after independence had been secured, didn't like that vision and didn't need it. Her scholarly moorings were far more in English. Yet she was certainly right that a religious unity for all of India was indeed what the idea of the bhakti movement proclaimed. Hindi—literally, "India-ish"—suited the task of its proclamation perfectly. No wonder Dvivedi's framing of the bhakti movement concept, being articulated in Hindi itself, carried the force it did.

Tagore and the Shantiniketan Circle

Even today, to come into Shantiniketan is to slip into a magical world—flat, lush, and peaceful as its name. Some do not like it for that reason (unsurprisingly, for example, Nirad Chaudhuri),[11] but for most, Tagore's simple utopia has a beguiling appeal. This was certainly so for Hazariprasad Dvivedi. He arrived in early November 1930, when Tagore—Gurudev to the many who surrounded him—was just about to complete the seventh decade of his life, and he came at the Guru's own behest. In a letter written years later Dvivedi described his encounter with Tagore in the most dramatic way—as the time he became "twice born." He, a Brahmin, at last underwent his real *upanayana* ceremony—this time, with no visible sacred thread. In another letter he turned to English to convey his sense of this transformation. It was "the turning point of his life," Dvivedi said. True to the imagery of *guru-dīkṣā,* he reported a new sense of power coursing through him like the pure waters of the Ganges, and he attributed it directly to Tagore. To set eyes on such a person made him feel as if he was reaping the rewards of many past lives.[12] Strong words, these, and from a man not given to platitudes!

Tagore's special impact on Dvivedi's sense of the bhakti movement was, if powerful, nonetheless indirect. In a way the actual circumstances of Dvivedi's arrival in Shantiniketan symbolize this fact, for on that particular day in November, Tagore was half a world away. He was lecturing, thinking, and trying to fund-raise in New York. He would not return until 1931, by which time Dvivedi's classes on Hindi literature were well under way at Shantiniketan. Tagore's absence was testament to his individual standing—he was already very much a world traveler—but doubtless it signified a measure of loneliness, as well. In one private missive written from the bustle of New York he said he had "come to the conclusion that the only place which is safe for the eastern simpleton is his own remote corner of obscurity."[13] On the other hand, of course, his lecture itinerary was also a way to reconfirm, through friends in far-flung places, his convictions about the shared condition of humanity, which was the subject of his Hibbert Lectures given at Oxford in May, 1930, and published in the following year as *The Religion of Man.* But the gesture to that "remote corner of obscurity," if it referred in part to Shantiniketan, was not a false one.

This may have been true in a special way in late 1930. Tagore's travels had taken him to Russia, where he had seen the immense strides that Communist rule had made in securing education for the common people. It became something of a cause célèbre when Tagore celebrated this fact to reporters who interviewed him even before he was safely moored in New York harbor. That the Russian experience should have touched him so deeply was no surprise, however. Education was the core of Tagore's vision for India, insofar as he had a consistent vision of that sort, and the "ascetics' grove" *(tapovan)* he had built about himself in Shantiniketan was its physical form.

The other stream of events that had a major impact on Tagore in 1930 came from India itself: news of the noncooperation movement, Gandhi's salt march, his imprisonment, and the adoption of martial law by the British. Not that Tagore entirely abandoned his hope for a meeting of the best minds of East and West, some of it surely at Shantiniketan, but for the first time, from 1931 onward, he joined Gandhi and others in advocating political independence for his country.[14] For the poet and cosmopolitan that he was, this was a momentous shift. It gave a somewhat new shape to the Gurudev whom Dvivedi would have met when Tagore returned from his long sojourn abroad—a man who lent his force to the nationalist cause in a new (if still cerebral and local) way, putting to the side his long-standing concern about nationalism's "arrogant" habit of perverting the cause of true education.[15] He was also a man still digesting the lessons to be learned from seeing what could happen when a vastly tiered society like czarist Russia turned egalitarian.[16]

Shantiniketan was never to become an outpost of the Soviet Union in anything like the Marxist sense that appealed to a number of intellectuals in Calcutta, but Tagore's engagement with caste took on a new color. In this he was much influenced by what he knew of the *sādhu-sants* or *sādhak-kavis* of the "medieval period"—as he, like just about everyone else, conceptualized it.[17] These medieval bhakti saints were hardly new to Tagore. Rameshwar Mishra, a great authority on the subject, guesses that a curiosity about Nānak may already have germinated when Tagore accompanied his father on a trip to Amritsar as a boy of eleven in 1873; similarly for Tukārām on a Maharashtrian visit in 1878.[18] Tagore's famous poem "Prayer of Sūrdās"—in Bengali, like almost all the others—was penned in 1888, and his even more famous English translations of Kabīr, in which he collaborated with the Christian mystic Evelyn Underhill, emerged in 1914. But it was only in the early 1930s that his poetic imagination was stirred irresistibly by untouchability, and the bhakti poets—particularly relationships *between* those poets—were his primary vehicle. Discussions with Kshitimohan Sen, who was a specialist on these *sants* and whom Tagore had brought to teach at Shantiniketan already in 1908, undoubtedly helped to stimulate his interest; these had been under way for decades. Now Hazariprasad Dvivedi was added to the group. But Tagore also had access to the classic Hindi bhaktas through the Bengali translation of the *Bhaktamāl*, which he possessed. It included the narrative material supplied by the *Bhaktirasabodhinī* of Priyādās in the seamless way that had by then become normal.[19]

What emerged was a set of striking Bengali poems, some of which Tagore reconfigured into English so that they could appear on the front page of the fortnightly newspaper *Harijan*. *Harijan* began to be published in Pune 1933 during the period when Gandhi was in residence there and was about to undertake his three-week fast of self-purification as a way to focus his own and other people's attention on the atrocious practice of untouchability.[20] Gandhi and Tagore had long seen more closely eye to eye on this issue than many others, and Gandhi's renewed dedication prompted some of the same in Tagore. "Sweet Mercy," the poem from which we draw the title of this book and the one we quoted in its entirety on the first page of Chapter 1, was composed on the third day of Gandhi's fast—May 10, 1933. To fashion this poem, Tagore adapted the first of three stanzas in his Bengali poem "Premer-Sonā" (Love's Golden Treasure), which had appeared in the course of the previous year in his collection *Punaśca*.[21]

The poem is remarkable in more than one respect. To begin with, it takes the *Bhaktamāl*'s claim that Ravidās was a disciple of Rāmānand and provides that claim with a narrative line that relates it to the issue of temple admission. Rāmānand was on his way to the temple, Tagore tells us, when the encounter with Ravidās occurred. But even before the poem arrives at this momentous meeting, it transports us into the world established by Ravidās himself. Tagore takes as his starting point the very advertisement of caste and occupational status that Ravidās himself frequently adopts in poems that are remembered as having come from his lips: he speaks of himself as *ravidās camār* or *ravidās camārā*—a leatherworker.[22] Thus we seem to meet a version of Ravidās's own oral signature in the phrase "Raidas, the sweeper," which Tagore employs in beginning and ending, just as one might when a Ravidās poem is performed. In such a traditional performance the poem's refrain serves as both its introduction and conclusion. Interestingly, as Joel Lee has observed, to make Ravidās a sweeper as Tagore did is to thrust on him a caste identity beyond the leatherworking variety that he himself claimed, tying him to Dalits who are usually thought to occupy positions even lower than his own.[23]

Then, of course, there is Rāmānand: Tagore literally pulls the line in which he appears to the fore—farther to the left—than any other line. At the same time he implicitly expands the familiar story of Rāmānand's encounter with Kabīr, which happened on the steps leading down to the Ganges, in such a way that it can also encompass Ravidās: Rāmānand meets him on the way back from his daily morning bath.

> Master Ramananda was walking to the temple
> after his morning bath,
> when Raidas bowed himself down before him from a distance.

Finally, it is hard to avoid the feeling, when one hears this poem, that it also refers to Rabindranath himself. How often must he have found himself in the situation of being adored from afar as he walked around Shantiniketan or moved as such a noble, hallowed, utterly visible Brahmin presence through the streets of many an Indian town or city?

In a poem called "The Sacred Touch," published in *Harijan* two months earlier, Tagore draws even closer to the bathing motif that takes center stage in the great story of how Kabīr, lying on the steps leading down to the Ganges in the predawn gloom, cleverly arranged for an initiation-by-foot from Rāmānand as he made his way to his early morning bath. As in "Sweet Mercy," the light of grace bathes the guru—it is he who takes the initiative, not waiting for the lowly devotee—and this time we are given the words to express what he feels when he takes that devotee in his arms. It is as if Tagore himself finds the words to describe the full drama of religious practices and avoidances that have brought him to that moment. As for Ravidās, it is notable that he has become more than a single person in this version of the story. As if to generalize the "storm of songs" that issued from Ravidās's encounter with Rāmānand in "Sweet Mercy," the lowly devotee is here actually given the name "Song," for this is what Bhajan means. By rules of Sanskrit grammar *bhajan* is the more active form of the noun *bhakti*. I quote the last three stanzas of this poem, where it becomes clear that in Tagore's view the "sacred touch" of his title moves to the Brahmin from the Untouchable, although it is also true that the Brahmin's self-awareness makes the touch of that touch possible:

Ramananda drew him to his heart
  and Bhajan, his eyes filled with tears, cried in dismay,
    "Master, why bringest upon thee such pollution?"
And Master said "While on my way to my bath I shunned
  your village and thus my heart missed the blessings
    of the Ganges whose mother's love is for all.

Her own touch comes down at last upon me at the touch
  of your body with mine and I am purified,
I cried this morning to the Sun,
  'The Divine Person who is in thee is also within me
    but why do I not meet thee in my mind?'

I have met him at this moment when his light descends
  upon your forehead as well as on mine,
    and there is no need for me to-day
      to go to the temple."[24]

One can imagine the impact that a person capable of uttering such lines, so supremely attuned to encounter and at the same time so willing to act the part of the guru, might have had upon the youthful Dvivedi. As a poet, Tagore's habit was to establish a direct connection between himself and the bhakti world whose texts he had before him or whose lyrics he heard sung around him. His visits to various Baul *akhāḍās* located in the vicinity of Shantiniketan are legendary.

In consonance with the Gangetic theme that appears in the poem we have just quoted, Tagore often turned to the metaphor of a river to give a sense of how real communication happened in India from region to region and age to age, enabling the country to weave difference into a complex oneness over the centuries. What Dvivedi would call the bhakti movement was exemplary of the process, though Tagore typically named it by means of the shared spiritual discipline *(sādhanā)* of India's poets and saints rather than by "the people" *(jan)*, as Dvivedi would insist. Here is a formulation from 1908, in which the liquid metaphor takes a somewhat different turn. The passage, which comes from the essay "Rājāprajā" (Ruler and Subject), is in part oriented toward redressing the partitioning of Bengal into Hindu- and Muslim-majority halves, as British administrators had done in 1905, and therefore serves as yet another example of the contemporaneity of bhakti history as understood by Tagore:

> Finally, when the determined pursuit *(sādhanā)* of philosophical wisdom began to create chasms between the lettered and the unlettered and between those who had authority and those who did not, Chaitanya, Nānak, Dādū, and Kabīr took the disunity of castes in various regions of India and the disunity of their teachings and rained down the immortal nectar of the superlative unity of bhakti, to make them one. Nor were these men merely engaged in the task of healing, through love, the wounds that had been opened by India's regional religions *(prādeśik dharma)*. They were also the very persons who built a religious bridge *(dharmasetu)* to mediate between the natures of Hindus and Muslims.[25]

One hears in this formulation something not unlike the riverine metaphors that several literary historians would choose to characterize the movements of bhakti—its currents and streams. Dvivedi used them too, although his favorite image, as we recall, was the monsoon. And, of course, the matter of *rasa* was always relevant, even in practical terms. Rabindranath hoped to establish in Shantiniketan a mood that would make it a microcosm of universally shared experience *(rasa)* from the ground up. Sometimes the results went beyond mood to mystique, one that was frequently pilloried by outsiders who saw it as mostly affectation. For Dvivedi, though, it was real. Global in its vision and certainly intended to comprehend all of India *(viśva-bhāratī)*, Shantiniketan made Dvivedi a citizen of a world that was light-years away from the village of his birth and even, in a different way, from the Banaras of his higher education.[26] Not that any of that became irrelevant. He still had the self-confidence that came in childhood from his learned Brahmin background, the degrees in Sanskrit and astrology that he earned from Banaras Hindu University, and the contacts that he developed with Ramchandra Shukla, Lālā Bhagavān Dīn, and Śyāmsundar Dās in its new Hindi Department. These in turn tied him as well to the ongoing work of the Nāgarīpracāriṇī Sabhā, the institution most directly responsible for the creation of Modern Standard Hindi and the past it claimed. All of these were important, but at Shantiniketan they were folded into a greater pan-Indian whole—greater in aspiration yet at the same time, owing to scale and educational intent, more intimate. Dvivedi's sense of his tie to the Master epitomized the importance of the transformation he underwent once he arrived in Shantiniketan, both personally and intellectually. There were material changes, as well. For the first time in his life his income was, if not overgenerous, sufficient to his needs. That too must also have given Hazariprasad a sense that he was standing on a new kind of terra firma.

In addition to the guru dimension—the adoptive tie to his famous new "father"—there was also a brotherly one. This came forward in Dvivedi's contacts with the artists Nandalal Bose and Bimanbehari Mukherji and with other denizens of Shantiniketan such as Charles Andrews and his close friend Banarsidas Chaturvedi, and it was manifest particularly in Dvivedi's bond to the man who had done the most to deepen Tagore's knowledge of the *sants,* Kshitimohan Sen. It was Sen who gave Tagore a new appreciation for Nānak, Dādū, and Kabīr—the non-Bengali bhaktas who appear in the passage we have just quoted. It was also he who wrote the preface to Dvivedi's book on Sūrdās, and to whom Dvivedi dedicated his celebrated book on Kabīr. In many ways, then, Sen hovered like an elder brother over the bhakti movement as Dvivedi articulated and performed it. He was also a major interpreter of that phenomenon himself.

Kshitimohan Sen (1880–1960) was both Bengali and Banarsi. His grandparents had undertaken *kāśīvās,* the vow to end their lives in Banaras, which meant that he grew up in one of the many Bengali households that made up the Bangālī Ṭolā neighborhood of the city. The teacher whom he most revered was a man called Sudhākar Dvivedī, whose enthusiasm for the literature of the *sants* he quickly came to share, but he had other teachers, as well. In an autobiographical reflection he published at the age of seventy-five, Sen reached lovingly back to the memory of the driver of a simple two-wheeled horse-cart who came up behind him and two boyhood friends as they set out south of the city toward Ramnagar *ghāṭ.* He heard their boisterous conversation, and insisted they climb aboard for a ride. This man too became his guru, low caste and unlettered but rich in his knowledge of the *sants,* both their stories and their songs. He became Sen's "charioteer"—his *sūta,* in the exalted terminology of the *Mahābhārata*—introducing him to a whole network of *sādhus* in Banaras, and not only there but at the Kumbh Mela in Allahabad and at villages in between. This charioteer became the young Sen's conduit to the living world of bhakti song.[27]

At many points in his scholarly life at Shantiniketan and also in his individual writings, Sen tacked back and forth between the textual and the oral, giving both their due. We can see this in the way he approached his repeated trips to Rajasthan and the Punjab between 1925 and 1930. On the one hand, for example, he pursued a manuscript in the possession of *sādhus* at Ghomān, near Batala, that promised to shed a different light on Nāmdev than could be had in the well-known Sikh and Marathi sources.[28] On the other hand, noticing that there were no independent manuscript collections for Mīrābāī, he kept a record of everything he heard in her name, so as to capture the oral for the page. Ruefully he reports that somehow he managed to lose this manuscript the very day he planned to send it off for publication, thus keeping the oral Mīrābāī oral for yet a little while longer.[29]

Kshitimohan Sen was a scholar. He was sensitive to the possibility that adjustments to history could easily be made in both textual and oral mediums. Singers might misremember the song they sang, so he listened carefully for variants. And paper hardly diminished the chances for emendation. Sen thought that upper-caste redactors—in particular "*sāmpradāyik* Vaishnavas"—had habitually tried to appropriate the *sants* and *sādhaks* for their own purposes, wiping away their actual origins, whether Muslim or lower caste or both, so as to bring these poets in line with the redactors' ideas about who was eligible to receive the gift of inspired speech and who was not.[30]

One can see how such a critical sensibility would have meant a great deal to Dvivedi, who was twenty-seven years Sen's junior. To begin with, there was his teaching work at Shantiniketan itself. Sen's devotion to the *sants* and *sādhaks* he identified as belonging to the medieval period (a concept that was not to be questioned in any serious way for at least a half a century) had played a considerable role in making the study of Hindi at Shantiniketan a pursuit of precisely that register of the language. Tagore and Sen favored the down-to-earth speech of the medieval poet-saints not only for its own intrinsic merit but because they felt it naturally reached out to idioms of song and epigram that animated the lives of common people across north India and Bengal, as well. In the same spirit, both men also had a taste for the style of personal, plain-speaking scholarship that Dvivedi would hone to a fine art. Dvivedi must have felt their encouragement many times, as sympathizers and also as models.

Sen's scholarly accomplishments had brought him considerable fame by the time Dvivedi arrived at Shantiniketan. Decades before, Tagore had made clear the substantial debt he owed to Sen as he prepared his English translations of Kabīr. He urged Sen to publish the poetry of Kabīr that he had gathered from oral sources in four installments in 1910–1911, even through Sen was at first reticent to do so.[31] Sen returned the compliment by pointing out that if it had not been for the huge success of the English translations by Tagore and Underhill, which followed in 1914, Kabīr would never have been admitted by the gatekeepers of Hindi to the canon of its literary greats.

In the year immediately preceding Dvivedi's arrival on the scene in Shantiniketan, Sen achieved something that was to be at least as important to Dvivedi as his work on Kabīr. He had been asked to give the Adhar Mookerji Lectures at the University of Calcutta in 1929, a task he performed in Bengali under the title *Bhāratiya Madhyayuge Sādhanār Dhārā* (The Stream of Spiritual Dedication in India's Middle Ages). The two lectures were soon published with a preface by Tagore, and began to circulate widely in Bengal under the same title. They also began to be translated into English by Manomohan Ghosh, with the author himself closely involved. The result was *Medieval Mysticism of India,* published in 1936. As we recall, Dvivedi published his book on Sūrdās in the same year. It was there that he first laid out his conception of the bhakti movement, surveying much of the same terrain that Sen explored in his Calcutta lectures.

The structure of those two lectures was significant. Sen devoted his first to a group of authors he called *lokavedapanthī,* members of the "path" that discovered "the people's wisdom," or their Veda. He believed that this *lok-ved*—something he did not attempt to name until he looked back at the end of his second lecture—was a level of knowing that could be traced all the way back before the Vedas themselves came into being. This ancient Indian tradition of love and devotion *(premabhakti)* preceded and ungirded Veda in the more formal sense, creating a broad rubric that enabled Sen to write Islam intrinsically into the Indian record later on. With the Muslim presence in India was launched a complex history of humanistic religion that involved *sādhaks* who were both Hindu and Muslim, both poets and patrons. Sen pointedly used the same overarching term—*sādhanā (> sādhak),* the one Tagore also favored—to describe Hindus and Muslims alike, and he took a deep interest in the many ways these Hindu and Muslim understandings of *sādhanā* had interpenetrated over time.

Having accomplished that long historical exposition in his first lecture, Sen took a different tack in his second. Without meaning to single out a group of figures who were altogether different from those he had already analyzed, he focused this time on persons who "followed the path of realizing truth by means of their own experience" *(anubhausāc-panthī).* This time, he restricted himself to persons and groups who belonged to north India in the Middle Ages, beginning with Rāmānand and concluding in the eighteenth century with Tulsī Sāhib Hāthrasī, the poet-saint who stood at the head of the *sant* lineage specifically claimed by the Radhasoami Satsang. That organization, a major *nirguṇī* community with a progressive bourgeois constituency and a devotion to constructing utopian ashrams for laypeople, had been founded in mid-nineteenth-century Agra and spread throughout north India and the Punjab by the time Sen wrote.[32] Especially through the Belvedere Press, founded in Allahabad in 1900 by Bāleśvar Prasād Agarvāl, one of its most influential members, Radhasoami became a major force in popularizing the idea of *sant mat,* a term Radhasoami adherents used to designate the distinctive habit of mind that brought together more or less the same group of poet-saints that Sen called *sādhaks* and Ramchandra Shukla labeled *nirguṇīs.*[33] The difference between Sen and Shukla was that Sen's interest, like that of H. H. Wilson, J. N. Farquhar, and his Bengali predecessor Akshaykumar Dutta, was at least as religious as it was literary.[34] Moreover, by devoting his entire second lecture—almost one hundred pages of printed text—to this "truth by experience" group, he prioritized exactly the figures whom Shukla was busy sidelining as victims of what he called a "mystical" worldview *(rahasyavād).*[35] Sen specifically valorized this term by placing it in the title of the English version of his lectures, and he lavished his own special research attention on the groups and individuals he featured in this second lecture.

Dādū, Nānak, Ravidās, and Kabīr are obvious cases in point. Sen wrote multiple essays on each, with Dādū and the Dādū *panth* lying at the very center of his scholarly concern. Equally interesting with respect to his overall depiction of the bhakti movement, however, was the attention he gave to Mīrābāī. The essays in which she figures show how eager Sen was to take a saint others thought of as a paradigmatic example of *saguṇ bhakti* and recast her as the sort of *sādhak* he himself preferred—the *nirguṇ* variety. Sen was adamant in arguing that Mīrābāī herself made this transition. She moved from one dimension to the other as if "by a natural law," he said, leaving behind her devotion to Krishna and "transcending its confines" as she matured and aspired to the all-encompassing vision of a true *sādhak* instead. The defining moment came when Mīrā escaped the clutches of her Brahmin advisers and went in search of Ravidās, whom she accepted as her true guru.[36]

Sen felt perfectly confident making this assessment of Mīrābāī. It aligned him with certain earlier interpreters of Mīrā—the Sikhs, for example—but definitely put him in conflict with the majority of his own teachers and peers. He met the obvious challenge—the ubiquity of appeals to Krishna as Giridhar Gopāl and so forth in so much of Mīrā's poetry—by saying that all this was actually a smokescreen produced and maintained over the years by image-worshipping, sectarian *(sāmpradāyik)* Krishnapanthīs, who adjusted the textual record repeatedly to make Mīrā seem always one of theirs. He admits that the Rāmpanthīs, whom he thought of as a rival group in this regard, doubtless sometimes did the same in reverse, attempt to release Mīrā from her close association to Krishna. Yet upon discovering a striking variant in the Belvedere Press collection of Mīrābāī's poetry, where "the name of Rām" substitutes for the more usual "Giridhar Gopāl," Sen doesn't even consider the possibility that the alteration could have come from the *nirguṇ* or Rāmpanthī side rather than from the *saguṇ* or Krishnapanthī one.[37] Similarly he dismisses as "controversial" the idea found in the *Bhaktirasabodhinī* of Priyādās, to the effect that at one stage, at least, Mīrā might have sought out the very Krishna-focused Jīv Gosvāmī to be her guru.[38] For Sen it had to be Ravidās all the way.

Dvivedi alongside Kshitimohan Sen

One gets a sense, then, of Sen's style. Often workmanlike and straightforward, he displayed scholarly capabilities that gave him the confidence, especially when writing the essays that poured forth from Shaktiniketan publications, to assert truths about the medieval bhakti world that he did not always feel he had to prove. His great awareness of how texts could be contaminated and interpolated, together with his many ties to oral performers and faraway *maṭhs* little known to others, surely helped the cause along. It may not be accidental that Hazariprasad Dvivedi displayed the same sort of self-confidence when he offered his memorable portraits of Rāmānand and Kabīr only a few years later. In fact, he spoke even more powerfully than Sen, making it seem he could simply mainline his way into these *sants'* spiritual veins. Of course, Dvivedi too wove textual evidence into his exposition, but often his prose style makes one think less of dusty scholarship than of Tagore's poetic flights, or perhaps of the exhortatory tone one might hear from a *kathāvācak* determined to enliven the text he sings with his own enthusiastic exposition.

Consider the example of Rāmānand—telling because of his pivotal position in the story of how bhakti spread to north India (and *which* bhakti, at that), and telling because so little remains of his own poetry. Sen and Dvivedi see somewhat different Rāmānands, and with a fair sense of self-assurance on both their parts. Sen focuses on the skullduggeries of upper-caste and *sāmpradāyik* exegetes who, he thought, had labored hard to obscure Rāmānand's radical disavowal of caste. Sen emphasizes the contrast between the actual freethinking Rāmānand and the figure who was tamed to sectarian sobriety by later "orthodox" writers. He says Rāmānand gave up his "caste glory" so as to join on the "easy festival field" *(sahaj utsavakṣetra)* of dharma, which is also "the natural field of *prema* and *bhakti*."[39] There he joined with "persons of so-called 'low' family" who, by virtue of their very commonness, were "capable of generating newer spiritual light in all eras and in all countries of the world." Kabīr, Rāmānand's pupil, comes to light in this regard. He embodies this principle to such a degree, Sen says, that "it can easily be argued that the medieval period of India is his creation." Yet Sen also stresses the fact that this expansive demotic sensibility is the common bond of *sādhaks* north and south, from the *āḻvārs* forward. Rāmānand is the figure who creates a bridge between these two groups, making them a single spectrum, but he is also the figure who ushers in the radiant era of Kabīr, the time when the luminousness of the "low" could truly shine forth and therefore the moment that "so-called history" subsequently tried so hard to cover in darkness.[40]

These themes in Sen's exegesis were certainly not objectionable to Dvivedi, except perhaps his friend's failure to appreciate the story of how Rāmānand initiated Kabīr. There was also, however, a contrast. For Dvivedi, Rāmānand represented the principle of true guruship—the ability to touch a desiccated soul, drench it with love, and bring that soul to life. As guru, then, he led in a distinctive way, just as Tagore had done for Dvivedi himself, thoroughly relativizing any social location. This pertained not just to the vanities of high-caste birth but also to the lowly one that was of such importance to Sen. Dvivedi felt that the special gifts of perception that humble birth conferred were in the end also superseded by a bhakti consciousness. Rāmānand released his disciples, whoever they were, to a discovery of the intrinsically human genius that is potentially universal. As guru, he enabled a disciple with capabilities like Kabīr's to discover and embrace his own overwhelming humanity, thereby serving as an unforgettable herald of everyone else's.

Perhaps in some corner of consciousness it was important for Dvivedi to make a place under the umbrella of humanity for his own formation as a Brahmin, rather than to exclude that from the picture, as Sen seemed to do. Sen belonged by birth to one of the highly respected mercantile castes; the special struggle of the sensitive Brahmin to prove his authenticity was therefore not his birthright—or rather, birth curse. For Dvivedi it was a different matter. I hesitate to make too much of this caste-based disparity since so far as I know it is not directly reflected in the letters or memoirs of either man. Certainly these two "brothers," as Sen described them in his introduction to Dvivedi's *Sūr-Sāhitya,* were not far apart in many respects.[41] They were notably comparable in striking out for what Namvar Singh has called "a second tradition" *(dūsrī paramparā)*—the sort of lineage that moves away from the more obviously brahminical formulation of religious and literary history preferred by Ramchandra Shukla and toward the egalitarian, the un-Aryan, the nativist, the *sant.* Yet Dvivedi was able to embrace Vaishnavism in its broadest reaches (as against its doctrinaire expressions) and to see that Vaishnavism as coming very close to capturing the religion of the people, what Sen called *lok-ved* and Dvivedi often termed *lok-dharm* or perhaps "the life-force of Indian religious strivings" *(bhāratīya sādhanā kī jīvan-śakti).*[42] Sen could not go that far.

This contrast is synchronic, but there is a diachronic one, as well. Dvivedi was less focused on the series of reforms and renewals that caught Sen's eye—"neo" or *nava* this or that—than he was on perceiving one great movement that extended from the *āḻvārs* to present time: the *bhakti āndolan.* It had been Sen who first insisted on bringing the *āḻvārs* into the picture, thus extending the reach of southern bhakti beyond the classical acharyas of the four *sampradāys* with respect to both time and social level. Sen saw Āṇṭāḷ and her father Viṣṇucitta (Periyāḻvār) as being "from low caste" and said that they, like all the *āḻvārs,* based their "Neo-Bhakti cult" on "love and devotion [*premabhakti*] which are inherent in the human heart." As channeled by a series of successors who were, by implication, more systematic in their intentions—he names Nāthamuni, Yāmunācārya, and Piḷḷai Lokācārya—they founded a "Neo-Bhakti movement" that "progressed uniformly up to the time of Rāmānuja," but then became embroiled in issues of caste and commensality.[43]

Sen's use of the term "movement" is, of course, significant—the original Bengali had the more generic *dhārā* (stream, flow) instead—but equally significant is the way in which he inflects the term. In qualifying it as "neo," he was simply taking over the usage made popular by Bhandarkar, who had meant to contrast this new stage in the history of bhakti to what one gets in the *Bhagavad Gītā.*[44] But it is possible to detect a second dimension as well: Sen's appreciation of the fact that in this world, especially this sectarianizing world, things decay and wither, requiring renewal. The history he begins to sketch with Rāmūnuja is testimony to that fact, demanding a figure like Rāmānand to exercise that "neo-izing" force once again. Dvivedi, by contrast, was content with a simplification of language—and, I would argue, thought—that emphasized the element of continuity rather than of disruption. Dvivedi appreciated Sen's point that many of the *āḻvārs* had came from castes deemed untouchable,[45] but he was far less concerned than Sen to mark out the subsequent departures from and returns to the royal road of no-caste. For Dvivedi, as in a way for Tagore, it was bhakti's constant movement that made the greater difference, not the stammerings and near asphyxias that periodically caused *premabhakti* to have to regroup and draw new breath, as Sen had thought.

In regard to times closer at hand, as well, Sen occasionally used the term "movement," and again, as in the case of the *āḻvārs,* he embedded it in a complex picture of historical and social reality. Using the plural rather than the singular, he referred on the one hand to groups like the Nirañjanīs of northeastern India, whose effects had been felt in "the Indian Midland," he believed. On the other hand he indicated a range of "movements . . . and their many-sided ramifications" that he saw as crystallizing throughout

India in response to the "quest of salvation" represented by the "idealism" of *sādhanā,* his central concern. In this quest, he said, "The soul of India is, as it were, changing body after body and is taking new forms."[46] These several movements seem to occupy just the sort of space they would if a contemporary historian of European social and religious history had been using the term—movements, *mouvements, Bewegungen.* With Dvivedi, there was a shift to something more unifying, more expressive of a collectively active *Volk*—in his language, *jan* or *lok.*

Sen was an astute reader. He was perhaps the first modern scholar to notice the silences in Nābhādās's *Bhaktamāl* that attracted our attention in Chapter 3. Importantly, he pointed out, Nābhā had been unaware of the *āḻvārs.* He chalked this up to simple ignorance, which sounds innocent enough, but one wonders what Sen thought might have happened if Nābhā had known of the *āḻvārs'* existence. Would his sense of history have been less *sāmpradāyik,* less "orthodox"? In a similar way, Sen noticed that among the *sants* and *sādhaks* that interested Sen the most, Nābhādās mentioned only Ravidās and Kabīr. They were exceptions to the upper-caste "sectarian" rule, Sen thought—a rule to which figures such as Dādū, Nānak, and Rajjab would also have provided a challenge. As he says, "the Bhaktamāl deals mainly with *bhaktas* who are sectarian and pay respect to the *śāstras.*" For him, sect and *śāstra* went together. What Dādū, for example, established was something different: a "Brahma society," as he called it in one of the essays that he appended to the English version of his Calcutta lectures. Obviously the aura of the Brahmo Samaj, with its effort to obliterate sectarian boundaries, was on his mental screen. Sen wanted to advance its effort to rectify the historical record, and had already done a great deal in this regard. He had traveled far and wide to unearth memories of *sādhaks* that would challenge the constructions to which they had been subjected by "sectarian" interpreters in the *Bhaktamāl* tradition, and thereby, so to speak, expand the canon. But what Sen really hoped was that an army of young researchers would join him in the battle, ferreting out "similar biographical materials preserved in different *maṭhs* and sectarian head-quarters" that "when properly collected [would] furnish the basis of an excellent history of the *sādhakas* of the Mediaeval India."[47]

If Dvivedi provided a measure of contrast to this, it was not because he wanted to write a history of bhakti that would proceed simply in terms of *sampradāy,* as the great Banarsi scholar Śyāmsundar Dās had tended to do in his *Hindī Sāhitya* (1930).[48] But he was willing to accord *sampradāys* an explicit and unchallenged place in the history of Indian bhakti, letting them play their role in a broader story. *Sampradāy* was not a bad word for Dvivedi, as it was for Sen—the opponent in *sādhanā*'s constant struggle against rigidity, narrowness, and lethargy. In *Sūr-Sāhitya,* after Dvivedi throws down his epochal "monsoon" gauntlet on the road where Grierson was walking, he provides the following summary of what this singular, comprehensive bhakti movement was all about:

1. Love [*prem*] is the highest goal of life, not release [*mokṣa*]: *premā pumartho mahān.*[49]
2. With respect to God, love is a matter of greater importance than social standing [*kaulīnya,* "high birth"].
3. A God-focused person [*bhakta*] is even greater than God.
4. Without bhakti, book learning and formal erudition are worthless.
5. The verbal [*nām*] is even greater than the visual [*rūp*].

All this sounds conceptually radical—and it was. But Dvivedi goes on to make clear that the bhakti movement's radical message did not sever it from the ground on which it had sprouted. He immediately adds the following comment: "In sum, you could say that while this way of thinking was not opposed to Brahminical religion [*brāhmaṇ-dharm*], it also did not follow from it. The difference from Mahāyāna was that the latter was entirely opposed to Brahminical religion. Once having been a part of it, it became independent."[50]

The simultaneous connection and contrast to Mahāyāna continued to occupy Dvivedi's thoughts. It was at the basis of his "search for an alternate tradition," as Namvar Singh has put it. But in following that out, we should not forget that Dvivedi was also eager to validate a history of bhakti that was capable of embracing Brahmins like himself in a new sort of faith community, rather than having to send them away at the door. What Sen called "liberality" in the English version of his Mookerji Lectures, setting it clearly apart from "orthodoxy" (the Bengali is silent in both respects), was a development Dvivedi saw as occurring in a much less polarized field. He made this perspective clear in *Hindī Sāhitya kī Bhūmikā,* working steadily outward from the four *sampradāys* to the *nirguṇ panths* and then, further, to the Sufis. A little later, in his *Kabīr* book, he did allow higher fences to emerge on this common bhakti field—the contradictions represented by *nirguṇ* and *saguṇ* perspectives, Hindus and Muslims, warring yogis and Vaishnavas—but what enabled him to make this "sectarian" concession was the fact that he was about to announce the figure who would address precisely such contradictions as these. In a moving passage he described Kabīr as "the human counterpart of God's Man-Lion avatar. Like the Man-Lion, he came to earth at the point of contradiction in settings that seemed irreconcilable."[51]

With Kabīr as with Rāmānand—but even more so—one feels that charismatic kairos-force that was, in a word, the True Guru. Dvivedi contrasts this urgent mood with that of commentators who spent their hours trying to reconcile the new dispensation of love with what had been recorded in canonical texts. Many of these commentators, though *smārta,* had Vaishnava leanings, and rank-and-file *saguṇ bhaktas,* though catholic in their practice, also tended to gravitate toward the authority of a Vaishnava text, the *Bhāgavata Purāṇa.* Kabīr could hardly fit this mold. At the very least he was Vaishnava and non-Vaishnava at the same time. And yet, there too, Dvivedi reaches for a Vaishnava image to characterize Kabīr's earthshaking sensibility. He was Narsiṃha, the Man-Lion, in human form. *Nirguṇīs* were hardly the same as *saguṇīs* in his view, nor Kabīr the same as Sūrdās, and yet Dvivedi was committed to holding them in a single field—a field with a Vaishnava flavor. In the passage we have just been following, the theology that orchestrates this "festival field" (to borrow a phrase from Sen) was *līlā,* a basically Vaishnava concept, and as for the festival itself, it was *holī.*[52]

Elements of the historical picture that prepared for the epiphany of Kabīr that emerged in Dvivedi's *Kabīr* monograph were already present in his Sūrdās book—even the sense that Islam had brought to India something indigestible, incomparable. In *Sūr-Sāhitya* he described not just the political power of Islam but also the corrosive effect of its social generosity, which was capable of sweeping away the previously inescapable landscape of caste, creating a situation that could not be wished away by even a distinguished band of revisionist medieval Hindu commentators.[53] In *Kabīr* he fleshed out the point by describing how Islam had brought to India a new understanding of religion *(dharma)* itself: *mazhab,* an organized system of religious doctrine accompanied by a collectivized form of practice.[54] In both historical portraits, though—the one focused on Sūr and the one focused on Kabīr—it was the bhakti movement, based unquestionably in love and bubbling up from the south, that brought the resources India needed to deal with the problem. Earlier efforts had failed. Dvivedi mentioned in particular those of the *smārta* commentators whose attempts to produce a unified canon of Hindu practice that would be comparable to Islam actually yielded the concept "Hindu" in the first place. The religious movements *(dhārmik āndolan)* of Sufis and Nāth Yogīs also figured into the picture, attempting synthesis but achieving it only partially. Over and above these, however, it was the appearance of "Vedanta-inspired bhakti" as it spread from one corner of India to the other—the bhakti movement originating in the south—that carried the day.[55] It led from Vallabha to Sūrdās and especially from Rāmānand to Kabīr, and was the miracle of its time—Grierson's lightning.

We have seen how Dvivedi pulled Kabīr toward Rāmānand. In Sūr's case it was Vallabha instead, just as the paradigm of the four *sampradāys* had come to be seen as demanding. Although the figure of the guru was much less prominent in Sūr's poetry than in Kabīr's, Dvivedi saw no reason to doubt what the *Caurāsī Vaṣṇavan kī Vārtā* said was true: Sūr's transformation from being a poet of separation *(viraha)* to one who celebrated the *līlā* world of Krishna was achieved because of the moment when Vallabha made Sūr his pupil. No wonder, then, that Sūr's Radha should stand somewhat apart from her Bengali prototype. Despite a fair amount of evidence from the *Sūrsāgar* itself, Dvivedi saw her as fully woman and therefore fully Krishna's wife—not his paramour, as the Gauḍīyas insisted. This, he emphasized, was the common understanding in Braj, where she was typically addressed as Krishna's queen *(rānī)*.[56] To say as much was not to deny that the Bengalis had been very successful in spreading their devotional commitments much to the west of Bengal, or deny that these Bengalis also had a special genealogical connection to the Mahāyāna traditions of northeastern India. But however important this range, Dvivedi believed medieval Vaishnava religion drew more of its efficacy from the even broader "people's religion" *(lok-dharm)* that it succeeded in developing and purifying. Both Vallabha and Chaitanya had a hand in the process of intellectualization that went with it. Once a *śāstric* level of development had been achieved under their guidance, it flashed forth from one corner of the subcontinent to the other like lightning. In saying so, Dvivedi returned once again to the metaphor he had always championed.[57]

Dvivedi began *Sūr-Sāhitya* by speaking only of streams *(dhārā)* and traditions of practice *(sādhanā)*, but halfway through the book he added another dimension. He shifted toward the dominant idiom of his day and began to speak of movements *(āndolan)*: struggles in the cause of social betterment and national salvation that led up to Gandhi's great August *āndolan* or Quit India Movement of 1942. Such *āndolans* never made it into his prose explicitly when he was describing the long, broad sweep of India's literary and religious history, yet one feels them in the wings when Dvivedi says that the bhakti movement was the greatest of all *dhārmik* movements, bar none. Already in *Sūr-Sāhitya* and then again in *Hindī Sāhitya kī Bhūmikā* he affirms that the bhakti movement was even more immense than "the movement of [the] Buddhist religion"—again, notably, that northeastern Mahāyāna element he was trying to integrate into the subcontinental whole. This, by implication, meant that the bhakti movement was the ultimate source of India's strength—a strength so great as to make India stand out on the international scene. Addressing that scene in the person of George Grierson (see Chapter 1), Dvivedi says:

> This very scholar writes in another place, "No one who reads the Indian religious literature of the 15th and following centuries can fail to notice the gulf that lies between the old and the new [religious sensibilities]. We find ourselves in the face of the greatest religious revolution that India has ever seen—greater even that that of Buddhism, for its effects have persisted to the present day. Religion is no longer a question of knowledge. It is one of emotion. We visit a land of mysticism and rapture, and meet spirits akin, not to the giant schoolmen of Benares, but to the poets and mystics of mediaeval Europe, in sympathy with Bernard of Clairvaux, with Thomas à Kempis, with Eckhart, and with St. Theresa." With these two quotations from Dr. Grierson it becomes manifestly clear that the bhakti movement of the Indian Middle Ages is incomparable. As Doctor Sahib has said, this age has to do not with religion [*dharma*] and wisdom, but with emotion [*ras*]. In other words, we might say that in this period one cannot think of religion and art as two separate domains. Whether it be architecture, painting, poetry, dance, or music, everywhere a single reality comes into view, and it is this: that the entire Indian subcontinent, from one end to the other, was agitated by a powerful wave of bhakti—especially Vaishnava bhakti. The importance of this fact becomes even

> greater when we see that in this period of time India had become the pitiable prey of a foreign religion [*dharma*] and alien culture.
>
> It was not just Grierson but many scholars before him who suspected that the bhakti movement was actually a gift of Christianity . . . But when we try to deduce what might have been the dominant spring from which this bhakti movement suddenly emerged in the mysterious Middle Ages, we cannot say it was surprising that foreign scholars came to the conclusion that the bhakti element in India's spiritual practice [*sādhanā*] had been acquired from outside. Theirs was a natural error. But after all, it's a simple thing. Just as a person's life-force quickly awakens and springs back to life after one has been weak and afflicted with disease, so too did the life-force of Indian culture—that is, its spiritual discipline of bhakti [*bhakti-sādhanā*]—quickly awaken, in just this manner.[58]

Later, in his *Kabīr* book, Dvivedi lets his vision dilate in a similar way. He lifts his eye from the page before him and explores the broad question of what place we should assign to Kabīr in India's overarching tradition of religious discipline *(bhāratīya dharma-sādhanā).* He devotes a whole chapter to the subject, just as he had stopped for eighteen pages in the middle of his Sūrdās book to ponder the relationship between Hindi literature and the general phenomenon of Vaishnava religion. This time, however, as he moves to his conclusion, he slips out of history altogether and into another mode. Suddenly, after explaining Kabīr's remarkable accomplishment—preparing "a throne where one human being can meet another in that capacity alone"—he acknowledges that it may seem never to have borne fruit.[59] After all, do our struggles and rivalries not persist?

And then his thoughts turn to Tagore, who had died the year before Dvivedi published these lines. He remembers that his guru also nursed doubts about the slippage between promise and fulfillment, but he seems to profess that he himself—Hazariprasad Dvivedi—was living proof that a flower fallen to earth before blooming or a river that seems to disappear in the desert is still, nonetheless, not lost. Without saying so in so many words, he turns and addresses his guru with the following words of reassurance: "In life, even today, whatever has been left behind, whatever has been unfinished, I know well, even that has not been in vain. Whatever my future is, that which is even now untouched, all these things are being played on the strings of your *vīṇā*. I know well, they have not been lost."[60] These words, actually, are a Hindi paraphrase of words first uttered in a song composed by Tagore himself.[61] Dvivedi proceeds to quote them in

Bengali, thereby addressing not only his own personal, dearly missed guru but also the eternal guru whom Tagore himself addressed, the *satguru*. And the context, we recall, is all Kabīr, so he too becomes part of the chain. By that token perhaps we should include Rāmānand and the legacy of the south, as well.

As Dvivedi thought about the continuity of the bhakti movement, marveling at how it expressed itself ever and again from guru to pupil even when it seemed to disappear, he was himself tasting the results of the monsoon rains about which he insisted on speaking in every book he wrote. Drought and a need to wait for nourishment could be there, no doubt, but the moment of satisfaction ever returned, as if by its own mysterious volition. As he put it in his *Kabīr* book, responding yet again to Grierson's eternal challenge: *yah bhakti kā āndolan hai,* "This is the movement of bhakti."[62] That was near the beginning of the chapter from which we have just quoted. By the time Dvivedi finished it, it was clear that he had in mind not just the bhakti movement in some general sense, but a bhakti movement in which he himself participated. That was what made his exposition so powerful, so enduring: in Dvivedi's hands the bhakti movement was not just historiography; it was faith. Many people heard it and believed.

Brahmos and Bengalis

We have no record that Dvivedi ever made the personal acquaintance of the great Bengali nationalist Bipin Chandra Pal, but if he had, there would have been much to discuss. Pal was born in the eastern reaches of Bengal a year after the co-called Mutiny of 1857, became one of the founders of the Congress Party, served as the chief orator and propagandist of the Swadeshi movement both in English and in Bengali, was twice imprisoned as a seditionist by the British, then eventually "retreated" (as his biographers often say) to a more moderate and less popular position, becoming deeply suspicious of Gandhi's aspirations to "pontifical authority" in Congress.[63] He died after a period of seclusion and poverty—but great productivity as a writer—in Calcutta in 1932. Here was a man whose generation, background, and multiple involvements were quite different from Dvivedi's, yet in some respects their scholarly concerns and even their individual pasts were interestingly intertwined.

At the time of his death Pal had just finished a short book called *Bengal Vaishnavism,* written in English and published posthumously in 1933, in which some powerful notions of "a general *bhakti* movement" appear.[64] Pal's exposition of this "Vaishnavic Movement all over India" launches his penultimate chapter, the fifth, which he entitled "Social Reconstruction and Mass Movement in Bengal Vaishnavism."[65] As this title would suggest, the chapter's principal subject was not the south-to-north span that Dvivedi, Sen, or others had detailed. Instead Pal focused almost entirely on Chaitanya, as he had done since the book's very first pages. As background, and in self-consciously Hegelian fashion, he describes Krishna as "eternal subject" and "Eternal Will," Radha as the eternal object, Brindavan as "the social ideal" that emerges in the course of their encounter, and the encounter itself as a dialogical "Ultimate Reality" in which Krishna "rules only and absolutely through love."[66] Thus he unveils Chaitanya as "the Perfect Man," making him out to be "the realization or revelation of the age-long genius of the Bengalee people." He considers Chaitanya to have been inspired by that genius, but at the same time as he gave definitive personal and intellectual shape to this "Bengal *bhakti* cult," thus establishing what Pal called Chaitanya's "new *bhakti* movement." Chaitanya was a colossus, the Universal Man capable of converting the "old *bhakti* cult" whose philosophical precepts had been laid out in the *Śāndilya Bhakti Sūtras* into a new and definitive Bengali strain.[67]

Given this talk of bhakti and movements and the ultimate importance of it all—given too the Hegelian leanings—it is striking that Pal felt so little obliged to reach for a historical perspective on the matter of Chaitanya's own time. That, as we have said, came only at the beginning of chapter 5, but when it did, it was freighted with meanings we have so far encountered nowhere else:

> The Vaishnavic Movement over all India—that of Baba Nanak in the North-West or the Punjab, that of Kabir, Dadu, and Ramanand in Upper India, of Tukaram in the Deccan, and of Shree Chaitanya Mahaprabhu in Bengal, of the 15th and 16th centuries—was the result of the contact of ancient and mediaeval Hindu thought with the soul-compelling humanism of Islam as it was developed in its philosophy and poetry under the influence of the special culture of Persia . . . Islamic piety and Islamic poetry of Persia made a strong appeal to the spiritual endeavors and realizations of mediaeval Hinduism, and called for a reconstruction of Hindu thought and life; these found more or less organized expression in and through

> this continental Vaishnavic upheaval among us. These Vaishnavic Movements, though they did not completely cut themselves off from the thoughts and realizations of ancient and mediaeval India, were really movements of protest against the current religion, social economy and institutions of the Hindu people. In the Punjab this continental movement gave birth to a new religion, Sikhism. In the other Indian provinces this general *bhakti* movement over all India in the 15th and 16th centuries attempted a reconstruction of current Hindu thought and life with a view to make these an efficient vehicle of the new spiritual and social ideals. This was seen in a general movement of renaissance that became very marked in the domain of vernacular literature. Hindi in Upper India, Marathi in the Deccan, and Bengalee in our own province, received a new inspiration, becoming the vehicle of the new thought, creating a new body of religious and spiritual literature that had previously been practically confined to Sanskrit. These new creations at once helped to emancipate the genius of these various peoples from the domination of mediaeval Brahminism. In this way this general Vaishnava upheaval created a continental mass movement in India.[68]

A number of features that emerge in this passage are worthy of note—the treatment of Islam and Iran (his father had been trained in Persian); the attention to the vernacular and indeed, vernaculars; the oscillation between singular and plural uses of the term "movement"; the emphasis on protest, not only religious but also social and economic; and, of course, the forward-thinking resonances of concepts such as "upheaval," "propaganda," and "mass." Pal had been unabashed in devoting a whole section of his book *The Soul of India* to seeing "Some World Problems through Indian Specs."[69] Here, as if in counterpoint, he feels no hesitation about using modern European tools of social analysis to describe a past that had usually been understood in distinctively Indian terms. Unlike his Shantiniketan counterparts, he sees the "medieval" not as representing a noble, simple, potentially timeless sensibility that had been siphoned off and trodden down by reactionaries, but as the very enemy that the "Vaishnavic bhakti movement" tried to combat. (It was in part the "medievalism" in Gandhi's vision of the Non-Cooperation Movement that had repelled him.)[70] In his praise of the "genius" of particular peoples we hear the evocation of peoplehood that so fascinated him when, all the way back in the mid-1870s as a student at Presidency College, Calcutta, he had heard Surendranath Banerjea lecture on how Young Bengal could be its own version of Mazzini's Young Italy. Indeed, Surendranath had used his two prior lectures to describe what Pal calls in retrospect "the freedom movement among the Sikhs" and "the great socio-religious reform movement of Sree Chaitanya."[71] In a mode of thinking that allied Surendranath with Bankimchandra Chatterji and greatly impressed Pal, Surendranath had called attention to the enervative dangers that lay in wait if Indians allowed the British to do the job of history for them. No, every people must write its own.

In Pal's thinking the modernity of Chaitanya, expressing the genius of Bengal, was everywhere on display, and it was a very masculine modernity, well calculated to rebut colonial slurs about the effeminacy of Bengali men, of whom Chaitanya himself often served as symbol.[72] Pal argued, by contrast, that Chaitanya initiated "a great and wide mass movement among the Vaishnavas of Bengal" that delivered an utterly new "social message, the presence of the Lord in every human individually and collectively in the human society, and applied itself to secure both individual and social uplift." This was, as he called it in the last few pages of his book, the doctrine of "the apotheosis of man."[73] As such, it was an apotheosis of Bengali manhood, as well.

Education, first and foremost, was the frame. Pal explained that Chaitanya's Vaishnava followers had established a trio of "authoritative scripture"—a new Chaitanya *prasthāna trayī* composed of the *Caitanyamangal*, the *Caitanyabhāgavata*, and the *Caitanyacaritāmṛta*—that were written in Bengali and therefore demanded new and general patterns of literacy on the part of those who would study them, including both men and women. In establishing his "new community," as Pal called it, Chaitanya also effected a broader upheaval. He waged war against the caste system, accepting "so-called untouchable castes" into his company and creating a precedent that "had a tremendous influence in working [for] the uplift of the Bengalee masses, regardless of their birth." Not only that, he established new forms of organization—a cadre of teachers who, regardless of their backgrounds, were "all called Goswamis" and were given places of honor formerly reserved for Brahmins. He created a new set of laws that abolished for Vaishnavas the old rules against caste intermarriage and the remarriage of widows.[74] Following the great mid-nineteenth-century reforms that had made such marriages legally possible—and, as he was now to argue, following the message of Chaitanya himself—Pal had himself undertaken a marriage with such a widow.[75] Finally, Pal wished to emphasize, Chaitanya was moved by a sense of emotional connection rather than by matters of creed. This enabled him to spearhead a "large missionary movement in Hinduism" that produced, in its egalitarianism, "a silent revolution in the caste-ridden Brahminical social order."[76] To characterize it in this way was once again to evoke an aspect of Pal's own life, for he had spent months and years as a Brahmo missionary himself.

If any aspect of the history of Chaitanya's own time emerged as comparable to what the Master had done, it was in Pal's mind the "movement of freedom" that the Sikhs had also pursued.[77] But as we have just suggested, the more palpable parallels were not synchronic but diachronic. They were to be found in the movements to which Pal himself had been so fervently involved—the Swadeshi agitations starting in 1905, the New Party wing of the Congress, the New Movement philosophy that he espoused on the beaches of Madras, and the "enthusiastic," *sādhāraṇ* (plain), sometimes openly Vaishnava branch of the Brahmo Samaj. It was among the Sadharan Brahmos that Pal had found his own guru, Bijay Krishna Goswami. Looking back on the broad sweep of history, Pal felt that Bengali Vaishnavism had often succumbed to a superficial, ritualized, even Brahminized version of Chaitanya's religion that would deeply have disappointed the Master. At the other extreme, however, lay "the gross sensualism of the familiar Vaishnavic *bhakti* culture through the four *rasa*-s." Classical Brahmo reformers like Rammuhan Roy obviously did not have the stomach—or bowels, as he put it—to accept such a thing, yet Pal felt they had dismissed it too quickly. They had not taken to heart Rūp Gosvāmī's perception that *śānta rasa* (or as Pal says, *śānta bhāva*)—the fifth emotional condition, the meditative one—is really only the platform for the rest.[78] Thus they missed the sensate, emotional side of Chaitanya's truth, the affirmation that true religion is located in the body and in the common social fabric that contains it.

In the brief exposition of the history of the Brahmo Samaj that Pal offers near the end of *Bengal Vaishnavism,* where he reviews the well-known tension between the more rationalist and more emotional wings of the Samaj, he holds up Chaitanya as the criterion of full realization by which all others are to be judged. Chaitanya provides the standard by which the nondual and the aesthetic, the cerebral and the bodily, form a whole. With Chaitanya as his image of Universal Man, Pal found it unsurprising that the great Brahmo leaders, however cerebral they might be, nonetheless felt the need for a complementary bhakti element in their own lives. Rammohan Roy and Debendranath Tagore (Rabindranath's father) found it in what Pal calls the bhakti of Islam; Keshub Chandra Sen, somewhat later, in the bhakti of Christianity. But Pal felt a particular sympathy for the frustrations of more common people, who also hungered for this bhakti dimension of life but necessarily searched for its fulfillment in their own religious and cultural vocabulary, not in the habits of Christians or Muslims. "This want of the great bulk of the members of the Brahmo Samaj," said Pal, "was met by Pandit Bijay Krishna Goswami, who helped Keshub to inaugurate a new *bhakti* movement in the Brahmo Samaj, more or less filiated to the movement of Shree Chaitanya Mahaprabhu."[79] This "new *bhakti* movement" was launched against "the old Vedantic type of *bhakti*" represented by more austere Brahmos such as Debendranath Tagore. Because of the way he frames it, one senses that for Pal this represented the proper dialogical solution to the historical progression he describes—indeed, perhaps, the necessary one. And it had its physical base. In the autobiography Pal was writing at the same time, he points out that the man who championed this solution—Bijay Krishna Goswami, the warm-hearted Ananda who strode beside Keshub Chandra Sen's Buddha—actually emerged from a family that could claim a lineal connection to the circle of Chaitanya himself, via Advaita Acharya.[80]

Here too, then, as in the case of Dvivedi, we find the writer standing in the midst of the bhakti movement history he himself articulates. Pal seems to take the general idea of the bhakti movement, the medieval or early modern one, and map it onto the much later moment of renewal that drew him into the Brahmo Samaj. Similarly, like Dvivedi, there are strong nationalist overtones in parts of what he says. In other ways, however, their cases are quite different. Pal's bhakti movement has a distinctly Bengali flavor. It forms a part of his effort to display Chaitanya's eternal contemporaneity to his Bengali countrymen, and through them to the world. Bengal had long been the seat of colonial rule, and *bhadralok* Bengalis therefore had a much more self-confident grasp of themselves as cosmopolitans than was common elsewhere in India—and surer footing in institutions spawned under British rule. Hence they had less need for the sort of pan-Indian bhakti movement narrative that occupied the attentions of Hindi speakers such as Dvivedi. Actually, as we have seen, some of the most influential among Chaitanya's followers—we have just mentioned Rūp Gosvāmī—were deeply implicated in the new cosmopolitanism that was forged under Mughal rule, with its continent-wide aspirations. But this side of things rarely came through when Bengali Vaishnavas looked back at history in an effort to reconstruct the "historical Chaitanya" who would answer to their own needs and times. Perhaps it simply didn't have to.

Strikingly, the effort in Jaisingh's time to tie Chaitanya's movement to a deeper Mādhva past and thereby to a wider Indian history was also largely absent in these accounts. Who needed it? Modern Bengal, with its position of leadership in British India, provided a sufficiently generous mirror against which could be refracted the forward-looking, cosmopolitan, yet distinctively populist persona Chaitanya was held to represent. What Jīv Gosvāmī had long ago argued was also true for Pal: no connection to a guru's lineage would ever be adequate to the task of representing Mahaprabhu's global significance, his "gospel of Universal Humanity." To the extent that any lens was useful for Pal, it was supplied by the various facets of Bengaliness itself.[81] Thus Pal gave new inflections to the nativist historiographies of Chaitanya that began to emerge in Bengal in the 1880s, the most influential being the six-volume *Amiya Nimai Carit* of Sishir Kumar Ghosh and its English condensation, *Lord Gauranga*.[82] By focusing so determinedly on Chaitanya, of course, Pal was also acting out the "bhakti movement" side of the Brahmo Samaj itself, the side personified by Keshub Chandra Sen and Bijay Krishna Goswami.

This put Pal in quite a different position from that of Hazariprasad Dvivedi or Kshitimohan Sen—members, one might say, of the "Tagore *sampradāy*," which had its roots on the other side of the Brahmo ledger.[83] Both Sen and Dvivedi participated in the regular Brahmo assemblies that were held at Shantiniketan's Mandir each Wednesday morning, and both of them came to share, through Rabindranath, in a Brahmo history somewhat at variance from the one Pal discovered in the charismatic presence of Bijay Krishna Goswami when he met him at the Sadharan Brahmo Samaj in Calcutta. The Shantiniketan Brahmo heritage went back to the Adi (original) Brahmos—the sober rationalists against whom Keshub's "bhakti movement" represented such a sharp reformulation. Rabindranath Tagore's grandfather, Debendranath, had in his time been the sturdiest pillar of the Brahmo Samaj, and the man who, perhaps even more than

Rammohan Roy himself, actually made the Brahmo Samaj a force in history.[84] He was also the person who had acquired as a family estate the land on which Shantiniketan would be built, first by his son Dvijendranath and then by his famous grandson. Bipin Chandra Pal remembered Debendranath as the seniormost person in the leadership of the Brahmo Samaj during the years when he was trying to discover his own life's calling, but Debendranath's cool commitments to the Advaitan Upanishads and also to Islamic forms of piety rendered him, for Pal, a somewhat distant presence.[85] As mediated by his son and grandson, however, Debendranath's commitment to "Vedanta-inspired bhakti" was just the sort of approach that would ultimately inspire a sympathetic response in the young Hazariprasad Dvivedi, who was, as we know, the author of just this phrase, though in quite a different context.

It seems significant that the "mass movement" radicalism Pal perceived as standing at the core of the fifteenth- and sixteenth-century bhakti movement was not the element that appealed most deeply to Dvivedi. For him it was not so much Chaitanya and his crowd of followers but rather Sūrdās and Kabīr who captured the limelight. Part of their attraction for Dvivedi was simply linguistic, of course—Hindi as against Bengali—but that fact also had a deeper significance. The Brindavan that Dvivedi saw through the prism of Sūrdās's Radha, as he appraised her, was soberer and more "natural" than the ecstatic Brindavan conjured up by her Gauḍīya devotees; and the guru he saw through Kabīr's example was similarly soberer, more discriminating, less ecstatic than Chaitanya—in a word, less "Bengali." As we have seen, Dvivedi did make a concerted effort to draw in the great traditions of the Bengali east—Buddhist, Nāth, and Vaishnava—as he approached both Sūrdās and Kabīr, but he also saw them as belonging to a broader, pan-Indian whole. That shared "bhakti India" provided quite a different metaphor for the emergent modern nation than had been supplied by the struggles for self-rule that most deeply affected Bengalis—struggles that confirmed their sense that they were natural symbols of the nation as a whole. In Bengali nationalist writing, Bengal and India were often little distinguished; Bengal itself was "the nation."[86] By contrast to that self-confidence, one found among speakers and scholars of Hindi a certain insecurity. It surfaced in their self-conscious imitation of literary strides that Bengalis had already made and in their awareness that as a modern language, Hindi was the new kid on the block. This helps explain why Dvivedi, as he looked back to the "Middle Ages," needed the four *sampradāys* and all the anchorage it provided in a way that Pal simply did not—and, of course, the idea was readily available in important Hindi sources.

Pal, for his part, was happy to marshal a bhakti movement of his own, explicitly so called, which buttressed his conception of the great events of the fifteenth and sixteenth centuries in a different way. The impetus for his doing so can be traced back to the dramatic moment in 1867 when Keshub Chandra Sen tried to democratize and invigorate Brahmo liturgical practices through the introduction of Vaishnava *kīrtan* and enthusiastic *brahmotsav* celebrations in which he himself played a leading role. As we have seen, the impetus for these innovations had come from Keshub's associate and close adviser Bijay Krishna Goswami, and it was immediately in their wake that Pal himself discovered the Brahmo Samaj. In his autobiography, even more forcefully than in *Bengal Vaishnavism*, Pal refers to these developments as "this *Bhakti* movement in the Brahmo Samaj" and as "the new *Bhakti* movement in Bengal."[87]

He was hardly the first to do so. Several early attestations of this specifically nineteenth-century use of the phrase "bhakti movement" come from the pen of Sophia Dobson Collet, a New Zealander who explained from London at the end of 1872 to the "mixed Indian public" she had come to know while resident in Calcutta that she was writing as a "Trinitarian Christian."[88] This, she evidently hoped, would enable her to be perceived by readers who stood outside the Samaj as presenting an objective account of the rivalist events that began to unfold late in 1865. In *An Historical Sketch of the Brahmo Somaj,* printed in Calcutta in early 1873, she explains that "the first noteworthy phase in the development of the Brahmo Somaj of India"—the new name that was adopted by the group of young reformers whom Keshub led—"was what has been called 'the Bhakti movement.'" To be specific, "a number of the younger Brahmos quitted the Calcutta Somaj (leaving behind them all the accumulated property of the institution), and 'went out, not knowing whether they went.'" As if to deflect charges that Keshub Chandra Sen was building a personality cult around himself—"Keshub-worship," as his opponents called it—Collet makes clear that about a year had passed before Keshub organized these young Brahmo secessionists into the Brahmo Samaj of India, and that in it "no President was appointed; like the Scottish

Covenanters, they declared that the Lord alone was their Head; but Keshub Chunder Sen was chosen to be their Secretary."[89] She quotes from "a brief narrative of this period"—a report made by P. C. Mozoomdar (Protap Chandra Majumdar) in the *Indian Mirror,* a regular Brahmo publication, on July 1, 1868—to give a sense of the mood: "Sunday after Sunday, their devotional meetings presented such a scene as angels might visit with pride . . . Songs expressive of the most lowly humility, most vivid faith and dependence, were sung in choral rapture, giving rise to that new hymnal service of the Brahmos called by the name of Brahmo Saṃkīrtan . . . Thus originated the *Brahmotsav,* literally meaning 'Rejoicing in the Lord.' It is the festival of the Brahmos."[90]

The term *saṃkīrtan,* of course, locates this practice expressly in the lineage of Chaitanya, and that was the exact intent of Bijay Krishna Goswami, who, as we have seen, played a significant role in persuading Keshub Sen to adopt such practices.[91] Collet, however, proceeds to draw in a Christian idiom as she describes the *brahmotsavs* that transpired annually in the wake of the first: "In the last few anniversary festivals, large bodies of Brahmos have gone out, threading the streets and lanes of the native quarter of Calcutta, singing missionary hymns to win their Hindu countrymen to the service of the One True God." Thus she chronicles events that transpired in Progressive Brahmoism "since the Bhakti movement began."[92]

Evidently this "bhakti movement" coinage was not Collet's alone. In volume 1 of *The Brahmo Year-book,* published in 1876, she says:

> The unsealing of heavenly light and joy which commenced in the Brahmo Samaj with this "Bhakti movement," as it was called (from *Bhakti* or loving faith in God) has continued, more or less, ever since, and has, on the whole, fixed the average type of Brahmoism. The first Brahmotsab [the formalized ceremony that channeled the enthusiasms of the preceding two years] took place at the house of Keshub Chunder Sen, on the 24th of November, 1867. In the following April and June, two others were held at Monghyr; and the Brahmotsab soon became a regular institution. One of its features is the rapturous singing of hymns, which have increased and flourished greatly in the Brahmo Samaj since the rise of the Bhakti movement."[93]

Collet takes the phrase "bhakti movement" and makes it the heading of the passage in which it occurs. Thus it becomes the first topic to be considered among the "Religious Movements in the Brahmo Samaj" that she describes as part of her annual report. Once again, in fact, she quotes the passage from Mozoomdar and he, as if to return the favor, adopted her practice of headlining Keshub's bhakti movement when in 1882 he published his book *The Faith and Progress of the Brahmo Samaj,* which, as the title implies, presents an overview of the Samaj's history until that point in time. There again we meet the passage Collet had quoted, though its parts are distributed somewhat differently in the text.[94] In these circles, at least, that early description seems to have become iconic, somewhat after the fashion of Acts' description of Pentecost. At the level of headings we have now "The Bhakti or Devotional Movement in the Brahmo Samaj," which becomes sufficiently foundational that it also generates the title of a later chapter. That one, concerning "The Second Devotional Movement of the Brahmo Samaj," describes various measures that were taken in the late 1870s to give greater force and definition to the Samaj's missionary activities.

Because of Mozoomdar's importance in the Samaj—especially its Sadharan or, as Collet says, Progressive branch—*The Faith and Progress of the Brahmo Samaj* quickly became a major resource. It may well have been in the back of Bipin Chandra Pal's mind when he laid out the analogy between what he now saw as the *new* bhakti movement—Keshub Chandra Sen's—and the enthusiastic activities that Chaitanya himself initiated, which are by implication the original bhakti movement, their antetype. Of course, Pal also absorbed the broad evolution of English-language uses of the word "movement" that had occurred between the 1880s and the 1930s. Notably he incorporated vocabulary that would resonate in a post-Bolshevik world—"the masses," "propaganda," and the like. He may also have been heir to parallel conventions that developed—if not to quite the same extent—in Bengali. Sivanath Sastri's *Rāmtanu Lahari o Tatkālīn Bāṅgāsamāj* (Ramtanu Lahiri and Contemporary Bengali Society), which had a major impact on the narration of the "Bengal Renaissance" in the nineteenth century, refers to Keshub's innovations within the Brahmo Samaj as "waves of a movement" *(āndolaner tarang)* and speaks of the society of Calcutta and other major places in that period as being "rocked by many waves" *(nānā tarang āndolit).* The specific *bhakti āndolan* coinage is not there, and never did become dominant in Bengali, but one can certainly sense the general *āndolan* ambiance.[95]

Pal was not the only person to recognize a clear tie between "Shree Chaitanya's Movement," as he called it, and the renewing events of the 1860s and 1870s.[96] In a way the bond was intrinsic, since Chaitanya's signature *saṃkīrtan* was involved in both, but there was another dimension, too: in both cases to launch *saṃkīrtan* was do something fundamentally new. One of the Brahmo missionaries who went out into the world during the period of Keshub Chundra Sen's leadership seems to rely on this analogy, for he retrojects the language of "bhakti movement," which had apparently even then become common as a way to refer to events within the Brahmo Samaj, so that it could refer to the great prophetic moment almost four centuries earlier. The man in question was a Bengali Brahmo missionary named Pearee Mohun Chaudry, who says that he delivered the following text as part of an English address to an audience gathered at the Shiksha Sava Hall in Lahore on May 13, 1870. He explains how the "Law of Love" known to Jesus was later revealed to Muhammad and Chaitanya:

> And it is only 385 years back that this Kingdom of Love was revealed to Chaitanya. This enabled him to originate the *Bhakti* movement which regenerated thousands of men and women in Bengal.
>
> And almost simultaneously with his movement nearly 400 years ago the self-same scenes of *Bhakti* or devout love were enacted here; in this part of India, I mean, in the Panjab. Baba Nanak, the founder of the Sikh sect was born in the year 1539 A.D. in a place close to Lahore . . . During a long life of 70 years he labored to show that there is but one God who is the Father of all mankind. He attempted to amalgamate the Hindoo and Mahomedan creeds.[97]

It is fascinating that the Sikh connection appears here, even if only a fraternal relationship is claimed to have existed between its expression of bhakti and the bhakti movement specifically initiated by Chaitanya. As we have already seen in the thinking of Kshitimohan Sen and Bipin Chandra Pal, and as we will see again in the murals that were created to line the walls of Hindi Bhavan in Shantiniketan, Sikhs and the Punjab played a special role in the Bengali bhakti imaginary. That the latter-day missionary circuit linking Calcutta to Lahore was so strong—in the Brahmo Samaj and also in its Arya Samaj cousin—adds a further dimension to the picture. But even with all that being so, when Pearee Mohun

Chaudry and Bipin Chandra Pal, almost half a century apart, frame events of the early sixteenth century as "bhakti movement," they nonetheless preserve a vivid sense that what Chaitanya did mattered first and foremost in Bengal. That was how it came to play its role in the history of the Brahmo Samaj itself.

Because of this devotedly Bengali dimension there are obvious differences of emphasis between Bipin Chandra Pal's ideas about the medieval bhakti movement and those of Hazariprasad Dvivedi, yet in some way the Brahmo Samaj may provide a common tie. Very likely there were multiple copies of Mozoomdar's *Faith and Progress of the Brahmo Samaj* in Shantiniketan when Dvivedi was there; certainly Tagore would have had one. We do not know whether Dvivedi read the book and was affected by its prioritization of "the bhakti movement" as an organizational concept. If so, he transposed it to a rather different key as he worked out his own idea of *bhakti āndolan*. Yet it is hard to believe that he was not affected at least to some degree by the broader "movement" thinking that characterized the Brahmo Samaj's image of itself, since the Samaj was so much a part of Shantiniketan's background and ambience. Then too there were all those other *āndolans* that made their appeals to thinking people in the 1930s.

It was a harbinger of future developments in the history of the bhakti movement idea that the specific emphases of the Brahmo Samaj in this regard remained recessive in Hazariprasad Dvivedi's thinking. Yes, he took Chaitanya and Bengal quite seriously as he thought about medieval times, but despite the fact that he was living in Bengal he never let this eastern dimension take center stage. Instead he submerged it in the Nāths; and the Nāths, in turn, in Kabīr. Hindi thinkers and textbook writers followed his lead, and they had a considerable impact on what would happen in English. As one watches the drama develop, conscious of its nationalist theme, one cannot help wondering what would have happened if the capital had remained in Calcutta rather than shifting to Delhi in 1911. Would the bhakti movement, as generally perceived, have passed much more directly through Chaitanya than it now does? Would specifically Bengali forms of cultural nationalism have won the day? But that was not what happened. Calcutta yielded to Delhi—and that gave Dvivedi's perspective on the bhakti movement a resonance that for Pal remained confined to Bengal.

Kabīr and Sūrdās as Exemplars

In thinking about the bhakti movement, Hazariprasad Dvivedi often refers to his relation to the great Banarsi intellectual world out of which he came. Time and again he quotes Ramchandra Shukla—always with great respect—but in doing so, he sometimes reveals their differences, as well. We have already outlined some of these in Chapter 1. At that point we also saw how Shukla, when he published a second edition of his influential *Hindī Sāhitya kā Itihās* (History of Hindi Literature) two years before he died in 1942, adopted from Dvivedi the *āndolan* language that signaled one of the most important differences between himself and the younger scholar who was making a name for himself at Shantiniketan. It was an important step—a concession to a new way of thinking—but in a way it was just window dressing.

The core of Shukla's thoughts about "the development of bhakti" *(bhakti kā vikās)* were contained in a long essay of that title in which Shukla made no mention of movements at all—and scarcely even of the "streams" *(dhārāeṅ)* he had charted out in *Hindī Sāhitya kā Itihās*. He seems to have written the essay in the early 1930s, and considering the "development" in its title, it is a remarkably static document. Its main purpose was not to articulate a theory of how bhakti emerged in ancient India and subsequently changed, though one gets a hint or two along the way, but rather to contrast a distinctively Indian way of thinking about the relation between religion and human society with the characteristic mode that Shukla thought he detected in the West. In doing so, he sketched his own version of the contrast between Semitic and Aryan that was a leading preoccupation among European academics of the time. For Shukla the key difference was that in the Semitic or "mystical" *(rahasyātmak)* tradition—these two closely overlapped in his mind—great religious figures positioned themselves outside the general course of human behavior, supposing they could criticize it from an independent vantage point and therefore often preaching "at" it.[98] In India, by contrast, the most influential thinkers located themselves within the social net, expecting first and foremost to uphold and reweave that fabric, making it ever stronger. This had been the case, Shukla argued, ever since the era when the Upanishads were composed, and it remained so all the way through to the great founding figures of Hindi literature, including especially Tulsīdās and

Sūrdās. The key was always a "double sensibility" *(ubhayātmak bhāvanā)* that took account of both *nirguṇ* and *saguṇ* actualities, but because the *saguṇ* aspect was so closely tied to the phenomenal world and its conduct, it naturally emerged as the more important of the two.[99] According to Shukla it was the characteristic unwillingness of Indian thinkers to relinquish their enduring stake in the real *saguṇ* world that made them stand apart from their Western counterparts. It was the West, not India, therefore, that became the otherworldly partner in this comparison—exactly the reverse of what Europeans tended to affirm.

Because of the fabric-strengthening, expressly human context in which the greatest Indian seers characteristically worked, their overarching concern was dharma, Shukla said. Bhakti was to be understood as its inner face—"the heart of dharma" *(dharma kā hṛdaya)*.[100] Not surprisingly, bhakti's sometimes uneasy relation to caste and social inequity assumed for Shukla a distinctly secondary importance, and the Muslim challenge to *varṇāśrama dharma* meant far less to him as a component of bhakti's broader story than it did to Dvivedi or Sen.[101] For Shukla as a nationalist on the frontlines of cultural defense—a senior spokesman for a mode of thought and behavior he believed to have been radically misrepresented by foreigners past and present—first things had to come first. He was in the business of defining what was truly "Indian" *(bhāratīya)*.[102]

Dvivedi was different. Although he also wrote in the 1930s, he was a generation removed from Shukla. He could take for granted the bulwark Shukla and his Banarsi cohort had labored to build, which was not just conceptual but institutional: the canon-creating work of the Nāgarīpracāriṇī Sabhā and educational program of Banaras Hindu University. That meant he could also go beyond it. He could be a revolutionary in the Romantic mode, as Namvar Singh put it, taking more seriously than Shukla had done the social conditioning and social consciousness that is embedded even in what seems at first to be purely asocial or even antisocial protest—the sort of thing one encounters in the single-minded bhakti personalities of Malik Muhammad Jāyasī's Sufi hero or Sūrdās's gopis.[103] Shukla sometimes made provision for a bhakti that could productively inhabit its own realm—he thought the *Bhāgavata Purāṇa* achieved just this—but Dvivedi's sense of an ongoing, organic, untrammeled bhakti allowed it to come more naturally to the fore and assume its distinctive historical trajectories.

"Bhakti kā Vikās" was the product of Shukla's maturity—it remained on his desk at the time of his death—and the context in which he planned to publish it was an interesting one. Shukla saw it as forming the first part (some seventy-five pages) of his book on Sūrdās, which was posthumously edited by Viśvanāthprasād Miśra for publication in 1948. Shukla's chapters on Sūr, one of which had been published in the Nāgarīpracāriṇī Sabhā's monthly magazine in 1926, came at the end, and he created a bridge between this and "Bhakti kā Vikās" by inserting an intermediary section on Vallabhācārya. Vallabha served to link the timeless, foundational, civilizational "development of bhakti" component to the great *saguṇ* poets who stood at the high-water mark of Hindi's literary history. If for Dvivedi the great through-story of bhakti passed from Rāmūnuja to Rāmānand to Kabīr, for Shukla it remained in the *saguṇ* realm instead, passing from the *Bhāgavata Purāṇa* to Vallabha to Sūr. In "Bhakti kā Vikās," at least, this was less a historical progression than a scriptural one—a great Sanskrit text being mediated to the vernacular. The sense of bhakti's being an actual movement was not articulated as such. True, the word "history" appears in the title of Shukla's most frequently read work, *Hindī Sāhitya kā Itihās,* but in "Bhakti kā Vikās" we are talking less of history than of *Geist.*

A younger member of the Banaras circle saw things quite differently. Pitambar Datta Barthwal, a brilliant Brahmin from the Garhwal mountains with a delicate constitution that led to a tragically early death (1901–1944), studied at Banaras Hindu University in the late 1920s, where he worked especially closely with Śyāmsundar Dās. He wrote an M.A. thesis of such distinction that Dās immediately made him a lecturer in the Hindi Department, where he joined not only his own mentor but Ramchandra Shukla.[104] Before long he had also become the head of the research wing *(khoj vibhāg)* of the Nāgarīpracāriṇī Sabhā, dealing daily with the substantial corpus of manuscripts Sabhā scholars were amassing and studying, especially so as to create the score of critically edited texts that would form the basis of the Hindi literary canon from that time forward. Most of these works had religious meaning, and none was to prove more influential than the *Kabīr Granthāvalī* (Collected Works of Kabīr) that Śyāmsundar Dās published in 1928. Based principally on a Dādūpathī manuscript whose colophon declared it to have been copied in 1504 (V.S. 1561), this was the text that Hazariprasad Dvivedi quoted most frequently as he thought his way through his famous book on Kabīr.[105]

Kabīr also stood at the center of Barthwal's vision of what really counted in—let us use Shukla's term—the "development of bhakti." The title of his thesis, also submitted in 1928, was *The Nirguṇa School of Hindi Poetry: An Exposition of Medieval Indian Santa Mysticism.* Written in English, this thesis was published as a book of the same title in 1936. There Barthwal expressed his view that it was not the comprehensiveness of Hindu dharma that best enabled one to see that *nirguṇ* and *saguṇ* belonged together, but the eclecticism of what he called "the Nirguṇ school," that is, the ability of its adherents to live a life that disclaimed every specific "sectarianism" and benefited from a broad evolutionary "process of social mind" that necessarily went by different names and threw up different emphases in the course of time.[106] As Dvivedi also urged, these included Advaitans, Buddhists, Gorakhnāthīs, Sufis, and Vaishnavas, each adding something the other had been unable to conceive with full clarity. Barthwal put it thus: "If the individuals forming the mediate links between the remotest sources and the Nirguṇ-panth had not kept an open mind to all wholesome influences, how could we hope to get a perfect system like the Nirguṇ-panth? And as Kabīr himself is the most conspicuous link in that evolutionary process, his part cannot be too greatly stressed."[107]

Barthwal held that "the Nirguṇ School reformed the clumsy habits of the Śūdras, taught them to honor labor, opened wide the solace of devout knowledge for them and instilled into them a strong sense of self-respect." If this sounds patronizing, one must remember that it accords with the distaste for the undisciplined practices of Shāktas and Tāntriks that one finds so prominently in Kabīr's own verse—the sort of mood that made him "a Vaishṇava who did not worship Vishṇu, his Avatār or his idol." And Barthwal was quick to add that it also expressed his Muslimness—the "utter dislike of a Moslem for all caste distinctions."[108]

Barthwal thought Rāmānand, the vanguard of the "current of devotional religion" that welled up from the south, had "slackened the rigor" of caste prejudice, but fell short of the commitment to full social equality on which Kabīr insisted. Yet even in relation to Kabīr one feels the constraint of another concern that Barthwal deeply felt, perhaps thinking of his own time as well as Kabīr's: the need for concord as well as social justice. The "Nirguṇ movement" charged itself to achieve both—unity and equality. Kabīr becomes to Barthwal the pupil not only of Rāmānand but, as Muslim claimants to his body would insist, an associate of Shaikh

Tāqī as well—or if not always his disciple, then at least associated with him in some way. Similarly the *nirguṇ* movement as a whole was a "unifying movement" in more than one respect.[109] It drew on and consolidated an "eclectic" past that stretched beyond the *varṇāśrama dharma* that remained Shukla's guide, and it specifically dealt with tensions and complementarities between Muslims and Hindus that became manifest in north India in the period of Muslim rule.

In contrast to Dvivedi's view, this *nirguṇ* movement builds on and supersedes the "Vaishnava movement." Barthwal thinks of this earlier movement as something that did not have to face the "frown" of conquest and religious self-righteousness that the Muslim conquest entailed, but by the same token could not yet breathe the bracing fresh air of Muslim habits and convictions. The *nirguṇ* movement Kabīr and his cohort initiated was both the inheritor of the earlier Vaishnava movement, riding its "wave" *(lahar)*, and the expression of something fundamentally new.[110] Yes, there was also a socially inclusive aspect to the earlier Vaishnava moment. At one point Barthwal brings the example of the Untouchable *āḻvār* Tiruppāṇ to the fore. In fact, he spews out a whole list of southern bhaktas who were *śūdra* in origin.[111] Nonetheless he depicts the straightforwardly "reformist" agenda that went with Kabīr's *nirguṇ panth* as a major advance. This was doubtless one reason Barthwal held back from grouping the earlier "Vaishnava movement" and its later *nirguṇ* cousin under a single designation, even though the latter sank its roots into a long-standing "religion of single-minded love" *(aikāntik dharma)* that undergirded the southern Vaishnava movement, as well.[112] He avoids the term "bhakti movement" both in Hindi and in English, though he is perfectly comfortable speaking of movements and *āndolans* in other contexts. For Barthwal, finding a single bhakti movement was ultimately less important than showing how Kabīr and others—the *nirguṇīs*—stood out from it.

It is striking that important articulations of the idea of the bhakti movement arose so often in the context of excavations into the personalities and poetry of Sūrdās and Kabīr. This was true for Shukla and Dvivedi in regard to Sūrdās, and for Dvivedi and Barthwal in regard to Kabīr. Yet little is said in any of these discussions about the movement that lies just beneath the surface of both poets' justly famous names—the circulatory and archival processes that created and perpetuated personae like "Kabīr" and "Sūr" in the first place. Barthwal appends a detailed and sensitive bibliographical note to *The Nirguṇa School of Hindi Poetry,* addressing manuscript problems that have to be solved in getting at Kabīr, but the effect of these considerations on what he says in the text itself remains unclear. Like others, he needs his Kabīr to be Kabīr in some obvious way.

The truth is more difficult. Especially with poets like Kabīr and Sūrdās, who favored the short lyrics or couplets that most critics would place at the heart of the bhakti movement, the authorial voice we hear as "Kabīr" or "Sūr" is the result of a process that draws in other poets who stand at quite some distance from the original artists.[113] These poets compose in the names of the poets they admire, thus participating in the genre that goes by the name of a Sūr or a Kabīr. We hear almost nothing of this from the great bhakti movement theorists of the 1920s and 1930s, but it is actually critical to the creation of the literary and religious phenomenon that the bhakti movement describes. Sūr and Kabīr "move" with their poetry—that is, with the poetry that is performed in their names. Take Kabīr. Each of the three major recensions containing poetry attributed to him—a fourth, the Fatehpur manuscript largely devoted to Sūrdās (1582), has since come to light—shows how this is so: each has its own personality. And with Sūrdās one can see the same pattern in a different way, and even more dramatically. Some four hundred poems can be shown to have circulated in Sūr's name by the end of the sixteenth century, but by the time we get to the nineteenth century the number approaches ten thousand. It takes a remarkable leap of faith to believe that a single sixteenth-century poet could have composed them all, especially since their numbers increase rather than decrease over time.[114]

Undoubtedly there was a "real" Sūrdās around whom the Sūr collections first began to congeal, but when most people—including scholars such as Shukla and Dvivedi—report that Sūrdās said this or that, they are referring to a far wider corpus. The same is true for scholars of Kabīr, and again, though they try to be cautious, both Dvivedi and Barthwal would have to be counted in their number. In regard to a number of other bhakti works—a long, narrative work like Tulsīdās's *Rāmcaritmānas,* for example, or the bounded, internally connected collections of verse represented in the *Tiruppāvai* and *Nācciyār Tirumoḷi* of Āṇṭāḷ—the processual factor intrudes less markedly, but what has often intrigued scholars of the bhakti movement is the degree to which one poet's poems may sometimes be found under the signature of another, that is, in another poet's corpus. It may not be a complete poem, but only several lines—especially the interior ones—yet the pattern is very general, and at least as marked in performance as on the page.

Because of the way the personae of Sūr and Kabīr were constructed over time, the reason this often happens is plain. It's not that Sūr was copying Kabīr or vice versa, though in principle something like this could well occur, but that groups of poets contributed to both oeuvres. Thus the poets we know as Sūr or Kabīr are actually bhakti movements in themselves. Within the range these names represent, regional and sectarian preferences can exercise their sway. The Sikh Kabīr is not the same as the Dādūpathī one, and both stand at a certain distance from the Kabīr who is remembered in the Kabīr Panth headquartered at Banaras. Moreover, as David Lorenzen has shown, Kabīr's "greatest hits" as recognized toward the end of the twentieth century are hardly the same poems that seem to have fascinated people two or three centuries earlier.[115] In large part this is because the relevant poems had not yet been composed. So "Kabīr," to repeat, is a bhakti movement all his own—in his poetry and in his hagiography, as well. The same is true for Sūrdās and many others.

In Chapters 3 and 4 we alluded to the processes that made Sūr and especially Kabīr so famous so fast—the increased mobility and rapid advances in communication that Suri and Mughal administrations made possible in sixteenth-century north India. But what is especially noteworthy here is that these poets were not actually the property of any *sampradāy,* though in both cases they were later claimed to be so. The singers on whose lips they sang moved more freely than that, and perhaps they themselves did too. As his poems circulated in the sixteenth century, Kabīr came to be deemed essential to the institutional success of both the Sikh *panth* and its Dādū analogue. Sikhs and Dādūpathīs saw him as a major pillar that could be used to give stability to the anthological edifices they were constructing, or perhaps we should think of this more as the written consolidation of a tradition of performance. Either way, Kabīr's existence outside the local core leant a sense of range and relevance to the utterances of Nānak, Dādū, and their successors and disciples. Similarly the Dādūpathī anthologist Rajjab frequently drew Sūrdās's petitionary (*binati* or *vinaya*) poems into his vast *Sarvāngī,* although the great bulk of his poetry would surely have been remembered as *saguṇ* in spirit.[116] Perhaps this was because Sūr was regarded as the finest exemplar of Brajbhasha poetry—a literary motive—but whatever the reason was, it certainly had nothing to do with the assertion of a specific connection between Sūrdās and the Dādū *panth*. Dadūite hagiography makes no such point.

The bhakti theorists of the 1920s and 1930s paid little attention to boundary-challenging facts such as these, but these facts lend a crucial density to their project, suggesting how the bhakti movement actually moved. They also dispense some golden drops of poetic justice. They show how right it is that Sūr and Kabīr were asked to bear the structural weight they did, even as they simultaneously challenge the veracity of the Vallabhite and Rāmānandī sectarian lineages that were supposed to have borne this weight in the first place. It is no accident that these poets in particular—Sūr and Kabīr, a *saguṇī* and a *nirguṇī*—became sites for some of the most important early statements of the bhakti movement.

The Hindi Bhavan Murals

If there is a single document that best testifies to how the bhakti movement narrative crystallized in India's great era of preindependence cultural nationalism, perhaps we may find it not in a verbal medium, but a visual one. I am thinking of the frescoes that adorn the upper reaches of three walls in the central room of Hindi Bhavan at Shantiniketan, the room that was originally the focus of its library. Entitled *Medieval Saints*, these murals were created in 1946–1947 by the noted artist Binodbihari Mukherji, who worked with one or two art students also resident at Shantiniketan.[117] Obviously the spirit of Tagore is in the background—it was he who drew Mukherji to Shantiniketan in the first place and he who commissioned the murals that Nandalal Bose and Mukherji created for Hindi Bhavan's predecessor institution, Chīn Bhavan (China House)—but the figure who most directly inspired *Medieval Saints* was surely the scholar who served as director of Hindi Bhavan at the time, Hazariprasad Dvivedi.

Elsewhere in contemporary India one can see displays of poet-saints whose arrangement in relation to one another suggests the subcontinental spread of bhakti. Sculpted in marble along the walls of the manuscript depository in the great Hanumān temple at Mahalakshmipuram near

Figure 5. Hindi Bhavan murals by Binodbihari Mukherji, south wall showing Rāmānuja and possibly Rāmānand (1946–1947). Courtesy of Viśva-Bhāratī and the Vadehra Art Gallery.

Bangalore, for instance, one finds an array of Karnataka saints, including Śaṃkarācārya, Tyāgarāja, and Kanakadāsa, who are joined by others from Maharashtra (Tukārām and Jñāneśvar), Bengal (Rāmakṛṣṇa and his wife Sāradādevī), and the north (Tulsīdās). The regional logic is not quite perfect: somehow Tulsīdās, the Banarsi Vaishnava, has been positioned next to Mahādevīakkā, the female Shaiva saint from Karnataka. At the eight-storey Bharat Mata temple built in 1983 by the Vishva Hindu Parishad (World Hindu Council) at Haridvar, one can see a much more elaborate display of saints from all over India. This time they are grouped by gender. Images of *mātās* (mothers, as they are called) line the walls of a floor just below that of the *sants,* while other floors feature political heroes, gods, and Mother India herself. In the Hindi Bhavan at Shantiniketan, however, by contrast to either of these, one has not just the collocation of "medieval saints" that Binodbihari's murals promises, but a real narrative. It represents the bhakti movement as *movement.*

Figure 6. Hindi Bhavan murals, south wall continued, showing Kabīr. Courtesy of Viśva-Bhāratī and the Vadehra Art Gallery.

The geography of it suits the cause. When the idea of these murals was first proposed, Binodbihari had assumed he would have all four of the room's walls to work with, but as it happened the mural on the eastern wall was soon assigned to Kripal Singh Shekhawat, a pupil of Nandalal Bose's. There he rendered themes from the *Rāmcaritmānas* of Tulsīdās. That left only three sides for Binodbihari, but the reduction proved providential. Moving clockwise in the traditionally auspicious direction of *pradakṣiṇā,* Binodbihari started in the south—or to be precise, the southeast. Day by day he and his helpers applied the wet paste and painted it before it dried, laying out the narrative as they did. Thus they themselves slowly accomplished the three-fourths' circumambulatory journey they laid out for the eyes of those who would later see the murals. But if they were pioneers in this way, they too had their guide. Their journey approximated the one Bhakti herself is said to have accomplished in the *Bhāgavata Māhātmya.*

Figure 7. Hindi Bhavan murals, west wall. Courtesy of Viśva-Bhāratī and the Vadehra Art Gallery. Figure continued on the facing page.

Like her, they began in the Tamil country—or rather, a Tamil location is the first that can be singled out with clarity in the scene that Binodbihari created. Knowledgeable viewers know they are gazing at the deep south because of the elongated figure who appears at the very center of the southern panel. He is Rāmūnuja, and he is surrounded by a cluster of disciples (Figure 5). The acharya's hair is pulled back into a bun as if Binodbihari had modeled him after one of the Śrī Vaishnava Brahmins who serve as priests in Srirangam to this day. Some interpreters of the scene have thought this central figure might be Rāmānand instead, but K. G. Subrahmanyam, who joined Binodbihari in the project as he reached the northern wall, is positive that his mentor intended it to be Rāmūnuja. Rāmānand, however,

is not absent. He can be seen two figures to the right, probably separated from the great preceptor by his own teacher, Rāghavānand. Subrahmanyam recalls in regard to Rāmānand, "We didn't know how he looked"; they therefore decided to depict his face in a way that would suggest the nineteenth-century Bengali saint Rāmakṛṣṇa Paramahaṃsa.[118] His characteristic beard and open, placid expression are famous in Bengal and elsewhere. The connection they provide to the land where the murals were fashioned and to Mukherji's own family past is a lovely, subtle touch in a narrative that otherwise might not mandate Bengal's presence.

As we have seen, Dvivedi also leaned toward Bengal in various aspects of his work, though he hewed to the four-*sampradāy* template—even its

Figure 8. Hindi Bhavan murals, north wall. Courtesy of Viśva-Bhāratī and the Vadehra Art Gallery.

explicitly Rāmānandī version—in his formal representation of the *bhakti āndolan* itself. In that connection it is significant that as one's eye travels further along the southern wall, Kabīr comes into view (Figure 6). He is seated soberly some distance to the right of Rāmānand, surrounded by an assembly in which music plays its part. He is bearded—apparently Muslim. One sees an Indian violin in the hands of an accompanist who sits just opposite the saint.

This is the point at which the southern wall yields to the one on the west, and Kabīr's position at just this juncture has special meaning. The entirety of the western wall is devoted to Banaras, Kabīr's home town (Figure 7), so he mediates between the bhakti movement's southern origins and its outworking further north. A nest of closely built Banarsi houses opens onto the Ganges, where a boatful of bhaktas sing their *bhajans*. They in turn lead forward to two large figures who dominate the western wall: Hanumān and Tulsīdās. Hanumān, disguised as an ordinary *sādhu* in accordance with a popular story about how he vouchsafed himself to Tulsīdās, conveys his divine inspiration with an extravagant teaching gesture that will be familiar to anyone who has ever visited north India. His hand is raised aloft in a flourish of rhetorical triumph: he's made his point. Tulsīdās, just to the right, is depicted in profile, as is traditional. He positions his hands in manner that suggests he is receiving something valuable but invisible—presumably what the mysterious *sādhu* has just delivered.

Binodbihari has made brilliant use of the Ganges. Not only does the river enact the current-wise metaphor so familiar in talk of bhakti and its movement; it also accurately represents the flow of the Ganges as it sweeps by the ancient city that set the stage for so much in bhakti history. Banaras marks the one point along the river's ordinarily southeastern course where it turns abruptly and flows north, just as it does on the western wall of Hindi Bhavan. One might have asked to see other bhakti saints who lived in Banaras or visited it—Ravidās and Mīrābāī in particular—but they are absent. If one wants to have a glimpse of Mukherji's Mīrābāī, one has to travel to the Kirti Mandir in Baroda, where she is featured in a mural Mukherji finished in 1940.

Soon after one has seen Tulsīdās, one turns the final corner and finds oneself in the north (Figure 8). Here is Sūrdās—shown blind, of course, and being led about by a young boy who holds his iconic one-stringed *ektār*. Perhaps the inclusion of the boating motif on the western extremity of the northern wall is intended this time to represent the Jamuna, not the

Ganges; after all, they are sisters. And is the pair of figures just to Sūrdās's right—a woman and her son joined in a simple embrace—intended to conjure up the *vātsalya bhāva* (parental emotion) for which the poet became so famous? Both mother and son seem to wait for him to sing.

Finally, there is the remarkable presence of a turbaned figure on horseback—clearly Guru Gobind Singh, accompanied by members of the *khālsā*. One might have thought that Binodbihari would choose to depict Guru Nānak instead, but very likely we are expected to have developed a sense of temporal progression by this time. Guru Gobind Singh brings us appropriately to the beginning of the eighteenth century—the time when one normally stops counting poets of "the bhakti era" and the time when the medieval yields conclusively to the modern, if one periodizes things in such a way. Commenting on Mukherji's motive for including the tenth Sikh guru rather than the first, however, K. G. Subrahmanyam emphasized the specifically artistic aspect. Binodbihari had to have "something dramatic" at the climax of the tale, he said, and the style he chose to achieve it was strongly influenced by a Turkish miniature he had once seen. Perhaps we may also see traces of a deep interest in the Sikhs on the part of Tagore himself. As we have mentioned, he had traveled to Amritsar with his father as a boy.[119]

Subrahmanyam reflected on a further dimension, as well: the balance that Mukherji sought to achieve between the political and the popular. With Gobind Singh and his mounted troops one cannot miss the political side. Considering that India's independence was ever more clearly on the horizon in the spring months of 1947, one wonders whether we are seeing an evocation of the bhakti movement's specific contribution to the creation of national unity, but Subrahmanyam said he thought this would be overreading. Rather, he emphasized the popular dimension: the way in which, throughout the murals, the monumental figures—those with names—are made to emerge from the much more numerous smaller figures who surround them: the nameless ones, the people.

The genius of the bhakti movement in many people's view was its ability to sustain this relationship between great and small. Hence the culmination of the entire visual epic, like its beginning, is actually not one of the larger-than-life figures who stand at the center of the south and north panels—Guru Gobind Singh answering to Rāmūnuja—but a series of smaller ones. An anonymous seer in a mountain cave watches over the first scene, in the southeast corner. If this is a gesture to the Himalayas, that answers poorly to the fact that this renunciant appears on Hindi Bhavan's southern wall. At the other end of the mural the geography works better. There, in the northeast corner, we have Mukherji's most specific evocation of the peculiar ambience of a Bengali village. From Subrahmanyam's vantage point the "sea of humanity" that the mural represents here achieves a certain telos in a moment of social and religious "democratization" that has been implicit throughout. No major figure appears, no one with a name. Yet perhaps we should not minimize the force of the political message that Guru Gobind Singh almost inevitably conveys in the scene just prior. A political message and an aesthetic one, too. We know that bhakti poetry was sung at Gobind Singh's court—and not just Sikh poetry at that. Similarly the dignified yet militant pose assumed by Guru Gobind Singh seems to convey a message that resonates well beyond the Sikh part of bhakti's kingdom.

Yet I bow to Subrahmanyam's wisdom. He did not want to stress this too much, and he so nicely draws attention to the interpenetration of folk and great in bhakti modes—just the sort of thing we also saw in the contributions that all those little Sūrdāses and Kabīrs made to the ever-evolving personae of the big ones. When we see couplets attributed to Kabīr, Tulsī, and Sūr at the top of the northern wall, we would be right to reflect on the question of who might have been their authors: the "original" poets those names imply or a member of the adoring, enveloping crowd? It is also appropriate that they be bunched together as they are—a bhakti constellation that lies behind the bhakti movement.

K. G. Subrahmanyam cautions against attributing the design of these murals in too great detail to Hazariprasad Dvivedi. He says that Dvivedi gave Mukherji free rein. Yet the moment of their fashioning, just before independence; the way they participate in the larger cultural program of Shantiniketan; and their location in a place where Hindi would be studied in its canonical "medieval" forms—each of these factors suggests a vector that made Dvivedi's contribution to the formulization and institutionalization of the idea of the bhakti movement so powerful, perhaps even unique. Dvivedi's voice was hardly the only one to have articulated the vision of the bhakti movement that became standard in India's public discourse from the time of independence onward. We have seen throughout this chapter that he was surrounded by a little cloud of others, yet no one's voice was more important than his. If anyone's individual sense of the bhakti movement is represented on the walls of Hindi Bhavan—aside from that of the artist himself—surely it was Dvivedi's. For the little world of Shantiniketan this makes obvious sense, but it also makes sense for the much larger world to which Shantiniketan belonged, and for which it hoped.

7

What Should the Bhakti Movement Be?

Contestations

IN THE DECADES THAT have elapsed since the earthshaking events of 1947, the idea of the bhakti movement has become gospel, but that doesn't mean it always broadcasts the same good news. Late in 1992, as is well known, mobs of young men assembled from all over India and bivouacked on the outskirts of Ayodhya, the city whose name proclaims it to be the place from which Rām once ruled his kingdom. Then on the morning of December 6 they surged through the streets toward the mosque that had been built in 1528 by a lieutenant of the Mughal emperor Babur: the Hindu right had turned it into a symbol of foreign Muslim domination in Indian history. As they raced down Ayodhya's narrow lanes, they passed a series of wall paintings urging them on. One of these, which seemed to speak for all the rest, showed a commanding Rām holding his great bow. It bore the simple slogan *rām kī bhakti rāṣṭra kī śakti hai* (the love of Rām is the strength of the nation).

Ayodhya, being in Avadh, inhabits a region with a major Muslim population, one whose cultural influence over much of the rest of the country is quite legendary. The strike against the Babri Mosque was also a strike against Islam both past and present. Many thinkers who contributed to the development of the *bhakti āndolan* story after the time of Jaisingh, however, were far less eager than these right-wing militants to pry apart Muslim and Hindu sides of the story. They strove instead to make a place for Sufis in the bhakti movement narrative. But this remained one of the narrative's most unstable components, subject to argument, emphasis, or elision. The ideologues of the Vishva Hindu Parishad (VHP) and the Bharatiya Janata Party (BJP) who masterminded the Ayodhya attack of 1992 could build on this uncertainty as they attempted effectively to blot out Islamic contributions to the history that produced the bhakti movement. In doing so, they directly challenged a local religious culture in which Sufi monuments like the tomb of Sisle Hazrat Islam, on the outskirts of Ayodhya, played a major role. On its annual *'urs,* this shrine had played host to as many Hindu bhaktas as Muslim ones. That was something that the great mobs who attacked the Babri Mosque either could not or did not want to see. Hence a group of them, returning from their victory downtown, turned their sticks and axes on the tomb of Sisle Hazrat Islam and the mosque associated with it. It probably did not help that tomb's dome bore a certain resemblance to the domes of the Babri Mosque. In January 1993, when I visited, it was half rubble.[1]

By now we know that bhakti institutions in Galtā, Brindavan, and elsewhere were deeply dependent on the Mughal-Kachvaha axis of power for support and patronage. And in the large view, too, political power and even state-sanctioned violence play a role in the long history of Indian bhakti. Attacks on Buddhists and especially Jains were a notable feature of first-millennium Tamil bhakti rhetoric, especially on the Shaiva side,[2] and competitions for royal patronage such as are registered in the story of Vallabha's visit to Vijayanagar were not just legends but realities in the history of bhakti *maṭhs* and temple institutions. But in recent centuries it was Muslims who came to be perceived as the great enemies of Hindu bhakti. We saw how Ishwari Prasad, who put forward the first full English-language articulation of the bhakti movement idea in 1925, envisioned the great bhaktas of Mughal north India as paragons of Hindu manhood, forces of resistance to Islamicate culture. Two years earlier, in a tract called *Hindutva: Who Is a Hindu?,* the celebrated nationalist Vinayak Damodar Savarkar had gone further. He reached beneath what he regarded as the distortions of the concept of Hinduism to argue for a sense of Hinduness—*hindutva*—that would embrace all who regarded Bhāratvarṣ (India) as fatherland and holy land. This would include not only Hindus in the sense that has become ordinary, but also Jains, Sikhs, and native Buddhists and Christians.[3] Savarkar did not work with the idea of the bhakti movement as such, but he folded figures such as Chaitanya, Basava, Nānak, and the Marathi saints Cakradhar and Rāmdās into his triumphant narrative and connected them to much more recent figures, as well. Against these, Muslims became the hated other. Personified in the figure of Muhammad, they had crossed the Indus, invaded India's sacred turf, and "century after century [waged a] ghastly conflict."[4]

Savarkar's tract became the single most important document defining the worldview of the Hindu right. He avoided the language of bhakti—*hindutva* was its substitute—but he integrated the idea of a nationally shared bhakti history into his vision, especially its Rāmaite aspect. It was not far from there to what the militants shouted in 1992: "Bhakti to Rām is what makes the nation strong." Islam, the force behind partition, was what had made it weak.

Such views are widespread. At a much less sophisticated level, the head of the Rāmānandī monastic community headquartered in the spacious Rām Bāgh compound at Bansībaṭ in Brindavan, a genial man of many years, represents the overriding framework of Rām's activities in the *kaliyug* as his struggle against Islam. According to *mahant* Raghunāth Bhūṣaṇācārya, the four brothers in Rām's family, viewing world affairs from their perch in heavenly Vaikuṇṭh, were deeply concerned by what they saw. They therefore expressed themselves as human beings and fanned out to the four directions to do so. Shatrughna became Chaitanya in Navadvīp, the east; Lakṣmaṇ became Rāmūnuja in Srirangam, the south; Bharat became Nānak in Sindh, the west; and Rām himself became Rāmānand in the north.[5] Obviously we have here a loose connection to the idea of the four *sampradāys* and to some of the most important figures in the bhakti movement narrative, but what is striking is that this whole history is understood as being an effort to beat back the attack of Islam on Hindu religion and culture. No wonder it was a Rāmānandī ascetic who played the most crucial local role in orchestrating the attack on the Babri Mosque in 1992. There is something eerie about the fact that this man, *mahant* Nṛtya Gopāl Dās of the Rāmānandī establishment in Ayodhya, hailed from the very Braj region from which Raghunāth Bhūṣaṇācārya spoke.

Fortunately, a sense of shared bhakti history has also been enlisted on the opposite side of the Ayodhya confrontation, and again, explicitly, under the banner of the bhakti movement. SAHMAT (Accord, the Safdar Hashmi Memorial Trust), an artists' collective based in Delhi, responded to the VHP's efforts to demonize Muslims by developing a graphic

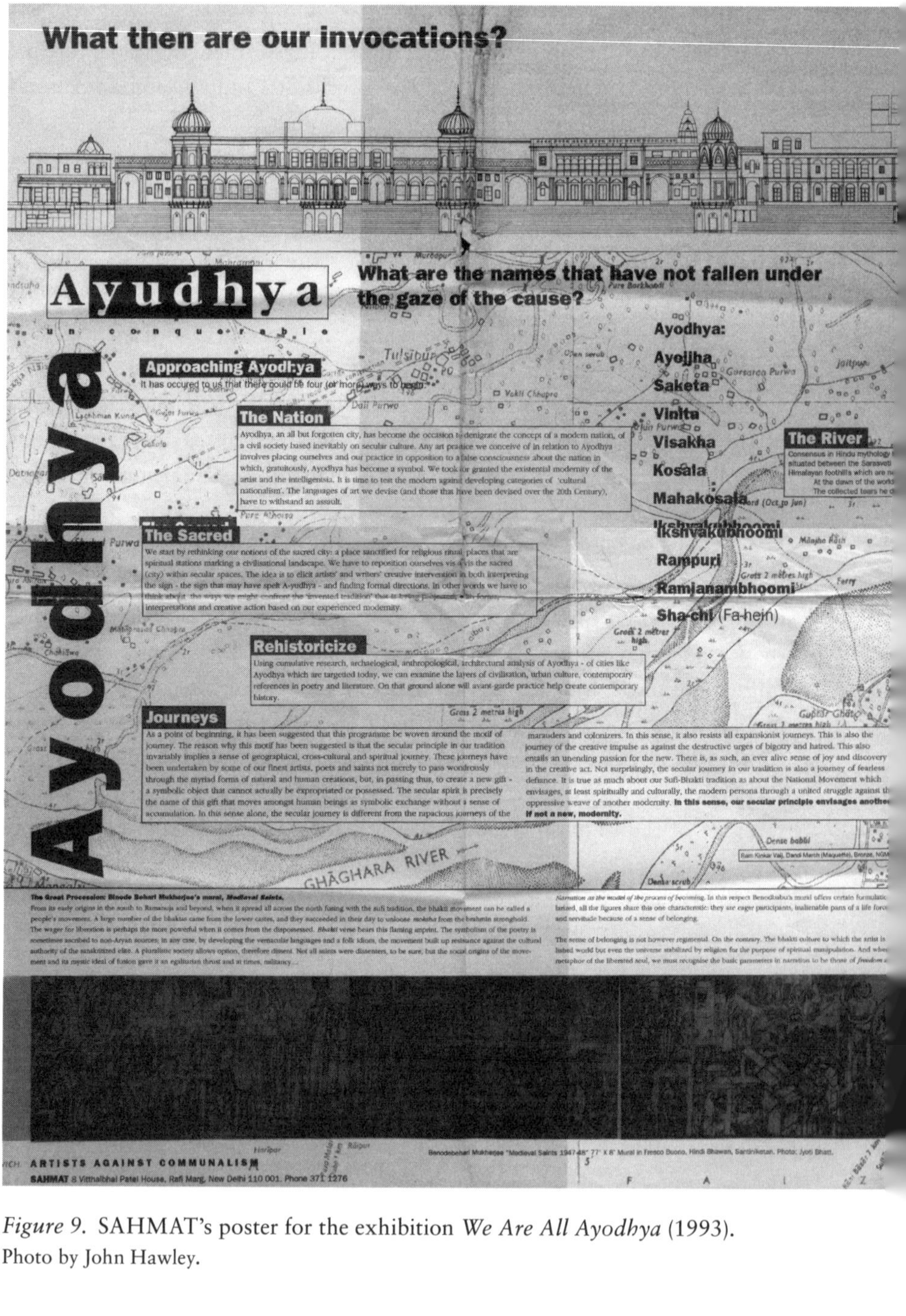

Figure 9. SAHMAT's poster for the exhibition *We Are All Ayodhya* (1993). Photo by John Hawley.

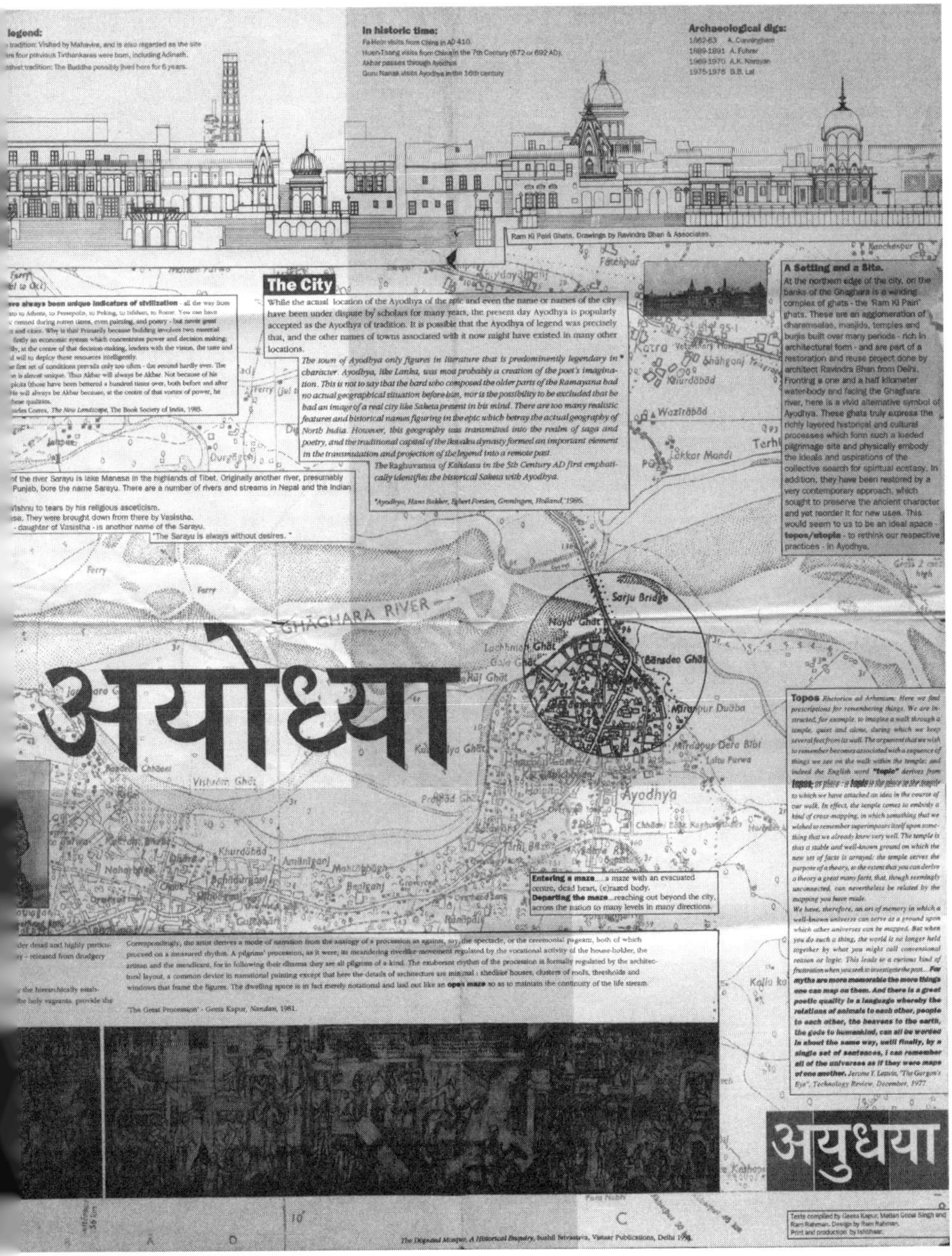
legend:
tradition: The Buddha possibly lived here for 6 years.
In historic time:
Fa-Hein visits from China in AD 410
Huen-Tsang visits from China in the 7th Century (672 or 692 AD).
Akbar passes through Ayodhya
Guru Nanak visits Ayodhya in the 16th century
Archaeological digs:
1862-63 A. Cunningham
1889-1891 A. Fuhrer
1969-1970 A.K. Narayan
1975-1976 B.B. Lal
Ram Ki Pairi Ghats. Drawings by Ravindra Bhan & Associates.
The City
While the actual location of the Ayodhya of the epic and even the name or names of the city have been under dispute by scholars for many years, the present day Ayodhya is popularly accepted as the Ayodhya of tradition. It is possible that the Ayodhya of legend was precisely that, and the other names of towns associated with it now might have existed in many other locations.
*The town of Ayodhya only figures in literature that is predominently legendary in character. Ayodhya, like Lanka, was most probably a creation of the poet's imagination. This is not to say that the bard who composed the older parts of the Ramayana had no actual geographical situation before him, nor is the possibility to be excluded that he had an image of a real city like Saketa present in his mind. There are too many realistic features and historical names figuring in the epic which betray the actual geography of North India. However, this geography was transmitted into the realm of saga and poetry, and the traditional capital of the Iksvaku dynasty formed an important element in the transmutation and projection of the legend into a remote past.**
The Raghuvamsa *of Kalidasa in the 5th Century AD first emphatically identifies the historical Saketa with Ayodhya.*
**Ayodhya*, Hans Bakker, Egbert Forsten, Groningen, Holland, 1986.
A Setting and a Site.
At the northern edge of the city, on the banks of the Ghaghara is a winding complex of ghats - the 'Ram Ki Pairi' ghats. These are an agglomeration of dharamsalas, masjids, temples and burjis built over many periods - rich in architectural form - and are part of a restoration and reuse project done by architect Ravindra Bhan from Delhi. Fronting a one and a half kilometer waterbody and facing the Ghaghara river, here is a vivid alternative symbol of Ayodhya. These ghats truly express the richly layered historical and cultural processes which form such a loaded pilgrimage site and physically embody the ideals and aspirations of the collective search for spiritual ecstasy. In addition, they have been restored by a very contemporary approach, which sought to preserve the ancient character and yet reorder it for new uses. This would seem to us to be an ideal space - **topos/utopia** - to rethink our respective practices - in Ayodhya.
The New Landscape, The Book Society of India, 1985.
Punjab, bore the name Sarayu. There are a number of rivers and streams in Nepal and the Indian
- daughter of Vasistha - is another name of the Sarayu.
"The Sarayu is always without desires."
GHAGHARA RIVER
Sarju Bridge
Naya Ghat
Lachhman Ghat
Bansdeo Ghat
अयोध्या
Ayodhya
Khurdabad
Amaniganj
Entering a maze.....a maze with an evacuated centre, dead heart, (e)razed body.
Departing the maze...reaching out beyond the city, across the nation to many levels in many directions.
Topos *Rhetorica ad Arhenium: Here we find prescriptions for remembering things. We are instructed, for example, to imagine a walk through a temple, quiet and alone, during which we keep several feet from its wall. The argument that we wish to remember becomes associated with a sequence of things we see on the walk within the temple: and indeed the English word* **"topic"** *derives from* **topos**, *or place - a* **topic** *is the place in the temple to which we have attached an idea in the course of our walk. In effect, the temple comes to embody a kind of cross-mapping, in which something that we wished to remember superimposes itself upon something that we already knew very well. The temple is thus a stable and well-known ground on which the new set of facts is arrayed: the temple serves the purpose of a theory, to the extent that you can derive a theory a great many facts, that, though seemingly unconnected, can nevertheless be related by the mapping you have made.*
We have, therefore, an art of memory in which a well-known universe can serve as a ground upon which other universes can be mapped. But when you do such a thing, the world is no longer held together by what you might call conventional reason or logic. This leads to a curious kind of frustration when you seek to investigate the past.... **For myths are more memorable the more things one can map on them. And there is a great poetic quality in a language whereby the relations of animals to each other, people to each other, the heavens to the earth, the gods to humankind, can all be worked in about the same way, until finally, by a single set of sentences, I can remember all of the universes as if they were maps of one another.** *Jerome Y. Lettvin, "The Gorgon's Eye", Technology Review, December, 1977*
Correspondingly, the artist derives a mode of narration from the analogy of a procession as against, say, the spectacle, or the ceremonial pageant, both of which proceed on a measured rhythm. A pilgrims' procession, as it were, its meandering riverlike movement regulated by the vocational activity of the house-holder, the artisan and the mendicant, for in following their dharma they are all pilgrims of a kind. The exuberant rhythm of the procession is formally regulated by the architectural layout, a common device in narrational painting except that here the details of architecture are minimal : shedlike houses, clusters of roofs, thresholds and windows that frame the figures. The dwelling space is in fact merely notational and laid out like an **open maze** so as to maintain the continuity of the life stream.
'The Great Procession' - Geeta Kapur, *Nandan*, 1981.
अयुधया
Texts compiled by Geeta Kapur, Madan Gopal Singh and Ram Rahman. Design by Ram Rahman.
Print and production by Ishtihaar.
The Disputed Mosque, A Historical Enquiry, Sushil Srivastava, Vistaar Publications, Delhi 1991.

campaign of its own. Describing themselves as "artists against communalism," they marked the first-year anniversary of the demolition of the Babri Mosque by mounting an exhibit that premiered in Delhi and New York under the title *Ham Sab Ayodhyā,* "We are all Ayodhya." They showed that the city the rightists claimed to be exclusively Hindu property, since it was Rām's birthplace and later his capital, had served in the course of actual history as the common terrain of Hindus, Buddhists, Jains, and Muslims.[6] To make this point they designed a huge poster depicting Ayodhya's varied past, and across the bottom, anchoring the whole, they laid out photographs of Binodbihari Mukherji's murals (Figure 9). These they introduced with a passage written by the well-known art critic Geeta Kapur, which began as follows:

> From its early origins in the south to Rāmūnuja and beyond, when it spread all across the north fusing with the sufi tradition, the bhakti movement can be called a people's movement. A large number of the bhaktas came from the lower castes, and they succeeded in their day to unloose *moksha* [liberation] from the Brahmin stronghold. The wager for liberation is perhaps the more powerful when it comes from the dispossessed. Bhakti verse bears this flaming imprint . . . A pluralistic society allows option, therefore dissent. Not all saints were dissenters, to be sure, but the social origins of the moment and its mystic ideal of fusion gave it an egalitarian thrust and at times, militancy.[7]

SAHMAT's message was clear. *That* bhakti movement—the bhakti-Sufi people's movement of dissent and liberation—represents the true essence of India's bhakti heritage, not the sort that attacked the Babri Mosque.

Such contestations had their precedents. When Ishwari Prasad saw the medieval bhakti movement as the expression of an indomitable Hindu manhood pitted against its Mughal overlords, he was hardly on the same page as his contemporary Tagore, who spoke of bhakti as a "religious bridge" *(dharmasetu)* connecting Hindus and Muslims. When Nābhādās refrained from including a single Muslim in his digest of some eight hundred bhaktas (unless one counts Kabīr), he was articulating a different sort of bhakti community than Bharatendu Harishchandra envisioned when he composed his sequel to Nābhā's *Bhaktamāl.* As Bharatendu began, he took pains to say that Muslim servants of Hari *(musalamān harijanan)* could have a value exceeding that of countless Hindus.[8] Similarly, as we remember, Bipin Chandra Pal pressed this inclusive cause when he explained that "the general bhakti movement" was a protest deeply colored by "the soul-compelling humanism of Islam." In the thinking of Ramchandra Shukla, however, we feel an element of internal divide.[9] When Shukla wrote his enduringly influential *Hindī Sāhitya kā Itihās* (History of Hindi Literature), he made it a point to highlight differences between Sufi compositions and the poetry of Kabīr, while still making a place for the Sufi school (or branch: *śākhā*), which he called *prem mārgī* (path of love), under the great, general canopy of "the bhakti era." This allowed Sufis to take a place structurally parallel to schools peopled by *nirguṇīs* and Rām or Krishna bhaktas, but he devoted far more attention to Hindu bhakti poets than to Sufi ones.

As these examples show, and as we have seen throughout the book, the bhakti movement idea contains a certain element of indeterminacy. It can mean many things to many people—by region, by caste, by community, by faith. It can be region-specific, as when the Maharashtrian Organization for the Eradication of Superstition claims Jñāneśvar, Tukārām, and other poet-saints of the Vārkarī movement as their predecessors in the struggle against religious supernaturalism.[10] (Their opponents claim the Vārkarīs on the other side of this debate.) Or it can be specifically panregional, as in the many doctoral dissertations that analyze, for example, the relationship between the Hindi-speaking bhakti movement and its Kannada or Tamil analogues. It can have a Marxist ring, as when it became a rubric for memorializing the work of a long-serving chair of the History Department at Aligarh Muslim University who went on to a career in national government. Given the orientation of the department it was natural that in this Aligarh-focused volume, *Bhakti Āndolan: Itihās aur Saṃskṛti* (The Bhakti Movement: History and Culture), issues of Marxist interpretation should find an important place, but this is by no means always true when Hindu-Muslim contacts are at the forefront of bhakti movement thinking. A conference held in Delhi in 2005 under the banner of "Sufism and Bhakti Movement: Eternal Relevance" often had a mellower, less theoretical tone. And then one has the massive government-sponsored *History of Science, Philosophy, and Culture in Indian Civilization,* whose volume *Theistic Vedānta* finds a place for two lengthy, elegant chapters on the bhakti movement, south and north: little trace of Islam there.[11] Simply at the level of books and conferences, then, one sees that the bhakti movement idea is capable of considerable variety, yet its persistence is testimony to the belief in a center that holds. Fluid yet compelling, this center holds against the sort of extremism that would exclude any major portion of India's citizenry. More often than not, in a mood that may seem amnesiac, it casts away the sharper edges that also form a part of the bhakti heritage: Kabīr's rhetorical attacks on pundits and *qāzīs*, for example, or the *Basava Purāṇa*'s recommendation that Brahmin villages be burned and Jains slaughtered. In the years following India's independence there have been many efforts to relate this mild, principled, and proudly aggregate religiosity to the secular, political center that rules from Delhi.

That political center speaks a distinctively Indian language. Fifteen years after Ayodhya—in December 2007—there occurred an event that may seem remarkable to readers accustomed to a constitution that enshrines the separation of church and state. On that occasion the Indian Council of Philosophical Research, an agency wholly funded by the federal government, teamed up with the body that administers India' s wealthiest and most influential temple, the Tirumala Tirupati Devasthanams, to sponsor a conference called "Celestial Love: Bhakti in Indian Tradition." It was held at Tirupati itself, in the shadow of the great temple and on the campus of the university it has spawned. In India the idea of secularity tends to mean something rather different from what it does in the United States. When Indians use the word "secular," it is not with the expectation that the state will stand back from any expression of religion, but to insist that the government be evenhanded in deferring to them all. Furthermore, since bhakti refers to felt religion, and since the bhakti movement is believed precisely to have challenged any institutional strangleholds on popular religiosity, a conference featuring it was seen to be perfectly appropriate for state funding. Here was a notion capacious enough to include in principle all religious groups—Hindu, Muslim, Sikh, Christian, Jain—and all classes of people.

The brochure accompanying the Tirupati conference spoke of the bhakti movement as simple, self-evident fact: "The bhakti movement began in South India around the fifth century CE, and in the next thousand years it spread northward through the subcontinent, taking on individual and distinctive forms as it moved from one area to another." Its hallmarks were equality, accessibility, and community. Elsewhere in the brochure we read, "The Bhakti movement in medieval India is responsible for the many rites and rituals associated with the worship of God by Hindus, Muslims, Sikhs, and other religious traditions in the Indian subcontinent. For example, Kirtan at a Hindu Temple, Qawalli [sic] at a Dargah by Muslims, and singing of Gurbani [on the part of Sikhs] are all derived from the Bhakti movement of medieval India (800–1700)." Such affirmations, we now know, are the product of a complex and interesting history—largely speaking, a northern history. Hence the enactment of that history at Tirupati—in many ways the very symbol of the south—was an event of major significance.

I had the good fortune to be there, but I was disappointed to find that despite the affirmations made in its brochure, the conference had not succeeded in attracting many scholars of non-Hindu backgrounds. To my knowledge only one paper was presented on a topic having to do with Sufism—interestingly, by a scholar based at Shantiniketan. So here too the potential inclusiveness of the bhakti movement remained an issue—not in concept, perhaps, but in practice and perception. Other issues also arose. When I spoke in a plenary session about some of the subjects we have explored in this book—the historical contingency of the idea of the bhakti movement in general and the relationship between Grierson and Dvivedi in particular—there was a chorus of disapproval.[12] Several speakers felt that I had been too narrow. In approaching the question of the bhakti movement the way I did, they said, I had ignored the core reality that this idea was intended to represent: bhakti itself. Being an outsider, I had mistaken the periphery for the center. I had focused too closely on *bhakti āndolan* as a concept that emerged at a particular point in time and had failed to appreciate the fact that this formulation was, as one person put it, *"bhakti kī lahar kā āvirbhāv,"* only one "manifestation of the wave of bhakti" that has coursed through Indian consciousness and religious practice for centuries, even millennia. From this point of view—and many shared it—the title Prema Nandakumar gave to the essay she contributed to the conference was far more felicitous and accurate: "Bhakti in Indian Tradition: A Perennial Stream."

Other participants pressed the point further. Some thought I had entirely missed the dimension of "bhakti history" that expresses itself as *sādhanā,* personal discipline. Ordinary people, they said, are not capable of such *sādhanā;* they simply participate in bhakti at the level of shared common practice. Others, to their good fortune, have been given the social and educational circumstances or have personally struggled to develop the capacities that enable them to take bhakti to a higher level. But common or elite, bhakti was to be understood as a perennial presence. One person seemed to bridge this gap between elite and common by suggesting that *sādhanā* need not be merely individual; it can also be collective. This is an argument that Tagore and others made about the genius of the Indian nation, and as such it brings us back to a certain sense of India's national history. At the same time, however, it sidelines any impetus to speak of bhakti as if it could be subject to the vagaries of history, as I had done. It was the organic presence of bhakti in Indian history that fascinated Tagore, not any concern about the way in which the idea of bhakti as a historiographical tool might have emerged at a certain point in the course of history itself. In this, many conference participants stood with him. As one man put it, bhakti is here today and it will still be here a hundred years from now.

Perhaps, others suggested, my line of argument was simply to be expected—the sort of unfortunate thing that often happens when Westerners permit themselves to make observations about Indian religion. One speaker brought forward the example of the Vārkarīs of Maharashtra, saying that Westerners had always been reductive in their interpretations of these saints, failing to appreciate the bhakti core. He noted that I came from a culture in which the church confined religion within clear institutional boundaries and forced upon it centralized structures of authority, so it would be hard for me to appreciate how protean, various, and unconstrained are the expressions of bhakti in India's religious history. Another participant argued that the structure of Christian religion led naturally in the direction of conversion campaigns: a monarch might be expected to try to extend the range of his hegemony by using religion as a tool. But bhakti orients religious life in an entirely different way, he explained, and for that reason conversion campaigns (at the mention of this concept I thought of Chaitanya) have never been part of bhakti's history. Given this considerable disparity between European and Indian history, he felt it was no wonder I had projected Western notions of how religion operates onto India's alien landscape, plotting the origins of the idea of the bhakti movement against developments in India's social and political history.

In what I said at Tirupati and at greater length in this book, I have indeed emphasized the importance of history and of ideas about how history has been shaped—religiously. In doing so, I have necessarily entered the historical process, as did everyone who joined the discussion that morning in Tirupati. It is a weighty history. My ethnic and religious forebears said some very demeaning things about features of Hindu religion that are intimately associated with bhakti—first and foremost, the worship of the Deity in image form—and when they said these things, they were often protected by the fact that they or theirs occupied positions of power that allowed them to do so with impunity. I hope that by speaking seriously about history, especially the history that lies behind ideas, I have not followed the example that some of these earlier Westerners set. I hope that the bhakti movement, as an idea *about* history, can be dislodged from the level of assumed fact and thereby rise to the level of being treated *as* history. And I hope that this can be done without minimizing or misrepresenting the transhistorical, transcendental commitments to which it refers.

The Bhakti Network

This has been a book about a story. We have tried to understand the historical process by means of which a master narrative of India's religious past emerged—a past that would be broad enough and subjectively real enough that no one would be excluded from its range by sectarian identification, geographical location, or social station. Often in the course of doing so, however, we have had to look back over our shoulder and wonder how adequately the idea of the bhakti movement, at whatever stage, captures the contours of "real" history. If the Hindi and Bengali usages of the term *āndolan* suggest agitation—agitations of the sort that laborers make in pursuit of better working conditions, or citizens in pursuit of firmer rights—then we must concede that this progressive struggle has not always been a part of the *bhakti āndolan*. If the English term "movement" implies a well-considered goal, then that sense of implicit teleology is also often absent. If it implies a necessarily oblique relation to patronage and the state—a people's agenda, not something imposed from above—then that too, on occasion, seems a difficulty: states have been directly involved in our story. So the *āndolan* and the movement that are built into the composite notion of the bhakti movement have their uncertainties. Furthermore there is the difficulty of having to account for the fact that the bhakti movement, so conceived, often failed to achieve the promises it seemed to make, namely, to override differences between Hindus and Muslims and to advance the cause of the poor and despised. How can we deal with these issues?

One way is to step back and consider whether a different sort of master narrative could be told—a narrative that is actually not a narrative but something more like a flow chart, a diagram, a network. A major aim of network theory is to displace the illusion that individual actors are the engines of history, and this surely resonates with bhakti despite its personalist focus. Along our way we have witnessed remarkable acts of individual creativity—think of Kabīr's "dictatorial" rhetoric, the ecstasies of the erstwhile grammarian Chaitanya, the poetic concision of the *pads* early attributed to Sūrdās—but even in these cases the logic has proved cumulative: each of these is also a case of collective authorship, a construction of collective memory. With Annamayya or Tulsīdās we can be more assured that we are hearing the voice of an individual poetic actor—in Annamayya's case, a real iconoclast—but there too we are dependent on the energies of networks: the temple leaders, including members of Annamayya's family, who saw to it that thousands of his poems were inscribed on copper plates and preserved for posterity, and the copyists who gave us part or all of the *Rāmcaritmānas,* beginning in Tulsīdās's own lifetime.[13] We must remember also that acts of bhakti creativity do not always occur at the beginning of a chain: think of the entrepreneurial genius of Viṭṭhalnāth, without which Vallabha would certainly not have the standing he has today. And as we have seen, the chain itself, the *sampradāy,* is often a thing claimed well after the fact. Perhaps it is no accident that Nābhādās, apostle of *sampradāys,* preferred in the end to speak of a garland.

Consider, too, the musical idiom. Isn't it striking that the principal nodes in bhakti's remembered network—the bhaktas of this world—are communicators who operated in a universe where ordinary words ride frequencies of sound that set them apart from their quotidian existence? Here is a mode of interpersonal connection whose very existence depends upon auditory frameworks that set it apart from conversational speech. In this realm of heightened feedback antiphons are frequent, refrains are repeated, and audiences are not only implied but participate in the work of the singer. The way we know who Mīrābāī or Nāmdev "is" is to enter into the world they are believed to have created. We pipe into the patterns of vibration—songs—that end with the announcing of their names. Because we do so, this musical network is never really past; it is always present. The fact that these bhakti songs are so often addressed to God, giving plot to divine actions or otherwise relating the *bhakta* to *bhagavān* through a process of "puranic" recycling, creates a shortcut for memory. It invites the hearer to act as a character in the story—to reenter it, absorb it, and in a way become the story itself. Thereby, as Christian Novetzke has pointed out, the singer-saint in question turns out to be, on closer inspection, a public.

The paradigmatic bhaktas who are the heroes of the bhakti movement are in large part creations of song. They are remembered not just *because* of what they have sung or are believed to have sung, but precisely *as* what they have sung. In Hindi, Bengali, or Gujarati *pads;* in Marathi *abhangs;* in Kannada, Telugu, and Tamil *padas, padams,* and *patikams,* these songs give tone and collective meaning to the oral signatures affixed thereto. No wonder the Ravidās look-alike whom Rāmānand encounters in Tagore's poem is called Bhajan. No wonder that the life of Allama Prabhu, written out in the fifteenth-century Kannada *Śūnyasampādane,* develops by means of a process in which poems attributed to him are laid end to end. No wonder that, in the following century, the oldest celebration of Bābā Nānak's life, the *Purātan Janamsākhī,* is half made up of his poems. Only later in the development of the *janam sākhī* tradition does the constitutive work performed by poems internalized as music fade from view in the lives of Sikhism's gurus and bhakti greats. One cannot say that every bhakti hagiography is musical or poetic in its genesis, but it is notable how many are.

Another indication of the network-like quality of these life stories is that they so vividly interconnect. It often seems as if the life of a given saint is assembled from the lives of all the others, whether by direct copying or by paraphrase. In Priyādās's Hindi *Bhaktirasabodhinī* (1712), which becomes an important template for Mahīpati's even more massive Marathi *Bhaktavijaya* only half a century after its composition, various saints meet or refuse to meet emperors, repel the attacks of murderous Brahmins, and are upbraided by their relatives for earning nothing, only to have God supply an abundance. Perhaps these overlaps are no surprise. Both the *Bhaktirasabodhinī* and the *Bhaktavijaya* were and still are declaimed in performance, and as every teller of tales knows, certain plots have more power with an audience than others. Moreover, echoes among these stories reinforce the reassuring sense that a coherent bhakti universe is being described. It is perhaps not so much that the bhaktas marshal the episodes that mark their lives, but that these archetypal vignettes search out ever new subjects upon which to enact themselves, making them thus ever old. Shiva makes his temple face a different direction to hear Nāmdev sing; Krishna as an image in Udupi turns on his pedestal when Kanakadāsa is prevented from entering the temple to worship him; when Nānak visits a mosque in Mecca, the *mihrāb* moves around so that it can stay aligned with his feet; and Sufi *tazkirās* sometimes report that the Ka'aba is willing to travel so that Sufis of distant lands can circumambulate it.[14] I do not mean to imply that every hagiographical collection or tradition is the same. There are certainly regional and sectarian specificities. But what makes it possible to speak of the bhakti movement as a movement is that there are so many overlaps between them. In a broad sense, one could make the case that it is a single network. Within that network there is plenty of movement, but it is hardly always directed chronologically from south to north.

The same can be said for poems. Genres and tropes are broadly shared between languages and centuries. On the genre side the remarkable fact with which to reckon is the way the relatively short sung lyric known as *pad, pada, padam,* or *abhang* came to define the field more or less throughout the subcontinent by the end of the sixteenth century. Other forms are also relevant, of course. Across north India one thinks particularly of the *caupāī* meter, which serves as the backbone for religious narrative poetry familiarly called *carit,* and of the *dohā* couplets that sometimes punctuate long *caupāī* sequences with moments of relief or summary reflection yet sometimes stand on their own, vying with the *pad* as the dominant means of communication in an entire anthology. But when it comes to lyrics in which the Deity is directly addressed, the *pad* and its variants stand out. This is the medium in which Narsī Mehtā, for example, finds his primal speech *(ādya vāṇī)* revealed to him. Much later writers, following his lead, fashioned Narsī as the originary poet *(ādikavi)* of the Gujarati language, meaning not only that he spoke uniquely for himself in the poems he composed but that he did so in a way that did not require being bilingual in Sanskrit.[15] This sense of a poetic point of origin for a new kind of bhakti speech—the self-contained *pad*—was something

Gujarati shared with other languages emerging into written view at just about that point in time.

We can trace the *pad* form back to the *Gītagovinda* of Jayadev, which was apparently composed during the reign of Lakṣmaṇasen in Bengal toward the end of the twelfth century and, ironically, in Sanskrit. The *padāvalī* to which Jayadev himself refers in that work—a sequence of *pads*—is, however, so unusual in Sanskrit that many feel it was probably uploaded from a vernacular idiom. As in a series of earlier Tamil examples that are loosely analogous, Jayadev's *padāvalīs* culminate in a final *pad* that bears the poet's name or signature. In the *Gītagovinda* there are typically eight to the set; in Tamil, ten plus one. What aligns the *Gītagovinda* more strongly with the *pad* form that comes later to be so widely used in the fifteenth and sixteenth centuries is that, unlike its Tamil cousin, it announces a refrain at the beginning and repeats it at intervals in the course of its performance.[16] These elements remain in the early modern period, but they undergo a characteristic compression. The Telugu *padam* form that Annamayya developed in fifteenth-century Tirupati arches over far fewer stanzas, and in the *bhāṣā* (later called Brajbhasha) *pads* of Sūrdās the poet tends to veer away from a sequence of rhymed couplets, which would be typical in a longer composition but also possible for shorter ones such as the fifteenth-century Maithili *pads* of Vidyāpati. Instead of that, Sūr generally settles on a single rhyme scheme that lasts throughout the *pad*'s six to ten rhymed verses.

In both Telugu and Brajbhasha the refrain announced at the beginning may have a longer or a shorter form, while in Marathi and Gujarati the shorter form predominates. In either case one sees a remarkable uniformity across languages, a shared grid that must have enabled performers from one linguistic area, whether professional or lay, to "speak" to those who hailed from elsewhere and be understood as they traveled from place to place. Sumit Guha, referring to the dramatic Marathi form known as *bhāruḍ*, has emphasized the "loaning" of words from one language or dialect to another, and the fact that in premodern India many more villages were to be found on a performer's route than after the railroads were built.[17] But whether *pads* or *padams* were more or less linguistically "chaste," the formal analogies they shared across regions became impressive in the period Francesca Orsini and Samira Sheikh have called the long fifteenth century (long indeed: it extends through more than half of the sixteenth).[18] Here was a *dolce stil nuovo* that, while hardly emerging from out of the blue, constituted something like the sort of newness that sixteenth- and seventeenth-century philosophers felt about the times in which they lived.[19] The tropes and motifs that these *pads* shared added density to a widely spread musical bhakti network that must have made communication not only possible but exciting across regional, linguistic, and social barriers.

To give a comprehensive list of such tropes would require far more space than we have or perhaps want, but we could offer a few suggestions just for starters. Everywhere there are poems of lovers' separation *(viraha),* shared across the line between *nirguṇ* and *saguṇ* modes, but what is striking is that within that broad domain we also find an array of more particular conceits and motifs that are also widely shared. Perhaps the idea of a broken heart is so universal that it attracts no particular attention, but the fact that a male poet takes on the voice of a woman to ask specifically why his heart does not burst is more arresting. This happens in poems of Narsī Mehtā or Sūrdās, for example.[20]

Within the narrative world of Krishna, so fundamental to much that goes under the heading of the bhakti movement, we meet an array of particular connections that cannot be explained as vernacular transubstantiations of motifs that occur in the *Bhāgavata Purāṇa,* that admittedly omnipresent Sanskrit text, since they do not appear there. In such instances we must apparently imagine that paths of transmission from one spoken language to another made it possible for these echoes to occur. In more than one regional language, for instance, the gopis ask Krishna's flute, Murali, what ascetical feat she has performed to earn her enviable intimacy with the great lover—something about which the *Bhāgavata*'s gopis remain silent. To this question the flute, their female rival, responds by explaining how painful it was to endure the regimen that bored those holes in her side. Or again, we hear a hundred ways in which the churning of butter in mythic Braj can be compared to the primordial churning of the Milk Ocean. Does this sound too general to have to be explained by one poet's knowledge of a motif that another poet employed in a language different from his own? Consider, then, the fact that, in a poem that circulated in Sūrdās's name in the sixteenth century, Krishna's foster mother, Yashoda, is heard trying to distract her peevish son by drawing his attention to the moon, as reflected in the shallow dish of water that is before him. This, says Yashoda, is a gift she's offering him. But is it a secondhand gift? This moon-in-dish motif, apparently unknown in Sanskrit, corresponds closely to appeals to the moon that Tamil poets are required to make on behalf of mothers with small children as a part of the *piḷḷaitamiḻ* genre that became so fashionable in the fourteenth or fifteenth century. There are echoes in a Telugu poem attributed to Annamayya and we meet it in Gujarati with Narsī Mehtā as the author.[21]

We could mention many similar examples. All around India, poets singing *pads* revel in the fact that they are "number one among idiots," as Annamayya says, or "best of sinners," as Sūrdās boasts.[22] Similarly, in the genre known as *nindāstuti* they go on to lambast the Deity for failing to rescue them, as would be required if he were faithful to the many names by which he is touted as Savior of the Fallen. For such a reputation, indeed, he is indebted to his human devotees, and now he defaults precisely with respect to them.[23] Such motifs are not necessarily restricted to the *pad* genre and its close analogues or, for that matter, to vernacular poetry, but the mutual resonances become particularly striking there, giving hearers in far-dispersed regional idioms closely related experiences. Knowingly or unknowingly, the audiences of these *pads* tune in on a vast network as soon as they pipe into any of these familiar conceits.

There are other resonances from region to region, too. One of the most appealing of these involves stories in which the poets who operate as parts of this common network are said to have actually met one another in the flesh. Typically these encounters are organized by region or language. In Tamil we have the story of how the *āḻvārs* became *āḻvārs* in the first place: the first three of them took refuge from a torrential downpour by making their way into a little hut—first Poykai, then Bhūtam, then Pey. With one there would have been room to lie down and rest; with two, at least to sit; but by the time the third came along there was only room to stand, and so they stood there singing the night away. Thus a tradition was born: those who are drenched *(āḻvār)* in the Lord. Other connections are also affirmed within the wider *āḻvār* group. Āṇṭāḷ, the only female among them, refers to herself as the daughter *(kotai)* of Viṣṇucitta, that is, Periyāḻvār, but does this mean she was his biological offspring, or does it mark a more spiritual connection, expressing a need to be taken in by an *āḻvār* male?[24] By the thirteenth century, rituals were put in place among Śrī Vaishnavas that would keep this sense of *āḻvār* unity alive, but even when Āṇṭāḷ is refused admission to the list of *āḻvārs* whose poems were mandated to be performed, her connection to Viṣṇucitta is affirmed.

Similar things happen elsewhere, but it is perhaps Maharashtra that presents us with the exemplary case—certainly the most complex. In a series of texts that begin to emerge in manuscripts dating to the late sixteenth century, we are led to believe that the two great originators of the Vārkarī tradition, Jñāndev and Nāmdev, traveled together throughout India; that Nāmdev was a friend of the *mahār* saint Cokhāmeḷā; and that the female poet Janābaī was not only his disciple but his domestic servant. As in the case of Eknāth, we also hear that he had a guru who was a Nāth Yogī—Visobā Khecar—and learn about his own biological family. There is a tendency for the web of connections to tighten over time. The older of the two accounts that report on Nāmdev's travels speaks, as it were, in his own voice, while the joint pilgrimage with Jñāndev comes somewhat later. Of course, Pandharpur and Viṭṭhal serve as great organizing geographical principles, enabling devotees to read back to the Vārkarī saints themselves the journeys to Pandharpur that they undertake in the present day, and Viṭṭhal does his part personally by longing for each of his exemplary bhaktas in turn, thus manifesting from the divine side the strength of the ties that bind them to him and to one another.[25] By the time we get to the great hagiographer Mahīpati in the second half of the eighteenth century, the networkness of it all is expressed in a new way. Following the general example of Kavikarṇapūra, other early Gauḍīyas, and in a different way the Vallabhite Harirāy, Mahīpati creates antetypes for the bhaktas of this age by telling us that Vishnu makes an avatar of himself in Jñāndev, Shiva becomes Narsī Mehtā, Ādimāyā becomes Jñāndev's sister Muktābaī, Śuk becomes Kabīr, and so forth. In doing so he effectively apotheosizes the networking effect that can be seen in the history he describes, reading it as an expression of potentialities that are ever-present and in that way divine.[26]

One can extend the story to north India, as well. There, utterly against fact, Nandadās and Tulsīdās become brothers, and Tulsī travels to Braj to meet Sūrdās or Nābhādās. Meanwhile, back home in Banaras, Kabīr plays host to Nānak and Ravidās. And later on fans of Tulsīdās feel that really it is Sūrdās who ought to have made the trip to Banaras to see their idol rather than the other way around, so off he goes.[27] The legend of Mīrābāī is particularly pliable. In the *parcaīs* of Anantadās, our earliest account, she travels from Chittor to Banaras so as to make Ravidās her guru, but in that story she is not called Mīrābāī but rather the Jhālī queen. A century later, by the time the *Premāmbodh* was written to be performed at the court of Guru Gobind Singh, she makes that journey explicitly as Mīrābāī. Anantadās hilariously weaves Kabīr into the story as the guru whose actual presence didn't live up to the reputation he had earned at a distance: seen up close by the Rajasthani queen, he is too forbiddingly poor, too unkempt. She turns with relief to Ravidās.[28] In the *Bhaktirasabodhinī,* Mira faces down the ascetical self-seriousness of Jīv Gosvāmī, and in the Vallabhite *vārtās* Kṛṣṇadās Adhikārī makes it a point not to accept any temple donations from her and her own personal Brahmin Rāmdās deserts her. Never mind: by the time we get to the nineteenth century she can take all her troubles to Tulsīdās in a soulful epistolary exchange.[29]

This is a fabric with wonderful textures, and it extends well beyond the plains of north India. In Kashmir, for instance, Sheikh Nuruddīn—or as he is familiarly called, Nand Ṛṣi—is brought into a relationship with the radical Shaivite female ascetic Lālded. They exchange spiritual songs; they play blind man's bluff; one time she even jumps into a baker's oven so as not to show him her nakedness.[30] In Tirupati, Purandaradāsa hears an aging Annamayya sing for Venkaṭeśvara, and Annamayya invites the younger musician home and to hear him sing in return.[31] In Rajasthan, Mīrābāī takes it upon herself to write a life of Narsī Mehtā.[32] One could build a very long list of such encounters, and some of them have a less than totally amicable twist. In the *Caitanyacaritāmṛta* and earlier Gauḍīya accounts, for example, Chaitanya is reported to have met Vallabha and to have outshone him, but if one reads the Vallabhite hagiographies one learns that the result was exactly opposite.[33] In general the *saṃvād* or *goṣṭhī* (debate, meeting) genre makes it possible for competing groups to talk with—or past—each another in the personae of the leaders they acclaim.

As a final dimension of this network we should notice that on occasion whole poems seem able to pass through the osmotic membrane that separates poets, languages, and centuries so as to manifest themselves at more than one point along the great bhakti grid. In Kannada, for instance, Basava and his nephew Cennabasava alternate with fair ease, and other poets may also be involved; verses travel between poets even when whole poems do not.[34] Similarly, a Hindi poem may be remembered in one collection as having been sung by Hit Harivaṃś or Tulsīdās; in another collection, by Sūrdās.[35] In such instances only the phrase surrounding the signature alters, making it sound like a case of mistaken identity, but there are others in which the same poem is no longer so "same" once it passes into the orbit of another poet.

One of these is particularly intriguing, since it seems to follow exactly the trajectory the concept of the bhakti movement leads us to expect. This poem, woven from milk, water, and flowers, belongs first to Basava (Karnataka, twelfth century), then to Nāmdev (Maharashtra, fourteenth century), then finally to Ravidās (north India, sixteenth century). It seems to move with the bhakti movement, adapting itself to the life circumstances of three individual bhaktas as it does:

(1) *Basava*

Milk is left over
From the calves.
Water is left over
from the fishes,
flowers from the bees.

How can I worship you,
O Śiva, with such offal?
But it's not for me
to despise left-overs,
so take what comes,

lord of the meeting rivers.[36]

(2) *Nāmdev*

You brought a pitcher of water
  to bathe the Lord:
Forty-two lakhs of beings live in that water:
  why do you pollute Vitthala?

  Wherever I look,
    there is Vitthala:
  In perfect Joy
    He sports forever!

You brought flowers and you wove a garland
  as an offering to the Lord—

But the Blackbee had sipped the nectar already:
  why do you pollute Vitthala?

You brought milk and you prepared sweet rice,
  as an offering to the Lord—
But the calf had already lapped the milk:
  why do you pollute Vitthala?

Vitthala is here, Vitthala is there,
  no place in the world where He is not!
In every and each spot, Nāmā renders Him homage—
  everywhere He is present in plenitude.[37]

(3) *Ravidās*

Mother, she asks, with what can I worship?
  All the pure is impure. Can I offer milk?
The calf has dirtied it in sucking its mother's teat.
  Water, the fish have muddied; flowers, the bees—
No other flowers could be offered than these.
  The sandalwood tree, where the snake has coiled, is spoiled.
The same act formed both nectar and poison.
  Everything's tainted—candles, incense, rice—
But still I can worship with my body and my mind
  and I have the guru's grace to find the formless Lord.
Rituals and offerings—I can't do any of these.
  What, says Ravidās, will you do with me?[38]

Actually, this textbook example of how the bhakti movement moves is not as self-evident as it seems. When we look with a critical eye, it becomes clear that we do not really know that the poem was first composed by Basava and then traveled northward, as we have supposed. We can be sure that the Nāmdev and Ravidās versions were in circulation in the sixteenth century, since both of them appear in the Sikhs' *Kartārpur Pothī,* dated 1604, but we do not know whether a more purely Marathi version of Nāmdev's poem circulated before then.[39] The situation with Basava is equally complex. So far as we know, it was only in the early fifteenth century that Basava's *vacanas* were collected, along with the utterances of other early Vīraśaiva greats, by a man named Mahalingadeva, and current scholarship does not permit us to ascertain from printed materials whether this particular composition takes its place among the 934 that Mahalingadeva initially anthologized.[40] Basava's naming of Shiva as

Kūḍalasangamadeva (lord of the meeting rivers) is the characteristic indication of his own identity—his signature—but knowing what we do about collective authorship and the well-accepted practice that allowed poets to invent new compositions and "sign" them with a venerable name, we cannot assume that the historical Basava composed this poem in the twelfth century. Not surprisingly, present-day collections of *vacanas* are exponentially larger than Mahalingadeva's. What we are left with, then, is not a progression of the sort that a unified bhakti movement would suggest, with Basava leading the charge, but an interlocking set of poems whose exact historical logic is at present hard to describe. Until pre-fifteenth-century manuscripts emerge—an unlikely prospect—or additional critical methods are trained on the corpus we already have, we simply do not know how "original" this poem is, any more than we know Nāmdev composed his in the fourteenth century.

The one thing we do know is that the poem is alive and well today, and still seeking new poets to give it voice. When I mentioned its theme to the Saurashtrian scholar Niranjan Rajyaguru, he immediately broke into song. This time the language of the poem was Gujarati, and the poet through whom it spoke was Gorakhnāth, a figure whose panregional reputation makes him seem particularly appropriate under present circumstances. Gorakh in turn mentions his own guru Matsyendranāth, anchoring the composition in quite a different lineage of inspiration from Basava's and dedicating it to his own chosen deity. Yet knowing the parallels as we do, it is clear that we are ultimately dealing not with specific lineages or devotional communities but with broad networks. Those networks also serve as background for the "new" verses that appear toward the end. The fly that befouls the food is a common and venerable motif, not one that any specific Gorakhnāth may have devised:

> Accept my service, elephant-trunk Master,
>   Accept my worship, Ganapati Lord.
>   Open my poor heart. Take the lock away.
> Suppose I offer water, Lord—that water isn't clean:
>   A fish has soiled the water. Take my service, Lord.
> Suppose I offer a flower, Lord—that flower isn't clean.
>   A bee has soiled the flower. Take my service, Lord.
> Suppose I offer milk, Lord—that milk isn't clean.
>   A calf has soiled the milk. Take my service, Lord.

Suppose I offer sandal, Lord—that sandal isn't clean.
  A snake has soiled the sandal. Take my service, Lord.
Suppose I offer food, Lord—that food isn't clean.
  A fly has soiled the food. Take my service, Lord.
By the energy of Maysendra the ascetic Gorakh speaks:
  Accept my humble bow.
    I've looked inside and found a man.
      Take my service, Lord.[41]

The chronology of this poem, like many others similar to it, is so far impossible to reconstruct.[42] Relevant inscriptions that would help us nail down dates are few, manuscripts go back only so far, there are oral sources to be considered, and we cannot trust that the way a poem is sung now accurately reflects the way it would have been sung way back when. Our Gujarati example and the one invoking Nāmdev suggest that coastal connections can be helpful transmitters, but in many other instances the Vindhyas are apt to get in the way—or more to the point, the general if not watertight division of Indian languages into Indo-Aryan and Dravidian groups, each characterized by a set of interrelated scripts. North of the Vindhyas, by the sixteenth century—was it *pax mughalica?*—there was a certain sense of connectivity from sea to sea. Sūrdās remembers Nāmdev in a poem we know to have circulated in the sixteenth century, and so do the anthologizers of the *Kartārpur Pothī,* who include the Bengali Jayadev, as well.[43] Poems of Narsī Mehtā also mention Nāmdev and Jayadev.[44] But neither in poetic compositions nor in the story literature that goes with them do we find any knowledge of the *nāyaṉmārs* or the *āḻvārs* or the Vīraśaivas. There is no sense of Annamayya or Purandaradāsa or Kanakadāsa, or even Nāmdev's supposed companion Jñāndev. Instead we confront a wall of south-north silence—just the silence that Nābhādās sought to break by claiming that Rāghavānand and Rāmānand had created a bridge from south to north. He wanted to suggest something similar for each of his four *sampradāys.*

As we saw in Chapter 4, there is some evidence of south-to-north movements relevant to bhakti in the fifteenth and sixteenth century, but the record is slim and elite: an affair of Brahmin Bhaṭṭs, largely speaking, and not one that corresponds at all with the picture Nābhādās gives us. In the seventeenth and eighteenth centuries we can in addition trace the movement of poets who traveled from court to court, all through the north and sometimes well south of the Vindhyas.[45] They performed in a widely understood Brajbhasha, but largely in an aestheticized *alaṃkāra* idiom that often rides "above" (though it sometimes connects with) the sort of bhakti poetry that animated non-court settings. It is hard to imagine that a more broadly accessible bhakti network such as we have been describing did not exist at and around the courts where these professional poets were employed, but to document it in historically satisfying ways is often difficult. Allison Busch reads the remembered poetry of Nāmdev and Tukārām as showing that there was an easy bilingualism along "the literary frontier" between Hindi and Marathi, and this may largely be so, but Monika Horstmann reports having seen a manuscript in the Dādūpathī collection at Narainā in which Marathi Nāmdev poems had been given interlinear glosses in Hindi so that unaccustomed readers could understand their contents.[46]

So on the whole, the northerly and southerly realms remained surprisingly distinct. If there was some flow from south to north, in conformity with the bhakti movement paradigm, there was at least as much momentum in the other direction, as the Mughal-Rajput core expanded outward to Golkonda and the Marathas later pressed their way south to Thanjavur. Indeed these new linkages created settings where we know that bhakti poems from various regions were performed. The Thanjavur court of Serfoji II and his successors, together with the Rāmdāsī *maṭhs* established in that city, provides a leading and interestingly complex example, where the embracing and expanding of a cosmopolitan Marathi, with its northern affiliates, coincided with an effort to inscribe a more local and Dravidian Chola past.[47]

Yet largely speaking we must be satisfied with more general networks such as we have been describing, not the sort of history to which names and dates can be affixed. How shall we envision these connections being built? In Gujarat, say, a group of ten or twenty ascetics making a circuit around the region's renowned pilgrimage places passes through a certain village along the way, or perhaps another performing group—even a single individual—comes through. Each will be welcomed and an evening's entertainment arranged, in which the visitors interact with local people, singing back one another's songs in turn, lodging them in memory. The network so created is not entirely oral. Today literacy is quite widespread—an interested someone may be taking notes—and in earlier times too there were various possibilities for the creation of written text. Merchants as a class, their own networks widespread, have always benefitted from being able to write things down, which has meant that not just the singers but those who heard them undoubtedly served as agents in the process of literarization, particularly along well-traveled commercial routes.

Tyler Williams has shown how this happened in Didwana, a town connected to major trading routes in central Rajasthan. There in the course of the later sixteenth century Bihani Maheshvari merchants became the principal patrons of a new religious community that was eventually to be called the Nirañjanī *sampradāy.* The Maheshvaris' trade connections in and beyond the immediate region connected these fledgling Nirañjanīs with Sikhs and especially the Dādū Panth, to which some of them belonged. In the first decades of the seventeenth century, as we recall, these two latter communities produced the expansive *nirguṇ bhakti* anthologies *(Gurū Granth, Pañcvāṇī, Sarvāṅgī)* that, along with a parallel hagiographical literature, became major sources for our knowledge about some of the Mughal-period developments we detailed in the central chapters of this book. A Nirañjanī anthology of the same type *(vāṇī)* took shape toward the end of that century.[48]

In their mercantile lives Maheshvaris certainly had to interact with the armed force and administrative protocols of the Mughals and Kachvahas, and one place they did so was in Fatehpur, which also played host to a major Dādūpathī community. It was in Fatehpur that a local Kachvaha chieftain commissioned for his son's benefit the oldest dated bhakti anthology to have come down to us in all of north India (1582), the one with Sūrdās at its center. Now we begin to suspect that it may have been surrounded by a number of other collections of bhakti poetry, probably smaller and more ephemeral, that would have circulated in networks of merchants like the Maheshvaris and been kept in their homes. Similarly it was a range of actors—merchants, Brahmins, farmers, and landowners—who joined the Vallabhite community along the trade routes that ran through Rajasthan connecting Braj to Gujarat.[49] By the mid-seventeenth century, Vallabhite intellectuals had isolated the eight Krishna-oriented poets *(aṣṭachāp)* who thereafter came to serve as the community's sole devotional focus. Dādūpathīs and Sikhs, *nirguṇ* by contrast, were dependent on Khatris and Jats, who represented a mix of mercantile and agrarian occupations. Dādū, as we have seen, was a cotton carder *(piñjārī),* while

Nānak, who came from a Khatri merchant family, was the son of a revenue official *(parvārī)*. Vallabha and Viṭṭhalnāth, of course, were Brahmins.

In many places—Didwana and Fatehpur included—Jains may have served as models for this literarizing activity and the efforts of circulation and archiving that it entailed. Indeed, Jains recorded not only Jain compositions but also the devotional poems of others; in all cases they reaped the merit associated with preserving sacred utterance.[50] Furthermore, as Williams points out, it cannot be coincidental that important Sufi *dargāhs*, with their own networks and canons of literate communication and book production, existed in rough proximity to places like Didwana and Fatehpur—most famously at Nagaur and Ajmer.[51] This was an important fact of life not just in Rajasthan but across north India and into the Deccan. We can see the impact of Brahmins on the bhakti traditions that developed in many places, but it is crucial to keep in mind the non-Brahmin networks as well. Let us not forget, in addition to the above, that *sādhus* were often traders—and sometimes fighters; they too had their bhakti connections.[52] Thus we are able to glimpse a complex network of networks that sustained bhakti transmission in the early modern period—a theater of religious performance and literacy that intersects with, sometimes mimics, yet certainly contrasts with what one might expect in settings that we think of broadly as "court." Narayana Rao has observed that the saints depicted in the *Basava Purāṇa* come entirely from the "left-hand," that is, nonlanded castes, by contrast to the bulk of saints who fill the pages of the Chola-championed *Periya Purāṇa,* upon which it draws.[53]

This is a crazy quilt. To describe it all as a movement serves in only the most general way to capture its full logic. This is true with respect to the south-north momentum that the idea of the bhakti movement classically seeks to promote, what we might call its first major aspect. It also applies to a second aspect that is typically inscribed within the bhakti movement ideal—the movement from low to high, the rebellious push from society's less privileged members toward and sometimes against their "betters." Yes, we do have many non-court and non-Brahmin actors, but we must also be conscious of the fact that in Karnataka, for example, the egalitarian, caste-questioning rhetoric of Basava's *vacanas* was later subsumed and therefore muted by the specific caste and sectarian location of the Lingayat community that claimed to be its realization. Similarly, few Chaitanyites these days follow the precedent of the master's close associate

Haridās in coming from Muslim backgrounds. As for Maharashtra, Christian Novetzke has proposed that the "quotidian revolution" Jñāndev helped initiate there—the embracing of Marathi vernacularity for the sake of (in Jñāndev's words) "women, low castes, and others"—produced already in that very same person a desire to "limit the effects of allowing the everyday to reorder the core of the public world."[54] Thus the strong sense of movement that is implied in many articulations of the bhakti movement idea is hardly as unstoppable and universally shared as its proponents have sometimes led us to believe, even if the radical example of some of the greatest bhaktas still continues to inspire.

Finally, we have a third development that is often folded into the idea of the bhakti movement—the idea that the bhakti movement is the underlying cause for the adoption of vernacular tongues as literary domains in the course of Indian history. Obviously this aspect too has to be questioned. Sheldon Pollock has persuasively shown that if our literary and epigraphic record is to be believed, it was not primarily in streets, homes, festivals, or temples but at court that vernacular speech first made its literary breakthrough. Kannada, Gujarati, Assamese, Malayalam, and Telugu are evidence of this. Each of these vernacular literary domains first took shape as a vehicle of political purpose and reflection, typically by reproducing rather than challenging the classical idioms that Sanskrit had established as appropriate for literary endeavor, especially epic ones.[55] And yet, this was not universally the case. In an even larger group of languages, as Christian Novetzke has observed, the clear impress of regional courts is not so clear—Marathi, Punjabi, Hindavi, Dingal, Bengali, Urdu—and even in court settings such as these (e.g., Maithili, Punjabi) the religious and even specifically bhakti element may be more prominent than Pollock's generalization might lead us to suspect.[56] Tamil, being an ancient literary language, is a special case, and it was not originally "bhakti" in tone, as Pollock correctly observes. Yet by the time we come to the period to which the idea of the bhakti movement applies, literary Tamil had undergone an internal proliferation and, as suggested by *Bhāgavata Māhātmya,* spoke the language of bhakti eloquently if not exclusively. The same is true for the very different and much more recent Nirañjanī world that Tyler Williams has explored, where we also see an interpenetration of religious and secular genres but this time with the bhakti poetry committed to writing at the outset.

Three cautions are in order when considering issues of vernacularization such as these. First, the emergence of a spoken language onto the stage of literature may only seem to have happened at court because it was there that one had the resources to produce durable literate/literary records. Second, we must be sure that we are not defining literature in such a way that it excludes ipso facto large swaths of vernacular speech—poetic utterances of the more humble *sants,* for example, or of Nāth Yogīs. Pollock himself observes this caution. Or if we do accept such a delimitation of the literary domain, we need to keep in mind that more "common" *(laukika)* registers of speech also served as vehicles of highly patterned vernacular expressivity.[57] Finally, it is significant that in languages where the earliest literary remains are associated with court settings, these court texts seem often to have been less valued over the long haul as marks of vernacular literary productivity than texts of a more religious nature, which followed somewhat later. This is the case with Pampa's and Viṣṇudās's vernacular versions of the *Mahābhārata* in Kannada and Gvaliyari (i.e., Brajbhasha) respectively—texts for which only a few manuscripts are preserved but that are critically important for Pollock as he makes his argument.[58] Recognizing this fact, Pollock argues that Kannada's Vīraśaivas and Haridāsas and the poets grouped together in Brajbhasha's earliest anthologies constituted a "second vernacular revolution."[59] That was the one that tended to stick, its poetic products being widely distributed from that point onward and celebrated as the literary basis of the language.

Such celebrations, especially when they involve the positing of a premodern "bhakti period," may unfairly play down the contributions of court culture to the literary debut of many Indian vernaculars, but they do suggest that the bhakti idiom matters far more in the emergence and patterning of India's vernacular languages than might be guessed from reading Pollock's peerlessly expansive work. Yet I am no more eager than he to argue that an India-encompassing bhakti movement makes sequential sense of the subcontinent's vernacular history. The whole thrust of this book works against such a view. I have grasped onto the notion of a far-reaching bhakti network as an alternative, but it precisely cannot do the kind of historical heavy lifting that the idea of the bhakti movement was intended to perform.

Kabīr and the Early Modern Self

So then, let's make a shift. Let's address the question of what the idea of the bhakti movement ought to mean by looking at it from a fresh perspective. Rather than focusing on how vernaculars came to compete with Sanskrit and Persian as literary domains, or assessing how patterns of south Indian bhakti might have been transferred to the north, as Nābhādās asserted, we could look toward the present rather than the past. Innovations made during the reign of Akbar did indeed mark a sea change in the history of north India—not absolute, of course, but so substantial that they had a great deal to do with the formation of Nābhādās's conception in the first place.[60] If we redirect our focus presentward, we will be letting go of one of the major ways in which earlier generations made use of the idea of the bhakti movement, namely, as a narrative serving to connect India's ancient period with its modern one. In that usage the bhakti movement served as a centerpiece of "the medieval," tying the sixth century with the sixteenth and replacing the other great preoccupation in British historiography of the middle period, "the age of Islam." In our revised perspective, we would let go of all this. We would portray the bhakti movement not as medieval but as early modern, following the logic of the fact that the core and precursor of the idea of the bhakti movement—the concept of the four *sampradāys*—was indeed a product of the period we have come to think of as early modern.

We can get a sense of what would be involved in making this shift by focusing on Kabīr. He more than any other figure identified with the bhakti movement has seemed to speak without mediation to modern sensibilities, and a good case can be made for freeing him from the historiographical ties that might otherwise bind him to the earlier reaches of medievalness. It was Nābhādās who first articulated these, anchoring Kabīr and the circle he was felt to inhabit—Dhannā, Sen, Ravidās, Pīpā—via Rāghavānand and Rāmānand to the Śrī Vaishnava south, and thereby to a deep historical past. Purushottam Agrawal, undoubtedly one of the most eloquent interpreters of Kabīr living in India today, has been vigorous in his defense of the Kabīr-Rāmānand link, although he is far less interested in defending that for which it stands: a lineage that would make it possible for Kabīr to channel southern forebears. To the contrary, Agrawal demonstrates that the only Rāmānand we know speaks entirely in Hindi, not in ageless Sanskrit. This makes it possible for Agrawal to affirm Kabīr's "early modernity" without qualification: his is a forward-looking perspective, openly conscious of the role Kabīr can and does play in shaping a sense of appropriate modernity in contemporary north India.[61]

I feel Agrawal's job can be made far more straightforward by loosing Kabīr from the fetter of Rāmānand, if I dare call it that. Agrawal has proposed that the Rāmānand-Kabīr link was not just a Rāmānandī concoction but a matter of widespread agreement in the sixteenth century—a "universal medieval consensus," to use his term—but I do not believe his argument holds.[62] At first the *Dabistān-i Mazāhib,* which accepts this view that Rāmānand was Kabīr's guru, seems an attractively neutral witness, since its author was merely a traveler on the Indian scene. But Mūbad Shāh is only repeating what he heard from a Rāmānandī at Lahore in 1642: he does us the favor of reporting his source.[63] That leaves Harirāmvyās as the sole remaining non-Rāmānandī witness, and his testimony proves ambiguous. On a common reading Vyās seems to use the term *sevak* (servant) to describe Kabīr's relation to Rāmānand—Kabīr serves the latter, his guru—but there is something odd about the fact that Kabīr comes up in an additional five poems in Heidi Pauwels's edition of Harirāmvyās, while Rāmānand is absent from each of them. If the pupil is so important, why not the teacher? An answer may well be found in the Rāmānand poem itself. The phrase that Vyās uses to describe Kabīr's relation to him is *jā kau sevaka kabīra dhīra,* which we might well translate as meaning "whose servant is steadfast Kabīr," and yet it is not clear that the possessive adjective *jā* does indeed refer to Rāmānand. Agrawal evidently takes it in this sense—Rāmānand appears in the refrain, so this is a good possibility—but one could also take this *jā* as referring to Hari, who is the subject of the line just preceding.[64]

Thus Harirāmvyās's witness is not at all the crucial fact that confirms Nābhādās's view of a relationship that proved crucially important in its turn. Rather, it is ambiguous. And when we put that together with everything else we know, we see that it makes much more sense to let Kabīr stand on his own two feet than try to link him to any guru. It was clearly Kabīr, not Rāmānand, who unleashed an absolute whirlwind into the religious consciousness of sixteenth-century north India, and he has retained that prominence in centuries since—in the proliferation of branches of the

Kabīr Panth, in the minds of the creative thinkers who gathered at Shantiniketan, in the seminal book of Krishna Sharma, in the poetry of Robert Bly, in the Dalit claim laid to him by the freethinking journalist Dharamvir in the 1990s, in the films of Shabnam Virmani and the activities of The Kabīr Project, and in the writing of living scholars such as Linda Hess, Milind Wakankar, Ananya Vajpeyi, and, of course, Purushottam Agrawal.

In his own time too, if ever there was a bona fide bhakti movement, it surely had Kabīr's name on it. He appears twice in Abu'l Fazl, for starters, and poems bearing his name are the most numerous of any of the bhaktas included in the *Gurū Granth,* taking a place that is second only to that of the Sikh gurus themselves. In Rajab's *Sarvāngī,* similarly, Kabīr's poems follow only those of Dādū in frequency, and it was evidently Kabīr after whom Dādū wanted to fashion himself:

> The one who was husband to Kabīr—I choose him as my groom too.
> In mind and word and action there's nothing else I'll do.[65]

If anyone functions as the go-to person in hagiographies that circulated in north India from the sixteenth century forward, it was Kabīr. Understandably, because of his own loyalties, Anantadās reserves this role for Rāmānand (though he does not actually compose a biography for him), but elsewhere Kabīr's prestige is clear. In accounts that circulated from the seventeenth century onward Nānak comes to him, Ravidās comes to him, even Mīrābāī eventually appears on his doorstep. And already in the middle of the seventeenth century, in a painting that may have been produced in an atelier patronized by Dara Shukoh, Kabīr sits at the head of one of two rows of non-Sufi divines who help frame a scene that focuses on a set of dancing Sufis, perhaps imagined as they might have been seen at Ajmer (Figure 10).

In the background, which appears at the top, major figures of the Chishtiya and Qadiri orders observe their ecstasy, but at the bottom Kabīr and those who sit behind him, to our left, balance a series of Shaiva ascetics headed by Matsyendranāth and Gorakhnāth, at the right. This bottom register is a kind of who's who. The figures sitting behind Kabīr seem to have been gathered from earlier, independent portraits—Kabīr himself is posed as he often is when weaving (Figure 11)—and the same is true for the Shaivas sitting opposite. Labels have been added to identify

Figure 10. Assembly of Sufis and bhaktas, Victoria and Albert Museum (ca. 1650?). Photo courtesy of the Victoria and Albert Museum.

them all, as if their images might not have been as familiar to potential viewers as those who people the Islamic registers just above.

I would argue that the painter understands Kabīr to be the preeminent figure among Vaishnavas, although of course the group he heads consists entirely of *nirguṇīs* or *sants*. (One among them is labeled *aughar,* but there is nothing Shaiva in his appearance: the Shaivas are sitting across the way.) This is the "vulgate Vaishnavism" to which we referred in Chapter 3, and it connects Kabīr to Nāmdev in hagiological imagination. Indeed, Nāmdev sits four behind Kabīr in this painting.[66] Nāmdev suggests the south, and as Maharashtrian warrior-rulers pushed south across the Deccan in the course of the late seventeenth and early eighteenth centuries, they evidently carried with them a tradition of Kabīr performance, so that by the time their most illustrious ruler, Serfoji II, made a pilgrimage to Banaras under the protection and with the encouragement of the British, he returned to Thanjavur not only with a horde of Sanskrit manuscripts but with some that preserved the songs and couplets of Kabīr. Telugu was a prominent language at Serfoji's court and elsewhere, and of late there has also been an effort to integrate Telugu speakers into the all-India bhakti canon by representing the low-caste Telugu poet Vemana as a homegrown analogue to Kabīr.[67] Such is Kabīr's prestige on the current national scene.

Ananya Vajpeyi has written sensitively about how the repeated urge to confront Kabīr was driven by the thirst for a new sense of Indian selfhood that occupied the minds of key intellectuals who lived in the decades that led up to the creation of an independent India. In a book focused on five major figures whose work stretches from 1885 to 1947—Gandhi, two Tagores, Nehru, and Ambedkar—Vajpeyi finds that Kabīr takes his place as the implicit, omnipresent sixth: "For modern India, Kabir represents the ultimate telos—an ability to simultaneously acknowledge irreducible differences and overcome them; an unflickering flame of faith that burnishes the gold of an equally precious skepticism; the strength to stand firm in a stance of confident rationality even while gazing unblinking into the abyss of violence. To proceed toward an enlightened, humane, inclusive nationhood even with its almost unbearable burdens of caste conflict, communal hatred, and sectarian prejudice, India itself has to approximate to the condition of Kabir—the coherent, charismatic, autotelic Self."[68]

Purushottam Agrawal approaches things from the other side, focusing less on the Kabīr of memory than on the Kabīr who actually lived in early modern times. Kabīr's sensibility was truly modern, he argues, but at the same time it reached forward to modernity in a distinctively indigenous way. Developing this perspective, Agrawal invites us to move beyond the sort of reading that Hazariprasad Dvivedi and P. D. Barthwal pioneered, which locates Kabīr in a social group with ties to the Nath *sampradāy* recently converted to Islam. Although he joins Marxist historians of the Aligarh school in seeing Kabīr in class terms—as an artisan—Agrawal presses for a more flexible understanding of the economics of things: a public sphere that crucially involved urban trade and exchange and basked in its own newly public voice. This ties Kabīr the "author" to the networks of performers, traders, and soldiers that must have been active in spreading his word so rapidly throughout upper India and thereby accommodates an important text-critical truth. It helps derail the question we always ask, given the dispersed and diverse manuscripts where his utterances were first recorded: what did Kabīr himself say, and what was attributed to him later on? Rather, it sees Kabīr as being intrinsically a part of the shared *satsang* context that perpetuated and doubtless expanded him in memory.[69]

All this suggests that while initially the realities of collective authorship may seem to frustrate any search for a singular self in Kabīr, in actuality they do not. The only Kabīr we know is the one who comes to us through something like a bhakti movement—or a bhakti network, if you like—but the movement that names and claims him would have been very hard to imagine if some great soul did not stand behind it and contribute to it. Yes, the Kabīr who comes down to us is inextricably a construction of those who received him, sang his songs, performed his words, and added their own already in the early modern period. In fact, our recensions give us several distinctively different Kabīrs, attesting in this way to the vibrancy of the Master's voice. Yet the fact that they listened so attentively and constituted by 1600 a bhakti network that was utterly novel in its range, both geographically and religiously, seems testimony to the perception that they were hearing something new, something deep yet appropriate to the age (how often mention is made of the *kaliyug!*), something upon which a self shared in *satsang* could actually, believably be based.

Of course, Kabīr was not the only self to be so "produced." As we have seen, Sūrdās too, by virtue of the collective authorship in which he is embedded, was in his way a movement. But that makes our point even more strongly. It's a network thing—a matter of call, answer, and recall—and the importance of the network neither removes the economic and social contexts that made it possible nor takes away the importance of the original voice that resounds through it. With Kabīr this voice is especially hard to miss, but it is also to be found in Sūr. One becomes ever more strongly convinced of Sūr's individuality the more one separates the earliest manuscripts in which his poems circulated from those that swirled around his name later on.[70] In the great composite selves we call Kabīr and Sūrdās, like the one called Nāmdev farther west, we feel the pulse of something we can label, without too much distortion, the bhakti movement. Because of his artistry, Sūrdās calls out to connoisseurs. Because of his reputed blindness, he calls out to blind performers. But there is something about Kabīr that calls out with special clarity, since he often speaks through the spare *nirguṇ* voice of the streets. We can still imagine the cosmopolitan urban network that was his—the shops and looms that lined the streets of Banaras, the *qāzīs* and pundits who gathered crowds there—and in part because his voice is so strong and so constitutive of the language Hindi speakers still use today, his words and grammatical constructions have not slipped too far back into old age.

Listen to how they call to Agrawal. In his book *Akath Kahānī Prem kī* (Love's Untold Story, a phrase from Kabīr), toward the end of the biographically oriented third chapter ("There Once Was a Weaver Who Lived in Banaras"), we come to a passage in which Agrawal takes up the famous moment when Kabīr decides to leave Kashi—that is, Banaras—behind. He dispenses with his liberation-dispensing birthright—he never believed all that Brahmin cant anyway—and goes off to live in godforsaken Magahar not far away. There he is visited by Gorakhnāth, who challenges him to a battle of theory and method—or rather, miracle. Agrawal tells us with obvious delight how Gorakh suspended a trident in midair and the weaver outdid him by throwing up a piece of thread and standing on it. Then Gorakh dispensed five hundred potfuls of water to quench the thirst of five hundred deities in image form *(mūrtis)*, in response to which Kabīr simply opened a well. Still not conclusive enough? That's when Purushottam Agrawal himself walks onstage. He tells us the well is still there today: "I visited it in April of 1987, and the water is very sweet."[71]

In autumn 2010 I happened to be in Delhi just after *Akath Kahānī Prem kī* had been released. There was lots of buzz in Delhi's literary circles, and a seminar was organized at the India International Centre under the chairmanship of Ashok Vajpeyi, the director of Sangit Natak Academy. I particularly remember a moment when the historian Sudhir Chandra picked up the book and began to read. The passage he chose was only a page before the one whose content I have just been describing. Magahar is already in the air, and Agrawal is following out the meaning of the well-known *pad* whose refrain—also the first line—goes *Vai kyoṅ kāsī tajaiṅ murārī:*

> Why should they leave behind Kashi, Murārī?
> That's where they've cheated you of serving you, Banvārī.[72]
> Yogis, renouncers, celibates, ascetics—
> they crowd the *maṭhs* and temples for the sake of touching Kashi.
> Three times a day they bathe their bodies
> but inside, they never get the news.
> Temple to temple they make their daily rounds
> but never sound the spotless name of God.
> I'll never set foot in famous Kashi, says Kabīr.
> I'd rather go to hell.[73]

In the commentary that follows this defiant poem, Agrawal rejects the notion that it expresses either a *nirguṇ* preacher's self-satisfaction at rejecting the puffed-up claims of Kashi's elites and entrepreneurs or a revolutionary's self-loathing as expressed by pooh-poohing the sort of bhakti that might regard Kashi and Magahar as equally worthless. No, he says, beneath both of these one has to deal with the poem's simple humanity. To rip that away would be inhumane:

> All right, for Kabīr Kashi was no guarantee of heaven, but it was the memory of his childhood, his youth, every love or pain [*rāg-virāg*] he ever had. Wherever a person is born, grows up, that city or town isn't just a feature of some external geography, it lives inside you, under your skin . . . However much you try to show you don't care, however much you label it ridiculous or even horrible, this city of yours carries all that ridicule and horror with it as it travels with you to the other side of the world—in dreams, in memories, in words, and most offensive to the "alienation" you project, in your tears.
>
> And when all your searches are over—incomplete and complete, fruitless and fruitful both—that's the time when your city especially calls you. However much you've cursed it in the course of being alive, on life's last shore you want to love it—you toss and turn for it like a fish out of water.

> From such moments of tossing and turning comes, in this poem of Kabīr, Kashi—for someone else Lahore; for someone else Delhi; for someone else Faridabad; for someone else, yes, Gwalior.[74]

Gwalior! Who do you suppose comes from Gwalior? Yes, it is Purushottam Agrawal himself, moved to an expression of his own selfhood by the selfhood he finds in Kabīr. Is it bhakti that causes this movement from age to age and person to person? I believe that is as good a way to name it as any.

Scholars of south India have discerned a similarly modern sensibility in Annamayya. The voice is quite different from Kabīr's, yet its doubting, deeply reflective mode also feels like "self" from the perspective of the twenty-first century. Here is what Velcheru Narayana Rao and David Shulman affirm:

> In a sense, Annamayya shows us a Tirupati close to the one we know today—a highly dynamic and successful entrepreneurial system built around a god of individual, subjective temperament, responsive to each of his visitors. By composing some thirty-two thousand Telugu *padam*-poems to this god (if we are to believe the figure given by his grandson, Cinnanna), Annamayya invented a style of lyrical intimacy that became a form of worship . . . There is an acute awareness of the finite nature of time given to human beings and of the poet's utter inability to use this gift that has been lavished, or rather wasted, upon him. What is more, this existential perception is the very condition of the poet's self-awareness. Knowing himself as a single subject, he knows, first, this consistent failure.[75]

Narayana Rao and Shulman give us an exemplary *padam* to support this conclusion:

> Where is my wisdom?
> Where is my good sense?
> Time is lost, like an offering
> poured in the dust. . . .
>
> *an offering poured in the dust.*
>
> I'm sure I'll be happy here, or maybe over there,
> So I keep moving from place to place.
> I don't even see the god right next to me.
> Time goes, like empty talk,
>
> *an offering poured in the dust.*[76]

David Shulman, Velcheru Narayana Rao, and Sanjay Subrahmanyam correlate such utterances with "the rise of a new elite, drawn largely from the so-called left-hand castes of warrior-merchants and other nonlanded groups that sought to profit from an increasingly cash-oriented economy with its new opportunities for self-made men, free from ascription determination."[77] They see it taking root not just in Tirupati, though that is a very important node, but all over south India in the fifteenth and following centuries: the Vijayanagar and later Nayaka domains. Other scholars—for example, John Richards, Sheldon Pollock, Allison Busch, and Purushottam Agrawal—have argued that a distinctive "early modernity" also emerges in the Mughal realms, and it is not hard to find echoes of Annamayya, individual as he is, in that singer of Mughal *pads,* Sūrdās.[78] Like Annamayya, Sūr also traverses the distance between the narrative world of Vishnu/Krishna and a realm that, while still marked by convention, is intended to seem—and does seem—more distinctively personal:

> Everyone has long stopped loving me.
> Oh Gopāl! My body is gripped by age
>   and I wither away inch by inch.
> The horoscope that once structured my life—
>   my zodiac, my lunar sign, my natal day and date—
> These no longer signify a thing.
>   The days are over when I tried to win the world.
> Money, mansion, lineage, name,
>   everything I worked so hard to make:
> I see them now the way a dog looks at a face—
>   motionless, staring from afar.
> With all the days and years I've grown old.
>   Soon they'll be writing my horoscope again,
> And the thought of all that unabated fault, Lord of Sūr,
>   makes me turn to you, Hari, for care.[79]

There are differences between Sūr's *pad* and Annamayya's—that goes without saying. But it would not be tampering with the evidence to notice that one could perfectly well insert a periodic refrain into the Sūrdās *pad,* just as Narayana Rao and Shulman have done in the Telugu: "Everyone has long stopped loving me," or simply "long stopped loving me." Then the two poems would look as alike on the page as they actually are. But historically, what could the real connection be? The Mughal poet never acknowledges his Vijayanagar predecessor, nor does anyone else in the world of which he was a part, despite the fact that later on, at least, we have hints of interregional ties: one of our earliest Sūrdās manuscripts was copied far to the south, at Burhanpur in the Deccan, in 1624, and we know that other Brajbhasha poems were performed in the Deccan.[80] This silence echoes from the southern side, as well: Telugu, Kannada, and Tamil poets make no reference to anything that might have happened in the north. Of course, to speak about such ties was not really the job of a poet speaking in a bhakti mode—not the sort of thing one might occasionally expect from poets with professional court connections, though the boundary was not hard and fast.[81] So in an obvious sense, it is overreaching to speak of Annamayya, Kabīr, and Sūrdās as belonging to a single bhakti movement, and yet the formal and personal resonances are compelling. We have seen that one *pad* of Sūrdās sounds as if Annamayya could have spoken it; there are a number of others, too. And many share their tropes with Kabīr.[82]

Such poems belong unquestionably to a single, widely dispersed bhakti environment. In them, as in the West at just this time, early modern selfhood emerges with special clarity; it emerges in a tussle with God.[83] By the time we get to Tukārām in early seventeenth-century Maharashtra, the battle is intense indeed—and intensely personal. Today's writers are often eager to rip off the rhetorical shell and see such contestations as revealing an independently standing, secular self that cries to be released from the religious trappings that encase it. I doubt that that can or should be done. The bhakti shell is deeply connected to the living organism it protects—or projects—and the species as a whole is largely visible only by comparing the patterns on the shells and feeling our way inward to the ligatures that tie the shells to their contents.

Prithvi Datta Chandra Shobhi has argued this point in relation to the great Vīraśaivas of the twelfth century, begging us to recognize that their utterances are not just "speaking of Śiva," as Ramanujan's famous title proclaimed, but "speaking *to* Śiva."[84] He comes to this formulation as part of his critique of the manner in which contemporary Lingayat organizations in their anti-Brahmin rhetoric have sought to portray Basava and his contemporaries as apostles of egalitarianism pure and simple—fully modern Enlightenment beings who long ago inveighed against caste society but were suppressed, unheard. Chandra Shobhi argues that their messages were far more intimately involved with the specific *vacana* medium, and notes that it was only in the fifteenth century that these *vacanas* were aligned with individual saints in coherent biographies, producing the paradigmatic individuals that a modern sensibility requires. He wants to render these *vacanas* accessible as "sources of the self" and mediums of practice to persons who do not wish to align themselves with the criteria demanded by "Lingayat identity politics"—Dalits especially. He emphasizes the quality of spontaneity that the *vacanas* so often express, "captur[ing] a momentary thought in an independent and autonomous stanza, which is complete itself," and he underscores their "more devotional element, self examination and inner conflict, rich personal experience and general heart."[85]

If these are significant markers of early modernity, then it would seem we have to press the age back to the twelfth century—the urbanity of fabled Kalyāṇa. Yet as we have suggested, and as Chandra Shobhi also demonstrates, a true sense of the individuals giving utterance to these sentiments emerges only in the Vijayanagar period, toward the middle of the fifteenth century. It was then that Vīraśaiva *maṭhs* emerged as powerful forces at Vijayanagar and delineated a whole series of "symbolic characters" such as Basava, Allama Prabhu, and Mahādevīakkā, who would serve to represent the militant mysticism their *virakta* inhabitants wished to cultivate. In that regard and also with respect to the variety of social locations they comprised, these ideal individuals align nicely with the early modernity that emerges in a similarly dynastic context farther north in the course of the sixteenth century.[86] Contemporarily similar things happened in a Vaishnava mode, as at Annamayya's Tirupati.

Are we really looking at a single movement, then? In the narrow, specific sense, probably not. To avoid chasing after such a chimera we have taken refuge in the metaphor of a network. But the network has its specific tones and tensions. For one thing, as the fifteenth century yielded to the sixteenth, it became overwhelmingly oriented to Krishna or Rām. As we have seen, Śrī Vaishnavism became an increasingly powerful institutional reality in the Vijayanagar domains, but elsewhere too there was a characteristic turning away from Shaivism. The widely accepted poetic protocols of "Mughal Vaishnavism" seem naturally to supersede it.[87] As we know, this trend toward Vaishnava sensibilities was not monolithic. The Vīraśaivas remain an important exception, and the Shaiva *maṭhs* who newly claimed

Śaṃkara as their founder consolidated their multiregional identity in just this period. But in Maharashtra and Gujarat, individual Vaishnava poets—Jñāndev, Nāmdev, Narsī Mehtā—are remembered as having had Shaivas or Shiva himself for gurus; they turned away from that earlier mooring toward Vishnu in one of his several forms. Similarly, in the Tailangana country independent temples to Vishnu begin to emerge only in the fifteenth century, creating some sort of bridge between Jagannāth in Puri and Purandaradāsa far to the south in Tirupati.[88] Crucially, this was a region that sent emigrants to Braj.

In the realm of high culture too, where Brahmins debated with one another for a living, there was a perceptible shift in the period about which we are speaking. It is not just that Advaitan intellectuals of Banaras and Madurai, most prominently Madhusūdan Sarasvatī and Appayya Dīkṣita, suddenly felt they had to repel the advances of the militant Mādhvite Vaishnava theism articulated by Vyāsatīrtha, but that, as Anand Venkatkrishnan has emphasized, certain of these intellectuals now felt the need to build bridges between their own philosophical and devotional selves. Venkatkrishnan has shown how the Advaitan philosopher Anantadev, whose family migrated to Banaras from Maharashtra in the course of the sixteenth century, responded in new ways as a philosopher to the chanting of the divine name that evidently formed the core of his personal devotional practice. Anantadev's sense that it was urgent to pull together these two worlds—professional philosophizing on the one hand and bhakti practice on the other—seems to have been relatively new for intellectuals of his ilk. Textually speaking it pays special attention to the *Bhagavānnāmakaumudī* (Comment on the Name of God) of Lakṣmīdhara, written in the first half of the fifteenth century, but contextually Anantadev shows an awareness that he lives in a city where "singing the name" (*nāmakīrtan* or *saṃkīrtan*) has become a lively force. Whether he means specifically the sort of chanting that Chaitanya enacted, we cannot say, but his general awareness of the phenomenon is striking.[89]

Let's think about that Banaras. Sheldon Pollock, Rosalind O'Hanlon, and Christopher Minkowski have drawn attention to the ways in which the Brahmin intellectuals who lived there constituted a new sort of Indian cosmopolitanism in the seventeenth century, but patterns of migration that brought a series of southerners there began already in the sixteenth. Was their Banaras under the spell of a unified bhakti movement? If so, it is probably safe to say that they largely reacted to it rather than making it. As the rapid proliferation of manuscripts of the *Rāmcaritmānas* attests, Tulsīdās surely became a major bhakti force when he adopted the Avadhi medium of the great Sufi *premākhyān* romances and reclaimed the *Rāmāyaṇa* themes they had echoed—the exilic journey to Lankā, the fatally attractive golden deer—for a *Rāmāyaṇa* of his own.[90] The very concept of the name of Rām *(rām nām),* which he celebrated there, may well also have derived some of its cogency from the utterance of the names of Allah and indeed, of that one as the pinnacle of ninety-nine others. As Brajbhasha became increasingly prized in Mughal/Kachvaha circles, Tulsīdās kept pace by turning to that medium instead. To hear Tulsīdās tell it, these acts of forward-looking engagement in the *paurāṇik* world of performance where he thrived made him the object of considerable resentment on the part of more conservative Banarsi Brahmins.[91]

Yet that was not the only tension in his world. Perhaps Tulsīdās was indeed the sort of "slave of Rām"—he uses a familiar Persian-derived word in shaping the phrase *rām gulām*—who could survive by begging and sleeping in mosques.[92] But these common man's proclivities made him no less eager to approve the *nirguṇ* (or as he says, *nirūp*) forms of bhakti that intruded on the integrity of his performative domain—the *sākhīs, śabdas,* and *dohās* that were the characteristic forms of expression when Kabīr or other *sants* like him began to speak. Tulsīdās derides the "bad paths" *(kupanth)* such people form, communities that deny the saliency of caste, demean the Vedas and Puranas, and tear apart the meaningful whole that makes dharma what it is—but the fact that he mounts these attacks with such vigor attests to more than simple irritation.[93] It also signals an awareness that somehow he and those he criticizes belong to a shared new world, a *kali yug* that fairly shouts its corrosive modernity. This newly intensified network of bhakti connections impinges on Tulsīdās whether he likes it or not, and there he joins Kabīr, Ravidās, and Anantadev. Cosmopolitan as Banaras undoubtedly was, however, we have no indication that this complex conversation significantly bridged the south/north gap except in the case of the last man on our list—and that, only if one counts Maharashtra as "south."

Alas, with few exceptions, we are able to tune in on this shared bhakti conversation only by inference. The writings of these major bhakti "authors" rarely address one another by name or even circumstantial description. Largely speaking it remains for hagiographers to connect the dots—Anantadās, Nābhādās, Jangopāl, Kṛṣṇadās Kavirāj, Gokulnāth, Priyādās, and the authors of the *Premāmbodh* and of the Sikh and Dādūpathī *janamsākhīs*. Anthologizers also contributed to this effort by placing the bhaktas' poetry in common vessels. Some worked on a grand scale with *sāmpradāyik* aims in mind—the architects of the *Gurū Granth* or the *Pañcvāṇī* and *Sarvāngī* on the *nirguṇ* side, or those who formed the Krishnaite collections of Braj in a *saguṇ* vein. Other anthologizers assembled much humbler collections of bhakti poetry for a single patron, often mixing *nirguṇ* and *saguṇ* poems as if they didn't see any difference between the two. Even the substantial Fatehpur collection of 1582, focused on Sūrdās, makes us wonder whether *nirguṇ* and *saguṇ* poems were characteristically seen as bhakti expressions that should be kept apart. In the second anthology of the three brought together in that manuscript, Kabīr and Ravidās are archived alongside the likes of Sūr, Paramānand, and Nāmdev, and the two anthologizers who were responsible for fusing these three earlier anthologies apparently saw no problem in retaining the *nirguṇīs* as part of their composite, predominantly Sūr-themed document. As certain editorial revisions to the Sikh *Gurū Granth* reveal, acts of sectarian clarification typically happened as refinements to a more inchoate flood of sung poetry rather than the other way around. Tulsīdās may have been exercised over the differences, but others did not necessarily agree. There was a strong sense that they shared their vernacularity—looking back, an early modern sense.

Bhakti Movements in the Plural

Effectively siding with Tulsīdās, however, some recent writers have argued that it is folly to claim anything like a broad, singly identifiable bhakti movement: the internal fissures are simply too deep. Such scholars insist that the idea of a unitary bhakti movement needs to be dismantled in favor of one or more independently constituted bhakti clusters. Often they have called these bhakti movements, but they do so, quite pointedly, in the plural.[94] In this regard consider, for example, the Sikhs. The role that their scriptures played in preserving a shared bhakti repertory that extended from Bengal (with Jayadev) to Multan (with Bābā Farīd) and perhaps even to Maharashtra (with Nāmdev) is by now familiar to us, but this resource for singing hardly amounts to a movement in the cohesive, institutionally savvy way that some of the best scholars believe characterized the early Sikh community itself. The creation and retention of Gurmukhi as a distinctive script—the very vessel in which the *Gurū Granth*'s anthology is contained—serves as only the most obvious outward sign of an emerging social, liturgical, and eventually political reality that has proved, over time, to be quite distinct.[95]

Maharashtra with its Vārkarī tradition, reinforced by twice-yearly pilgrimages to Pandharpur, and Bengal with its Gauḍīya tradition are also candidates for the idea of bhakti movements in the plural. Both have specific regional and linguistic identities, though both have at least some open borders with Hindi and the north. Nāmdev bridges this gap in the Vārkarī case, since a body of literature in Hindi is also ascribed to him, and one too often forgets that there were quite a number of Gauḍīya (i.e., "Bengali") poets composing in Brajbhasha.[96] Still, both the Vārkarī and Gauḍīya traditions bear signs of an after-the-fact consolidation that occurred in the early modern period itself—in the one case, as Eknāth edited Jñāndev; in the other, as Kṛṣṇadās Kavirāj brought Chaitanya's earlier biographers within the scope of a single narrative work.

The sense that we should be talking about an in-built plurality of bhakti movements rather than a single one becomes even more pronounced when we move from regional distinctions to those imposed by social and economic disparities—by class and, especially, by caste. Scholars like David Lorenzen have long argued that there is a very high wall separating early modern bhaktas who accept caste hierarchies or pay them no mind, on the one hand, from those who in some way foreground and reject caste as part of their own bhakti stance.[97] Braj Ranjan Mani, writing from a similarly engaged perspective in a book he calls *Debrahminizing History,* takes a different line. He feels compelled to acknowledge that the crossovers are more dense and habitual in certain regions—Maharashtra more than the north or south, he thinks—but still, he argues that the true engine of motion comes from the protests of the poor and disenfranchised. He characterizes upper-caste bhaktas who worked against social discrimination as being mere "fellow travelers." Sometimes he goes so far as to say that "flag-bearers of the institutionalized brahmanical religion joined the movement to contest and sabotage from within the ideals of the *nirguṇ* saint-poets who had 'challenged the tenets of feudalism in a feudal age.' " Which movement? Mani entitles the chapter from which we are quoting "Medieval Mukti [i.e., liberation] Movements of the Subaltern Poet-Saints," as if these movements were a thing unto themselves, but throughout the book he is also content to speak of the bhakti movement in the singular, provided one realize that subaltern leaders who "wielded devotionalism as a cultural weapon against caste" stood "at the heart of the movement."[98]

For a time the internationally trained Dalit intellectual and jurist B. R. Ambedkar embraced a similar perspective. In 1951, when an Eknath Research Society was founded in Aurangabad, Ambedkar sent a note of congratulations in which he remarked, "In my young days I was very fond of the literary works of the Maharashtra Saints and I can say how great a contribution the reading of this literature can make to the moral rearmament of man."[99] By 1954, however, he had definitively charted a new course. In that year he persuaded a group of Maharashtrians not to install an image of the Dalit saint Cokhāmeḷā in the temple they had built for him, but to dedicate it to the Buddha instead, thus moving beyond the whole orbit of Hinduism.[100] Other Ambedkarites have followed suit, for instance, the Lucknow-based intellectual Jijñāsu in relation to Ravidās. Not long after Ambedkar's dramatic public turn to Buddhism, Jijñāsu reconfigured the traditional stories about Ravidās by claiming that they had taken hold only when the *camār* saint, who was actually Buddhist, was Hinduized by Brahmins and other members of the Hindu elites.[101]

As Ambedkarites broke away from Hinduism, they were acting out their own kind of bhakti movement—a Buddhist bhakti movement that quickly came to focus on Ambedkar himself. Either they rejected the bhakti past altogether or they concentrated only on the Dalit saints, leaving aside the rest and thus enacting an independent narrative of their own making. But the very class of beings whom they claimed had in large part been created by the bhakti hagiography they rejected. The transvaluation of the poor and despised was part of that multicaste narrative too.

When we survey the life stories of Ravidās in the north, Cokhāmeḷā in the west, and Tiruppāṇ and Nantaṉār in the deep south—all Vaishnava except the last—we find that they share important motifs. For example, the latter three are all said to long from afar for a temple-enshrined god and to do so in the immediate vicinity of the holiest of holy places: Pandharpur, Srirangam, and Chidambaram. The deity pines for each in return, but the evil Brahmins submit them to bodily attack as if to make sure the distance between *bhakti* and *bhagavān* is not collapsed. With Cokhāmeḷā and Tiruppāṇ, we learn that the wound these Brahmins inflict is registered simultaneously on the body of the deity himself—his image. That is the bhakti message: a loving relationship to God is what counts, not the status of the body that expresses it. Of course, Dalit critics were right to observe that stories such as these, in saying the body doesn't matter, actually failed to address frontally the scourge of imagined untouchability. In the end Nantaṉār must be transvalued into a Brahmin if he is to enter the Chidambaram temple, and when Tiruppāṇ is lifted into the temple of Lord Ranganāth on the shoulders of his erstwhile Brahmin tormenters, his own feet still fail to touch the temple floor, leaving it "pure." Nantaṉār, similarly, is drawn to Shiva through a fire that the Brahmins have built at the entrance of the Chidambaram temple to keep him out. He makes it through unscathed, but emerges on the other side not in his own body but in that of a Brahmin.[102] As for Cokhāmeḷā, he is still ardently worshipped in a little shrine outside the temple of Viṭṭhal despite the fact that he is believed to have ended his life by being absorbed into the image that stands at the temple's heart.

We do not know how these Dalit bhaktas from different regions came to be grouped so closely in story and, to an extent, in their own poetry. Was it a common narrative stereotyping imposed from the outside, or is it possible that a role was also played by networks of itinerant trader-singers who traveled between villages where Dalits lived? These are the model for the *banjārā* whom Ravidās addresses in four memorably connected *pads:* the *banjārā*'s trials are the trials life poses from birth to death, and all of us travel his path.[103] It is just this universal vision—especially salient when glimpsed from below—that is falsified by any attempt to give it caste. Sometimes, at least, bhakti has served as the means by which society faces up to its unitary, organic status and recognizes that what it sometimes despises as leftovers are actually integral to the social whole—parts of its own body and esteemed parts, at that. But do broadly based bhakti communities accomplish this freely and completely, or only under pressure and for a time? If the latter, they not only allow the profane world to go on being as profane as it always was, but make it feel better for having taken a temporary bhakti break. No wonder Jijñāsu was determined to turn the curse of untouchability back on its perpetrators in its own terms. He urged his readers to abandon Hinduism in the same way one eliminates feces and urine.[104]

Figure 11. Kabīr and Ravidās (?), National Museum, Delhi (eighteenth century?). Photo by Neeraja Poddar.

Historically speaking, it is crucial that a vast amount of bhakti energy has been generated from below, both socially and in rhetorical terms. But that does not mean these so called low-caste saints are remembered as being essentially indistinguishable, the same. Ravidās needs Kabīr's gritty voice to be the man-for-all-men that tradition wants him to be, and Kabīr needs Ravidās to be grounded in the grittiest aspects of social reality. Hence, in the *goṣṭhī* or *saṃvād* (dialogue, debate) format, they are brought into direct contact with one another. They parry and thrust, with the winner being declared by the partisans of one saint or the other as they write their independent reports. As these saints are made to bicker after the fact—there's no evidence that they actually met in person—they continually reconstitute what is in some special way the "people's" side of the bhakti movement.

Some art historians have speculated that we find a visual record of the encounter between Ravidās and Kabīr in a Mughal-style miniature painting they date to the third decade of the seventeenth century (Figure 11). Not incidentally, this painting is displayed and so captioned in India's

National Museum. Other scholars are skeptical about the seventeenth-century date, estimating that it can be no earlier than the eighteenth.[105] Here the representation of Kabīr is clear—his image is the same as the one that appears in the "Dara Shukoh" painting that we have already seen (Figure 10)—but the portrait of Ravidās is different. The string of beads held in the hand of the man who visits Kabīr could as easily signal a Sufi identity as a Vaishnava one. If so, it evokes the Muslim ambience that probably did encourage the articulation of a shared, openly low-caste bhakti comradeship that we see develop in the early modern period—what Barthwal called "the Nirguṇa School." What is significant is that in the course of time someone supposed this unidentified, turbaned figure must be Ravidās, as if he and Kabīr shared a bhakti movement of their own, with Kabīr in the lead just as the textbooks say he should be.

Elsewhere, though, the lens widens. In Maharashtra the Brahmin Eknāth has been remembered for his determination to share the food Dalits ate. Jon Keune has proposed that the anomaly of this Brahmin-Dalit commensality—its entertainment value—may have been a great measure of what kept this story so persistently before the public eye. This suggests a complicated, perhaps grudging response on the part of certain members of the audience, but as Keune also observes, that is surely only part of the story. Similarly, *pace* Braj Ranjan Mani, we should resist being dismissive every time we see high-caste people projecting themselves into a Dalit bhakti milieu.[106] In one ongoing performance tradition this has been happening since the middle of the nineteenth century by means of a series of dance-dramas, plays, and films depicting the life of Nantaṉār. The drama that started the ball rolling was composed by the great Tamil poet-musician Gopalakrishna Bharati in the *kālakṣepa* mode mixing prose, poetry, and dramatic gesture. Bharati went back to Cēkkiḻār's *Periya Purāṇa* when he did so, quoting from this old and specifically Tamil tradition but augmenting and reshaping it as he went.[107] In that way he, born a Brahmin, contributed to the notion that real bhakti flows from the bottom up.

Yet was the sense of collective selfhood that he cultivated an aspect of a pan-Indian Dalit sensibility, or was it actually more regional by nature? And if regional, how would one square it with the middle- or upper-class, often Brahmin-majority bhakti practices—*bhajan* singing groups—that became such a distinctive part of urban Tamil religious culture in the course of the twentieth century? These groups are lineally connected to the history of bhakti performance that V. Raghavan inherited, and they often espouse his vision of bhakti equality, but they have tended nonetheless to remain bourgeois institutions where a person of low-caste background would feel ill at ease. Christopher Fuller has suggested analogies for "devotionalist" communities elsewhere in modern India and in the Hindu diaspora where bhakti has a distinctly middle-class feel. These include, importantly, the Swaminarayan *sampradāy,* whose members sometimes see the bhakti movement as an important part of the historical context out of which their founder emerged.[108]

It can all be very different for Dalits themselves. In the north Indian city of Lucknow, as Joel Lee has explained, sanitation workers generally find it hard to connect at a very deep level even with Ravidās, much less any other figure in the bhakti movement story. This is both despite and because of the fact that Ravidās has come to be seen as their bhakti ambassador to a group in which they feel they do not participate—Hindus.[109] Among *camārs*, who generally occupy a social position somewhat above these sanitation workers, there is a still stronger sense of ambivalence. Ravidās is their caste fellow, to be sure, but many *camārs* follow the lead of Ambedkar and Jijñāsu in rejecting the sense of broader kinship that the idea of the bhakti movement implies. Their Ravidās is a very different person from the humble, supple Ravidās whom Tagore was eager to sweep into the great bhakti stream—or so they are determined to make him be.

The Bhakti Movement of "the Bhakti Movement"

The bhakti movement is a modern idea. It has roots in the early modern period, it answers to a modern search for nationhood and self, and it has crystallized only in the course of the last one hundred years. In fact, as we have just seen, it is unfinished, ongoing. It continues to build upon itself, ever asking, implicitly: what should the bhakti movement be?

Sometimes this question can seem easier to answer in the negative than in the positive. To start with, bhakti should never be confused with what happened at Ayodhya in 1992. The narrative of the bhakti movement achieved its definitive force as an aspect of *deś bhakti*—love of one's country—but the country whose religious history is so represented is not a specifically Hindu country. Thus on the twentieth anniversary of the assault on the Babri Mosque, SAHMAT issued a commemorative book celebrating the exhibit *We Are All Ayodhya* and affirming its message all over again. At a gathering in Delhi where the book was launched, its primary author, Ram Rahman, an imaginative and well-known photographer who has often split his time between Delhi and New York, spoke about how in historical fact Ayodhya is a place where the mosque domes mixed with temple spires and Muslim *darveshes* lived cheek by jowl with Hindu priests.[110] Some in the audience remembered that when *We Are All Ayodhya* had its American premiere at Columbia University in December 1993 and a conference was organized to mark the moment, a small group of attendees with BJP affiliations had shouted their contempt for Ram Rahman and challenged his right to speak because his first name was Hindu and his last name was Muslim. A fistfight broke out. This time the mood was calmer. Unlike the Columbia event, no one insisted that the BJP be invited to articulate its point of view.

Yet the BJP was hardly absent from the scene more broadly speaking. In late 2012 Narendra Modi, the BJP chief minister of Gujarat—the man who would become prime minister of the whole country a year and a half later—was running for reelection in Gujarat with the Congress Party as his primary opponent. Modi had been the man in charge at the state level when fire broke out on a train carrying a group of Gujaratis back home after a pilgrimage to Ayodhya in 2002. Muslims at the Godhra station were accused of setting the fire, but for a time, at least, the courts concluded the allegation was false. Modi never conceded the point, and many hold him directly or indirectly responsible for the ensuing bloodbath that killed thousands of Muslims and displaced many more from their homes. Nonetheless he received continuing public acclaim in his home state, not only because of his probusiness stance but because of his tough-talking *hindutva* rhetoric, something he would attempt to downplay in the national campaign that followed. When I visited SAHMAT's office on December 7, 2012, the award-winning civil rights activist Teesta Setalwad, who had come for the inaugural functions the previous evening, was off to work on behalf of the Congress Party in the Gujarat elections, hoping to help unseat him. She was accompanied by armed guards. Setalwad offered the opinion that, however much the Hindu right might try to lay claim to the hero-poets of the bhakti movement, they would never be able to swallow Kabīr.

We shall see. But this, at least, can be said: until now Kabīr reigns powerfully over new iterations of the bhakti movement. In 2003, for example, The Kabir Project was launched by the Bangalore-based filmmaker Shabnam Virmani. Since then she and an enthusiastic dedicated team of performers and coworkers have produced four documentary films that are now freely accessible on the Web. In their words, "We glimpsed not one but many Kabirs, tantalizingly present in seemingly opposing spaces—Hindu and Muslim, secular and sacred, folk and classical, *des* (home land) and *pardes* (foreign lands). Kabir walked with us into that unstable dividing line between all these dualities, and each journey became a film."[111] That momentum continues in a new Virmani project called Ajab Shahar, that is, Wondrous City. The phrase comes from a poem of Kabīr, but here the Kabir Project expands to include many other bhakti poets, mostly of the *nirguṇ* sort, as they are sung in the folk traditions of north India. To these, in turn, are added the Baul poets of Bengal and Sufi poets as they are heard in both India and Pakistan. Financial support comes from a small group of Indian NGOs and the Ford Foundation. Ajab Shahar is an interactive Web-based "wondrous city" enabling users to see, hear, search, combine, and extrapolate elements from some 450 *pads* and 250 *dohās,* having as an added resource hundreds of reflections from the performers themselves. Based in as many regional languages as the songs themselves are sung, Ajab Shahar is fully bilingual in Hindi and English in the translations and commentarial materials it provides. It refrains from employing the rhetoric of the bhakti movement per se, but it is hard not to feel the moving, integrative, border-crossing spirit that has long been associated with that idea.[112]

Kabīr is not the only defiant figure whose bhakti voice continues to be heard.[113] In 1989, to mark its tenth anniversary, the pioneering feminist journal *Manushi* published a special double issue called "Women Bhakta Poets." *Manushi* had been widely celebrated as inaugurating the beginning of a new era—an openly feminist era in Indian history—but its founder, the prominent intellectual activist Madhu Kishwar, thought it was important not to succumb to the delusory hype of doing everything for the first time, but to claim the roots of its progressivism in Indian women's history. She found these most markedly among the bhakti saints—in Tamilnadu, Āṇṭāḷ; in Karnataka, Mahādevīakkā; in Kashmir, Lālded; and in Rajasthan and Gujarat, Mīrābāī.[114] Kishwar's own involvement with Mīrābāī is crucial to her identity as an activist. The most formative moment in her childhood, she says, came when she went to the birthday party of a teenage aunt at the age of five or six and saw her dance in the Kathak style to the most famous song attributed to Mīrābāī, *mere to giridhar gopāl dūsaro na koi* (Mine is the cowherd Mountain Lifter—he and no one else). It is a song of defiance, in which Mīrā says she has given up all social conventions for the sake of Krishna, the one to whom she is devoted. What could anyone do to make her someone who she's not? That sense of self-knowing, forthrightness, and independence of mind, fostered in the person of a female bhakti saint, has been Kishwar's watchword ever since, expressing itself at every turn, including her controversial support for Narendra Modi in the 2014 elections.[115]

One of the essays that appeared in *Manushi*'s tenth-anniversary issue was A. K. Ramanujan's "Talking to God in the Mother Tongue," and thanks to Kishwar that same phrase became the title of a spectacular four-evening series of performances by almost exclusively female musicians and dancers from around the country in November, 2012. In organizing this event, *Manushi* joined the Delhi International Arts Festival and the Indian Council on Cultural Religions, an agency of the national government like the one that had participated in the Tirupati conference, in sponsoring the event. The bhakti movement was not specifically mentioned in the publicity that announced the program, but one could easily detect its presence. These performances were heralded as "a festival of dance and music to celebrate the lives and poetic compositions of women bhaktas and sufis (6th to 18th century AD)." Only one male musician was involved, and he too performed an entirely female repertoire in this distinctively gendered application of the bhakti movement ideal.

Finally in the realm of live performance we should mention what's called "the season" in Chennai—a veritable orgy of music and dance that consumes the cultural life of the city each December. There singers of Karnatak music, the iconically southern classical genre, are expected to bring their displays of virtuosity to a rousing conclusion by performing a series of popular pieces called *ṭukaḍās*. Given the fact that the basic language of Karnatak music is Telugu, it may seem surprising that the word *ṭukaḍā* is taken over from Hindi/Urdu. The better the vocalist, the more gifted she (or he) will be in choosing songs from around the country to display her range: Marathi *abhangs* first and foremost, as if to acknowledge the enduring imprint of the Thanjavur court on musical traditions in this part of the country, but also Kannada, Hindi, Bengali, and, of course, Tamil. We hear Tukārām, Mīrābāī, Kabīr, Sūrdās, and many more. The list of such *ṭukaḍās* grows year by year, and as it does, the bhakti movement keeps on moving—not just in Chennai, but wherever Karnatak music is performed: Singapore, Dubai, Cleveland.[116]

These interregional *ṭukaḍās* have roots in the multilingual bhakti singing traditions that V. Raghavan encountered in his boyhood, which date back to the eighteenth century, but they also connect with a more popular register, nicely symbolized by the moment in 1945 when M. S. Subbulakshmi performed the title role of Mīrābāī in an unforgettable Tamil film called *Meera*. As the film starts, we see Mīrābāī as a child even younger than Madhu Kishwar was when the enduringly famous "Giridhar Gopāl" song captured her imagination. In an explicit north-south connection, this Tamil Mīrā cites the example of Āṇṭāḷ's marriage to Krishna to justify her own determination. Later, as the plot develops, Subbulakshmi appears as the adult Mīrā, and the Mīrā songs she sings—all Tamil—were composed specifically for the occasion. As the film became famous and Subbulakshmi's own reputation as a bhakta continued to grow, this Tamil vision of Mīrābāī was transposed "back" into Hindi (in 1947), and at that point *mere to giridhar gopāl* reappeared among the lyrics she sang.[117] *Manushi* perpetuated and amplified transregional resonances such as these when it launched its Delhi performance of 2012.

These current expressions of the bhakti movement should not be seen as unalloyed, unproblematic celebrations of a shared spiritual identity that makes India the vibrant force it is today. As we have seen, there are many fissures and dark sides. Responding to these, a group of concerned academics organized an international seminar at Mangalore University in spring 2013 called "Rethinking Bhakti." Without naming political names, they noted that "dominant historical ways of studying Bhakti in India" as "a movement and a tradition traceable to medieval times" have rendered bhakti "vulnerable to appropriation by aggressive forms of cultural nationalism."[118] They did not want to see it as something hardwired into Indian identity, something that could easily become a tool of the state. They were particularly apprehensive about the BJP government that came to power in Karnataka in 2008, fearing that it intended to exploit the caste identities of several bhakti poet-saints, including the sixteenth-century singer Kanakadāsa after whom their own research center is named, so as to consolidate a regional constituency that would support a national Hinduizing agenda.

The seminar ranged widely, but its most dramatic moment came when Rajaram Hegde, a professor from Kuvempu University in Shankarghatta, Shimoga, stepped to the podium. It was a category mistake, he said, to conceive of the bhakti movement as a movement of social reform, and it was certainly an "Orientalist mistake" to think of it as religion. The whole narrative of bhakti as a movement aimed at combating the supposed degradation of an originally pure religion—pristine ancient Hinduism—was utterly misguided, something fobbed off on India by foreigners who had been blinded by their own reflection. The image of antibrahmanical bhakti that such Orientalists formed was actually just a mirror of the Protestant struggle against Catholicism in European history. In truth, rather, bhakti traditions formed but one aspect of the *ādhyātmik* (spiritual) mentality that had always made India so different from the Christian West. In India, said Hegde, everyone has always agreed on the nature of the world we live in. It is illusorily constructed by *māyā,* and our task through repeated births is to pierce the veil, discovering with a guru's guidance the regimen of practice that will enable us to see beyond the ignorance *(avidyā)* that is our individual lot. This was what Basava was trying to do, and one could only represent him as a social reformer, as many have done, by cherry-picking particular songs from a much larger and quite differently oriented corpus. In one poem, Basava explicitly resists this, Hegde pointed out, saying you shouldn't worry about someone else's sorrows. Every person has equal access to this *ādhyātmik* tradition, which is eternal—as eternal for Basava as for any enlightened soul. What possibility is there for it to be corrupted and therefore needing reform?[119]

When Hegde finished speaking, people rushed to seize the microphone. Valerian Rodrigues of Jawaharlal Nehru University in Delhi called Hegde's argument a huge collapsing of a complex tradition—reductionism plain and simple. He pointed to the characteristic concern among bhakti poets for the common people *(lok)* and their common social lot. Vijayakumar Boratti of Mysore objected on other grounds. He explained that from the nineteenth century to the present there had been many voices vying to interpret Basava in their own way—no self-evident truth—and that itself was consonant with what one sees in the diverse bhakti movement as a whole.[120] Prabhakar Joshi, a Mangalore participant, conceded that much about the interaction between Protestants and Catholics was specific to European history, but argued that other aspects of these contestations—

bhakti contestations—were universal. Madhva, for example, today the representative of time-honored orthodoxy in the Mangalore region, actually launched his distinctively dualist philosophical initiative because he believed the theorists who preceded him had polluted the original truth of the canonical texts.[121] His bhakti was an effort to redress a history of what he saw as degradation. On many sides, thus, Hegde was accused of the same sort of cherry-picking he had condemned in others. It was only that he had picked different cherries.

Why did it matter? It mattered for the truth of history, of course, but it also mattered because of the political truth in Karnataka today—the ongoing need for justice and diversity and the danger that the state might succeed in suppressing those concerns by enacting a uniform Hinduism of its own design. A scholar who refers to himself as Dr. Dominic D railed at the way low-caste youths who serve as construction works for Bangalore's new high-tech economy have been recruited into syndicated forms of religious life authorized by the Hindu right. In his view it was the RSS—parent organization to the BJP and the incubator of many of its leaders, including Narendra Modi—that stood behind these efforts. Not long ago such youths left their jobs for a month, donning distinctive black robes and walking barefoot to the mountain shrine of Ayyappa. Now, however, they only wore the necklace of the god Dattātreya, and only for an eight-day retreat. Abandoning Ayyappa, they had become pilgrims to a shrine much closer to Bangalore—a great savings of labor for their employers—and unwitting participants in the RSS's effort to transform a shrine where a Sufi *pīr* had once been venerated by both Hindus and Muslims into a place of worship that was unambiguously Hindu, a temple to Dattātreya alone. Dr. Dominic D implied that this RSS determination to homogenize Hindu religion was simply another expression of the *ādhyātmik* uniformity Hegde was championing. Both ran directly counter to the historic openness and variousness of the bhakti movement.

And so it continues. By arguing about the true meaning of the bhakti movement—and even whether there was one—and by performing it in a host of different ways, the citizens of today's India keep that idea alive. They turn to the resources of their own regions and languages to discern the new-old meanings of the bhakti experience for the world in which they live. In Karnataka this is apt to mean an argument about Basava. It is Basava who is said to have established a Pavilion of Experience *(anubhava maṇḍapa)* in Kalyāṇa, a place where the meanings and implications of bhakti insight could be exchanged and debated by people of many backgrounds and both sexes, and where the experience itself could thus be inculcated. This hall is remembered as a place of speaking *(vacana)*, the sort of speech that could serve as an alternative to the palaver one heard in temples or royal courts.[122] No wonder, then, that it was an interpretation of Basava that made so many participants in the Mangalore conference jump from their seats in protest. In that way he is the southern Kabīr, a lightning rod of Indian modernity. And not just Indian. The organizers of the Mangalore conference and the architects of The Kabir Project believe that the issues at stake are more than Indian. They matter in every society across the globe.

Real Religion

We live in a time when reality is under siege. Nations no longer function as the sovereign beings they proclaim themselves to be, virtuality encroaches on intimacy, and the pillars of tradition are riddled with cracks. Religion tries to provide solace with a deep view of the past and perhaps an expansive view of the future, but it too often wavers uncertainly. Political leaders shout till they are hoarse. Onto this stage walks bhakti, a form of engagement that says it breaks all the molds—anything the state could trumpet, merchants sell, or priests intone from the other side of whatever barrier separates them from people like you and me. Bhakti is religion beyond religion. It's connection as religion. It's a sharing that makes you wonder if all those boundaries people spend such effort defining and defending ever really existed. It's a storm that wipes all that away—a storm of songs.

What does it mean for a nation to claim this kind of religion as its own, as was done in India when the idea of the bhakti movement crystallized in the 1920s and 1930s and was promoted by national institutions after independence? It means acknowledging the uncomfortable alliance between songs of protest—cries from the street *(nirguṇ)*—and songs of reassurance that transport you to an imagined realm of color, taste, and limitless good *(saguṇ)*. It means refusing to hover above such contradictions with an intellectualist empyrean nondualism. It means appealing to God—what else can we do?—while knowing only the name, the song. It means talking to God in the mother tongue—and understanding that mothers speak different languages. It means rescuing Kanakadāsa or Āṇṭāḷ or Tulsīdās from the clutches of caste solidarity and vote banks. It means knowing that the saint many Indians hold dearest—Kabīr—emerged from a population that would in part secede from India to form a separate state. It means acknowledging that politics are important, but they aren't everything.

The idea of the bhakti movement carries a message of simultaneous acclaim and subjugation. It was formulated in the early twentieth century as an admiring gesture from north to south, from upper caste to lower caste, and from Hindus to Muslims, yet it proved to have a smothering aspect too, one that many southerners and Dalits and Muslims have reframed or rejected. How can one live the belief that India's real religion is more than Hinduism or Hindutva? How can one fully claim the perception that it flows in the actual workings of history—and that we ourselves, looking backward and forward, are the very makers of that history? These are the challenges that the idea of the bhakti movement poses, not just to India or South Asia but to the world.

Every nation requires a narrative of itself. This one, incubated in a nation, pushes well beyond that nation. It touches and tests every heart.

Notes

Introduction

1. Tagore 1933b. Further, see Chapter 6. I am grateful to Joel Lee for making me aware of this publication and providing me with a scanned text (New York, June, 2011).
2. On bhakti "publics," see Novetzke 2008: 10–23.
3. Ramanujan 1973: 40.
4. Ibid.
5. Grierson 1908: 11–12; Grierson 1910: 539–540; less so, Monier Williams on Vaishnavism as "the only real religion of the Hindūs," 1882: 295–296.
6. Pechilis 1999: 22–24, particularly 24n36; cf. Hara 1964:124–132.
7. van Buitenen 1981: 24.
8. Cort 2002: 62.
9. Ibid., 85; cf. Frederick Smith 2006.
10. Cort 2002: 86.
11. Brian Smith 1987; Lipner 2010: 27–87.
12. Further, Hawley 1988; Naim 1974: 181–182; Zelliot and Mokashi-Punekar 2005: 13–15.
13. Christian Novetzke offers a discursive, performance-based analysis of evolving Brahmin agency with respect to bhakti in his notion of "the Brahmin double" (Novetzke 2011).
14. This too is an idea with a specific location in time: see Hawley 2009d.
15. Pollock 2006: 423–424.
16. Ibid., 402–408, 413.
17. Ibid., 427–429.

1. The Bhakti Movement and Its Discontents

1. Basic resources are Caturvedī 1972; Callewaert and Snell 1994; Nandakumar 2003; Schelling 2011.

2. Anderson 1991 [1983]; Hobsbawm and Ranger 1983. For a fine analysis of the related literature on collective memory, see Castelli 2004; also Novetzke 2008.
3. The details, varying by region, period, and language, are of course more complicated and sometimes divergent. On Anderson and the larger frame and a set of specific Bengali responses, see Partha Chatterjee 2010: 23–36, 59–90; on Maharashtra, also with reference to Anderson, Prachi Deshpande 2007: 94–150, especially 130–135; on northern India, similarly, Dalmia 1997: 1–20, 35–42, 338–429. For Tamilnadu, rather differently, see Champakalakshmi 2011: 1–50.
4. Callewaert and Friedlander 1992: 197, *Gurū Granth* version. The second verse is the refrain.
5. Hawley and Juergensmeyer, 2004 [1988]: 24, cf. 25. On the mythic status of the connection between Chamars and leather, see Rawat 2011: 1–12, 54–116.
6. Ramanujan 1981: 21.
7. Ramanujan 1973: 131.
8. Hawley 2009b: 125.
9. Ramanujan 1981: 33.
10. *Rāmcaritmānas* 1.8.1, with thanks to Rupert Snell for highlighting this passage and for a translation that contributes to my own.
11. Behl 2007: 322–324.
12. Raghavan 1966: 9–10.
13. Ibid., 15, 26, 50.
14. Ibid., 33.
15. The lectures themselves were delivered on December 11–12, 1964, starting at 6:00 p.m., in sessions lasting some two or two and a half hours each. Four half-hour broadcasts were prepared on the basis of these lectures and broadcast throughout the country over All India Radio from 9:30 to 10:00 p.m. on December 11–14, 1964. I am grateful to Smt. Nandini Ramani, Dr. Raghavan's daughter and the managing trustee of the V. Raghavan Centre for Performing Arts, for her help in reconstructing these circumstances on the basis of records left by Professor Raghavan himself, and for allowing me the privilege of looking at those records (Chennai, December 2, 2009).
16. Raghavan 1966: 9.
17. Ibid., 48. See also Gurumurthy 1994; Soneji 2014.
18. Raghavan 1966: 17.
19. Ibid., 46.
20. Others have been more determinedly proletarian, e.g., Lele 1980; Omvedt 2008.
21. Raghavan 1966: 31–32, 47, 16.
22. Ibid., 20.

23. Others in the ministry had hoped K. M. Munshi, the founder of Bharatiya Vidya Bhavan, would deliver the lectures. I do not know whether Munshi's active involvement in the restoration of the great Hindu temple at Somnath, reputedly the target of Muslim violence over the centuries, played a role in dissuading Indira Gandhi from that choice. A letter from her to Raghavan on August 25, 1964, alludes to the difference of opinion but does not clarify the issues involved, if any (Gandhi 1964).
24. Raghavan 1966: 19, 20.
25. Ibid., 21.
26. Ibid., 24. The *pada* (e.g., Telugu *padam,* Hindi *pad*) is a relatively short lyrical composition that appears in various Indian vernacular languages and is a primary vehicle for bhakti. In singing, the opening verse or a portion thereof serves as a refrain.
27. Ibid., 25–26.
28. Laine 2003, especially 52.
29. Raghavan 1966: 26–27.
30. Novetzke 2008; Schultz 2013.
31. Raghavan 1966: 28.
32. The claim that Tulsīdās and Kabīr were pupils of Rāmānand is almost surely false in the first case and very dubious in the second. See below, pp. 119, 314–315.
33. Raghavan 1966: 29.
34. Ibid., 48.
35. Ibid., 49.
36. Toynbee 1960.
37. Raghavan 1966: 100.
38. Ibid., 33.
39. Ranade 1961 [1900]: 72.
40. Ibid., 71–72.
41. Ibid., 70.
42. Ibid., 70–71.
43. Ibid., 69. A major revision of this caste-neutral portrait emerged in Karve 1962; cf. Keune 2010.
44. Ranade 1961 [1900]: 72, 67.
45. Ibid., vii, 7, 8, 12, 76. Other historians have distinguished more sharply between the confederacy that took shape in the years following 1761 and the empire that preceded it.
46. Ibid., 76.
47. Ibid., 73, 76.
48. Ibid., 7.
49. Ibid., 64–65.
50. Krishna Sharma 1987: 78–81, 86–91.
51. Ibid., 87.

52. Ibid., 70, 76, 87–88
53. Krishna Sharma 1965, under the supervision of A. L. Basham. I am grateful to Prof. Prabha Dixit, Sharma's junior colleague in the Department of History at Miranda House, for discussions on this and related matters (Delhi, November 27 and 30, 2009).
54. Krishna Sharma 1987: 78–80, 81n3, 84–85.
55. Ibid., 85.
56. Grierson 1910: 547–548.
57. Ibid., 548. In the spirit of Macaulay's famous "minute," the use of the Christian term "saint" to describe Hindu counterparts was anathema to Europeans such as Henry Shea (Stark 2010: 172–173), but Grierson persisted in appealing to such parallels, hoping to broaden his audience's vision (Grierson 1920 [1918]).
58. Krishna Sharma 1987: 87. The quotation marks are hers.
59. Grierson 1910: 544–547.
60. Ibid., 548–549. Other Europeans framed similar hypotheses (e.g., Constable 1997: 326–328).
61. Ibid., 550. *Mahāprasāda* evidently refers, in this context, to the *caukā* ceremony of the Kabīr Panth as practiced at Kabīr Chaurā in Banaras. Grierson refers to Westcott 1907: 127, i.e., 127–133.
62. Chandra 1978; Thapar 1988a; Thapar 1988b.
63. A group of important conflicts concerning NCERT and its ideological orientation were ushered in with the accession to power of the BJP as the leading party in the central government in 1998. See Nussbaum 2007: 231–234, 265–267. Since the return to power of the Congress Party and its allies in 2004, a third generation of NCERT texts has been published (2007) under the general title *Themes in Indian History* or, in Hindi, *Bhāratīya Itihās ke Kuch Viṣay*.
64. Jain 2002: 121; Jain 2003: 123.
65. K. N. Pannikar (2007: 261) has implicitly pointed to the absence of a parallel section on *nirguṇ bhakti* by observing that the *nirguṇ bhaktas* Kabīr and Ravidās are absent from Jain's texts. His point is an important one, but only partially correct: Jain omits any mention of Ravidās, but she does include a sentence on Kabīr (Jain 2002: 122; Jain 2003: 124).
66. Jain 2002: 121; Jain 2003: 124.
67. Jain 2002: 121; Jain 2003: 123.
68. Jain 2002: 120, 124; Jain 2003: 122, 123, 127.
69. Raghavan 1966: 76.
70. No author is listed for *Themes in Indian History* or, in Hindi, *Bhāratīya Itihās ke Kuch Viṣay* (2007), but the chairperson of the advisory committee is Hari Vasudevan of the University of Calcutta and the chief advisor is Neeladri Bhattacharya of Jawaharlal Nehru University. In both languages, Theme Six is treated in volume 2: 140–169. The fact that, even in the Hindi

version, suggestions for further reading consist entirely of books written in English underscores the fact that the text was first composed in that language.

71. Jain 2002: 121; Jain 2003: 123.
72. King 1974; King 1994; Rai 2001; Busch 2011: 220–239; Orsini 2010.
73. Pāṭhak 2004: 57.
74. Ibid.
75. Shukla 1969 [1948]: 38–40, 77. It is not known exactly when Shukla composed *Bhakti kā Vikās,* but his daughter, Kusum Chaturvedi, believes that it was probably about 1932 (interview, Banaras, February 26, 2004).
76. Shukla 1969 [1948]: 31–50, 61.
77. Ibid., 34–36.
78. Ibid., 36, 52.
79. Macnicol 1917: 116; Shukla 1969 [1948]: 77.
80. In the course of this exposition Pāṭhak (2004: 57–58) quotes Dvivedi directly on two occasions. He worked from the chapter in Dvivedi's relatively recent *Hindi Sāhitya: Uskā Udbhav aur Vikās* called "Bhakti Literature: The Beginning of Real Hindi Literature" without feeling the need to provide exact page references (Dvivedi 1964: 58, 66; compare Dvivedi 1991[1940]: 52–53). I am grateful to Dalpat Rajpurohit for spotting the source (email communication, June 28, 2014).
81. Pāṭhak 2004: 59; cf. Dvivedi 1991 [1940]: 52 (discussed also in Chapter 6).
82. Krishna Sharma 1987: 24n2, cf. 34–35. Tyler Williams (2013), however, has traced the notion of a *nirguṇ/saguṇ* distinction as far back as the Dādūpathī poet Sundardās, writing in the first quarter of the seventeenth century.
83. Krishna Sharma 1987: 25, cf. 197. In actuality the situation is considerably more complicated: Hawley 2005: 70–86; Tyler Williams 2007.
84. Krishna Sharma 1987: 29–31; Ranajit Guha 1989.
85. Krishna Sharma 1987: 30–31. Sharma asserts (33n1) that Muhammad Habib was the first to articulate the analysis followed out by Irfan Habib, in his introduction to volume 2 of Elliott 1967 [1867–1877].
86. Krishna Sharma 1987: 31 (in relation to K. A. Nizami), and 33.
87. Ibid., 195–196; cf. also Barthwal 1936.
88. Krishna Sharma 1987: 18, 194.
89. Ibid., 184, 195.
90. Barthwal 1936: v. The essay to which he refers is "Hindī Kavitā meṅ Yog Pravāh" (1930).
91. Krishna Sharma 1987: 73, 185–186.
92. Ibid., 87.
93. Dvivedi 1973 [1936]: 80; Dvivedi 1991 [1940 (2nd ed. 1954)]: 52; Dvivedi 1976 [1942]: 183. That Dvivedi addressed this same Grierson passage in three different books—*Sūr-Sāhitya, Hindī Sāhitya kī Bhūmikā,* and *Kabīr*—

is, of course, significant. Others, certainly, noted its importance for Dvivedi (Namvar Singh 2005 [1982]: 62). The first edition of *Hindī Sāhitya kī Bhūmikā* differs occasionally from the second, which is cited here, but not in this passage.

94. Grierson 1907: 313.
95. Ibid., 314.
96. Grierson 1910: 548; Dvivedi 1991 [1940]: 52. In the latter passage, to be precise, Dvivedi said that this *dhārmik āndolan* of bhakti was *bauddh dharm ke āndolan se bhī adhik viśāl*. Cf. also Dvivedi 1973 [1936]: 80–81.
97. Dvivedi 1973 [1936]: 90–91.
98. But compare the ordinary "movement" usage of *āndolan* in Shukla 2001 [1940]: 322.
99. Shukla 1929: 154; Shukla 2001 [1940]: 102.
100. Dvivedi 1973 [1936]: 80, 97.
101. Hemant Śarmā 1987: 863–872.
102. Shukla 2001 [1940]: 41.
103. Farquhar 1920: 234, 302; Farquhar 1912 [1911]: 135; Farquhar 1915: 1.
104. When Farquhar discusses such matters in *The Crown of Hinduism,* he speaks interchangeably of sects, cults, movements, and even systems as playing into "the Vishṇuite Church" (1913: 384–396). He apparently uses the term "movement" only once (384), in the plural.
105. Keay 1920: 19–21; Keay 2003: 24–26.
106. Ainslie T. Embree, personal communication, New York, June 30, 2011. Later, after independence, when the curriculum of a university like Allahabad's was conducted far more in Hindi, several versions of Prasad's work, complete or abridged, appeared in that language, too: *Bhāratīya Madhya Yug kā Itihās, Madhyayug kā Saṃkṣipt Itihās,* and *Madhyayugīn Bhārat kā Saṃkṣipt Itihās.*
107. Prasad 1925: 575–576. We recall that, like Prasad, M. G. Ranade had also connected bhakti leaders with an assertion of manliness (1961 [1900]: 67). The affirmation of Indian virility in the face of external challenges was a familiar concern in the colonial period (Sinha 1995).
108. Prasad 1925: 547.
109. "A great impetus was given to the Hindi literature by the growth of the Bhakti movement in northern India" (ibid., 553).
110. I am grateful to C. B. Tripathi, who was a student of Prasad's and also taught medieval Indian history at Allahabad University, for a vivid portrait of intellectual and personal relationships in the department in its halcyon days (interview, Allahabad, December 15, 2010), and for the presence of Arvind Krishna Mehrotra of the English department in that interview. Subsequent discussions with Prof. Tripathi (January 16, 2013) and Profs. Vinaya Chand Pandey, Heramb Chaturvedi, and Yogeshwar Tewari, all of

the History Department at Allahabad University (January 15, 2013), added many helpful perspectives.

111. Grierson 1910: 546; cf. Pinch 2003.
112. I owe this information to interviews with C. B. Tripathi (Allahabad, December 15, 2010) and A. D. Pant (Gurgaon, January 3, 2012).
113. Vasudha Dalmia has argued this point in a somewhat different way (1997: 338–429; 410 in relation to Krishna Sharma).

2. *The Transit of Bhakti*

1. *utpannā draviḍe sāham vṛddhim karṇāṭake gatā*
kvacit kvacin mahārāṣṭre gurjari jīrṇatām gatā
tatra ghorakaler yogāt pākhaṇḍaiḥ khaṇḍitāṅgakā
durbalāham ciram yātā putrābhyām saha mandatām
vṛndāvanam punaḥ prāpya navīn eva surūpinī
jātāham yuvatī samyak preṣṭharūpā tu sāmpratam.
(*Bhāgavata Māhātmya* 1.48–50)

Unless otherwise stated, I follow the Gita Press edition (*Bhāgavata Mahāpurāṇa* 1995 [1971]), which prints the *Bhāgavata Māhātmya* as if it were a preface to the *Bhāgavata Purāṇa*. The name *Bhāgavata Māhātmya* can be used to refer to more than one text. This one—the standard, best-known one—is the one that is associated with the final book of the *Padma Purāṇa,* which is given in the Ānandāśrama Saṃskṛtagranthāvalī (fascicle 131) as chapters 189–195. In the oldest manuscripts, however, the *Bhāgavata Māhātmya* appears not as part of the *Padma Purāṇa* but as an independent text, even if the document itself claims to belong to the *Padma Purāṇa.* See Rocher 1986: 211–212. (Hereafter, the abbreviations BM, BhP, and BG will be used to refer to verse numbers in the *Bhāgavata Māhātmya, Bhāgavata Purāṇa,* and *Bhagavad Gītā.*)

2. These apparently contrast to the two traditional lines of transmission described by K. T. Pandurangi—one emerging from Nārāyana (Vishnu) via Brahmā > Nārada > Vyāsa > Śuka, whence the dialogue between Parīkṣit and Sūta emerges, and the other one via Śeṣa and others to Vidura. See Pandurangi 1997: iv–v.
3. *sanakādyaiḥ,* BM 1.21–22. In this passage it is stressed that what Nārada particularly learns in this exchange with the sons of Brahmā is the value of a seven-day recitation rather than one that lasts throughout the rainy season. See Tagare 1976–1978, 1: 46–47.
4. I have seen—and seen references to—several manuscripts called *Bhāgavata Māhātmya* that comprise only the sixth book. An example is Rajasthan Oriental Research Institute acc. no. 2597. Its date, V.S. 1781 (1724 C.E.), makes it one of the earliest manuscripts we have.

5. Hawley 2009a; Lochtefeld 1992: 124–125. Cf. Krishna Sharma 1987: 310–311; Filliozat 1962: 75–77; Prentiss 1999: 34–35. But the broader background of meditations on the relationship between *jñāna, vairāgya,* and *bhakti,* following the cue of the *Bhāgavata Purāṇa* itself, is also relevant, as in Anantadev's *Kṛṣṇabhakticandrikā* (Upādhyay 1936; Granoff 2005: 163–167; Venkatkrishnan, forthcoming).
6. Chanchani, forthcoming.
7. Hein 1972: 223–230.
8. *Gurū Granth, āsā dī vār,* in *Bhāgavata Mahāpurāṇa* 1995 [1971]: 465; cf. Hein 1972: 116–117.
9. Orsini 2014a: 213–214; Pauwels 2012: 40; Pauwels 2013.
10. Śarmā and Śāstrī 1963; McGregor 1984: 96.
11. Pauwels 1996; McGregor 1973.
12. Nandadās says he is conveying the luminosity of the *Bhāgavata* into *bhāṣā* (Vrajaratnadās 1957 [1949], 2: 2).
13. Niemann 1980; Niemann1983.
14. Archer 1958: 12; Poddar 2014. I am also grateful to Monika Horstmann (London, June 8, 2009) for information about this text.
15. From the Nirañjanī Bhagavāndās (Tyler Williams 2014: 220n468).
16. Majumdar 1961, with cautions about the need for manuscript work on a number of figures he mentions. In regard to the accuracy of attributing a Persian rendering of the *Bhāgavata* to Sheikh Abū'l Faiz Faizī, Akbar's poet laureate, see Stark 2007b: 493. On the recitation of Puranas in relation to "social uncertainties" and the consequent defense of specific Brahmin identities in early modernity, see O'Hanlon 2013b: 96–99.
17. Śarmā and Śāstrī 1963: 7–9.
18. Yadunāth [attrib.] 1985 [1904, 1906], 1: 11; 2: 95. The text dates itself to V.S. 1658 (1601 C.E.), but the *New Catalogus Catalogorum* (forthcoming, 28: 216, 234) reveals that not a single manuscript version of the *Vallabhadigvijaya* exists in all the catalogues it surveys. The first printed edition emerged from the Venkateshwar Press, Bombay, in 1904, followed shortly afterward by another from the Rajanagara Press, Ahmedabad, in 1906. I am indebted to Prof. Seniruddha Dash and his staff, who showed me a preprint version of the *New Catalogus Catalogorum,* volume 28, in Chennai (December 2, 2009).
19. *Caurāsī Baiṭhak Carit, baiṭhak* 84, in Gokulnāth [attrib.] 1967 [V.S. 2024]: 191. See also Shyam Das 1985: 83. The seventeenth-century figure Gokulnāth is traditionally claimed to be the compiler of the *Caurāsī Baiṭhak Carit,* but this seems impossible (Entwistle 1987: 263–264). Shandip Saha points out that the *Caurāsī Vaiṣṇavan kī Vārtā,* which is almost certainly earlier than the *Caurāsī Baiṭhak Carit,* makes no mention of Vallabha performing *bhāgavat saptāh* (email communication, April 9, 2008).
20. *Caitanyacaritāmṛta* 3.125, trans. Dimock and Stewart 1999: 924.

21. Goswami (personal communication, March 17, 2009). See also Swapna Sharma 2008: 31.
22. Eck 1982: 354–355; Hawley 2009e: 244–246.
23. Hawley 2009c.
24. I am deeply grateful to Vidvan Samba Dikshita for explaining this and other facets of his family's performative practice (interviews, December 23 and 25, 2007) and to his son Gajanan Dikshita for a supplementary conversation (December 25, 2007). I owe to Frederick Smith my information about the family's connection to Udupi (Montreal, November 8, 2009). See Vartak 2009 for an exposition of the *Bhāgavata*'s embryological expertise.
25. See Horstmann 1999; Case 1996.
26. Mukherjee and Habib 1988: 240–241, articles 4.6–4.8.
27. Vaudeville 1976.
28. Mukherjee and Habib 1988: 235.
29. *Caitanyacaritāmṛta* 3.125, trans. Dimock and Stewart, 1999: 924.
30. The most massive structure anchoring Gauḍīya practice in the Govardhan area—but far from the only one—is the Haridev temple (ca. 1570), also patronized by Bhagavāndās of Āmer. See Thakur 1996: 16, fig. 2.9; cf. Burton-Page 1996: 125. On the dating of the Vallabhite-Bengali controversy, see Entwistle 1987: 153–154, but the matter is still far from being clearly understood.
31. Entwistle 1987: 149.
32. For a somewhat more extended treatment of this subject than I offer here, see Hawley 2009e.
33. George Michell, personal communication, Sernabatim, Goa, January 11, 2012.
34. Thakur and Beeche 1996: figs 2.63–64; Hawley 2009e: 243, fig. 11.6.
35. Burton-Page 1996: 123, 127; Michell 1996: 119. The relevant inscriptions are reproduced and translated by Bahura 1996: 200–202. An example of an architectural detail on the temple of Govindadev that resonates with the Gujarati style is the canopy over the *jagmohan*. See Goswami 1996: 75, cf. fig. 3.24.
36. Verghese 2000: 170–198.
37. Michell 1996: 119–120; Michell, personal communication, December 26, 2007.
38. Ghosh 2005: 188–189.
39. These traditions come to us through the written records—Rāmānuja's biographies and the history of the Srirangam temple *(Koil Oḻuku)*—but important questions have been raised about the absence of any corroboration from the temple's generous inscriptional record. See Orr 1995: 109–110, 121–129.
40. On Madhva's life and dates see B. N. K. Sharma 1961: 75–89.
41. Novetzke, forthcoming: chs. 1–2.

42. I am grateful to Christian Novetzke for clarifications on this point (email communication, January 13, 2010); cf. Novetzke 2008: 87–90. In other forms, however, the tradition is much older: see Deleury 1960: 7–8; Tulpule 1979: 327–329; Feldhaus 2003: 215–218.
43. Keune 2010.
44. The earliest known manuscript in which Narsī Mehtā's poetry appears dates only to 1611 (Shukla-Bhatt 2014: 12), so the sixteenth century is also conceivable.
45. Vishnudatt Rakesh, interview, Haridvar, July 8, 2007.
46. Shukla-Bhatt 2007: 280–281, in reference to Kardamrishi Shastri 1998: 6–7.
47. Pollock 2001: especially 13–14.
48. Goswami, oral communication, New York, February 8, 2003; Sheikh 2012.
49. Ajay Rao 2006; Ajay Rao 2011; Ajay Rao 2013; Verghese 1995: 69–84.
50. Wagoner 1993. We will have more to say about Vijayanagar in Chapter 5.
51. Filliozat 1962: 77.
52. Kasdorf 2006.
53. Prithvi Datta Chandra Shobhi, interview, Mysore, January 4, 2013.
54. Ben-Herut 2013: 51–52, 60–61; Ben-Herut 2014.
55. Narayana Rao 1990: 14–15. Conversely, Tamil Shaivas were interested in the north (Monius 2013).
56. Peterson 1989: 8–18; Dehejia 1988: 18–20; Raman 2007: 58–60; Narayanan 2011: 560–561; Venkatesan 2010: 5–6. On the limits of this sense of parallelism, see Champakalakshmi 2006.
57. Halbfass 1988: 172–196.
58. Ibid., 186–187, 513; Nicholson 2010: 185–186.
59. The operative term, occurring in Madhusūdan's *Prasthānabheda,* is *mlecchādiprasthānavat.* See Nicholson 2010: 231, cf. 163–164, 195–196; and in a somewhat different light, Minkowski 2011: 222–223, 228.
60. On the permeable boundaries between these two sorts of literature, most invariably labeled *rīti* and *bhakti* in Hindi literary criticism, see Busch 2011: 65–101, 226–231.
61. Cf. Halbfass 1988: 193, referring especially to M. S. Golwalkar and V. D. Savarkar. Cf. Savarkar 1969 [1923]: 6–8, 42–44.
62. Ernst 2004 [1992]: 24–26.
63. Bhagwat 2008: 77–93, especially 81; Zelliot 1987: 91–109; Keune forthcoming.
64. E.g., Hawley and Juergensmeyer 2004 [1988]: 54; Vaudeville 1993: 216–218, 233. But the background for this specifically religious counterposition is more complex: see O'Connell 1973; Talbot 1995.
65. Selections from their poetry appear in Snell 1991b: 39–41, 110–127. On Rahīm, see Busch 2010: 282–284; Busch 2011: 138–140. On Raskhān, see Snell 1989. On Mughal bhakti, see Hawley 2013c.

66. Pellò 2014b. It was Lakṣmīnārāyan "Shafīq" (d. 1808) whose *Taẕkira-yi Gul-i Ra'nā* devoted its first volume to Muslims, the second to Hindus. His name suggests that he grew up in a Vaishnava family. Similarly, later, Bhagavāndās "Hindī" (Pellò 2014a).
67. Behl 2003: 205. Thomas de Bruijn (2010: 136–141) has conversely shown, under the heading of "dialogism," how directly Tulsīdās responds in his *Rāmcaritmānas* to the language and framing of Malik Muhammad Jāyasī's *Padmāvat*. More broadly, Busch 2014.
68. Most important among these is the *Haqā'iq-i Hindī* (India's Truths) of 'Abd al-Wahīd Bilgrāmī (1566), on which see Alam 2004: 93; also Orsini 2014a; Orsini 2014b. The bibliography in this area is vast, but particularly helpful for present purposes are Francesca Orsini's discussion of overlapping genres and repertoires that have varying linguistic, cultural, and religious associations (e.g., Orsini 2006: 1–29) and Tony Stewart's work on translation, complementarity, mutual intimacy, and the subjunctive mood (Stewart 2001; Stewart 2013; Stewart, forthcoming).
69. Chand 1936: 137–138.
70. Ibid., i, 240–241, 243.
71. Ibid., 115–116, 129. On the Vīraśaivas in a similar vein, see also Hunashal 1947: 186–194.
72. Hedayetullah 1977: 75, 119.
73. Iraqi 2009: 105–106.
74. Ibid., 258–259, 104–105, 245–253.
75. Kuṅvarpāl Siṃh 1995: 278–281.
76. Allison Busch offers examples from Kavīndrācārya Sarasvatī in Busch 2009: 10–11; Busch 2010: 290–291.
77. Busch 2011: 23–64. The verse in question is *Jahāngīrjascandrikā* 163, discussed on p. 60.
78. Bangha 2000; Bangha 2007, especially 333–348.
79. Pauwels 2013. See also Orsini, 2014a: 195–197, 213–214, 227–230; Orsini, forthcoming, on manuscripts and on "the divide"; de Bruijn 1996: 76–78.
80. de Bruijn 2012; Bronner 2013; Bronner and Shulman 2006; Hopkins, forthcoming; Bader 2000; Clark 2006: 148–159. See further, Chapter 5.
81. Dasgupta 1940: 63.

3. The Four Sampradāys and the Commonwealth of Love

1. Clémentin-Ojha 2001: 185.
2. The work and its title are strikingly novel, but it is intriguing that the term *bhaktamāli* (or perhaps *bhaktimāli*) occurs in an inscription of the Yādava king Rāmchandra (r. 1273–1277), where it apparently means "devotional assembly" or "assembly of bhaktas." The inscription records a gift of

flowers, so perhaps the "garland" valence is also intended—long, long before Nābhādās (Novetzke 2014a).

3. Jhā 1978, part 2: 10, §§27–28. The symbol § refers to the *chappays* and *dohās* that structure the work.
4. Ibid., part 2: 2, §7.1.
5. *Pīpā Parcaī* 35.25, in Callewaert 2000a: 276. The word *kul* (family) is often used in the case of a *sampradāy* whose leaders form a bloodline succession, as familiarly with the *vallabh-kul*. It may also have a more general meaning, however. The sixteenth-century Brindavan poet Harirāmvyās speaks of the *kul* of Rūp and Sanātan Gosvāmī, whom he explicitly designates as *sādhus* (Pauwels 2002: 82–83).
6. Jhā 1978, part 2: 11, §31.1.
7. Sen 1936a [1929–1930]: 49–50; Dvivedi 1991 [1940]: 58.
8. Cf. Upādhyay 1978: 64–65, 145, 241–242; Horstmann 2009: 57.
9. The Nimbārkī scholar Brindāvan Bihārī emphasized instead the importance of Harivyāsdev (Brindāvan Bihārī, interview, Brindavan, March 1, 2009). In regard to Keśav Kāśmīrī Bhaṭṭ, see Clémentin-Ojha 1990: 338–342.
10. Dvivedi 1991 [1940]: 54.
11. Ibid., 53–54.
12. Ibid., 54.
13. Priyādās, *Bhaktirasabodhinī, kavitt* 138, in Rūpkalā 1969 [1910]): 262.
14. This bifurcation became distinct and conclusive only much later (Raman 2007: 9–11).
15. Dvivedi 1991 [1940]: 53.
16. Rāmānuj Harivardās, *Haribhakti-Prakāśikā,* 1875, quoted in Dvivedi 1991 [1940]: 54–55.
17. Ibid., 55.
18. Ibid., 54.
19. Jhā 1978, part 2: 18, §45. See Chapter 5.
20. Dvivedi 1991 [1940]: 59, 90.
21. Ibid., 62–63.
22. Sen 1936a [1929–1930]: 4, 46–51. I am grateful to Rachel McDermott and Hena Bose for the analysis and translation that have enabled me to compare aspects of the Bengali version of this book with what appears in its English counterpart.
23. Sen 1936a [1929–1930]: 66.
24. Bhandarkar 1913: 77.
25. Farquhar 1912 [1911]: 149.
26. Miśra 1913 [V.S. 1970], 1: 266–267; cf. 1956 [1913]: 187–188.
27. Miśra 1956 [1913]: 310–312.
28. Shukla 1929: 64, 155; Shukla 2001 [1940]: 35, 103.
29. Published posthumously as part of Ramchandra Shukla's *Sūrdās* (1969 [1948]: 82; Shukla 2002 [V.S. 2059]: 48–49).

30. Hemant Śarmā 1987: 863–868. See also Dalmia 1997: 379–381.
31. Dalmia-Lüderitz 1992.
32. James Mallinson has pointed out that the terms "Nāthyogī" and "Nāthpanthī," though familiar in the present day, apparently were not standard in the period to which we are referring and emerged only in the early eighteenth century (Mallinson 2011: 411). Before then, the simple designation "Yogī" was in force, although Gorakhnāth was certainly understood as having played a formative role in shaping the tradition. In what follows I largely retain the terms "Nāth Yogī" and "Nāthpanthī" to describe this Yogī tradition.
33. I am indebted to Patton Burchett for a vivid retelling of the confrontation between Tārānāth and Kṛṣṇadās, including the phrase "What a jackass!" (Burchett 2012b: 350). The encounter does not appear in the *Bhaktamāl* itself or in its *Bhaktirasabodhinī* commentary, but does have a wider circulation than the Rāmānandi location might indicate. In relation to Haridās Nirañjanī, see Tyler Williams 2014: 167–168.
34. When Sītārāmśaraṇ Bhagavānprasād "Rūpkalā" gives this account, he credits it to his distinguished uncle Tursīrām Agravāl, originally of Ambala, then Delhi, then Brindavan, who published his *Bhagatmāl* in Urdu in 1854. See Rūpkalā 1969 [1910]: 43; Stark 2007a: 401.
35. Jhā 1978, part 2: 15, §§4, 40.5.
36. Horstmann 2002c: 145. Horstmann presents an example of such usage—from the years preceding 1734—in translation on p. 161.
37. Ibid., 154–155. Horstmann reports the exposition of *mahant* Avadesh Kumar Mishra. A copy of this painting exists in the main Galtā temple where the *mahant* resides (Patton Burchett, email communication, September 19, 2010).
38. Specifically, from Kedār Rājā, who served Rājā Pratāpāditya of Jesar (Jessore), ca. 1600. See R. N. Prasad 1966: 101–102, 134.
39. See Nath 1996: 160, fig. 7.1.
40. Horstmann 2002c: 157. The document is a confirmation of Akbar's grants, dated 1640.
41. Clark 2006: 114–115, 131, 224–226. I am indebted to Matthew Clark for an email reviewing main aspects of his argument about the emergence of the Saṃnyāsī *Maṭhāmnayas* (July 15, 2009). On Vidyāraṇya as the after-the-fact architect of the institution of the "Śaṃkara *maṭh*" in the fourteenth century, see Hacker 1995 [1964]: 28–30.
42. Pinch 2006: 19–21, 211–212.
43. Pinch 1999: 395.
44. Priyādās, *Bhaktirasabodhinī, kavitt* 16, in Rūpkalā 1969 [1910]: 43.
45. Menāriyā 1999 [1958]: 51, to which I have been directed by Patton Burchett (email communication, October 2, 2010). Also H. H. Wilson 1846 [1828, 1832]: 60, reprinted 1972: 31, to which Jhā refers in a more comprehensive

discussion (1978, part 1: 25). Hare 2011: 31–34 provides a helpful review of this and related matters.

46. Pinch 1999: 397.
47. Hare 2007a: 185.
48. Jhā reviews the entire matter as a background to his critical edition (1978, part 1: 181–251).
49. Nābhādās uses the phrase *śrī mārag* to characterize Rāmānuja's line at §33.1, and *paddhati* apparently to characterize his philosophical approach in §34.1.
50. Rūpkalā apparently understands Braj-Vallabh to be one and the same as Vallabhācārya, but he remembers him as the guru of Nārāyaṇ Bhaṭṭ, which continues to muddy the waters (Rūpkalā 1969 [1910]: 590–591).
51. I explore some of the musical implications of Nābhādās's portrait of the *kabi* Sūrdās (§72) in Hawley 1984a.
52. These include, in addition to Pīpā, Kabīr and Raidās (east), Nāmdev (south), Dhannā (north), and the following bhaktas who are mentioned without specific directional referents: Bīthal, Sen, Angad, Bhuvan, Mādhavdās Jagannāthī, Trilochan, Mīrābāī, Rankā and Bankā, and Chaturbhuj and his wife. Anantadās himself invokes the number sixteen as he comes to the end of the list (35.17).
53. A sample is in Callewaert 2000a: 23–25; cf. Lorenzen, Kumar, and Thukral 1991: 73–78. The great manuscript libraries of Rajasthan contain many more.
54. These stories are reported in *Raidās Parcaī* 7.1–18 and *Pīpā Parcaī* 6.6–18, 10.5–10, and 35.1–10 (Callewaert 2000a: 153–154, 161–162, 222–223, 236, 240–241, 274–275, 320–322, 346–347).
55. I am grateful to Patton Burchett for a photograph of the lintel above the doorway of the *maṭh* at Raivāsā, whose text makes this clear, and for a supplementary email communication from Dalpat Rajpurohit underlining that fact (August 29, 2010). On the debate about whether Agradās can, as locally claimed, be associated with the founding of the Raivāsā monastery, see Burchett 2012a: 191–200.
56. Jhā 1978, part 2: 15, §40.3.
57. Balabhadra Tivārī 1985: 49–57. See also McGregor 1983; McGregor 1984: 107–108.
58. This aspect of Nābhādās is explored under the heading of "Vaishnava Catholicism" in Pinch 1999: 394–399. Monika Horstmann traces it back to Agradās in Horstmann 2002c: 152–153, speaking of the latter's "impressive versatility."
59. E.g., Richards 1993; Richards 1997; Pollock 2011: 1–48; Agrawal 2009a: 79–95; Hawley 2010; Busch 2011: 12, 245–246; Partha Chatterjee 2012: 73–76.
60. *Pīpā Parcaī* 35.14–15, in Callewaert 2000a: 275.

61. Shukla 1929: 72–93 (part 2, chapter 2: "Nirguṇ Dhārā"); Barthwal 1936: 14–17, *passim*.
62. Hawley and Mann 2008: 199–203.
63. I do not mean to imply that humor is absent in the *parcaīs* of Anantadās. Ample evidence to the contrary can be found, for instance, in Anantadās's depiction of the Jhālī queen's adventures in Banaras; see *Raidās Parcaī* 7.9–18, 8.4–7, in Callewaert 2000a: 321–323, 346–348.
64. Hawley and Mann 2014.
65. Tyler Williams has brilliantly explored this theme in Williams 2008, 2013, and 2014.
66. On the Guru Harsahāy Pothī, which consists exclusively of poetry attributed to Nānak, and may preexist all other collections in which his poetry appears, see Mann 2001: 32–40.
67. These have been collected in Callewaert 2000a: 405–408. A crucial reconsideration of historiographical issues connected with Rāmānand is Agrawal 2009b; also Agrawal 2009a: 235–310.
68. Burchett 2012a: 215–230. The suggestion about the connection to Nandadās is owed to McGregor 1983: 237, 241–242.
69. Anthologies such as these have been studied by Tyler Williams (2007).
70. Iraqi 1985: 37–60; Callewaert 1978: 21–75; Rajpurohit 2013.
71. Horstmann 2006b: especially 170–171, 175; Callewaert 1988: 79, 120, §15.4. Horstmann concedes that we have "virtually no details" in regard to early Dādūpanthī preaching practice (2006b: 175), but of its existence and importance there can be no doubt.
72. Horstmann 2000a: 544; Hastings 2002: 46; cf. Rajpurohit 2013: 58.
73. In the Dādūpanthī case, this would mean the *Dādūvāṇī* of Mohandās, while the Sikhs' *Kartārpur Bīr* contained the compositions of several gurus and some *bhagats*. Horstmann suggests, however, that the *Dādūvāṇī* and broader anthologies may have been in simultaneous use from early on (Horstmann 2006b: 167–169; on *dvārās*, Horstmann 2000a: 522, 530).
74. Gurinder Singh Mann, email and personal communications, August 31 and September 4, 2010.
75. *jana nānaka dādūdayāla rāgho ravi sasi jyūṅ dipai*, in Nahta 1965: 176, §344.6.
76. On connotations of the terms *sampradāy* and *panth*, see Khan 2004: 22. On Rāghavdās in relation to Nābhādās, see Dube 1968: 98–116.
77. Rajpurohit 2007: 8–10; Rajpurohit, email communication, January 19, 2014.
78. Horstmann 2000 a: 515n9.
79. Nahta 1965: 176, §348.5. All subsequent citations of Rāghavdas's *Bhaktamāl* will be to this edition. Winand Callewaert's arguments as to the plausibility of the date V.S. 1777 on strictly linguistic grounds are also worth

considering (Callewaert 1994: 96; Callewaert 2000a: 28–29). A comment by Rupert Snell on a metrical problem is also to be noted (Snell 1991a: 23n1).

80. Hawley 1984b: 14–22; Hawley 2005: 181–193.
81. Khan 1997: 29–96; Khan 2004: 48–50.
82. *hindū turaka pramāna ramainī śabdī sākhī,* in Jhā 1978, part 2: 22, §59.4.
83. Horstmann 2012.
84. I am grateful to Monika Horstmann for directing me to this verse, which is *bicār kau aṅg* 27 and may be found in R. C. Mishra 1992: 907.
85. Orsini and Pellò 2010. The authors note that this is one of several examples of such Persian *Bhaktamāls,* and that multiple copies of Rām Sonī's *Bhaktamāl* exist (p. 8). I am grateful for further conversations with Stefano Pellò (New York, autumn 2010).
86. Folio 6b in the *Bhagat Mālā* preserved in the University of Punjab Library in Lahore, no. 4300/1247, copied in Delhi in 1826 (A.H. 1242). Translated by Orsini and Pellò 2010: 8n18.
87. Orsini and Pellò 2010: 8–13.
88. Further on the question of whether the *tazkirā* tradition may have served as a powerful impetus for the creation of Nābhādās's *Bhaktamāl,* see Hawley 2012.
89. It is notable, for example, that the *Dasam Granth,* recording compositions associated with the Anandpur court, contains a *Zafarnāmā* (Book of Victory) written in Persian verse in the form of a letter addressed by Guru Gobind Singh to the Mughal emperor Aurangzeb.
90. Behl 2010: 113–123; cf. Behl 2011. Behl, in turn, is indebted to a lineage of scholarship that stretches back to Anthony Troyer and includes prominently Askari 1977; Digby 1993; Athar Ali 1999.
91. I follow the translation of Shea and Troyer (1843, 2: 184–185). Joel Lee, checking this translation against the 1875 Bombay edition of the *Dabistān,* suggests that the phrase "profess to be Vaishnavas" might also be rendered "take themselves to be Vaishnavas" (New York, June 13–14, 2009).
92. Shea and Troyer 1843, 2: 185–186. Joel Lee has suggested, more literally, "according to what preceded" (New York, July 14, 2009).
93. Based on Shea and Troyer 1843, 2: 179–185, with spellings altered to match the 1875 Bombay *Dabistān.*
94. The term "Harbyāsī" (cf. Harbayāntī), designating adherents of the Nimbārka *sampradāy* by means of the acharya Harivyās (ca. 1600), apparently also surfaced in conversations with ascetics and laypersons held by Matthew Clark in 2001 (Clark 2006: 54).
95. Shea and Troyer 1843, 2: 182.
96. Shea and Troyer (1843, 2: 193–194) report this name as Nārāin Dāsī, but the feminine ending does not appear in the 1875 Bombay edition (Joel Lee, New York, June 14, 2009).

97. Shea and Troyer 1843, 2: 196.
98. Shea and Troyer evidently misconstrued "Nāmdev" as "the name Dāyū" (1843, 2: 192), as Joel Lee points out (New York, June 14, 2009).
99. Shea and Troyer 1843, 2: 195–196.
100. Speaking with only a little exaggeration, James Hare says of Priyādās that "the entire *Bhaktamāl* tradition flows through him." Hare points out that only six of the approximately fifty manuscripts examined by Narendra Jhā fail to couple Nābhādās's text with that of Priyādās (Hare 2013: 74, 76).
101. H. H. Wilson 1846 [1828, 1832]: 6–7, reprinted 1972: 5.
102. Priyādās, *Bhaktirasabodhinī, kavitts* 137–140, in Rūpkalā 1969 [1910]: 262–264.
103. For a general treatment of this motif, see William Smith 2000b: 199–227; William Smith 2003: 195–224. On Priyādās's conservatism in regard to caste, see Hare 2011: 125–128.
104. R. D. Gupta 1969: especially 62–63.
105. *ina musalamāna harijanana pai koṭikina hinduna vāriyai,* in Dalmia-Lüderitz 1992: 289.

4. *The View from Brindavan*

1. On which, in the present day, see Horstmann 1986.
2. Hare 2011: 79–84; cf. Pollet 1963: 188–197.
3. Habib 2010–2011: 293.
4. Ibid., 296, 298. There is a reference to a tank or pond *(kuṇḍa)* named after Radha in the twelfth-century *Mathurā Māhātmya* of Lakṣmīdhara, but it is unclear whether it refers to this spot or not (Entwistle 1987: 48, cf. 228–229).
5. Habib 2010–2011: 297–298; Habib 2009.
6. Vaudeville 1976: 203, reprinted 1996: 58.
7. Habib 2010–2012: 301.
8. Mukherjee and Habib 1988: 241, article 4.8.
9. Ibid., 239–240.
10. Michell 1996: 116, 120–122. There is an alternate theory that the temple remained unfinished (e.g., Entwistle 1987: 410), but it would in that case be difficult to account for the absence of the *garbhagṛha,* the most important component of the structure overall. See Goswami 1996: 271–272, 274; Delmonico 1993: 139.
11. Mītal 1966, 1: 133; Vaudeville 1976: 207, reprinted 1996: 64. The presence of Vṛndādevī on that spot is recognized by means of a shrine that forms a part of the Govindadev temple itself: Case 1996: figs. 2.67–2.70.
12. Joshi 1989: 165–170, fig. 18.1. In regard to necessary cautions about identifying this site with the ancient or continuing worship of Vishnu or Krishna, however, see Thapar 1989: 15; Pauwels 2011: 279–281.

13. Hoyland and Banerjee 1922: 93.
14. Mukherjee and Habib 1988: 242.
15. Pauwels 2011: 279.
16. Michell 1996: 120; Rothfarb 2012: 78–88.
17. I.e., eighteen leagues. Manucci in Irvine 1990 [1907], 2: 154. Quoted by Pauwels 2011: 289.
18. Hermansen 1997: 325, quoting from the *Kalimāt-al Ṣādiqīn* of Muhammad Ṣādiq Dihlavī Kaśmīrī Hamidānī, which dates to the seventeenth century. Also Hermansen and Lawrence 2002: 166–167.
19. *vṛndāvane mahāsadma . . . govindasya,* §392 in Bhūmipati Dāsa, n.d.: 130; cf. Entwistle 1987: 236. On the alteration of the old *Mathurā Māhātmya,* whose first datable version is found in the twelfth-century writings of Lakṣmīdhara, to respond to the new demands of the sixteenth century, see Entwistle 1990.
20. So specified in *Mahāprabhvādi Prākaṭyasaṃvatsarāṇi,* quoted by Bahura 1996: 199. The text is apparently undated, but venerable enough to have become a part of the Khās Mohar collection of the Jaipur *pothīkhānā* (no. 5171). On Rūp and the *Mathurā Māhātmya,* see Entwistle 1990: 11, 21. Rembert Lutjeharms cautions that several signals in the text make one wonder if Rūp may have been writing it at a distance from Braj—before he arrived—and with an imperfect knowledge of the Braj landscape, but even if this document is more conceptual than documentary, the terms Govind and Govindadev remain significant (email communication, July 15, 2014).
21. Principally the *Mān Prakāś* of Murārīdās. See Bahura 1976: 29–30, 33; Bahura 1996: 199–200; Bahura 1984: 13–16; Goswami 1996: 272n6. For a different view, see Snell 1991b: 32n2.
22. De 1961: 163; Habib 1996: 156.
23. Kolff 1990: 54–70.
24. Mukherjee and Habib 1988: 236; Habib 1996: 140. This is evidently in addition to the two hundred *bīghās* conferred to him in a *farmān* of 1565.
25. Entwistle 1987: 160. On his possible association with the temple of Madanmohan and the poet Sūrdās Madanmohan, see Bansal 1980: 231–236.
26. Mītal 1968b: 187. Cf. also Mītal 1967, 2: 150.
27. This is an extraordinarily difficult subject. A concise, well-balanced statement addressing relevant issues can be found in Yajneshwar Shastri 2003: 277–282, 299–301. Further, see Hawley, forthcoming-a.
28. Priyādās, *Bhaktirasabodhinī, kavitt* 135, in Rūpkalā 1969 [1910]: 259.
29. A crucial document in this transformation is the *Mahāvāṇī* of Harivyāsdev, whom Mītal estimates to have lived from about 1550–1630, and for whom we have an entry in the *Bhaktamāl* of Nābhādas (§74). See Entwistle 1987: 171; Mītal 1968b: 347–348.
30. Clémentin-Ojha 1990: 334–335, 339, 342. This contrasts with the fourteenth-century dating often given within the Nimbārka *sampradāy,* but

accords with the fact that Rāghavdās offers only names in the order's genealogy of *mahants* until he comes to Keśav Kāśmīrī Bhaṭṭ and his successors, whom he describes substantively (§§244ff.).

31. Priyādās, *Bhaktirasabodhinī, kavitts* 408–411, in Rūpkalā 1969 [1910]: 560–562. Mention of this encounter is also made by Vṛndāvandās in verses 1.13.1–209 of his *Caitanya Bhāgavata* (Vṛndāvandās 1997, 1: 375–409), which is later adopted in the *Caitanyacaritāmṛta* of Kṛṣṇadās Kavirāj (1.16.26–104, trans. Dimock and Stewart 1999: 307–312); cf. De 1961: 73–74.
32. Priyādās, *Bhaktirasabodhinī, chappay* 92, in Rūpkalā 1969 [1910]: 559–560.
33. Ibid., *kavitt* 412, p. 563.
34. Ibid., pp. 563–564.
35. Pauwels 2011: 281. The record comes from al-Badāyūnī, *Muntakhabu-t-Tawārīkh* 1973 [1899]: 127–128.
36. Cf. Clémentin-Ojha 1990: 338.
37. Brindavan Bihari confirms that this structure is not more than two hundred years old (personal communication, Brindavan, December 7, 2010).
38. *Pad* 114, in Bahura and Bryant 1982 [1984]: 160.
39. Goswami, forthcoming. Another connection to the Sri Vaisnava past is provided by the family that cares for the image of Gataśram Nārāyaṇ directly above Viśrām Ghāṭ in Mathura, who consider themselves Teṅkalai and who maintain ritual practices corresponding to those of the Śrī Vaishnava Rangjī Temple in Brindavan. But the image is no longer present and the family's sense of its history focuses on the grant of its land by the *rājā* of Gwalior some two hundred years ago, not on an earlier period. (Rāghav Ācārya, interview, Mathura, December 20, 2012). All one safely can say is that Gataśram Nārāyaṇ and those who serve him do not seem to have figured importantly in the major religious changes that occurred in sixteenth-century Brindavan.
40. Hudson 2009: 12, 70–74.
41. Entwistle 1987: 149, who refers to Nārāyaṇ Bhaṭṭ's *Vrajotsavacandrikā*, pp. 228–230, and Jānakīprasād's *Nārāyaṇabhaṭṭacaritāmṛta*, 1.45–54.
42. Entwistle 1987: 253.
43. *jñāna samārata paccha ko nāhina kou khaṅḍana biyau*, in Jhā 1978, part 2: 31, §83. Cf. *chappay* 442 in Rūpkalā 1969 [1910]: 59.
44. Delmonico 1993: 147–149.
45. *Kṛṣṇadās kī Vārtā, prasang* 2, in Gokulnāth [attrib.], 1970 [V.S. 2027]: 536, trans. Barz 1976: 218. Cf. Pauwels 2002: 151–152.
46. *Caitanyacaritāmṛta* 2.1.165, 2.1.174, trans. Dimock and Stewart 1999: 346; Delmonico 1993: 137n21, who credits Jānā 1970: 37.
47. *Caitanyacaritāmṛta* 2.1.179, trans. Dimock and Stewart 1999: 346. Cf. 2.1.183, p. 347.

48. Cakravartī *Bhaktiratnākara* 1.592–594, trans. Kuśakrantha dāsa 2006: 53–54.
49. E.g., *Caitanyacaritāmṛta* 2.1.179–193, 2.20.51, 54, 93.
50. Haynes 1974: 58; Rosenstein 1997: 34; Snell 1991a: 19–20, 36–37. Cf. Brzezinski 1998: 22–23; Packert 2010: 78–81; Pauwels 2002: 128–140. Rosenstein (1997: 6) parries the possibility of an association between Haridās and Viṣṇusvāmī, as might seem implied by Nābhādās.
51. *Pads* 41–45, in Pauwels 2002: 99–105.
52. Ibid., 158–166.
53. *Pads* 31–32, in Pauwels 2002: 84–85; cf. Hermansen 1997: 318, 322.
54. E.g., Tillich 1963 (vol. 3): 369–372; 1951 (vol. 1): 136.
55. Dimock and Stewart 1999: 29–31; Stewart 2010: 304. For cautions, nonetheless, on their use as historical documents, see Mumme 1997.
56. So *Caitanya Bhāgavata* 2.26.216–217, *Caitanyacaritāmṛta* 1.7.7, 2.1.11.
57. Murārī Gupta *Kṛṣṇacaitanyacaritāmṛta* 4.2, trans. Bhakti Vedanta Bhagavata 2006: 584–591; Entwistle 1987: 256.
58. Rūp Gosvāmī, *Padyāvalī* 22, 31, 32, 71, 93, 94, 324, 337, collected as the *śikṣāṣṭakam* in *Caitanyacaritāmṛta* 3.20.9–37. Cf. De 2002 [1934]: 9ff.
59. Murārī Gupta, *Kṛṣṇacaitanyacaritāmṛta* 2.1.19, trans. Stewart 2010: 82.
60. *Bhāgavata Purāṇa* 11.14.23–24, trans. Holdrege 2014: 82. Cf. 11.2.40.
61. *mṛgīvyādhi*, *Caitanyacaritāmṛta* 2.18.174, trans. Dimock and Stewart 1999: 606.
62. *Caitanya Bhāgavata* 1.8.67–83, trans. Dimock and Stewart 1999: 313–314.
63. More than a few scholars have offered comments on Chaitanya's experiences of possession in relation to their philosophical and scriptural anchoring—or lack thereof. See especially Hein 1976: 15–32; Frederick Smith 2006: 345–362.
64. This has been beautifully documented by Ghosh 2005.
65. Pauwels 2002: 127–168; Pauwels 2009.
66. *Haribhaktivilāsa* 1.39, 1.78, 1.214, 5.171, 5.174, 6.42, 8.110, 17.5, trans. Gopāl Bhaṭṭ 2002, 1: 14, 24, 63, 376–377; 2: 11–12, 215; 5: 2. Clémentin-Ojha 1990: 358–360 and Vijay Ramnarace accept the Nimbārkī identification of the *Kramadīpikā*, but Jan Brzezinski doubts it (email communication, June 30, 2009). Ramnarace has discovered a copy in the royal library of Nepal that dates to 1556 (email communication, February 10, 2012).
67. Premlatā Śarmā 1998: 102 and 112, verses 1.2.269 and 1.2.309. Cf. Horstmann and Mishra 2013.
68. Deshpande 2010.
69. Tony Stewart, email communication, October 24, 2010.
70. *Caitanyacaritāmṛta* 2.1.83, trans. Dimock and Stewart 1999: 342.
71. Ibid., 2.1.110–111, trans. Dimock and Stewart 1999: 343.
72. Ibid., 2.3.139–147, 2.3.176–184, trans. Dimock and Stewart 1999: 376, 378.

73. Ibid., 2.7–9, 2.17–18, trans. Dimock and Stewart 1999: 423–482, 581–610.
74. Kavikarṇapura, *Caitanyacandrodaya* 7.7, trans. Rāmcandra Miśra 1966: 235–237; *Caitanyacaritāmṛta* 2.8, especially 2.8.2, 2.8.214–242, trans. Dimock and Stewart 1999: 431, 457–459. Cf. Stewart 2010: 174–175, 337.
75. Sukumar Sen 1935:1–5, 23–28; William Smith 2000a.
76. *Caitanyacaritāmṛta* 2.8.150–156, trans. Dimock and Stewart 1999: 451.
77. Ibid., 3.1.105–137, trans. Dimock and Stewart 1999: 788–797.
78. This would account for the mention of this commissioning in the opening scene, along with the date of 1572 (*śaka* 1494).
79. A list of *ślokas* quoted from the *Caitanyacandrodaya* by Kṛṣṇadās Kavirāj appears in Dimock and Stewart 1999: 1085–1086.
80. *Caitanyacaritāmṛta* 1.14.18–58, trans. Dimock and Stewart 1999: 293–296.
81. Stewart 2010: 170.
82. Haberman 2003: xlix–lxvii.
83. Stewart 2010: 167–175.
84. As dramatized in *vārtās* 69 and 84 of the *Caurāsī Vaiṣṇavan kī Vārtā* (Gokulnāth [attrib.] 1970 [V.S. 2027]: 343–344, 563–565).
85. On the terminological issue, contrast Sukumar Sen 1935: 3 and William Smith 2000a: 398.
86. *Caurāsī Vaiṣṇavan kī Vārtā,* *vārtā* 84, in Gokulnāth [attrib.] 1970 [V.S. 2027]: 553–554; cf. Barz 1976: 237.
87. *Caurāsī Vaiṣṇavan kī Vārtā,* *vārtā* 84, in Gokulnāth [attrib.] 1970 [V.S. 2027]: 546–549; cf. Barz 1976: 228–229. The phrase used to introduce this girl is *ek vesyā apanī chorī ko nṛtya sikhāvat hutī,* so a biological relationship seems to exist between the courtesan and the girl she is teaching to dance. She is *apanī chorī,* her own girl.
88. *Caurāsī Vaiṣṇavan kī Vārtā,* *vārtā* 84, in Gokulnāth [attrib.] 1970 [V.S. 2027]: 547–548; cf. Barz 1976: 229–230. Of course, there are analogies to be drawn with what the Chaitanyites did when they sought out prototypes in Krishna's world for the cast of characters who gathered around Chaitanya in this one. See Chapter 5 on the *Gauragaṇoddeśadīpikā.*
89. Dalmia 2011; Barz 1994: 43–64: and, as if in response, Kaṇṭhamaṇi Śāstrī 1952: 1–13. Justin Ben-Hain points out that the number 84 was assigned by Harirāy, not Gokulnāth; the number 252 apparently does not appear within the *vārtās* themselves. Internally, one can ferret out a logic by which the *vārtās* accumulated, but it does not match the 84/252 scheme (Ben-Hain 2014; Ben-Hain, email communication, June 3, 2014).
90. Tarapada Mukherjee and Irfan Habib (1990: 237–238) point out that occasionally an element of historical fabrication can also be seen on the Chaitanyite side of the ledger, to wit, in respect to deeds that were drawn up for Jīv Gosvāmī in the 1580s.

91. McGregor 1984: 85–86; cf. Dīndayāl Gupta 1970, 1: 371. Also see McGregor 1973: 41–44; cf. Entwistle 1987: 165–166.
92. Hawley 1984b: 35–52; Hawley 2005: 201–203.
93. Hawley 2005: 186–188; cf. Bryant and Hawley 2015: §420.
94. Hawley 1984b: 21–22.
95. In regard to the Fatehpur manuscript, see Bahura and Bryant 1982: 76–221. In regard to early Dādūpathī collections, see Rajpurohit 2013: 57–63. In K. M. Hindi Institute accession no. 1057, dating to V.S. 1713 (1656 C.E.), we do find that a collection of Sūrdās poems has been placed before Nandadās's *Rāspañcādhyayī,* suggesting a Vallabhite connection. The difficulty is that it follows a *Hit Caurāsī,* which challenges the sectarian bond.
96. Jhaveri 1928: *farmān* 1. Cf. *farmān* 2, dated 1581.
97. Doubts have been raised about the authenticity of two subsequent *farmāns* presented by Jhaveri (§§4–5), both of which are dated 1593. They continue in the same vein, but expand. Mukherjee and Habib (1988: 238, 248–249) draw attention to "the quality of their writing, especially in the titles *(tughra)* and the ignorance of the scribe as to the simple requirement that a *farman* had to begin with two half-lines."
98. The *Siddhāntarahasyam* is numbered fifth among sixteen short treatises of Vallabha that have been grouped together as the "Sixteen Books" (*Śoḍaśagranthāḥ,* trans. Redington 2000). The verse in question is 5.2 (Redington 2000: 64). All other references in this paragraph pertain to the *Ṣoḍaśagranthāḥ.*
99. The exact date of the composition of the *Śrī Govardhannāthjī kī Prākaṭya Vārtā* is not given in the text, but it has to be after 1685 (V.S. 1742), a date it reports in its final chapter. See Harirāy [attrib.] 1905: 4; 2007: 55; cf. Entwistle 1987: 262.
100. The C.E. year is often given as 1479, but since the exact time is specified to be the eleventh day of the dark half of Vaiśākh in V.S. 1535, this does not seem possible (*Śrīnāthjī kī Prākaṭya Vārtā,* 2). The followers of Gokulnāth hew to a different tradition, favoring the date 1473 (Mītal 1968a: 3–4; Ṭaṇḍan 1960: 548–551). No date is given when allusions to Vallabha's birth are made in the *Caurāsī Vaiṣṇavan kī Vārtā* itself.
101. The *Śrīnāthjī kī Prākaṭya Vārtā* (p. 2) gives Agnikuṇḍ as the place Vallabha was born—or rather, "made manifest" *(prākaṭya),* using the same term it employs to designate the appearance of the deity at the same time. The earliest allusion to his birth in the Campā forest, if its date is to believed, would be the *Sampradāyapradīpa* of Gadādhar Bhaṭṭ, on which see Chapter 5.
102. *Caurāsī Vaiṣṇavan kī Vārtā,* *vārtā* 73, in Gokulnāth [attrib.] 1970 [V.S. 2027]: 357.
103. Dalmia (2001: 136–137, 146) has drawn attention to several moments in the *Caurāsī Vaiṣṇavan kī Vārtā* when the stature of the guru is regarded as such that he is effectively equated with his god or even exalted above him.

104. *Śrīnāthjī kī Prākaṭya Vārtā,* p. 7, also Harirāy [attrib.] 1905: 10; *Caurāsī Vaiṣṇavan kī Vārtā, vārtā* 73, in Gokulnāth [attrib.] 1970 [V.S. 2027]: 357–358.

105. This estimation of historical reality is at great variance with accounts given by Puṣṭimārgīs themselves. They may have trouble reconciling the dates proposed in the traditional *digvijay* accounts (e.g., Mītal 1968a: 5–7), but they rarely question the documents themselves (except Shyam Manohar Goswami: see Chapter 5). The oldest manuscript yet to have emerged for the *Caurāsī Vaiṣṇavan kī Vārtā* bears the date 1640 as the year in which it was copied. Earlier Vrajeśvar Varmā and I had questioned this date (Varmā, n.d.: 30–31; Hawley 1984b: 7), but owing to the kindness of Vallabhite authorities, Emilia Bachrach has recently viewed the manuscript and sees no obstacle to accepting its date as authentic (email communication, April 25, 2012).

5. Victory in the Cities of Victory

1. Lutgendorf 1997: especially 37–42.
2. Biman Bihari Majumdar, on whom see Elkman 1986: 33; De 1961: 46.
3. Manring 1989: 70–71, *Gauragaṇoddeśadīpikā* §24, based on Asiatic Society of Bengal manuscript G-677, no. 8745. I cite Manring's verse order throughout. Printed editions typically differ, however. §24, e.g., appears as §22 in Kavikarṇapūra 1950: 10–11; Kavikarṇapūra 2004: 15–17.
4. Lutjeharms 2009: 34, citing *Bhaktiratnākara* 9.196.
5. The operative terms are *antaraṅga* and *pārśadāgryaṃ: Caitanyacaritāmṛta* 1.10.54, as cited in Lutjeharms 2009: 30n80, and *Gauragaṇoddeśadīpikā* §24.
6. Lutjeharms 2009: 31–34, 58.
7. A classic study by Friedhelm Hardy (1974) connects Mādhavendra Purī to south India not via Madhva but rather via the philosopher Śrīdhar, author of the most influential commentary on the *Bhāgavata Purāṇa,* and Bilvamangal, author of the *Kṛṣṇakarṇāmṛta.*
8. Entwistle 1987: 137–140; Vaudeville 1980: 6–12. On Mādhavendra Purī (a.k.a. Mādhavānand) in the *Śrināthjī kī Prākaṭya Vārtā,* see Vaudeville 1980: 22, 31, 43.
9. Hawley 2013a, with its supporting bibliography. On the last point, Lutjeharms, personal conversation, Oxford, July 10, 2010, somewhat by contrast to Lutjeharms 2009: 43.
10. Horstmann 2002c: 160–162, 168; Horstmann 2006c: 26–28, 31.
11. Horstmann 2006c: 14, 17; O'Hanlon 2010a; O'Hanlon 2010b; O'Hanlon 2011. Generally, cf. Pollock 2001.
12. Another prominent interlocutor, Harekṛṣṇa Bhaṭṭ, may also have been Vallabhite (Horstmann 2006c: 16–17; Horstmann 2009: 37–38).

13. Horstmann 2006c: 28.
14. Schwartz 2012: 4–5.
15. Sumit Guha 2009: 279.
16. Ajay Rao 2007.
17. Horstmann 2003: 1, 10; Horstmann 2006c: 22–26; Horstmann 2009: 158–179. Cf. Horstmann 2011.
18. Sachdev and Tillotson 2002: 11–56.
19. On the dates, see Burton 2000: 83–85.
20. For an English translation of the *Govindabhāṣya,* see Vasu 1912. The Sanskrit *Prameyaratnāvalī* with an English translation by M. D. Basu appears as Appendix II of the same work. The dates of these two works are not secure. The *Prameyaratnāvalī* bears no date itself, but a commentary associated with it is traditionally attributed to Kṛṣṇadev Bhaṭṭācārya, who died before 1749; the *Prameyaratnāvalī,* in turn, gives evidence of the existence of the *Govindabhāṣya* in its first verse (Burton 2000: 84).
21. Monika Horstmann, oral communication, July 24, 2009. Baladev states at several points that he regards Viśvanāth as his mentor, possibly but not necessarily involving formal mantraic initiation (Burton 2000: 82).
22. Burton 2000: 116–118.
23. Mītal 1968b: 422–423; Horstmann 2000b: 43; Entwistle 1987: 194; Snātak 1968: 121–125.
24. Jīv Gosvāmī, *Sarvasaṃvādinī* commentary on the *mangalācaraṇa* of the *Tattvasandarbha* (Burton 2000: 120).
25. Jaipur Kapaddvārā no. 1519 (trans. Burton 2000: 121–122), with spellings altered to conform to general usage in this book. Note the identification of Chaitanya's companions as manifestations of the weapons of Krishna. On the Gauḍīya affiliation of the temple of Gopināth, see Entwistle 1987: 149.
26. *Caitanyacaritāmṛta* 2.9.249–250, building upon 2.9.228ff., trans. Dimock and Stewart 1999: 475–478.
27. Shrivatsa Goswami, personal communication, Brindavan, December 5, 2010, referring, for example, to *Tattvasandarbha* 27, 28, and 50 (Jīv Gosvāmī 1995: 141, 144–146, 257); Goswami, forthcoming; Brzezinski 2007: 64, 78.
28. Burton 2000: 82–90; cf. Elkman 1986: 25–26.
29. Horstmann 2009: 57–58; the letter itself, 287. See also Horstmann 2000b: 43–44, 52n5.
30. Also depicted in the frescoes that line the entrance to the *bhojanśālā* at Āmer (Figure 1).
31. Bhatnagar, V.S. 2002 [1974]: 342 and 342n88; Horstmann 2000b: 47–49, but cf. Horstmann 2002c: 162–163. On irony, Entwistle 1987: 191; Horstmann 2000b: 47.
32. Hastings 2002: 78, 152–158; cf. Clark 2006: 248.
33. Clémentin-Ojha 1999: 212–234, passim.

34. Clark 2006: 55n7; Maclean 2003; Maclean 2007; Lochtefeld 2004. In regard to more recent practice see Sinha and Saraswati 1978: 115–137, 155–157.
35. Horstmann, forthcoming.
36. He is therefore not to be confused with two important figures in the Chaitanya *sampradāy* who also bear that name. These are familiarly called Gadādhar Dās and Gadādhar Paṇḍit, and they seem to have sometimes been confused by Chaitanyites themselves. See Stewart 2010: 285–286.
37. Convenient summaries of what we know are provided by Bhatt 1935; Dasgupta 1975, 4: 382–383.
38. von Glasenapp 1933–1934: 326–327, reprinted 1934: 244–245. On Lālūbhaṭṭ's exposition of the term *tāmasa* in Vallabha's usage, widely accepted in the Puṣṭimārgīya *sampradāy,* see Redington 1983: 19–23.
39. Bhatt 1935: 460; Bhatt 1937: 326–327.
40. For a somewhat more detailed but slightly superseded account, see Hawley 2011.
41. Vallabha's *puṣṭimārg* attains the "qualitylessness" of its "pure nonduality" *(śuddhādvaita)* since it is a path characterized entirely by a love that presumes self-surrendering participation *(ātmanivedanapūrva[kam] premaiva bhaktimārgaḥ)*: Śāstrī 1935, 2: 61; cf. 1: 88 (Baroda 11580, 27a). In rendering this passage into Hindi, Śāstrī supplies the *nirguṇ* gloss explicitly.
42. Śāstrī 1935 2: 57–58n8.
43. Verghese 1995: 3, citing *Epigraphia Indica,* vol. 7, pp. 17–22.
44. These epigraphic records do not, however, confirm that Vyāsatīrtha was the *rājguru* of Kṛṣṇadevarāya, although this is what is claimed in the *Vyāsayogicarita* (Verghese 1995: 8–9; cf. Clark 2006: 201n84). Rather, Ajay Rao has made clear the extent to which the sympathies of Kṛṣṇadevarāya were principally with the Śrī Vaishnavas (Rao 2011; Rao 2013).
45. Śāstrī 1935, 2: 59.
46. *sampradāyatraye,* in Śāstrī 1935, 2: 59 (Baroda 9570, 23b; Baroda 11580, 27a).
47. This formula appears at the end of every chapter in the Śāstrī edition, and at the end of chapters 1 and 3 in Baroda manuscripts 9570 and 11580. E.g., Śāstrī 1935, 2: 13 (Baroda 9570, 7a; Baroda 11580, 7ab).
48. Nābhādās also comes close to juxtaposing these two (Jhā 1978, part 2: 15–17).
49. Śāstrī 1935, 2: 31 (Baroda 7590, 13b; Baroda 11580, 14b–15a).
50. Frances Wilson 1975: 16–17.
51. *Caitanyacaritāmṛta* 2.1.111, trans. Dimock and Stewart 1999: 343.
52. Horstmann and Mishra 2013.
53. *Śrīkṛṣṇāśraya* 1, 9–11, in Redington 2000: 109–111.
54. Śāstrī 1935, 2: 48 (Baroda 9570, 20b; Baroda 11580, 23b).
55. Ibid., 2: 80 (Baroda 9570, 30b; Baroda 11580, 33ab).

56. Satīś Candrācārya Bhagavatbhūṣaṇ, interview, Govardhan, December 19, 2012. Cf. Mītal 1968b: 151–152; Entwistle 1987: 344; Toomey 1994: 61–62.
57. Entwistle 1987: 263n130.
58. Shyam Manohar Goswami, interview, Mumbai, December 12, 2009. No manuscripts at all—only printed books—are cited in connection with entries given for the *Vallabhadigvijaya* in the *New Catalogus Catalogorum* (forthcoming, 27: 219, 234).
59. Nārāyaṇ Śāstrī, interview, Nāthdvārā, April 1, 2009, who thus contrasts with Shandip Saha's careful attempt to isolate elements of the accounts of Vallabha's travels that bear the mark of historical probability (Saha 2004: 107–118).
60. *Caurāsī Vaiṣṇavan kī Vārtā,* in Gokulnāth [attrib.] 1970 [V.S. 2027]: 564–565. Of course, this claim may come from a later period. On the witness of Vyās, see Pauwels 2002: 84–85, 105–106, 180–181.
61. Mukherjee and Habib 1988: 240–241, §§4.6–4.8. Compare Habib 2011: 223.
62. Swapna Sharma 2008.
63. G. H. Bhatt 1935: 460.
64. On the dating of the *Sampradāyabodhinī* of Manohardās, where the notion of the four *sampradāys* also appears, see Bansal 1980: 309. The text itself is published by Kṛṣṇadās Bābā (Mathura, 1953 [V.S. 2016]).
65. Srinivasachari 1970: 539–540; Subramaniam 2014: 36–37.
66. Thackston 1993, 3: 581, written in A.H. 932 (1525/26 C.E.). Cf. Wagoner 1993: 33, 52.
67. Shyam Manohar Goswami, interview, Mumbai, December 12, 2010.
68. Hemant Śarmā 1987: 864; cf. Dalmia 1997: 379–381. The title *Viṣṇusvāmīcaritāmṛta* does not appear in the collection of Bharatendu Harishchandra's own books, as bequeathed to Bharat Kala Bhavan at Banaras Hindu University, nor is it to be found in the library of the Kāśīrāj Trust at Ramnagar, the residence of the Maharaja of Banaras (December 13, 2010). There is also no record of it in the *New Catalogus Catalagorum* (forthcoming).
69. *Hinduism Today,* July–September 2008: 44. A more formal anticipation of this quintet—also quite recent—can be found in Tapasyānanda 1990.
70. Clark 2006: 243–244.
71. Mann 2001: 42–44; Mann 1996: 28, 155.
72. Horstmann 1990: 478–490; Horstmann 2009: 57. It is Horstmann who has convincingly established the 1734 date.
73. Clark 2006: 173–176, 227, 232–235, 246; cf. Pinch 1996: 27–28; Mallinson 2013: 75–80.
74. Jhā 1978, part 2: 15, §41.

75. Clark 2006: 114ff. More broadly, however, the institution of the *maṭh* is much older (Champakalakshmi 2011: 286–318).
76. Clark 2006: 118–122, 224–225, 246.
77. Michell 1995: 55–56, figs. 28–29; cf. Clark 2006: 204.
78. Stoker 2014: 265–266.
79. Minkowski 2011: 219–220, 223; variously, cf. Sanjukta Gupta 2006.
80. As evidenced particularly in his translation of fifty-two Upanishads as *Sirr-i Akbar* and his *Majma' al-Bahrayn* (2006, trans. Mahfuz-ul-Haq). Cf. Ahmad 1964: 191–196.
81. Sharma and Patkar 1939; Minkowski 2011: 217–218.
82. On the Shaivization of Advaita Vedanta at Madurai in the sixteenth and especially seventeenth centuries—its "sectarianization"—see Fisher 2012; Fisher 2013. Fisher has also noticed direct correspondence between Smārta Shaiva intellectuals at Madurai and their counterparts in Banaras (2013: 48).
83. Minkowski addresses this theme in regard to Madhusūdan Sarasvatī, citing especially his dismissal of *mlecchas* as *nāstikas,* although in passing (2011: 222–223, 228n72).
84. Stoker 2011b; Stoker 2014; Narayanan 2007: 246–251.
85. Alam 1996: 164–191.
86. On Rahīm, see Busch 2011: 93–95, 136–140; on Tulsīdās, see Behl 2007; on the *rām rasiks,* Bhagavatī Prasād Siṃh 1957 [V.S. 2014]: 32–138; Burchett 2012a: 176–246; and their relation to Tulsīdās, Paramasivan 2010.
87. Pellò 2008; Pellò 2014b. The work in question is *Safina-yi Khwushgū* (Khwushgū's Vessel), compiled between 1724 and 1734.
88. Hawley 2012.
89. Wagoner 1996: 856–861.
90. Bryant and Hawley 2015: §378.9.
91. Orr 1947: 71–78; Callewaert 1988: 37, 49, 81, 83, 92, 99, 122–123; Horstmann 2000a [2001]: 519; Horstmann 1983: 109, 117.
92. Bahura and Bryant 1982 [1984]: 76–220.
93. Williams 2007; Hawley 2005: 70–86.
94. For information on the anonymous *Sikhāṅ dī Bhagatmālā* (MS 185, Balbir Singh Sahit Kendar, Dehradun), whose earliest manuscript is dated 1798, I am indebted to Gurinder Singh Mann (email communication, November 13, 2010). Mann believes the text was written no earlier than 1765. Another Gurmukhi manuscript pertaining to the *Bhaktamāl,* in the possession of Tirlochan Singh Bedi of Manimajara, claims to have been written by a certain Nārāyaṇdās upon hearing Priyādās recite his *"kathā"* on it—presumably a reference to the *Bhaktirasabodhinī*—at the court of Savāī Mānsingh [sic] in 1712 (V.S. 1769), that is, the year in which the *Bhaktirasabodhinī* was composed (Mann, email communication, June 3, 2014).
95. Monika Horstmann, email communication, November 3, 2012.

96. These include prominently Sital Singh and Mathuranath of Banaras and Tarini Charan Mitr of Calcutta. See H. H. Wilson 1846 [1828, 1832]: 5, reprinted 1972: 4–5; Mitr and Price 1827, 1: ix; Morgenstern Fuerst 2012: 151–154; Hare 2011: 183–200.

6. A Nation of Bhaktas

1. Dvivedi 1976 [1942]: 221.
2. Dvivedi 1991 [1940]: 55–57.
3. Ramchandra Shukla 1923.
4. Mitr and Price 1827, 1: vi; 2: 84–134.
5. Partha Chatterjee 1993: 5–6.
6. Rai 2001: 53–58; Jordens 1978: 83, 86.
7. Dvivedi 1973 [1936]: 95–96.
8. Krishna Sharma 1987: 4; Prabha Dixit, interviews, Delhi, November 27 and 30, 2009.
9. Krishna Sharma 1987: 21n1.
10. *Ūpar hamne jo kuch kahā hai uskā sārāṅś yah hai ki vaiṣṇav dharm śāstrīya dharm kī apekṣā lok-dharm adhik hai,* in Dvivedi 1973 [1936]: 97.
11. Dutta and Robinson 1995: 326.
12. Letters to Śivmangal Siṃh "Suman" (October 23, 1973) and Banarsidas Chaturvedi (September 19, 1945), quoted in Viśvanāth Prasād Tivārī 1989: 11–12. Dvivedi's understanding of his relationship to Tagore has been beautifully studied in Horstmann 2002a: especially 122–124.
13. Dutta and Robinson 1995: 299.
14. Ibid., 290–291.
15. Tagore 1961 [1921]: 249.
16. Dutta and Robinson 1995: 299.
17. These terms appear, for instance, in passages from Tagore quoted in Rameshwar Mishra 1989: 69, 71.
18. Rameshwar Mishra 1989: 86–87.
19. Ibid., 60; Jhā 1978, part 1: 125; Hare 2011: 141–159.
20. It would be fascinating to know whether *Harijan*'s parent organization, the Harijan Sevak Sangh (The Servants of Untouchables Society) founded by Gandhi in 1932, adopted some such conception as the bhakti movement in its work with Dalits, especially in connection with the *bhajan*-singing sessions it sponsored throughout the country in the course of the 1930s (Lee 2014, chapter 4).
21. Tagore 2010 [1962], 8: 307–308. The Bengali source for the English phrase "storm of songs" is *gītavasanter hāoyā,* meaning literally "wind of song-spring." Brian Hatcher, to whom I am indebted for tracking down the Bengali original (email communication, March 24–25, 2014), points out that this phrase calls up the "sudden spring thunderstorms that pop up in

Bengal around the turn of the Bengali new year" and that the *prāṇer kuñja-vane* (bower of life-breath) of Ravidās that receives this squall suggests, by its phrasing, the romantic setting Vaishnavas would likely associate with the world of Krishna in Brindavan.

22. E.g., *Gurū Granth* §§3–5, 19, cf. 20, in Padam Gurcaran Siṃh 1977. 162–163, 197–198.
23. Joel Lee, personal communication, New York, June 16, 2011. This was an idea Tagore shared with Kshitimohan Sen (Sen 2009 [1935], in Mukhopādhyāy 2009 [2003]: 200).
24. Tagore 1933a; cf. Dutta and Robinson 1997: 422. On the Bengali "Snān-Samāpan," from which this poem derives (1932), see Tagore 2010 [1962], 8: 308–309; Miśra 1989: 74. Compare "Śuci" (Tagore 2010 [1987], 8: 301–303), originally composed in 1932, where Rāmānand encounters Kabīr and Nābhādās. The latter appears as a *caṇḍāl* associated with the work of cremating the dead, apparently a reference to the idea that Nābhādās was a member of the *ḍom* caste.
25. Rameshwar Mishra 1989: 67; cf. Tagore 2010 [1987], 5: 621–688.
26. Namvar Singh 2005 [1982]: 15.
27. Sen 2009 [1955], in Mukhopādhyāy 2009 [2003].
28. Sen 1936a: 55–56. Similarly, in regard to the question of the relationship between the *pads* included in Sen's anthology of Kabīr and those published in the preexisting Belvedere Press collection of Bāleśvar Prasād Agravāl, see Friedlander 2014: 13–24; Mehrotra 2011: xxvi–xxvii.
29. Sen 2009 [1935]: 194.
30. Ibid., 201; cf. Sen 2009 [1939]: 298, where Sen emphasizes the degree to which the "histories" to which we are heir are dependent on such latter-day fabrications.
31. Sen 2009 [1953]: 240, referring to Sen 1910–1911.
32. Sen 1929: 128; Sen 1936a: 167; Juergensmeyer 1991: 3–55, 183–194.
33. Friedlander, 2014: 24–25; Schomer 1987: 3, 7.
34. Dutta's *Bhāratabarṣīya Upāsak-Sampradāy* (1987–1990 [1870–1882]), a major updating of Wilson's *Sketch of the Religious Sects of the Hindus* (1846 [1828, 1832]) and especially rich in figures and groups active in northeastern India, is a landmark in the field.
35. Shukla 1969 [1949]: 34–36; Shukla 2001 [1940]: 50 (absent from 1929: 75). Cf. Wakankar 2007 [2005]: 113.
36. Sen 2009 [1935]: 195, 200; Sen 2009 [1939]: 297.
37. Sen 2009 [1935]: 195
38. Sen 1936a: 54; cf. Priyādās, *Bhaktirasabodhinī, kavitt* 514, in Rūpkalā 1969 [1910]: 271.
39. Sen 1936a: 72 [in Bengali, Sen 1929: 63]. In Sen's authorized translation, Manomohan Ghosh renders *sahaj utsavakṣetra* as "natural festive ground

of spiritual culture," but "easy" perhaps captures something of the spontaneity connoted by *sahaj*.

40. Sen 2009 [1939]: 295–296.
41. Dvivedi 1973 [1936]: 3.
42. Ibid., 97–98, and much later Dvivedi 1981a [1978]: 152. Compare Namvar Singh 2005 [1982]: 70–84, although my perspective on the centrality of the bhakti movement in Dvivedi's thinking cuts somewhat across the grain of Namvar Singh's effort to see it as expressing for him a deeper, more all-embracing populism upon which it is based (e.g., pp. 79, 82). Milind Wakankar reads the latter as "secular, worldly individuality" (Wakankar 2007 [2005]:135–136; cf. Wakankar 2010: 47–50), about which I have some reservations, yet I am far from seeing Dvivedi as the "Brahminizer" others have sometimes labeled him (especially Dharmavīr 1998 [1997]: 73–96, cf. Callewaert 2000b: 15).
43. Sen 1936a: 46–47.
44. Ibid., 45.
45. Dvivedi 1991 [1940]: 53.
46. Sen 1936a: 69, 165–166.
47. Ibid., 66–67, 175.
48. Śyāmsundar Dās 1956 [1928]: e.g., 211–236.
49. The Sanskrit epigram is drawn from the opening verses of Śrīnāth Cakravartī's *Śrīcaitanyamatamañjūṣā* (§1.1.1), in which he cites the *Bhāgavata Purāṇa* and the witness of Chaitanya as proof of his conviction that "love is the supreme goal of life," surpassing the standard four *puruṣārthas*. I am grateful to Shrivatsa Goswami for locating and commenting on the reference (email communication, July 19–20, 2011).
50. Dvivedi 1973 [1936]: 91.
51. Dvivedi 1976 [1942]: 189.
52. Ibid., 183–189, trans. Lorenzen 2004b: 275–282. Cf. Dvivedi 1973 [1936]: 63–64, 169; Dvivedi 1991 [1940]: 62.
53. Dvivedi 1973 [1936]: 54ff. Dvivedi had in mind figures like Medhātithi, Vijñāneśvar, Raghunandan, Hemādri, and Kamalākar (p. 56).
54. Dvivedi 1976 [1942]: 179–180, 183, trans. Lorenzen 2004b: 271, 275.
55. Dvivedi 1976 [1942]: 181–183, trans. Lorenzen 2004b: 274–275.
56. Dvivedi 1973 [1936]: 96–97, 140.
57. Ibid., 96–98.
58. Ibid., 80–82. On the Krishna vs. Christ controversy, see Hawley 1981: 57–59.
59. Dvivedi 1976 [1942]: 192, trans. Lorenzen 2004b: 286.
60. Dvivedi 1976 [1942]: 193, trans. Lorenzen 2004b286.
61. Dvivedi (1976 [1942]:193) cites it as coming from the *Gītāñjalī*, but it also appears as *Gītabitan* 296 (Tagore 2010 [1962]: 124).
62. Dvivedi (1976 [1942]:183.

63. Chakravarti 1998: 125.
64. Pal 1962 [1933]: 99.
65. Ibid., 88–103.
66. Ibid., 7, 16–17, 32–33; cf. Sartori 2008: 149–152.
67. Pal 1962 [1933]: 28–29, 34, 63.
68. Ibid., 88–90.
69. Pal 1911, part 2: 1–93.
70. Saggi 1962: 243, 246–247, 251.
71. Pal 1973 [1932]: 197; Banerjee 1979: 54, 63; cf. Saggi 1962: 353. For the Mazzini speech, see Palit 1880: 75–92.
72. In this, too, Pal followed the example of Surendranath Banerjea (Pal 1973 [1932]: 197).
73. Pal 1962 [1933]: 88, 91, 112.
74. Ibid., 91–93.
75. To appreciate the context and consequences, see Hatcher 2011b.
76. Pal 1962 [1933]: 102–103.
77. Pal 1973 [1932]: 196.
78. Pal 1962 [1933]: 109–111.
79. Ibid., 110.
80. Pal 1973 [1932]: 504–506, 519; cf. Manring 2005.
81. Pal 1962 [1933]: 114.
82. Ghosh 1985–1911; Ghosh 1897–1898.
83. I owe this term to a helpful email of Richard H. Davis (July 15, 2002).
84. Hatcher 2006: especially 73–74.
85. On the special charge of those same Vedantic commitments as they were passed down in the Tagore family, however, see Hatcher 2011a.
86. E.g., Haridās Gosvāmī 1914: 3, as quoted by Bhatia 2008: 348: "The life of Shri Gauranga is the national history [of the Bengalis]." Sudipta Kaviraj offers a more complex meditation on this indeterminacy in Kaviraj 1995: 112, 128–129.
87. Pal 1973 [1932]: 505.
88. Collet 1873: iv.
89. Ibid., 12–13, 19.
90. Ibid., 14–15.
91. Kopf 1979: 222–223.
92. Collet 1873: 18.
93. Collet 1876: 18.
94. Mozoomdar 1882: 217–218, 220.
95. Sastri 1983 [1903]: 224, 231. I am indebted to Brian Hatcher for the Bengali (email communication, July 26, 2011). In the parallel account that appears in Sastri's widely read *History of the Brahmo Samaj*, we hear of "the public inauguration of the *Bhakti* or devotional movement in the Brahmo Samaj, which had such strange developments within a short time" (Sastri 1919:

221). Hatcher has noticed an earlier usage that is similar but possibly more generic (email communication, July 9, 2014). Writing to his son Ganendranath in 1858 from Bareilly, Debendranath Tagore speaks of how the *brahmadharma* has created "a great stir" or "great movement" (*mahā āndolan*) there (1989: App. 2).

96. Pal 1973 [1932]: 98–101.
97. Chaudry 1877: 5.
98. Shukla 1969 [1949]: 71.
99. Ibid., 13, 35.
100. Ibid., 72.
101. Cf. ibid., 36–37, 75.
102. Phrases such as *bhāratīya bhaktimārg, bhāratīya bhakti,* and *hamāre yahāṅ kā bhaktimārg* occur repeatedly (e.g., ibid., 69–71, 76–78).
103. Namvar Singh 2005 [1982]: 64–65.
104. Further biographical details and critical appraisals can be found in Rākeś 2001: especially 9–38, 66–74; Caturvedī 1995 [1950]; Caturvedī 1969; Ḍhauṅḍiyāl 1982: 1–9.
105. The date 1504 is improbably—one is tempted to say impossibly—early, though this was precisely the reason Śyāmsundar Dās acclaimed it. Such a date would have placed this manuscript within the lifespan traditionally ascribed to Kabīr. See Callewaert 2000b: 13–14; Barthwal 1936: 276–277.
106. Barthwal 1936: 195, 208, 214–215.
107. Ibid., 204. Compare Agrawal 2011: 7–9.
108. Ibid., 17, 180–181, 198–199.
109. Ibid., 7–8, 15–17, 252–253; on Shaikh Tāqī, see also Barthwal 1934: 28; on Rāmānand, Barthwal 1954 [V.S. 2012].
110. Barthwal 1934 [V.S. 1991]: 24–25; 1936: 17.
111. Ibid., 11–12. To judge by his footnotes, Barthwal's access to poet-saints of the south seems to have been mediated principally through English.
112. Ibid., 5.
113. Barthwal denies this in the case of the *nirguṇīs* (1936: 274).
114. On Kabīr see Hess 1987; Agrawal 2009b: 42–47; Callewaert 2000b: 1–26. On Sūr, see Hawley 2005: 194–207, 268–271, 279–304; Bryant and Hawley 2015: xii–xv.
115. Lorenzen 1996.
116. Rajpurohit 2013: 58, 64–66. Similarly in Gopāldās's *Sarvāṅgī,* Sūrdās is the most frequently anthologized poet after Dādū, Kabīr, and Nāmdev (Callewaert 1993: 5).
117. Also spelled Binode Behari or Benodebehari Mukherjee. Photographs of these murals can be seen in Chakrabarti, Siva Kumar, and Nag 1995: pls. 34–45; and Gulammohammed Sheikh and Siva Kumar 2007: 52–57. A discussion of their contents by R. Siva Kumar appears in Chakrabarti, Siva Kumar, and Nag 1995: 5–78; and by Gulammohammed Sheikh in Sheikh

and Siva Kumar 2007: 31–47. Further, Ajay Sinha, 2007: 66–91; Rameshwar Mishra 2008b. My interpretations largely agree with those of Mishra, to whom I am indebted for a conversation at Hindi Bhavan on December 28, 2007, but they sometimes differ from Sinha's and Sheikh's.

118. K. G. Subrahmanyam, interview, Baroda, December 17, 2010. All subsequent references to Subrahmanyam's view refer to this interview, for which I am deeply grateful.
119. Chhanda Chatterjee 2014.

7. *What Should the Bhakti Movement Be?*

1. Hawley 2006 [1993]: 262–263.
2. Champakalakshmi 2011: 218–221, 438–460.
3. Savarkar 1969 [1923]: 102–107. Savarkar was not the first to use the term *hindutva* (Bordeaux 2014, chapter 5), but he was certainly responsible for its wide deployment.
4. Ibid., 43–44, 111–113, 135.
5. Raghunāth Bhūṣaṇācārya, interview, Brindavan, December 19, 2012; I am grateful to Anup Sharma and Rasik Sharma for facilitating it. Raghunāth Bhūṣaṇācārya's mention of Sindh evidently refers to the fact that Sindhi Hindus typically integrate the *Gurū Granth Sāhib* into their worship practices (Ramey 2008).
6. Cf. Bakker 1986; Bakker 1987.
7. Rahman et al. 1993; Rahman et al. 2012: 5.
8. Dalmia-Lüderitz 1992: 289.
9. Pal 1962 [1933]: 88.
10. Mahārāśtra Andhaśraddhā Nirmūlan Samiti, as in Quack 2012: x–xi, 53–56.
11. Hiranmay 1959; Mohammad 1964; Kuṅvarpāl Siṃh 1995; Hussain 2007; Nandakumar 2003. Nandakumar on Sufis: 890–891.
12. Hawley 2007.
13. On Annamayya see Narayana Rao and Shulman 2005: 104–107; Shulman 2012: 147–152. On Tulsīdās see Vaudeville 1955: xii–xiii; Mātāprasād Gupta 1965: 207–225; Bangha 2011: 141, 151–152.
14. Abbott and Godbole 1982 [1933–1934], 1: 201; McLeod 1980: 137; Aquil 2009: 171.
15. Yashaschandra 2003: 587–588.
16. Miller 1977: 20; Knutson 2011. Knutson responds to Herman Tieken's proposal of a strong connection with early Tamil poetry (Tieken 2001: ch. 10) on p. 134.
17. Sumit Guha 2007.
18. Orsini and Sheikh 2014:1–2.
19. Narayana Rao, Shulman, and Subrahmanyam 1992: 113–168; Pollock 2001; Shulman 2012; Fisher 2013.

20. For Narsī Mehtā, Jesalpura 1981: 223, trans. Shukla-Bhatt 2003: 208. For Sūrdās, Nāgarīpracāriṇī Sabhā edition §3623 ("Ratnākar" et al. 2: 283), first attested in a dated manuscript (B2) in 1624.
21. Ate 2011: 78–80; Richman 1997: 27–30; Jackson 1998: 46 (Annamayya 1977: §20); Bryant and Hawley 2015: 34–35, §18; Jesalpura 2003: 15, §8. For a possible fifth-century antecedent, see Bakker 2000.
22. Shulman 2012: 150; Bryant and Hawley 2015: §397, cf. "Ratnākar" et al., 1: 45–48: 137–149; Hawley 1984b: 151–156. Strikingly, Sūrdās and Annamayya are also noticeably silent about any flaws they might have as poets, which flaws are often formulaically confessed at the beginning of a *kāvya*-type utterance. Sometimes, in fact, to the contrary (Bryant and Hawley 2015: 120–121, §68).
23. Such charges also appear in the Sanskrit *Stutikusumāñjali* of the fourteenth-century Shaiva poet Jagaddhara, e.g., 11.66 in Stainton 2013: 347. Similarly Tukārām, as in Keune and Novetzke 2011: 621. For a quite different example from eighteenth-century Brindavan, see Richard Williams, forthcoming.
24. Bharati Jagannathan, would choose the former option (Jagannathan, email communication, March 16, 2013); Archana Venkatesan, the latter (2010: 5–6).
25. Novetzke 2008: 42–43, 68–70, *passim.*
26. Mahīpati, *Bhaktavijaya,* 1: 87–109, in Abbott and Godbole 1982 [1933–1934]: 8–10.
27. Rūpkalā 1969 [1910]: 771; McGregor 1973: 33–34; Hawley and Juergensmeyer 2004 [1988]: 45–46, 158.
28. Callewaert 2000a: 346–347, cf. 321–322.
29. Barz 1976: 211–212; Rousseva Sokolova 2013: 98–99; Hawley and Juergensmeyer 2004 [1988]: 126, 158, 203, 211.
30. Kaul 1973: 18–20.
31. Jackson 1998: 69–70.
32. Trivedi 1972.
33. *Caitanyacaritāmṛta* 3.7.2–156, trans. Dimock and Stewart 1999: 870–880; *Sampradāyapradīpa,* trans. Kaṇṭhamaṇi Śāstrī 1935, 2: 80.
34. Chandra Shobhi 2005: 111–112, 181–182.
35. Hawley 2005: 207.
36. Ramanujan 1973: 90.
37. *Gurū Granth, rāg āsā,* folio 377b = Sehgal 1980, 2: 406, trans. Vaudeville 1993: 331, with minor alterations. Cf. Singh et al. 2000 [1960]: 224.
38. *Gurū Granth, rāg gujrī,* folio 409 = Padam Gurcaran Siṃh 1977: 195 §13, trans. Hawley and Juergensmeyer 2004 [1988]: 26.
39. The problem of explaining the wide dispersion of the Nāmdev corpus and the relationship of its parts is as yet, in my mind, unsolved (Callewaert and Lath 1989: 3–10; Novetzke 2008: 137, 157–160; Prill 2009).

40. Chandra Shobhi 2005: 127–128, 166ff. I am deeply grateful to Prithvi Datta Chandra Shobhi for a series of conversations in Mysore (January 2–4, 2013) in which he explained many dimensions of Vīraśaiva textual scholarship, including the fact that none of today's working scholarly editions, however vast and carefully conceived, enables one to move from the printed text to the exact manuscript basis for any given printed *vacana*. At present, therefore, we can only be sure that this *vacana* appears in the standard editions of both Basavaraju (1990: §480) and Kalburgi (1970: §886).
41. Niranjan Rajyaguru, interview, Goghavadar, Gujarat, December 22, 2012. Rajyaguru cautions against thinking of this as a written text, but it can be found in Rajyaguru 2012: 81, §78.
42. Another version to consider—more distant—is attributed to Kanakadāsa (*Hari Bhakti Sara* 101, in Jackson 2013: 6).
43. Bryant and Hawley 2015: 650–651, §378.
44. In regard to Jaydev, see Kothari 1997: 9, 60, based on manuscripts dated 1611 and 1643. In regard to Nāmdev, see Jesalpura 1981: 48, based on a manuscript dated 1618. I am grateful to Niranjan Rajyaguru (interview, Goghavadar, December 21, 2012) and Neelima Shukla-Bhatt (email communication, June 25, 2013) for these references.
45. Busch 2011: 159–161, 188–196.
46. Ibid., 195; Horstmann, personal communication, Jaipur, December 11, 2012.
47. Peterson 2011; Soneji 2012: 50–52; Soneji 2014.
48. Williams 2014: 196–214, 273–304.
49. Dalmia 2001; Saha 2004: 113–115.
50. Gurinder Singh Mann, personal conversation, November 26, 2012; Niranjan Rajyaguru, personal conversation, Goghavadar, December 21, 2012; Williams 2014: 246.
51. Williams 2014: 76–94, 139.
52. Pinch 2006; Pinch 2009.
53. Narayana Rao 1990: 14–15.
54. Novetzke 2014b: 7.
55. Pollock 2006: 394–395, 413 ("geopolity") –423, 479–480.
56. Novetzke, email communication, March 19, 2014; Williams 2014: 67–69; Freeman 2003: 457–462.
57. Pollock 2006: 300–302 (on Someśvara's twelfth-century *Mānasollāsa*), 393.
58. Ibid., 316.
59. Ibid., 432–436.
60. Aquil 2012 [2007]; Orsini and Sheikh 2014.
61. *Ārambhik ādhuniktā* (Agrawal 2009a: 203); cf. *deśaj ādhuniktā,* or indigenous modernity—as against colonial modernity (Agrawal 2009a: 27–36).
62. Agrawal 2009b: 155.

63. Shea and Troyer 1843, 2: 193–194.
64. Pauwels 2002: 97–105. The crucial poem is §46: see 160–161, especially note 49.
65. Dās and Svāmī 2008: 355 §20.9. Cf. Jangopāl 1.17, 2.3–4, in Callewaert 1988: 36–37, 92.
66. Gadon 1987: 415–421; Novetzke 2008: 50.
67. Subbaya 1986; Rohitasva 1987; Murthy 1991; Sujātāreḍḍi 1993. I am indebted to Aruna Magier for related discussions (New York, March, 2011) and for pursuing these sources.
68. Vajpeyi 2012: 45–46.
69. Broadly, see de Bruijn and Busch 2014.
70. Hawley 1984b: 52–63; Hawley 2009b: 24–28, 443.
71. Agrawal 2009a: 198.
72. This line is omitted in ibid., 196, probably inadvertently. It appears in Mātāprasād Gupta 1985 [1969]: 319, which is cited as the reference.
73. Possibly the last line should instead be read as follows: "I'll never cede to Kashi the fame your feet deserve. / Kabīr says, I'd rather go to hell."
74. Agrawal 2009a: 197.
75. Narayana Rao and Shulman 2005: 99, 101.
76. Ibid., 99–100.
77. Shulman 2012: 152; Narayana Rao, Shulman, and Subrahmanyam 1992: 53–56, 73–82; Shulman 1993: 50–51.
78. Richards 1997; Subrahmanyam 1997; Subrahmanyam 1998; Subrahmanyam 2001: 260–265; Agrawal 2009a: 27–36, 65–146, 203; Pollock 2011: 1–48; Busch 2011: 11–22; O'Hanlon 2013a: especially 765–774; contra Goldstone 1998, cf. Koselleck 2002: 154–169.
79. Bryant and Hawley 2015: 714–717, §413; cf. Jesalpura 2003: 78, §35.
80. Busch 2011: 194–196.
81. Ibid., 87–88, 188–201, 226–231.
82. Hawley 1984b: 130–148.
83. Simultaneous "selfhood" developments at court are also relevant, however (Shulman 2008).
84. Chandra Shobhi 2005: 184, following the Kannada writer Chandrashekhar Kambar, who had been a student of Ramanujan's.
85. Ibid., 88, 154, 157.
86. Ibid., 145, 327.
87. Sanderson 2009; Vaudeville 1976; Pinch 2009; Burchett 2012a: 247–319; Sheikh 2012.
88. I am grateful to Phillip Wagoner for this realization (New York, September 28–29, 2012).
89. Venkatkrishnan 2011; Venkatkrishnan 2012: 15–18; Venkatkrishnan, forthcoming.
90. Behl 2007; de Bruijn 2010: 125–141.

91. Tulsīdās, *Vinaya-Patrikā* 8.3, in Shukla, Bhagavāndīn, and Brajratnadās 1976 [1923], 2: 383; cf. Lutgendorf 1991: 128–129 on the *Gautamcandrikā*.
92. Tulsīdās, *Kavitavali* 7.106, in Shukla, Bhagavāndīn, and Brajratnadās 1976 [1923], 2: 187.
93. Tulsīdās, *Dohāvalī* 551–557, in Shukla, Bhagavāndīn, and Brajratnadās 1976 [1923], 2: 126.
94. Notably, Lorenzen 2004b: 198–209; Omvedt 2008: 130–131.
95. Mann 2004: 22–28.
96. Goyal 1990.
97. Lorenzen 1991: 13–21.
98. Mani 2005: 181–183. An obvious example of the "sabotage" to which he refers is provided by Anantadās's and Priyādās's stories of how Ravidās had actually been a Brahmin in a former life (Jijñāsu 1984 [1959]: 2–3; cf. Hawley and Juergensmeyer 2004 [1988]: 15–16, 23).
99. Ambedkar 1952, to which I have access thanks to Jon Keune (email communication, November 21, 2012).
100. Zelliot and Mokashi-Punekar 2005: 42.
101. Jijñāsu 1984 [1959]: 9–11, 74–78; Lochtefeld 2005.
102. Or, as the story is also told, a spotless ascetic, and therefore someone from whom the question of caste has been removed altogether (Raman, forthcoming). A different but comparable story, told in the *Āmuktamālyada* of Kṛṣṇadevarāya, concerns a leather-wearing outcaste *(maladāsari)* whose meritorious devotion to Krishna/Vishnu, expressed though singing, causes a Brahmin demon *(brahmarākṣasa)* to regain his former Brahmin status, yet without altering that of his Dalit savior (Sistla 2010: 392–431). Cf. Burchett 2009.
103. Hawley and Juergensmeyer 2004 [1988]: 30–31.
104. Jijñāsu 1984 [1959]: 10.
105. *Saint Kabir with Saint Ravidasaji, ca. 1620–30* (New Delhi: National Museum, acc. no. 79.444); photograph by Neeraja Poddar. Molly Emma Aitken has proposed the eighteenth-century *terminus a quo* (email communication, December 1, 2012). In illustrations that accompany the Sikh *janamsākhīs,* Kabīr first appears in a manuscript dated 1733, being absent from the twenty-eight pictures that accompany the *Bālā Janam Sākhī* manuscript dated 1658 (Gurinder Singh Mann, email communication, December 7, 2012).
106. Keune 2011: 323–324, 354–364.
107. Pechilis 2005: 105–106; Zvelebil 1974: 227–228; Parthasarathy 2003; Raman, forthcoming, especially in regard to the impact of this drama on Ramalinga Swamigal.
108. Fuller 2004 [1992]: 155–181; "Sahajananad Swami and the Swaminarayan Sampraday" 2013.
109. Lee 2013.

110. Cf. Rahman et al. 2012; Ali 2012.
111. "The Films," The Kabir Project, accessed January 17, 2014, http://www.kabirproject.org/the%20films.
112. Ajab Shahar, accessed July 27, 2014, http://www.ajabshahar.org/. I am grateful to Shabnam Virmani, Smriti Chanchani, and Linda Hess for email communications of January 5–6, 2014.
113. Zecchini 2013.
114. Cf. Mullatti 1989; Vijaya Ramaswamy1996; Rekha Pande 2010.
115. Madhu Kishwar, interview, Delhi, December 10, 2012; Kishwar 2013.
116. Vasudha Narayanan, interview, Bangalore, December 31, 2012. Cf. Hansen 1996. Shiv Subramaniam (email communication, January 7, 2014) has drawn my attention to the fact that among purists the great increase in the importance of *ṭukaḍās* can signify the decline of Karnatak music, on account of its lack of depth, its dilution of Dravidian purity, its frequent use by female performers, and its overly strong bhakti flavor (Krishna 2013: 181–182).
117. I am indebted to Siddhartha Shah for a perceptive study of the Ellis Dungan Tamil film starring Subbulakshmi, contrasting it with the 1979 Bollywood version of Gulzar (Shah 2014), and to an email on the former from S. Theodore Bhaskaran (May 8, 2014).
118. Shetty, Tolpady, and Parinitha 2013.
119. Hegde 2013.
120. Cf. Boratti 2012: 29–52; Boratti 2013.
121. On the *Mahābhārata* in this regard, see Sarma 1998: 53–54. I am grateful to Deepak Sarma for the reference.
122. So far, the concept *anubhava maṇḍapa* has not been traced back farther than a sixteenth-century version of the *Śūnyasampādane*. It is preceded in Harihara's thirteenth-century *Ragaḷegaḷu* by the idea of a *śivagoṣṭhi* (Shiva discussion), a term whose explicit discursiveness contrasts with the non- or superverbal rhetoric of *anubhava* but does not challenge the emphasis on interiority that is at the root of Vīraśaiva ideology (Ben-Herut 2013: 35–36, 43–44, 273–274).

Bibliography

Abbott, Justin E., and Narhar R. Godbole. 1982 [1933–1934]. *Stories of Indian Saints: Translation of Mahipati's Marathi Bhaktavijaya.* 2 vols. Delhi: Motilal Banarsidass.

Agrawal, Madan Mohan. 2005. *Nimbārka Philosophical Tradition.* Delhi: Chaukhamba Sanskrit Pratishthan.

Agrawal, Purushottam. 2009a. *Akath Kahānī Prem kī: Kabīr kī Kavitā aur unkā Samay.* Delhi: Rājkamal Prakāśan.

———. 2009b. "In Search of Ramanand: The Guru of Kabir and Others." In Banerjee-Dube and Dube, eds., *Ancient to Modern,* 135–170.

———. 2011. "The Naths in Hindi Literature." In David N. Lorenzen and Adrián Muñoz, eds., *Yogi Heroes and Poets: Histories and Legends of the Nāths.* Albany: State University of New York Press, 3–17.

Ahmad, Aziz. 1964. *Studies in Islamic Culture in the Indian Environment.* Oxford: Clarendon Press.

Alam, Muzaffar. 1996. "Assimilation from a Distance: Confrontation and Sufi Accommodation in Awadh Society." In R. Champakalakshmi and S. Gopal, eds. *Tradition, Dissent, and Ideology: Essays in Honour of Romila Thapar.* Delhi: Oxford University Press, 164–191.

———. 2004. *The Languages of Political Islam: India 1200–1800.* Chicago: University of Chicago Press.

al-Badāyūnī. 1973 [1899]. *Muntakhabu-t-Tawārīkh,* vol. 3, trans. and ed. T. Wolseley Haig. Delhi: Idarah-i Adabiyat-i Delli.

Ali, Mohammad. 2012. "Concern over 'Creeping Fascism' in Popular Discourse of the Country." *Hindu,* December 7.

Ambedkar, Bhim Rao. 1952. Introduction to *Eknāth Darśan Khaṇḍa.* Aurangabad: Eknāth Saṃśodhan Mandir.

Anderson, Benedict. 1991 [1983]. *Imagined Communities: Reflections on the Origin and Spread of Nationalism.* London: Verso.

Annamayya. 1977. *Annamācāryula Kīrtaṇalu*. Tirupati: Tirumala Tirupati Devasthanams.

Aquil, Raziuddin. 2012 [2007]. *Sufism, Culture, and Politics: Afghans and Islam in Medieval North India*. Delhi: Oxford University Press.

———. 2009. *In the Name of Allah: Understanding Islam and Indian History*. Delhi: Viking.

Archer, W. G. 1958. *Central Indian Painting*. London: Faber and Faber.

Asher, Catherine B. 1992. *Architecture of Mughal India. The New Cambridge History of India*. Cambridge: Cambridge University Press, 1: 4.

Askari, S. H. 1977. "Dabistan-i-Mazahib and Diwan-i-Mubad." In Fathullah Mujtabai, ed., *Indo-Iranian Studies Presented for the Golden Jubilee of the Pahlavi Dynasty of Iran*. New Delhi: Indo-Iran Society, 85–104.

Ate, Lynn. 2011. *Yaśodā's Songs to Her Playful Son, Kṛṣṇa: Periāḻvār's 9th Century Tamil Tirumoḻi*. Woodland Hills, CA: South Asian Studies Association.

Athar Ali, M. 1999. "Pursuing an Elusive Seeker of Universal Truth: The Identity and Environment of the Author of the *Dabistān-ī Mazāhib*." *Journal of the Royal Asiatic Society*, 3rd ser., 9: 365–373.

Bader, Jonathan. 2000. *Conquest of the Four Quarters: Traditional Accounts of the Life of Śaṅkara*. New Delhi: Aditya Prakashan.

Bahura, Gopal Narayan. 1976. *Literary Heritage of the Rulers of Amber and Jaipur*. Jaipur: Maharaja Sawai Man Singh II Museum.

———. 1984. *Catalogue of Manuscripts in the Maharaja Sawai Man Singh II Museum*. Jaipur: Maharaja Sawai Man Singh II Museum.

———. 1996. "Śrī Govinda Gāthā." In Case, ed., *Govindadeva*, 195–214.

Bahura, Gopal Narayan, and Kenneth E. Bryant, eds. 1982 [1984]. *Pad Sūrdāsjī kā/The Padas of Sūrdās*. Jaipur: Maharaja Sawai Man Singh II Museum.

Bailey, G. M., and I. Kesarcodi Watson, eds. 1992. *Bhakti Studies*. Bangalore: Sterling.

Bakker, Hans. 1986. *Ayodhyā*. Groningen: Egbert Forsten.

———. 1987. "Reflections on the Evolution of Rāma Devotion in the Light of Textual and Archaeological Evidence." *Wiener Zeitschrift für die Kunde Südasiens* 31: 9–42.

———. 2000. "Little Kṛṣṇa's Play with the Moon." In Offredi, ed., *Banyan Tree*, 2: 353–362.

Balasubramanian, R., ed. 2003. *Theistic Vedānta*, vol. 2, part 3 of D. P. Chattopadhyaya, gen. ed., *History of Science, Philosophy and Culture in Indian Civilization*. New Delhi: Centre for Studies in Civilizations.

Banerjea, Surendra Nath. 1870. *Speeches of Surendra Nath Banerjea*. Calcutta: Indian Association.

Banerjee, Bani. 1979. *Surendranath Banerjea and History of Modern India (1848–1925)*. New Delhi: Metropolitan Book.

Banerjee-Dube, Ishita, and Saurabh Dube, eds. 2009. *Ancient to Modern: Religion, Power, and Community in India.* Delhi: Oxford University Press.

Bangha, Imre. 2000. "Mundane and Divine Love in Ānandghan's Poetry: An Eighteenth Century Literary Debate." In Offredi, ed., *Banyan Tree,* 2: 523–537.

———. 2007. "Courtly and Religious Communities as Centres of Literary Activity in Eighteenth-Century India: Ānandghan's Contacts with the Princely Court of Kishangarh-Rūpnagar and with the Maṭh of the Nimbārka Sampradāy in Salemabad." In Csaba Dezsö, ed., *Indian Languages and Texts through the Ages: Studies by Hungarian Indologists in Honour of Prof. Csaba Töttössy.* Delhi: Manohar, 307–353.

———. 2011. "Writing Devotion: The Dynamics of Textual Transmission in the *Kavitāvalī* of Tulsīdās." In Pollock, ed., *Forms of Knowledge in Early Modern South Asia,* 140–170.

———, ed. 2013. *Bhakti beyond the Forest: Current Research on Early Modern Literatures in North India, 2003–2009.* Delhi: Manohar.

Bansal, Naresh Chandra. 1980. *Caitanya-Sampradāy: Siddhānt aur Sāhitya.* Agra: Vinod Pustak Mandir.

Barthwal, Pitambar Datta. 1930 [V.S. 1987]. "Hindī Kavitā meṅ Yog Pravāh." *Nāgarīpracāriṇī Patrikā* 11: 385–405.

———. 1934 [V.S. 1991]. "Hindī Kāvya meṅ Nirguṇ Sampradāy." *Nāgarīpracāriṇī Patrikā* 15: 1–32

———. 1936. *The Nirguna School of Hindi Poetry: An Exposition of Medieval Indian Santa Mysticism.* Banaras: Indian Bookshop.

———. 1995 [1950]. *Hindī Kāvya kī Nirguṇ Dhārā.* Delhi: Takṣaśilā Prakāśan.

———. 1954 [V.S. 2012]. *Rāmānand kī Hindī Racanāeṅ.* Banaras: Nāgarīpracāriṇī Sabhā.

———. 1969. *Hindī Kāvya meṅ Nirguṇ Sampradāy.* Lucknow: Avadh Publishing House.

Barz, Richard. 1976. *The Bhakti Sect of Vallabhācārya.* Faridabad: Thomson Press.

———. 1994. "The *Caurāsī Vaiṣṇavan kī Vārtā* and the Hagiography of the Puṣṭimārg." In Callewaert and Snell, eds., *According to Tradition,* 43–64.

Basavaraju, L. 1990. *Śivadāsagītāñjali,* 2nd ed. Mysore: Jagadguru Sri Shivaratrisvara Granthamala.

Behl, Aditya. 2003. "The Magic Doe: Desire and Narrative in a Hindavi Sufi Romance, circa 1503." In Richard M. Eaton, ed., *India's Islamic Traditions, 711–1750.* Delhi: Oxford University Press, 180–208.

———. 2007. "Presence and Absence in *Bhakti:* An Afterword." *International Journal of Hindu Studies* 11: 319–324.

———. 2010. "Pages from the Book of Religions: Comparing Self and Other in Mughal India." In Laurie L. Patton and David L. Haberman, eds., *Notes from a Mandala: Essays in Honor of Wendy Doniger.* Newark: University of Delaware Press, 113–121.

———. 2011. "Pages from the Book of Religions: Encountering Difference in Mughal India." In Pollock, ed., *Forms of Knowledge in Early Modern Asia,* 210–239.

———. 2012. *Love's Subtle Magic: An Indian Islamic Literary Tradition, 1379–1545,* ed. Wendy Doniger. New York: Oxford University Press.

Ben-Hain, Justin. 2014. "Harirāy's Encompassment and Renovation of Vallabhite Vārtās." M.A. thesis, Columbia University.

Ben-Herut, Gil. 2013. "Narrating Devotion: Representation and Prescriptions of the Early Kannada *Śivabhakti* Tradition according to Harihara's *Śivaśaraṇara Ragaḷĕgaḷu.*" Ph.D. dissertation, Emory University.

———. Forthcoming. "Figuring the South-Indian Śivabhakti Movement: Early Kannada Hagiographic Literature in Its Broader Narrative Context." *Journal of Hindu Studies.*

Benson, James. 2001. "Śamkarabhaṭṭa's Family Chronicle: The *Gādhivaṃśavarṇana.*" In Alex Michaels, ed., *The Pandit: Traditional Scholarship in India.* Delhi: Manohar, 105–118.

Bhāgavata Mahāpurāṇa, with English translation by C. L. Goswami. 1995 [1971]. Gorakhpur: Gita Press.

Bhāgavata Māhātmya, with Brajbhāṣā translation. n.d. Jaipur: Maharaja Sawai Man Singh II Museum, accession no. 3224(1).

Bhagwat, Vidyut. 2008. "Hindu-Muslim Dialogue: A Rereading of Sant Eknath and Sant Shaikh Muhammad." In M. Naito, I. Shima, and H. Kotani, eds., *Mārga: Ways of Liberation, Empowerment, and Social Change in Maharashtra.* Delhi: Manohar, 77–93.

Bhandarkar, Ramkrishna Gopal. 1913. *Vaiṣṇavism, Śaivism, and Minor Religious Systems.* Strassburg: K. J. Trübner.

Bhatia, Varuni. 2008. "Devotional Tradition and National Culture: Recovering Gauriya Vaishnavism in Colonial Bengal." Ph.D. dissertation, Columbia University.

Bhatnagar, V. S. 2002 [1974]. *Life and Times of Sawai Jai Singh, 1688–1743.* Jodhpur: Book Treasures.

Bhatt, G. H. 1935. "Viṣṇusvāmī and Vallabhācārya." In *Proceedings and Transactions of the Seventh All-India Oriental Conference, December, 1933.* Baroda: Oriental Institute, 449–458.

———. 1937. "A Further Note on Vishṇusvāmi and Vallabhāchārya." In *Proceedings and Transactions of the Eighth All-India Oriental Conference, December, 1935.* Bangalore: Government Press, 326–327.

Bhattacharyya, N. N., ed. 1989. *Medieval Bhakti Movements in India: Śrī Caitanya Quincentenary Commemoration Volume.* New Delhi: Munshiram Manoharlal.

Bhūmipati Dāsa, trans. n.d. *Śrī Mathurā Māhātmya: The Glories of Mathurā Maṇḍala.* Brindavan: Rasbihari and Sons.

Boratti, Vijayakumar M. 2012. *The "Discovery" of Vachanas: Halakatti and the Medieval Kannada Literature in Colonial Karnataka*. Hampi: Kannada University.

———. 2013. "Bhakti, Community, and Vachanas in Colonial Karnataka. Paper presented at the conference "Rethinking Bhakti," Mangalore University, March 29.

Bordeaux, Joel. 2014. "The Mythic King: Raja Krishnacandra and Early Modern Bengal." Ph.D. dissertation, Columbia University.

Bronner, Yigal. 2013. "Birds of a Feather: Vāmana Bhaṭṭa Bāṇa's *Haṃsasandeśa* and Its Intertexts." *Journal of the American Oriental Society* 133: 495–526.

Bronner, Yigal, Whitney Cox, and Lawrence J. McCrea, eds. 2011. *South Asian Texts in History: Critical Engagements with Sheldon Pollock*. Ann Arbor: Association for Asian Studies.

Bronner, Yigal, and David Shulman. 2006. " 'A Cloud Turned Goose': Sanskrit in the Vernacular Millennium." *Indian Economic and Social History Review* 43: 1–30.

Bryant, Edwin F. 2002. "The Date and Provenance of the Bhāgavata Purāṇa." *Journal of Vaishnava Studies* 11: 51–80.

Bryant, Kenneth E., and John Stratton Hawley. 2015. *Sur's Ocean: Poems from the Early Tradition*. Cambridge, MA: Harvard University Press.

Brzezinski, Jan K. 1998. "Prabodhānanda, Hita Harivaṃśa, and the *Rādhā-rasa-sudhā-nidhi*." *Journal of Vaishnava Studies* 7: 19–61.

———. 2007. "Jiva Goswami: Biography and Bibliography." *Journal of Vaishnava Studies* 15: 51–80.

Buchta, David. 2007. "Complexity in Hindu Biography: Baladeva Vidyābhūṣaṇa's Multi-regional Influences." *Journal of Vaishnava Studies* 15: 81–93.

Burchett, Patton Elliot. 2009. "*Bhakti* Rhetoric in the Hagiography of 'Untouchable' Saints: Discerning *Bhakti*'s Ambivalence on Caste and Brahminhood." *International Journal of Hindu Studies* 13: 115–141.

———. 2012a. "Bhakti Religion and Tantric Magic in Mughal India: Kacchwāhas, Rāmānandīs, and Nāths, ca. 1500–1750." Ph.D. dissertation, Columbia University.

———. 2012b. "My Miracle Trumps Your Magic: Confrontations with Yogis in Sufi and Bhakti Hagiographical Literature." In Knut Jacobsen, ed., *Yoga Powers*. Leiden: E. J. Brill, 345–380.

Burton, Adrian. 2000. "Temples, Texts, and Taxes: The Bhagavad-gītā and the Politico-Religious Identity of the Caitanya Sect." Ph.D. dissertation, Australian National University.

Burton-Page, John. 1996. "The Early Vṛndāvana Temples: The 'Hindu-Muslim Synthesis' Rejected." In Case, ed., *Govindadeva*, 123–127.

Busch, Allison. 2003. "The Courtly Vernacular: The Transformation of Brajbhāṣā Literary Culture (1590–1690)." Ph.D. dissertation, University of Chicago.

———. 2009. "Braj beyond Braj: Classical Hindi in the Mughal World." Delhi: India International Centre Occasional Publication 12.

———. 2010. "Hidden in Plain View: Brajbhasha Poets at the Mughal Court." *Modern Asian Studies* 44: 267–309.

———. 2011. *Poetry of Kings: The Classical Hindi Literature of Mughal India.* New York: Oxford University Press.

———. 2014. "Poetry in Motion: Literary Circulation in Mughal India." In de Bruijn and Busch, eds., *Culture and Circulation,* 186–221.

Cakravartī, Narahari. 2006. *Bhaktiratnākara,* trans. Kuśakrantha dāsa as *The Jewel-filled Ocean of Devotional Service.* Brindavan: Ras Biharilal and Sons.

Callewaert, Winand M. 1978. *The Sarvāṅgī of the Dādūpanthī Rajab.* Leuven: Departement Oriëntalistiek, Katholieke Unversiteit Leuven.

———. 1988. *The Hindī Biography of Dādū Dayāl.* Delhi: Motilal Banarsidass.

———. 1991. "The 'Earliest' Song of Mira (1503–1546)." *Orientalia Lovaniensia Periodica* 22: 201–214.

———. 1993. *The Sarvāṅgī of Gopāldās: A 17th Century Anthology of Bhakti Literature.* Delhi: Manohar.

———. 1994. "Bhagatmāls and Parcaīs in Rajasthan." In Callewaert and Snell, eds., *According to Tradition,* 87–98.

———. 2000a. *The Hagiographies of Anantadās.* Richmond, Surrey: Curzon Press.

———. 2000b. In collaboration with Swapna Sharma and Dieter Taillieu. *The Millennium Kabīr Vāṇī: A Collection of Pads.* Delhi: Manohar.

———. 2009. With the assistance of Swapna Sharma. *Dictionary of Bhakti: North-Indian Bhakti Texts into Khaṛī Bolī Hindī and English.* 3 vols. New Delhi: D. K. Printworld.

Callewaert, Winand M., and Peter G. Friedlander. 1992. *The Life and Works of Raidās.* Delhi: Manohar.

Callewaert, Winand M., and Mukund Lath. 1989. *The Hindī Songs of Nāmdev.* Leuven: Departement Oriëntalistiek, Katholieke Unversiteit Leuven.

Callewaert, Winand M., and Rupert Snell, eds. 1994. *According to Tradition: Hagiographical Writing in India.* Wiesbaden: Harrassowitz.

Case, Margaret H., ed. 1996. With photographs by Robyn Beeche. *Govindadeva: A Dialogue in Stone.* New Delhi: Indira Gandhi National Centre for the Arts.

———. 2000. *Seeing Krishna: The Religious World of a Brahman Family in Vrindaban.* New York: Oxford University Press.

Castelli, Elizabeth. 2004. *Martyrdom and Memory: Early Christian Culture-Making.* New York: Columbia University Press.

Cātak, Govind, ed. 1978. *Dr. Pītāmbardatt Baḍthvāl ke Śreṣṭh Nibandh.* New Delhi: Takṣaśīlā Prakāśan.

Caturvedī, Paraśurām. 1995 [1950]. Introduction to P. D. Barthwal, *Hindī Kāvya kī Nirguṇ Dhārā*. Delhi: Takṣaśilā Prakāśan, 20–38.

———. 1969. Introduction to P. D. Barthwal, *Hindī Kāvya meṅ Nirguṇ Sampradāy*. Lucknow: Avadh Publishing House, 16–54.

———. 1972. *Uttarī Bhārat kī Sant-Paramparā*. Allahabad: Leader Press.

Chakrabarti, Jayanta, R. Siva Kumar, and Arun K. Nag. 1995. *The Santiniketan Murals*. Calcutta: Seagull Books.

Chakravarti, Aroop. 1998. *Bipin Chandra Pal: Nationalist Politics and Ideology*. Lucknow: C. M. Bajaj.

Champakalakshmi, R. 2006. "Bhakti and Tamil Textual Tradition." *Tattvabodha: Essays from the Lecture Series of the National Mission for Manuscripts*, vol. 1. Delhi: National Mission for Manuscripts and Munshiram Manoharlal, 81–108.

———. 2011. *Religion, Tradition, and Ideology: Pre-colonial South India*. Delhi: Oxford University Press.

Chanchani, Nachiket. Forthcoming. "Pandukeshwar, Architectural Knowledge, and an Idea of India." *Ars Orientalis* 45.

Chand, Tara. 1936. *Influence of Islam on Indian Culture*. Allahabad: Indian Press.

Chandra, Satish. 1978. *Medieval India: A Textbook for Classes XI–XII*. New Delhi: National Council of Educational Research and Training.

Chandra Shobhi, Prithvi Datta. 2005. "Pre-modern Communities and Modern Histories: Narrating Vīraśaiva and Lingayat Selves." Ph.D. dissertation, University of Chicago.

Chatterjee, Chhanda. 2014. *Tagore and the Sikh Gurus: A Search for an Indiagenous Modernity*. Delhi: Manohar.

Chatterjee, Kumkum. 2009. "Cultural Flows and Cosmopolitanism in Mughal India: The Bishnupur Kingdom." *Indian Economic and Social History Review* 46: 147–182.

Chatterjee, Partha. 1993. *The Nation and Its Fragments: Colonial and Postcolonial Histories*. Princeton: Princeton University Press.

———. 2010. *Empire and Nation: Selected Essays*. New York: Columbia University Press.

———. 2012. *The Black Hole of Empire: History of a Global Practice of Power*. Princeton: Princeton University Press.

Chaudry, Pearee Mohun. 1877. *Sermons and Essays by a Missionary of the Brahmo Samaj in India*. Calcutta: Sucharu Press.

Clark, Matthew. 2006. *The Daśanāmī Saṃnyāsīs: The Integration of Ascetic Lineages into an Order*. Leiden: E. J. Brill.

Clémentin-Ojha, Catherine. 1990. "La Renaissance du Nimbārka Sampradāya: Contribution a l'étude d'une secte kṛṣṇaïte." *Journal Asiatique* 258, nos. 3–4: 328–376.

———. 1999. *Le Trident sur le palais: Une Cabale anti-Vishnouite dans un royaume hindou á l'époque colonial.* Paris: École Française d'Extrême Orient.

———. 2001. "A Mid-Nineteenth-Century Controversy over Religious Authority." In Dalmia, Malinar, and Christof, eds., *Charisma and Canon,* 183–201.

Collet, Sophia Dobson. 1873. *An Historical Sketch of the Brahmo Somaj.* Calcutta: Calcutta Central Press.

———. 1876. *The Brahmo Year-book, Brief Records of Work and Life in the Theistic Churches of India.* London: Williams and Norgate.

Constable, Philip. 1997. "Early Dalit Literature and Culture in Late Nineteenth- and Early Twentieth-Century Western India." *Modern Asian Studies* 31: 317–338.

Corcoran, Maura. 1995. *Vṛndāvana in Vaiṣṇava Literature: History—Mythology—Symbolism.* Brindavan: Vrindaban Research Institute.

Cort, John. 2002. "Bhakti in the Early Jain Tradition: Understanding Devotional Religion in South Asia." *History of Religions* 42: 59–86.

Cutler, Norman. 1987. *Songs of Experience: The Poetics of Tamil Devotion.* Bloomington: Indiana University Press.

Dalmia, Vasudha., ed. 1996. *Myths, Saints, and Legends in Medieval India.* Delhi: Oxford University Press

———. 1997. *The Nationalization of Hindu Traditions: Bhāratendu Hariśchandra and Nineteenth-Century Banaras.* Delhi: Oxford University Press.

———. 2001. "Forging Community: The Guru in a Seventeenth-Century Vaiṣṇava Hagiography." In Dalmia, Malinar, and Christof, eds., *Charisma and Canon,* 129–154.

———. 2006. "The 'Other' in the World of the Faithful." In Horstmann, ed., *Bhakti in Current Research, 2001–2003,* 115–138.

———. 2011. "Lives of Brajbhasa Poets: Generic Types or Individuals?" Paper presented at the seminar "Alternative Modernities: Views from Pre-Colonial India," Banaras Hindu University, December 11.

———. See also Dalmia-Lüderitz, Vasudha.

Dalmia, Vasudha, and Munis Faruqui, eds. 2014. *Religious Interactions in Mughal India.* Delhi: Oxford University Press.

Dalmia, Vasudha, Angelika Malinar, and Martin Christof, eds. 2001. *Charisma and Canon: Essays on the Religious History of the Indian Subcontinent.* Delhi: Oxford University Press.

Dalmia-Lüderitz, Vasudha. 1992. "Hariścandra of Banaras and the Reassessment of Vaiṣṇava Bhakti in the Late Nineteenth Century." In R. S. McGregor, ed., *Devotional Literature in South Asia: Current Research, 1985–1988.* Cambridge: Cambridge University Press, 281–297.

Dara Shikuh. 2006. *Sirr-i Akbar* and *Majma' al-Bahrayn,* trans. M. Mahfuz-ul-Haq. Gurgaon: Hope India.

Dās, Rāmprasād, and Aśok Svāmī, eds. 2008 [V.S. 2063]. *Śrī Dādū Vāṇī.* Jaipur: Śrī Dādū Dayāl Mahāsabhā.
Dās, Śyāmsundar. 1956 [1930]. *Hindī Sāhitya.* Allahabad: Indian Press.
———.1962 [1928]. *Kabīr Granthāvalī.* Banaras: Nāgarīpracāriṇī Sabhā.
Dasgupta, Surendranath. 1940, 1949. *A History of Indian Philosophy,* vols. 3–4. Cambridge: Cambridge University Press.
Das Gupta, Uma. 2004. *Rabindranath Tagore: A Biography.* Delhi: Oxford University Press.
De, S. K., ed. 2002 [1934]. *The Padyāvalī of Rūpa Gosvāmin.* Calcutta: Sanskrit Book Depot.
———. 1961. *Early History of the Vaisnava Faith and Movement in Bengal from Sanskrit and Bengali Sources.* Calcutta: K. L. Mukhopadhyay.
de Bruijn, Thomas 1996. "The Ruby Hidden in the Dust: Study of the Poetics of Malik Muḥammad Jāyasī's Padmāvat." Ph.D. dissertation, University of Leiden.
———. 2010. "Dialogism in a Medieval Center: The Case of the Avadhi Epics." In Orsini, ed., *Before the Divide,* 121–141.
———. 2012. *The Ruby in the Dust: Poetry and History in Padmāvat by the South Asian Sufi Poet Muḥammad Jāyasī.* Leiden: Leiden University Press.
de Bruijn, Thomas, and Allison Busch, eds. 2014. *Culture and Circulation: Literature in Motion in Early Modern India.* Leiden: E. J. Brill.
Dehejia, Vidya. 1988. *Slaves of the Lord: The Path of the Tamil Saints.* Delhi: Munshiram Manoharlal.
———. 1990. *Āṇṭāḷ and Her Path of Love: Poems of a Woman Saint from South India.* Albany: State University of New York Press.
Deleury, G. A. 1960. *The Cult of Viṭhobā.* Poona: Deccan College Postgraduate and Research Institute.
Delmonico, Neal. 1993. "Rūpa Gosvāmin: His Life, Family, and Early Vraja Commentators." *Journal of Vaishnava Studies* 1: 133–157.
Desai, Sangeeta. 2009. "Audience Is King: Audience as Performers in Seven-Day Ritual Narrations of the *Bhāgavata Purāṇa.*" Paper presented at the American Academy of Religion, Montreal, November 8.
Deshpande, Madhav M. 2010. "Pañca Gauḍa and Pañca Drāviḍa: Contested Borders or a Traditional Classification." *Studia Orientalia* 108: 29–58.
Deshpande, Prachi. 2007. *Creative Pasts: Historical Memory and Identity in Western India, 1700–1960.* New York: Columbia University Press.
Dharmavīr. *Kabīr ke Ālocak.* 1998 [1997]. Delhi: Vāṇī Prakāśan.
Ḍhauṅḍiyāl, Nandakiśor "Aruṇ." 1982. *Dr. Pītāmbar Datt Baḍthvāl: Saṃkṣipt Paricay.* Koṭdvār: Kālevar Press.
Dhere, Ramchandra Chintaman. 2011. *The Rise of a Folk God: Viṭṭhal of Pandharpur,* ed. and trans. Anne Feldhaus. New York: Oxford University Press. Originally published as *Śrīviṭṭhal: Ek Mahāsamanvay,* 1984. Pune: Śrīvidyā Prakāśan.

Digby, Simon. 1993. "Some Asian Wanderers in Seventeenth Century India: An Examination of Sources in Persian." *Studies in History*, n.s., 9: 247–264.

Dimock, Edward C., Jr., and Tony K. Stewart, eds. 1999. *Caitanya Caritāmṛta of Kṛṣṇadās Kavirāja: A Translation and Commentary*. Harvard Oriental Series. Cambridge, MA: Harvard University Press.

Dube, Lāltā Prasād. 1968. *Hindī Bhakta-Vārtā Sāhitya*. Dehradun: Sāhitya Sadan.

Dutta, Akshaykumar. 1987–1990 [1870–1882]. *Bhāratabarṣīẏa Upāsak-Sampradāẏ* Calcutta: Karuṇā Prakāśanī.

Dutta, Krishna, and Andrew Robinson. 1995. *Rabindranath Tagore: The Myriad-Minded Man*. London: Bloomsbury Press.

———. 1997. *Selected Letters of Rabindranath Tagore*. Cambridge: Cambridge University Press.

Dvivedi, Hazariprasad (Hazārīprasād Dvivedī). 1973 [1936]. *Sūr-Sāhitya*. New Delhi: Rājkamal Prakāśan.

———. 1991 [1940]. *Hindī Sāhitya kī Bhūmikā*. New Delhi: Rājkamal Prakāśan. Originally Bombay: Hindī Granth Karyālay. Reprint, 1997.

———. 1976 [1942]. *Kabīr (Kabīr ke Vyaktitva, Sāhitya, aur Dārśanik Vicāroṅ kī Ālocanā)*. New Delhi: Rājkamal Prakāśan.

———. 1950. *Nāth Sampradāy*. Allahabad: Hindustani Academy.

———. 1952. *Madhyakālīn Dharma-Sādhanā*. Allahabad: Sāhitya Bhavan.

———. 1964. *Hindī Sāhitya: Uskā Udbhav aur Vikās*. Delhi: Attarcand Kapūr and Sons.

———. 1981a [1978]. "Sūr-kāvya: Preraṇā aur Srot." In Dvivedī, ed., *Hazārīprasād Dvivedī Granthāvalī*, 4: 147–160.

———. 1981b. *Hazārīprasād Dvivedī Granthāvalī*, ed. Mukund Dvivedī. New Delhi: Rājkamal Prakāśan.

———.1994. *Hazarīprasād Dvivedī ke Patra*, vol. 1, ed. Mukund Dvivedī. New Delhi: Indirā Gāndhī Rāṣṭrīya Kalā Kendra.

Eck, Diana L. 1982. *Banaras: City of Light*. New York: Alfred A. Knopf.

———. 2012. *India: A Sacred Geography*. New York: Harmony Books.

Elkman, Stuart Mark. 1986. *Jīva Gosvāmin's Tattvasandarbha: A Study on the Philosophical and Sectarian Development of the Gauḍīya Vaiṣṇava Movement*. Delhi: Motilal Banarsidass.

Elliott, H. M. 1967 [1867–1877]. *The History of India, as Told by Its Own Historians*, ed. John Dowson. 8 volumes. Aligarh: Progressive.

Entwistle, Alan W. 1987. *Braj, Centre of Krishna Pilgrimage*. Groningen: Egbert Forsten.

———. 1990. "Māhātmya Sources on the Pilgrimage Circuit of Mathurā." In Hans Bakker, ed., *The History of Sacred Places in India as Reflected in Traditional Literature: Papers on Pilgrimage in South Asia*. Leiden: E. J. Brill, 5–28.

Ernst, Carl W. 2004 [1992]. *Eternal Garden: Mysticism, History, and Politics at a South Asian Sufi Center*, 2nd ed. Delhi: Oxford University Press.

Farquhar, J. N. 1912 [1911]. *A Primer of Hinduism*. London: Oxford University Press.
———. 1913. *The Crown of Hinduism*. London: Oxford University Press.
———. 1915. *Modern Religious Movements in India*. New York: Macmillan.
———. 1920. *An Outline of the Religious Literature of India*. London: Oxford University Press.
Feldhaus, Anne. 1986. "Maharashtra as a Holy Land: A Sectarian Tradition." *Bulletin of the School of Oriental and African Studies* 49: 532–548.
———. 2003. *Connected Places: Region, Pilgrimage, and Geographical Imagination in India*. New York: Palgrave Macmillan.
Filliozat, Jean. 1962. "Les Dates du Bhāgavatapurāṇa et du Bhāgavata-māhātmya." In Ernest Bender, ed., *Indological Studies in Honor of W. Norman Brown*. New Haven: American Oriental Society, 70–77.
Fisher, Elaine. 2012. "Just Like Kālidāsa: The Śākta Intellectuals of Seventeenth-Century South India." *Journal of Hindu Studies* 5: 172–192.
———. 2013. "A New Public Theology. Sanskrit and Society in Seventeenth-Century South India." Ph.D. dissertation, Columbia University.
Freeman, Rich. 2003. "Genre and Society: The Literary Culture of Premodern Kerala." In Pollock, ed., *Literary Cultures in History*, 437–500.
Friedlander, Peter. 2014. "A Fountain in Mid-Air: Kabīr's Songs, Traditions, and Translations." Unpublished manuscript.
Fritz, John. 2014. "Krishnadevaraya in the Popular Imagination." In Verghese, ed., *Krishnadevaraya and His Times*, 375–402.
Fuller, Christopher. 2004 [1992]. *The Camphor Flame: Popular Hinduism and Society in India*. Princeton: Princeton University Press.
Gadon, Elinor. 1987. "Note on the Frontispiece." In Schomer and McLeod, eds., *Sants*, 415–421.
Gandhi, Indira. 1964. Letter to V. Raghavan, August 25. Chennai: V. Raghavan Centre for Performing Arts.
Ghosh, Pika. 2005. *Temple to Love: Architecture and Devotion in Seventeenth-Century Bengal*. Bloomington: Indiana University Press.
Ghosh, Sisir. 1985–1911. *Amiya Nimai Carit*. Calcutta: Bishvabani Prakashini.
———. 1897–1898. *Lord Gauranga, or Salvation for All*. Calcutta: Golap Lal Ghose, "Patrika" Office.
Ghurye, G. S. 1964 [1953]. *Indian Sadhus*, 2nd ed. Bombay: Popular Prakashan.
Gokulnāth [attrib.]. 1970 [V.S. 2027; orig. 1948]. *Caurāsī Vaiṣṇavan kī Vārtā [Tīn Janma kī Līlā Bhāvanā Vālī]*, ed. Dvārkādās Parīkh. Mathura: Śrī Bajarang Pustakālay.
———. 1951–1953. *Do Sau Bāvan Vaiṣṇavan kī Vārtā*, ed. Brajbhūṣaṇ Śarmā and Dvārkādās Parīkh, Kankaroli: Śuddhādvaita Academy.
———. 1965. *Dosau Bāvan Vaiṣṇavan kī Vārtā*, ed. Niranjandev Śarmā. Mathura: Bajaraṅg Pustakālay.

———. 1967 [V.S. 2024]. *Caurāsī Baiṭhak Carit.* Mathura: Śrī Govardhan Granthamālā Kāryālay.

Goldstone, Jack A. 1998. "The Problem of the 'Early Modern' World." *Journal of the Economic and Social History of the Orient* 41: 249–284.

Gonda, Jan. 1977. "Bhakti." In Gonda, *Medieval Religious Literature in Sanskrit.* Wiesbaden: Otto Harrassowitz, 10–38.

Gopāl Bhaṭṭ [misattributed to Sanatān Goswāmī]. 2005. *Haribhaktivilāsa,* with an English translation by Bhūmipati Dāsa. 5 vols. Vrindaban: Rasbihari Lal Sons.

Gosvāmī, Haridās. 1914. *Bāṅgālīr Ṭhākur Śrī Gaurāṅga.* Bhopal: n.p.

Goswami, Shrivatsa. 1996. "Govinda Darśana: Lotus in Stone." In Case, ed., *Govindadeva,* 269–277.

———. Forthcoming. "Gopal Bhatt: Carrier of Bhakti to the North." In Williams, Malhotra, and Hawley, eds., *Early Modern Literatures in North India.*

Goyal, Usha. 1990. *Caitanya-Sampradāy kā Brajbhāṣā-kāvya.* New Delhi: National Publishing House.

Granoff, Phyllis. 2003. "Pilgrimage as Revelation: Śaṅkaradeva's Journey to Jagannātha Purī." In Phyllis Granoff and Koichi Shinohara, eds., *Pilgrims, Patrons, and Place: Localizing Sanctity in Asian Religions.* Vancouver: University of British Columbia Press, 181–202.

———. 2005. "Playing with the Winds: The Place of Yoga in the Vaisnava Movement of Śankaradeva of Assam." *Journal of Vaishnava Studies* 14: 155–171.

Grierson, George A. 1889. *The Modern Vernacular Literature of Hindustan.* Calcutta: Asiatic Society.

———. 1907. "Modern Hinduism and Its Debt to the Nestorians." *Journal of the Royal Asiatic Society* 39, no. 2: 311–335.

———. 1908. *The Monotheistic Religion of Ancient India and Its Descendant, the Modern Hindu Doctrine of Faith.* Oxford: Third International Congress for the History of Religions.

———. 1909–1910. "Gleanings from the Bhakta-Mala." *Journal of the Royal Asiatic Society* 1909: 607–644; 1910: 87–109, 269–306.

———. 1910. "Bhakti-Mārga." In James Hastings, ed., *Encyclopaedia of Religion and Ethics.* Edinburgh: T. and T. Clark, 2: 539–551.

———. 1920 [orally, 1918]. "The Popular Literature of Northern India." *Bulletin of the School of Oriental Studies* 1: 87–122.

Growse, Frederic Salmon. 1883 [1874]. *Mathurá: A District Memoir,* 3rd ed. Allahabad: North-Western Provinces and Oudh Government Press.

Guha, Ranajit. 1989. "Dominance without Hegemony and Its Historiography." In Ranajit Guha, ed., *Subaltern Studies VI: Writings on South Asian History and Society.* Delhi: Oxford University Press, 210–309.

Guha, Sumit. 2007. "Northerners in the Bharuds of Ekanatha." Paper presented at the conference "Circulatory Processes between North and South India in the Early Modern Period," Columbia University, January 28.

———. 2009. "The Frontiers of Memory: What the Marathas Remembered of Vijayanagara." *Modern Asian Studies* 43: 269–288.

Guptā, Āśā. 1970. *Madhyayugīn Saguṇ aur Nirguṇ Hindī Sāhitya kā Tulnātmak Adhyayan*. Allahabad: Hindī Sāhitya Sammelan.

Gupta, Dīndayāl. 1970. *Aṣṭachāp aur Vallabh Sampradāy*, vol. 1. Allahabad: Hindi Sāhitya Sammelan.

Gupta, Kiśorīlāl, ed. 1965. *Nāgarīdās: Granthāvalī*. Varanasi: Nāgarīpracāriṇī Sabhā.

Gupta, Mātāprasād. 1965. *Tulsīdās*. Allahabad: Allahabad University Hindi Department.

———. 1985 [1969]. *Kabīr Granthāvalī*. Allahabad: Sāhitya Bhavan.

Gupta, Murārī. 2006. *Kṛṣṇacaitanyacaritāmṛta*, trans. Bhakti Vedanta Bhagavata. Brindavan: Ras Biharilal and Sons.

Gupta, R. D. 1969. "Priyā Dās, Author of the *Bhaktirasabodhinī*." *Bulletin of the School of Oriental and African Studies* 32: 57–70.

Gupta, Ravi M., and Kenneth R. Valpey, eds. 2013. *The Bhāgavata Purāṇa: Sacred Text and Living Tradition*. New York: Columbia University Press.

Gupta, Sanjukta. 2006. *Advaita Vedānta and Vaiṣṇavism: The Philosophy of Madhusūdana Sarasvatī*. London: Routledge.

Gurumurthy, Prameela. 1994. *Kathakalaksepa: A Study*. Madras: International Society for the Investigation of Ancient Civilizations.

Haberman, David L. 1988. *Acting as a Way of Salvation: A Study of Rāgānugā Bhakti Sādhana*. New York: Oxford University Press.

———. 2003. *The Bhaktirasāmṛtasindhu of Rūpa Gosvāmin*. New Delhi: Indira Gandhi National Centre for the Arts.

Habib, Irfan. 1967 . Introduction to Elliott, *History of India, as Told by Its Own Historians*.

———. 1996. "A Documentary History of the Gosā'ins (Gosvāmīs) of the Caitanya Sect at Vṛndāvana." In Case, ed., *Govindadeva*, 131–160.

———. 2009. "Braj Itihas Dhara." Paper presented at the Braj Mahotsav, Indira Gandhi National Centre for the Arts, New Delhi, November 24.

———. 2010–2011. "Braj Bhūm in Mughal Times." In Irfan Habib, ed., *Proceedings of the Indian Historical Congress, Seventeenth Session*. Aligarh: Aligarh Historians Society, 292–308.

———. 2011. "From Ariṭh to Rādhākund: The History of a Braj Village in Mughal Times." *Indian Historical Review* 38: 211–224.

Hacker, Paul. 1995 [1964]. "On Śaṅkara and Advaitism," trans. J. L. Mehta. In Wilhelm Halbfass, ed., *Philology and Confrontation: Paul Hacker on Traditional and Modern Vedanta*. Albany: State University of New York Press, 27–32.

Halbfass, Wilhelm. 1988. *India and Europe: An Essay in Understanding*. Albany: State University of New York Press.

Hansen, Kathryn. 1996. "Performing Identities: Tyagaraja Music Festivals in North America." *South Asia Research* 16: 155–174.

Hara, Minoru. 1964. “Note on Two Sanskrit Religious Terms: Bhakti and Śraddhā.” *Indo-Iranian Journal* 7: 124–145.
Hardy, Friedhelm. 1974. “Mādhavêndra Purī: A Link between Bengal Vaiṣṇavism and South Indian Bhakti.” *Journal of the Royal Asiatic Society,* facs. 1: 23–41.
———. 1983. *Viraha-Bhakti: The Early History of Kṛṣṇa Devotion in South India.* Delhi: Oxford University Press.
Hare, James P. 2007a. “A Contested Community: Priyādās and the Re-imagining of Nābhādās’s *Bhaktamāl.*” *Sikh Formations: Religion, Culture, Theory* 3: 185–198.
———. 2007b. “Garlanding Hinduism: Nabhadas’s *Bhaktamāl* in the Colonial Context.” Paper presented at the American Academy of Religion, San Diego, November 17.
———. 2011. “The Garland of Devotees: Nābhādās’s *Bhaktamāl* and Modern Hinduism.” Ph.D. dissertation, Columbia University.
———. 2013. “Nabhadas’s *Bhaktamāl* and Manuscript Culture.” In Bangha, ed., *Bhakti beyond the Forest,* 73–89.
Harirāy [attrib.]. 1905. *Śrī Govardhannāthjī ke Prākaṭya kī Vārtā,* ed. Mohanlāl Viṣṇulāl Paṇḍyā. Bombay: Sri Venkateshwar Press.
———. 2007 [V.S. 2064]. *Śrīnāthjī kī Prākaṭya Vārtā.* Nathdvara: Vidyāvibhāg Mandir Maṇḍal.
Hastings, James M. 2002. “Poets, Sants, and Warriors: The Dadu Panth, Religious Change, and Identity Formation in Jaipur State circa 1562–1860 CE.” Ph.D. dissertation, University of Wisconsin–Madison.
Hatcher, Brian A. 2006. “Remembering Rammohian: An Essay on the (Re-)Emergence of Modern Hinduism.” *History of Religions* 46: 50–80.
———. 2011a. “Father, Son, and Holy Text: Rabindranath Tagore and the Upaniṣads.” *Journal of Hindu Studies* 4: 119–143.
———. 2011b. *Hindu Widow Marriage: Ishvarchandra Vidyasagar.* New York: Columbia University Press.
Hawley, John Stratton. 1981. In association with Shrivatsa Goswami. *At Play with Krishna: Pilgrimage Dramas from Brindavan.* Princeton: Princeton University Press.
———. 1983. *Krishna, the Butter Thief.* Princeton: Princeton University Press.
———. 1984a. “The Music in Faith and Morality.” *Journal of the American Academy of Religion* 52: 243–262.
———. 1984b. *Sūr Dās: Poet, Singer, Saint.* Seattle: University of Washington Press.
———. 1988. “Bhakti.” In Ainslie T. Embree et al., eds., *Encyclopedia of Asian History.* New York: Charles Scribner’s Sons, 1: 154–157.
———. 2005. *Three Bhakti Voices: Mirabai, Surdas, and Kabir in Their Time and Ours.* Delhi: Oxford University Press.
———. 2006 [1993]. “Militant Hinduism: Ayodhya and the Momentum of Hindu Nationalism.” In J. S. Hawley and Vasudha Narayanan,

eds. *The Life of Hinduism*. Berkeley: University of California Press, 257–265.

———. 2007. "The Bhakti Movement—Since When?" *Journal of the Indian Council of Philosophical Research* 24: 69–90.

———. 2009a. "The *Bhāgavata Māhātmya* in Context." In Heidi R. M. Pauwels, ed., *Patronage and Popularisation, Pilgrimage and Procession: Channels of Transcultural Translation and Transmission in Early Modern South Asia. Papers in Honor of Monika Horstmann*. Wiesbaden: Harrassowitz, 81–100.

———. 2009b. *The Memory of Love: Sūrdās Sings to Krishna*. New York: Oxford University Press.

———. 2009c. "Performing the *Bhagavata Purana:* The Great Prescription." Paper presented at the American Academy of Religion, Montreal, November 8.

———. 2009d. "Sanātana Dharma as the Twentieth Century Began: Two Textbooks, Two Worlds." In Banerjee-Dube and Dube, eds., *Ancient to Modern*, 312–336.

———. 2009e. "Seeing the Bhakti Movement." In Himanshu Prabha Ray, ed., *Archaeology and Text: The Temple in South Asia*. Delhi: Oxford University Press, 232–267.

———. 2010. "The Bhakti Movement in Early Modernity." Paper presented at the international seminar "Alternative Modernities: Views from Pre-colonial India," Banaras Hindu University, December 12.

———. 2011. "The Four *Sampradāyas:* Ordering the Religious Past in Mughal North India." In O'Hanlon and Washbrook, eds., "Religious Cultures in Early Modern India," 160–183.

———. 2012. "The Commonwealth of Love and Its Limits." Paper presented at the workshop "Religion, Conflict, and Accommodation in Indian History: The Medieval Period," Columbia University, September 28–29.

———. 2013a. "How Do the Gauḍīyas Belong? Kavikarṇapūra, Jaisingh II, and the Question of Sampradāy," *Journal of Hindu Studies* 6: 114–130.

———. 2013b. "How Vallabhacharya Met Krishnadevaraya." In Verghese, ed., *Krishnadevaraya and His Times*, 81–96.

———. 2013c. "Mughal Bhakti, a Response." *Journal of Hindu Studies* 6: 73–81.

———. Forthcoming-a. "Bhaṭṭs in Braj." In Williams, Malhotra, and Hawley, eds., *Early Modern Literatures in North India*.

———. Forthcoming-b. *Into Sūr's Ocean: Poetry, Context, and Commentary*. Harvard Oriental Series. Cambridge, MA: Harvard University Press.

Hawley, John Stratton, and Mark Juergensmeyer. 2004 [1988]. *Songs of the Saints of India*, 2nd rev. ed. Delhi: Oxford University Press.

Hawley, John Stratton, and Gurinder Singh Mann. 2008. "Mirabai in the *Pothi Prem Ambodh*." *Journal of Punjab Studies* 15, nos. 1–2: 199–226.

———. 2014. "Mirabai at the Court of Guru Gobind Singh." In de Bruijn and Busch, eds. *Culture and Circulation,* 107–138.

Haynes, Richard. 1974. "Svāmī Haridās and the Haridāsī Sampradāy." Ph.D. dissertation, University of Pennsylvania.

Hedayetullah, Muhammad. 1977. *Kabir: The Apostle of Hindu-Muslim Unity.* Delhi: Motilal Banarsidass.

Hegde, Rajaram. 2013. "Towards Understanding Bhakti Literature." Paper presented at the international seminar "Rethinking Bhakti," Kanakadasa Adhyayana Peeta, Mangalore University, March 29.

Hein, Norvin. 1972. *The Miracle Plays of Mathurā.* New Haven: Yale University Press.

———. 1976. "Caitanya's Ecstasies and the Theology of the Name." In Bardwell Smith, ed., *Hinduism: New Essays in the History of Religions.* Leiden: E. J. Brill.

Hermansen, Marcia K. 1997. "Religious Literature and the Inscription of Identity: The Sufi Tazkira Tradition in Muslim South Asia." *Muslim World* 87, nos. 3–4: 315–329.

Hermansen, Marcia K., and Bruce B. Lawrence. 2002. "Indo-Persian Tazkiras as Memorative Communications." In David Gilmartin and Bruce B. Lawrence, eds., *Beyond Hindu and Turk: Rethinking Religious Identities in Islamicate South Asia.* New Delhi: India Research Press, 149–175.

Hess, Linda. 1987. "Three Kabir Collections." In Schomer and McLeod, eds., *Sants,* 111–142

———. 2009. "Fighting over Kabir's Dead Body." In Banerjee-Dube and Dube, eds., *Ancient to Modern,* 171–206.

Hiranmay. 1959. *Hindī aur Kannaḍa meṅ Bhakti-Andolan kā Tulnātmak Adhyayan.* Agra: Vinod Pustak Mandir.

Hobsbawm, Eric, and Terence Ranger, eds. 1983. *The Invention of Tradition.* Cambridge: Cambridge University Press.

Holdrege, Barbara A. 2014. *Bhakti and Embodiment: Fashioning Divine Bodies and Devotional Bodies in Kṛṣṇa Bhakti.* New York: Routledge.

Hopkins, Steven. Forthcoming. "Bodies of Desire, Bodies of Lament: Marking Emotion in a South Indian Vaishnava Messenger Poem." In Barbara A. Holdrege and Karen Pechilis, eds., *Refiguring the Body: Embodiment in South Asian Religions.* Albany: State University of New York Press.

Horstmann, Monika. 1983. *Crossing the Ocean of Existence: Braj Bhāṣā Religious Poetry from Rajasthan.* Wiesbaden: Otto Harrassowitz.

———. 1986. *Symbiotic Antinomy: The Social Organization of a North Indian Sect.* Canberra: Australian National University.

———. 1990. "Die Kriegermönsche Rajasthans: Jai Singh II. und das Bālānand-Problem." In Werner Diem and Abdoljaved Falaturi, eds., vol. 24, *Deutscher Orientalistentag . . . 1988 in Köln: Ausgewälte Vorträge.* Stuttgart: Franz Steiner, 478–490.

———. 1999. In collaboration with Heike Bill. *In Favor of Govindadevji: Historical Documents relating to a Deity of Vrindaban and Eastern Rajasthan*. New Delhi: Indira Gandhi National Centre for the Arts.
———. 2000a. "The Flow of Grace: Food and Feast in the Hagiography and History of the Dādūpanth," *Zeitschrift der Deutschen Morgenländischen Gesellschaft* 150: 513–566.
———. 2000b. "Warrior Ascetics in 18th Century Rajasthan and the Religious Policy of Jai Singh II." In M. K. Gautam and G. H. Schokker, eds., *Bhakti in Current Research, 1982–85*. Lucknow: Indo-European, 43–55.
———. 2002a. "Hazārīprasād Dvivedī's Kabīr." In Horstmann, ed., *Images of Kabīr*. Delhi: Manohar, 115–126.
———, ed. 2002b. *Images of Kabīr*. Delhi: Manohar.
———. 2002c. "The Rāmānandīs of Galtā (Jaipur, Rajasthan)." In Lawrence A. Babb, Varsha Joshi, and Michael W. Meister, eds., *Multiple Histories: Culture and Society in the Study of Rajasthan*. Jaipur: Rawat Publications, 141–197.
———. 2003. "Sectarian Disputes at Jaisingh's Court." Paper presented at the conference "Jaisingh's Jaipur: Scientific, Religious, and Artistic Mediations at Court," Columbia University, February 7–9.
———, ed. 2006a. *Bhakti in Current Research, 2001–2003: Proceedings of the Ninth International Conference on Early Devotional Literature in New Indo-Aryan Languages, Heidelberg, 23–26 July 2003*. Delhi: Manohar.
———.2006b. "Dādūpanthī Anthologies of the Eighteenth and Nineteenth Centuries." In Horstmann, ed., *Bhakti in Current Research, 2001–2003*, 163–177.
———. 2006c. *Visions of Kingship in the Twilight of Mughal Rule*. Amsterdam: Royal Netherlands Academy of Arts and Sciences.
———. 2009. *Der Zusammenhalt der Welt: Religiöse Herrschaftslegitimation und Religionspolitik Mahārāja Savāī Jaisinghs (1700–1743)*. Wiesbaden: Harrassowitz.
———. 2011. "Theology and Statecraft." *South Asian History and Culture* 2: 184–204.
———. 2012. "Approaching Sant Satire." In Horstmann and Pauwels, eds., *Indian Satire in the Period of First Modernity*, 95–115.
———. Forthcoming. "Power and Status: Ramanandi Warrior Ascetics in 18th-Century Rajasthan." In Peter Flügel and Gustaaf Houtman, eds., *Asceticism and Power in South and Southeast Asia*. London: Routledge.
———. See also Thiel-Horstmann, Monika.
Horstmann, Monika, and Anand Mishra. 2013. "Vaiṣṇava Sampradāys on the Importance of Ritual: A Comparison of the Two Contemporaneous Approaches by Viṭṭhalanātha and Jīv Gosvāmī." In Bangha, ed., *Bhakti beyond the Forest*, 155–176.

Horstmann, Monika, and Heidi R. M. Pauwels, eds. 2012. *Indian Satire in the Period of First Modernity*. Wiesbaden: Harrassowitz.

Hoyland, J. S., and S. N. Banerjee. 1922. *The Commentary of Father Monserrate, S. J., on His Journey to the Court of Akbar*. London: Oxford University Press.

Hudson, D. Dennis. 2009. *Krishna's Mandala: Bhagavata Religion and Beyond*, ed. J. S. Hawley. Delhi: Oxford University Press.

Hunashal, S. M. 1947. *The Lingayat Movement: A Social Revolution in Karnatak*. Dharwar: Karnatak Sahitya Mandira.

Hussain, Hamid, ed. 2007. *Sufism and Bhakti Movement: Eternal Relevance*. New Delhi: ManakPublications.

Iraqi, Shahabuddin. 1985. *Rajjabdās kī Sarbaṅgī: The Sarbangi of Rajjabdas (A Dadupanthi Source of the 17th Century)*. Aligarh: Granthayan.

———. 2009. *Bhakti Movement in Medieval India: Social and Political Perspectives*. Aligarh: Centre of Advanced Study, Department of History.

Irvine, William, trans. 1990 [1907]. *Mogul India, 1653–1708, or, Storia do Mogor by Niccolao Manucci, Venetian*. 4 vols. New Delhi: Low Price Publications.

Jackson, William J. 1998. *Songs of Three Great South Indian Saints*. Delhi: Oxford University Press.

———. 2013. "Kanakadasa Confronted Caste Prejudice." Paper submitted to the symposium "Rethinking Bhakti," Mangalore University, March 27–30.

Jacobsen, Knut et al., eds. 2011. *Brill's Encyclopedia of Hinduism*, vol. 3, *Society, Religious Specialists, Religious Traditions, Philosophy*. Leiden: Brill.

Jagannathan, Bharati. 2014. *Approaching the Divine: The Integration of Āḻvār Bhakti in Śrīvaiṣṇavism*. Delhi: Primus Books.

Jain, Meenakshi. 2002. *Medieval India: A Textbook for Class XI*. New Delhi: National Council of Educational Research and Training.

———. 2003. *Madhyakālīn Bhārat: Kakṣā 11 ke lie Pāṭhyapustak*. New Delhi: National Council of Educational Research and Training.

Jānā, Nareścandra. 1970. *Vṛndāvaner Chaya Gosvāmī*. Calcutta: Calcutta University.

Jesalpura, Shivlal, ed. 1981. *Narasiṃḥ Mehtā ni Kāvya Kṛtio*. Ahmedabad: Sahitya-Sanshodhan Prakashan.

———. 2003. *Songs of Narasinh Mehta*. Ahmedabad: Sahitya-Sanshodhan Prakashan.

Jhā, Narendra. 1978. *Bhaktamāl: Pāṭhānuśīlan evam Vivecan*. Bhagalpur: Bhāgalpur Viśvavidyālaya.

Jha, Subhadra. 1954. *The Songs of Vidyapati or Vidyāpati-Gīt-Sangrah*. Banaras: Motilal Banarsidass.

Jhaveri, Krishnalal Mohanlal. 1928. *Imperial Farmans (A.D. 1577 to A.D. 1804) Granted to the Ancestors of His Holiness the Tikayat* [sic] *Maharaj*. Bombay: News Printing Press.

Jijñāsu. 1984 [1959]. *Sant Pravar Ravidās Sāheb*. Lucknow: Bahujan Kalyāṇ Prakāśan.

Jīv Gosvāmī. 1995. *Śrī Tattva-sandarbha*, ed. and trans. Satya Nārāyaṇa Dāsa and Kuṇḍinī Dāsa. Brindavan: Jīva Institute for Vaisnava Studies.

Jordens, J. T. F. 1978. *Dayānanda Sarasvatī: His Life and Ideas*. Delhi: Oxford University Press.

Joshi, M. C. 1989. "Mathurā as an Ancient Settlement." In Srinivasan, ed., *Mathurā*, 165–170.

Juergensmeyer, Mark. 1991. *Radhasoami Reality: The Logic of a Modern Faith*. Princeton: Princeton University Press.

Kalburgi, M. M. 1970. *Śāsanagaḷalli Śivaśaraṇaru*. Dharwad: Karnataka University.

———. 1993. *Basavannanavara Vacanasamputa*. Bangalore: Kannada and Culture Department, Government of Karnataka.

Kalyāṇ. 1952. *Bhakta-Caritāṅk*. Gorakhpur: Gita Press.

Karve, Irawati. 1962. "On the Road: A Maharashtrian Pilgrimage," trans. D. D. Karve and Franklin Southworth. *Journal of Asian Studies* 22: 13–29.

Kasdorf, Katherine. 2006. "Images of Divinity and Legitimation: Rāmānuja, Hoysala Imperialism, and Sri Vaisnava Narrative." Unpublished paper, Columbia University.

Kaul, Jayalal. 1973. *Lal Ded*. New Delhi: Sahitya Akademi.

Kavikarṇapūra. 1950. *Śrī gauragaṇoddeśa-dīpikā*, ed. Bhaktiprajñān Keśav Gosvāmī. Mathura: Gauḍīya Maṭh.

———. 1966. *Caitanyacandrodayanāṭakam*, with a Hindi translation by Rāmcandra Miśra. Varanasi: Chaukhamba Sanskrit Series.

———. 2004. *Śrī Gaura-gaṇoddesśa dīpikā*, ed. Pūrṇaprajña Dāsa, trans. Bhūmipati Dāsa. Brindavan: Ras Biharilal Sons.

Kaviraj, Sudipta. 1995. *The Unhappy Consciousness: Bankimchandra Chattopadhyay and the Formation of Nationalist Discourse in India*. Delhi: Oxford University Press.

Keay, F. E. 1920. *A History of Hindi Literature*. Calcutta: Association Press.

———. 2003 [1920]. *A History of Hindi Literature*. New Delhi: Rupa.

———. 1931. *Kabir and His Followers*. Calcutta: Association Press.

Kennedy, Melville T. 1925. *The Chaitanya Movement: A Study of the Vaishṇavism of Bengal*. Calcutta: Association Press.

Keśavakāśmīrī Bhaṭṭ. 1989. *Kramadīpikā*, ed. and trans. [into Hindi] Sudhakar Malaviya. Varanasi: Krishnadas Academy.

———. 1994. *Kramadīpikā*, ed. Hariśaraṇ Upādhyay. Ajmer: Akhil Bhāratīya Śrīnimbārkācāryapīṭha Śikṣā Samiti.

Keune, Jon Milton. 2010. "Varkari Pilgrimages and Local Traditions in Marathwada (Central Maharashtra)." Paper presented at the Annual Meeting of the American Academy of Religion, Atlanta, November 1.

———. 2011. "Eknāth Remembered and Reformed: Bhakti, Brahmans, and Untouchables in Marathi Historiography." Ph.D. dissertation, Columbia University.

———. Forthcoming. "Eknāth in Context: The Literary, Social, and Political Milieus of an Early Modern Saint-Poet." *South Asian History and Culture* 6, no. 1.

Keune, Jon, and Christian Lee Novetzke. 2011. "Vārkarī Sampradāy." In Jacobsen et al., eds. *Brill's Encyclopedia of Hinduism*, 3: 616–626.

Khan, Dominique-Sila. 1997. *Conversions and Shifting Identities: Ramdev Pir and the Ismailis in Rajasthan*. Delhi: Manohar.

———. 2004. *Crossing the Threshold: Understanding Religious Identities in South Asia*. London: I. B. Tauris.

King, Christopher R. 1974. "The Nagari Pracharini Sabha (Society for the Promotion of the Nagari Script and Language) of Benares, 1893–1914: A Study in the Social and Political History of the Hindi Language." Ph.D. dissertation, University of Wisconsin–Madison.

———. 1994. *One Language, Two Scripts: The Hindi Movement in Nineteenth Century North India*. Bombay: Oxford University Press.

Kishwar, Madhu. 2013. "Modi Nama 1." Accessed March 30, 2013. www.manushi.in.

Knutson, Jesse Ross. 2011. "The Vernacular Cosmopolitan: Jayadeva's *Gītagovinda*." In Bronner, Cox, and McCrea, eds., *South Asian Texts in History*, 125–149.

Kolff, Dirk H. A. 1990. *Naukar, Rajput, and Sepoy: The Ethnohistory of the Military Labor Market in Hindustan, 1450–1850*. Cambridge: Cambridge University Press.

Kopf, David. 1979. *The Brahmo Samaj and the Shaping of the Modern Indian Mind*. Princeton: Princeton University Press.

Koselleck, Reinhart. 2002. *The Practice of Conceptual History: Timing History, Spacing Concepts*, trans. Todd Presner, Kerstin Behnke, and Jobst Welge. Stanford: Stanford University Press.

Kothari, Jayant. 1997. With Darshana Dholakia. *Narasiṃh Padmālā*. Ahmedabad: Gurjar.

Krishna, T. M. 2013. *A Southern Music: The Karnatik Story*. Noida: HarperCollins.

Laine, James W. 2003. *Shivaji: Hindu King in Islamic India*. Delhi: Oxford University Press.

Lal, Vinay. 2003. *The History of History: Politics and Scholarship in Modern India*. Delhi: Oxford University Press.

Lee, Joel. "Ravidas and Dalit Religion." Lecture given at Barnard College, Columbia University, April 25, 2013.

———. 2014. "Sweeping the Nation: Dalit Religion, Sanitation Labor, and Untouchability in Modern India." Ph.D. dissertation, Columbia University.

Lele, Jayant. 1980. "The *Bhakti* Movement in India: A Critical Introduction." *Journal of Asian and African Studies* 15, nos. 1–2: 1–15.

Lipner, Julius. 2010. *Hindus: Their Religious Beliefs and Practices,* 2nd rev. ed. London: Routledge.

Lochtefeld, James G. 1992. "Haridwara, Haradwara, Gangadwara: The Construction of Identity and Meaning in a Hindu Pilgrimage Place." Ph.D. dissertation, Columbia University.

———. 2004. "The Construction of the Kumbha Mela." *South Asian Popular Culture* 2: 103–126.

———. 2005. "The Saintly Chamar: Perspectives on the Life of Ravidas." In Zelliot and Mokashi-Punekar, eds., *Untouchable Saints,* 208–212.

———. 2010. *God's Gateway: Identity and Meaning in a Hindu Pilgrimage Place.* New York: Oxford University Press.

Lorenzen, David N., ed. 1991. *Bhakti Religion in North India: Community Identity and Political Action.* Albany: State University of New York Press.

———. ed. 1995. *Bhakti Religion in North India: Community Identity and Political Action.* Albany: State University of New York Press.

———. 1996. "Kabir's Most Popular Songs." In Lorenzen, *Praises to a Formless God: Nirguṇī Texts from North India.* Albany: State University of New York Press, 205–223.

———. 2004a. "Bhakti." In Sushil Mittal and Gene Thursby, eds., *The Hindu World.* New York: Routledge, 199–208.

———, ed. 2004b. *Religious Movements in South Asia, 600–1800.* Delhi: Oxford University Press.

Lorenzen, David N., Jadish Kumar, and Uma Thukral. 1991. *Kabir Legends and Anantadas's Kabir Parachai.* Albany: State University of New York Press.

Lutgendorf, Philip. 1991. *The Life of a Text: Performing the Rāmcaritmānas of Tulsidas.* Berkeley: University of California Press.

———. 1997. "Imagining Ayodhyā: Utopia and Its Shadows in a Hindu Landscape." *International Journal of Hindu Studies* 1: 19–54.

———. 2008. "The 'Mira Trope' in Mainstream Hindi Cinema. Three Examples from Notable Films." In Stefania Cavaliere, ed., *Gurumala: Papers in Honour of Shyam Manohar Pandey.* Annali: Rivista del Seminario di studi asiatici e del Seminario di studi africani/Istituto universitario orientale 68. Naples: Annali dell' Università degli Studi di Napoli L'Orientale, 123–143.

Lutjeharms, Rembert. 2009. "Splendor of Speech: The Theology of Kavikarṇapūra's Poetics." Ph.D. dissertation, University of Oxford.

Maclean, Kama. 2003. "Making the Colonial State Work for You: The Modern Beginnings of the Ancient Kumbha Mela in Allahabad." *Journal of Asian Studies* 62: 873–905.

———. 2007. "On the Modern Kumbh Mela." In Arvind Krishna Mehrotra, ed., *The Last Bungalow: Writings on Allahabad*. New Delhi: Penguin Books, 285–306.

Macnicol, Nicol. 1917. "Mysticism (Hindu)." In James Hastings, ed., *Encyclopaedia of Religion and Ethics*. Edinburgh: T. and T. Clark, 9: 1113–1117.

Majumdar, A. K. 1979 [1965]. *Bhakti Renaissance*. Bombay: Bharatiya Vidya Bhavan.

Majumdar, Bimanbehari. 1961. "The Bhāgavata Purāṇa and Its Influence in the Sixteenth Century." *Journal of the Bihar Research Society* 47, nos. 1–4: 381–393.

Malinar, Angelika. 2011. "Sampradāya." In Jacobsen et al., eds., *Brill's Encyclopedia of Hinduism*, 3: 156–164.

Mallinson, James. 2011. "Nāth Sampradāya." In Jacobsen et al., eds., *Brill's Encyclopedia of Hinduism*, 3: 409–428.

———. 2013. "Yogis in Mughal India." In Debra Diamond, ed., *Yoga: The Art of Transformation*. Washington: Freer Gallery of Art and Arthur M. Sackler Gallery, Smithsonian Institution, 69–83.

———. 2014. "The Yogis' Latest Trick." *Journal of the Royal Asiatic Society* 24, no. 1: 165–180.

Mallison, Francoise. 2011. "The Teaching of Braj, Gujarati, and Bardic Poetry at the Court of Kutch: The Bhuj Brajbhāṣā Pāṭhśālā (1749–1948)." In Pollock, ed., *Forms of Knowledge in Early Modern South Asia*, 171–182.

Mani, Braj Ranjan. 2005. *Debrahmanizing History: Dominance and Resistance in Indian Society*. Delhi: Manohar.

Mann, Gurinder Singh. 1996. *The Goindval Pothis: The Earliest Extant Source of the Sikh Canon*. Harvard Oriental Series. Cambridge, MA: Harvard University Press.

———. 2001. *The Making of Sikh Scripture*. New York: Oxford University Press.

———. 2004. *Sikhism*. Upper Saddle River, NJ: Prentice Hall.

———. 2010. "Guru Nanak's Life and Legacy: An Appraisal." *Journal of Punjab Studies* 17, nos. 1–2: 3–44.

———. 2012. "Guru Nanak's Life and Legacy: An Appraisal." In Anshu Malhotra and Farina Mir, eds., *Punjab Reconsidered: History, Culture, and Practice*. Delhi: Oxford University Press, 116–160.

———. 2014. "Early Textual Sources for Sikh Studies." Paper presented at the conference "Sikh Studies in the 21st Century," University of California, Santa Barbara, May 16.

Manohardās. 1953 [V.S. 2016]. *Sampradāyabodhinī*. Mathura: Kṛṣṇadās Bābā.

Manring, Rebecca Jane. 1989. "Kavikarṇapūra's *Gauragaṇoddeśadīpikā* (an Elucidation Regarding the Associates of Caitanya): A Translation and Preliminary Edition." M.A. thesis, University of Washington.

———. 2005. *Reconstructing Tradition: Advaita Ācārya and Gauḍīya Vaiṣṇavism at the Cusp of the Twentieth Century*. New York: Columbia University Press. McGregor, Ronald Stuart. 1973. *Nanddas: The Round Dance of Krishna and Uddhav's Message*. London: Luzac.
———. 1983. "The Dhyān-Mañjarī of Agradās." In Thiel-Horstmann, ed., *Bhakti in Current Research, 1979–1982*, 237–244.
———. 1984. *Hindi Literature from Its Beginnings to the Nineteenth Century*. Weisbaden: Otto Harrassowitz.
McLeod, W. H. 1980. *Early Sikh Tradition: A Study of the Janam-sākhīs*. Oxford: Clarendon Press.
Mehrotra, Arvind Krishna. 2011. *Songs of Kabir*. New York: New York Review of Books.
Menāriyā, Motilāl. 1999 [1958]. *Rājasthān kā Pingal Sāhitya: Rājasthān ke Kaviyoṅ dvārā racit Brajabhāṣā Sāhitya kā Itihās*. Jodhpur: Rājasthānī Granthāgār.
Michell, George. 1995. *Architecture and Art of Southern India*. Cambridge: Cambridge University Press.
———. 1996. "The Missing Sanctuary." In Case, *Govindadeva*, 115–122.
Miller, Barbara Stoler. 1977. *Love Song of the Dark Lord: Jayadeva's Gītagovinda*. New York: Columbia University Press.
Minhāj-i Sirāj. 1970 [1881]. *Ṭabaqāt-i Nāṣirī*, trans. H. G. Raverty. New Delhi: Oriental Books Reprint.
Minkowski, Christopher. 2011. "Advaita Vedānta in Early Modern History." *South Asian History and Culture* 2: 205–231.
Mishra, R. C., ed. 1992. *Sundar-Granthāvalī*. New Delhi: Kitābghar.
Mishra, Rameshwar (Rāmeśvar Miśra). 1989. *Madhyayugīn Hindī Sant Sāhitya aur Ravīndranāth*. Allahabad: Viśvavidyālay Prakāśan.
———, ed. 2008a. *Apnī Bāt: Viśvabhāratī Patrikā: Hazārīprasād Dvivedī—1942–47 Sampādakīya evam Anyanya Ṭipaṇiyāṅ*. Calcutta: Viśvabhāratī Granthanvibhāg.
———. 2008b. "Bhitticitra: Sāhityik Pṛṣṭibhūmi." In Rameshwar Mishra, ed., *Śāntiniketan kā Hindī-Bhavan—Hajārīprasād Dvivedī: Janmaśatī Prakāśan*. Calcutta: Viśvabhāratī Granthanvibhāg, 176–185.
Mishra, Umesha. 1940. *Nimbārka School of Vedānta*. Allahabad: University of Allahabad.
Miśra, Gaṇeśvihārī, Śyāmvihārī Miśra, and Śukdevvihārī Miśra. 1910. *Hindī-Navaratna, arthāt Hindī-Sahitya ke Nav Sarvottam Kavi*. Allahabad: Hindī-Granth-Pracārak Maṇḍalī.
———. 1913 [V.S. 1970]. *Miśrabandhuvinod athavā Hindī Sāhitya kā Itihās tathā Kavi-Kīrttani*. 3 vols. Khaṇḍavā: Hindī Granth-Prasārak Maṇḍalī.
———. 1956 [1913]. *Miśrabandhuvinod athavā Hindī Sāhitya kā Itihās tathā Kavi-Kīrttan*. 5th ed. Lucknow: Gangā-Granthāgār.
Mītal, Prabhudayāl. 1966. *Braj kā Sāṅskṛtik Itihās*, parts 1–2. Delhi: Rājkamal Prakāśan.

———. 1968a. *Brajasth Ballabh Sampradāy kā Itihās.* Mathura: Sāhitya Saṅsthān.

———. 1968b. *Braj ke Dharma-Sampradāyoṅ kā Itihās.* Delhi: National Publications House.

Mitr, Tarini Charan, and William Price. 1827. *Hindee and Hindoostanee Selections: to which are prefixed the Rudiments of Hindoostanee and Braj Bhakha Grammar.* Calcutta: Hindoostanee Press.

Mohammad, Malik. 1964. *Ālvār Bhaktoṅ kā Tamil-Prabandham aur Hindī Kṛṣṇa-Kāvya.* Agra: Vinod Pustak Mandir.

Moin, A. Azfar. 2012. *The Millennial Sovereign: Sacred Kingship and Sainthood in Islam.* New York: Columbia University Press.

Monius, Anne E. 2013. "Linguistic Anxiety and Geographical Aspiration in the Tamiḻ Śaiva Literary World." Paper presented at the Annual Meeting of the American Academy of Religion, Baltimore, November 26.

Morgenstein Fuerst, Ilyse R. 2012. "Religions of Empire: Islamicate Texts, Imperial Taxomonies, and South Asian Definitions of Religion." Ph.D. dissertation, University of North Carolina at Chapel Hill.

Mozoomdar, P. C. 1882. *The Faith and Progress of the Brahmo Samaj.* Calcutta: Calcutta Central Press.

Mukherjee, Prabhat. 1981 [1940]. *The History of Medieval Vaishnavism in Orissa.* New Delhi: Asian Educational Services.

Mukherjee, Tarapada, and Irfan Habib. 1988. "Akbar and the Temples of Mathura and Its Environs." In *Proceedings of the Indian History Congress,* 48th Session. Panaji: Goa University, 234–250.

———. 1989. "The Mughal Administration and the Temples of Vrindavan during the Reigns of Jahangir and Shahjahan." In *Proceedings of the Indian History Congress,* 49th Session. Dharwad: Karnataka University, 287–300.

———. 1990. "Land Rights in the Reign of Akbar: The Evidence of the Sale-Deeds of Vrindaban and Aritha." In *Proceedings of the Indian History Congress,* 50th Session. Gorakhpur: Gorakhpur University, 236–255.

Mukhopādhyāy, Praṇati. 1999. *Kshitimohan Sen o Ardhaśatābdīr Śāntiniketan.* Calcutta: Paścimabaṅga Bāṃlā Ākādemi.

———. ed. 2009 [2003]. *Kṣitimohan Sen: Sādhak o Sādhanā.* Koltaka: Punaśca.

Mullatti, Leela. 1989. *The Bhakti Movement and the Status of Women: A Case Study of Virasaivism.* New Delhi: Abhinav Publications.

Mumme, Patricia Y. 1997. "History, Myth, and Śrīvaiṣṇava Hagiography: Lessons from Biblical Scholarship." *Journal of Vaishnava Studies* 5: 157–184.

Murthy, Yenneti Veda Sesha Satya Narayana. 1991. *A Comparative Study of Kabir and Vemana as Social Reformers.* Madras: Pragati Prakasan.

Nābhādās. See Jhā, Narendra; "Rūpkalā," Sītārāmśaraṇ Bhagavānprasād.

Nagaraj, D. R. 1993. *The Flaming Feet.* Bangalore: South Forum Press.

———. 2010. *The Flaming Feet and Other Essays*, ed. P. D. Chandra Shobhi. Delhi: Permanent Black.

Nāhar, Ratibhānu Siṃh. n.d. [1968?]. *Bhakti-Andolan kā Adhyayan*. Allahabad: Kitāb Mahal.

Nahta, Agar Chand, ed. 1965. *Rāghavdās kṛt Bhaktamāl*. Jodhpur: Rajasthan Oriental Research Institute.

Naikar, Basavaraj. 2001. *Kanakadasa: The Golden Servant of Lord Hari*. Delhi: National Book Trust.

Naim, C. M. 1974. "*Ghazal* and *Taghazzul:* The Lyric, Personal and Social." In Edward C. Dimock, Jr., et al., eds., *The Literatures of India: An Introduction*. Chicago: University of Chicago Press, 181–197.

Nandakumar, Prema. 2003. "The Bhakti Movement in South India" and "The Bhakti Movement in North India." In R. Balasubramanian, ed. *Theistic Vedānta,* vol. 2, part 3, 790–904.

Nandimukh, S. C. 1979 [1942]. *A Handbook of Vīraśaivism*. Delhi: Motilal Banarsidass.

Narayana Rao, Velcheru. 1990. Assisted by Gene H. Roghair. *Śiva's Warriors: The Basava Purāṇa of Pālkuriki Somanātha*. Princeton: Princeton University Press.

Narayana Rao, Velcheru, and David Shulman. 2005. *God on the Hill: Temple Poems from Tirupati*. New York: Oxford University Press.

Narayana Rao, Velcheru, David Shulman, and Sanjay Subrahmanyam. 1992. *Symbols of Substance: Court and State in Nāyaka-Period Tamilnadu*. Delhi: Oxford University Press.

———. 2003. *Textures of Time: Writing History in South India, 1600–1800*. New York: Other Press.

Narayanan, Vasudha. 2007. "'With the Earth as a Lamp and the Sun as the Flame': Lighting Devotion in South India." *International Journal of Hindu Studies* 11: 227–253.

———. 2011. "Śrīvaiṣṇavism." In Jacobsen et al., eds., *Brill's Encyclopedia of Hinduism,* 3: 556–573.

Natarajan, B., B. Venkataraman, and B. Ramachandran. 1988–1990. *Sri Krishna Leela Tarangini by Narayana Tirtha*., 2 vols. Madras: Mudgala Trust.

Nath, R. 1996. "Śrī Govindadeva's Itinerary from Vṛndāvana to Jayapura, c. 1534–1727." In Case, ed., *Govindadeva*, 161–184.

New Catalogus Catalogorum: An Alphabetical Register of Sanskrit and Allied Works and Authors. 1949–. Chennai: University of Madras.

Nicholson, Andrew J. 2010. *Unifying Hinduism: Philosophy and Identity in Indian Intellectual History*. New York: Columbia University Press.

Niemann, Grahame. 1980. "The Bhāgavat Daśam Skandh of Bhūpati." *IAVRI Bulletin* 8: 3–9.

———. 1983. "Bhūpati's *Bhāgavat* and the Hindi *Bhāgavat* Genre." In Thiel-Horstmann, ed., *Bhakti in Current Research, 1979–1982*, 257–267.

Novetzke, Christian Lee. 2007. "Bhakti and Its Public." *International Journal of Hindu Studies* 11: 255–272.

———. 2008. *Religion and Public Memory: A Cultural History of Saint Namdev in India*. New York: Columbia University Press.

———. 2011. "The Brahmin Double: The Brahminical Construction of Anti-Brahminism and Anti-caste Sentiment in the Religious Cultures of Precolonial Maharashtra." In O'Hanlon and Washbrook, eds., "Religious Cultures in Early Modern India," 232–252.

———. 2014a. "The Language of Men in the World of Gods: Religion, Vernacularization, and Everyday Life in Medieval India." Paper presented at the workshop "Bhakti Literature between the Elite and the Popular," Harvard University, May 19.

———. 2014b. "The Vernacular Millennium: Vernacularization, Religion, and Everyday Life in Medieval India." Précis.

———. Forthcoming. *The Vernacular Millennium: Vernacularization, Religion, and Everyday Life in Medieval India*. New York: Columbia University Press.

Nussbaum, Martha C. 2007. *The Clash Within: Democracy, Religious Violence, and India's Future*. Cambridge, MA: Harvard University Press.

O'Connell, Joseph T. 1973. "The Word 'Hindu' in Gauḍīya Vaiṣṇava Texts." *Journal of the American Oriental Society* 93: 340–344.

Offredi, Mariola, ed. *The Banyan Tree: Essays on Early Literature in New Indo-Aryan Languages*. 2 vols. Delhi: Manohar and Venice: Department of Eurasiatic Studies, University of Venice.

O'Hanlon, Rosalind. 2010a. "Letters Home: Banaras Pandits and the Maratha Regions in Early Modern India." *Modern Asian Studies* 44, no. 2: 201–240.

———. 2010b. "The Social Worth of Scribes: Brahmins, Kāyasthas, and the Social Order in Early Modern India." *Indian Social and Economic History Review* 47, no. 2: 563–595.

———. 2011. "Speaking from Siva's Temple: Banaras Scholar Households and the Brahman 'Ecumene' of Mughal India." *South Asian History and Culture* 2, no. 2: 253–277.

———. 2013a. "Contested Conjunctures: Brahman Communities and 'Early Modernity' in India." *American Historical Review* 118, no. 3: 765–787.

———. 2013b. "Performance in a World of Paper: Puranic Histories and Social Communication in Early Modern India." *Past and Present* 219: 87–126.

O'Hanlon, Rosalind, and Christopher Minkowski. 2008. "What Makes People Who They Are? Pandit Networks and the Problem of Livelihoods in Early Modern Western India." *Indian Economic and Social History Review* 45: 381–416.

O'Hanlon, Rosalind, and David Washbrook, eds. 2011. "Religious Cultures in Early Modern India: New Perspectives." Special issue, *South Asian History and Culture* 2: 160–183.

Okita, Kiyokazu. 2014. *Hindu Theology in Early Modern South Asia: The Rise of Devotionalism and the Politics of Genealogy*. Oxford: Oxford University Press.

Omvedt, Gail. 2008. *Seeking Begumpura: The Social Vision of Anticaste Intellectuals*. New Delhi: Navayana.

Orr, Leslie C. 1995. "The Vaiṣṇava Community at Śrīraīgam: The Testimony of the Early Medieval Inscriptions." *Journal of Vaishnava Studies* 3: 109–136.

Orr, W. G. 1947. *A Sixteenth-Century Indian Mystic: Dadu and His Followers*. London: Lutterworth.

Orsini, Francesca. 2002. *The Hindi Public Sphere: Language and Literature in the Age of Nationalism*. Delhi: Oxford University Press.

———, ed. 2006. *Love in South Asia: A Cultural History*. Cambridge: Cambridge University Press.

———. 2009. "Kathās as Sites of Religious Interchange: Sufis and Krishna Bhaktas in Awadh." Paper presented at Oxford University, June 5.

———, ed. 2010. *Before the Divide: Hindi and Urdu Literary Culture*. Hyderabad: Orient Blackswan.

———. 2014a. "Inflected Kathas: Sufis and Krishna Bhaktas in Awadh." In Dalmia and Faruqui, eds., *Religious Interactions in Mughal India*, 195–232.

———. 2014b. "Krishna Is the Truth of Man: Mir 'Abdul Wahid Bilgrami's Haqā'iq-e Hindī (Indian Truths) and the Circulation of Dhrupad and Bishnupad." In de Bruijn and Busch, eds., *Culture and Circulation*, 222–246.

———. Forthcoming "The Multilingual Local in World Literature." *Comparative Literature*.

Orsini, Francesca, and Stefano Pellò. 2010. "Bhakti in Persian." Paper presented at the 21st European Conference on Modern South Asian Studies, Bonn, July 27.

Orsini, Francesca, and Sumira Sheikh, eds. 2014. *After Timur Left: Culture and Circulation in Fifteenth-Century North India*. Delhi: Oxford University Press 2014.

Packert, Cynthia. 2010. *The Art of Loving Krishna: Ornamentation and Devotion*. Bloomington: Indiana University Press.

Padmanabhacharya, C. M. 1970. *Life and Teachings of Sri Madhvacharya*. Udipi: Paryaya Sri Palimar Mutt.

Padma Purāṇa. 1724. Jodhpur: Rajasthan Oriental Research Institute, Jodhpur [earlier, Rājasthān Purātattva Mandir, Jaipur], accession no. 2597.

Pal, Bipin Chandra. 1911. *The Soul of India: A Constructive Study of Indian Thoughts and Ideals*. Calcutta: Chaudhury and Chaudhury.

———. 1973 [1932]. *Memories of My Life and Times*. Calcutta: Bipinchandra Pal Institute.

———. 1962 [1933]. *Bengal Vaishnavism.* Calcutta: Yugayatri Prakashak.
Palit, R. C., ed. 1880. *Speeches of Babu Surendranath Banerjea,* vol. 1. Calcutta: Bose Press.
Pande, Rekha. 2010. *Divine Sounds from the Heart—Singing Unfettered in Their Own Voices: The Bhakti Movement and Its Women Saints (12th to 17th Century).* Newcastle-upon-Tyne: Cambridge Scholars.
Pande, Susmita. 1982. *Birth of Bhakti in Indian Religions and Art.* New Delhi: Books and Books.
———. 1989. *Medieval Bhakti Movement (Its History and Philosophy).* Meerut: Kusumanjali Prakashan.
Pandurangi. 1997. *Śrīmad Bhāgavatam.* Bangalore: Dvaita Vedanta Studies and Research Foundation.
Pannikar, K. N. 2007. *Colonialism, Culture, and Resistance.* Delhi: Oxford University Press.
Paramasivan, Vasudha. 2010. "Between Text and Sect: Early Nineteenth Century Shifts in the Theology of Ram." Ph.D. dissertation, University of California, Berkeley.
Parīkh, Dvārakādās. 1960. *Vārtā-Sāhitya (Ek Bṛhat Adhyayan).* Aligarh: Bhārat Prakāśan Mandir.
———. 1948, 1951–1953. See Gokulnāth [attrib.].
Parthasarathy, Indira. 2003. *The Legend of Nandan: Nandan Kathai,* trans. C. T. Indra. Delhi: Oxford University Press.
Pāṭhak, Śiv Mūrti. 2004. *Navīn Hindī Gāiḍ.* Allahabad: Ajantā Prakāśan.
Pauwels, Heidi R. M. 1996. *Kṛṣṇa's Round Dance Reconsidered.* Richmond, Surrey: Curzon.
———. 2002. *In Praise of Holy Men: Hagiographic Poems by and about Harirām Vyās.* Groningen: Egbert Forsten.
———. 2005. "Romancing Rādhā: Nāgrīdās's Royal Appropriations of Bhakti Themes." *South Asia Research* 15: 55–78.
———. 2009. "Imagining Religious Communities in the Sixteenth Century: Harirām Vyās and the Haritrayī." *International Journal of Hindu Studies* 13: 143–161.
———. 2010. "Hagiography and Community Formation: The Case of a Lost Community of Sixteenth-Century Vrindāvan." *Journal of Hindu Studies* 3, no. 1: 53–90.
———. 2011. "A Tale of Two Temples: Mathurā's Keśavadeva and Orchhā's Caturbhujadeva." *South Asian History and Culture* 2: 278–299.
———. 2012. "Whose Satire? Gorakhnāth Confronts Krishna in *Kanhāvat.*" In Horstmann and Pauwels, eds., *Indian Satire in the Period of First Modernity,* 35–64.
———. 2013. "When a Sufi Tells about Krishna's Doom: The Case of *Kanhāvat* (1540?)." *Journal of Hindu Studies* 6: 21–36.

Pechilis, Karen. 2005. "The Story of Nandanar: Contesting the Order of Things." In Zelliot and Mokashi-Punekar, eds., *Untouchable Saints*, 95–107.

———. See also Prentiss, Karen Pechilis.

Pellò, Stefano. 2008. "Safina-ye Košgu." *Encyclopaedia Iranica*. Accessed August 17, 2014. http://www.iranicaonline.org/articles/safina-ye-kosgu.

———. 2014a. "'Drowned in the Sea of Mercy': The Textual Identification of Hindu Persian Poets from Shi'i Lucknow in the *Tazkira* of Bhagwān Dās 'Hindī.'" In Dalmia and Faruqui, eds., *Religious Interactions in Mughal India*, 135–158.

———. 2014b. "Persian as a Passe-Partout: The Case of Mīrzā 'Abd al-Qādir Bīdal and His Hindu Disciples." In de Bruijn and Busch, eds., *Culture and Circulation*, 21–46.

Pemārām. 1977. *Madhyayugīn Rājasthān meṅ Dhārmik Āndolan*. Ajmer: Arcanā Prakāśan.

Peterson, Indira Viswanathan. 1982. "Singing of a Place: Pilgrimage as Metaphor and Motif in the Tēvāram Songs of the Tamil Śaivite Saints." *Journal of the American Oriental Society* 102, no. 1: 69–90.

———. 1983. "Lives of the Wandering Singers: Pilgrimage and Poetry in Tamil Śaivite Hagiography." *History of Religions* 22, no. 4: 338–360.

———. 1989. *Poems to Śiva: The Hymns of the Tamil Saints*. Princeton: Princeton University Press.

———. 2011. "Multilingual Dramas at the Tanjavur Maratha Court and Literary Cultures in Early Modern South India." *Medieval History Journal* 14, no. 2: 285–321.

Phukan, Shantanu. 2000. "Through a Persian Prism: Hindi and Padmāvat in the Mughal Imagination." Ph.D. dissertation, University of Chicago.

Pinch, Vijay (William R.). 1996. *Peasants and Monks in British India*. Berkeley: University of California Press.

———. 1999. "History, Devotion, and the Search for Nabhadas of Galta." In Daud Ali, ed., *Invoking the Past: The Uses of History in South Asia*. Delhi: Oxford University Press, 367–399.

———. 2003. "*Bhakti* and the British Empire." *Past and Present* 179: 159–196.

———. 2006. *Warrior Ascetics and Indian Empires*. Cambridge: Cambridge University Press.

———. 2009. "Mughal Vaishnavas, Rajputs, and Religion in Early Modern India, 1450–1800." Paper presented at the World History Association, Salem, Massachusetts, June 27.

Poddar, Neeraja. 2014. "Krishna in His Myriad Forms: Narration, Translation, and Variation in Illustrated Manuscripts of the Latter Half of the Tenth Book of the Bhāgavata Purana." Ph.D. dissertation, Columbia University.

Pollet, Gilbert. 1963. "Studies in the Bhakta Mâla of Nâbhâ Dâsa." Ph.D. dissertation, School of Oriental and African Studies, University of London.

Pollock, Sheldon. 2001. "New Intellectuals in Seventeenth-Century India," *Indian Economic and Social History Review* 38: 3–31.

———, ed. 2003. *Literary Cultures in History: Reconstructions from South Asia*. Berkeley: University of California Press.

———. 2006. *The Language of the Gods in the World of Men*. Berkeley: University of California Press.

———. 2008. "Is There an Indian Intellectual History?" Introduction to "Theory and Method in Indian Intellectual History." Special issue, *Journal of Indian Philosophy* 36: 533–542.

———, ed. 2011. *Forms of Knowledge in Early Modern South Asia: Explorations in the Intellectual History of India and Tibet, 1500–1800*. Delhi: Manohar.

Prasad, Ishwari. 1925. *History of Medieval India from 647 A.D. to the Mughal Conquest*. Allahabad: Indian Press.

———. 1936. *A History of the Qaraunah Turks in India*, vol. 1. Allahabad: Indian Press.

Prasad, R. N. 1966. *Raja Man Singh of Amber*. Calcutta: World Press.

Prentiss, Karen Pechilis. 1999. *The Embodiment of Bhakti*. New York: Oxford University Press.

———. See also Pechilis, Karen.

Prill, Susan. 2009. "Representing Sainthood in India: Sikh and Hindu Visions of Namdev." *Material Religion* 5: 155–178.

Quack, Johannes. 2012. *Disenchanting India: Organized Rationalism and Criticism of Religion in India*. New York: Oxford University Press.

Raghavan, V. 1966. *The Great Integrators: The Singer-Saints of India*. New Delhi: Publications Division, Ministry of Information and Broadcasting.

Rahman, Ram et al. 1993. "Ayodhya: What Then Are Our Invocations?" Delhi: Broadside.

———. 2012. *Ham Sab Ayudhyā / Hum Sab Ayodhya*. Delhi: SAHMAT in conjunction with the Aligarh Historians Society.

Rai, Alok. 2001. *Hindi Nationalism*. Hyderabad: Orient Longman.

Rajpurohit, Dalpat. 2007. "Rajjab aur Gopāldās kī Sarvangī kā Tulnātmak Adhyayan." M.Phil. dissertation, Jawaharlal Nehru University.

———. 2013. "The Dādūpanth and the Sarvangī Literature." In Bangha, ed., *Bhakti beyond the Forest*, 51–72.

Rajyaguru, Niranjan. 2012. *Madhyakālīn Gujarātī Bhakti-Kavitā Saṃcay*. Delhi: Sahitya Academy.

Rākeś, Viṣṇudatt. 2001. *Pītāmbar Datt Baḍthvāl*. New Delhi: Sahitya Academy.

Ramachandra Dikshitar, V. R. 1995. *The Purana Index*. Delhi: Motilal Banarsidass.

Raman, Srilata. 2007. *Self-Surrender (Prapatti) to God in Śrīvaiṣṇavism: Tamil Cats and Sanskrit Monkeys*. London: Routledge.
———. Forthcoming. *The Transformation of Tamil Religion: Ramalinga Swamigal and Modern Dravidian Sainthood*. New York: Routledge.
Ramanujan, A. K. 1973. *Speaking of Śiva*. Baltimore: Penguin.
———. 1981. *Hymns for the Drowning: Poems for Viṣṇu by Nammāḻvār*. Princeton: Princeton University Press.
Ramaswamy, Sumathi. 2010. *The Goddess and the Nation: Mapping Mother India*. Durham: Duke University Press.
Ramaswamy, Vijaya. 1996. *Divinity and Deviance: Women in Virasaivism*. Delhi: Oxford University Press.
Ramey, Steven W. 2008. *Hindu, Sufi, or Sikh: Contested Practices and Identifications of Sindhi Hindus in India and Beyond*. New York: Palgrave Macmillan.
Ranade, M. G. 1961 [1900]. *Rise of the Maratha Power*. New Delhi: Publications Division, Ministry of Information and Broadcasting.
Rao, Ajay K. 2006. "Srivaisnavas and the Royal Rama Cult at Vijayanagara." Paper presented at the conference "Sacred Cows and False Prophets: Traversing History and Religion in South Asia," University of Chicago, April 22.
———. 2011. "A New Perspective on the Royal Rāma Cult at Vijayanagara." In Bronner, Cox, and McCrea, eds., *South Asian Texts in History*, 25–44.
———. 2013. *Re-figuring the Rāmāyaṇa as Theology: A History of Reception in Premodern India*. New York: Routledge.
"Ratnākar," Jagannāthdās, Nandadulāre Vājpeyī, et al. 1972, 1976 [1948]. *Sūrsāgar*. 2 vols. Varanasi: Kāśī Nāgarīpracāriṇī Sabhā.
Rawat, Ramnarayan S. 2011. *Reconsidering Untouchability: Chamars and Dalit History in North India*. Bloomington: Indiana University Press.
Redington, James D. 1983. *Vallabhācārya on the Love Games of Kṛṣṇa*. Delhi: Motilal Banarsidass.
———. 2000. *The Grace of Lord Krishna: The Sixteen Verse-Treatises (Ṣodaśagranthāḥ) of Vallabhacharya*. Delhi: Sri Satguru Publications.
Renard, John. 2008. *Friends of God: Islamic Images of Piety, Commitment, and Servanthood*. Berkeley: University of California Press.
Richards, John F. 1993. *The Mughal Empire*. Cambridge: Cambridge University Press.
———. 1997. "Early Modern India and World History." *Journal of World History* 8: 197–209.
Richman, Paula. 1997. *Extraordinary Child: Poems from a South Indian Devotional Genre*. Honolulu: University of Hawai'i Press.
Rocher, Ludo. 1986. *The Purāṇas*. Wiesbaden: Otto Harrassowitz.
Rohitasva. 1987. *Kabīr evam Vemanā: Ek Adhyayan*. Hyderabad: Ālocanā Prakāśan.

Rosenstein, Lucy L. 1997. *The Devotional Poetry of Svāmī Hiridās*. Groningen: Egbert Forsten.

Rothfarb, Edward Leland. 2012. *Orccha and Beyond: Design at the Court of Raja Bir Singh Dev Bundela*. Mumbai: Marg Foundation.

Rousseva-Sokolova, Galina. 2013. "Sainthood Revisited: Two Printed Versions of the *Lives of the Eighty-four Vaishnavas* by Gokulnāth." In Bangha, ed., *Bhakti beyond the Forest*, 91–103.

"Rūpkalā," Sītārāmśaraṇ Bhagavānprasād. 1969 [1910]. *Śrī Bhaktamāl* with the *Bhaktirasabodhinī* commentary of Priyādās. Lucknow: Tejkumār Press.

Sachdev, Vibhuti, and Giles Tillotson. 2002. *Building Jaipur: The Making of a City*. Delhi: Oxford University Press.

Sadana, Rashmi. 2003. "Reading Delhi: Englishwallahs, Hindiwallahs, and the Politics of Language and Literary Production." Ph.D. dissertation, University of California, Berkeley.

Saggi, P. D. 1962. *Life and Works of Lal, Bal, and Pal*. New Delhi: Overseas Publishing House.

Saha, Shandip. 2004. "Creating a Community of Grace: A History of the Puṣṭi Mārga in Northern and Western India (1493–1905)." Ph.D. dissertation, University of Ottawa.

———. 2007. "The Movement of *Bhakti* along a North-West Axis: Tracing the History of the Puṣṭimārga between the Sixteenth and Nineteenth Centuries." *International Journal of Hindu Studies* 11: 299–318.

"Sahajananad Swami and the Swaminarayan Sampraday: Historical, Social, and Cultural Perspectives." 2013. Conference held in New Delhi, August 2–4.

Sanderson, Alexis. 2009. *The Śaiva Age: The Rise and Dominance of Śaivism during the Early Medieval Period*. In Shingo Einoo, ed., *The Genesis and Development of Tantrism*. Tokyo: Institute of Oriental Culture, University of Tokyo, 41–350.

Sarma, Deepak. 1998. "Exclusivist Strategies in Madhva Vedanta." Ph.D. dissertation, University of Chicago.

Śarmā, Hemant, ed. 1987. *Bhāratendu Samagra*. Varanasi: Hindī Pracārak Publications.

Śarmā, Munśīrām. 1979. *Bhakti kā Vikās (Vaidik Bhakti evam Bhāgavat Bhakti tathā Hindī ke Bhaktikālīn Kāvya meṅ uskī Abhivyakti)*. Varanasi: Caukhambā Vidyābhavan.

Śarmā, Nalinavilocan, and Śrirāmanārāyaṇ Śāstrī, eds. 1963. *Lālacdās-racit Avadhī-Kāvya Haricarit*. Patna: Bihār-Rāṣṭrabhāṣā-Pariṣad.

Śarmā, Nārāyaṇadatt. 1964. *Nimbārk Sampradāy aur uske Kṛṣna Hindī Kavi*, vol. 1. Mathura: Aśok Prakāśan.

Śarmā, Premlatā, ed. and trans. [into Hindi]. 1998. *Śrī Śrī Rūpagosvāmiprabhupādapraṇītaḥ Śrī Śrī Bhaktirasāmṛtasindhuḥ*. New Delhi: Indira Gandhi National Centre for the Arts.

Śarmā, Rāmvilās. 2003. *Ācārya Rāmcandra Śukla aur Hindī Ālocanā*. New Delhi: Rājkamal Prakāśan.
Śarmā, Suman. 1974. *Madhyakālīn Bhakti-Andolan kā Sāmājik Vivecan*. Varanasi: Viśvavidyālay Prakāśan.
Sartori, Andrew. 2008. *Bengal in Global Concept History: Culturalism in the Age of Capital*. Chicago: University of Chicago Press.
Śāstrī, Kaṇṭhamaṇi. 1935. *Sampradāyapradīpa*, with Hindi translation. Kankaroli: Vidyā-Vibhāg. Reprinted, with Gujarati translation by Jaṭāśaṃkar Śāstrī, Kankaroli: Vidyā-Vibhāg, 1936.
———.1952. *Aṣṭachāp kī Vārtā*, vol. 1. Kankaroli: Vidyā-Vibhāg.
Sastri, Sivanath. 1907 [1903]. *Rāmtanu Lahari o Tatkālīn Bāngāsamaj* [Ramtanu Lahiri and Contemporary Bengali Society], trans. Roper Lethbridge as *Ramtanu Lahiri, Brahman and Reformer: A History of the Renaissance in Bengal*. London: Swan Sonnenschein.
———. 1983 [1903]. *Rāmtanu Lahari o Tatkālīn Bāngāsamaj*. Calcutta: New Age Publishers.
———. 1919. *History of the Brahmo Samaj*, vol. 1, 2nd ed. [1st ed., 1912]. Calcutta: R. Chatterjee.
Sastry, R. Ananta Krishna, ed. 1921. *Kavīndrācāryasūcipatram: Kavindracharya List*. Baroda: Central Library.
Satyanand, Joseph. 1997. *Nimbārka, a Pre-Śaṃkara Vedāntin and His Philosophy*. New Delhi: Munshiram Manoharlal.
Savarkar, Vinayak Damodar. 1969 [1923]. *Hindutva: Who Is a Hindu?* Bombay: Veer Savarjar Prakashan.
Schelling, Andrew, ed. 2011. *The Oxford Anthology of Bhakti Literature*. Delhi: Oxford University Press.
Schomer, Karine. 1987. Introduction to Schomer and McLeod, eds., *Sants*, 1–17.
Schomer, Karine, and W. H. McLeod, eds. 1987. *The Sants: Studies in a Devotional Tradition of India*. Berkeley: Berkeley Religious Studies Series.
Schultz, Anna. 2013. *Singing a Hindu Nation: Marathi Devotional Performance and Nationalism*. New York: Oxford University Press.
Schwartz, Jason. 2012. "Caught in the Net of Śāstra: Devotion and Its Limits in an Evolving Śaiva Corpus." *Journal of Hindu Studies* 5: 210–231.
Sehgal, Manmohan. 1980. *Śrī Gurū Granth Sāhib*, vol. 2. Lucknow: Bhuvan Vāṇī Trust.
Selby, Martha Ann, and Indira Viswanathan Peterson, eds. 2008. *Tamil Geographies: Cultural Constructions of Space and Place in Tamil South India*. Albany: State University of New York Press.
Sen, Kshitimohan. 1910–1911. *Kabīr*. Bolpur: Brahmacaryāśram.
———. 1929. *Bhāratīya Madhyayuge Sādhanār Dhārā*. Calcutta: Lekhak Samavāy Samiti and Calcutta Viśvavidyālay.
———. 2009 [1935]. "Mīrā's Songs and the Spring Festival" [*Mīrār Gān o Vasantotsav*]. In Mukhopādhyāy, ed., *Kṣitimohan Sen*, 194–208.

———. 1936a [1929–1930]. *Medieval Mysticism of India,* trans. Manomohan Ghosh. London: Luzac. Reprinted New Delhi: Oriental Books Reprint Corp., 1974.

———. 1987 [1936b]. *Dādū.* Shantiniketan: Viśva Bhāratī Gaveṣaṇā Prakāśan Vibhāg.

———. 2009 [1939] "Bhakta Ravidās." In Mukhopādhyāy, ed., *Kṣitimohan Sen,* 295–306.

———. 2009 [1953]. "My Story" [*Amar Kathā*]. In Mukhopādhyāy, ed., *Kṣitimohan Sen,* 232–245.

———. 2009 [1955] "Bhakta Ravidas's Spring Festival" [*Bhakta Ravidaser Vasantotsav*]. In Mukhopadhyaya, ed., *Kṣitimohan Sen,* 388–393.

Sen, Sukumar. 1935. *A History of Brajabuli Literature.* Calcutta: University of Calcutta.

Shah, Siddhartha. 2014. "Meera vs. Meera: The Life of Mirabai in Performative Translation." Unpublished paper, Columbia University.

Shankar, D. A. 2007. *Golden Flock: Raama Dhaanya Charite and Other Works of Kanakadasa.* Hampi: Kannada University.

Sharma, Arvind. 2003. *Hinduism and Its Sense of History.* Delhi: Oxford University Press.

Sharma, B. N. K. 1961. *History of the Dvaita School of Vedānta and Its Literature from the Earliest Beginnings to Our Own Times.* Delhi: Motilal Banarsidass.

Sharma, Har Dutt, and M. M. Patkar, eds. 1939. *Kavīndracandrodaya* [*A Collection of Addresses Presented to Kavīndrācārya by Some of His Contemporary Scholars during Shah Jehan's Reign*]. Poona: Oriental Book Agency.

Sharma, Krishna. 1965. "Ancient Indian Bhakti with Special Reference to Kabir." Ph.D. dissertation, School of Oriental and African Studies, University of London.

———. 1987. *Bhakti and the Bhakti Movement: A New Perspective.* New Delhi: Munshiram Manoharlal.

Sharma, Swapna. 2008. *Gadādhar Bhaṭṭ: Paramparā aur Sāhitya.* Vrindaban: Vrajagaurav Prakāśan.

Shastri, Kardamrishi. 1998. *Śrīmad Bhāgavat Piyuṣ.* Ahmedabad: Śrī Kṛṣṇanidhi.

Shastri, Yajneshwar S. 2003. "Svābhāvika-bhedābheda of Nimbārka." In R. Balasubramanian, ed., *Theistic Vedānta,* vol. 2, part 3, 277–305.

Shea, David, and Anthony Troyer. 1843. *The Dabistan, or School of Manners.* 3 vols. Paris: Allen.

Sheikh, Gulammohammed, and R. Siva Kumar, eds. 2007. *Benodebehari Mukherjee (1904–1980): Centenary Retrospective.* New Delhi: Vadehra Art Gallery and National Gallery of Modern Art.

Sheikh, Samira. 2012. "The Rise of Vaishnavism in Sultanate and Mughal Gujarat." Paper presented at the workshop "Religion, Conflict, and

Accommodation in Indian History: The Medieval Period," Columbia University, September 28–29.

Shetty, R. Shivarama, Rajaram Tolpady, and Parinitha. 2013. "Call for Papers: Rethinking Bhakthi [sic]." Kanakadasa Adhyayana Peeta and Kanakadasa Samshodhana Kendra, Mangalore University. Email communication announcing a seminar held on March 27–30.

Shima, Iwao, Teiji Sakata, and Katsuyuki Ida, eds. 2011. *The Historical Development of the Bhakti Movement in India: Theory and Practice.* Delhi: Manohar.

Shobha, Savitri Chandra. 1996. *Medieval India and Hindi Bhakti Poetry: A Socio-cultural Study.* New Delhi: Har-Anand Publications.

Shukla, Ramchandra (Rāmcandra Śukla). 1923. *Gosvāmī Tulsīdās.* Banaras: Nāgarīpracāriṇī Sabhā.

———. 1929. *Hindī Sāhitya kā Itihās.* Banaras: Nāgarīpracāriṇī Sabhā.

———. 2001 [1940]. *Hindī Sāhitya kā Itihās,* 2nd ed. Allahabad: A to Zed Publications.

———. 1969 [1948 = V.S. 2005]. *Sūrdās,* ed. Viśvanāthprasād Miśra. Banaras: Sarasvatī Bhaṇḍār.

———. 2002 [V.S. 2059]. *Sūrdās,* ed. Viśvanāthprasād Miśra. Banaras: Nāgarīpracāriṇī Sabhā.

Shukla, Ramchandra, Bhagavāndīn, and Brajratnadās, eds. 1976 [1923]. *Tulsī Granthāvalī.* Banaras: Nāgarīpracāriṇī Sabhā.

Shukla-Bhatt, Neelima. 2003. "Nectar of Devotion: Bhakti-rasa in the Tradition of Gujarati Saint-Poet Narasinha Mehta." Ph.D. dissertation, Harvard University.

———. 2007. "Performance as Translation: Mīrā in Gujarat." *International Journal of Hindu Studies* 11: 273–298.

———. 2014. *Narasinha Mehta of Gujarat: A Legacy of Bhakti in Songs and Stories.* New York: Oxford University Press.

Shulman, David. 1984. "The Enemy Within: Idealism and Dissent in South Indian Hinduism." In S. N. Eisenstadt, Reuven Kahane, and David Shulman, eds., *Orthodoxy, Heterodoxy, and Dissent in India.* Berlin: Mouton, 11–55.

———. 1993. *The Hungry God: Hindu Tales of Filicide and Devotion.* Chicago: University of Chicago Press.

———. 2008. "Glimpses of the Unitary Self in Sixteenth-Century Tamil Literature." Paper delivered to the Tamil Studies Conference, Toronto, May 17.

———. 2012. *More Than Real: A History of the Imagination in South India.* Cambridge, MA: Harvard University Press.

Shyam Das. 1985. *Chaurasi Baithak: Eightyfour* [sic] *Seats of Shri Vallabhacharya.* Baroda: Shri Vallabha Publications.

Siṃh, Bhagavatī Prasād. 1957 [V.S. 2014]. *Rāmbhakti meṅ Rasik Sampradāy.* Balarampur: Avadh-Sāhitya-Mandir.

Siṃh, Durgāvatī. 1998. *Ācārya Hajārīprasād Dvivedī ke Sāhityetihās Granthoṅ meṅ Itihās-cetanā kā Anuśīlan*. Delhi: Nirmal Publications.
Siṃh, Gopeśvar, ed. 2005. *Madhyakālīn Bhakti-Āndolan kā Sāmājik Svarūp*. New Delhi: Bhāratīya Prakāśan Sansthān.
Siṃh, Kuṅvarpāl. 1995. "Bhakti Āndolan: Navīn Bhautik Paristhitiāṅ aur Caritra." In Kuṅvarpāl Siṃh, ed., *Bhakti Āndolan: Itihās aur Saṃskṛti*. New Delhi: Vāṇī Prakāśan, 274–286.
Siṃh, Padam Gurcaran. 1977. *Sant Ravidās: Vicārak aur Kavi*. Jalandhar: Nav-Cintan Prakāśan.
Simon, Robert Leopold. 2007. *Spiritual Aspects of Indian Music*. Delhi: Sundeep Prakashan.
Singh, Namvar. 2005 [1982]. *Dūsrī Paramparā kī Khoj*. Delhi: Rājkamal Prakāśan.
Singh, Trilochan, Jodh Singh, Kapur Singh, Bawa Harikishen Singh, and Kushwant Singh. 2000 [1960]. *Selections from the Sacred Writings of the Sikhs*. New Delhi: Orient Longman.
Sinha, Ajay. 2007. "Against Allegory: Binode Bihari Mukherjee's *Medieval Saints* at Shantiniketan." In Richard H. Davis, ed., *Picturing the Nation: Iconographies of Modern India*. Hyderabad: Orient Longman, 66–91.
Sinha, Mrinalini. 1995. *Colonial Masculinity: The "Manly Englishman" and the "Effeminate Bengali" in the Late Nineteenth Century*. Manchester: Manchester University Press.
Sinha, Surajit, and Baiyanath Saraswati. 1978. *Ascetics of Kashi: An Anthropological Exploration*. Varanasi: N. K. Bose Foundation.
Sircar, D. C., ed. 1970. *The Bhakti Cult and Ancient Indian Geography*. Calcutta: University of Calcutta.
Sistla, Srinivas. 2010. *Sri Krishna Deva Raya: Āmuktamālyada*. Vishakhapatnam: Drusya Kala Deepika.
Sivaramkrishna, M., and Sumita Roy, eds. 1996. *Poet-Saints of India*. New Delhi: Sterling.
Smith, Brian K. 1987. "Exorcizing the Transcendent: Strategies for Defining Hinduism and Religion." *History of Religions* 21: 32–55.
Smith, Frederick. 2006. *The Self Possessed: Deity and Spirit Possession in South Asian Literature and Civilization*. New York: Columbia University Press.
Smith, Travis L. 2000. "Translating Bhakti: Reading Nābhādās and His Commentaries." Unpublished paper, Columbia University.
Smith, William L. 2000a. "Inventing Brajabuli." *Archiv Orientální* 68: 387–398.
———. 2000b. *Patterns in North Indian Hagiography*. Stockholm: Department of Indology, University of Stockholm.
———. 2003. *Patterns in Indian Hagiography*. Gawahati: Srikrishna Prakashan.

Snātak, Vijayendra. 1968. *Rādhāvallabh Sampradāy: Siddhānt aur Sāhitya*. Delhi: National Publishing House.
Snell, Rupert. 1989. "Raskhān the Neophyte: Hindu Perspectives on a Muslim Vaishnava." In Christopher Shackle, ed., *Urdu and Muslim South Asia: Studies in Honor of Ralph Russell*. Delhi: Oxford University Press, 29–37.
———. 1991a. *The Eighty-Four Hymns of Hita Harivaṃśa*. Delhi: Motilal Banarsidass.
———. 1991b. *The Hindi Classical Tradition: A Brajbhāṣā Reader*. London: School of Oriental and African Studies.
Soneji, Davesh. 2012. *Unfinished Gestures: Devadāsīs, Memory, and Modernity in South India*. Chicago: University of Chicago Press.
———. 2014. "The Powers of Polyglossia: Marathi *Kīrtan*, Multilingualism, and the Making of a South Indian Devotional Tradition." *International Journal of Hindu Studies* 17: 339–369.
Srinivasachari, P. N. 1970. *The Philosophy of Viśiṣṭādvaita*. Madras: Adyar Library and Research Centre.
Srinivasan, Doris Meth, ed., 1989. *Mathurā: The Cultural Heritage*. Delhi: American Institute of Indian Studies.
Stainton, Hamsa. 2013. "Poetry, Praise and Prayer: Stotras in the Religious and Literary History of Kashmir." Ph.D. dissertation, Columbia University.
Stark, Ulrike. 2007a. *An Empire of Books: The Naval Kishore Press and the Diffusion of the Printed Word in Colonial India*. Delhi: Permanent Black.
———. 2007b. "Makkhanlal's *Sukhsāgar* (1846/1847: The First Complete Version of the *Bhāgavata Purāṇa* in Modern Hindi Prose?" In Konrad Klaus and Jens-Uwe Hartmann, eds., *Indica et Tibetica: Festschrift für Michael Hahn*. Wien: Arbeitskreis für Tibetische und Buddhistische Studien, Universität Wien, 491–506.
———. 2010. "Translation, Book History, and the Afterlife of a Text: Growse's *The Rámáyana of Tulsi Dás*." In Maya Burger and Picola Pozza, eds., *India in Translation through Hindi Literature: A Plurality of Voices*. Bern: Peter Lang, 155–180.
Starr, Jason. 2012. "The Movement beyond Basava's Revolution." Unpublished paper, Columbia University.
Stewart, Tony K. 2001. "In Search of Equivalence: Conceiving Muslim-Hindu Encounter through Translation Theory." *History of Religions* 40: 260–287.
———. 2010. *The Final Word: The Caitanya Caritāmṛta and the Grammar of Religious Tradition*. New York: Oxford University Press.
———. 2013. "Religion in the Subjunctive: Vaiṣṇava Narrative, Sufi Counter-Narrative in Early Modern Bengal." *Journal of Hindu Studies* 6: 52–72.
———. Forthcoming. "Jaban Haridās: The Sufi Who Practiced Kṛṣṇa *Jikir*." In *Romance of the Pīrs: Fictive Discourse in Early Modern Bengali Sufism*.

Stoker, Valerie. 2011a. "Hindu Sectarian Identity in 16th-Century Vijayanagara: Vyāsatīrtha and the Śrī Vaiṣṇavas at Tirupati." Paper presented at the conference "Religion, Conflict, and Accommodation in India," Columbia University, November 5.

———. 2011b. "Polemics and Patronage in Sixteenth-Century Vijayanagara: Vyāsatīrtha and the Dynamics of Hindu Sectarian Relations." *History of Religions* 51: 129–155.

———. 2014. "Krishnadevaraya and the Patronage of Vyasatirtha: Royal and Religious Authority in Sixteenth-Century Vijayanagara Sources." In Verghese, ed., *Krishnadevaraya and His Times*, 262–277.

Subbaya, Tati. 1986. *Vemanā aur Kabīr kī Sāmājik Vicārdhārā*. Patna: Bihār Rāṣṭrabhāṣā Pariṣad.

Subrahmanyam, Sanjay. 1995. "An Eastern El Dorado: The Tirumala-Tirupati Temple Complex in Early European Views and Ambitions, 1540–1660." In David Shulman, ed., *Syllables of Sky: Studies in South Indian Civilization in Honor of Velcheru Narayana Rao*. Delhi: Oxford University Press, 338–390.

———. 1997. "Connected Histories: Notes towards a Reconfiguration of Early Modern Eurasia." *Modern Asian Studies* 31: 735–762.

———. 1998. "Hearing Voices: Vignettes of Early Modernity in South Asia, 1400–1750." *Daedalus* 127: 75–104.

———. 2001. *Penumbral Visions: Making Polities in Early Modern South India*. Ann Arbor: University of Michigan Press.

Subramaniam, Shiv Kaushik. 2014. "On the Poetry and Poetics of Vedāntadeśika." M.A. thesis, Columbia University.

Sujātāreḍḍi, Mudigaṇṭi. 1993. *Vémana-Nātha Sampradāyaṃ*. Hyderabad: Pratulaku, Mudigaṇṭi Sujātāreḍḍi.

Śukla, Dineś Candra, and Oṃkār Nārāyaṇ Siṃh. 2004. *Rājasthān kī Bhakti-Paramparā tathā Saṃskṛti*. Jodhpur: Rājasthānī Granthāgār.

Surdas. See Bahura, Gopal Narayan, and Kenneth E. Bryant; Bryant, Kenneth E., and John Stratton Hawley; "Ratnākar," Jagannāthdās, Nandadulāre Vājpeyī, et al.

Tagare, Ganesh Vasudeo, trans. 1976–1978. *The Bhāgavata-Purāṇa*. 5 vols. Delhi: Motilal Banarsidass.

Tagore, Debendranath. 1989. *Mahārṣi Debendranāth Ṭhākurer Ātmajīvani*. Reprinted by Arabinda Mitra and Ashim Amed [sic], Calcutta: Chariot International.

Tagore, Rabindranath. 1961 [1921]. "The Unity of Education" [*Shikshar Milan*]. In *Towards Universal Man*. Bombay: Asia Publishing House, 231–251.

———. 1933a. "The Sacred Touch." *Harijan* 1, no. 7: 1. Pune: The Servants of Untouchables Society, March 25.

———. 1933b. "Sweet Mercy." *Harijan* 1, no. 15: 1. Pune: The Servants of Untouchables Society, May 20.

———. 2010 [1962]. *Rabīndra-racanābalī*. 15 vols. Calcutta: Viśva-Bhāratī.

Talbot, Cynthia. 1995. "Inscribing the Other, Inscribing the Self: Hindu-Muslim Identities in Pre-colonial India." *Comparative Studies in Society and History* 37: 692–722.

Ṭaṇḍan, Hariharnāth. 1960. *Vārtā-Sāhitya [Ek Bṛhat Adhyayan]*. Aligarh: Bhārat Prakāśan Mandir.

Tapasyānanda, Svāmī. 1990. *Bhakti Schools of Vedānta* [Lives and Philosophies of Rāmānuja, Nimbārka, Madhva, Vallabha, and Caitanya]. Madras: Sri Ramakrishna Math.

Thackston, Wheeler M., Jr. 1993. *Zahiruddin Muhammad Babur Mirza: Bāburnāma*, part 3. Cambridge, MA: Harvard University, Department of Near Eastern Languages and Civilizations.

Thakur, Nalini, with photographs by Robyn Beeche. 1996. "The Building of Govindadeva." In Case, ed., *Govindadeva*, 11–68.

Thapar, Romila. 1988a. *Madhyakālīn Bhārat*. New Delhi: National Council of Educational Research and Training.

———. 1988b. *Medieval India: A Textbook for Class VII*. New Delhi: National Council of Educational Research and Training.

———. 1989. "The Early History of Mathurā: Up to and Including the Mauryan Period." In Srinivasan, ed., *Mathurā*, 12–18.

Thayanithy, Maithili. 2010. "The Concept of Living Liberation in the Tirumantiram." Ph.D. dissertation, University of Toronto.

Thiel-Horstmann, Monika, ed. 1983. *Bhakti in Current Research, 1979–1982*. Berlin: Dietrich Weimer.

Tieken, Herman. 2001. *Kāvya in South India: Old Tamil Caṅkam Poetry*. Groningen: Egbert Forsten.

Tillich, Paul. 1951, 1963. *Systematic Theology*, vols. 1, 3. Chicago: University of Chicago Press.

Tivārī, Balabhadra, ed. 1985. *Agradās Granthāvalī*. Allahabad: Satyendra Prakāśan.

Tivārī, Viśvanāth Prasād. 1989. *Hazārīprasād Dvivedī*. New Delhi: Sahitya Academy.

Tolpady, Rajaram. 2003. "The Dynamics of Hindutva Politics: The Case of Dakshina Kannada." In B. Surendra Rao and K. Chinnappa Gowda, eds., *The Retrieved Acre: Nature and Culture in the World of the Tuluva*. Mangalore: Mangalore University, 164–180.

Toomey, Paul M. 1994. *Food from the Mouth of Krishna: Feasts and Festivities in a North Indian Pilgrimage Center*. Delhi: Hindustan Publishing House.

Toynbee, Arnold. 1960. *One World and India*. New Delhi: Indian Council for Cultural Relations and Orient Longmans.

Trivedi, Jethalal N., ed. 1972. *Narsījī ro Māhero*. Jodhpur: Rajasthan Oriental Research Institute.

Tulpule, S. G. 1979. *Classical Marāṭhī Literature*. Wiesbaden: Otto Harrassowitz.

———. 2000. Introduction to S. G. Tulpule and Anne Feldhaus, *A Dictionary of Old Marathi*. New York: Oxford University Press, xi–xxxiii.
Tulsīdās. See Ramchandra Shukla et al.
Upādhyay, Baldev. 1936. "A Devotional Drama in Sanskrit." *Indian Historical Quarterly* 12: 721–729.
———. 1978. *Vaiṣṇav Sampradāyoṅ kā Sāhitya aur Siddhānt*. Varanasi: Caukhambā Amarabhāratī Prakāśan.
Vajpeyi, Ananya. 2012. *Righteous Republic: The Political Foundations of Modern India*. Cambridge, MA: Harvard University Press.
van Buitenen, J. A. B. 1981. *The Bhagavadgītā in the Mahābhārata*. Chicago: University of Chicago Press.
Varmā, Vrajeśvar. n.d. *Sūr Mīmāṃsā*. New Delhi: Oriental Book Depot.
Vartak, Padmakar Vishnu. 2009. "Embryology and Chromosomes from Śrīmad Bhāgavatam." Paper presented at the national seminar "Śrīmad Bhāgavatam: Its Philosophical, Religious, and Social Themes," Mumbai, Ananthacharya Indological Research Institute, March 28.
Vasu, Rai Bahadur Śrīśa Chandra. 1912. *The Vedânta-Sûtras of Bâdarâyaṇa, with the Commentary of Baladeva*. Allahabad: Pâṇiṇi Office.
Vasudevan, Hari, and Neeladri Bhattacharya, eds. 2007a. *Bhāratīya Itihās ke Kuch Viṣay*. New Delhi: National Council of Educational Research and Training.
———. eds. 2007b. *Themes in Indian History*. New Delhi: National Council of Educational Research and Training.
Vaudeville, Charlotte. 1955. *Étude sur les sources et la composition du Rāmāyaṇa de Tulsī Dās*. Paris: Librairie d'Amérique et d'Orient.
———. 1976. "Braj, Lost and Found." *Indo-Iranian Journal* 18, nos. 3–4: 195–213. Reprinted 1996 in Dalmia, ed., *Myths, Saints, and Legends*, 47–71.
———. 1980. "The Govardhan Myth in Northern India" *Indo-Iranian Journal* 22: 1–45. Reprinted 1996 in Dalmia, ed., *Myths, Saints, and Legends*, 72–139.
———. 1993. *A Weaver Named Kabir: Selected Verses with a Detailed Biographical and Historical Introduction*. Delhi: Oxford University Press.
Venkatesan, Archana. 2010. *The Secret Garland: Āṇṭāḷ's Tiruppāvai and Nācciyār Tirumoḻi*. New York: Oxford University Press.
———. 2013. "A Different Kind of Āṇṭāḷ Story: The *Divyasūricaritam* of Garuḍavāhana Paṇḍita." *Journal of Hindu Studies* 6, no. 3: 243–272.
Venkatkrishnan, Anand. 2011. "Āpadeva and the 'Vedānticization' of Mīmāṃsā." Unpublished paper, Columbia University.
———. 2012. "Mīmāṃsā, Vedanta, and the Bhakti Movement." Unpublished paper, Columbia University.
———. Forthcoming. "Ritual, Reflection, and Religion: The Devas of Banaras." In "Scholar-Intellectuals in Early Modern India," ed. Rosalind O'Hanlon, Christopher Minkowski, and Anand Venkatkrishnan. Special issue, *Journal of South Asian History and Culture* 6, no. 1.

Verghese, Anila. 1995. *Religious Traditions at Vijayanagara as Revealed through Its Monuments.* New Delhi: American Institute of Indian Studies.

———. 2000. *Archaeology, Art, and Religion: New Perspectives on Vijayanagara.* Delhi: Oxford University Press.

———. 2002. *Hampi.* Delhi: Oxford University Press.

———, ed. 2013. *Krishnadevaraya and His Times.* Mumbai: K. R. Cama Oriental Institute.

von Glasenapp, Helmuth. 1933–1934. "Die Lehre Vallabhācāryas." *Zeitschrift für Indologie und Iranistik* 9: 268–334. Reprinted in von Glasenapp, *Von Buddha zu Gandhi: Indisches Denken im Wandel der Jahrhunderte,* Wiesbaden: Otto Harrassowitz, 1962 [1934]: 193–248. Citations refer to the Harrassowitz edition.

Vrajaratnadās, ed. 1957 [1949]. *Nandadās Granthāvalī.* 2 vols. Banaras: Nāgarīpracāriṇī Sabhā.

Vṛndāvandās. 1997–2003. *Śrīśrīcaitanyabhāgavata.* 3 vols. Brindavan: Śrīcaitanya Gauḍīya Maṭh.

Wagoner, Phillip B. 1993. *Tidings of the King: A Translation and Ethnohistorical Analysis of the Rāyavacakamu.* Honolulu: University of Hawai'i Press.

———. 1996. "'Sultan among Hindu Kings': Dress, Titles, and the Islamicization of Hindu Culture at Vijayanagara." *Journal of Asian Studies* 55: 851–880.

Wakankar, Milind. 2002. "The Moment of Criticism in Indian Nationalist Thought: Ramchandra Shukla and the Poetics of a Hindi Responsibility." *South Atlantic Quarterly* 101: 987–1011.

———. 2007 [2005]. "The Anomaly of Kabir: Caste and Canonicity in Indian Modernity." In Shail Mayaram, M. S. S. Pandian, and Ajay Skaria, eds., *Muslims, Dalits, and the Fabrications of History.* Subaltern Studies 12. Delhi: Permanent Black, 99–139.

———. 2010. *Subalternity and Religion: The Prehistory of Dalit Empowerment in South Asia.* London: Routledge.

Westcott, G. H. 1907. *Kabīr and the Kabīr Panth.* Cawnpore [Kanpur]: Christ Church Mission Press.

Williams, Monier. 1882. "The Vaishṇava Religion, with special reference to the Sikshā-patrī of the Modern Sect called Svāmi-Nāyāyaṇa. *Journal of the Royal Asiatic Society,* n.s., 14: 289–316.

Williams, Richard. Forthcoming. "Krishna's Neglected Responsibilities: Religious Devotion and Social Critique in Eighteenth-Century North India." *Modern Asian Studies.*

Williams, Tyler Walker. 2007. "Bhakti Kāvya meṅ Nirguṇ-Saguṇ Vibjājan kā Aitihāsik Adhyayan." M.Phil. dissertation, Jawaharlal Nehru University.

———. 2008. "Libraries in Early Modern North India." Unpublished paper, Columbia University.

———. 2009. "Nirgun and Sagun in the Discourse of Literary Historiography: The Creation of Two Traditions." Paper presented at the Tenth International Bhakti Conference: "Early Modern Literatures in North India," Miercurea Ciuc, Romania, July 22–24.

———. 2013. "From Sacred Sound to Sacred Book in the Sant Tradition of North India." Paper presented at the conference "Rethinking Bhakti," Mangalore University, March 29.

———. 2014. "Sacred Sounds and Sacred Books: A History of Writing in Hindi." Ph.D. dissertation, Columbia University.

———. Forthcoming. "Commentary as Translation: The *Vairāgya Vṛnd* of Bhagvandas Niranjani." In Williams, Malhotra, and Hawley, eds. *Early Modern Literatures in North India.*

Williams, Tyler, Anshu Malhotra, and John Stratton Hawley, eds. Forthcoming. *Early Modern Literatures in North India.* Delhi: Indian Institute for Advanced Study and Oxford University Press.

Wilson, Frances. 1975. *The Love of Krishna: The Kṛṣṇakarṇāmṛta of Līlāśuka Bilvamaṅgala.* Philadelphia: University of Pennsylvania Press.

Wilson, H. H. 1846 [1828, 1832]. *Sketch of the Religious Sects of the Hindus.* Calcutta: Bishop's College Press. Reprint, Banaras: Indological Book House, 1972.

Yadunāth [attrib.]. 1985 [1904, 1906]. *Śrīvallabhadigvijaya,* with a Hindi translation by Paraśurām Śarmā Caturvedī. Baroda: Shri Vallabha Publications.

Yashaschandra, Sitamshu. 2003. "From Hemacandra to *Hind Svarāj:* Region and Power in Gujarati Literary Culture." In Pollock, ed., *Literary Cultures in History,* 567–611.

Zecchini, Laetitia. 2013. "Contemporary *Bhakti* Recastings: Recovering a Demotic Tradition, Challenging Nativism, Fashioning Modernism in Indian Poetry." *Interventions* 16, no. 2: 257–276

Zelliot, Eleanor. 1976. "The Bhakti Movement in History: An Essay on the Literature in English." In Bardwell L. Smith, ed., *Hinduism: New Essays in the History of Religions.* Leiden: E. J. Brill.

———. 1987. "Eknath's *Bhāruḍs:* The Sant as a Link between Cultures." In Schomer and McLeod, eds., *Sants,* 91–110.

Zelliot, Eleanor, and Rohini Mokashi-Punekar, eds. 2005. *Untouchable Saints: An Indian Phenomenon.* Delhi: Manohar.

Zvelebil, Kamil V. 1974. *Tamil Literature.* Wiesbaden: Otto Harrassowitz.

———. 1984. *The Lord of the Meeting Rivers: Devotional Poems of Basavaṇṇa.* Delhi: Motilal Banarsidass.

Zydenbos, Robert. 1994. "Some Examples from Mādhva Hagiography." In Callewaert and Snell, eds., *According to Tradition,* 169–189.

Index

Abd al-Qādir "Bīdil," Mīrzā, 91, 225
Abhang, 297–298, 336
Acyutarayā, 222
Adhar Mookerji Lectures, 243
Adi Brahmos, 261
Ādhyātmik, 338–339
Advaitācārya, 194
Advaitans, 90, 104, 222, 223–224, 262, 271. *See also* Madhusūdan Sarasvāti Śaṃkara
Afghans, 30, 156, 173, 186
Agarvāl, Bāleśvar Prasād, 244
Agra, 78, 154–156, 160, 201, 244
Agradās, 113, 116, 118, 123–124, 225
Agrawal, Purushottam: on early modernity, 313–315, 317–318, 319, 322; Kabīr poem, 320–321
Ajab Shahar (Wondrous City), 335
Akath Kahānī Prem kī (Love's Untold Story, a phrase from Kabīr) (Agrawal), 319
Akbar (Emperor), 79, 115, 151, 152; Brindavan and, 75; rule of, 76, 78, 156–157, 166, 186
Alam, Muzaffar, 225
Allahabad University, 42, 45, 47, 56
All India Radio, 6, 23, 34
"All of India." *See* Viśva Bhāratī
Āḻvārs, 26, 83, 87, 105, 246–247
Ambedkar, B. R., 317, 329, 333
Amiya Nimai Carit (Ghosh, S. K.), 261
Ānandghan, 95–96
Anantadās, 101–102, 114, 138, 146, 315, 327; Galtā and, 120–125; on four *sampradāys*, 122–123, 126
Anantadev, 325–326
Anderson, Benedict, 13
Andrews, Charles, 241
Angad, 122–123
Annamayya, 324; Bhakti network and, 296, 299, 301, 303, 307; influence, 321–323
Āṇṭāḷ, 2, 248, 301–302
Anubhava maṇḍapa, 339–340, 341
Anyāśraya (taking refuge with another), 211
Architecture: of temples, 75–76, 78, 79, 144; in Brindavan, 152–153
Archive. *See* Bhakti archive
Āsānand, 72
Aṣṭachāp. *See* "Eight Seals"
Aurangzeb (Emperor), 10, 138, 151, 160, 217
Avatars, 101, 121, 132, 142, 251, 302
Ayyaṅkār, Kantāṭai Rāmūṉuja, 224
Ayyappa, 339

Babur (King), 166
Babri Mosque, 4, 285, 286, 287, 290, 334
Bahādur, Tegh, 125
Bāṅvarī *panth*, 91
Bālānand, 205
Balarām, 179
Baladev Vidyābhūṣaṇ, 199–200, 202–203, 212
Banaras, 69, 71, 73, 102, 110, 156
Banaras Hindu University, 43, 55, 240, 269, 270
Banerjea, Surendranath, 257–258
banjārā, 330

Barthwal, Pitambar Datta, 125, 270, 272–273, 318; Kabīr and, 50, 271; Nirguṇa School and, 332
Basava, 303, 304, 305–306, 323, 324
al-Basri, Hasan, 219
Bauls, 94, 239, 335
Behl, Aditya, 58, 91
Belvedere Press, 244, 245
Bengali, 58, 71, 106, 172, 236, 265; Chaitanyites and, 180; Rabindranath Tagore and, 233
Bengalis, 173, 211, 252; Brindavan and, 78, 171; Brahmos and, 255–267
Bengal Vaishnavism (Pal), 256, 259, 263
Bernard of Clairvaux, 253
Bhagavad Gītā, 39, 60, 63, 64
Bhagavān (God who shares), 5, 53, 297, 330
Bhagavāndās (or Bhagavantdās), (Rājā of Āmer), 75, 114, 136, 151, 213
Bhagavān Dīn, Lālā, 240
Bhagavānnāmakaumudī (Comment on the Name of God) (Lakṣmīdhara), 325
Bhagavānprasād, Sītārāmśaraṇ "Rūpkalā," 110, 119
Bhāgavata Māhātmya: Bhāgavata Purāṇa in, 61, 62, 64–65, 66, 67; Bhakti in, 61–68, 75, 78; Krishna in, 62, 64, 65, 67; Nārada in, 62, 63–65, 67; women in, 63–64; geography and time of, 68–74; Haridvar and, 70; Brahmins as author of, 73–74; "born in Dravida" and, 74, 105; Hindu allusions in, 81–89; Vārkarī pilgrimage and, 84; Muslim exclusions from, 89–98
Bhāgavata Purāṇa, 10, 17, 60, 158, 169; in *Bhāgavata Māhātmya*, 61, 62, 64–65, 66, 67; as growth industry, 70; Brahmins and, 72, 73; Vallabha on, 206
Bhāgavat Dasam Skandh, 71
Bhajan (Tagore), 297
Bhajans, 128, 239, 281, 332
Bhaktamāl (Nābhādās), 105, 111, 117, 119–120, 125; *chappays*, 100–101, 121, 131; *dohās*, 101–102, 121, 127; influence of, 128–129, 130–131, 143, 232; Keśav Kāśmīrī Bhaṭṭ and, 159; silences in, 249, 307
Bhaktamāl (Rāghavdās), 128–129, 133, 136, 138, 216
Bhaktamāl (Rām Sonī), 140
Bhakti: defined, 2, 5–6; poetry, songs and, 2; etymology of, 5–6; as liberation for Brahmins, 7; as history, 32–36; Hinduism and, 39; as protest language, 48, 94, 291; Kabīr and, 50–51, 105, 106, 119; as feminine in gender, 59–60; with "born in Dravida" narrative, 59–61, 66, 74, 82, 83, 85–86, 97, 100, 105, 231; in *Bhāgavata Māhātmya*, 61–68, 75, 78; in Brindavan, 78, 79, 98; in Gujarat, 79; lyrics and Muslims, 91; "Neo-Bhakti cult," 108; distance and, 122; *mādhurya*, 124; *nirguṇ*, 133, 335; Chaitanyites and, 165–166; *deś*, 333; "Rethinking Bhakti," 337. *See also* Mughal bhakti
Bhakti āndolan, 11, 37–38, 51–54, 58, 231
Bhakti and the Bhakti Movement: A New Perspective (Sharma), 32
Bhakti archive: political unification and, 13–19
"Bhakti in Indian Tradition: A Perennial Stream" (Nandakumar), 293
Bhakti kā Vikās (The Development of Bhakti) (Shukla), 43–44, 54
Bhakti movement: idea of, 2–4, 6; Tamil as root of, 3; as unifying force, 3, 6, 13–14; Muslims and, 3–4, 46, 61; religion and, 3–4, 6, 8–9, 34–36; themes, 6–7; personal experience and, 7, 15–16, 324; today, 12; bhakti archive and, 13–19; great integrators, 19–28; three trajectories of, 21; major figures in narrative of, 22; legacy in English, 29–37, 58; Grierson and, 33–36, 50–53, 103–104, 253–254; in education, 37–39; Hindi and, 37–49, 58, 232; misimpressions of, 39–40, 43–44; Islam and, 43, 45, 61, 287; Shukla and, 54–55, 125, 291; narrative with four *sampradāys*, 103–111; of Gauḍīyas, 165–179; Dvivedi on, 49–58, 250; Pal with, 262–263, 265, 290–291; Collet on, 264–265; in Hindi Bhavan murals, 276–277; contestations, 285–295, 338–339; bhakti network and, 295–312; with Kabīr and early modernity, 313–327; in plural, 327–333; of "The Bhakti Movement," 333–340; real religion and, 340–341
Bhakti Movement in Medieval India: Social and Political Perspectives (Iraqi), 93–94

Bhakti network: bhakti movementas, 295–312; Annamayya and, 296, 299, 301, 303, 307; network theory and, 296; musical idioms and, 296–297; poems interconnected in, 297–298, 304–305, 307; stories interconnected in, 297 298, 302; *pad* form and, 298–300, 301
Bhakti poetry: songs and, 2; contrasting aspects of, 17; at Gurū Gobind Singh's court, 283
Bhakti poets: language of, 2–3; as saints, 6; women, 16. *See also specific bhakti poets*
Bhaktirasabodhinī (Priyādās), 110, 123
Bhandarkar, Ramakrishna Gopal, 33, 108, 109, 248
Bharati, Gopalakrishna, 332
Bhāratī, Keśav, 166
Bharatiya Janata Party (BJP), 38, 40, 286, 334, 337, 339
Bharat Mata temple, 276
Bhāṣā Dasam Skandh (Nandadās), 71
Bhaṭṭ, Gadādhar. *See* Dvivedī, Gadādhar Bhaṭṭ
Bhatt, G. H., 206–207, 215
Bhaṭṭ, Gopāl, 115, 161, 171–172, 180, 202
Bhaṭṭ, Jānakīprasād, 161
Bhaṭṭ, Keśav Kāśmīrī, 72, 103, 158–160, 176
Bhaṭṭ, Lālū, 196
Bhaṭṭ, Ratnākar, 196
Bhaṭṭ, Śrī, 158, 161
Bhaṭṭ, Śrīnivās, 197
Bhaṭṭ, Viśvanāth, 196
Bhaṭṭācārya, Gāngal, 158
Bhaṭṭācārya, Kṛṣṇadās, 196, 203
Bhūpati, 71–72
Bhūṣaṇācārya, Raghunāth, 287
Bibi, Madhava, 94
Bīdil. *See* Abd al-Qādir "Bīdil," Mīrzā
Bihari, Brindavan, 161
Bilvamangal, Līlāśuk, 120, 135, 208–209, 210–212, 214
Biṣṇupurī, 119
Biṣṇusvāmī, 119. *See also* Viṣṇusvāmī
Bittideva (King), 87
BJP. *See* Bharatiya Janata Party
Bliss. *See* Forest of bliss
Bly, Robert, 315
Bodies, gendered, 16
Books: textbooks, 37–38, 42, 59; as cultural capital, 126–127
Boratti, Vijayakumar, 338
"Born in Dravida" narrative, 59, 66, 83, 85–86, 97; in public consciousness, 60; origins, 61, 82; *Bhāgavata Māhātmya* and, 74, 105; Brindavan and, 74; with south-to-north flow, 100; Dvivedi and, 231
Bose, Nandalal, 241, 275
Brahmā (deity), 62, 65, 68
Brahmacārī, Kṛṣṇadās, 162
Brahmasambandh ("becoming Brahman"), 186
Brahmins, 4, 25, 27, 64, 69, 145–146, 153, 164, 250, 325; bhakti as liberation for, 7; Dalits and, 2, 3; Vedic traditions of, 6, 7; in Banaras, 69; in Haridvar, 69; *Bhāgavata Purāṇa* and, 72, 73; as authors of *Bhāgavata Māhātmya,* 73–74; Maharashtrian, 196, 197, 329; bhakti movements and, 329–330
Brahmo Samaj, 11, 249, 255–267; Adi, 261; Shantiniketan, 261
Braj, 161–162, 177, 179, 185, 187; pilgrimage, 78; Nimbārka in, 158–159; Rūp Gosvāmī in, 163–164; Puri and, 174, 195; Vallabha in, 188–189
Brajbhasha, 95, 100, 119, 125, 180, 299
Braj ke Dharma-Sampradāyoṅ kā Itihās (History of the Religious Communities of Braj) (Mītal), 158
Brindavan, 10, 61, 148–149, 190, 225; in "born in Dravida" narrative, 74; Mughal bhakti and, 74–81, 91, 150–157; Akbar and, 75; Bengalis and, 78, 171; Bhakti in, 78, 79, 98; as forest, 150, 190; history of, 150–151; temples in, 151–154; architecture in, 152–153; as garden, 154, 190, 192; Mathura and rivalry with, 154; immigrants from south, 157–164; Puri and, 173–174; Vallabhites and, 179–189; Krishna in, 194
Brindāvandās, 225
Buddhism, 3, 6, 25, 53, 253, 286, 329–330
Bundelā, Vīrsingh (King), 153, 154
Burton, Adrian, 200, 203
Burton-Page, John, 78
Busch, Allison, 308, 322
Butter, churning of, 138, 300

Caitanyacandrodaya (Kavikarṇapūra), 177–178, 192
Caitanyacaritāmṛta (Kavirāj), 164, 167, 170, 171, 176; influence, 166; play within the play, 178–179
Cakravartī, Viśvanāth, 200, 212
Caliphs, 219
Callewaert, Winand, 129
Camārs, 333
Caṇḍīdās, 233
Capital, books as cultural, 126–127
Cār panth, 216
Caste system, 147, 248, 294, 309–310; in poems, 14–15, 16; democracy and, 27; tyranny of, 39–40, 48, 341; Muslims and, 45; Rāmānand and, 246; Dādū Dayāl and, 309; nonlanded castes, 310, 322; as regards bhakti movement in plural, 328–330. *See also specific caste categories*
Caturdās, 71
Caurāsī Baiṭhak Caritra, 72, 213–214
Caurāsī Vaiṣṇavan kī Vārtā, 134, 135, 185
Cēkkiḻār, 88, 332
"Celestial Love: Bhakti in Indian Tradition," 292
Celibacy, 161, 203, 204, 320
Cennabasava, 303
Chaitanya, 20, 27, 48, 70, 130, 161; Madhva linked to, 103, 106, 109, 195; Keśav Kāśmīrī Bhaṭṭ and, 159; conversion of, 166–167; legacy, 167–179; with epilepsy, 169; Kṛṣṇadās Kavirāj on, 173–175; influence of, 193, 233; Kavikarṇapūra on, 193–194; "Five Elements" and, 194; lineage, 194, 212; divinity of, 200–201; Gadādhar Bhaṭṭ Dvivedī on, 211–212; B. C. Pal on, 255–261, 266
Chaitanyites, 72–73, 76, 78; bhakti and, 165–166; Bengali and, 180; Vallabhites and, 180, 211, 303
Chamars. *See Camārs*
Chand, Tara, 43, 92–93, 95
Chandra, Satish, 38
Chandra, Sudhir, 320
Chappay, 100–101, 119, 121, 131
Chatterjee, Partha, 232
Chatterji, Bankimchandra, 258, 233
Chaturvedi, Banarsidas, 241
Chaudry, Pearee Mohun, 266
Chennai, 23, 336–337
Chidambaram, 173, 329–330
Chīn Bhavan, murals of, 275
Christianity, 4, 33, 35–36, 166, 234
Churning. *See* Butter, churning of
Circumcision, 160
Cities of victory. *See* Brindavan; Jaipur; Vijayanagar
Clark, Matthew, 221–222
Clothing, 16, 89
Cokhāmeḷā, 302, 329–330
Collet, Sophia Dobson, 263–265
Columbia University, 334
Comment on the Name of God. *See Bhagavānnāmakaumudī*
Commonwealth of love, 100, 124–127
Congress Party, 255, 334
Construction: temples, 75, 78, 114, 155; roads, 156; mosques, 160, 226
Contestations, 323; between Advaitans and Mādhvites, 222; of bhakti movement, 285–295, 338–339
Conversions: to Islam, 39–40; to Vaishnavism, 87; of Chaitanya, 166–167; of Baladev Vidyābhūṣan, 203
Cort, John, 5–6
Cruelty, of Hinduism, 7
Culture, books as cultural capital, 126–127

Dabistān-i-Mazābib (School of Religions) (Shāh, M.), 139–141, 219, 314
Dādū Dayāl, 106, 127–128, 136, 309, 315
Dādū Panth, 91, 129, 244, 275, 309
Dādūpathīs, 38, 148–149, 218; Sikhs and, 27, 228; influence of, 204; Kabīr and, 274
Dalits (Untouchables), 1, 2, 3, 11, 239
Dāmodar, Svarūp, 193
Dara Shukoh, 217, 223, 315, 332
Dās, Nārāin, 141
Dās, Nṛtya Gopāl, 287
Dās, Paramānand, 193
Dās, Raghunāth, 150
Dās, Śyāmsundar, 240, 249–250
Dās, Vrindāvan, 193
Dāsas, 27
Dasgupta, Surendranath, 97–98
Dattātreya (god), 339
Debrahminizing History (Mani), 328
Delhi International Arts Festival, 336

Democracy: India and, 24; caste system and, 27
Deś bhakti, 333
The Development of Bhakti. *See Bhakti kā Vikās*
Devotional Enjoyments of Braj. *See Vrajabhaktivilāsa*
Devotional hymns, 38
Dhannā, 126
Dharamvir, 315
Dhundhukārī, 67, 68, 74
Didwana, 309–310
Dīkṣita, Appaya, 223, 325
Distance, bhakti and, 122
Divine stories. *See Līlā*
Divinity, 200–201, 219
Divisions, of time, 219
Divyaprabandham, 26
Dohā, 101–102, 121, 127
Doubleness, 184, 269
Dravida. *See* "Born in Dravida" narrative
Dr. Dominic D, 339
Dutta, Akshaykumar, 244
Dvārā, 128
Dvivedī, Gadādhar Bhaṭṭ, 73, 191, 194, 216, 205–210, 216, 222; on Chaitanya, 211–212; origins of, 213. *See also Sampradāyapradīpa*
Dvivedi, Hazariprasad, 10, 11, 43, 44, 59, 110; on Islam, 45; Ganga-Jamuna sari and, 49–58; influence of, 50–51, 57, 230–234; on Grierson, 51–53, 103–104, 253–254, 293; on four *sampradāys*, 99–100, 103, 104–108; and the "born in Dravida" narrative, 231; with Rabindranath Tagore, 235, 236–237, 241, 247; in Shantiniketan, 235, 240, 241, 243; with Kshitimohan Sen, 245–255; on bhakti movement, 250; with Hindi Bhavan murals, 275
Dvivedī, Sudhākar, 241

Early modernity: explanation of, 313; with Kabīr and Rāmānand link, 313–315; with Kabīr and bhakti movement, 313–327; *vacanas* and, 324; with bhakti movement, 333–340
Eckhart, 35, 253
Education: NCERT, 37, 40–41; language in, 37–38, 42, 55; textbooks in, 37–38, 42, 59; bhakti movement in, 37–39
"Eight seals," 106–107, 135, 182–183
Eknāth, 71, 84, 90, 302, 328, 332
Eknath Research Society, 329
Encyclopedia of Religion and Ethics (Hastings), 34
English: bhakti movement legacy in, 29–37, 58; Raghavan and, 31–32; Hinglish and, 37; Hindi and, 37–38, 41, 53, 55, 234; Rabindranath Tagore and, 233
Entwistle, Alan, 162
Epic texts, 17–19
Epilepsy, 169
Ernst, Carl, 90
Exclusions, Muslims, 89–98

The Faith and Progress of the Brahmo Samaj (Sen, K. C.), 265
Farīd, Bābā, 139, 327
Farquhar, J. N., 9, 55, 58, 109, 111, 244
Fazl, Abu'l, 152, 171, 216, 315
Feminine, bhakti as, 59–60
Filliozat, Jean, 87, 92
The Final Word (Stewart), 170
"Five Elements," 193–194
Flutes, 18, 300
Ford Foundation, 335
Forest, Brindavan as, 150, 190
Forest of bliss, 68, 81
Fourness: Mughal bhakti and, 217–229; importance of, 219; with scripture, 220
The Fragrance of the Heavenly Tree of Vedānta. *See Vedāntapārijātasaurabha*
Frescoes. *See* Hindi Bhavan, murals of
Fuller, Christopher, 333

Gadādhar. *See* Dvivedī, Gadādhar Bhaṭṭ
Gadākhya, 216
Galtā, 10; Nābhādās at, 111–121, 123, 124; Payahārī and Tārānāth at, 112, 113; four *sampradāys* and, 113, 116, 120–127; Kachvahas and, 115–116; sphere of influence, 120–127
Gandhi, Indira, 19, 25
Gandhi, Mahatma, 1, 28, 32, 236, 237, 253
Ganga-Jamuna sari, Dvivedi and, 49–58
Ganges, 46, 65, 235, 238, 281–282
Garden, Brindavan as, 154, 190, 192

Gauḍīyas, 114–115, 130, 134, 199; Mādhva-Gauḍīya link, 135, 196, 199–200, 203, 222; bhakti movement of, 165–179; Vallabhites and, 179–180, 211; within four *sampradāys,* 195, 199, 219. *See also* Chaitanyites
Gauragaṇoddeśadīpikā (A Lamp to Explicate the Companions of the Golden One) (Kavikarṇapūra), 192–193
Gender: clothing and gendered bodies, 16; of bhakti, 59–60
Geography: *Bhāgavata Māhātmya* with time and, 68–74; sacred, 162
Ghamaṇḍī, 70, 78, 161–163
Ghosh, Manomohan, 243
Ghosh, Pika, 80
Ghosh, Sishir Kumar, 261
Gibbon, Edward, 58
Giridhar, 119
Gītagovinda (Jayadev), 299
Gita Press, 60
Glasenapp, Helmuth von, 206–207
God, 32, 44, 49, 104, 323, 325
Godhra station, 334
God who shares. *See Bhagavān*
Gokarṇa, 67, 68, 73–74, 89
Gokulnāth, 119, 180, 182, 214, 326
Gold, 208, 215
Gopīnāth, 187
Gorakhnāth, 25, 44, 50, 136, 232, 306
goṣṭhī, 303, 331
Gosvāmī, Jīv, 150, 157, 163, 170, 171, 193
Gosvāmī, Raghunāth Bhaṭṭ, 72–73, 75–76, 157
Gosvāmī, Rūp, 72–73, 171, 177; legacy, 75–76, 155, 157; in Braj, 163–164
Gosvāmī, Sanātan, 115, 157, 162, 163–164, 177
Gosvāmī, Śivānand, 197
Goswami, Bijay Krishna, 259, 260–264
Goswami, Shrivatsa, 85, 202
Goswami, Shyam Manohar, 217
Govindadev, 75–76, 78, 151, 152, 155, 190, 198
Grants, land, 75, 154, 157, 186
Great Britain, 14, 40
Great Hindi Dictionary, 42
Great integrators: bhakti movement and, 19–28; three trajectories, 21; major figures among, 22; Mahatma Gandhi among, 28
Grierson, George, 4, 9, 27, 43, 109, 229; bhakti movement and, 33–36, 50–53, 103–104, 253–254; Dvivedi on, 51–53, 103–104, 253–254, 293; influence of, 55–56; on the four *sampradāys,* 99; Christianity and, 234
Growse, Frederic Salmon, 108
Guha, Ranajit, 48
Guha, Sumit, 197
Gujarat, 79, 84–85, 134, 306, 307
Guṇas, 133, 206
Gupta, Murārī, 167–169, 179, 193
Gurbani, 293
Gurmukhi script, 125, 328
Gurū Granth, 315, 326, 328
Guru (Sikh: Gurū), 2, 20, 109, 116, 128, 130. *See also specific gurus*

Habib, Irfan, 48, 50, 75, 150
Halbfass, Wilhelm, 89
Hanumān, 281
Hardās, Bābā Banvārī, 128
Hare, James, 118
Haridās, 129, 134, 165
Haridāsas (servants of Hari), 26–27, 83
Haridvar, 68, 70, 73, 74, 81, 276
Harihara, 87
Harijan, 237, 238
Harirāmvyās, 135, 165–166, 171, 215, 228, 314
Harirāy, 183–184, 187, 189
Harishchandra, Bharatendu, 147, 205, 218; Shukla and, 54, 110–111; on Muslims and Hindus, 290
Harivaṃś, Hit, 103, 107, 135, 141, 165, 304
Harivardās, Rāmānuj, 105
Harkishan (Gurū), 129–130
Hastings, James, 34, 52
Hastings Encyclopedia of Religion and Ethics, 44, 52, 99
Hāthrasī, Tulsī Sāhib, 244
Havṃīr, Vīr, 170
Hedayatullah, Muhammad, 93
Hegde, Rajaram, 338, 339
Hermits, 167
Hess, Linda, 315
Hibbert Lectures, 235
Hindi, 2, 3, 56, 105, 233, 240; *bhakti āndolan* and, 11, 37–38, 51–54, 58, 231; Hinglish and, 37; English and, 37–38, 41, 53, 55, 234; bhakti movement and,

37–49, 58, 232; standardization of, 41; history of, 42; lyrics, 90, 139; Banaras and, 110; Bengali and, 233
Hindi Bhavan, murals of, 266, 275–284; Binodbihari Mukherji and, 275, 277–278, 281–282, 290; Dvivedi and, 275; Rāmānand in, 278–279; south and, 278–279, 281, 283; Kabīr in, 281, 283; Sūrdās in, 281–282; Gobind Singh in, 282
Hindī Sāhitya kā Itihās (History of Hindi Literature) (Shukla), 42, 47, 49, 54, 59, 110
Hindī Sāhitya kī Bhūmikā (Dvivedi), 110, 231
Hinduism, 6, 25, 51–52, 55, 109; Muslims and, 4, 56, 75, 90–95, 97–98, 104, 137, 160, 220, 223, 243–244, 286–287, 290, 291, 335; cruelty of, 7; bhakti and, 39; Banaras Hindu University, 43, 55, 240, 269, 270; Yavanas and, 80; *Bhāgavata Māhātmya* and allusions to, 81–89; VHP, 276, 286, 287, 290
Hinduism Today, 218
Hindutva: Who Is a Hindu? (Savarkar), 286
Hinglish, 37
An Historical Sketch of the Brahmo Somaj (Collet), 263
History, 158, 328; India, 14; bhakti as, 32–36; of Hindi, 42; Brindavan, 150–151
History of Hindi Literature. *See Hindī Sāhitya kā Itihās*
History of Medieval India (Prasad), 56, 57
History of Science, Philosophy, and Culture in Indian Civilization, 291
History of the Religious Communities of Braj. *See Braj ke Dharma-Sampradāyoṅ kā Itihās*
Hobsbawm, Eric, 13
Holy mendicancy, 27, 28
Honey love. *See Mādhurya bhakti*
Horstmann, Monika, 128, 129, 130, 203, 211, 308
Humor, 13, 125, 180, 181
Husain, Abid, 43
Hymns, 38, 83

Idea, of Bhakti movement, 2–4, 6
Illusionism, 39, 209
Imagined Communities (Anderson), 13
Immigrants, Brindavan and, 157–164. *See also* Migration
Independence: for India, 4, 9, 27, 282, 317; for Pakistan, 4
India, 39, 55–57, 92, 93–94; with bhakti movement as unifying force, 3, 6, 13–14; independence for, 4, 9, 27, 282, 317; All India Radio, 6, 23, 34; Viśva Bhāratī, 11, 100; history of, 14; democracy and, 24; Linguistic Survey of India, 27, 53; Middle Ages of, 107; Quit India Movement, 253. *See also Medieval India; Medieval Mysticism of India; The Soul of India*
India International Centre, 320
Indian Council of Philosophical Research, 292
Indian Council on Cultural Religions, 336
Indian Mirror, 264
Indologists, 32–33
Influence of Islam on Indian Culture (Chand), 92
Integrators. *See* Great integrators
Interconnectedness: of poems, 297–298, 304–305, 307; of stories, 297–298, 302; with language and loaning of words, 299
Introduction to Hindi Literature (Keay), 55–56
The Invention of Tradition (Hobsbawm and Ranger), 13
Iraqi, Shahabuddin, 93–94
Islam, 14, 89, 92, 285, 286; conversions to, 39–40; bhakti movement and, 43, 45, 61, 287; spread of, 90
Ismaīlīs, Nizāmī, 136–137
"I've never known how to tan or sew" (Ravidās), 15, 16

Jagannāth Puri, 144–145
Jagannāth Samrāṭ, 196
Jagatguru, Sarvajña, 163
Jahāngīr (Emperor), 153
Jain, Meenakshi, 38–41, 43
Jainism, 5, 6, 25, 286, 292, 310
Jaipur, 111, 198–199, 207, 220
Jaisingh, Savāī II (Rājā), 10–11, 69, 110, 114, 141; policies of, 146, 196, 200–201, 203–204; legacy of, 151, 190; with Kavikarṇapūra and *sampradāys,* 192–205
Janābaī, 302

Jāṭs, 123, 217, 309
Jayadev, 20, 126, 134, 210, 233, 299, 327
Jāyasī, Malik Muhammad, 70, 95, 107, 225
Jesus, 166, 266
Jhā, Narendra, 118, 119
Jijñāsu, 329–330, 333
Jīv. *See* Gosvāmī, Jīv
Jīvā, 120
Jñāna, 64, 65, 66, 67, 98
Jñāndev, 31–32, 84, 106, 134, 291, 302, 311
Jñāneśvar. *See* Jñāndev
Jones, Rufus, 44
Joshi, Prabhakar, 338

Kabīr, 2, 26, 27, 36, 44, 49; Barthwal and, 50, 271; bhakti and, 50–51, 105, 106, 119; on Hindus and Muslims, 90; *panth,* 91, 129, 274, 315; on pilgrimage, 122; influence of, 126, 142, 231; Nābhādās on, 137; as exemplar, 268–275; Dādūpathīs and, 274; Sikhs and, 274; in Hindi Bhavan murals, 281, 283; Rāmānand and, 313–315; as early modern, 313–327; Dādū Dayāl and, 315; Ravidās and, 331–332
Kabīr (Dvivedi), 50, 51
Kabir, Humayun, 43
Kabir: The Apostle of Hindu-Muslim Unity (Hedayatullah), 93
The Kabir Project, 315, 335, 340
Kachvaha, Rāmdās, 152
Kachvahas, 10, 148; Galtā and, 115–116; Mughals and, 151, 155, 224. *See also* Bhagavāndās; Jai Singh; Mānsingh
Kairos, 166, 251
Kaivān, Parrah, 142
Kālakṣepa, 23, 332
Kalyāṇa, 87, 324, 340
Kamāl, 106
Kampaṉ, 19
Kanakadāsa, 87, 276, 298, 307, 337, 341
Kanhāvat (Jāyasī), 70
Kannada, 8, 71, 83, 291, 297, 311
Kapur, Geeta, 290
Karma, 64
Karnataka saints, 276. *See also* Basava; Kanakadāsa; Purandaradāsa
Karnatak music, 23, 336–337
Kartārpur Pothī, 305
Kāśī Nāgarīpracāriṇī Sabhā. *See* Nāgarīpracāriṇī Sabhā
Kāśmīrī, Keśav. *See* Bhaṭṭ, Keśav Kāśmīrī
Kavicandra, Viśveśvara, 163
Kavikarṇapūra, 177–179; with Jaisingh II and *sampradāys,* 192–205; on Chaitanya, 193–194
Kavīndrācārya Sarasvatī, 223–224
Kavirāj, Kṛṣṇadās. *See* Kṛṣṇadās Kavirāj
Kāyasth, 72
Keay, Frank Ernest, 55–56, 58
Keith, Arthur Berriedale, 43
Keśavdās, 95, 135, 215
Keśav Kāśmīrī. *See* Bhaṭṭ, Keśav Kāśmīrī
Keune, Jon, 332
Khālsā, 128
Khan, Abdunnabi, 217
Khan, Dominique-Sila, 136
Khān, Mukhtār, 150
Khān, Rajab Ali, 136, 315
Khānkhānā, Abdurrahīm, 225
Khatrīs, 48, 156, 225, 309–310
Khecar, Visobā, 302
Kīlhadev, 124
Kīrtan, 23, 27, 263, 293
Kishwar, Madhu, 335–336, 337
Kosambi, D. D., 48
Krishna, 5, 17, 39, 59, 125, 179; in *Bhāgavata Māhātmya,* 62, 64, 65, 67; stories, 70, 177–179, 182; in Brindavan, 194; divinity of, 200–201; B C. Pal on, 256; flute of, 300
Kṛṣṇacaitanyacaritāmṛta (Murari Gupta), 167
Kṛṣṇadās Kavirāj, 163, 164, 167, 170, 171, 176, 328; legacy, 166; on Chaitanya, 173–175
Kṛṣṇadevarāya (King), 86, 149, 176, 190, 191, 208, 217
Kumbha, Rāṇā, 197
Kumbh Mela celebrations, 204–205

Lakṣmī, 144
Lakṣmīdhara, 325
Lāl, Bābā, 138
Lālac "Halvāī," 71, 72
Lālded, 94, 303
A Lamp to Explicate the Companions of the Golden One. *See Gauragaṇoddeśa-dīpikā*

Land: grants, 75, 154, 157, 186; purchases, 150–151; nonlanded castes, 310, 322
Languages, 27, 53, 105, 307; of bhakti poets, 2–3; with politics and religion, 8–9; in education, 37–38, 42, 55; history of Hindi, 42; bhakti as protest, 48, 94, 291; Vallabhites and Chaitanyites, 180; loaning of words between, 299; Telugu as musical, 336. *See also* Vernacularization; *specific languages*
The Language of the Gods in the World of Men (Pollock), 8–9
"The Latter Half of the *Bhaktamāl*" (Harishchandra), 111
Lee, Joel, 238, 333
Liberality, 133, 146, 250
Libraries, 126–127, 275
Light. *See Nūr*
Līlā, 17, 63, 121, 173–182, 251–252. *See also rās līlā*
Lineage: Madhva, 83, 199–203; Rāmānuja, 104; Vallabha, 106–107; Viṣṇusvāmī 106–107, 119; Nāth, 136, 306; Rāmānand, 165; Chaitanya, 194, 212. *See also Sampradāys, individual lineages*
Linguistic Survey of India, 27, 53
"linked families of cultural practice," 91
Loaning, of words, 299
Lodi, Ibrahim, 157
Lokācārya, Piḷḷai, 248
Lok-dharm, 247
Lok-ved, 243, 247
Lorenzen, David, 328
Lorinser, Franz, 33
Love, 124, 176, 250, 300, 319. *See also* Commonwealth of love; *Premāmbodh*
Love's Golden Treasure. *See* "Premer-Sonā"
Love's Untold Story. *See Akath Kahānī Prem kī*
Luminous Array of Festivals in Braj. *See Vrajotsavacandrikā*
Lutjeharms, Rembert, 193
Lyrics, 23, 95, 176, 239, 321; *pada,* 26, 273, 298; Hindi, 90, 139; Muslims and bhakti, 91. *See also Pad* and parallel forms

Macnicol, Nicol, 43–44
Madanmohan, Sūrdās, 134–135
Madanmohan temple, 75
Mādhodās, 143
Madhupuri, Madhvācārya, 196
Mādhurya bhakti, 124
Madhusūdan Sarasvatī, 90, 223, 227, 325
Madhva (Madhvācārya), 83–84, 86, 106, 339; within four *sampradāys,* 35, 46, 49; Chaitanya linked to, 103, 106, 109, 195; Mādhva-Gauḍīya link, 135, 196, 199–200, 203, 222
Mādhvites, 83, 142, 162, 222–223, 325
Magahar, 319–320
Mahābhārata, 16
Mahādevīakkā (poet-saint), 16, 17, 276, 324
Mahalingadeva, 305
Maharaja Libel Case of 1861, 141
Maharashtrian Brahmins, 196, 197, 329
Maharashtrian Organization for the Eradication of Superstition, 291
Maithili, 176–177
Mangalore, 83; University, 337–340
Mani, Braj Ranjan, 328–329, 332
Māṇikkavācakar, 26, 88
Manjhan, 225
Man-Lion, 112, 251
Mann, Gurinder Singh, 220
Manohardās, 146, 217
Mānsingh (King), 85, 136, 171, 190, 223; temple construction by, 75, 78, 114, 155; legacy of, 115, 199, 223; land purchase by, 150–151
Manucci, Niccolao, 154
Manushi, 335–337
Marathas, 30–31, 217
Marathi, 2, 71, 83, 106, 257, 297
Marxists, 48, 94, 236, 291
Mathura, 73, 80, 152, 154, 159, 162
Mathurā: A District Memoir (Growse), 108
Mathurā Māhātmya, 155
Matsyendranāth, 136, 306, 315
Māyāvādīs, 207–208. *See also* Śaṃkara
Medieval India, 37–38
Medieval Mysticism of India (Ghosh, M.), 243
Medieval Saints (murals), 275. *See also* Hindi Bhavan, murals of
Meera (film), 337

Mehtā, Narsī, 71, 84, 134, 301, 303, 307
Mendicancy. *See* Holy mendicancy
Michell, George, 78, 80
Middle Ages, of India, 107
Migration, 74, 78, 150, 162–163, 325
Milk, 188, 304, 305, 306
Milk Ocean, 300
Minkowski, Christopher, 325
Mīrābāī, 2, 122, 125, 126, 134, 242, 336; Kshitimohan Sen on, 244–245; mural of, 281; stories, 302–303; songs, 336; in *Meera,* 337
Mishra, Anand, 211
Mishra, Rameshwar, 236
Miśra, Viśvambhar. *See* Chaitanya
Miśrabandhuvinod (Miśra brothers), 109
Miśra brothers, 109–110, 111
Mītal, Prabhudayāl, 158, 213
Mitra, Rajendralal, 233
"Modern Hinduism and Its Debt to the Nestorians" (Grierson), 51–52
Modern Religious Movements in India (Farquhar), 55
Modern Standard Hindi, 240
The Modern Vernacular Literature of Hindustan (Grierson), 33, 56
Modi, Narendra, 334, 339
Monarch-as-bhakta, 112–114, 148–149
Monasteries, 83, 95, 124
Monastics, 148
Mongols, 90
Monserrate, Antonio, 153–154
Mookerji Lectures, 250
Mosques, 160, 226, 298, 326. *See also* Babri Mosque
"Movement," 248–249, 265, 276–277, 295. *See also* Bhakti movement; Quit India Movement; Vaishnavic Movements
Mozoomdar, P. C., 264, 265
Mughal bhakti, 91; Brindavan and, 74–81, 91, 150–157; fourness and, 217–229
Mughals, 10, 38; Kachvahas and, 151, 155, 224; rule of, 156, 186
Muhammad, 219, 266, 287
Mukherjee, Tarapada, 75
Mukherji, Bhudev, 233
Mukherji, Bimanbehari, 241
Mukherji, Binodbihari, 275, 277–278, 281–282, 290
Murals, 281. *See also* Chīn Bhavan, murals of; Hindi Bhavan, murals of
Music: Karnatak, 23, 336–337; *saṅkīrtan,* 27; Muslims and Hindus with shared traditions in, 91
Musical idioms, 296–297
Muslims, 3, 11, 79, 147; bhakti movement and, 3–4, 46, 61; Hinduism and, 4, 56, 75, 90–95, 97–98, 104, 137, 160, 220, 223, 243–244, 286–287, 290, 291, 335; caste system and, 45; as *yavana,* 64; exclusions, 89–98; bhakti lyrics and, 91; circumcision and, 160; Vaishnavas and, 224–225, 226; VHP and, 287, 290; at Godhra station, 334
Mutiny of 1857, 255
"Mystical" worldview, 244
Mysticism, 43–44, 243, 253, 271, 324

Nābhādās, 100–102, 105, 106, 159, 218, 327; at Galtā, 111–121, 123, 124; on four *sampradāys,* 120, 121–123, 134–136; commonwealth of love and, 126, 127; influence of, 128–129, 130–131, 143, 232; on Kabīr, 137. *See also Bhaktamāl*
Nāgarīpracāriṇī Sabhā, 41, 240, 269–270
Nahta, Agar Chand, 129
Nāmdev, 2, 106, 126, 134, 302, 327–328; influence, 27; Sufis and, 93; poems, 304–305, 307
Nammāḻvār (poet-saint), 2, 15–16, 17, 18, 88
Nānak (Gurū), 107, 127, 128, 129, 136, 310; as Bābā Nānak, 2, 256, 266, 297
Nandadās, 71, 127, 183, 192
Nandakumar, Prema, 293
Nantaṉār, 330, 332
Nārada, 62, 63–65, 67, 79
Narahariānand, 119
Naraharitīrtha, 83
Nārāyaṇ Bhaṭṭ. *See* Ghamaṇḍī
Narayana Rao, Velcheru, 310, 321–322
Narratives: major figures in bhakti movement, 22; "born in Dravida," 59–61, 66, 74, 82, 83, 85–86, 97, 100, 105, 231; four *sampradāys* and bhakti movement, 103–111
Narsiṃha, 251
Narsiṃha, Saluva (King), 224
Nāth Yogīs, 136, 234, 252, 302, 312; *see also* Gorakhnāth; Matsyendranāth; Tārānāth
Nāthamuni, 46, 83, 248
Nāth Sampradāy (Dvivedi), 50

National Council of Educational Research and Training (NCERT), 37, 40–41
Navīn Hindī Gāiḍ (New Hindi Guide), 42
Nāyaṉmārs, 26, 87, 307
NCERT. *See* National Council of Educational Research and Training
"Neo-Bhakti cult," 108
Nestorians, 36, 51–52
Network. *See* Bhakti network
Network theory, 296
New Catalogus Catalogorum, 217
New Hindi Guide. *See Navīn Hindī Gāiḍ*
New Party (Congress), 259
NGOs, 335
Nimbārka (Nimbārkācārya), 69; within four *sampradāys*, 35, 46, 49, 103, 135; in Braj, 158–159
Nirguṇ (without attributes), 17, 38, 47, 48, 125, 137, 300, 317–320, 326–328, 335, 340; *panth*, 49, 250–251, 271–272; kind of bhakti, 133, 136, 148, 228, 234, 244–245, 269, 309; as movement, 271–272; and Sufis, 291
Nirguṇa School, 94, 332
The Nirguṇa School of Hindi Poetry: An Exposition of Medieval Indian Santa Mysticism (Barthwal), 271, 273
Nityānand, 179, 194
Nonlanded castes, 310, 322
North: southern flow toward, 100–103; immigration to, 157–164; 307–308; Hindi Bhavan murals and, 281–283
Novetzke, Christian, 84, 297, 311
Nūr (light), 131–132, 133
Nuruddīin (Sheikh), 94, 303

The Ocean of Love. See Premāmbodh
O'Hanlon, Rosalind, 325
Orsini, Francesca, 138, 299
An Outline of the Religious Literature of India (Farquhar), 55

Padmāvat (Jāyasī), 107
Pad and parallel forms, 26, 127, 273, 298–300, 301, 321
Pakistan, 4, 335
Pal, Bipin Chandra: with Chaitanya, 255–261, 266; on Krishna, 256; on bhakti movement, 262–263, 265, 290–291
Pañcvāṇī, 327
Pāṇḍe, Saḍḍū, 188
Pandharpur, 30, 79, 83–84, 175, 302, 328–329
Panini, 5
Panth, 204, 228; *nirguṇ*, 49, 250, 271–272; Banvārī, 91; Dādū, 91, 129, 244, 275, 309; Kabīr, 91, 129, 274, 315; Rāghavdās and four, 127–138; *khālsā* and *dvārā*, 128; Sikh, 128, 274; Haridās, 129; Nānak, 129, 136; *cār*, 216; Nāth, 234
Paramānanddās, 135
Patel Lectures. *See* Sardar Vallabhbhai Patel Memorial Lectures
Pāṭhak, Śiv Mūrti, 43, 44, 46
Pauwels, Heidi, 314
Pavilion of Experience, 339–340
Pavilions, 197, 339
Payahārī, Kṛṣṇadās, 112, 113, 116–117, 119, 124
Pellò, Stefano, 138
Periya Purāṇa (Cēkkiḻār), 332
Persian, 71, 90–91; four *sampradāys* in, 138–147; *tazkirā*, 139
Personal experience, 7, 15–16, 324
Personal signatures, in poems, 17–18
Pilgrimages, 28, 31, 151, 153–154, 328; Vārkarī, 30, 83–84; Shaiva, 73; Braj, 78; Rāmānand and Kabīr on, 122
Pinch, Vijay, 116–117, 118
Pīpā Parcaī (Anantadās), 120–123
Play within the play, 178–179
Plural, bhakti movement in, 331–333; Sikhs and, 327–328; caste and, 328–330; Brahmins and, 329–330
Poems: caste system in, 14–15, 16; by Nammāḻvār, 15–16; personas and personal signatures in, 17–18, 299; women in, 17–18, 181–182, 300; interconnectedness of, 297–298, 304–305, 307; by Nāmdev, 304–305, 307; Agrawal, 320–321. *See also specific poems and genres*
Poetry. *See* Bhakti poetry
Poets. *See* Bhakti poets; Poet-saints
Poet-saints, 17; as great integrators, 19–28; devotional hymns of, 38. *See also specific poet-saints*
Politics, 40; language and, 8–9; four *sampradāys* and, 10–11; of Great Britain in India, 14. *See also specific political parties*

Pollock, Sheldon, 29, 84, 85, 311; on vernacularization, 8–9; on early modernity, 322, 325
Powers, 29, 59; royal, 148–149, 191; yogic, 194
Prabhu, Allama, 297, 324
Prasad, Ishwari, 56–57, 58, 95, 108, 229; influence of, 286; bhakti movement for, 290
Pratāparudra (King), 176, 177, 178
"Prayer of Sūrdās" (Tagore, R.), 236
Premākhyān genre, 44, 91, 96, 107, 139, 225
Premāmbodh (The Ocean of Love), 125–126, 139–140
"Premer-Sonā" (Love's Golden Treasure) (Tagore, R.), 237–238
A Primer of Hinduism (Farquhar), 55, 109
Priyādās, 110, 123, 159; on the four *sampradāys*, 143–147; Keśav Kāśmīrī Bhaṭṭ and, 159–160
Progressive Writers' Association, 54
Protestant Reformation, 29, 30, 31, 32
Protestants, 2, 338
Protests: songs of, 13, 340; bhakti as language of, 48, 94, 291; Vaishnavic Movements and, 257
Pṛthvīrāj (King), 112–114
Punjabi, 2, 47, 96, 126, 228
Purandaradāsa, 23, 87, 303, 307, 325
Purchases, land, 150–151
Puri, 175–176, 193, 194; Brindavan and, 173–174; Braj and, 174, 195
Purī, Īśvara, 166, 193, 194
Purī, Mādhavendra, 194–195
Puṣṭimārgīs, 134, 135, 179–180, 185, 213. *See also* Vallabhites

Qawwali, 293
Quit India Movement, 253
Qutban, 225

Radha, 80, 124, 154, 158, 167, 256
Radhasoami Satsang, 27, 244
Rādhāvallabhīs, 107, 141
Raghavan, V., 43, 59, 105, 333, 337; Patel Lectures of, 19–20, 23, 25–27, 60; on democracy, 24, 27; on singer-saints, 28; on vernacularization, 29; English and, 31–32
Rāghavānand, 102, 105
Rāghavdās, 191, 216; on four *panths* and *sampradāys*, 127–138; *nirguṇ bhakti* and, 133, 137; *saguṇ bhakti* and, 133. *See also Bhaktamāl*
Rāghavdās kṛt Bhaktamāl (Nahta), 129
Rahman, Ram, 334
Raidās, 122, 126, 145. *See also* Ravidās
Rajab. *See* Khān, Rajab Ali
Rājasūya sacrifice, 226
Rajyaguru, Niranjan, 306
Rām (god), 4, 36, 112, 113, 123, 124; *Rāmcaritmānas*, 19; rituals, 198; wall painting, 285; Tulsīdās as slave of, 326
Rāmakṛṣṇa Paramahaṃsa, 279
Ramā (Śrī), 101, 130, 132
Rāmānand, 7, 26, 27, 35, 102, 119; influence of, 15, 55–56, 106, 138, 231, 287; vernacular usage, 105; on pilgrimage, 122; lineage, 165; Ravidās as disciple of, 237; caste system and, 246; in Hindi Bhavan murals, 278–279; Kabīr and, 313–315
Rāmānandīs, 112–113, 127, 220, 225; among four *sampradāys*, 110, 115–120, 199, 205; as monastics, 148; royal power and, 148–149
Rāmānuja, 35, 46, 49, 56, 82–83, 87, 101–105, 108–110, 117, 130, 132, 141, 144–146, 161, 165, 202, 206, 212, 224, 248, 270, 276, 278, 282, 287, 290; four *sampradāys* and, 35, 46, 49; lineage of, 104
Ramanujan, A. K., 3, 15, 87, 336
Rāmāyaṇa, 16, 19, 326
Rāmcaritmānas (Spiritual Lake of the Acts of Rām) (Tulsīdās), 19
Rāmdās, 27, 30, 286
Rāmprasād (poet-saint), 20
Rām Sonī, 138, 140, 225, 228
Rāmtanu Lahari o Tatkālīn Bāngāsamāj (Ramtanu Lahiri and Contemporary Bengali Society) (Sastri), 265
Ranade, Mahadeo Govind, 29–32, 59, 84
Ranger, Terence, 13
Rao, Ajay, 197
Rao, Velcheru Narayana. *See* Narayana Rao, Velcheru
rās līlā, 17, 70, 89, 180
Rāspañcādhyayī (Nandadās), 71

Ravidās (poet-saint), 17, 305; influence of, 1–2, 7; Rabindranath Tagore on, 1–2, 15; on caste system, 14–15, 16; Rāmānand and, 237; Kabīr and, 331–332. *See also* "I've never known how to tan or sew"; Raidās; "You and Me"
Rāy, Rāmānand, 174, 176, 177
Reformation. *See* Protestant Reformation
Religion, 44, 140, 336; bhakti movement and, 3–4, 6, 8–9, 34–36; language and, 8–9; *Encyclopedia of Religion and Ethics,* 34; *sādhanā,* 39, 41; *Dabistān-i-Mazābib,* 139–141, 219, 314; bhakti movement and real, 340–341. *See also specific religions*
The Religion of Man, 235
Religious pursuit. *See Sādhanā*
"Rethinking Bhakti," 337
Richards, John, 322
Rise and Fall of the Roman Empire (Gibbon), 58
Rise of the Maratha Power (Ranade), 29, 59
Rituals, 198, 293
Roads, 156
Rodrigues, Valerian, 338
Roman Catholic Church, 30, 338
Roy, Rammohan, 11, 259, 260, 262
Royal power, 148–149, 191
Rudra, 103, 106, 218
Rule: of Akbar, 76, 78, 156–157, 166, 186; Mughals, 156, 186
Rūp. *See* Gosvāmī, Rūp

Sacred geography, 162
"The Sacred Touch" (Tagore, R.), 238
Sādhanā (religious discipline), 39, 41, 294
Saguṇ (with attributes), 17, 19, 38, 44, 45, 47, 49
SAHMAT (Accord, the Safdar Hashmi Memorial Trust), 287, 290, 334
Saints, 6, 30, 45, 275–276. *See also* Poet-saints; Singer-saints; *specific saints*
Saints' path. *See Sant Mārg*
Śaṃkarācārya, 26, 39, 49, 82, 220, 221, 222
Saṃkīrtan, 166, 168, 264, 266, 325
Sāṃkrityāyan, Rāhul, 57
Sampradāyabodhinī (Manohardās), 217
Sampradāyapariśuddhi (Vedantadeśika), 217
Sampradāyapradīpa (Dvivedī, G. B.), 72, 205, 209, 212, 215–216, 218
Sampradāys, four (traditions of teaching and reception), 15, 70; politics and, 10–11; Madhva and, 35, 46, 49; Nimbārka, 35, 46, 49, 103, 135; Rāmānuja and, 35, 46, 49; Viṣṇusvāmī and, 35, 106, 110; Vallabha and, 46, 49, 106–107, 108; Grierson and, 99; Dvivedi on, 99–100, 103, 104–108; explanation of, 99–100; three-storey house of, 100–103; time-structure of, 103; Vaishnava and, 103; within bhakti movement narrative, 103–111; Shukla and, 109, 110; Rāmānandīs and, 110, 115–120, 199, 205; Galtā and, 113, 116, 120–127; Nābhādās on, 120, 121–123, 134–136; Anantadās on, 122–123, 126; with commonwealth of love, 124–127; with four *panths,* 127–138; in Persia, 138–147; Priyādās and, 143–147; with Kavikarṇapūra and Jaisingh II, 192–205; Gauḍīyas and, 195, 199, 219; Vaishnava, 221. *See also* Lineage; *Panth*
saṃvād, 90, 303, 331
"Sanaka and the rest," 62, 103, 132
Sandstone, red, 80
Saṅkīrtan, 27. *See also Saṃkīrtan*
Sanskrit, 8–9, 23–24, 29–30
Sant Mārg (saints' path), 45
Sarasvatī, Kavīndrācārya. *See* Kavīndrācārya Sarasvatī
Sarasvatī, Madhusūdan. *See* Madhusūdan Sarasvatī
Sardar Vallabhbhai Patel Memorial Lectures (Patel Lectures), 19–20, 23, 25–27, 60
Sarvāṅgī (or Sarvangī), 309, 315, 327
Śāstrī, Jaṭāśaṃkar, 214
Śāstrī, Kaṇṭhamaṇi, 214–215
Śāstrī, Nārāyaṇ, 214
Sastri, Sivanath, 265
Savarkar, Vinayak Damodar, 286–287
School of Religions. *See Dabistān-i-Mazābib*
Scripture, four categories of, 220
"Second tradition" (Dvivedī), 247
Sen, Keshub Chandra, 260, 261, 263–264, 265, 266

Sen, Kshitimohan, 54, 100, 103, 104, 108, 126; influence of, 237, 241; in Shantiniketan, 242–243; on Mīrābāī, 244–245; Dvivedi and, 245–255; on silences in Nābhādās, 249
Sen, Śivānand, 192
Serfoji II (King), 28, 308, 317
Servants of Hari. *See* Haridāsas
Setalwad, Teesta, 334
Shāh, Bahādur (Emperor), 128
Shāh, Husain, 164, 177
Shāh, Islām, 156
Shāh, Mūbad, 139, 140–143, 219, 314
Shāh, Sher, 156
Shaivas, 6, 25, 73, 204, 220–221; *see also* Shiva
Shakti, 17, 28, 130
Shantiniketan, 11, 55, 100; Rabindranath Tagore and, 233, 235–245, 275; Dvivedi in, 235, 240, 241, 243; Kshitimohan Sen in, 242–243; Brahmos, 261; Hindi Bhavan murals at, 275–284
Sharma, Krishna, 42, 47, 76, 234, 315; on bhakti as history, 32–36; on *nirguṇ bhakti,* 48–49; Dvivedi's influence on, 50–51; on Grierson, 51
Sharma, R. S., 48
Sheikh, Samira, 299
Shekhawat, Kripal Singh, 277
Shiva, 17, 38, 155, 298, 302, 305–306, 325; *see also* Shaivas
Shobhi, Prithvi Datta Chandra, 323–324
Shukla, Pundit Ramchandra, 42, 43–44, 47, 49, 59; Harishchandra and, 54, 110–111; bhakti movement and, 54–55, 125, 291; on four *sampradāys,* 109, 110; Banaras and, 110; influence of, 230–231, 233, 247
Shulman, David, 321–322
Signatures. *See* Personal signatures, in poems
Sikhs, 125, 131, 220, 245, 266; Gurus, 2, 20, 128, 130; Dādūpathīs and, 27, 127–128, 228; songs, 126; *khālsā* and *dvārā,* 128; *panth,* 128, 274; Kabīr and, 274; Gurbani and, 293; bhakti movements and, 327–328
Silences, 89. 136, 168, 216, 249, 307
Siṃhabhūpāla (King), 163
Singer-saints, 25; holy mendicancy of, 27, 28; Vārkarī pilgrimage and, 30, 83–84. *See also specific singer-saints*
Singh, Bisan, 197
Singh, Gobind (Gurū), 125, 128, 130, 139–140, 282, 303
Singh, Namvar, 247, 250
Sisle Hazrat Islam, 286
Sītā, 124
Sītārāmjī (deity), 112
Śivājī (King), 27
Snake, 305, 306, 307
Social classification, 219
Social health, 64
Songs: bhakti poetry and, 2; of protest, 13, 340; Sikhs and, 126; musical idioms and, 296–297; Mīrābāī, 336. *See also* Hymns; Lyrics; Music
The Soul of India (Pal), 257
South: northern flow from, 100–103, 307–308; Brindavan and immigrants from, 157–164; Hindi Bhavan murals and, 278–279, 281, 283. *See also* "Born in Dravida" narrative
Soviet Union, 236
Speaking of Śiva (Ramanujan), 87
Spiritual Lake of the Acts of Rām. *See Rāmcaritmānas*
Śrī. *See* Lakṣmī, Ramā, Śrī Vaishnavas
Śrījī temple, 161
Śrīkṛṣṇakarṇāmṛta (Bilvamangal), 210–211
Śrīnāthjī, 188
Śrīnivās, 194
Śrī Vaishnavas, 86, 97
Standardization, of Hindi, 41
Stewart, Tony, 170, 178
Stories, 319; Krishna, 70, 177–179, 182; interconnectedness of, 297–298, 302; Mīrābāī, 302–303. *See also Līlā; Vārtā*
Subbulakshmi, M. S., 337
Subrahmanyam, K. G., 278–279, 282–283
Subrahmanyam, Sanjay, 322
"Sub-sects," 111
Sufis, 3, 18, 44, 139, 219–220; epic texts, 19; movement, 40, 94; Nāmdev and, 93; Vaishnavas and, 95–96. *See also Premākhān* genre
"Sufism and Bhakti Movement: Eternal Relevance," 291
Sukhānand, 119
Sundardās, 137–138, 216
Supernaturalism, 291
Surasurānand, 119

Surasurī, 119
Sūrdās, 2, 28, 106, 134, 135, 228; personal signature in poems, 17–18; legacy, 183–184; influence of, 233, 236, 318; as exemplar, 268–275; in Hindi Bhavan murals, 281–282; as early modern, 322–323
Sūrya, 111
Śvetāśvatara Upaniṣad, 39
Swadeshi movement, 255, 259
"Sweet Mercy" (Tagore), 1, 15, 237–238
Śyāmcaraṇdās, 201

Tagore, Debendranath, 238, 260
Tagore, Rabindranath, 7, 100, 229; on Ravidās, 1–2, 15; Viśva Bhāratī and, 11; in English and Bengali, 233; Shantiniketan and, 233, 235–245, 275; Dvivedi and, 235, 236–237, 241, 247. *See also* "Sweet Mercy"
Taking refuge with another. *See Anyāśraya*
"Talking to God in the Mother Tongue" (Ramanujan), 336
Tamil, 2, 311; as root of bhakti movement, 3; *pad* and, 299
Tārānāth, 112, 113
Tattva, 120
Tattvavādīs, 206, 207–208
Tazkirā, 91, 139, 165, 225–226, 298
Telugu, 299, 317, 336
Temples, 203; construction of, 75, 78, 114, 155; architecture of, 75–76, 78, 79, 144; with red sandstone, 80; Vishnu temple at Srirangam, 82; Govindadev, 151, 152, 155, 190, 198; in Brindavan, 151–154; land for, 157; Śrījī, 161; Bharat Mata, 276; Tirumala Tirupati Devasthanams, 292
Teṉkalais, 105
Tevāram, 26
Textbooks, 37–38, 42, 59
Thanjavur, 27–28, 308, 317, 336
Texts: epic, 17–19; written, 309
Thapar, Romila, 38
Time: *Bhāgavata Māhātmya* on geography and, 68–74; structure of four *sampradāys,* 103; divisions of, 219
Tirumala Tirupati Devasthanams, 292
Tirupati, 80, 86, 173, 224, 292–295, 299, 303, 321–325, 336
Tiruppāṇ, 272, 329–330
Ṭodarmal, 156–157
Toynbee, Arnold, 28, 32
Traditions of teaching and reception. *See Sampradāys,* four
Trilocan, 106, 126, 134
Tripathi, R. P., 57
Ṭukaḍā, 336–337
Tukārām, 2, 291
Tulsīdās, 19, 106, 134, 281, 326 ,341; influence, 30, 42, 44, 46, 231; *premākhyān* genre and, 225; as slave of Rām, 326
Tyranny, of caste system, 39–40, 48, 341

Ubhayavedānta ("the Vedanta of both"), 82
Underhill, Evelyn, 237, 243
Unification: bhakti movement as force of, 3, 6, 13–14; bhakti archive and, 13–16, 19; with poet-saints as great integrators, 19–28
Untouchables. *See* Dalits
Urdu language, 3
Uttarādhās, 128

Vacana, 27, 87, 305–306, 310, 324, 340
Vairāgya (renunciation, self-control), 64–67, 98
Vaishnavas, 6, 10, 25, 103, 220; Sufis and, 95–96; four *sampradāys* and, 221; Muslims and, 224–225, 226. *See also* Vaishnavism
Vaishnavic Movements (B. C. Pal), 257
Vaishnavism, 92, 109, 129, 218; conversion to, 87; vulgate, 134, 140, 317
Vaiṣṇavism, Śaivism, and Minor Religious Systems (Bhandarkar), 108, 109
"Vaiṣṇav Sarvasva" (Harishchandra), 218
Vajpeyi, Ananya, 315, 317
Vajpeyi, Ashok, 320
Vallabha (Vallabhācārya), 28, 69, 103, 109, 119, 158, 180, 185, 207, 214; in four *sampradāys,* 46, 49, 106–107, 108; "becoming Brahman" formula of, 186; legacy, 187, 189; birth of, 188; in Braj, 188–189; on *Bhāgavata Purāṇa,* 206; Vijayanagar and, 207–208; caste system and, 310
Vallabhadigvijaya (Yadunāth), 72, 214

Vallabhites, 76, 205; Gauḍīyas or Chaitanyites and, 179–180, 211, 303; Brindavan and, 179–189; *vartā* genre and, 180; Vijayanagar and, 205–217; *anyāśraya* and, 211. *See also* Puṣṭimārgīs
Vālmīki, 134
Van Buitenen, J. A. B., 5
Vārkarī pilgrimage, 30, 83–84, 328
Vārtā, 180–185
Vaṭakalais, 105
Vaudeville, Charlotte, 151
Vedanta, 26, 51, 82, 252, 262
Vedantadeśika, 217
Vedāntapārijātasaurabha (The Fragrance of the Heavenly Tree of Vedānta) (Nimbārka), 158–159
"the Vedanta of both." *See Ubhayavedānta*
Vedic traditions, 6, 7
Vemana, 317
Venkatkrishnan, Anand, 325
Vernacularization, 33, 56, 311–312; of Sanskrit, 8–9, 23–24, 29–30; vernacular-to-vernacular transmission process, 24; in writing, 90
VHP. *See* Vishva Hindu Parishad
Vidyābhūṣaṇ, Baladev. *See* Baladev Vidyābhūṣaṇ
"Vidyābhūṣaṇ Svāmī," 203. *See also* Baladev Vidyābhūṣaṇ
Vidyāpati, 176–177, 233
Vijayanagar, 190, 222; Vallabhites and, 205–217; Vallabha and, 207–208
Vinod, 121
Vīraśaivas, 26–27.*See also* Basava; Mahādevīakkā; Prabhu, Allama, *vacana*
Virmani, Shabnam, 315, 335
Vishnu, 114, 121, 197, 325; temple at Srirangam, 82; as Narsiṃha, 112. *See also* Vaishnavas, Vaishnavism
Vishva Hindu Parishad (VHP), 276, 286, 287, 290
Viṣṇusvāmī, 206–207, 213; in four *sampradāys,* 35, 106, 110
Viṣṇusvāmīcaritāmṛta (source for Harishchandra), 218
Viśrām Ghāṭ, 160
Viśva Bhāratī ("All of India"), 11, 100
Viṭṭhalnāth, 106–107, 119, 180, 186, 206
Vrajabhaktivilāsa (Devotional Enjoyments of Braj) (Nārāyaṇ Bhaṭṭ), 161–162
Vrajotsavacandrikā (Luminous Array of Festivals in Braj) (Nārāyaṇ Bhaṭṭ), 161
Vṛndā (goddess), 152
Vulgate Vaishnava, 134, 140, 317
Vyās, 165, 171, 185, 314
Vyāsatīrtha, 83, 223

Wakankar, Milind, 315
Wall paintings, 285. *See also* Hindi Bhavan, murals of
We Are All Ayodhya (SAHMAT), 334
Weber, Albrecht, 33, 43
Williams, Monier, 33
Williams, Tyler, 309, 310, 311
Wilson, Horace Hyman, 33, 43, 109, 118, 144, 229
With attributes. *See Saguṇ*
Without attributes. *See Nirguṇ*
Women, 203, 311; bhakti poets, 16; in poems, 17–18, 181–182, 300; Bhakti as feminine, 59–60; in *Bhāgavata Māhātmya,* 63–64
Wondrous City. *See* Ajab Shahar
Words, loaning of, 299
Writing: vernacularization in, 90; texts, 309

Xenology, 89

Yadunāth, 72, 214
Yāmuna (Yāmunācārya), 82, 248
Yashoda, 300–301
Yavanas, 63, 79–80
Yoga, 25, 194
Yogīs, Nāth, 136, 252, 302, 312
"You and Me" (Ravidās), 14, 15
Yudhiṣṭhira, 207

Zoroastrian Pārsī community, 140